SRA Handbook

OCTOBER 2014 EDITION

Other titles available from Law Society Publishing:

Alternative Business Structures
Iain Miller and Mark Pardoe

Anti-Bribery Toolkit
Amy Bell

Anti-Money Laundering Toolkit
Alison Matthews

COFAs Toolkit
Jeremy Black and Florence Perret du Cray

COLPs Toolkit
Michelle Garlick

Complaints Handling Toolkit
Vicky Ling and Fiona Westwood

Conveyancing Protocol
The Law Society

Conveyancing Quality Scheme Toolkit (2nd edition)
The Law Society

Data Protection Toolkit
Alison Matthews

Equality and Diversity Toolkit
Mark Lomas

In-house Lawyers' Toolkit
Richard Tapp and Ann Page

Outcomes-Focused Regulation
Andrew Hopper QC and Gregory Treverton-Jones QC

The Solicitor's Handbook 2015 (eBook also available)
Andrew Hopper QC and Gregory Treverton-Jones QC

Wills and Inheritance Protocol
The Law Society

Wills and Inheritance Quality Scheme Toolkit
The Law Society

Titles from Law Society Publishing can be ordered from all good bookshops or direct (telephone 0370 850 1422, email **lawsociety@prolog.uk.com** or visit our online shop at **www.lawsociety.org.uk/bookshop**).

SRA HANDBOOK

OCTOBER 2014 EDITION

Solicitors Regulation Authority

The Law Society

© The Law Society 2014

ISBN: 978-1-78446-016-7

First print edition published 2011 (website version 1)
Second print edition published 2012 (website version 5)
Third print edition published 2013 (website version 8)
Fourth print edition published 2014 (website version 9)

This edition (website version 12) published in 2014 by the Law Society
113 Chancery Lane, London WC2A 1PL

Reprinted 2015

Typeset by Columns Design XML Ltd, Reading
Printed by TJ International Ltd, Padstow, Cornwall

FSC
www.fsc.org
MIX
Paper from
responsible sources
FSC® C013056

The paper used for the text pages of this book is FSC certified. FSC (the Forest Stewardship Council) is an international network to promote responsible management of the world's forests.

Contents

CONTENTS

[A]   Introduction

[A.1] **Introduction to the SRA Handbook**

Contents

1 Consumer interests and the general public interest are the key justifications for any regulatory scheme. Users of legal services are, therefore, the focus of the Solicitors Regulation Authority's (SRA's) regulatory framework.

2 This Handbook sets out the standards and requirements which we expect our regulated community to achieve and observe, for the benefit of the clients they serve and in the general public interest. Our approach to regulation (i.e. authorisation, supervision and enforcement) is outcomes-focused and risk-based so that clients receive services in a manner which best suits their own particular needs, and depending on how services are provided (e.g. whether in-house or through private practice).

3 Our Handbook brings together the key regulatory elements in the following sections:

(a) SRA **Principles** – these are the ten Principles which are mandatory and apply to all those we regulate and underpin all aspects of practice. They define the fundamental ethical and professional standards that we expect of all firms (including owners who may not be lawyers) and individuals when providing legal services. In some circumstances they apply outside practice.

(b) SRA **Code of Conduct ("the Code")** – this section contains the "Outcomes" we require which, when achieved, benefit users of legal services and the public at large. These Outcomes are mandatory and, when achieved, will help ensure compliance with the Principles in the particular contexts covered by the various chapters in the Code. We recognise that these mandatory Outcomes may be achieved in a variety of ways depending on the particular circumstances, and we have supplemented the mandatory Outcomes with non-mandatory "Indicative Behaviours" to aid compliance. The Indicative Behaviours which we set out are not exhaustive: the Outcomes can be achieved in other ways. We encourage firms to consider how they can best achieve the Outcomes taking into account the nature of the firm, the particular circumstances and, crucially, the needs of their particular clients.

   (i) Introduction

   (ii) SRA Code of Conduct

(c) **Accounts** – this section contains the SRA Accounts Rules – requirements aimed at protecting client money.

   (i) Introduction

   (ii) SRA Accounts Rules

(d) **Authorisation and Practising Requirements** – this section includes key requirements for the training and admission for individuals intending to become solicitors; exercising higher rights of audience; acting as advocates in the criminal courts; for individuals and firms setting up in practice and for holding certain roles in a practice.

   (i) Introduction

   (ii) SRA Practice Framework Rules

   (iii) SRA Authorisation Rules for Legal Services Bodies and Licensable Bodies

   (iv) SRA Practising Regulations

   (v) Solicitors Keeping of the Roll Regulations

   (vi) SRA Training Regulations:

      (A) 2014 – Qualification and Training Provider Regulations

      (B) 2011 Part 3 – CPD Regulations

   (vii) SRA Admission Regulations

   (viii) SRA Qualified Lawyers Transfer Scheme Regulations

   (ix) SRA Higher Rights of Audience Regulations

   (x) SRA Quality Assurance Scheme for Advocates (Crime) Regulations

   (xi) SRA Suitability Test

(e) **Client Protection** – this section contains key elements for the financial protection of clients.

   (i) Introduction

   (ii) SRA Indemnity Insurance Rules

   (iii) SRA Indemnity (Enactment) Rules and SRA Indemnity Rules

   (iv) SRA Compensation Fund Rules

   (v) SRA Intervention Powers (Statutory Trust) Rules

(f) **Discipline and Costs Recovery** – this section contains provisions upon which our disciplinary and costs recovery powers are based.

   (i) Introduction

   (ii) SRA Disciplinary Procedure Rules

   (iii) SRA Cost of Investigations Regulations

(g) **Overseas Rules**

   (i) Introduction

   (ii) Overseas Rules

(h) **Specialist Services** – this section contains provisions which are only applicable when certain services are being provided to clients.

   (i)   Introduction

   (ii) SRA Property Selling Rules

   (iii) SRA Financial Services (Scope) Rules

   (iv) SRA Financial Services (Conduct of Business) Rules

   (v)   SRA European Cross-border Practice Rules

   (vi) SRA Insolvency Practice Rules

(i) **Glossary** – The Glossary is central to all the rules and regulations within the SRA Handbook. It comprises all terms used throughout the Handbook which are shown in italics, and sets out their definitions. The same terms in the SRA Handbook may appear as italicised text in some cases but not in others. Where they are not italicised, for reasons relating to the specific context, they are not being used in their defined sense and take their natural meaning in that context. The Glossary also contains interpretation and transitional provisions.

Additional information

1   Non-mandatory guidance and notes appear, as appropriate, throughout the Handbook as an aid to compliance.

2   Our approach to regulation has two elements: firm-based requirements and individual requirements. It focuses on the practices of regulated entities as well as the conduct and competence of regulated individuals. This approach allows us to take regulatory action against firms or individuals, or both, in appropriate cases. This could include action against anyone in the firm including non-lawyer owners, managers and employees. We exercise our regulatory powers in a proportionate manner, focusing on risk and outcomes for clients.

3   Firms will need to ensure that all employees (even if non-qualified and non-fee earners) receive appropriate training on the requirements in the Handbook, but only to the extent necessary for the role they undertake in the firm. For example, all staff will need to understand that they should keep clients' affairs confidential and behave with integrity; however it is likely that only those in fee-earning roles need be aware of the procedures required for checking for conflicts of interests and giving undertakings.

4   Although firms now have greater freedom in the way they offer services (e.g. outsourcing certain functions), they may not abrogate responsibility for compliance with regulatory requirements.

5   We are confident that the contents of this Handbook, coupled with our modern, outcomes-focused, risk-based approach to authorisation, supervision and effective enforcement will:

(a) benefit the public interest;

(b) support the rule of law;

(c) improve access to justice;

(d) benefit consumers' interests;

(e) promote competition;

(f) encourage an independent, strong, diverse and effective legal profession;

(g) increase understanding of legal rights and duties; and

(h) promote adherence to the professional principles set out in the Legal Services Act 2007.

6 The Handbook will, therefore, support not only consumers of legal services, but will also support the independence of the legal profession and its unique role in safeguarding the legal rights of those it serves.

7 These regulatory objectives can only be achieved if we and our regulated community work together in a spirit of mutual trust for the benefit of clients and the ultimate public interest.

[B] Principles

Principles

PREAMBLE

The SRA Principles dated 17 June 2011 commencing 6 October 2011 made by the Solicitors Regulation Authority Board under sections 31, 79 and 80 of the Solicitors Act 1974, sections 9 and 9A of the Administration of Justice Act 1985 and section 83 of the Legal Services Act 2007, with the approval of the Legal Services Board under paragraph 19 of Schedule 4 to the Legal Services Act 2007, regulating the conduct of solicitors and their employees, registered European lawyers, recognised bodies and their managers and employees, and licensed bodies and their managers and employees.

PART 1: SRA PRINCIPLES

1: SRA Principles

These are mandatory *Principles* which apply to all.

You must:

1. uphold the rule of law and the proper administration of justice;

2. act with integrity;

3. not allow your independence to be compromised;

4. act in the best interests of each *client*;

5. provide a proper standard of service to your *clients*;

6. behave in a way that maintains the trust the public places in you and in the provision of legal services;

7. comply with your legal and regulatory obligations and deal with your regulators and ombudsmen in an open, timely and co-operative manner;

8. run your business or carry out your role in the business effectively and in accordance with proper governance and sound financial and risk management principles;

9. run your business or carry out your role in the business in a way that encourages equality of opportunity and respect for diversity; and

10. protect *client* money and *assets*.

2: SRA Principles – notes

2.1   The Principles embody the key ethical requirements on firms and individuals who are involved in the provision of legal services. You should always have regard to the Principles and use them as your starting point when faced with an ethical dilemma.

2.2   Where two or more Principles come into conflict, the Principle which takes precedence is the one which best serves the public interest in the particular circumstances, especially the public interest in the proper administration of justice.

2.3   These Principles:

(a)   apply to individuals and firms we regulate, whether traditional firms of solicitors or ABSs, in private practice or in-house. Where a firm or individual is *practising overseas*, the Overseas Principles apply;

(b)   will be breached by you if you permit another person to do anything on your behalf which if done by you would breach the Principles; and

(c)   apply to you to the fullest extent if a sole practitioner or manager in a firm, but still apply to you if you work within a firm or in-house and have no management responsibility (for example, even if you are not a manager you may have an opportunity to influence, adopt and implement measures to comply with Principles 8 and 9).

2.4   Compliance with the Principles is also subject to any overriding legal obligations.

Principle 1: You must uphold the rule of law and the proper administration of justice.

2.5   You have obligations not only to clients but also to the court and to third parties with whom you have dealings on your clients' behalf – see, e.g., Chapter 5 (Your client and the court) and Chapter 11 (Relations with third parties) of the Code.

Principle 2: You must act with integrity.

2.6   Personal integrity is central to your role as the client's trusted adviser and should characterise all your professional dealings with clients, the court, other lawyers and the public.

Principle 3: You must not allow your independence to be compromised.

2.7   "Independence" means your own and your firm's independence, and not merely your ability to give independent advice to a client. You should avoid situations which might put your independence at risk – e.g. giving control of your practice to a third party which is beyond the regulatory reach of the SRA or other approved regulator.

Principles

Principle 4: You must act in the best interests of each client.

2.8   You should always act in good faith and do your best for each of your clients. Most importantly, you should observe:

(a)   your duty of confidentiality to the client – see Chapter 4 (Confidentiality and disclosure) of the Code; and

(b)   your obligations with regard to conflicts of interests – see Chapter 3 (Conflicts of interests) of the Code.

Principle 5: You must provide a proper standard of service to your clients.

2.9   You should, e.g., provide a proper standard of client care and of work. This would include exercising competence, skill and diligence, and taking into account the individual needs and circumstances of each client.

Principle 6: You must behave in a way that maintains the trust the public places in you and in the provision of legal services.

2.10   Members of the public should be able to place their trust in you. Any behaviour either within or outside your professional practice which undermines this trust damages not only you, but also the ability of the legal profession as a whole to serve society.

Principle 7: You must comply with your legal and regulatory obligations and deal with your regulators and ombudsmen in an open, timely and co-operative manner.

2.11   You should, e.g., ensure that you comply with all the reporting and notification requirements – see Chapter 10 (You and your regulator) of the Code – and respond promptly and substantively to communications.

Principle 8: You must run your business or carry out your role in the business effectively and in accordance with proper governance and sound financial and risk management principles.

2.12   Whether you are a manager or an employee, you have a part to play in helping to ensure that your business is well run for the benefit of your clients and, e.g. in meeting the outcomes in Chapter 7 (Management of your business) of the Code.

Principle 9: You must run your business or carry out your role in the business in a way that encourages equality of opportunity and respect for diversity.

2.13   Whether you are a manager or an employee, you have a role to play in achieving the outcomes in Chapter 2 (Equality and diversity) of the Code. Note that a finding of unlawful discrimination outside practice could also amount to a breach of Principles 1 and 6.

Principle 10: You must protect client money and assets.

2.14   This Principle goes to the heart of the duty to act in the best interests of your clients. You should play your part in e.g. protecting money, documents or other property belonging to your clients which has been entrusted to you or your firm.

Breach of the Principles

2.15   Our approach to enforcement is proportionate, outcomes-focused and risk-based. Therefore, how we deal with failure to comply with the Principles will depend on all the particular circumstances of each case. Our primary aim is to achieve the right outcomes for clients.

PART 2: SRA PRINCIPLES – APPLICATION PROVISIONS

The *Principles* apply to you in the following circumstances (and "you" must be construed accordingly).

3: Application of the SRA Principles in England and Wales

3.1   Subject to paragraphs 3.2 to 6.1 below and any other provisions in the *SRA Code of Conduct*, the *Principles* apply to you, in relation to your activities carried out from an office in England and Wales, if you are:

(a)   a *solicitor*, *REL* or *RFL* who is *practising* as such, whether or not the entity through which you *practise* is subject to these *Principles*;

(b)   a *solicitor*, *REL* or *RFL* who is:

  (i)   a *manager*, *employee* or *owner* of a body which should be a *recognised body*, but has not been recognised by the *SRA*;

  (ii)   a *manager*, *employee* or *owner* of a body that is a *manager* or *owner* of a body that should be a *recognised body*, but has not been recognised by the *SRA*;

  (iii)   an *employee* of a *sole practitioner* which should be a *recognised sole practitioner*, but has not been recognised by the *SRA*;

  (iv)   an *owner* of an *authorised body* or of a body which should be a *recognised body* but has not been recognised by the *SRA*, even if you undertake no work for the body's *clients*;

  (v)   a *manager* or *employee* of an *authorised non-SRA firm*, or a *manager* of a body which is a *manager* of an *authorised non-SRA firm*, when doing work of a sort authorised by the *SRA*, for that firm;

(c)   an *authorised body*, or a body which should be a *recognised body* but has not been recognised by the *SRA*;

(d)   any other person who is a *manager*, or *employee* of an *authorised body*, or of a body which should be a *recognised body* but has not been recognised by the *SRA*;

(e) any other person who is an *employee* of a *recognised sole practitioner*, or of a *sole practitioner* who should be a *recognised sole practitioner* but has not been recognised by the *SRA*;

and "you" includes "your" as appropriate.

3.2 The *Principles* apply to you if you are a *solicitor*, *REL* or *RFL*, and you are:

(a) *practising* as a *manager* or *employee* of an *authorised non-SRA firm* when doing work of a sort authorised by the *authorised non-SRA firm's approved regulator* or carrying on any other activity that is not precluded by the terms of your authorisation from the firm's *approved regulator*; or

(b) an *owner* of an *authorised non-SRA firm* even if you undertake no work for the body's *clients*.

4: Application of the SRA Principles in relation to practice from an office outside England and Wales

4.1 The *Principles* apply to you if you are:

(a) a body practising from an office outside England and Wales only if you are required to be an *authorised body* as a result of the nature of your practice and you have been authorised by the *SRA* accordingly; or

(b) a *manager* of such a body.

Guidance note

(i) In most circumstances, overseas offices of authorised bodies based in England and Wales will not require authorisation with the SRA and will be governed by the SRA Overseas Rules. However, in some circumstances, because of the work that is being carried out from the overseas office, it will need to be authorised (see Rule 2.1(e) and have regard to Rule 2.1(g) of the SRA Overseas Rules). In those circumstances, the SRA Principles and Code of Conduct apply.

4.2 The *Principles* apply to you if you are an individual engaged in *temporary practice overseas*.

5: Application of the SRA Principles outside practice

5.1 In relation to activities which fall outside *practice*, whether undertaken as a *lawyer* or in some other business or private capacity, *Principles* 1, 2 and 6 apply to you if you are a *solicitor*, *REL* or *RFL*.

6: General provisions

6.1 You must comply with the *Principles* at all times, but the extent to which you are expected to implement the requirements of the *Principles* will depend on your role in the *firm*, or your way of *practising*. For example, those who are managing a business will be expected to have more influence on how the *firm* or business is run than those *practising* in-house but not managing a legal department, or those *practising* as *employees* of a *firm*.

PART 3: TRANSITIONAL PROVISIONS

7: Transitional provisions

7.1 For the avoidance of doubt, where a breach of any provision of the Solicitors' Code of Conduct 2007 comes to the attention of the *SRA* after 6 October 2011, this shall be subject to action by the *SRA* notwithstanding any repeal of the relevant provision.

7.2 From 31 March 2012 or the date on which an order made pursuant to section 69 of the *LSA* relating to the status of *sole practitioners* comes into force, whichever is the later, paragraph 3.1 shall have effect subject to the following amendments:

    (a) paragraph 3.1(b)(iii), and

    (b) paragraph 3.1(e)

shall be omitted.

7.3 The *Principles* shall not apply to *licensed bodies* until such time as the *Society* is designated as a *licensing authority* under Part 1 of Schedule 10 to the *LSA* and all definitions shall be construed accordingly.

7.4 References in the preamble to:

    (a) the *Principles* being made under section 83 of the Legal Services Act 2007, and

    (b) *licensed bodies* and their *managers* and *employees*,

shall have no effect until such time as the *Society* is designated as a *licensing authority* under Part 1 of Schedule 10 to the *LSA*.

PART 4: INTERPRETATION

8: Interpretation

8.1 The SRA Handbook Glossary 2012 shall apply to these rules and, unless the context otherwise requires:

    (a) all italicised terms within these rules shall be defined; and

    (b) terms within these rules shall be interpreted,

in accordance with the *Glossary*.

[C]   Code of Conduct

SRA Code of Conduct 2011

INTRODUCTION TO THE SRA CODE OF CONDUCT

Overview

Outcomes-focused regulation concentrates on providing positive outcomes which when achieved will benefit and protect *clients* and the public. The SRA Code of Conduct (the Code) sets out our outcomes-focused conduct requirements so that you can consider how best to achieve the right outcomes for your *clients* taking into account the way that your *firm* works and its *client* base. The Code is underpinned by effective, risk-based supervision and enforcement.

Those involved in providing legal advice and representation have long held the role of trusted adviser. There are fiduciary duties arising from this role and obligations owed to others, especially the *court*. No code can foresee or address every issue or ethical dilemma which may arise. You must strive to uphold the intention of the Code as well as its letter.

The Principles

The Code forms part of the Handbook, in which the 10 mandatory *Principles* are all-pervasive. They apply to all those we regulate and underpin all aspects of *practice*. They define the fundamental ethical and professional standards that we expect of all *firms* and individuals (including owners who may not be *lawyers*) when providing legal services. You should always have regard to the *Principles* and use them as your starting point when faced with an ethical dilemma.

Where two or more *Principles* come into conflict the one which takes precedence is the one which best serves the public interest in the particular circumstances, especially the public interest in the proper administration of justice. Compliance with the *Principles* is also subject to any overriding legal obligations.

You must:

1. uphold the rule of law and the proper administration of justice;

2. act with integrity;

3. not allow your independence to be compromised;

4. act in the best interests of each *client*;

5. provide a proper standard of service to your *clients*;

6. behave in a way that maintains the trust the public places in you and in the provision of legal services;

7. comply with your legal and regulatory obligations and deal with your regulators and ombudsmen in an open, timely and co-operative manner;

8. run your business or carry out your role in the business effectively and in accordance with proper governance and sound financial and risk management principles;

9. run your business or carry out your role in the business in a way that encourages equality of opportunity and respect for diversity; and

10. protect *client* money and *assets*.

Structure of the Code

The Code is divided into 5 sections:

- You and your client
- You and your business
- You and your regulator
- You and others
- Application, waivers and interpretation

Each section is divided into chapters dealing with particular regulatory issues, for example, client care, *conflicts of interests*, and *publicity*.

These chapters show how the *Principles* apply in certain contexts through mandatory and non-mandatory provisions.

Mandatory provisions

The following provisions are mandatory:

- the outcomes;
- the application and waivers provisions in Chapters 13 and 13A;
- the interpretations; and
- the transitional provisions in Chapter 15.

The outcomes describe what *firms* and individuals are expected to achieve in order to comply with the relevant *Principles* in the context of the relevant chapter. In the case of *in-house practice*, we have set out at the end of each chapter which outcomes apply and in some cases have specified different outcomes.

In respect of *in-house practice*, different outcomes may apply depending on whether you are acting for your employer or for a *client* other than your employer as permitted by rules 4.1 to 4.10 of the *SRA Practice Framework Rules*.

The outcomes contained in each chapter are not an exhaustive list of the application of all the *Principles*. We have tried to make them as helpful as possible.

Non-mandatory provisions

The following provisions are non-mandatory:

- indicative behaviours;

- notes.

The outcomes are supplemented by indicative behaviours. The indicative behaviours specify, but do not constitute an exhaustive list of, the kind of behaviour which may establish compliance with, or contravention of the *Principles*. These are not mandatory but they may help us to decide whether an outcome has been achieved in compliance with the *Principles*.

We recognise that there may be other ways of achieving the outcomes. Where you have chosen a different method from those we have described as indicative behaviours, we might require you to demonstrate how you have nevertheless achieved the outcome. We encourage *firms* to consider how they can best achieve the outcomes, taking into account the nature of the *firm*, the particular circumstances of the matter and, crucially, the needs of their particular *clients*.

Waivers

Due to the flexibility of approach this structure allows, we do not anticipate receiving many applications for waivers from the mandatory outcomes. The *SRA*, nonetheless, reserves power to waive a provision in exceptional circumstances.

Interpretation

Words shown in italics are defined in the *Glossary*.

Sources of help

You can access the Code and other elements of the Handbook and find information on particular issues on the *SRA* website. You can also seek guidance on professional conduct from our Professional Ethics Guidance Team.

List of contents of the Code

1st section: You and your client

Chapter 1 Client care
Chapter 2 Equality and diversity
Chapter 3 Conflicts of interests
Chapter 4 Confidentiality and disclosure
Chapter 5 Your client and the court
Chapter 6 Your client and introductions to third parties

2nd section: You and your business

Chapter 7 Management of your business
Chapter 8 Publicity
Chapter 9 Fee sharing and referrals

3rd section: You and your regulator

Chapter 10 You and your regulator

4th section: You and others

Chapter 11 Relations with third parties
Chapter 12 Separate businesses

5th section: Application, waivers and interpretation

Chapter 13 Application and waivers provisions
Chapter 13A Practice Overseas
Chapter 14 Interpretation
Chapter 15 Transitional provisions

PREAMBLE

The SRA Code of Conduct dated 17 June 2011 commencing 6 October 2011 made by the Solicitors Regulation Authority Board under sections 31, 79 and 80 of the Solicitors Act 1974, sections 9 and 9A of the Administration of Justice Act 1985 and section 83 of the Legal Services Act 2007, with the approval of the Legal Services Board under paragraph 19 of Schedule 4 to the Legal Services Act 2007, regulating the conduct of solicitors and their employees, registered European lawyers and their employees, registered foreign lawyers, recognised bodies and their managers and employees and licensed bodies and their managers and employees.

1ST SECTION: YOU AND YOUR CLIENT

Chapter 1: Client care

This chapter is about providing a proper standard of service, which takes into account the individual needs and circumstances of each *client*. This includes providing *clients* with the information they need to make informed decisions about the services they need, how these will be delivered and how much they will cost. This will enable you and your *client* to understand each other's expectations and responsibilities. This chapter is also about ensuring that if *clients* are not happy with the service they have received they know how to make a *complaint* and that all *complaints* are dealt with promptly and fairly.

Your relationship with your *client* is a contractual one which carries with it legal, as well as conduct, obligations. This chapter focuses on your obligations in conduct.

You are generally free to decide whether or not to accept instructions in any matter, provided you do not discriminate unlawfully (see Chapter 2).

The outcomes in this chapter show how the *Principles* apply in the context of client care.

Outcomes

You must achieve these outcomes:

O(1.1)   you treat your *clients* fairly;

O(1.2)   you provide services to your *clients* in a manner which protects their interests in their matter, subject to the proper administration of justice;

O(1.3)   when deciding whether to act, or terminate your instructions, you comply with the law and the Code;

O(1.4)   you have the resources, skills and procedures to carry out your *clients'* instructions;

O(1.5)   the service you provide to *clients* is competent, delivered in a timely manner and takes account of your *clients'* needs and circumstances;

O(1.6)   you only enter into fee agreements with your *clients* that are legal, and which you consider are suitable for the *client's* needs and take account of the *client's* best interests;

O(1.7)   you inform *clients* whether and how the services you provide are regulated and how this affects the protections available to the *client*;

O(1.8)   *clients* have the benefit of your *compulsory professional indemnity insurance* and you do not exclude or attempt to exclude liability below the minimum level of cover required by the *SRA Indemnity Insurance Rules*;

O(1.9)   *clients* are informed in writing at the outset of their matter of their right to complain and how *complaints* can be made;

O(1.10)   *clients* are informed in writing, both at the time of engagement and at the conclusion of your *complaints* procedure, of their right to complain to the *Legal Ombudsman*, the time frame for doing so and full details of how to contact the *Legal Ombudsman*;

O(1.11)   *clients' complaints* are dealt with promptly, fairly, openly and effectively;

O(1.12)   *clients* are in a position to make informed decisions about the services they need, how their matter will be handled and the options available to them;

O(1.13)   *clients* receive the best possible information, both at the time of engagement and when appropriate as their matter progresses, about the likely overall cost of their matter;

O(1.14)   *clients* are informed of their right to challenge or complain about your bill and the circumstances in which they may be liable to pay interest on an unpaid bill;

O(1.15)   you properly account to *clients* for any *financial benefit* you receive as a result of your instructions;

O(1.16)   you inform current *clients* if you discover any act or omission which could give rise to a claim by them against you.

Indicative behaviours

Acting in the following way(s) may tend to show that you have achieved these outcomes and therefore complied with the *Principles*:

DEALING WITH THE CLIENT'S MATTER

IB(1.1)   agreeing an appropriate level of service with your *client*, for example the type and frequency of communications;

IB(1.2)   explaining your responsibilities and those of the *client*;

IB(1.3)   ensuring that the *client* is told, in writing, the name and status of the person(s) dealing with the matter and the name and status of the person responsible for its overall supervision;

IB(1.4)   explaining any arrangements, such as fee sharing or *referral arrangements*, which are relevant to the *client's* instructions;

IB(1.5)   explaining any limitations or conditions on what you can do for the *client*, for example, because of the way the *client's* matter is funded;

IB(1.6)   in taking instructions and during the course of the retainer, having proper regard to your *client's* mental capacity or other vulnerability, such as incapacity or duress;

IB(1.7)   considering whether you should decline to act or cease to act because you cannot act in the *client's* best interests;

IB(1.8)   if you seek to limit your liability to your *client* to a level above the minimum required by the *SRA Indemnity Insurance Rules*, ensuring that this limitation is in writing and is brought to the *client's* attention;

IB(1.9)   refusing to act where your *client* proposes to make a gift of significant value to you or a member of your family, or a member of your *firm* or their family, unless the *client* takes independent legal advice;

IB(1.10)   if you have to cease acting for a *client*, explaining to the *client* their possible options for pursuing their matter;

IB(1.11)   you inform *clients* if they are not entitled to the protections of the SRA Compensation Fund;

IB(1.12) considering whether a *conflict of interests* has arisen or whether the *client* should be advised to obtain independent advice where the *client* notifies you of their intention to make a claim or if you discover an act or omission which might give rise to a claim;

FEE ARRANGEMENTS WITH YOUR CLIENT

IB(1.13) discussing whether the potential outcomes of the *client's* matter are likely to justify the expense or risk involved, including any risk of having to pay someone else's legal fees;

IB(1.14) clearly explaining your fees and if and when they are likely to change;

IB(1.15) warning about any other payments for which the *client* may be responsible;

IB(1.16) discussing how the *client* will pay, including whether public funding may be available, whether the *client* has insurance that might cover the fees, and whether the fees may be paid by someone else such as a trade union;

IB(1.17) where you are acting for a *client* under a fee arrangement governed by statute, such as a conditional fee agreement, giving the *client* all relevant information relating to that arrangement;

IB(1.18) where you are acting for a publicly funded *client*, explaining how their publicly funded status affects the costs;

IB(1.19) providing the information in a clear and accessible form which is appropriate to the needs and circumstances of the *client*;

IB(1.20) where you receive a *financial benefit* as a result of acting for a *client*, either:

    (a) paying it to the *client*;

    (b) offsetting it against your fees; or

    (c) keeping it only where you can justify keeping it, you have told the *client* the amount of the benefit (or an approximation if you do not know the exact amount) and the *client* has agreed that you can keep it;

IB(1.21) ensuring that *disbursements* included in your bill reflect the actual amount spent or to be spent on behalf of the *client*;

COMPLAINTS HANDLING

IB(1.22) having a written *complaints* procedure which:

    (a) is brought to *clients'* attention at the outset of the matter;

    (b) is easy for *clients* to use and understand, allowing for *complaints* to be made by any reasonable means;

    (c) is responsive to the needs of individual *clients*, especially those who are vulnerable;

    (d) enables *complaints* to be dealt with promptly and fairly, with decisions based on a sufficient investigation of the circumstances;

    (e) provides for appropriate remedies; and

    (f) does not involve any charges to *clients* for handling their *complaints*;

IB(1.23) providing the *client* with a copy of the *firm's complaints* procedure on request;

IB(1.24) in the event that a *client* makes a *complaint*, providing them with all necessary information concerning the handling of the *complaint*.

Acting in the following way(s) may tend to show that you have not achieved these outcomes and therefore not complied with the *Principles*:

ACCEPTING AND REFUSING INSTRUCTIONS

IB(1.25) acting for a *client* when instructions are given by someone else, or by only one *client* when you act jointly for others unless you are satisfied that the *person* providing the instructions has the authority to do so on behalf of all of the *clients*;

IB(1.26) ceasing to act for a *client* without good reason and without providing reasonable notice;

IB(1.27) entering into unlawful fee arrangements such as an unlawful contingency fee;

IB(1.28) acting for a *client* when there are reasonable grounds for believing that the instructions are affected by duress or undue influence without satisfying yourself that they represent the *client's* wishes.

In-house practice

Outcomes 1.1 to 1.5, 1.7, 1.15 and 1.16 apply to your *in-house practice*.

Outcomes 1.6 and 1.9 to 1.14 apply to your *in-house practice* where you act for someone other than your employer unless it is clear that the outcome is not relevant to your particular circumstances.

IHP(1.1) Instead of Outcome 1.8 you comply with the *SRA Practice Framework Rules* in relation to professional indemnity insurance.

Notes

(i) The information you give to *clients* will vary according to the needs and circumstances of the individual *client* and the type of work you are doing for them, for example an individual instructing you on a conveyancing matter is unlikely to need the same information as a sophisticated commercial *client* who instructs you on a regular basis.

(ii)   Information about the *Legal Ombudsman*, including the scheme rules, contact details and time limits, can be found at **www.legalombudsman.org.uk**.

Chapter 2: Equality and diversity

This chapter is about encouraging equality of opportunity and respect for diversity, and preventing unlawful discrimination, in your relationship with your *clients* and others. The requirements apply in relation to age, disability, gender reassignment, marriage and civil partnership, pregnancy and maternity, race, religion or belief, sex and sexual orientation.

Everyone needs to contribute to compliance with these requirements, for example by treating each other, and *clients*, fairly and with respect, by embedding such values in the workplace and by challenging inappropriate behaviour and processes. Your role in embedding these values will vary depending on your role.

As a matter of general law you must comply with requirements set out in legislation – including the Equality Act 2010 – as well as the conduct duties contained in this chapter.

The outcomes in this chapter show how the *Principles* apply in the context of equality and diversity.

Outcomes

You must achieve these outcomes:

O(2.1)   you do not discriminate unlawfully, or victimise or harass anyone, in the course of your professional dealings;

O(2.2)   you provide services to *clients* in a way that respects diversity;

O(2.3)   you make reasonable adjustments to ensure that disabled *clients*, *employees* or *managers* are not placed at a substantial disadvantage compared to those who are not disabled, and you do not pass on the costs of these adjustments to these disabled *clients*, *employees* or *managers*;

O(2.4)   your approach to recruitment and employment encourages equality of opportunity and respect for diversity;

O(2.5)   *complaints* of discrimination are dealt with promptly, fairly, openly, and effectively.

Indicative behaviours

Acting in the following way(s) may tend to show that you have achieved these outcomes and therefore complied with the *Principles*:

IB(2.1)   having a written equality and diversity policy which is appropriate to the size and nature of the *firm* and includes the following features:

   (a)   a commitment to the principles of equality and diversity and legislative requirements;

   (b)   a requirement that all *employees* and *managers* comply with the outcomes;

   (c)   provisions to encompass your recruitment and interview processes;

   (d)   details of how the *firm* will implement, monitor, evaluate and update the policy;

   (e)   details of how the *firm* will ensure equality in relation to the treatment of *employees*, *managers*, *clients* and third parties instructed in connection with *client* matters;

   (f)   details of how *complaints* and disciplinary issues are to be dealt with;

   (g)   details of the *firm's* arrangements for workforce diversity monitoring; and

   (h)   details of how the *firm* will communicate the policy to *employees*, *managers* and *clients*;

IB(2.2)   providing *employees* and *managers* with training and information about complying with equality and diversity requirements;

IB(2.3)   monitoring and responding to issues identified by your policy and reviewing and updating your policy.

Acting in the following way(s) may tend to show that you have not achieved these outcomes and therefore not complied with the *Principles*:

IB(2.4)   being subject to any decision of a court or tribunal of the *UK*, that you have committed, or are to be treated as having committed, an unlawful act of discrimination;

IB(2.5)   discriminating unlawfully when accepting or refusing instructions to act for a *client*.

In-house practice

Outcomes 2.1 and 2.2 apply to all *in-house practice*.

Instead of outcomes 2.3 to 2.5 you must achieve the following outcome:

IHP(2.1)   if you have management responsibilities you take all reasonable steps to encourage equality of opportunity and respect for diversity in your workplace.

   Notes

   (i)   The obligations in this chapter closely mirror your legal obligations. You can obtain further information from the Equality and Human Rights Commission, **www.equalityhumanrights.com.**

(ii)   See also Chapter 1 (Client care) for the handling of *client complaints*.

(iii)   See also Chapter 7 (Management of your business) for your obligation to have in place appropriate systems and controls for complying with the outcomes in this chapter.

Chapter 3: Conflicts of interests

This chapter deals with the proper handling of *conflicts of interests*, which is a critical public protection. It is important to have in place systems that enable you to identify and deal with potential conflicts.

Conflicts of interests can arise between:

1.   you and current *clients* ("*own interest conflict*"); and

2.   two or more current *clients* ("*client conflict*").

You can never act where there is a conflict, or a significant risk of conflict, between you and your *client*.

If there is a conflict, or a significant risk of a conflict, between two or more current *clients*, you must not act for all or both of them unless the matter falls within the scope of the limited exceptions set out at Outcomes 3.6 or 3.7. In deciding whether to act in these limited circumstances, the overriding consideration will be the best interests of each of the *clients* concerned and, in particular, whether the benefits to the *clients* of you acting for all or both of the *clients* outweigh the risks.

You should also bear in mind that *conflicts of interests* may affect your duties of confidentiality and disclosure which are dealt with in Chapter 4.

The outcomes in this chapter show how the *Principles* apply in the context of *conflicts of interests*.

Outcomes

You must achieve these outcomes:

SYSTEMS

O(3.1)   you have effective systems and controls in place to enable you to identify and assess potential *conflicts of interests*;

O(3.2)   your systems and controls for identifying *own interest conflicts* are appropriate to the size and complexity of the *firm* and the nature of the work undertaken, and enable you to assess all the relevant circumstances, including whether your ability as an individual, or that of anyone within your *firm*, to act in the best interests of the *client(s)*, is impaired by:

(a)   any financial interest;

(b)   a personal relationship;

(c)   the appointment of you, or a member of your *firm* or family, to public office;

(d)   commercial relationships; or

(e)   your employment;

O(3.3)   your systems and controls for identifying *client conflicts* are appropriate to the size and complexity of the *firm* and the nature of the work undertaken, and enable you to assess all relevant circumstances, including whether:

(a)   the *clients'* interests are different;

(b)   your ability to give independent advice to the *clients* may be fettered;

(c)   there is a need to negotiate between the *clients*;

(d)   there is an imbalance in bargaining power between the *clients*; or

(e)   any *client* is vulnerable;

PROHIBITION ON ACTING IN CONFLICT SITUATIONS

O(3.4)   you do not act if there is an *own interest conflict* or a significant risk of an *own interest conflict*;

O(3.5)   you do not act if there is a *client conflict*, or a significant risk of a *client conflict*, unless the circumstances set out in Outcomes 3.6 or 3.7 apply;

EXCEPTIONS WHERE YOU MAY ACT, WITH APPROPRIATE SAFEGUARDS, WHERE THERE IS A CLIENT CONFLICT

O(3.6)   where there is a *client conflict* and the *clients* have a *substantially common interest* in relation to a matter or a particular aspect of it, you only act if:

(a)   you have explained the relevant issues and risks to the *clients* and you have a reasonable belief that they understand those issues and risks;

(b)   all the *clients* have given informed consent in writing to you acting;

(c)   you are satisfied that it is reasonable for you to act for all the *clients* and that it is in their best interests; and

(d)   you are satisfied that the benefits to the *clients* of you doing so outweigh the risks;

O(3.7)   where there is a *client conflict* and the *clients* are *competing for the same objective*, you only act if:

(a)   you have explained the relevant issues and risks to the *clients* and you have a reasonable belief that they understand those issues and risks;

(b)   the *clients* have confirmed in writing that they want you to act, in the knowledge that you act, or may act, for one or more other *clients* who are *competing for the same objective*;

(c)   there is no other *client conflict* in relation to that matter;

(d) unless the *clients* specifically agree, no individual acts for, or is responsible for the supervision of work done for, more than one of the *clients* in that matter; and

(e) you are satisfied that it is reasonable for you to act for all the *clients* and that the benefits to the *clients* of you doing so outweigh the risks.

Indicative behaviours

Acting in the following way(s) may tend to show that you have achieved these outcomes and therefore complied with the *Principles*:

IB(3.1) training *employees* and *managers* to identify and assess potential *conflicts of interests*;

IB(3.2) declining to act for *clients* whose interests are in direct conflict, for example claimant and defendant in litigation;

IB(3.3) declining to act for *clients* where you may need to negotiate on matters of substance on their behalf, for example negotiating on price between a buyer and seller of a property;

IB(3.4) declining to act where there is unequal bargaining power between the *clients*, for example acting for a seller and buyer where a builder is selling to a non-commercial *client*;

IB(3.5) declining to act for *clients* under Outcome 3.6 (*substantially common interest*) or Outcome 3.7 (*competing for the same objective*) where the *clients* cannot be represented even-handedly, or will be prejudiced by lack of separate representation;

IB(3.6) acting for *clients* under Outcome 3.7 (*competing for the same objective*) only where the *clients* are sophisticated users of legal services;

IB(3.7) acting for *clients* who are the lender and borrower on the grant of a mortgage of land only where:

(a) the mortgage is a standard mortgage (i.e. one provided in the normal course of the lender's activities, where a significant part of the lender's activities consists of lending and the mortgage is on standard terms) of property to be used as the borrower's private residence;

(b) you are satisfied that it is reasonable and in the *clients'* best interests for you to act; and

(c) the certificate of title required by the lender is in the form approved by the *Society* and the Council of Mortgage Lenders.

Acting in the following way(s) may tend to show that you have not achieved these outcomes and therefore not complied with the *Principles*:

IB(3.8) in a personal capacity, selling to or buying from, lending to or borrowing from a *client*, unless the *client* has obtained independent legal advice;

IB(3.9) advising a *client* to invest in a business, in which you have an interest which affects your ability to provide impartial advice;

IB(3.10) where you hold a power of attorney for a *client*, using that power to gain a benefit for yourself which in your professional capacity you would not have been prepared to allow to a third party;

IB(3.11) acting for two or more *clients* in a *conflict of interests* under Outcome 3.6 (*substantially common interest*) where the *clients'* interests in the end result are not the same, for example one partner buying out the interest of the other partner in their joint business or a seller transferring a property to a buyer;

IB(3.12) acting for two or more *clients* in a *conflict of interests* under Outcome 3.6 (*substantially common interest*) where it is unreasonable to act because there is unequal bargaining power;

IB(3.13) acting for two buyers where there is a *conflict of interests* under Outcome 3.7 (*competing for the same objective*), for example where two buyers are competing for a residential property;

IB(3.14) acting for a buyer (including a lessee) and seller (including a lessor) in a transaction relating to the transfer of land for value, the grant or assignment of a lease or some other interest in land for value.

In-house practice

Outcomes 3.4 to 3.7 apply to your *in-house practice*.

Outcomes 3.1 to 3.3 apply if you have management responsibilities.

Chapter 4: Confidentiality and disclosure

This chapter is about the protection of *clients'* confidential information and the disclosure of material information to *clients*.

Protection of confidential information is a fundamental feature of your relationship with *clients*. It exists as a concept both as a matter of law and as a matter of conduct. This duty continues despite the end of the retainer and even after the death of the *client*.

It is important to distinguish the conduct duties from the concept of law known as legal professional privilege.

Bear in mind that all members of the *firm* or *in-house practice*, including support staff, consultants and locums, owe a duty of confidentiality to your *clients*.

The duty of confidentiality to all *clients* must be reconciled with the duty of disclosure to *clients*. This duty of disclosure is limited to information of which you are aware which is material to your *client's* matter. Where you cannot reconcile these two duties, then the protection of confidential information is paramount. You should not continue to act for a *client* for whom you cannot disclose material information, except in very limited circumstances, where safeguards are in place. Such situations often also give rise to a *conflict of interests* which is discussed in Chapter 3.

The outcomes in this chapter show how the *Principles* apply in the context of confidentiality and disclosure.

Outcomes

You must achieve these outcomes:

O(4.1)   you keep the affairs of *clients* confidential unless disclosure is required or permitted by law or the *client* consents;

O(4.2)   any individual who is advising a *client* makes that *client* aware of all information material to that retainer of which the individual has personal knowledge;

O(4.3)   you ensure that where your duty of confidentiality to one *client* comes into conflict with your duty of disclosure to another *client*, your duty of confidentiality takes precedence;

O(4.4)   you do not act for A in a matter where A has an interest adverse to B, and B is a *client* for whom you hold confidential information which is material to A in that matter, unless the confidential information can be protected by the use of safeguards, and:

(a)   you reasonably believe that A is aware of, and understands, the relevant issues and gives informed consent;

(b)   either:

(i)   B gives informed consent and you agree with B the safeguards to protect B's information; or

(ii)   where this is not possible, you put in place effective safeguards including information barriers which comply with the common law; and

(c)   it is reasonable in all the circumstances to act for A with such safeguards in place;

O(4.5)   you have effective systems and controls in place to enable you to identify risks to *client* confidentiality and to mitigate those risks.

Indicative behaviours

Acting in the following way(s) may tend to show that you have achieved these outcomes and therefore complied with the *Principles*:

IB(4.1)   your systems and controls for identifying risks to *client* confidentiality are appropriate to the size and complexity of the *firm* or *in-house practice* and the nature of the work undertaken, and enable you to assess all the relevant circumstances;

IB(4.2) you comply with the law in respect of your fiduciary duties in relation to confidentiality and disclosure;

IB(4.3) you only outsource services when you are satisfied that the provider has taken all appropriate steps to ensure that your *clients'* confidential information will be protected;

IB(4.4) where you are an individual who has responsibility for acting for a *client* or supervising a *client's* matter, you disclose to the *client* all information material to the *client's* matter of which you are personally aware, except when:

    (a) the *client* gives specific informed consent to non-disclosure or a different standard of disclosure arises;

    (b) there is evidence that serious physical or mental injury will be caused to a person(s) if the information is disclosed to the *client*;

    (c) legal restrictions effectively prohibit you from passing the information to the *client*, such as the provisions in the money-laundering and anti-terrorism legislation;

    (d) it is obvious that privileged documents have been mistakenly disclosed to you;

    (e) you come into possession of information relating to state security or intelligence matters to which the Official Secrets Act 1989 applies;

IB(4.5) not acting for A where B is a *client* for whom you hold confidential information which is material to A unless the confidential information can be protected.

Acting in the following way(s) may tend to show that you have not achieved these outcomes and therefore not complied with the *Principles*:

IB(4.6) disclosing the content of a will on the death of a *client* unless consent has been provided by the personal representatives for the content to be released;

IB(4.7) disclosing details of bills sent to *clients* to third parties, such as debt factoring companies in relation to the collection of book debts, unless the *client* has consented.

In-house practice

The outcomes listed above apply to your *in-house practice*.

    Notes

    (i) The protection of confidential information may be at particular risk where:

        (a) two or more *firms* merge;

        (b) when you leave one *firm* and join another, such as if you join a *firm* acting against one of your former *clients*.

(ii) The following circumstances may make it difficult to implement effective safeguards and information barriers:

> (a) you are a small *firm*;
>
> (b) the physical structure or layout of the *firm* means that it will be difficult to preserve confidentiality; or
>
> (c) the *clients* are not sophisticated users of legal services.

Chapter 5: Your client and the court

This chapter is about your duties to your *client* and to the *court* if you are exercising a right to conduct litigation or acting as an advocate. The outcomes apply to both litigation and advocacy but there are some indicative behaviours which may be relevant only when you are acting as an advocate.

The outcomes in this chapter show how the *Principles* apply in the context of your *client* and the *court*.

Outcomes

You must achieve these outcomes:

O(5.1)   you do not attempt to deceive or knowingly or recklessly mislead the *court*;

O(5.2)   you are not complicit in another *person* deceiving or misleading the *court*;

O(5.3)   you comply with *court* orders which place obligations on you;

O(5.4)   you do not place yourself in contempt of *court*;

O(5.5)   where relevant, *clients* are informed of the circumstances in which your duties to the *court* outweigh your obligations to your *client*;

O(5.6)   you comply with your duties to the *court*;

O(5.7)   you ensure that evidence relating to sensitive issues is not misused;

O(5.8)   you do not make or offer to make payments to witnesses dependent upon their evidence or the outcome of the case.

Indicative behaviours

Acting in the following way(s) may tend to show that you have achieved these outcomes and therefore complied with the *Principles*:

IB(5.1)   advising your *clients* to comply with *court* orders made against them, and advising them of the consequences of failing to comply;

IB(5.2)   drawing the *court's* attention to relevant cases and statutory provisions, and any material procedural irregularity;

IB(5.3) ensuring child witness evidence is kept securely and not released to *clients* or third parties;

IB(5.4) immediately informing the *court*, with your *client's* consent, if during the course of proceedings you become aware that you have inadvertently misled the *court*, or ceasing to act if the *client* does not consent to you informing the *court*;

IB(5.5) refusing to continue acting for a *client* if you become aware they have committed perjury or misled the *court*, or attempted to mislead the *court*, in any material matter unless the *client* agrees to disclose the truth to the *court*;

IB(5.6) not appearing as an advocate, or acting in litigation, if it is clear that you, or anyone within your *firm*, will be called as a witness in the matter unless you are satisfied that this will not prejudice your independence as an advocate, or litigator, or the interests of your *clients* or the interests of justice.

Acting in the following way(s) may tend to show that you have not achieved these outcomes and therefore not complied with the *Principles*:

IB(5.7) constructing facts supporting your *client's* case or drafting any documents relating to any proceedings containing:

    (a) any contention which you do not consider to be properly arguable; or

    (b) any allegation of fraud, unless you are instructed to do so and you have material which you reasonably believe shows, on the face of it, a case of fraud;

IB(5.8) suggesting that any *person* is guilty of a crime, fraud or misconduct unless such allegations:

    (a) go to a matter in issue which is material to your own *client's* case; and

    (b) appear to you to be supported by reasonable grounds;

IB(5.9) calling a witness whose evidence you know is untrue;

IB(5.10) attempting to influence a witness, when taking a statement from that witness, with regard to the contents of their statement;

IB(5.11) tampering with evidence or seeking to persuade a witness to change their evidence;

IB(5.12) when acting as an advocate, naming in open *court* any third party whose character would thereby be called into question, unless it is necessary for the proper conduct of the case;

IB(5.13) when acting as an advocate, calling into question the character of a witness you have cross-examined unless the witness has had the opportunity to answer the allegations during cross-examination.

In-house practice

The outcomes in this chapter apply to your *in-house practice*.

Notes

(i) If you are a litigator or an advocate there may be occasions when your obligation to act in the best interests of a *client* may conflict with your duty to the *court*. In such situations you may need to consider whether the public interest is best served by the proper administration of justice and should take precedence over the interests of your *client*.

Chapter 6: Your client and introductions to third parties

There may be circumstances in which you wish to refer your *clients* to third parties, perhaps to another *lawyer* or a financial services provider. This chapter describes the conduct duties which arise in respect of such introductions. It is important that you retain your independence when recommending third parties to your *client* and that you act in the *client's* best interests.

The outcomes in this chapter show how the *Principles* apply in the context of your *client* and introductions to third parties.

Outcomes

You must achieve these outcomes:

O(6.1)   whenever you recommend that a *client* uses a particular *person* or business, your recommendation is in the best interests of the *client* and does not compromise your independence;

O(6.2)   *clients* are fully informed of any financial or other interest which you have in referring the *client* to another *person* or business;

O(6.3)   *clients* are in a position to make informed decisions about how to pursue their matter;

O(6.4)   you are not *paid* a *prohibited referral fee*.

Indicative behaviours

Acting in the following way(s) may tend to show that you have achieved these outcomes and therefore complied with the *Principles*:

IB(6.1)   any *arrangement* you enter into in respect of *regulated mortgage contracts*, *general insurance contracts* (including after the event insurance) or *pure protection contracts*, provides that referrals will only be made where this is in the best interests of the particular *client* and the contract is suitable for the needs of that *client*;

IB(6.2)   any referral to a third party that can only offer products from one source is made only after the *client* has been informed of this limitation;

IB(6.3) having effective systems in place for assessing whether any *arrangement* complies with the statutory and regulatory requirements;

IB(6.4) retaining records and management information to enable you to demonstrate that any *payments* you receive are not *prohibited referral fees*.

Acting in the following way(s) may tend to show that you have not achieved these outcomes and therefore not complied with the *Principles*:

IB(6.5) entering into any *arrangement* which restricts your freedom to recommend any particular business, except in respect of *regulated mortgage contracts*, *general insurance contracts* or *pure protection contracts*;

IB(6.6) being an *appointed representative*.

In-house practice

The outcomes in this chapter apply to your *in-house practice*.

Notes

(i) See Outcome 1.15, in relation to *financial benefits* that you may receive in respect of introductions to third parties.

(ii) If the introduction is in connection with the provision of financial services, and your *firm* is not authorised by the Financial Conduct Authority, you will need to comply with the SRA Financial Services (Scope) Rules 2001 and the SRA Financial Services (Conduct of Business) Rules 2001. Where an introduction is not a *regulated activity* because you can rely on an exclusion in the *Regulated Activities Order*, you will need nevertheless to consider Outcome 1.15.

(iii) This chapter should be read in conjunction with Chapter 12 (Separate businesses).

2ND SECTION: YOU AND YOUR BUSINESS

Chapter 7: Management of your business

This chapter is about the management and supervision of your *firm* or *in-house practice*.

Everyone has a role to play in the efficient running of a business, although of course that role will depend on the individual's position within the organisation. However, over-arching responsibility for the management of the business in the broadest sense rests with the *manager(s)*. The *manager(s)* should determine what arrangements are appropriate to meet the outcomes. Factors to be taken into account will include the size and complexity of the business; the number, experience and qualifications of the *employees*; the number of offices; and the nature of the work undertaken.

Where you are using a third party to provide services that you could provide, (often described as "outsourcing"), this chapter sets out the outcomes you need to achieve.

The outcomes in this chapter show how the *Principles* apply in the context of the management of your business.

Outcomes

You must achieve these outcomes:

O(7.1)   you have a clear and effective governance structure and reporting lines;

O(7.2)   you have effective systems and controls in place to achieve and comply with all the *Principles*, rules and outcomes and other requirements of the Handbook, where applicable;

O(7.3)   you identify, monitor and manage risks to compliance with all the *Principles*, rules and outcomes and other requirements of the Handbook, if applicable to you, and take steps to address issues identified;

O(7.4)   you maintain systems and controls for monitoring the financial stability of your *firm* and risks to money and *assets* entrusted to you by *clients* and others, and you take steps to address issues identified;

O(7.5)   you comply with legislation applicable to your business, including anti-money laundering and data protection legislation;

O(7.6)   you train individuals working in the *firm* to maintain a level of competence appropriate to their work and level of responsibility;

O(7.7)   you comply with the statutory requirements for the direction and supervision of *reserved legal activities* and *immigration work*;

O(7.8)   you have a system for supervising *clients'* matters, to include the regular checking of the quality of work by suitably competent and experienced people;

O(7.9)   you do not outsource *reserved legal activities* to a *person* who is not authorised to conduct such activities;

O(7.10)   subject to Outcome 7.9, where you outsource *legal activities* or any operational functions that are critical to the delivery of any *legal activities*, you ensure such outsourcing:

(a)   does not adversely affect your ability to comply with, or the *SRA's* ability to monitor your compliance with, your obligations in the Handbook;

(b)   is subject to contractual arrangements that enable the *SRA* or its agent to obtain information from, inspect the records (including electronic records) of, or enter the premises of, the third party, in relation to the outsourced activities or functions;

(c)   does not alter your obligations towards your *clients*; and

(d) does not cause you to breach the conditions with which you must comply in order to be authorised and to remain so;

O(7.11) you identify, monitor and manage the compliance of your *overseas practices* with the SRA Overseas Rules;

O(7.12) you identify, monitor and manage all risks to your business which may arise from your *connected practices*.

Indicative behaviours

Acting in the following way(s) may tend to show that you have achieved these outcomes and therefore complied with the *Principles*:

IB(7.1) safekeeping of documents and *assets* entrusted to the *firm*;

IB(7.2) controlling budgets, expenditure and cash flow;

IB(7.3) identifying and monitoring financial, operational and business continuity risks including *complaints*, credit risks and exposure, claims under legislation relating to matters such as data protection, IT failures and abuses, and damage to offices;

IB(7.4) making arrangements for the continuation of your *firm* in the event of absences and emergencies, for example holiday or sick leave, with the minimum interruption to *clients'* business;

IB(7.5) you maintain systems and controls for managing the risks posed by any financial inter-dependence which exists with your *connected practices*;

IB(7.6) you take appropriate action to control the use of your brand by any body or individual outside of England and Wales which is not an *overseas practice*.

In-house practice

Outcomes 7.5 and 7.7 apply to your *in-house practice*.

Outcomes 7.1 to 7.3, and 7.6 and 7.8 to 7.10 apply to you if you have management responsibilities.

Notes

(i) All of the chapters in the Code will be relevant to the management of your business, in particular those which require you to have systems and controls in place.

(ii) This chapter should also be read with the *SRA Authorisation Rules*, the SRA Financial Services (Conduct of Business) Rules 2001 and the *SRA Indemnity Insurance Rules*.

Chapter 8: Publicity

This chapter is about the manner in which you publicise your *firm* or *in-house practice* or any other businesses. The overriding concern is that *publicity* is not misleading and is sufficiently informative to ensure that *clients* and others can make informed choices.

In your *publicity*, you must comply with statutory requirements and have regard to voluntary codes.

The outcomes in this chapter show how the *Principles* apply in the context of *publicity*.

Outcomes

You must achieve these outcomes:

O(8.1)   your *publicity* in relation to your *firm* or *in-house practice* or for any other business is accurate and not misleading, and is not likely to diminish the trust the public places in you and in the provision of legal services;

O(8.2)   your *publicity* relating to charges is clearly expressed and identifies whether VAT and *disbursements* are included;

O(8.3)   you do not make unsolicited approaches in person or by telephone to *members of the public* in order to publicise your *firm* or *in-house practice* or another business;

O(8.4)   *clients* and the public have appropriate information about you, your *firm* and how you are regulated;

O(8.5)   your letterhead, website and e-mails show the words "authorised and regulated by the Solicitors Regulation Authority" and either the *firm's* registered name and number if it is an *LLP* or *company* or, if the *firm* is a *partnership* or *sole practitioner*, the name under which it is licensed/authorised by the *SRA* and the number allocated to it by the *SRA*.

Indicative behaviours

Acting in the following way(s) may tend to show that you have achieved these outcomes and therefore complied with the *Principles*:

IB(8.1)   where you conduct other regulated activities your *publicity* discloses the manner in which you are regulated in relation to those activities;

IB(8.2)   where your *firm* is an *MDP*, any *publicity* in relation to that *practice* makes clear which services are regulated legal services and which are not;

IB(8.3)   any *publicity* intended for a jurisdiction outside England and Wales complies with the *Principles*, voluntary codes and the rules in force in that jurisdiction concerning *publicity*;

IB(8.4)   where you and another business jointly market services, the nature of the services provided by each business is clear.

Acting in the following way(s) may tend to show that you have not achieved these outcomes and therefore not complied with the *Principles*:

IB(8.5) approaching people in the street, at ports of entry, in hospital or at the scene of an accident; including approaching people to conduct a survey which involves collecting contact details of potential *clients*, or otherwise promotes your *firm* or *in-house practice*;

IB(8.6) allowing any other *person* to conduct *publicity* for your *firm* or *in-house practice* in a way that would breach the *Principles*;

IB(8.7) advertising an estimated fee which is pitched at an unrealistically low level;

IB(8.8) describing overheads of your *firm* (such a normal postage, telephone calls and charges arising in respect of *client* due diligence under the Money Laundering Regulations 2007) as *disbursements* in your advertisements;

IB(8.9) advertising an estimated or fixed fee without making it clear that additional charges may be payable, if that is the case;

IB(8.10) using a name or description of your *firm* or *in-house practice* that includes the word "solicitor(s)" if none of the *managers* are *solicitors*;

IB(8.11) advertising your *firm* or *in-house practice* in a way that suggests that services provided by another business are provided by your *firm* or *in-house practice*;

IB(8.12) producing misleading information concerning the professional status of any *manager* or *employee* of your *firm* or *in-house practice*.

In-house practice

Outcomes 8.1 to 8.4 apply to your *in-house practice* unless it is clear from the context that the outcome is not relevant in your particular circumstances.

Notes

(i) This chapter should be read in conjunction with Chapters 1 and 9.

Chapter 9: Fee sharing and referrals

This chapter is about protecting *clients'* interests where you have *arrangements* with third parties who introduce business to you and/or with whom you share your fees. The relationship between *clients* and *firms* should be built on trust, and any such *arrangement* should not jeopardise that trust by, for example, compromising your independence or professional judgement.

The outcomes in this chapter show how the *Principles* apply in the context of fee sharing and *referrals*.

Outcomes

You must achieve these outcomes:

O(9.1)   your independence and your professional judgement are not prejudiced by virtue of any *arrangement* with another *person*;

O(9.2)   your *clients'* interests are protected regardless of the interests of an *introducer* or *fee sharer* or your interest in receiving *referrals*;

O(9.3)   *clients* are in a position to make informed decisions about how to pursue their matter;

O(9.4)   *clients* are informed of any financial or other interest which an *introducer* has in referring the *client* to you;

O(9.5)   *clients* are informed of any fee sharing *arrangement* that is relevant to their matter;

O(9.6)   you do not make payments to an *introducer* in respect of *clients* who are the subject of criminal proceedings or who have the benefit of public funding;

O(9.7)   where you enter into a financial *arrangement* with an *introducer* you ensure that the agreement is in writing;

O(9.8)   you do not *pay* a *prohibited referral fee*.

Indicative behaviours

Acting in the following way(s) may tend to show that you have achieved these outcomes and therefore complied with the *Principles*:

IB(9.1)   only entering into *arrangements* with reputable third parties and monitoring the outcome of those *arrangements* to ensure that *clients* are treated fairly;

IB(9.2)   in any case where a *client* has entered into, or is proposing to enter into, an *arrangement* with an *introducer* in connection with their matter, which is not in their best interests, advising the *client* that this is the case;

IB(9.3)   terminating any *arrangement* with an *introducer* or *fee sharer* which is causing you to breach the *Principles* or any requirements of the Code;

IB(9.4)   being satisfied that any *client* referred by an *introducer* has not been acquired as a result of marketing or other activities which, if done by a *person* regulated by the *SRA*, would be contrary to the *Principles* or any requirements of the Code;

IB(9.5)   drawing the *client's* attention to any payments you make, or other consideration you provide, in connection with any *referral*;

IB(9.6)   where information needs to be given to a *client*, ensuring the information is clear and in writing or in a form appropriate to the *client's* needs;

IB(9.7)   having effective systems in place for assessing whether any *arrangement* complies with statutory and regulatory requirements;

IB(9.8)   ensuring that any *payments* you make for services, such as marketing, do not amount to the *payment* of *prohibited referral fees*;

IB(9.9)   retaining records and management information to enable you to demonstrate that any *payments* you make are not *prohibited referral fees*.

Acting in the following way(s) may tend to show that you have not achieved these outcomes and therefore not complied with the *Principles*:

IB(9.10)   entering into any type of business relationship with a third party, such as an unauthorised *partnership*, which places you in breach of the *SRA Authorisation Rules* or any other regulatory requirements in the Handbook;

IB(9.11)   allowing an *introducer* or *fee sharer* to influence the advice you give to *clients*;

IB(9.12)   accepting *referrals* where you have reason to believe that *clients* have been pressurised or misled into instructing you.

In-house practice

Outcomes 9.1 to 9.3 apply to your *in-house practice*.

Outcomes 9.4 to 9.8 apply unless it is clear from the context that the outcome is not relevant to your particular circumstances.

Notes

(i)   This chapter should be read in conjunction with:

(a)   Chapter 1 (Client care)

(b)   Chapter 4 (Confidentiality and disclosure)

(c)   Chapter 8 (Publicity)

(d)   The *SRA Authorisation Rules*

(e)   The *SRA European Cross-Border Practice Rules*

3RD SECTION: YOU AND YOUR REGULATOR

Chapter 10: You and your regulator

This chapter is about co-operation with your regulators and ombudsmen, primarily the *SRA* and the *Legal Ombudsman*.

The information which we request from you will help us understand any risks to *clients*, and the public interest more generally.

The outcomes in this chapter show how the *Principles* apply in the context of you and your regulator.

Outcomes

You must achieve these outcomes:

O(10.1) you ensure that you comply with all the reporting and notification requirements in the Handbook that apply to you;

O(10.2) you provide the *SRA* with information to enable the *SRA* to decide upon any application you make, such as for a practising certificate, registration, recognition or a licence and whether any conditions should apply;

O(10.3) you notify the *SRA* promptly of any material changes to relevant information about you including serious financial difficulty, action taken against you by another regulator and serious failure to comply with or achieve the *Principles*, rules, outcomes and other requirements of the Handbook;

O(10.4) you report to the *SRA* promptly, serious misconduct by any person or *firm* authorised by the *SRA*, or any *employee*, *manager* or *owner* of any such *firm* (taking into account, where necessary, your duty of confidentiality to your *client*);

O(10.5) you ensure that the *SRA* is in a position to assess whether any persons requiring prior approval are fit and proper at the point of approval and remain so;

O(10.6) you co-operate fully with the *SRA* and the *Legal Ombudsman* at all times including in relation to any investigation about a *claim for redress* against you;

O(10.7) you do not attempt to prevent anyone from providing information to the *SRA* or the *Legal Ombudsman*;

O(10.8) you comply promptly with any written notice from the *SRA*;

O(10.9) pursuant to a notice under Outcome 10.8, you:

(a) produce for inspection by the *SRA documents* held by you, or held under your control;

(b) provide all information and explanations requested; and

(c) comply with all requests from the *SRA* as to the form in which you produce any *documents* you hold electronically, and for photocopies of any *documents* to take away;

in connection with your *practice* or in connection with any trust of which you are, or formerly were, a trustee;

O(10.10) you provide any necessary permissions for information to be given, so as to enable the *SRA* to:

(a) prepare a report on any *documents* produced; and

(b) seek verification from *clients*, staff and the banks, building societies or other financial institutions used by you;

O(10.11) when required by the *SRA* in relation to a matter specified by the *SRA*, you:

(a) act promptly to investigate whether any *person* may have a *claim for redress* against you;

(b) provide the *SRA* with a report on the outcome of such an investigation, identifying *persons* who may have such a claim;

(c) notify *persons* that they may have a right of redress against you, providing them with information as to the nature of the possible claim, about the *firm's complaints* procedure and about the *Legal Ombudsman*; and

(d) ensure, where you have identified a *person* who may have a *claim for redress*, that the matter is dealt with under the *firm's complaints* procedure as if that *person* had made a *complaint*;

O(10.12) you do not attempt to abrogate to any third party your regulatory responsibilities in the Handbook, including the role of Compliance Officer for Legal Practice (*COLP*) or Compliance Officer for Finance and Administration (*COFA*);

O(10.13) once you are aware that your *firm* will cease to *practise*, you effect the orderly and transparent wind-down of activities, including informing the *SRA* before the *firm* closes.

Indicative behaviours

Acting in the following way(s) may tend to show that you have achieved these outcomes and therefore complied with the *Principles*:

IB(10.1) actively monitoring your achievement of the outcomes in order to improve standards and identify non-achievement of the outcomes;

IB(10.2) actively monitoring your financial stability and viability in order to identify and mitigate any risks to the public;

IB(10.3) notifying the *SRA* promptly of any indicators of serious financial difficulty, such as inability to pay your professional indemnity insurance premium, or rent or salaries, or breach of bank covenants;

IB(10.4) notifying the *SRA* promptly when you become aware that your business may not be financially viable to continue trading as a going concern, for example because of difficult trading conditions, poor cash flow, increasing overheads, loss of *managers* or *employees* and/or loss of sources of revenue;

IB(10.5)   notifying the *SRA* of any serious issues identified as a result of monitoring referred to in IB10.1 and IB10.2 above, and producing a plan for remedying issues that have been identified;

IB(10.6)   responding appropriately to any serious issues identified concerning competence and fitness and propriety of your *employees*, *managers* and *owners*;

IB(10.7)   reporting disciplinary action taken against you by another regulator;

IB(10.8)   informing the *SRA* promptly when you become aware of a significant change to your *firm*, for example:

 (a)   key personnel, such as a *manager*, *COLP* or *COFA*, joining or leaving the *firm*;

 (b)   a merger with, or an acquisition by or of, another *firm*;

IB(10.9)   having appropriate arrangements for the orderly transfer of *clients'* property to another *authorised body* if your *firm* closes;

IB(10.10)   having a "whistle-blowing" policy.

Acting in the following way(s) may tend to show that you have not achieved these outcomes and therefore not complied with the *Principles*:

IB(10.11)   entering into an agreement which would attempt to preclude the *SRA* or the *Legal Ombudsman* from investigating any actual or potential *complaint* or allegation of professional misconduct;

IB(10.12)   unless you can properly allege malice, issuing defamation proceedings in respect of a *complaint* to the *SRA*.

In-house practice

The outcomes in this chapter apply to your *in-house practice*.

 Notes

 (i)   A notice under this chapter is deemed to be duly served:

  (a)   on the date on which it is delivered to or left at your last notified *practising* address;

  (b)   on the date on which it is sent electronically to your e-mail or fax address; or

  (c)   seven days after it has been sent by post or document exchange to your last notified *practising* address.

 (ii)   The outcomes in this chapter should be considered in conjunction with the following:

  (a)   Chapter 7 (Management of your business) – requirements for risk management procedures; and

(b) note (xv) to Rule 8 of the *SRA Authorisation Rules*.

4TH SECTION: YOU AND OTHERS

Chapter 11: Relations with third parties

This chapter is about ensuring you do not take unfair advantage of those you deal with and that you act in a manner which promotes the proper operation of the legal system.

This includes your conduct in relation to *undertakings*; there is no obligation to give or receive an *undertaking* on behalf of a *client* but, if you do, you must ensure that you achieve the outcomes listed in this chapter.

The conduct requirements in this area extend beyond professional and business matters. They apply in any circumstances in which you may use your professional title to advance your personal interests.

The outcomes in this chapter show how the *Principles* apply in the context of your relations with third parties.

Outcomes

You must achieve these outcomes:

O(11.1) you do not take unfair advantage of third parties in either your professional or personal capacity;

O(11.2) you perform all *undertakings* given by you within an agreed timescale or within a reasonable amount of time;

O(11.3) where you act for a seller of land, you inform all buyers immediately of the seller's intention to deal with more than one buyer;

O(11.4) you properly administer oaths, affirmations or declarations where you are authorised to do so.

Indicative behaviours

Acting in the following way(s) may tend to show that you have achieved these outcomes and therefore complied with the *Principles*:

IB(11.1) providing sufficient time and information to enable the costs in any matter to be agreed;

IB(11.2) returning documents or money sent subject to an express condition if you are unable to comply with that condition;

IB(11.3) returning documents or money on demand if they are sent on condition that they are held to the sender's order;

IB(11.4) ensuring that you do not communicate with another party when you are aware that the other party has retained a *lawyer* in a matter, except:

(a) to request the name and address of the other party's *lawyer*; or

(b) the other party's *lawyer* consents to you communicating with the *client*; or

(c) where there are exceptional circumstances;

IB(11.5) maintaining an effective system which records when *undertakings* have been given and when they have been discharged;

IB(11.6) where an *undertaking* is given which is dependent upon the happening of a future event and it becomes apparent the future event will not occur, notifying the recipient of this.

Acting in the following way(s) may tend to show that you have not achieved these outcomes and therefore not complied with the *Principles*:

IB(11.7) taking unfair advantage of an opposing party's lack of legal knowledge where they have not instructed a *lawyer*;

IB(11.8) demanding anything for yourself or on behalf of your *client*, that is not legally recoverable, such as when you are instructed to collect a simple debt, demanding from the debtor the cost of the letter of claim since it cannot be said at that stage that such a cost is legally recoverable;

IB(11.9) using your professional status or qualification to take unfair advantage of another *person* in order to advance your personal interests;

IB(11.10) taking unfair advantage of a public office held by you, or a member of your family, or a member of your *firm* or their family.

In-house practice

The outcomes in this chapter apply to your *in-house practice*.

Notes

(i) This chapter should be read in conjunction with Chapter 7 (Management of your business) in relation to the system you will need to have in place to control *undertakings*.

Chapter 12: Separate businesses

The purpose of this chapter is to ensure *clients* are protected when they obtain mainstream legal services from a *firm* regulated by the *SRA*. This is accomplished by restricting the services that can be provided through a *separate business* that is not authorised by the *SRA* or another *approved regulator*.

This chapter addresses two kinds of services:

1. those which you cannot offer through a *separate business* ("*prohibited separate business activities*"). These are "mainstream" legal services which members of the public would expect you to offer as a *lawyer* regulated by the *SRA* or another *approved regulator*; and

2. those which you can offer either through a *separate business* ("a *permitted separate business*"), or through an *authorised body*. These are the kind of services a member of the public would not necessarily expect to be provided only by a *lawyer* regulated by the *SRA* or another *approved regulator*, but which are "solicitor-like" services.

Clients of a *permitted separate business* will not have the same statutory protections as *clients* of an *authorised body* and it is important that this is clear to *clients* of the *separate business*, particularly where they are being referred from one business to the other.

The outcomes in this chapter show how the *Principles* apply in the context of *separate businesses*.

Outcomes

You must achieve these outcomes:

O(12.1)   you do not:

    (a)   *own*; or

    (b)   *actively participate in*,

a *separate business* which conducts *prohibited separate business activities*;

O(12.2)   if you are a *firm* you are not:

    (a)   *owned by*; or

    (b)   *connected with*,

a *separate business* which conducts *prohibited separate business activities*;

O(12.3)   where you:

    (a)   *actively participate in*;

    (b)   *own*; or

    (c)   are a *firm* and *owned by* or *connected with*,

a *permitted separate business*, you have safeguards in place to ensure that *clients* are not misled about the extent to which the services that you and the *separate business* offer are regulated;

O(12.4)   you do not represent any *permitted separate business* as being regulated by the *SRA* or any of its activities as being provided by an individual who is regulated by the *SRA*;

O(12.5)   you are only *connected with* reputable *separate businesses*;

O(12.6) you are only *connected with* a *permitted separate business* which is an *appointed representative* if it is an *appointed representative* of an *independent financial adviser*.

Indicative behaviours

Acting in the following way(s) may tend to show that you have achieved these outcomes and therefore complied with the *Principles*:

IB(12.1) ensuring that *client* information and records are not disclosed to the *permitted separate business*, without the express consent of the *client*;

IB(12.2) complying with the *SRA Accounts Rules* and not allowing the *client account* to be used to hold money for the *permitted separate business*;

IB(12.3) where you are referring a *client* to a *permitted separate business*, informing the *client* of your interest in the *separate business*;

IB(12.4) terminating any connection with a *permitted separate business* where you have reason to doubt the integrity or competence of that *separate business*.

In-house practice

Outcomes 12.1 and 12.3 to 12.6 in this chapter apply to your *in-house practice*.

Notes

(i) It is important that *clients* are not misled or confused about the regulatory status of a *permitted separate business*, the services it provides and the people working within it. Particular care needs to be taken regarding:

(a) the name or branding of the *separate business*;

(b) misleading *publicity*; and

(c) the proximity of the *permitted separate business* to your *firm*, particularly if you share premises.

(ii) This chapter should be read in conjunction with:

(a) Chapter 3 (Conflicts of interests)

(b) Chapter 6 (Your client and introductions to third parties); and

(c) Chapter 8 (Publicity).

5TH SECTION: APPLICATION, WAIVERS AND INTERPRETATION

Chapter 13: Application and waivers provisions

The SRA Code of Conduct applies to you in the following circumstances (and "you" must be construed accordingly):

Application of the SRA Code of Conduct in England and Wales

13.1   Subject to paragraphs 13.2 and 13.7 to 13.11 below and any other provisions in this Code, this Code applies to you, in relation to your activities carried out from an office in England and Wales, if you are:

    (a) a *solicitor*, *REL* or *RFL*, and you are *practising* as such, whether or not the entity through which you *practise* is subject to this Code;

    (b) a *solicitor*, *REL* or *RFL* who is:

        (i)   a *manager*, *employee* or *owner* of a body which should be a *recognised body*, but has not been recognised by the *SRA*;

        (ii) a *manager*, *employee* or *owner* of a body that is a *manager* or *owner* of a body that should be a *recognised body*, but has not been recognised by the *SRA*;

        (iii) an *employee* of a *sole practitioner* who should be a *recognised sole practitioner*, but has not been recognised by the *SRA*;

        (iv) an *owner* of an *authorised body* or a body which should be a *recognised body* but has not been recognised by the *SRA*, even if you undertake no work for the body's *clients*; or

        (v)   a *manager* or *employee* of an *authorised non-SRA firm*, or a *manager* of a body which is a *manager* of an *authorised non-SRA firm*, when doing work of a sort authorised by the *SRA*, for that firm;

    (c) an *authorised body*, or a body which should be a *recognised body* but has not been recognised by the *SRA*;

    (d) any other person who is a *manager* or *employee* of an *authorised body*, or of a body which should be a *recognised body* but has not been recognised by the *SRA*;

    (e) any other person who is an *employee* of a *recognised sole practitioner*, or of a *sole practitioner* who should be a *recognised sole practitioner* but has not been recognised by the *SRA*;

and "you" includes "your" as appropriate.

13.2   Chapters 10, 12, 13, 14 and 15 of the Code apply to you if you are a *solicitor*, *REL* or *RFL* and you are:

    (a) *practising* as a *manager* or *employee* of an *authorised non-SRA firm* when doing work of a sort authorised by the *authorised non-SRA firm's approved regulator*; or

    (b) an *owner* of an *authorised non-SRA firm* even if you undertake no work for the body's *clients*.

Application of the SRA Code of Conduct in relation to practice from an office outside England and Wales

13.3 [Deleted]

13.4 [Deleted]

13.5 [Deleted]

13.6 [Deleted]

Application of the SRA Code of Conduct outside practice

13.7 In relation to activities which fall outside *practice*, whether undertaken as a *lawyer* or in some other business or private capacity, the following apply to you if you are a *solicitor*, or *REL*:

(a) Outcome 11.1; and

(b) Outcome 11.2.

General Provisions

13.8 The extent to which you are expected to implement the requirements of the Code will depend on your role in the *firm*, or your way of *practising*. For example, those who are managing the business will be expected to have more influence on how the *firm* or business is run than those *practising* in-house but not managing a legal department, or those *practising* as *employees* of a *firm*.

13.9 You must deliver all outcomes which are relevant to you and your situation.

13.10 Where in accordance with this chapter, the requirements of the Code apply to a *licensed body*, this Code applies to the *regulated activities* carried on by the body.

13.11 Where the *licensed body* is an *MDP*, the Code applies to the body, any *solicitor*, *REL* or *RFL* who is a *manager*, *employee* or *owner* of the body and any other person who is a *manager* or *employee* of the body as follows:

(a) in relation to any *regulated activities*; and

(b) in relation to any other *non-reserved legal activities*:

(i) outcomes 1.7, 1.9 to 1.11 and 10.6 apply to the body; and

(ii) outcomes 1.7, 1.9 to 1.11, chapters 4, 10, 11 and 13 to 15, apply to a *solicitor*, *REL* or *RFL* who is a *manager*, *employee* or *owner* of the body.

Waivers

In any particular case or cases the *SRA* Board shall have the power, in exceptional circumstances, to waive in writing the provisions of these outcomes for a particular purpose or purposes expressed in such waiver, to place conditions on and to revoke such a waiver.

Chapter 13A: Practice Overseas

13A.1   If you are an individual or body *practising overseas*, the Code does not apply to you, but you must comply with the SRA Overseas Rules.

13A.2   However, if the following circumstances apply then you must comply with the provisions of the Code that are applicable to you as set out in 13A.3 to 13.A.6 below:

  (a)   a body practising from an office outside England and Wales, only if you are required to be an *authorised body* as a result of the nature of your practice and you have been authorised by the *SRA* accordingly;

  (b)   a *manager* of such a body; or

  (c)   an individual engaged in *temporary practice overseas*;

  (d)   a *regulated individual practising overseas* who is providing *reserved legal activities* to clients in England and Wales on an occasional basis, in accordance with rule 2(e)(i) of the *SRA Overseas Rules*.

13A.3   The following provisions of the Code apply:

  (a)   chapter 3 (conflicts of interests);

  (b)   chapter 4 (confidentiality and disclosure);

  (c)   chapter 5 (your client and the court), to the extent that your practice relates to litigation or advocacy conducted before a court, tribunal or enquiry in England and Wales or a British court martial;

  (d)   outcomes 6.1 to 6.3 (your client and introductions to third parties);

  (e)   chapter 7 (management of your business);

  (f)   outcomes 8.1 and 8.4 (publicity);

  (g)   outcomes 9.1 to 9.7 (fee sharing and referrals), except where they conflict with the *SRA European Cross-Border Practice Rules*, in which case the latter will prevail;

  (h)   chapter 10 (you and your regulator);

  (i)   chapter 11 (relations with third parties), except that Outcome 11.3 only applies if the land in question is situated in England and Wales; and

  (j)   outcomes 12.3 to 12.6 (separate businesses).

13A.4   In addition, you must meet the following outcomes:

O(**13A.1**) you properly account to your *clients* for any *financial benefit* you receive as a result of your instructions unless it is the prevailing custom of your local jurisdiction to deal with *financial benefits* in a different way;

O(**13A.2**) *clients* have the benefit of insurance or other indemnity in relation to professional liabilities which takes account of:

(a) the nature and extent of the risks you incur in your practice overseas;

(b) the local conditions in the jurisdiction in which you are *practising*; and

(c) the terms upon which insurance is available;

and you have not attempted to exclude liability below the minimum level required for practice in the local jurisdiction;

O(**13A.3**) you do not enter into unlawful contingency fee arrangements;

O(**13A.4**) you do not discriminate unlawfully according to the jurisdiction in which you are practising; and

O(**13A.5**) publicity intended for a jurisdiction outside England and Wales must comply with any applicable law or rules regarding lawyers' publicity in the jurisdiction in which your office is based and the jurisdiction for which the publicity is intended.

13A.5   you must be aware of the local laws and regulations governing your practice in an overseas jurisdiction;

13A.6   if compliance with any outcome in the Code would result in your breaching local laws or regulations you may disregard that outcome to the extent necessary to comply with that local law or regulation.

Chapter 14: Interpretation

14.1   The SRA Handbook Glossary 2012 shall apply and, unless the context otherwise requires:

(a) all italicised terms shall be defined; and

(b) all terms shall be interpreted,

in accordance with the *Glossary*.

Chapter 15: Transitional provisions

15.1   For the avoidance of doubt, where a breach of any provision of the Solicitors' Code of Conduct 2007 comes to the attention of the *SRA* after 6 October 2011, this shall be subject to action by the *SRA* notwithstanding any repeal of the relevant provision.

15.2   The SRA Code of Conduct shall not apply to *licensed bodies* until such time as the *Society* is designated as a *licensing authority* under Part 1 of Schedule 10 to the *LSA* and all definitions shall be construed accordingly.

Code of Conduct

15.3   References:

    (a) in the preamble, to:

        (i)   the Code being made under section 83 of the Legal Services Act 2007, and

        (ii) licensed bodies and their managers and employees, and

    (b) in Chapter 10, to:

        (i)   an application for a licence (O(10.2)), and

        (ii) the role of *COLP* and *COFA* (O(10.12) and IB(10.8)),

shall have no effect until such time as the *Society* is designated as a *licensing authority* under Part 1 to Schedule 10 of the *LSA*.

15.4   In Chapter 8, the provision in IB(8.2) relating to multi-disciplinary practices, shall have no effect until such time as the *Society* is designated as a *licensing authority* under Part 1 of Schedule 10 to the *LSA*.

[D] Accounts Rules

SRA Accounts Rules 2011

PREAMBLE

Authority: made by the Solicitors Regulation Authority Board under sections 32, 33A, 34, 37, 79 and 80 of the Solicitors Act 1974, section 9 of the Administration of Justice Act 1985, section 83(5)(h) of, and paragraph 20 of Schedule 11 to, the Legal Services Act 2007 with the approval of the Legal Services Board;

date: 6 October 2011;

replacing: the Solicitors' Accounts Rules 1998;

regulating: the accounts of solicitors and their employees, registered European lawyers and their employees, registered foreign lawyers, recognised bodies and their managers and employees, and licensed bodies and their managers and employees, in respect of practice in England and Wales; and

regulating: the accounts of solicitors, lawyer-controlled bodies and their managers, lawyers of England and Wales who are managers of overseas law firms controlled by lawyers of England and Wales, solicitors who are named trustees, and managers of a lawyer-controlled body who are named trustees, in respect of practice outside the UK; and

regulating: the accounts of solicitors and registered European lawyers, lawyer-controlled and registered European lawyer-controlled bodies and their managers, lawyer of England and Wales and registered European lawyer managers of overseas law firms controlled by lawyers of England and Wales and/or registered European lawyers, solicitors and registered European lawyers who are named trustees, and managers of a lawyer-controlled body or a registered European lawyer-controlled body who are named trustees, in respect of practice from Scotland or Northern Ireland.

For the definition of words in italics in Parts 1–6, see rule 2 – Interpretation. For the definition of words in italics in Part 7 see rule 48 – Application and Interpretation (overseas provisions).

INTRODUCTION

The Principles set out in the Handbook apply to all aspects of practice, including the handling of client money. Those which are particularly relevant to these rules are that you must:

* protect client money and assets;

* act with integrity;

* behave in a way that maintains the trust the public places in you and in the provision of legal services;

- comply with your legal and regulatory obligations and deal with your regulators and ombudsmen in an open, timely and co-operative manner; and

- run your business or carry out your role in the business effectively and in accordance with proper governance and sound financial and risk management principles.

The desired outcomes which apply to these rules are that:

- client money is safe;

- clients and the public have confidence that client money held by firms will be safe;

- firms are managed in such a way, and with appropriate systems and procedures in place, so as to safeguard client money;

- client accounts are used for appropriate purposes only; and

- the SRA is aware of issues in a firm relevant to the protection of client money.

Underlying principles which are specific to the accounts rules are set out in rule 1 below.

These rules apply to all those who carry on or work in a firm and to the firm itself (see rules 4 and 5). In relation to a multi-disciplinary practice, the rules apply only in respect of those activities for which the practice is regulated by the SRA, and are concerned only with money handled by the practice which relates to those regulated activities.

PART 1: GENERAL

Rule 1: The overarching objective and underlying principles

1.1   The purpose of these rules is to keep *client money* safe. This aim must always be borne in mind in the application of these rules.

1.2   *You* must comply with the Principles set out in the Handbook, and the outcomes in Chapter 7 of the *SRA Code of Conduct* in relation to the effective financial management of the *firm*, and in particular must:

(a) keep other people's money separate from money belonging to *you* or *your firm*;

(b) keep other people's money safely in a *bank* or *building society* account identifiable as a *client account* (except when the rules specifically provide otherwise);

(c) use each *client's* money for that *client's* matters only;

(d) use money held as *trustee* of a *trust* for the purposes of that *trust* only;

(e) establish and maintain proper accounting systems, and proper internal controls over those systems, to ensure compliance with the rules;

(f) keep proper accounting records to show accurately the position with regard to the money held for each *client* and *trust*;

(g) account for *interest* on other people's money in accordance with the rules;

(h)   co-operate with the *SRA* in checking compliance with the rules; and

(i)   deliver annual accountant's reports as required by the rules.

Rule 2: Interpretation

2.1   The guidance notes do not form part of the rules.

2.2   The SRA Handbook Glossary 2012 shall apply and, unless the context otherwise requires:

(a)   all italicised terms shall be defined; and

(b)   all terms shall be interpreted,

in accordance with the *Glossary*.

2.3   References to the Legal Aid Agency are to be read, where appropriate, as including the Legal Services Commission.

Guidance notes

(i)   The effect of the definition of "you" is that the rules apply equally to all those who carry on or work in a firm and to the firm itself. See also rule 4 (persons governed by the rules) and rule 5 (persons exempt from the rules).

(ii)   The general definition of "office account" is wide. However, rule 17.1(b) (receipt and transfer of costs) and rule 19.1(b) and 19.2(b) (payments from the Legal Aid Agency) specify that certain money is to be placed in an office account at a bank or building society. Out-of-scope money can be held in an office account (which could be an account regulated by another regulator); it must not be held in a client account.

(iii)   For a flowchart summarising the effect of the rules, see Appendix 1. For more details of the treatment of different types of money, see the chart "Special situations – what applies" at Appendix 2. These two appendices do not form part of the rules but are included to help solicitors and their staff find their way about the rules.

Rule 3: Geographical scope

3.1   Parts 1 to 6 of these rules apply to practice carried on from an office in England and Wales. Part 7 of these rules applies to practice carried on from an office outside England and Wales.

Rule 4: Persons governed by the rules

4.1   Save as provided in rule 4.2 below, Parts 1 to 6 of these rules apply to *you*.

4.2   In relation to an *MDP*, the rules apply to *you* only in respect of your *regulated activities*.

4.3   Part 6 of the rules (accountants' reports) also applies to reporting accountants.

4.4   If *you* have held or received *client money*, but no longer do so, whether or not *you* continue in practice, *you* continue to be bound by some of the rules.

Guidance notes

(i)   "You" is defined in the Glossary. All employees of a recognised body or licensed body are directly subject to the rules, following changes made by the Legal Services Act 2007. All employees of a recognised sole practitioner are also directly subject to the rules under sections 1B and 34A of the Solicitors Act 1974. Non-compliance by any member of staff will also lead to the principals being in breach of the rules – see rule 6. Misconduct by an employee can also lead to an order of the SRA or the Solicitors Disciplinary Tribunal under section 43 of the Solicitors Act 1974 imposing restrictions on his or her employment.

(ii)   Rules which continue to apply to you where you no longer hold client money include:

(a)   rule 7 (duty to remedy breaches);

(b)   rule 17.2 and 17.8, rule 29.15 to 29.24 and rule 30 (retention of records);

(c)   rule 31 (production of documents, information and explanations);

(d)   Part 6 (accountants' reports), and in particular rule 32 and rule 33.5 (delivery of final report), and rule 35.2 and rule 43 (completion of checklist).

(iii)   The rules do not cover trusteeships carried on in a purely personal capacity outside any legal practice. It will normally be clear from the terms of the appointment whether you are being appointed in a purely personal capacity or in your professional capacity. If you are charging for the work, it is clearly being done in a professional capacity. Use of professional stationery may also indicate that the work is being done in a professional capacity.

(iv)   A solicitor who wishes to retire from private practice will need to make a decision about any professional trusteeship. There are three possibilities:

(a)   continue to act as a professional trustee (as evidenced by, for instance, charging for work done, or by continuing to use the title "solicitor" in connection with the trust). In this case, the solicitor must continue to hold a practising certificate, and money subject to the trust must continue to be dealt with in accordance with the rules.

(b)   continue to act as trustee, but in a purely personal capacity. In this case, the solicitor must stop charging for the work, and must not be held out as a solicitor (unless this is qualified by words such as "non-practising" or "retired") in connection with the trust.

(c)   cease to be a trustee.

(v)   A licensed body may undertake a range of services, comprising both "traditional" legal services and other, related, services of a non-legal nature, for example, where a solicitor, estate agent and surveyor set up in practice together. Where a licensed body practises in this way (an MDP), only some of the services it provides (reserved and other legal activities, and other activities which are subject to one or more conditions on the body's licence) are within the regulatory reach of the SRA. Other, "non-legal", activities of the licensed body may be regulated by another regulator, and some activities may not fall within the regulatory ambit of any regulator.

Rule 5: Persons exempt from the rules

5.1   The rules do not apply to *you* when:

(a)   practising as an employee of:

(i)   a *local authority*;

(ii)   *statutory undertakers*;

(iii)   a body whose accounts are audited by the Comptroller and Auditor General;

(iv)   the Duchy of Lancaster;

(v)   the Duchy of Cornwall; or

(vi)   the Church Commissioners; or

(b)   practising as the Solicitor of the City of London; or

(c)   carrying out the functions of:

(i)   a coroner or other judicial office; or

(ii)   a sheriff or under-sheriff; or

(d)   practising as a *manager* or employee of an *authorised non-SRA firm*, and acting within the scope of that *firm's* authorisation to practise.

Guidance note

(i)   A person practising as a manager or employee of an authorised non-SRA firm is exempt from the Accounts Rules when acting within the scope of the firm's authorisation. Thus if a solicitor is a partner or employee in a firm authorised by the Council for Licensed Conveyancers, the rules will not apply to any money received by the solicitor in connection with conveyancing work. However if the solicitor does in-house litigation work – say collecting money owed to the firm – the Accounts Rules will apply to any money received by the solicitor in that context. This is because, whilst in-house litigation work is within the scope of the solicitor's authorisation as an individual, it is outside the scope of authorisation of the firm.

Rule 6: Principals' responsibility for compliance

6.1   All the *principals* in a *firm* must ensure compliance with the rules by the *principals* themselves and by everyone employed in the *firm*. This duty also extends to the *directors* of a *recognised body* or *licensed body* which is a *company*, or to the members of a *recognised body* or *licensed body* which is an *LLP*. It also extends to the *COFA* of a *firm* (whether a *manager* or non-*manager*).

Guidance note

(i)   Rule 8.5(d) of the SRA Authorisation Rules requires all firms to have a COFA. The appointment of a COFA satisfies the requirement under section 92 of the Legal Services Act 2007 for a licensed body to appoint a Head of Finance and Administration. Under rule 6 of the accounts rules, the COFA must ensure compliance with the accounts rules. This obligation is in addition to, not instead of, the duty of all the principals to ensure compliance (the COFA may be subject to this duty both as COFA and as a principal). Under rule 8.5(e) of the SRA Authorisation Rules, the COFA of a licensed body must report any breaches, and the COFA of a recognised body must report material breaches, of the accounts rules to the SRA as soon as reasonably practicable. The COFA of a recognised sole practitioner has a duty to report material breaches under regulation 4.8(e) of the SRA Practising Regulations. All COFAs must record any breaches and make those records available to the SRA on request. (See also outcomes 10.3 and 10.4 of Chapter 10 of the SRA Code of Conduct in relation to the general duty to report serious financial difficulty or serious misconduct.)

Rule 7: Duty to remedy breaches

7.1   Any breach of the rules must be remedied promptly upon discovery. This includes the replacement of any money improperly withheld or withdrawn from a *client account*.

7.2   In a private practice, the duty to remedy breaches rests not only on the person causing the breach, but also on all the *principals* in the *firm*. This duty extends to replacing missing *client money* from the *principals'* own resources, even if the money has been misappropriated by an employee or another *principal*, and whether or not a claim is subsequently made on the *firm's* insurance or the Compensation Fund.

Rule 8: Liquidators, trustees in bankruptcy, Court of Protection deputies and trustees of occupational pension schemes

8.1   If in the course of practice *you* act as:

(a)   a liquidator,

(b)   a trustee in bankruptcy,

(c)   a *Court of Protection deputy*, or

(d)   a trustee of an occupational pension scheme which is subject to section 47(1)(a) of the Pensions Act 1995 (appointment of an auditor) and section 49(1) (separate bank account) and regulations under section 49(2)(b) (books and records),

you must comply with:

(i)   the appropriate statutory rules or regulations;

(ii) the Principles referred to, and the underlying principles set out, in rule 1; and

(iii) the requirements of rule 8.2 to 8.4 below;

and will then be deemed to have satisfactorily complied with the Accounts Rules.

8.2   In respect of any records kept under the appropriate statutory rules, there must also be compliance with:

(a)   rule 29.15 – bills and notifications of costs;

(b)   rule 29.17(c) – retention of records;

(c)   rule 29.20 – centrally kept records;

(d)   rule 31 – production of documents, information and explanations; and

(e)   rule 39.1(l) and (p) – reporting accountant to check compliance.

8.3   If a liquidator or trustee in bankruptcy uses any of the *firm's client accounts* for holding money pending transfer to the Insolvency Services Account or to a local bank account authorised by the Secretary of State, he or she must comply with the Accounts Rules in all respects whilst the money is held in the *client account*.

8.4   If the appropriate statutory rules or regulations do not govern the holding or receipt of *client money* in a particular situation (for example, money below a certain limit), *you* must comply with the Accounts Rules in all respects in relation to that money.

Guidance notes

(i)   The Insolvency Regulations 1994 (S.I. 1994 no. 2507) regulate liquidators and trustees in bankruptcy.

(ii)   The Court of Protection Rules 2007 (S.I. 2007 no. 1744 (L.12)) regulate Court of Protection deputies.

(iii)   Money held or received by liquidators, trustees in bankruptcy, Court of Protection deputies and trustees of occupational pension schemes is client money but, because of the statutory rules and rule 8.1, it will not normally be kept in a client account. If for any reason it is held in a client account, the Accounts Rules apply to that money for the time it is so held (see rule 8.3 and 8.4).

Rule 9: Joint accounts

9.1   If, when acting in a *client's* matter, *you* hold or receive money jointly with the *client*, another practice or another third party, the rules in general do not apply, but the following must be complied with:

(a)   rule 29.11 – statements from banks, building societies and other financial institutions;

(b)   rule 29.15 – bills and notifications of costs;

Accounts Rules

(c)   rule 29.17(b)(ii) – retention of statements and passbooks;

(d)   rule 29.21 – centrally kept records;

(e)   rule 31 – production of documents, information and explanations; and

(f)   rule 39.1(m) and (p) – reporting accountant to check compliance.

A joint account is not a *client account* but money held in a joint account is *client money*.

Operation of the joint account by you only

9.2   If the joint account is operated only by *you*, *you* must ensure that *you* receive the statements from the *bank*, *building society* or other financial institution in accordance with rule 29.11, and have possession of any passbooks.

Shared operation of the joint account

9.3   If *you* share the operation of the joint account with the *client*, another practice or another third party, *you* must:

(a)   ensure that *you* receive the statements or duplicate statements from the *bank*, *building society* or other financial institution in accordance with rule 29.11, and retain them in accordance with rule 29.17(b)(ii); and

(b)   ensure that *you* either have possession of any passbooks, or take copies of the passbook entries before handing any passbook to the other signatory, and retain them in accordance with rule 29.17(b)(ii).

Operation of the joint account by the other account holder

9.4   If the joint account is operated solely by the other account holder, *you* must ensure that *you* receive the statements or duplicate statements from the *bank*, *building society* or other financial institution in accordance with rule 29.11, and retain them in accordance with rule 29.17(b)(ii).

Rule 10: Operation of a client's own account

10.1   If, in the course of practice, *you* operate a *client's* own account as signatory (for example, as donee under a power of attorney), the rules in general do not apply, but the following must be complied with:

(a)   rule 30.1 to 30.4 – accounting records for clients' own accounts;

(b)   rule 31 – production of documents, information and explanations; and

(c)   rule 39.1(n) and (p) – reporting accountant to check compliance.

Operation by you only

10.2   If the account is operated by *you* only, *you* must ensure that *you* receive the statements from the *bank*, *building society* or other financial institution in accordance with rule 30, and have possession of any passbooks.

Shared operation of the account

10.3   If *you* share the operation of the account with the *client* or a co-attorney outside *your firm*, *you* must:

   (a)   ensure that *you* receive the statements or duplicate statements from the *bank*, *building society* or other financial institution and retain them in accordance with rule 30.1 to 30.4; and

   (b)   ensure that *you* either have possession of any passbooks, or take copies of the passbook entries before handing any passbook to the *client* or co-attorney, and retain them in accordance with rule 30.1 to 30.4.

Operation of the account for a limited purpose

10.4   If *you* are given authority (whether as attorney or otherwise) to operate the account for a limited purpose only, such as the taking up of a share rights issue during the *client's* temporary absence, *you* need not receive statements or possess passbooks, provided that *you* retain details of all cheques drawn or paid in, and retain copies of all passbook entries, relating to the transaction, and retain them in accordance with rule 30.1 to 30.3.

Application

10.5   This rule applies only to private practice. It does not cover money held or received by a donee of a power of attorney acting in a purely personal capacity outside any legal practice (see rule 4, guidance notes (iii)–(iv)).

10.6   A "*client's* own account" covers all accounts in a *client's* own name, whether opened by the *client* himself or herself, or by *you* on the *client's* instructions under rule 15.1(b). A "*client's* own account" also includes an account opened in the name of a person designated by the *client* under rule 15.1(b).

Guidance notes

   (i)   Money held in a client's own account (under a power of attorney or otherwise) is not "client money" for the purpose of the rules because it is not "held or received" by you. If you close the account and receive the closing balance, this becomes client money subject to all the rules.

   (ii)   Merely paying money into a client's own account, or helping the client to complete forms in relation to such an account, is not "operating" the account.

   (iii)   If as executor you operate the deceased's account (whether before or after the grant of probate), you will be subject to the limited requirements of rule 10. If the account is subsequently transferred into your name, or a new account is opened in your name, you will have "held or received" client money and are then subject to all the rules.

Rule 11: Firm's rights not affected

11.1   Nothing in these rules deprives *you* of any recourse or right, whether by way of lien, set off, counterclaim, charge or otherwise, against money standing to the credit of a *client account*.

Rule 12: Categories of money

12.1   These rules do not apply to *out-of-scope money*, save to the limited extent specified in the rules. All other money held or received in the course of practice falls into one or other of the following categories:

(a)   "client money" – money held or received for a *client* or as *trustee*, and all other money which is not *office money*; or

(b)   "office money" – money which belongs to *you* or *your firm*.

12.2   "Client money" includes money held or received:

(a)   as *trustee*;

(b)   as agent, bailee, stakeholder, or as the donee of a power of attorney, or as a liquidator, trustee in bankruptcy, *Court of Protection deputy* or trustee of an occupational pension scheme;

(c)   for payment of unpaid *professional disbursements*;

(d)   for payment of stamp duty land tax, Land Registry registration fees, telegraphic transfer fees and court fees (but see also guidance note (i));

(e)   as a payment on account of *costs* generally;

(f)   as a financial benefit paid in respect of a *client*, unless the *client* has given *you* prior authority to retain it (see Chapter 1, outcome 1.15 and indicative behaviour 1.20 of the *SRA Code of Conduct*);

(g)   jointly with another person outside the *firm*.

12.3   Money held to the sender's order is *client money*.

(a)   If money is accepted on such terms, it must be held in a *client account*.

(b)   However, a cheque or draft sent to *you* on terms that the cheque or draft (as opposed to the money) is held to the sender's order must not be presented for payment without the sender's consent.

(c)   The recipient is always subject to a professional obligation to return the money, or the cheque or draft, to the sender on demand.

12.4   An advance to a *client* which is paid into a *client account* under rule 14.2(b) becomes *client money*.

12.5   A cheque in respect of damages and *costs*, made payable to the *client* but paid into a *client account* under rule 14.2(e), becomes *client money*.

12.6   Endorsing a cheque or draft over to a *client* or employer in the course of practice amounts to receiving *client money*. Even if no other *client money* is held or received, *you* must comply with some provisions of the rules, e.g.:

(a) rule 7 (duty to remedy breaches);

(b) rule 29 (accounting records for client accounts, etc.);

(c) rule 31 (production of documents, information and explanations);

(d) rule 32 (delivery of accountants' reports).

12.7   "Office money" includes:

(a) money held or received in connection with running the *firm*; for example, PAYE, or VAT on the *firm's fees*;

(b) *interest* on *general client accounts*; the *bank* or *building society* should be instructed to credit such *interest* to the *office account* – but see also rule 14.2(d);

(c) payments received in respect of:

(i)   *fees* due to the *firm* against a bill or written notification of *costs* incurred, which has been given or sent in accordance with rule 17.2;

(ii) *disbursements* already paid by the *firm*;

(iii) *disbursements* incurred but not yet paid by the *firm*, but excluding unpaid *professional disbursements*;

(iv) money paid for or towards an *agreed fee*;

(d) money held in a *client account* and earmarked for *costs* under rule 17.3;

(e) money held or received from the Legal Aid Agency as a *regular payment* (see rule 19.2).

12.8   If a *firm* conducts a personal or office transaction – for instance, conveyancing – for a *principal* (or for a number of *principals*), money held or received on behalf of the *principal(s)* is *office money*. However, other circumstances may mean that the money is *client money*, for example:

(a) If the *firm* also acts for a lender, money held or received on behalf of the lender is *client money*.

(b) If the *firm* acts for a *principal* and, for example, his or her spouse jointly (assuming the spouse is not a *partner* in the practice), money received on their joint behalf is *client money*.

(c) If the *firm* acts for an assistant *solicitor*, consultant or non-solicitor employee, or (if it is a *company*) a *director*, or (if it is an *LLP*) a member, he or she is regarded as a *client* of the *firm*, and money received for him or her is *client money* – even if he or she conducts the matter personally.

Guidance notes

(i)   Money held or received for payment of stamp duty land tax, Land Registry registration fees, telegraphic transfer fees and court fees is not office money because you have not incurred an obligation to HMRC, the Land Registry, the bank or the court to pay the duty or fee; (on the other hand, if you have already paid the duty or fee out of your own resources, or have received the service on credit, or the bank's charge for a telegraphic transfer forms part of your profit costs, payment subsequently received from the client will be office money);

(ii)   Money held:

   (a) by liquidators, trustees in bankruptcy, Court of Protection deputies and trustees of occupational pension schemes;

   (b) jointly with another person outside the practice (for example, with a lay trustee, or with another firm);

is client money, subject to a limited application of the rules – see rules 8 and 9. The donee of a power of attorney, who operates the donor's own account, is also subject to a limited application of the rules (see rule 10), although money kept in the donor's own account is not "client money" because it is not "held or received" by the donee.

(iii)   If the SRA intervenes in a practice, money from the practice is held or received by the SRA's intervention agent subject to a trust under Schedule 1 paragraph 7(1) of the Solicitors Act 1974, and is therefore client money. The same provision requires the agent to pay the money into a client account.

(iv)   Money held or received in the course of employment when practising in one of the capacities listed in rule 5 (persons exempt from the rules) is not "client money" for the purpose of the rules, because the rules do not apply at all.

(v)   The receipt of out-of-scope money of an MDP which is mixed with other types of money is dealt with in rules 17 and 18.

(vi)   See Appendices 1 and 2 (which do not form part of the rules) for a summary of the effect of the rules and the treatment of different types of money.

PART 2: CLIENT MONEY AND OPERATION OF A CLIENT ACCOUNT

Rule 13: Client accounts

13.1   If *you* hold or receive *client money*, *you* must keep one or more *client accounts* (unless all the *client money* is always dealt with outside any *client account* in accordance with rule 8, rule 9, rule 15 or rule 16).

13.2   A "client account" is an account of a practice kept at a *bank* or *building society* for holding *client money*, in accordance with the requirements of this part of the rules.

13.3   The *client account(s)* of:

(a)   a *sole practitioner* must be in the name under which the *sole practitioner* is recognised by the *SRA*, whether that is the *sole practitioner's* own name or the *firm* name;

(b)   a *partnership* must be in the name under which the *partnership* is recognised by the *SRA*;

(c)   an incorporated practice must be in the company name, or the name of the *LLP*, as registered at Companies House;

(d)   in-house *solicitors* or *RELs* must be in the name of the current *principal solicitor/REL* or *solicitors/RELs*;

(e)   *trustees*, where all the *trustees* of a *trust* are *managers* and/or employees of the same *recognised body* or *licensed body*, must be either in the name of the *recognised body/licensed body* or in the name of the *trustee(s)*;

(f)   *trustees*, where all the *trustees* of a *trust* are the *sole practitioner* and/or his or her employees, must be either in the name under which the *sole practitioner* is recognised by the *SRA* or in the name of the *trustee(s)*;

and the name of the account must also include the word "client" in full (an abbreviation is not acceptable).

13.4   A *client account* must be:

(a)   a *bank* account at a branch (or a *bank's* head office) in England and Wales; or

(b)   a *building society* account at a branch (or a society's head office) in England and Wales.

13.5   There are two types of *client account*:

(a)   a "separate designated client account", which is an account for money relating to a single *client*, other person or *trust*, and which includes in its title, in addition to the requirements of rule 13.3 above, a reference to the identity of the *client*, other person or *trust*; and

(b)   a "general client account", which is any other *client account*.

13.6   [Deleted]

13.7   The *clients* of a *licensed body* must be informed at the outset of the retainer, or during the course of the retainer as appropriate, if the *licensed body* is (or becomes) owned by a *bank* or *building society* and its *client account* is held at that *bank* or *building society* (or another *bank* or *building society* in the same group).

13.8   Money held in a *client account* must be immediately available, even at the sacrifice of *interest*, unless the *client* otherwise instructs, or the circumstances clearly indicate otherwise.

Guidance notes

(i)   In the case of in-house practice, any client account should include the names of all solicitors or registered European lawyers held out on the notepaper as principals. The names of other employees who are solicitors or registered European lawyers may also be included if so desired. Any person whose name is included will have to be included on the accountant's report.

(ii)   A firm may have any number of separate designated client accounts and general client accounts.

(iii)   Compliance with rule 13.1 to 13.4 ensures that clients, as well as the bank or building society, have the protection afforded by section 85 of the Solicitors Act 1974 or article 4 of the Legal Services Act 2007 (Designation as a Licensing Authority) (No. 2) Order 2011 as appropriate.

Rule 14: Use of a client account

14.1   *Client money* must *without delay* be paid into a *client account*, and must be held in a *client account*, except when the rules provide to the contrary (see rules 8, 9, 15, 16, 17 and 19).

14.2   Only *client money* may be paid into or held in a *client account*, except:

(a)   an amount of the *firm's* own money required to open or maintain the account;

(b)   an advance from the *firm* to fund a payment on behalf of a *client* or *trust* in excess of funds held for that *client* or *trust*; the sum becomes *client money* on payment into the account (for *interest* on *client money*, see rule 22.2(c));

(c)   money to replace any sum which for any reason has been drawn from the account in breach of rule 20; the replacement money becomes *client money* on payment into the account;

(d)   *interest* which is paid into a *client account* to enable payment from the *client account* of all money owed to the *client*; and

(e)   a cheque in respect of damages and *costs*, made payable to the *client*, which is paid into the *client account* pursuant to the *Society's* Conditional Fee Agreement; the sum becomes *client money* on payment into the account (but see rule 17.1(e) for the transfer of the *costs* element from *client account*);

and except when the rules provide to the contrary (see guidance note (ii) below).

14.3   *Client money* must be returned to the *client* (or other person on whose behalf the money is held) promptly, as soon as there is no longer any proper reason to retain those funds. Payments received after *you* have already accounted to the *client*, for example by way of a refund, must be paid to the *client* promptly.

14.4   *You* must promptly inform a *client* (or other person on whose behalf the money is held) in writing of the amount of any *client money* retained at the end of a matter (or the substantial conclusion of a matter), and the reason for that retention. *You* must inform the *client* (or other person) in writing at least once every twelve months thereafter of the amount of *client money* still held and the reason for the retention, for as long as *you* continue to hold that money.

14.5   *You* must not provide banking facilities through a *client account*. Payments into, and transfers or withdrawals from, a *client account* must be in respect of instructions relating to an underlying transaction (and the funds arising therefrom) or to a service forming part of *your* normal regulated activities.

Guidance notes

(i)   Exceptions to rule 14.1 (client money must be paid into a client account) can be found in:

(a)   rule 8 – liquidators, trustees in bankruptcy, Court of Protection deputies and trustees of occupational pension schemes;

(b)   rule 9 – joint accounts;

(c)   rule 15 – client's instructions;

(d)   rule 16 – cash paid straight to client, beneficiary or third party;

(A)   cheque endorsed to client, beneficiary or third party;

(B)   money withheld from client account on the SRA's authority;

(C)   money withheld from client account in accordance with a trustee's powers;

(e)   rule 17.1(b) – receipt and transfer of costs;

(f)   rule 19.1 – payments by the Legal Aid Agency.

(ii)   Rule 14.2(a) to (e) provides for exceptions to the principle that only client money may be paid into a client account. Additional exceptions can be found in:

(a)   rule 17.1(c) – receipt and transfer of costs;

(b)   rule 18.2(b) – receipt of mixed payments;

(c)   rule 19.2(c)(ii) – transfer to client account of a sum for unpaid professional disbursements, where regular payments are received from the Legal Aid Agency.

(iii)   Only a nominal sum will be required to open or maintain an account. In practice, banks will usually open (and, if instructed, keep open) accounts with nil balances.

(iv)   If client money is invested in the purchase of assets other than money – such as stocks or shares – it ceases to be client money, because it is no longer money held by the firm. If the investment is subsequently sold, the money received is, again, client money. The records kept under rule 29 will need to include entries to show the purchase or sale of investments.

(v)   Rule 14.5 reflects decisions of the Solicitors Disciplinary Tribunal that it is not a proper part of a solicitor's everyday business or practice to operate a banking facility for third parties, whether they are clients of the firm or not. It should be noted that any exemption under the Financial Services and Markets Act 2000 is likely to be lost if a deposit is taken in circumstances which do not form part of your practice. It should also be borne in mind that there are criminal sanctions against assisting money launderers.

(vi)   As with rule 7 (Duty to remedy breaches), "promptly" in rule 14.3 and 14.4 is not defined but should be given its natural meaning in the particular circumstances. Accounting to a client for any surplus funds will often fall naturally at the end of a matter. Other retainers may be more protracted and, even when the principal work has been completed, funds may still be needed, for example, to cover outstanding work in a conveyancing transaction or to meet a tax liability. (See also paragraphs 4.8 and 4.9 of the Guidelines for accounting procedures and systems at Appendix 3.)

(vii)   There may be some instances when, during the course of a retainer, the specific purpose for which particular funds were paid no longer exists, for example, the need to instruct counsel or a medical expert. Rule 14.3 is concerned with returning funds to clients at the end of a matter (or the substantial conclusion of a matter) and is not intended to apply to ongoing retainers. However, in order to act in the best interests of your client, you may need to take instructions in such circumstances to ascertain, for instance, whether the money should be returned to the client or retained to cover the general funding or other aspects of the case.

(viii)   See rule 20.1(j)–(k) for withdrawals from a client account when the rightful owner of funds cannot be traced. The obligation to report regularly under rule 14.4 ceases to apply if you are no longer able to trace the client, at which point rule 20.1(j) or (k) would apply.

Rule 15: Client money withheld from client account on client's instructions

15.1   *Client money* may be:

    (a)   held by *you* outside a *client account* by, for example, retaining it in the *firm's* safe in the form of cash, or placing it in an account in the *firm's* name which is not a *client account*, such as an account outside England and Wales; or

    (b)   paid into an account at a *bank*, *building society* or other financial institution opened in the name of the *client* or of a person designated by the *client*;

but only if the *client* instructs *you* to that effect for the *client's* own convenience, and only if the instructions are given in writing, or are given by other means and confirmed by *you* to the *client* in writing.

15.2   It is improper to seek blanket agreements, through standard terms of business or otherwise, to hold *client money* outside a *client account*.

15.3   If a *client* instructs *you* to hold part only of a payment in accordance with rule 15.1(a) or (b), the entire payment must first be placed in a *client account*, before transferring the relevant part out and dealing with it in accordance with the *client's* instructions.

15.4   A payment on account of *costs* received from a person who is funding all or part of *your fees* may be withheld from a *client account* on the instructions of that person given in accordance with rule 15.1.

Guidance notes

(i)   Money withheld from a client account under rule 15.1(a) remains client money, and all the record-keeping provisions of rule 29 will apply.

(ii)   Once money has been paid into an account set up under rule 15.1(b), it ceases to be client money. Until that time, the money is client money and, under rule 29, a record is required of your receipt of the money, and its payment into the account in the name of the client or designated person. If you can operate the account, rule 10 (operating a client's own account) and rule 30 (accounting records for clients' own accounts) will apply. In the absence of instructions to the contrary, rule 14.1 requires any money withdrawn to be paid into a client account.

(iii)   Rule 29.17(d) requires clients' instructions under rule 15.1 to be kept for at least six years.

Rule 16: Other client money withheld from a client account

16.1   The following categories of *client money* may be withheld from a *client account*:

(a)   cash received and *without delay* paid in cash in the ordinary course of business to the *client* or, on the *client's* behalf, to a third party, or paid in cash in the execution of a *trust* to a beneficiary or third party;

(b)   a cheque or draft received and endorsed over in the ordinary course of business to the *client* or, on the *client's* behalf, to a third party, or *without delay* endorsed over in the execution of a *trust* to a beneficiary or third party;

(c)   money withheld from a *client account* on instructions under rule 15;

(d)   money which, in accordance with a *trustee's* powers, is paid into or retained in an account of the *trustee* which is not a *client account* (for example, an account outside England and Wales), or properly retained in cash in the performance of the *trustee's* duties;

(e)   unpaid *professional disbursements* included in a payment of *costs* dealt with under rule 17.1(b);

(f)   in respect of payments from the Legal Aid Agency:

(i)   advance payments from the Legal Aid Agency withheld from *client account* (see rule 19.1(a)); and

(ii)   unpaid *professional disbursements* included in a payment of *costs* from the Legal Aid Agency (see rule 19.1(b)); and

(g)   money withheld from a *client account* on the written authorisation of the *SRA*. The *SRA* may impose a condition that the money is paid to a charity which gives an indemnity against any legitimate claim subsequently made for the sum received.

Guidance notes

(i)   If money is withheld from a client account under rule 16.1(a) or (b), rule 29 requires records to be kept of the receipt of the money and the payment out.

(ii)   If money is withheld from a client account under rule 16.1(d), rule 29 requires a record to be kept of the receipt of the money, and requires the inclusion of the money in the monthly reconciliations. (Money held by a trustee jointly with another party is subject only to the limited requirements of rule 9.)

(iii)   It makes no difference, for the purpose of the rules, whether an endorsement is effected by signature in the normal way or by some other arrangement with the bank.

(iv)   The circumstances in which authorisation would be given under rule 16.1(g) must be extremely rare. Applications for authorisation should be made to the Professional Ethics Guidance Team.

Rule 17: Receipt and transfer of costs

17.1   When *you* receive money paid in full or part settlement of *your* bill (or other notification of *costs*) *you* **must follow one of the following five options:**

(a)   **determine the composition of the payment without delay, and deal with the money accordingly:**

(i)   if the sum comprises *office money* and/or *out-of-scope money* only, it must be placed in an *office account*;

(ii)   if the sum comprises only *client money*, the entire sum must be placed in a *client account*;

(iii)   if the sum includes both *office money* and *client money*, or *client money* and *out-of-scope money*, or *client money*, *out-of-scope money* and *office money*, *you* must follow rule 18 (receipt of mixed payments); or

(b)   **ascertain that the payment comprises only *office money* and/or *out-of-scope money*, and/or *client money* in the form of *professional disbursements* incurred but not yet paid, and deal with the payment as follows:**

(i) place the entire sum in an *office account* at a *bank* or *building society* branch (or head office) in England and Wales; and

(ii) by the end of the second working day following receipt, either pay any unpaid *professional disbursement*, or transfer a sum for its settlement to a *client account*; **or**

(c) pay the entire sum into a *client account* (regardless of its composition), and transfer any *office money* and/or *out-of-scope money* out of the *client account* within 14 days of receipt; or

(d) on receipt of *costs* from the Legal Aid Agency, follow the option in rule 19.1(b); or

(e) in relation to a cheque paid into a *client account* under rule 14.2(e), transfer the *costs* element out of the *client account* within 14 days of receipt.

17.2 If *you* properly require payment of *your fees* from money held for a *client* or *trust* in a *client account*, *you* must first give or send a bill of *costs*, or other written notification of the *costs* incurred, to the *client* or the paying party.

17.3 Once *you* have complied with rule 17.2 above, the money earmarked for *costs* becomes *office money* and must be transferred out of the *client account* within 14 days.

17.4 A payment on account of *costs* generally in respect of those activities for which the practice is regulated by the *SRA* is *client money*, and must be held in a *client account* until *you* have complied with rule 17.2 above. (For an exception in the case of legal aid payments, see rule 19.1(a). See also rule 18 on dealing with mixed payments of *client money* and/or *out-of-scope money* when part of a payment on account of *costs* relates to activities not regulated by the *SRA*.)

17.5 A payment for an *agreed fee* must be paid into an *office account*. An "agreed fee" is one that is fixed – not a *fee* that can be varied upwards, nor a *fee* that is dependent on the transaction being completed. An *agreed fee* must be evidenced in writing.

17.6 *You* will not be in breach of rule 17 as a result of a misdirected electronic payment or other direct transfer from a *client* or paying third party, provided:

(a) appropriate systems are in place to ensure compliance;

(b) appropriate instructions were given to the *client* or paying third party;

(c) the *client's* or paying third party's mistake is remedied promptly upon discovery; and

(d) appropriate steps are taken to avoid future errors by the *client* or paying third party.

17.7 *Costs* transferred out of a *client account* in accordance with rule 17.2 and 17.3 must be specific sums relating to the bill or other written notification of *costs*, and covered by the amount held for the particular *client* or *trust*. Round sum withdrawals on account of *costs* are a breach of the rules.

Accounts Rules

17.8   In the case of a *trust* of which the only *trustee(s)* are within the *firm*, the paying party will be the *trustee(s)* themselves. *You* must keep the original bill or notification of *costs* on the file, in addition to complying with rule 29.15 (central record or file of copy bills, etc.).

17.9   Undrawn *costs* must not remain in a *client account* as a "cushion" against any future errors which could result in a shortage on that account, and cannot be regarded as available to set off against any general shortage on *client account*.

Guidance notes

(i)   This note lists types of disbursement and how they are categorised:

  (a) Money received for paid disbursements is office money.

  (b) Money received for unpaid professional disbursements is client money.

  (c) Money received for other unpaid disbursements for which you have incurred a liability to the payee (for example, travel agents' charges, taxi fares, courier charges or Land Registry search fees, payable on credit) is office money.

  (d) Money received for disbursements anticipated but not yet incurred is a payment on account, and is therefore client money.

(ii)   The option in rule 17.1(a) allows you to place all payments in the correct account in the first instance. The option in rule 17.1(b) allows the prompt banking into an office account of an invoice payment when the only uncertainty is whether or not the payment includes some client money in the form of unpaid professional disbursements. The option in rule 17.1(c) allows the prompt banking into a client account of any invoice payment in advance of determining whether the payment is a mixture of office and client money (of whatever description), or client money and out-of-scope money, or client money, out-of-scope money and office money, or is only office money and/or out-of-scope money.

(iii)   If you are not in a position to comply with the requirements of rule 17.1(b), you cannot take advantage of that option.

(iv)   The option in rule 17.1(b) cannot be used if the money received includes a payment on account – for example, a payment for a professional disbursement anticipated but not yet incurred.

(v)   In order to be able to use the option in rule 17.1(b) for electronic payments or other direct transfers from clients, you may choose to establish a system whereby clients are given an office account number for payment of costs. The system must be capable of ensuring that, when invoices are sent to the client, no request is made for any client money, with the sole exception of money for professional disbursements already incurred but not yet paid.

(vi)   Rule 17.1(c) allows clients to be given a single account number for making direct payments by electronic or other means – under this option, it has to be a client account.

(vii)   "Properly" in rule 17.2 implies that the work has actually been done, whether at the end of the matter or at an interim stage, and that you are entitled to appropriate the money for costs. For example, the costs set out in a completion statement in a conveyancing transaction will become due on completion and should be transferred out of the client account within 14 days of completion in accordance with rule 17.3. The requirement to transfer costs out of the client account within a set time is intended to prevent costs being left on client account to conceal a shortage.

(viii)   Money is "earmarked" for costs under rule 17.2 and 17.3 when you decide to use funds already held in client account to settle your bill. If you wish to obtain the client's prior approval, you will need to agree the amount to be taken with your client before issuing the bill to avoid the possibility of failing to meet the 14 day time limit for making the transfer out of client account. If you wish to retain the funds, for example, as money on account of costs on another matter, you will need to ask the client to send the full amount in settlement of the bill. If, when submitting a bill, you fail to indicate whether you intend to take your costs from client account, or expect the client to make a payment, you will be regarded as having "earmarked" your costs.

(ix)   An amendment to section 69 of the Solicitors Act 1974 by the Legal Services Act 2007 permits a solicitor or recognised body to sue on a bill which has been signed electronically and which the client has agreed can be delivered electronically.

(x)   The rules do not require a bill of costs for an agreed fee, although your VAT position may mean that in practice a bill is needed. If there is no bill, the written evidence of the agreement must be filed as a written notification of costs under rule 29.15(b).

(xi)   The bill of an MDP may be in respect of costs for work of the SRA-regulated part of the practice, and also for work that falls outside the scope of SRA regulation. Money received in respect of the non-SRA regulated work, including money for disbursements, is out-of-scope money and must be dealt with in accordance with rule 17.

(xii)   See Chapter 1, indicative behaviour 1.21 of the SRA Code of Conduct in relation to ensuring that disbursements included in a bill reflect the actual amount spent or to be spent.

Rule 18: Receipt of mixed payments

18.1   A "mixed payment" is one which includes *client money* as well as *office money* and/or *out-of-scope money*.

18.2   A *mixed payment* must either:

    (a) be split between a *client account* and *office account* as appropriate; or

    (b) be placed *without delay* in a *client account*.

18.3   If the entire payment is placed in a *client account*, all *office money* and/or *out-of-scope money* must be transferred out of the *client account* within 14 days of receipt.

Guidance notes

(i)   See rule 17.1(b) and (c) for additional ways of dealing with (among other things) mixed payments received in response to a bill or other notification of costs.

(ii)   See rule 19.1(b) for (among other things) mixed payments received from the Legal Aid Agency.

(iii)   Some out-of-scope money may be subject to the rules of other regulators which may require an earlier withdrawal from the client account operated under these rules.

Rule 19: Treatment of payments to legal aid practitioners

Payments from the Legal Aid Agency

19.1   Two special dispensations apply to payments (other than *regular payments*) from the Legal Aid Agency:

    (a) An advance payment, which may include *client money*, may be placed in an *office account*, provided the Legal Aid Agency instructs in writing that this may be done.

    (b) A payment for *costs* (interim and/or final) may be paid into an *office account* at a *bank* or *building society* branch (or head office) in England and Wales, regardless of whether it consists wholly of *office money*, or is mixed with *client money* in the form of:

        (i) advance payments for *fees* or *disbursements*; or

        (ii) money for unpaid *professional disbursements*;

    provided all money for payment of *disbursements* is transferred to a *client account* (or the *disbursements* paid) within 14 days of receipt.

19.2   The following provisions apply to *regular payments* from the Legal Aid Agency:

    (a) "Regular payments" (which are *office money*) are:

        (i) standard monthly payments paid by the Legal Aid Agency under the civil legal aid contracting arrangements;

(ii)   standard monthly payments paid by the Legal Aid Agency under the criminal legal aid contracting arrangements; and

(iii)   any other payments for work done or to be done received from the Legal Aid Agency under an arrangement for payments on a regular basis.

(b)   *Regular payments* must be paid into an *office account* at a *bank* or *building society* branch (or head office) in England and Wales.

(c)   *You* must within 28 days of submitting a report to the Legal Aid Agency, notifying completion of a matter, either:

(i)   pay any unpaid *professional disbursement(s)*, or

(ii)   transfer to a *client account* a sum equivalent to the amount of any unpaid *professional disbursement(s)*,

relating to that matter.

(d)   In cases where the Legal Aid Agency permits *you* to submit reports at various stages during a matter rather than only at the end of a matter, the requirement in rule 19.2(c) above applies to any unpaid *professional disbursement(s)* included in each report so submitted.

Payments from a third party

19.3   If the Legal Aid Agency has paid any *costs* to *you* or a previously nominated *firm* in a matter (advice and assistance or legal help *costs*, advance payments or interim *costs*), or has paid *professional disbursements* direct, and *costs* are subsequently settled by a third party:

(a)   The entire third party payment must be paid into a *client account*.

(b)   A sum representing the payments made by the Legal Aid Agency must be retained in the *client account*.

(c)   Any balance belonging to *you* must be transferred to an *office account* within 14 days of *your* sending a report to the Legal Aid Agency containing details of the third party payment.

(d)   The sum retained in the *client account* as representing payments made by the Legal Aid Agency must be:

(i)   **either** recorded in the individual *client's* ledger account, and identified as the Legal Aid Agency's money;

(ii)   **or** recorded in a ledger account in the Legal Aid Agency's name, and identified by reference to the *client* or matter;

and kept in the *client account* until notification from the Legal Aid Agency that it has recouped an equivalent sum from subsequent payments due to *you*. The retained sum must be transferred to an *office account* within 14 days of notification.

19.4 Any part of a third party payment relating to unpaid *professional disbursements* or outstanding *costs* of the *client's* previous *firm* is *client money*, and must be kept in a *client account* until *you* pay the *professional disbursement* or outstanding *costs*.

Guidance notes

(i)   This rule deals with matters which specifically affect legal aid practitioners. It should not be read in isolation from the remainder of the rules which apply to everyone, including legal aid practitioners.

(ii)   In cases carried out under public funding certificates, firms can apply for advance payments ("Payments on Account" under the Standard Civil Contract). The Legal Aid Agency has agreed that these payments may be placed in office account.

(iii)   Rule 19.1(b) deals with the specific problems of legal aid practitioners by allowing a mixed or indeterminate payment of costs (or even a payment consisting entirely of unpaid professional disbursements) to be paid into an office account, which for the purpose of rule 19.1(b) must be an account at a bank or building society. However, it is always open to you to comply with rule 17.1(a) to (c), which are the options for everyone for the receipt of costs. For regular payments, see guidance notes (v)–(vii) below.

(iv)   Firms are required by the Legal Aid Agency to report promptly to the Legal Aid Agency on receipt of costs from a third party. It is advisable to keep a copy of the report on the file as proof of compliance with the Legal Aid Agency's requirements, as well as to demonstrate compliance with the rule.

(v)   Rule 19.2(c) permits a firm, which is required to transfer an amount to cover unpaid professional disbursements into a client account, to make the transfer from its own resources if the regular payments are insufficient.

(vi)   The 28 day time limit for paying, or transferring an amount to a client account for, unpaid professional disbursements is for the purposes of these rules only. An earlier deadline may be imposed by contract with the Legal Aid Agency or with counsel, agents or experts. On the other hand, you may have agreed to pay later than 28 days from the submission of the report notifying completion of a matter, in which case rule 19.2(c) will require a transfer of the appropriate amount to a client account (but not payment) within 28 days.

(vii)   For the appropriate accounting records for regular payments, see rule 29.7.

Rule 20: Withdrawals from a client account

20.1   *Client money* may only be withdrawn from a *client account* when it is:

   (a)   properly required for a payment to or on behalf of the *client* (or other person on whose behalf the money is being held);

   (b)   properly required for a payment in the execution of a particular *trust*, including the purchase of an investment (other than money) in accordance with the *trustee's* powers;

(c) properly required for payment of a *disbursement* on behalf of the *client* or *trust*;

(d) properly required in full or partial reimbursement of money spent by *you* on behalf of the *client* or *trust*;

(e) transferred to another *client account*;

(f) withdrawn on the *client's* instructions, provided the instructions are for the *client's* convenience and are given in writing, or are given by other means and confirmed by *you* to the *client* in writing;

(g) transferred to an account other than a *client account* (such as an account outside England and Wales), or retained in cash, by a *trustee* in the proper performance of his or her duties;

(h) a refund to *you* of an advance no longer required to fund a payment on behalf of a *client* or *trust* (see rule 14.2(b));

(i) money which has been paid into the account in breach of the rules (for example, money paid into the wrong *separate designated client account*) – see rule 20.5 below;

(j) money not covered by (a) to (i) above, where *you* comply with the conditions set out in rule 20.2; or

(k) money not covered by (a) to (i) above, withdrawn from the account on the written authorisation of the *SRA*. The *SRA* may impose a condition that *you* pay the money to a charity which gives an indemnity against any legitimate claim subsequently made for the sum received.

20.2 A withdrawal of *client money* under rule 20.1(j) above may be made only where the amount held does not exceed £500 in relation to any one individual *client* or *trust* matter and *you*:

(a) establish the identity of the owner of the money, or make reasonable attempts to do so;

(b) make adequate attempts to ascertain the proper destination of the money, and to return it to the rightful owner, unless the reasonable costs of doing so are likely to be excessive in relation to the amount held;

(c) pay the funds to a charity;

(d) record the steps taken in accordance with rule 20.2(a)–(c) above and retain those records, together with all relevant documentation (including receipts from the charity), in accordance with rule 29.16 and 29.17(a); and

(e) keep a central register in accordance with rule 29.22.

20.3 *Office money* may only be withdrawn from a *client account* when it is:

Accounts Rules

(a)   money properly paid into the account to open or maintain it under rule 14.2(a);

(b)   properly required for payment of *your costs* under rule 17.2 and 17.3;

(c)   the whole or part of a payment into a *client account* under rule 17.1(c);

(d)   part of a *mixed payment* placed in a *client account* under rule 18.2(b); or

(e)   money which has been paid into a *client account* in breach of the rules (for example, *interest* wrongly credited to a *general client account*) – see rule 20.5 below.

20.4   *Out-of-scope money* must be withdrawn from a *client account* in accordance with rules 17.1(a), 17.1(c) and 18 as appropriate.

20.5   Money which has been paid into a *client account* in breach of the rules must be withdrawn from the *client account* promptly upon discovery.

20.6   Money withdrawn in relation to a particular *client* or *trust* from a *general client account* must not exceed the money held on behalf of that *client* or *trust* in all *your general client accounts* (except as provided in rule 20.7 below).

20.7   *You* may make a payment in respect of a particular *client* or *trust* out of a *general client account*, even if no money (or insufficient money) is held for that *client* or *trust* in *your general client account(s)*, provided:

(a)   sufficient money is held for that *client* or *trust* in a *separate designated client account*; and

(b)   the appropriate transfer from the *separate designated client account* to a *general client account* is made immediately.

20.8   Money held for a *client* or *trust* in a *separate designated client account* must not be used for payments for another *client* or *trust*.

20.9   A *client account* must not be overdrawn, except in the following circumstances:

(a)   A *separate designated client account* operated in *your* capacity as *trustee* can be overdrawn if *you* make payments on behalf of the *trust* (for example, inheritance tax) before realising sufficient assets to cover the payments.

(b)   If a *sole practitioner* dies and his or her *client accounts* are frozen, overdrawn *client accounts* can be operated in accordance with the rules to the extent of the money held in the frozen accounts.

Guidance notes

(i)   Withdrawals in favour of firm, and for payment of disbursements

(a)   Disbursements to be paid direct from a client account, or already paid out of your own money, can be withdrawn under rule 20.1(c) or (d) in advance of preparing a bill of costs. Money to be withdrawn from a client account for the payment of costs (fees and disbursements) under rule 17.2 and 17.3 becomes office money and is dealt with under rule 20.3(b).

(b) Money is "spent" under rule 20.1(d) at the time when you despatch a cheque, unless the cheque is to be held to your order. Money is also regarded as "spent" by the use of a credit account, so that, for example, search fees, taxi fares and courier charges incurred in this way may be transferred to your office account.

(c) See rule 21.4 for the way in which a withdrawal from a client account in your favour must be effected.

(ii) Cheques payable to banks, building societies, etc.

(a) In order to protect client money against misappropriation when cheques are made payable to banks, building societies or other large institutions, it is strongly recommended that you add the name and number of the account after the payee's name.

(iii) Drawing against uncleared cheques

(a) You should use discretion in drawing against a cheque received from or on behalf of a client before it has been cleared. If the cheque is not met, other clients' money will have been used to make the payment in breach of the rules (see rule 7 (duty to remedy breaches)). You may be able to avoid a breach of the rules by instructing the bank or building society to charge all unpaid credits to your office or personal account.

(iv) Non-receipt of electronic payments

(a) If you withdraw money from a general client account on the strength of information that an electronic payment is on its way, but the electronic payment does not arrive, you will have used other clients' money in breach of the rules. See also rule 7 (duty to remedy breaches).

(v) Withdrawals on instructions

(a) One of the reasons why a client might authorise a withdrawal under rule 20.1(f) might be to have the money transferred to a type of account other than a client account. If so, the requirements of rule 15 must be complied with.

(vi) Withdrawals where the rightful owner cannot be traced, on the SRA's authorisation and without SRA authorisation

(a) Applications for authorisation under rule 20.1(k) should be made to the Professional Ethics Guidance Team, who can advise on the criteria which must normally be met for authorisation to be given. You may under rule 20.1(j) pay to a charity sums of £500 or less per client or trust matter without the SRA's authorisation, provided the safeguards set out in rule 20.2 are followed.

(b) You will need to apply to the SRA, whatever the amount involved, if the money to be withdrawn is not to be paid to a charity. This situation might arise, for example, if you have been unable to deliver a bill of costs because the client has become untraceable and so cannot make a transfer from client account to office account in accordance with rule 17.2–17.3.

(c) After a practice has been wound up, surplus balances are sometimes discovered in an old client account. This money remains subject to rule 20 and rule 21. An application can be made to the SRA under rule 20.1(k).

Rule 21: Method of and authority for withdrawals from client account

21.1   A withdrawal from a *client account* may be made only after a specific authority in respect of that withdrawal has been signed by an appropriate person or persons in accordance with the *firm's* procedures for signing on *client account*. An authority for withdrawals from *client account* may be signed electronically, subject to appropriate safeguards and controls.

21.2   *Firms* must put in place appropriate systems and procedures governing withdrawals from *client account*, including who should be permitted by the *firm* to sign on *client account*. A non-*manager* owner or a non-employee owner of a *licensed body* is not an appropriate person to be a signatory on *client account* and must not be permitted by the *firm* to act in this way.

21.3   There is no need to comply with rule 21.1 above when transferring money from one *general client account* to another *general client account* at the same *bank* or *building society*.

21.4   A withdrawal from a *client account* in *your* favour must be either by way of a cheque, or by way of a transfer to the *office account* or to *your* personal account. The withdrawal must not be made in cash.

Guidance notes

(i)   A firm should select suitable people to authorise withdrawals from the client account. Firms will wish to consider whether any employee should be able to sign on client account, and whether signing rights should be given to all managers of the practice or limited to those managers directly involved in providing legal services. Someone who has no day-to-day involvement in the business of the practice is unlikely to be regarded as a suitable signatory because of the lack of proximity to client matters. An appropriate understanding of the requirements of the rules is essential – see paragraph 4.2 of the Guidelines for accounting procedures and systems at Appendix 3.

(ii)   Instructions to the bank or building society to withdraw money from a client account (rule 21.1) may be given over the telephone, provided a specific authority has been signed in accordance with this rule before the instructions are given. It is of paramount importance that there are appropriate in-built safeguards, such as passwords, to give the greatest protection possible for client money. Suitable safeguards will also be needed for practices which operate a CHAPS terminal or other form of electronic instruction for payment.

(iii)　In the case of a withdrawal by cheque, the specific authority (rule 21.1) is usually a signature on the cheque itself. Signing a blank cheque is not a specific authority.

(iv)　A withdrawal from a client account by way of a private loan from one client to another can only be made if the provisions of rule 27.2 are complied with.

(v)　If, in your capacity as trustee, you instruct an outside administrator to run, or continue to run, on a day-to-day basis, the business or property portfolio of an estate or trust, you will not need to comply with rule 21.1, provided all cheques are retained in accordance with rule 29.18. (See also rule 29, guidance note (ii)(d).)

(vi)　You may set up a "direct debit" system of payment for Land Registry application fees on either the office account or a client account. If a direct debit payment is to be taken from a client account for the payment of Land Registry application fees, a signature, which complies with the firm's systems and procedures set up under rule 21, on the application for registration will constitute the specific authority required by rule 21.1. As with any other payment method, care must be taken to ensure that sufficient uncommitted funds are held in the client account for the particular client before signing the authority. You should also bear in mind that should the Land Registry take an incorrect amount in error from a firm's client account (for example, a duplicate payment), the firm will be in breach of the rules if other clients' money has been used as a result.

(vii)　If you fail to specify the correct Land Registry fee on the application for registration (either by specifying a lesser amount than that actually due, or failing to specify any fee at all), you will be in breach of rule 21.1 if the Land Registry takes a sum from your client account greater than that specified on the application, without a specific authority for the revised sum being in place as required by rule 21. In order that you can comply with the rules, the Land Registry will need to contact you before taking the revised amount, so that the necessary authority may be signed prior to the revised amount being taken.

(viii)　Where the Land Registry contacts you by telephone, and you wish to authorise an immediate payment by direct debit over the telephone, you will first need to check that there is sufficient money held in client account for the client and, if there is, that it is not committed to some other purpose.

(ix)　The specific authority required by rule 21.1 can be signed after the telephone call has ended but must be signed before the additional payment (or correct full payment) is taken by the Land Registry. It is advisable to sign the authority promptly and, in any event, on the same day as the telephone instruction is given to the Land Registry to take the additional (or correct full) amount. If you decide to fund any extra amount from the office account, the transfer of office money to the client account would need to be made, preferably on the same day but, in any event, before the direct debit is taken. Your internal procedures would need to make it clear how to deal with such situations; for example, who should be consulted before a direct debit for an amount other than that specified on the application can be authorised, and the mechanism for ensuring the new authority is signed by a person permitted by the firm to sign on client account.

(x) You may decide to set up a direct debit system of payment on the office account because, for example, you do not wish to allow the Land Registry to have access to the firm's client account. Provided you are in funds, a transfer from the client account to the office account may be made under rule 20.1(d) to reimburse you as soon as the direct debit has been taken.

(xi) Variable "direct debit" payments to the Land Registry, as described in guidance notes (vi)–(x) above, are not direct debits in the usual sense as each payment is authorised and confirmed individually. A traditional direct debit or standing order should not be set up on a client account because of the need for a specific authority for each withdrawal.

PART 3: INTEREST

Rule 22: When interest must be paid

22.1   When *you* hold money in a *client account* for a *client*, or for a person funding all or part of *your fees*, or for a *trust*, *you* must account to the *client* or that person or *trust* for *interest* when it is fair and reasonable to do so in all the circumstances. (This also applies if money should have been held in a *client account* but was not. It also applies to money held in an account in accordance with rule 15.1(a) (or which should have been held in such an account), or rule 16.1(d).)

22.2   *You* are not required to pay *interest*:

   (a) on money held for the payment of a *professional disbursement*, once counsel etc. has requested a delay in settlement;

   (b) on money held for the Legal Aid Agency;

   (c) on an advance from *you* under rule 14.2(b) to fund a payment on behalf of the *client* or *trust* in excess of funds held for that *client* or *trust*; or

   (d) if there is an agreement to contract out of the provisions of this rule under rule 25.

22.3   *You* must have a written policy on the payment of *interest*, which seeks to provide a fair outcome. The terms of the policy must be drawn to the attention of the *client* at the outset of a retainer, unless it is inappropriate to do so in the circumstances.

Guidance notes

   (i) Requirement to pay interest

      (a) Money is normally held for a client as a necessary, but incidental, part of the retainer, to facilitate the carrying out of the client's instructions. The main purpose of the rules is to keep that money safe and available for the purpose for which it was provided. The rules also seek to provide for the payment of a fair sum of interest, when appropriate, which is unlikely to be as high as that obtainable by the client depositing those funds.

(b) An outcomes-focused approach has been adopted in this area, allowing firms the flexibility to set their own interest policies in order to achieve a fair outcome for both the client and the firm.

(c) In addition to your obligation under rule 22.3, it is good practice to explain your interest arrangements to clients. These will usually be based on client money being held in an instant access account to facilitate a transaction. Clients are unlikely to receive as much interest as might have been obtained had they held and invested the money themselves. A failure to explain the firm's policy on interest may lead to unrealistic expectations and, possibly, a complaint to the Legal Ombudsman.

(d) The Legal Services Act 2007 has abolished the distinction in the Solicitors Act 1974 between interest earned on client money held in a general client account or a separate designated client account, meaning that interest earned on the latter type of account is, in theory, to be accounted for like interest on any other client money on a "fair and reasonable" basis. In practice, however, a firm which wishes to retain any part of the interest earned on client money will need to hold that money in a general client account and continue to have interest paid to the office account (see rule 12.7(b)). The tax regime still treats interest arising on money held in a separate designated client account as belonging to the client, and requires banks to deduct tax at source from that interest (subject to the tax status of the individual client) and credit the interest to the separate designated client account. This makes it impracticable for firms to retain any part of the interest earned on a separate designated client account.

(e) Some firms may wish to apply a de minimis by reference to the amount held and period for which it was held, for example, providing that no interest is payable if the amount calculated on the balance held is £20 or less. Any de minimis will need to be set at a reasonable level and regularly reviewed in the light of current interest rates.

(f) It is likely to be appropriate for firms to account for all interest earned in some circumstances, for example, where substantial sums of money are held for lengthy periods of time.

(g) If sums of money are held in relation to separate matters for the same client, it is normally appropriate to treat the money relating to the different matters separately but there may be cases when the matters are so closely related that they ought to be considered together, for example, when you are acting for a client in connection with numerous debt collection matters. Similarly, it may be fair and reasonable in the circumstances to aggregate sums of money held intermittently during the course of acting for a client.

Accounts Rules

    (h) There is no requirement to pay interest on money held on instructions under rule 15.1(a) in a manner which attracts no interest.

    (i) Accounts opened in the client's name under rule 15.1(b) (whether operated by you or not) are not subject to rule 22, as the money is not held by you. All interest earned belongs to the client. The same applies to any account in the client's own name operated by you as signatory under rule 10.

(ii) Interest policy (rule 22.3)

    (a) It is important that your clients should be aware of the terms of your interest policy. This should normally be covered at the outset of a retainer, although it may be unnecessary where you have acted for the client previously. It is open to you and your client to agree that interest will be dealt with in a different way (see rule 25).

(iii) Unpresented cheques

    (a) A client may fail to present a cheque to his or her bank for payment. Whether or not it is reasonable to recalculate the amount due will depend on all the circumstances of the case. A reasonable charge may be made for any extra work carried out if you are legally entitled to make such a charge.

(iv) Liquidators, trustees in bankruptcy, Court of Protection deputies and trustees of occupational pension schemes

    (a) Under rule 8, Part 3 of the rules does not normally apply to liquidators, etc. You must comply with the appropriate statutory rules and regulations, and rule 8.3 and 8.4 as appropriate.

(v) Joint accounts

    (a) Under rule 9, Part 3 of the rules does not apply to joint accounts. If you hold money jointly with a client, interest earned on the account will be for the benefit of the client unless otherwise agreed. If money is held jointly with another practice, the allocation of interest earned will depend on the agreement reached.

(vi) Failure to pay interest

    (a) A client, including one of joint clients, or a person funding all or part of your fees, may complain to the Legal Ombudsman if he or she believes that interest was due and has not been paid, or that the amount paid was insufficient. It is advisable for the client (or other person) to try to resolve the matter with you before approaching the Legal Ombudsman.

(vii) Role of the reporting accountant

    (a) Paragraph 2.8 of the Guidelines for accounting procedures and systems at Appendix 3 states the need for policies and systems in relation to the payment of interest.

(b) The reporting accountant does not check for compliance with the interest provisions but has a duty under rule 40 to report any substantial departures from the Guidelines discovered whilst carrying out work in preparation of the accountant's report. The accountant is not, however, required to determine the adequacy of a firm's interest policy (see rule 41.1(d)).

Rule 23: Amount of interest

23.1 The *interest* paid must be a fair and reasonable sum calculated over the whole period for which the money is held.

Guidance notes

(i) You will usually account to the client for interest at the conclusion of the client's matter, but might in some cases consider it appropriate to account to the client at intervals throughout.

(ii) The sum paid by way of interest need not necessarily reflect the highest rate of interest obtainable but it is unlikely to be appropriate to look only at the lowest rate of interest obtainable. A firm's policy on the calculation of interest will need to take into account factors such as:

(a) the amount held;

(b) the length of time for which cleared funds were held;

(c) the need for instant access to the funds;

(d) the rate of interest payable on the amount held in an instant access account at the bank or building society where the client account is kept;

(e) the practice of the bank or building society where the client account is kept in relation to how often interest is compounded.

(iii) A firm needs to have regard to the effect of the overall banking arrangements negotiated between it and the bank, on interest rates payable on individual balances. A fair sum of interest is unlikely to be achieved by applying interest rates which are set at an artificially low level to reflect, for example, more favourable terms in relation to the firm's office account.

(iv) A firm might decide to apply a fixed rate of interest by reference, for example, to the base rate. In setting that rate, the firm would need to consider (and regularly review) the level of interest it actually receives on its client accounts, but also take into account its overall banking arrangements so far as they affect the rates received.

(v) When looking at the period over which interest must be calculated, it will usually be unnecessary to check on actual clearance dates. When money is received by cheque and paid out by cheque, the normal clearance periods will usually cancel each other out, so that it will be satisfactory to look at the period between the dates when the incoming cheque is banked and the outgoing cheque is drawn.

(vi)   Different considerations apply when payments in and out are not both made by cheque. So, for example, the relevant periods would normally be:

   (a)   from the date when you receive incoming money in cash until the date when the outgoing cheque is sent;

   (b)   from the date when an incoming telegraphic transfer begins to earn interest until the date when the outgoing cheque is sent;

   (c)   from the date when an incoming cheque or banker's draft is or would normally be cleared until the date when the outgoing telegraphic transfer is made or banker's draft is obtained.

(vii)   Rule 13.8 requires that money held in a client account must be immediately available, even at the sacrifice of interest, unless the client otherwise instructs, or the circumstances clearly indicate otherwise. The need for access can be taken into account in assessing the appropriate rate for calculating interest to be paid.

(viii)   For failure to pay a sufficient sum by way of interest, see guidance note (vi)(a) to rule 22.

Rule 24: Interest on stakeholder money

24.1   When *you* hold money as stakeholder, *you* must pay *interest* on the basis set out in rule 22 to the person to whom the stake is paid, unless the parties have contracted out of this provision (see rule 25.3).

Rule 25: Contracting out

25.1   In appropriate circumstances *you* and *your client* may by a written agreement come to a different arrangement as to the matters dealt with in rule 22 (payment of interest).

25.2   *You* must act fairly towards *your clients* when entering into an agreement to depart from the *interest* provisions, including providing sufficient information at the outset to enable them to give informed consent.

25.3   When acting as stakeholder *you* may, by a written agreement with *your* own *client* and the other party to the transaction, come to a different arrangement as to the matters dealt with in rule 22.

Guidance notes

(i)   Whether it is appropriate to contract out depends on all the circumstances, for example, the size of the sum involved or the nature, status or bargaining position of the client. It might, for instance, be appropriate to contract out by standard terms of business if the client is a substantial commercial entity and the interest involved is modest in relation to the size of the transaction. The larger the sum of interest involved, the more there would be an onus on you to show that a client who had accepted a contracting out provision was properly informed and had been treated fairly.

(ii)   Contracting out which on the face of it appears to be against the client's interests is permissible where the client has given informed consent. For example, some clients may wish to contract out for reasons related to their tax position or to comply with their religious beliefs.

(iii)   A firm which decides not to receive or pay interest, due to the religious beliefs of its principals, will need to ensure that clients are informed at the outset, so that they can choose to instruct another firm if the lack of interest is an issue for them.

(iv)   Another example of contracting out is when the client stipulates, and the firm agrees, that all interest earned should be paid to the client despite the terms of the firm's interest policy.

(v)   In principle, you are entitled to make a reasonable charge to the client for acting as stakeholder in the client's matter.

(vi)   Alternatively, it may be appropriate to include a special provision in the contract that you retain the interest on the deposit to cover your charges for acting as stakeholder. This is only acceptable if it will provide a fair and reasonable payment for the work and risk involved in holding a stake. The contract could stipulate a maximum charge, with any interest earned above that figure being paid to the recipient of the stake.

(vii)   Any right to charge the client, or to stipulate for a charge which may fall on the client, would be excluded by, for instance, a prior agreement with the client for a fixed fee for the client's matter, or for an estimated fee which cannot be varied upwards in the absence of special circumstances. It is therefore not normal practice for a stakeholder in conveyancing transactions to receive a separate payment for holding the stake.

(viii)   A stakeholder who seeks an agreement to exclude the operation of rule 24 should be particularly careful not to take unfair advantage either of the client, or of the other party if unrepresented.

PART 4: ACCOUNTING SYSTEMS AND RECORDS

Rule 26: Guidelines for accounting procedures and systems

26.1   The *SRA* may from time to time publish guidelines for accounting procedures and systems to assist *you* to comply with Parts 1 to 4 of the rules, and *you* may be required to justify any departure from the guidelines.

Guidance notes

(i)   The current guidelines appear at Appendix 3.

(ii)   The reporting accountant does not carry out a detailed check for compliance, but has a duty to report on any substantial departures from the guidelines discovered whilst carrying out work in preparation of his or her report (see rules 40 and 41.1(e)).

Rule 27: Restrictions on transfers between clients

27.1   A paper transfer of money held in a *general client account* from the ledger of one *client* to the ledger of another *client* may only be made if:

(a)   it would have been permissible to withdraw that sum from the account under rule 20.1; and

(b)   it would have been permissible to pay that sum into the account under rule 14;

(but there is no requirement in the case of a paper transfer for a written authority under rule 21.1).

27.2   No sum in respect of a *private loan* from one *client* to another can be paid out of funds held for the lender either:

(a)   by a payment from one *client account* to another;

(b)   by a paper transfer from the ledger of the lender to that of the borrower; or

(c)   to the borrower directly,

except with the prior written authority of both *clients*.

27.3   If a *private loan* is to be made by (or to) joint *clients*, the consent of each *client* must be obtained.

Rule 28: Executor, trustee or nominee companies

28.1   If *your firm* owns all the shares in a *recognised body* or a *licensed body* which is an executor, trustee or nominee company, *your firm* and the *recognised body* or *licensed body* must not operate shared *client accounts*, but may:

(a)   use one set of accounting records for money held, received or paid by the *firm* and the *recognised body* or *licensed body*; and/or

(b)   deliver a single accountant's report for both the *firm* and the *recognised body* or *licensed body*.

28.2   If such a *recognised body* or *licensed body* as nominee receives a dividend cheque made out to the *recognised body* or *licensed body*, and forwards the cheque, either endorsed or subject to equivalent instructions, to the share-owner's *bank* or *building society*, etc., the *recognised body* or *licensed body* will have received (and paid) *client money*. One way of complying with rule 29 (accounting records) is to keep a copy of the letter to the share-owner's *bank* or *building society*, etc., on the file, and, in accordance with rule 29.23, to keep another copy in a central book of such letters. (See also rule 29.17(f) (retention of records for six years)).

Rule 29: Accounting records for client accounts, etc.

Accounting records which must be kept

29.1   *You* must at all times keep accounting records properly written up to show *your* dealings with:

(a)   *client money* received, held or paid by *you*; including *client money* held outside a *client account* under rule 15.1(a) or rule 16.1(d); and

(b)   any *office money* relating to any *client* or *trust* matter.

29.2   All dealings with *client money* must be appropriately recorded:

(a)   in a client cash account or in a record of sums transferred from one client ledger account to another; and

(b)   on the client side of a separate client ledger account for each *client* (or other person, or *trust*).

No other entries may be made in these records.

29.3   If *separate designated client accounts* are used:

(a)   a combined cash account must be kept in order to show the total amount held in *separate designated client accounts*; and

(b)   a record of the amount held for each *client* (or other person, or *trust*) must be made either in a deposit column of a client ledger account, or on the client side of a client ledger account kept specifically for a *separate designated client account*, for each *client* (or other person, or *trust*).

29.4   All dealings with *office money* relating to any *client* matter, or to any *trust* matter, must be appropriately recorded in an office cash account and on the office side of the appropriate client ledger account.

29.5   A cheque or draft received on behalf of a *client* and endorsed over, not passing through a *client account*, must be recorded in the books of account as a receipt and payment on behalf of the *client*. The same applies to cash received and not deposited in a *client account* but paid out to or on behalf of a *client*.

29.6   Money which has been paid into a *client account* under rule 17.1(c) (receipt of costs), or rule 18.2(b) (mixed money), and for the time being remains in a *client account*, is to be treated as *client money*; it must be appropriately identified and recorded on the client side of the client ledger account.

29.7   Money which has been paid into an *office account* under rule 17.1(b) (receipt of costs), rule 19.1(a) (advance payments from the Legal Aid Agency), or rule 19.1(b) (payment of costs from the Legal Aid Agency), and for the time being remains in an *office account* without breaching the rules, is to be treated as *office money*. Money paid into an *office account* under rule 19.2(b) (regular payments) is *office money*. All these payments must be appropriately identified and recorded on the office side of the client ledger account for the individual *client* or for the Legal Aid Agency.

29.8   *Client money* in a currency other than sterling must be held in a separate account for the appropriate currency, and *you* must keep separate books of account for that currency.

Current balance

29.9   The current balance on each client ledger account must always be shown, or be readily ascertainable, from the records kept in accordance with rule 29.2 and 29.3 above.

Acting for both lender and borrower

29.10   When acting for both lender and borrower on a mortgage advance, separate client ledger accounts for both *clients* need not be opened, provided that:

(a)   the funds belonging to each *client* are clearly identifiable; and

(b)   the lender is an institutional lender which provides mortgages on standard terms in the normal course of its activities.

Statements from banks, building societies and other financial institutions

29.11   *You* must, at least every 5 weeks:

(a)   obtain hard copy statements (or duplicate statements permitted in lieu of the originals by rule 9.3 or 9.4 from *banks, building societies* or other financial institutions, or

(b)   obtain and save in the *firm's* accounting records, in a format which cannot be altered, an electronic version of the *bank's, building society's* or other financial institution's on-line record,

in respect of:

(i)   any *general client account* or *separate designated client account*;

(ii)   any joint account held under rule 9;

(iii) any account which is not a *client account* but in which *you* hold *client money* under rule 15.1(a) or rule 16.1(d); and

(iv) any *office account* maintained in relation to the *firm*;

and each statement or electronic version must begin at the end of the previous statement.

This provision does not apply in respect of passbook-operated accounts, nor in respect of the *office accounts* of an *MDP* operated solely for activities not subject to *SRA* regulation.

Reconciliations

29.12   *You* must, at least once every five weeks:

(a)   compare the balance on the client cash account(s) with the balances shown on the statements and passbooks (after allowing for all unpresented items) of all *general client accounts* and *separate designated client accounts*, and of any account which is not a *client account* but in which *you* hold *client money* under rule 15.1(a) or rule 16.1(d), and any *client money* held by *you* in cash; and

(b)   as at the same date prepare a listing of all the balances shown by the client ledger accounts of the liabilities to *clients* (and other persons, and *trusts*) and compare the total of those balances with the balance on the client cash account; and also

(c)   prepare a reconciliation statement; this statement must show the cause of the difference, if any, shown by each of the above comparisons.

29.13   Reconciliations must be carried out as they fall due, or at the latest by the due date for the next reconciliation. In the case of a *separate designated client account* operated with a passbook, there is no need to ask the *bank*, *building society* or other financial institution for confirmation of the balance held. In the case of other *separate designated client accounts*, *you* must either obtain statements at least monthly or written confirmation of the balance direct from the *bank*, *building society* or other financial institution. There is no requirement to check that *interest* has been credited since the last statement, or the last entry in the passbook.

29.14   All shortages must be shown. In making the comparisons under rule 29.12(a) and (b), *you* must not, therefore, use credits of one *client* against debits of another when checking total client liabilities.

Bills and notifications of costs

29.15   *You* must keep readily accessible a central record or file of copies of:

(a)   all bills given or sent by *you* (other than those relating entirely to activities not regulated by the *SRA*); and

(b)   all other written notifications of *costs* given or sent by *you* (other than those relating entirely to activities not regulated by the *SRA*).

Withdrawals under rule 20.1(j)

29.16   If *you* withdraw *client money* under rule 20.1(j) *you* must keep a record of the steps taken in accordance with rule 20.2(a)–(c), together with all relevant documentation (including receipts from the charity).

Retention of records

29.17   *You* must retain for at least six years from the date of the last entry:

(a)   all documents or other records required by rule 29.1 to 29.10, 29.12, and 29.15 to 29.16 above;

(b)   all statements required by rule 29.11(a) above and passbooks, as printed and issued by the *bank*, *building society* or other financial institution; and/or all on-line records obtained and saved in electronic form under rule 29.11(b) above, for:

   (i)   any *general client account* or *separate designated client account*;

   (ii)   any joint account held under rule 9;

   (iii)   any account which is not a *client account* but in which *you* hold *client money* under rule 15.1(a) or rule 16.1(d); and

   (iv)   any *office account* maintained in relation to the practice, but not the *office accounts* of an *MDP* operated solely for activities not subject to *SRA* regulation;

(c)   any records kept under rule 8 (liquidators, trustees in bankruptcy, Court of Protection deputies and trustees of occupational pension schemes) including, as printed or otherwise issued, any statements, passbooks and other accounting records originating outside *your* office;

(d)   any written instructions to withhold *client money* from a *client account* (or a copy of *your* confirmation of oral instructions) in accordance with rule 15;

(e)   any central registers kept under rule 29.19 to 29.22 below; and

(f)   any copy letters kept centrally under rule 28.2 (dividend cheques endorsed over by nominee company).

29.18   *You* must retain for at least two years:

(a)   originals or copies of all authorities, other than cheques, for the withdrawal of money from a *client account*; and

(b)   all original paid cheques (or digital images of the front and back of all original paid cheques), unless there is a written arrangement with the *bank*, *building society* or other financial institution that:

   (i)   it will retain the original cheques on *your* behalf for that period; or

   (ii)   in the event of destruction of any original cheques, it will retain digital images of the front and back of those cheques on *your* behalf for that period and will, on demand by *you*, *your* reporting accountant or the *SRA*, produce copies of the digital images accompanied, when requested, by a certificate of verification signed by an authorised officer.

(c)   The requirement to keep paid cheques under rule 29.18(b) above extends to all cheques drawn on a *client account*, or on an account in which *client money* is held outside a *client account* under rule 15.1(a) or rule 16.1(d).

(d) Microfilmed copies of paid cheques are not acceptable for the purposes of rule 29.18(b) above. If a *bank*, *building society* or other financial institution is able to provide microfilmed copies only, *you* must obtain the original paid cheques from the *bank* etc. and retain them for at least two years.

Centrally kept records for certain accounts, etc.

29.19 Statements and passbooks for *client money* held outside a *client account* under rule 15.1(a) or rule 16.1(d) must be kept together centrally, or *you* must maintain a central register of these accounts.

29.20 Any records kept under rule 8 (liquidators, trustees in bankruptcy, Court of Protection deputies and trustees of occupational pension schemes) must be kept together centrally, or *you* must maintain a central register of the appointments.

29.21 The statements, passbooks, duplicate statements and copies of passbook entries relating to any joint account held under rule 9 must be kept together centrally, or *you* must maintain a central register of all joint accounts.

29.22 A central register of all withdrawals made under rule 20.1(j) must be kept, detailing the name of the *client*, other person or *trust* on whose behalf the money is held (if known), the amount, the name of the recipient charity and the date of the payment.

29.23 If a nominee company follows the option in rule 28.2 (keeping instruction letters for dividend payments), a central book must be kept of all instruction letters to the share-owner's *bank* or *building society*, etc.

Computerisation

29.24 Records required by this rule may be kept on a computerised system, apart from the following documents, which must be retained as printed or otherwise issued:

(a) original statements and passbooks retained under rule 29.17(b) above;

(b) original statements, passbooks and other accounting records retained under rule 29.17(c) above; and

(c) original cheques and original hard copy authorities retained under rule 29.18 above.

There is no obligation to keep a hard copy of computerised records. However, if no hard copy is kept, the information recorded must be capable of being reproduced reasonably quickly in printed form for at least six years, or for at least two years in the case of digital images of paid cheques retained under rule 29.18 above.

Suspense ledger accounts

29.25   Suspense client ledger accounts may be used only when *you* can justify their use; for instance, for temporary use on receipt of an unidentified payment, if time is needed to establish the nature of the payment or the identity of the *client*.

Guidance notes

(i)   It is strongly recommended that accounting records are written up at least weekly, even in the smallest practice, and daily in the case of larger firms.

(ii)   Rule 29.1 to 29.10 (general record-keeping requirements) and rule 29.12 (reconciliations) do not apply to:

(a)   liquidators, trustees in bankruptcy, Court of Protection deputies and trustees of occupational pension schemes operating in accordance with statutory rules or regulations under rule 8.1(i);

(b)   joint accounts operated under rule 9;

(c)   a client's own account operated under rule 10; the record-keeping requirements for this type of account are set out in rule 30;

(d)   you in your capacity as a trustee when you instruct an outside administrator to run, or continue to run, on a day-to-day basis, the business or property portfolio of an estate or trust, provided the administrator keeps and retains appropriate accounting records, which are available for inspection by the SRA in accordance with rule 31. (See also guidance note (v) to rule 21.)

(iii)   A cheque made payable to a client, which is forwarded to the client by you, is not client money and falls outside the rules, although it is advisable to record the action taken. See rule 14.2(e) for the treatment of a damages cheque, made payable to the client, which you pay into a client account under the Law Society's Conditional Fee Agreement.

(iv)   Some accounting systems do not retain a record of past daily balances. This does not put you in breach of rule 29.9.

(v)   "Clearly identifiable" in rule 29.10 means that by looking at the ledger account the nature and owner of the mortgage advance are unambiguously stated. For example, if a mortgage advance of £100,000 is received from the ABC Building Society, the entry should be recorded as "£100,000, mortgage advance, ABC Building Society". It is not enough to state that the money was received from the ABC Building Society without specifying the nature of the payment, or vice versa.

(vi)   Although you do not open a separate ledger account for the lender, the mortgage advance credited to that account belongs to the lender, not to the borrower, until completion takes place. Improper removal of these mortgage funds from a client account would be a breach of rule 20.

(vii)   Section 67 of the Solicitors Act 1974 permits a solicitor or recognised body to include on a bill of costs any disbursements which have been properly incurred but not paid before delivery of the bill, subject to those disbursements being described on the bill as unpaid.

(viii)   Rule 29.17(d) – retention of client's instructions to withhold money from a client account – does not require records to be kept centrally; however this may be prudent, to avoid losing the instructions if the file is passed to the client.

(ix)   You may enter into an arrangement whereby the bank keeps digital images of paid cheques in place of the originals. The bank should take an electronic image of the front and back of each cheque in black and white and agree to hold such images, and to make printed copies available on request, for at least two years. Alternatively, you may take and keep your own digital images of paid cheques.

(x)   Certificates of verification in relation to digital images of cheques may on occasion be required by the SRA when exercising its investigative and enforcement powers. The reporting accountant will not need to ask for a certificate of verification but will be able to rely on the printed copy of the digital image as if it were the original.

(xi)   These rules require an MDP to keep accounting records only in respect of those activities for which it is regulated by the SRA. Where an MDP acts for a client in a matter which includes activities regulated by the SRA, and activities outside the SRA's regulatory reach, the accounting records should record the MDP's dealings in respect of the SRA-regulated part of the client's matter. It may also be necessary to include in those records dealings with out-of-scope money where that money has been handled in connection with, or relates to, the SRA-regulated part of the transaction. An MDP is not required to maintain records in respect of client matters which relate entirely to activities not regulated by the SRA.

Rule 30: Accounting records for clients' own accounts

30.1   When *you* operate a *client's* own account as signatory under rule 10, *you* must retain, for at least six years from the date of the last entry, the statements or passbooks as printed and issued by the *bank*, *building society* or other financial institution, and/or the duplicate statements, copies of passbook entries and cheque details permitted in lieu of the originals by rule 10.3 or 10.4; and any central register kept under rule 30.2 below.

30.2   *You* must either keep these records together centrally, or maintain a central register of the accounts operated under rule 10.

30.3   If *you* use on-line records made available by the *bank*, *building society* or other financial institution, *you* must save an electronic version in the *firm's* accounting records in a format which cannot be altered. There is no obligation to keep a hard copy but the information recorded must be capable of being reproduced reasonably quickly in printed form for at least six years.

30.4 If, when *you* cease to operate the account, the *client* requests the original statements or passbooks, *you* must take photocopies and keep them in lieu of the originals.

30.5 This rule applies only to private practice.

PART 5: MONITORING AND INVESTIGATION BY THE SRA

Rule 31: Production of documents, information and explanations

31.1 *You* must at the time and place fixed by the *SRA* produce to any person appointed by the *SRA* any records, papers, *client* and *trust* matter files, financial accounts and other documents, and any other information, necessary to enable preparation of a report on compliance with the rules.

31.2 A requirement for production under rule 31.1 above must be in writing, and left at or sent by post or document exchange to the most recent address held by the *SRA's* Information Directorate, or sent electronically to the *firm's* e-mail or fax address, or delivered by the *SRA's* appointee. A notice under this rule is deemed to be duly served:

(a) on the date on which it is delivered to or left at *your* address;

(b) on the date on which it is sent electronically to *your* e-mail or fax address; or

(c) 48 hours (excluding Saturdays, Sundays and Bank Holidays) after it has been sent by post or document exchange.

31.3 Material kept electronically must be produced in the form required by the *SRA's* appointee.

31.4 The *SRA's* appointee is entitled to seek verification from *clients* and staff, and from the *banks*, *building societies* and other financial institutions used by *you*. *You* must, if necessary, provide written permission for the information to be given.

31.5 The *SRA's* appointee is not entitled to take original documents away but must be provided with photocopies on request.

31.6 *You* must be prepared to explain and justify any departures from the Guidelines for accounting procedures and systems published by the *SRA* (see rule 26).

31.7 Any report made by the *SRA's* appointee may, if appropriate, be sent to the Crown Prosecution Service or the Serious Fraud Office and/or used in proceedings before the Solicitors Disciplinary Tribunal. In the case of an *REL* or *RFL*, the report may also be sent to the competent authority in that lawyer's home state or states. In the case of a *solicitor* who is established in another state under the *Establishment Directive*, the report may also be sent to the competent authority in the host state. The report may also be sent to any of the accountancy bodies set out in rule 34.1(a) and/or taken into account by the *SRA* in relation to a possible disqualification of a reporting accountant under rule 34.3.

31.8   Without prejudice to rule 31.1 above, *you* must produce documents relating to any account kept by *you* at a *bank* or with a *building society*:

   (a)   in connection with *your* practice; or

   (b)   in connection with any *trust* of which *you* are or formerly were a *trustee*,

for inspection by a person appointed by the *SRA* for the purpose of preparing a report on compliance with the rules or on whether the account has been used for or in connection with a breach of any of the Principles or other SRA Handbook requirements made or issued by the *SRA*. Rules 31.2–31.7 above apply in relation to this paragraph in the same way as to rule 31.1.

Guidance notes

(i)   The SRA's powers override any confidence or privilege between you and the client.

(ii)   The SRA's monitoring and investigation powers are exercised by Forensic Investigations.

(iii)   The SRA will normally give a brief statement of the reasons for its investigations and inspections but not if the SRA considers that there is a risk that disclosure could:

   (a)   breach any duty of confidentiality;

   (b)   disclose, or risk disclosure of, a confidential source of information;

   (c)   significantly increase the risk that those under investigation may destroy evidence, seek to influence witnesses, default, or abscond; or

   (d)   otherwise prejudice or frustrate an investigation or other regulatory action.

PART 6: ACCOUNTANTS' REPORTS

Rule 32: Delivery of accountants' reports

32.1   Subject to rule 32.1A, if *you* have, at any time during an *accounting period*, held or received *client money*, or operated a *client's* own account as signatory, *you* must:-

   (a)   obtain an accountant's report for that *accounting period* within six months of the end of the *accounting period*; and

   (b)   if the report has been qualified, deliver it to the SRA within six months of the end of the *accounting period*.

This duty extends to the *directors* of a *company*, or the members of an *LLP*, which is subject to this rule.

32.1A   Subject to rule 32.2, you are not required to obtain or deliver an accountant's report if all of the *client money* held or received during an *accounting period* is money held or received from the Legal Aid Agency or in the circumstances set out in rule 19.3.

32.2   The *SRA* may require the delivery of an accountant's report in circumstances other than those set out in rule 32.1 and in the circumstances set out in rule 32.1A if the *SRA* has reason to believe that it is in the public interest to do so.

Guidance notes

(i)   A qualified accountant's report is a report prepared in accordance with rule 32.1(a) which the reporting accountant has found necessary to qualify. The form of the report is dealt with in rule 44. The circumstances in which the accountant will be required to qualify his or her report are set out in the form at Appendix 5 to these rules.

(ii)   Examples of situations under rule 32.2 include:

     (a)   when no report has been delivered but the SRA has reason to believe that a report should have been delivered;

     (b)   when a report has been delivered but the SRA has reason to believe that it may be inaccurate;

     (c)   when your conduct gives the SRA reason to believe that it would be appropriate to require earlier delivery of a report (for instance three months after the end of the accounting period);

     (d)   when your conduct gives the SRA reason to believe that it would be appropriate to require delivery in all circumstances or more frequent delivery of reports (for instance every six months);

     (e)   when the SRA has reason to believe that the regulatory risk justifies the imposition on a category of firm of a requirement to deliver reports earlier or at more frequent intervals;

     (f)   when a condition on a solicitor's practising certificate requires earlier delivery of reports or the delivery of reports at more frequent intervals.

(iii)   For accountant's reports of limited scope see rule 8 (liquidators, trustees in bankruptcy, Court of Protection deputies and trustees of occupational pension schemes), rule 9 (joint accounts) and rule 10 (operation of a client's own account). For exemption from the obligation to deliver a report, see rule 5 (persons exempt from the rules).

(iv)   The requirement in rule 32 for a registered foreign lawyer to deliver an accountant's report applies only to a registered foreign lawyer practising in one of the ways set out in paragraph (vi)(C) of the definition of "you" in the Glossary.

(v)   When client money is held or received by an unincorporated practice, the principals in the practice will have held or received client money. A salaried partner whose name appears in the list of partners on a firm's letterhead, even if the name appears under a separate heading of "salaried partners" or "associate partners", is a principal.

(vi)   In the case of an incorporated practice, it is the company or LLP (i.e. the recognised body or licensed body) which will have held or received client money. The recognised body/licensed body and its directors (in the case of a company) or members (in the case of an LLP) will have the duty to obtain the accountant's report and to deliver any such report to the SRA if it is qualified, although the directors or members will not usually have held client money.

(vii)   Assistant solicitors, consultants and other employees do not normally hold client money. An assistant solicitor or consultant might be a signatory for a firm's client account, but this does not constitute holding or receiving client money. If a client or third party hands cash to an assistant solicitor, consultant or other employee, it is the sole principal or the partners (rather than the assistant solicitor, consultant or other employee) who are regarded as having received and held the money. In the case of an incorporated practice, whether a company or an LLP, it would be the recognised body or licensed body itself which would be regarded as having held or received the money.

(viii)   If, exceptionally, an assistant solicitor, consultant or other employee has a client account (as a trustee), or operates a client's own account as signatory, the assistant solicitor, consultant or other employee will have to deliver an accountant's report. The assistant solicitor, consultant or other employee can be included in the report of the practice, but will need to ensure that his or her name is added, and an explanation given.

(ix)   If a cheque or draft is made out to you, and in the course of practice you endorse it over to a client or employer, you have received (and paid) client money. You will have to deliver an accountant's report, even if no other client money has been held or received.

(x)   Rule 32 does not apply to a solicitor or registered European lawyer, employed as an in-house lawyer by a non-solicitor employer, who operates the account of the employer or a related body of the employer.

(xi)   When only a small number of transactions is undertaken or a small volume of client money is handled in an accounting period, a waiver of the obligation to obtain a report may sometimes be granted. Applications should be made to the SRA.

(xii)   If a firm owns all the shares in a recognised body or licensed body which is an executor, trustee or nominee company, the firm and the recognised body/licensed body may deliver a single accountant's report (see rule 28.1(b)).

Rule 33: Accounting periods

The norm

33.1   An "accounting period" means the period for which *your* accounts are ordinarily made up, except that it must:

(a)   begin at the end of the previous *accounting period*; and

(b)   cover twelve months.

Rules 33.2 to 33.5 below set out exceptions.

First and resumed reports

33.2   If *you* are under a duty to deliver *your* first report, the *accounting period* must begin on the date when *you* first held or received *client money* (or operated a *client's* own account as signatory), and may cover less than twelve months.

33.3   If *you* are under a duty to deliver *your* first report after a break, the *accounting period* must begin on the date when *you* for the first time after the break held or received *client money* (or operated a *client's* own account as signatory), and may cover less than twelve months.

Change of accounting period

33.4   If *you* change the period for which *your* accounts are made up (for example, on a merger, or simply for convenience), the *accounting period* immediately preceding the change may be shorter than twelve months, or longer than twelve months up to a maximum of 18 months, provided that the *accounting period* shall not be changed to a period longer than twelve months unless the *SRA* receives written notice of the change before expiry of the deadline for delivery of the accountant's report which would have been expected on the basis of *your* old *accounting period*.

Final reports

33.5   If *you* for any reason stop holding or receiving *client money* (and operating any *client's* own account as signatory), *you* must deliver a final report. The *accounting period* must end on the date upon which *you* stopped holding or receiving *client money* (and operating any *client's* own account as signatory), and may cover less than twelve months.

Guidance notes

(i)   For a person who did not previously hold or receive client money, etc., and has become a principal in the firm, the report for the firm will represent, from the date of joining, that person's first report for the purpose of rule 33.2. For a person who was a principal in the firm and, on leaving, stops holding or receiving client money, etc., the report for the firm will represent, up to the date of leaving, that person's final report for the purpose of rule 33.5 above.

(ii)   When a partnership splits up, it is usually appropriate for the books to be made up as at the date of dissolution, and for an accountant's report to be delivered within six months of that date. If, however, the old partnership continues to hold or receive client money, etc., in connection with outstanding matters, accountant's reports will continue to be required for those matters; the books should then be made up on completion of the last of those matters and a report delivered within six months of that date. The same would be true for a sole practitioner winding up matters on retirement.

(iii)   When a practice is being wound up, you may be left with money which is unattributable, or belongs to a client who cannot be traced. It may be appropriate to apply to the SRA for authority to withdraw this money from the client account – see rule 20.1(k) and guidance note (vi)(a) to rule 20.

Rule 34: Qualifications for making a report

34.1   A report must be prepared and signed by an accountant

(a)   **who is a member of:**

(i)   the Institute of Chartered Accountants in England and Wales;

(ii)   the Institute of Chartered Accountants of Scotland;

(iii)   the Association of Chartered Certified Accountants;

(iv)   the Institute of Chartered Accountants in Ireland; or

(v)   the Association of Authorised Public Accountants; **and**

(b)   **who is also:**

(i)   an individual who is a registered auditor within the terms of section 1239 of the Companies Act 2006; or

(ii)   an employee of such an individual; or

(iii)   a *partner* in or employee of a *partnership* which is a registered auditor within the terms of section 1239 of the Companies Act 2006; or

(iv)   a director or employee of a company which is a registered auditor within the terms of section 1239 of the Companies Act 2006; or

(v)   a member or employee of an *LLP* which is a registered auditor within the terms of section 1239 of the Companies Act 2006.

34.2   An accountant is not qualified to make a report if:

(a)   at any time between the beginning of the *accounting period* to which the report relates, and the completion of the report:

(i)   he or she was a *partner* or employee, or an officer or employee (in the case of a company), or a member or employee (in the case of an *LLP*) in the *firm* to which the report relates; or

(ii)   he or she was employed by the same *non-solicitor employer* as the *solicitor* or *REL* for whom the report is being made; or

(iii)   he or she was a *partner* or employee, or an officer or employee (in the case of a company), or a member or employee (in the case of an *LLP*) in

Accounts Rules

an accountancy practice which had an ownership interest in, or was part of the group structure of, the *licensed body* to which the report relates; or

(b) he or she has been disqualified under rule 34.3 below and notice of disqualification has been given under rule 34.4 (and has not subsequently been withdrawn).

34.3   The *SRA* may disqualify an accountant from making any accountant's report if:

(a) the accountant has been found guilty by his or her professional body of professional misconduct or discreditable conduct; or

(b) the *SRA* is satisfied that *you* have not complied with the rules in respect of matters which the accountant has negligently failed to specify in a report.

In coming to a decision, the *SRA* will take into account any representations made by the accountant or his or her professional body.

34.4   Written notice of disqualification must be left at or sent by recorded delivery to the address of the accountant shown on an accountant's report or in the records of the accountant's professional body. If sent through the post, receipt will be deemed 48 hours (excluding Saturdays, Sundays and Bank Holidays) after posting.

34.5   An accountant's disqualification may be notified to any *firm* likely to be affected and may be printed in the *Society's* Gazette or other publication.

Guidance note

(i)   It is not a breach of the rules for you to retain an outside accountant to write up the books of account and to instruct the same accountant to prepare the accountant's report. However, the accountant will have to confirm that these circumstances do not affect his or her independence in preparing the report – see the form of report in Appendix 5.

Rule 35: Reporting accountant's rights and duties – letter of engagement

35.1   *You* must ensure that the reporting accountant's rights and duties are stated in a letter of engagement incorporating the following terms:

"In accordance with rule 35 of the SRA Accounts Rules 2011, you are instructed as follows:

(a) I/this firm/this company/this limited liability partnership recognises that, if during the course of preparing an accountant's report:

(i)   you discover evidence of fraud or theft in relation to money

(A)   held by a solicitor (or registered European lawyer, or registered foreign lawyer, or recognised body, or licensed body, or employee of a solicitor or registered European lawyer, or manager or employee of a recognised body or licensed body) for a client or any other person (including money held on trust), or

(B) held in an account of a client, or an account of another person, which is operated by a solicitor (or registered European lawyer, registered foreign lawyer, recognised body, licensed body, employee of a solicitor or registered European lawyer, or manager or employee of a recognised body or licensed body); or

(ii) you obtain information which you have reasonable cause to believe is likely to be of material significance in determining whether a solicitor (or registered European lawyer, or registered foreign lawyer, or recognised body, or licensed body, or employee of a solicitor or registered European lawyer, or manager or employee of a recognised body or licensed body) is a fit and proper person

(A) to hold money for clients or other persons (including money held on trust), or

(B) to operate an account of a client or an account of another person,

you must immediately give a report of the matter to the Solicitors Regulation Authority in accordance with section 34(9) of the Solicitors Act 1974 or article 3(1) of the Legal Services Act 2007 (Designation as a Licensing Authority) (No. 2) Order 2011 as appropriate;

(b) you may, and are encouraged to, make that report without prior reference to me/this firm/this company/this limited liability partnership;

(c) you are to report directly to the Solicitors Regulation Authority should your appointment be terminated following the issue of, or indication of intention to issue, a qualified accountant's report, or following the raising of concerns prior to the preparation of an accountant's report;

(d) you are to deliver to me/this firm/this company/this limited liability partnership with your report the completed checklist required by rule 43 of the SRA Accounts Rules 2011; to retain for at least three years from the date of signature a copy of the completed checklist; and to produce the copy to the Solicitors Regulation Authority on request;

(e) you are to retain these terms of engagement for at least three years after the termination of the retainer and to produce them to the Solicitors Regulation Authority on request; and

(f) following any direct report made to the Solicitors Regulation Authority under (a) or (c) above, you are to provide to the Solicitors Regulation Authority on request any further relevant information in your possession or in the possession of your firm.

To the extent necessary to enable you to comply with (a) to (f) above, I/we waive my/the firm's/the company's/the limited liability partnership's right of confidentiality. This waiver extends to any report made, document produced or information disclosed to the Solicitors Regulation Authority in good faith pursuant to these instructions, even though it may subsequently transpire that you were mistaken in your belief that there was cause for concern."

35.2   The letter of engagement and a copy must be signed by *you* and by the accountant. *You* must keep the copy of the signed letter of engagement for at least three years after the termination of the retainer and produce it to the *SRA* on request.

35.3   The specified terms may be included in a letter from the accountant to *you* setting out the terms of the engagement but the text must be adapted appropriately. The letter must be signed in duplicate by both parties, with *you* keeping the original and the accountant the copy.

Guidance note

(i)   Any direct report by the accountant to the SRA under rule 35.1(a) or (c) should be made to the Fraud and Confidential Intelligence Bureau.

Rule 36: Change of accountant

36.1   On instructing an accountancy practice to replace that previously instructed to produce accountant's reports, *you* must immediately notify the *SRA* of the change and provide the name and business address of the new accountancy practice.

Rule 37: Place of examination

37.1   Unless there are exceptional circumstances, the place of examination of *your* accounting records, files and other relevant documents must be *your* office and not the office of the accountant. This does not prevent an initial electronic transmission of data to the accountant for examination at the accountant's office with a view to reducing the time which needs to be spent at *your* office.

Rule 38: Provision of details of bank accounts, etc.

38.1   The accountant must request, and *you* must provide, details of all accounts kept or operated by *you* in connection with *your* practice at any *bank*, *building society* or other financial institution at any time during the *accounting period* to which the report relates. This includes *client accounts*, *office accounts*, accounts which are not *client accounts* but which contain *client money*, and *clients'* own accounts operated by *you* as signatory.

Rule 39: Test procedures

39.1   The accountant must examine *your* accounting records (including statements and passbooks), *client* and *trust* matter files selected by the accountant as and when appropriate, and other relevant documents, and make the following checks and tests:

   (a)   confirm that the accounting system in every office complies with:

      (i)   rule 29 – accounting records for client accounts, etc;

      (ii)   rule 30 – accounting records for clients' own accounts;

   and is so designed that:

      (A)   an appropriate client ledger account is kept for each *client* (or other person for whom *client money* is received, held or paid) or *trust*;

(B) the client ledger accounts show separately from other information details of all *client money* received, held or paid on account of each *client* (or other person for whom *client money* is received, held or paid) or *trust*; and

(C) transactions relating to *client money* and any other money dealt with through a *client account* are recorded in the accounting records in a way which distinguishes them from transactions relating to any other money received, held or paid by *you*;

(b) make test checks of postings to the client ledger accounts from records of receipts and payments of *client money*, and make test checks of the casts of these accounts and records;

(c) compare a sample of payments into and from the *client accounts* as shown in *bank* and *building society* or other financial institutions' statements or passbooks with *your* records of receipts and payments of *client money*, including paid cheques;

(d) test check the system of recording *costs* and of making transfers in respect of *costs* from the *client accounts*;

(e) make a test examination of a selection of documents requested from *you* in order to confirm:

(i) that the financial transactions (including those giving rise to transfers from one client ledger account to another) evidenced by such documents comply with Parts 1 and 2 of the rules, rule 27 (restrictions on transfers between clients) and rule 28 (executor, trustee or nominee companies); and

(ii) that the entries in the accounting records reflect those transactions in a manner complying with rule 29;

(f) subject to rule 39.2 below, extract (or check extractions of) balances on the client ledger accounts during the *accounting period* under review at not fewer than two dates selected by the accountant (one of which may be the last day of the *accounting period*), and at each date:

(i) compare the total shown by the client ledger accounts of the liabilities to the *clients* (and other persons for whom *client money* is held) and *trusts* with the cash account balance; and

(ii) reconcile that cash account balance with the balances held in the *client accounts*, and accounts which are not *client accounts* but in which *client money* is held, as confirmed direct to the accountant by the relevant *banks*, *building societies* and other financial institutions;

(g) confirm that reconciliation statements have been made and kept in accordance with rule 29.12 and 29.17(a);

(h) make a test examination of the client ledger accounts to see whether payments from the *client account* have been made on any individual account in excess of money held on behalf of that *client* (or other person for whom *client money* is held) or *trust*;

(i) check the office ledgers, office cash accounts and the statements provided by the *bank*, *building society* or other financial institution for any *office account* maintained by *you* in connection with the practice, to see whether any *client money* has been improperly paid into an *office account* or, if properly paid into an *office account* under rule 17.1(b) or rule 19.1, has been kept there in breach of the rules;

(j) check the accounting records kept under rule 29.17(d) and 29.19 for *client money* held outside a *client account* to ascertain what transactions have been effected in respect of this money and to confirm that the *client* has given appropriate instructions under rule 15.1(a);

(k) make a test examination of the client ledger accounts to see whether rule 29.10 (accounting records when acting for both lender and borrower) has been complied with;

(l) for liquidators, trustees in bankruptcy, *Court of Protection deputies* and trustees of occupational pension schemes, check that records are being kept in accordance with rule 29.15, 29.17(c) and 29.20, and cross-check transactions with *client* or *trust* matter files when appropriate;

(m) check that statements and passbooks and/or duplicate statements and copies of passbook entries are being kept in accordance with rule 29.17(b)(ii) and 29.21 (record-keeping requirements for joint accounts), and cross-check transactions with *client* matter files when appropriate;

(n) check that statements and passbooks and/or duplicate statements, copies of passbook entries and cheque details are being kept in accordance with rule 30 (record-keeping requirements for clients' own accounts), and cross-check transactions with *client* matter files when appropriate;

(o) for money withdrawn from *client account* under rule 20.1(j), check that records are being kept in accordance with rule 29.16, 29.17(a) and 29.22, and cross-check with *client* or *trust* matter files when appropriate;

(p) in the case of private practice only, check that for the period which will be covered by the accountant's report the *firm* was covered for the purposes of the *SRA's* indemnity insurance rules in respect of its offices in England and Wales by:

    (i) certificates of qualifying insurance outside the assigned risks pool; or

    (ii) a policy issued by the assigned risks pool manager; or

    (iii) certificates of indemnity cover under the professional requirements of an *REL's* home jurisdiction in accordance with paragraph 1 of Appendix 3 to those rules, together with the *SRA's* written grant of full exemption; or

    (iv) certificates of indemnity cover under the professional requirements of an *REL's* home jurisdiction plus certificates of a difference in conditions policy with a qualifying insurer under paragraph 2 of Appendix 3 to those rules, together with the *SRA's* written grant of partial exemption; and

(q) ask for any information and explanations required as a result of making the above checks and tests.

Extracting balances

39.2   For the purposes of rule 39.1(f) above, if *you* use a computerised or mechanised system of accounting which automatically produces an extraction of all client ledger balances, the accountant need not check all client ledger balances extracted on the list produced by the computer or machine against the individual records of client ledger accounts, provided the accountant:

(a) confirms that a satisfactory system of control is in operation and the accounting records are in balance;

(b) carries out a test check of the extraction against the individual records; and

(c) states in the report that he or she has relied on this exception.

Guidance notes

(i)   The rules do not require a complete audit of your accounts nor do they require the preparation of a profit and loss account or balance sheet.

(ii)   In making the comparisons under rule 39.1(f), some accountants improperly use credits of one client against debits of another when checking total client liabilities, thus failing to disclose a shortage. A debit balance on a client account when no funds are held for that client results in a shortage which must be disclosed as a result of the comparison.

(iii)   The main purpose of confirming balances direct with banks, etc., under rule 39.1(f)(ii) is to ensure that your records accurately reflect the sums held at the bank. The accountant is not expected to conduct an active search for undisclosed accounts.

(iv)   In checking compliance with rule 20.1(j), the accountant should check on a sample basis that you have complied with rule 20.2 and are keeping appropriate records in accordance with rule 29.16, 29.17(a) and 29.22. The accountant is not expected to judge the adequacy of the steps taken to establish the identity of, and to trace, the rightful owner of the money.

Rule 40: Departures from guidelines for accounting procedures and systems

40.1   The accountant should be aware of the *SRA's* guidelines for accounting procedures and systems (see rule 26), and must note in the accountant's report any substantial departures from the guidelines discovered whilst carrying out work in preparation of the report. (See also rule 41.1(e).)

Rule 41: Matters outside the accountant's remit

41.1   The accountant is not required:

(a)   to extend his or her enquiries beyond the information contained in the documents produced, supplemented by any information and explanations given by *you*;

(b)   to enquire into the stocks, shares, other securities or documents of title held by *you* on behalf of *your clients*;

(c)   to consider whether *your* accounting records have been properly written up at any time other than the time at which his or her examination of the accounting records takes place;

(d)   to check compliance with the provisions in rule 22 on *interest*, nor to determine the adequacy of *your interest* policy;

(e)   to make a detailed check on compliance with the guidelines for accounting procedures and systems (see rules 26 and 40); or

(f)   to determine the adequacy of the steps taken under paragraphs (a) and (b) of rule 20.2.

Rule 42: Privileged documents

42.1   When acting on a *client's* instructions, *you* will normally have the right on the grounds of privilege as between *solicitor* and *client* to decline to produce any document requested by the accountant for the purposes of his or her examination. In these circumstances, the accountant must qualify the report and set out the circumstances.

Guidance note

(i)   In a recognised body or licensed body with one or more managers who are not legally qualified, legal professional privilege may not attach to work which is neither done nor supervised by a legally qualified individual – see Legal Services Act 2007, section 190(3) to (7), and Schedule 22, paragraph 17.

Rule 43: Completion of checklist

43.1   The accountant should exercise his or her professional judgment in adopting a suitable "audit" programme, but must also complete and sign a checklist in the form published from time to time by the *SRA*. *You* must obtain the completed checklist, retain it for at least three years from the date of signature and produce it to the *SRA* on request.

Guidance notes

(i)   The current checklist appears at Appendix 4. It is issued by the SRA to firms at the appropriate time for completion by their reporting accountants.

(ii)   The letter of engagement required by rule 35 imposes a duty on the account-ant to hand the completed checklist to the firm, to keep a copy for three years and to produce the copy to the SRA on request.

Rule 44: Form of accountant's report

44.1   The accountant must complete and sign his or her report in the form published from time to time by the *SRA*. An explanation of any significant difference between liabilities to *clients* and *client money* held, as identified at section 2 of the report, must be given by either the accountant or *you*.

Guidance notes

(i)   The current form of accountant's report appears at Appendix 5. The report confirms if the accountant has found it necessary to qualify the report. If so, the report must be delivered to the SRA – see rule 32.1(b) and guidance note (i) to that rule.

(ii)   Separate reports can be obtained for each principal in a partnership but most firms choose to obtain one report in the name of all the principals. In either case, the report must be delivered to the SRA if it is qualified – see rule 32.1(b) and guidance note (i). For assistant solicitors, consultants and other employees, see rule 32, guidance notes (vii) and (viii).

(iii)   An incorporated practice will obtain only one report, on behalf of the company and its directors, or on behalf of the LLP and its members – see rule 32.1. The report must be delivered to the SRA if it is qualified – see rule 32.1(b) and guidance note (i) to that rule.

(iv)   Although it may be agreed that the accountant send any qualified reports direct to the SRA, the responsibility for delivery is that of the firm. The form of report requires the accountant to confirm that a copy of the report (whether qualified or unqualified) has been sent to the COFA on behalf of the firm to which it relates. The COFA should ensure that the report is seen by each of the managers of the firm.

(v)   A reporting accountant is not required to report on trivial breaches due to clerical errors or mistakes in book-keeping, provided that they have been rectified on discovery and the accountant is satisfied that no client suffered any loss as a result.

(vi)   In many practices, clerical and book-keeping errors will arise. In the majority of cases these may be classified by the reporting accountant as trivial breaches. However, a "trivial breach" cannot be precisely defined. The amount involved, the nature of the breach, whether the breach is deliberate or accidental, how often the same breach has occurred, and the time outstanding before correction (especially the replacement of any shortage) are all factors which should be considered by the accountant before deciding whether a breach is trivial.

(vii)   For direct reporting by the accountant to the SRA in cases of concern, see rule 35 and guidance note (i) to that rule.

Rule 45: Firms with two or more places of business

45.1   If a *firm* has two or more offices:

(a)   separate reports may be delivered in respect of the different offices; and

(b)   separate *accounting periods* may be adopted for different offices, provided that:

(i)   separate reports are delivered;

(ii)   every office is covered by a report delivered within six months of the end of its *accounting period*; and

(iii)   there are no gaps between the *accounting periods* covered by successive reports for any particular office or offices.

Rule 46: Waivers

46.1   The *SRA* may waive in writing in any particular case or cases any of the provisions of Part 6 of the rules, and may revoke any waiver.

Guidance note

(i)   Applications for waivers should be made to the SRA. In appropriate cases, firms may be granted a waiver of the obligation to obtain an accountant's report (see rule 32, and guidance note (xi) to that rule). The circumstances in which a waiver of any other provision of Part 6 would be given must be extremely rare.

PART 7: PRACTICE FROM AN OFFICE OUTSIDE ENGLAND AND WALES

Rule 47: Purpose of the overseas accounts provisions

47.1   The purpose of applying different accounts provisions to practice from an office outside England and Wales is to ensure similar protection for *client money (overseas)* but by way of rules which are more adaptable to conditions in other jurisdictions.

Rule 48: Application and Interpretation

48.1   Part 7 of these rules applies to your practice from an office outside England and Wales to the extent specified in each rule in this Part. If compliance with any applicable provision of Part 7 of these rules would result in your breaching local law, you may disregard that provision to the extent necessary to comply with that local law.

48.2   The SRA Handbook Glossary 2012 shall apply and, unless the context otherwise requires:

(a)   all italicised terms shall be defined; and

(b)   all terms shall be interpreted,

in accordance with the *Glossary*.

Rule 49: Interest

49.1   You must comply with rule 49.2 below, if you hold *client money (overseas)* and you are:

(a)   a *solicitor sole practitioner practising from an office* outside England and Wales, or an *REL sole practitioner practising from an office* in Scotland or Northern Ireland;

(b)   a *lawyer-controlled body* or (in relation to *practice from an office* in Scotland or Northern Ireland) a *lawyer-controlled body*, or an *REL-controlled body*;

(c)   a *lawyer of England and Wales* who is a *manager (overseas)* of a *firm (overseas)* which is *practising from an office* outside the *UK*, and *lawyers of England and Wales* control the *firm (overseas)*, either directly as *partners*, members or *owners*, or indirectly by their ownership of *bodies corporate* which are *partners*, members or *owners*; or

(d)   a *lawyer of England and Wales* or *REL* who is a *manager (overseas)* of a *firm (overseas)* which is *practising from an office* in Scotland or Northern Ireland, and *lawyers of England and Wales* and/or *RELs* control the *firm (overseas)*, either directly as *partners*, members or *owners*, or indirectly by their ownership of *bodies corporate* which are *partners*, members or *owners*.

49.2   If it is fair and reasonable for interest to be earned for the client on that *client money (overseas)*, you must ensure that:

(a)   the *client money (overseas)* is dealt with so that fair and reasonable interest is earned upon it, and that the interest is paid to the client;

(b)   the client is paid a sum equivalent to the interest that would have been earned if the *client money (overseas)* had earned fair and reasonable interest; or

(c)   any alternative written agreement with the client setting out arrangements regarding the payment of interest on that money is carried out.

49.3   In deciding whether it is fair and reasonable for interest to be earned for a client on *client money (overseas)*, you must have regard to all the circumstances, including:

(a)   the amount of the money;

(b)   the length of time for which you are likely to hold the money; and

(c)   the law and prevailing custom of lawyers practising in the jurisdiction in which you are practising.

Rule 50: Accounts

Practice from an office outside the UK

50.1   You must comply with rule 50.3 and 50.4 below in relation to *practice from an office* outside the *UK* if you are:

- (a)   a *solicitor sole practitioner* who has held or received *client money (overseas)*;

- (b)   a *lawyer-controlled body* which has held or received *client money (overseas)* as a *firm (overseas)*;

- (c)   a *lawyer of England and Wales*, or a *non-lawyer*, who is a *manager (overseas)* of a *lawyer-controlled body* which holds or receives *client money (overseas)*;

- (d)   a *lawyer of England and Wales* who is a *manager (overseas)* of any other *firm (overseas)* which is controlled by *lawyers of England and Wales*, either directly as *partners*, members or *owners*, or indirectly by their ownership of *bodies corporate* which are *partners*, members or *owners*, if the *firm (overseas)* holds or receives *client money (overseas)*;

- (e)   a *solicitor* who holds or receives *client money (overseas)* as a named *trustee*;

- (f)   a *lawyer of England and Wales*, or a *non-lawyer*, who is a *manager (overseas)* of a *lawyer-controlled body* and who holds or receives *client money (overseas)* as a named *trustee*.

Practice from an office in Scotland or Northern Ireland

50.2   You must comply with rule 50.3 and 50.4 below in relation to *practice from an office* in Scotland or Northern Ireland if you are:

- (a)   a *solicitor* or *REL sole practitioner* who has held or received *client money (overseas)*;

- (b)   a *lawyer-controlled body*, or an *REL-controlled body*, which has held or received *client money (overseas)* as a *firm (overseas)*;

- (c)   a *lawyer of England and Wales*, an *REL*, a European lawyer registered with the *BSB* or a *non-lawyer*, who is a *manager (overseas)* of a *lawyer-controlled body*, or an *REL-controlled body*, which holds or receives *client money (overseas)*;

- (d)   a *lawyer of England and Wales* or *REL* who is a *manager (overseas)* of any other *firm (overseas)* which is controlled by *lawyers of England and Wales* and/or *RELs*, either directly as *partners*, members or *owners*, or indirectly by their ownership of *bodies corporate* which are *partners*, members or *owners*, if the *firm (overseas)* holds or receives *client money (overseas)*;

- (e)   a *solicitor* or *REL* who holds or receives *client money (overseas)* as a named *trustee*;

- (f)   a *lawyer of England and Wales*, a European lawyer registered with the *BSB* or a *non-lawyer*, who is a *manager (overseas)* of a *lawyer-controlled body*, or an *REL-controlled body*, and who holds or receives *client money (overseas)* as a named *trustee*.

Dealings with client money

50.3 In all dealings with *client money (overseas)*, you must ensure that:

(a) it is kept in a *client account (overseas)*, separate from money which is not *client money (overseas)*;

(b) on receipt, it is paid without delay into a *client account (overseas)* and kept there, unless the client has expressly or by implication agreed that the money shall be dealt with otherwise or you pay it straight over to a third party in the execution of a *trust* under which it is held;

(c) it is not paid or withdrawn from a *client account (overseas)* except:

   (i) on the specific authority of the client;

   (ii) where the payment or withdrawal is properly required:

   (A) for a payment to or on behalf of the client;

   (B) for or towards payment of a debt due to the *firm (overseas)* from the client or in reimbursement of money expended by the *firm (overseas)* on behalf of the client; or

   (C) for or towards payment of costs due to the *firm (overseas)* from the client, provided that a bill of costs or other written intimation of the amount of the costs incurred has been delivered to the client and it has thereby (or otherwise in writing) been made clear to the client that the money held will be applied in payment of the costs due; or

   (iii) in proper execution of a *trust* under which it is held;

(d) accounts are kept at all times, whether by written, electronic, mechanical or other means, to:

   (i) record all dealings with *client money (overseas)* in any *client account (overseas)*;

   (ii) show all *client money (overseas)* received, held or paid, distinct from any other money, and separately in respect of each client or *trust*; and

   (iii) ensure that the *firm (overseas)* is able at all times to account, without delay, to each and every client or *trust* for all money received, held or paid on behalf of that client or *trust*; and

(e) all accounts, books, ledgers and records kept in relation to the *firm's (overseas) client account(s) (overseas)* are preserved for at least six years from the date of the last entry therein.

Accountants' reports

50.4 You must deliver an accountant's report in respect of any period during which you or your *firm (overseas)* have held or received *client money (overseas)* and you were subject to rule 50.3 above, within six months of the end of that period.

50.5 The accountant's report must be signed by the reporting accountant, who must be an accountant qualified in England and Wales or in the overseas jurisdiction where your office is based, or by such other person as the *SRA* may think fit. The *SRA* may for reasonable cause disqualify a person from signing accountants' reports.

50.6 The accountant's report must be based on a sufficient examination of the relevant documents to give the reporting accountant a reasonable indication whether or not you have complied with rule 50.3 above during the period covered by the report, and must include the following:

(a) your name, practising address(es) and practising style and the name(s) of the *firm's (overseas) managers (overseas)*;

(b) the name, address and qualification of the reporting accountant;

(c) an indication of the nature and extent of the examination the reporting accountant has made of the relevant documents;

(d) a statement of the total amount of money held at banks or similar institutions on behalf of clients and *trusts*, and of the total liabilities to clients and *trusts*, on any date selected by the reporting accountant (including the last day), falling within the period under review; and an explanation of any difference between the total amount of money held for clients and *trusts* and the total liabilities to clients and *trusts*;

(e) if the reporting accountant is satisfied that (so far as may be ascertained from the examination) you have complied with rule 50.3 above during the period covered by the report, except for trivial breaches, or situations where you have been bound by a local rule not to comply, a statement to that effect; and

(f) if the reporting accountant is not sufficiently satisfied to give a statement under (e) above, details of any matters in respect of which it appears to the reporting accountant that you have not complied with rule 50.3 above.

Rule 51: Production of documents, information and explanations

51.1 You must promptly comply with:

(a) a written notice from the *SRA* that you must produce for inspection by the appointee of the *SRA* all documents held by you or held under your control and all information and explanations requested:

(i) in connection with your practice; or

(ii) in connection with any *trust* of which you are, or formerly were, a *trustee*;

for the purpose of ascertaining whether any person subject to Part 7 of these rules is complying with or has complied with any provision of this Part of these rules, or on whether the account has been used for or in connection with a breach of any of the Principles or other SRA Handbook requirements made or issued by the *SRA*; and

(b) a notice given by the *SRA* in accordance with section 44B or 44BA of the *LSA* or section 93 of the *LSA* for the provision of documents, information or explanations.

51.2 You must provide any necessary permissions for information to be given so as to enable the appointee of the *SRA* to:

(a) prepare a report on the documents produced under rule 51.1 above; and

(b) seek verification from clients, staff and the banks, building societies or other financial institutions used by you.

51.3 You must comply with all requests from the *SRA* or its appointee as to:

(a) the form in which you produce any documents you hold electronically; and

(b) photocopies of any documents to take away.

51.4 A notice under this rule is deemed to be duly served:

(a) on the date on which it is delivered to or left at your address;

(b) on the date on which it is sent electronically to your e-mail or fax address; or

(c) 48 hours (excluding Saturdays, Sundays and Bank Holidays) after it has been sent by post or document exchange to your last notified practising address.

Guidance notes

(i) If your firm has offices in and outside England and Wales, a single accountant's report may be submitted covering your practice from offices both in, and outside, England and Wales – such a report must cover compliance both with Parts 1 to 6 of these rules, and with Part 7 of these rules.

(ii) The accounting requirements and the obligation to deliver an accountant's report in this part of the rules are designed to apply to you in relation to money held or received by your firm unless it is primarily the practice of lawyers of other jurisdictions. The fact that they do not apply in certain cases is not intended to allow a lower standard of care in the handling of client money – simply to prevent the "domestic provisions" applying "by the back door" in a disproportionate or inappropriate way.

(iii) In deciding whether interest ought, in fairness, to be paid to a client, the fact that the interest is or would be negligible, or it is customary in that jurisdiction to deal with interest in a different way, may mean that interest is not payable under rule 49.2.

Rule 52: Waivers

52.1   The *SRA* may waive in writing in any particular case or cases any of the provisions of Part 7 of the rules, may place conditions on, and may revoke, any waiver.

Guidance note

(i)   Applications for waivers should be made to the Professional Ethics Guidance Team. You will need to show that your circumstances are exceptional in order for a waiver to be granted.

PART 8:

[Deleted]

APPENDIX 1: FLOWCHART – EFFECT OF SRA ACCOUNTS RULES 2011

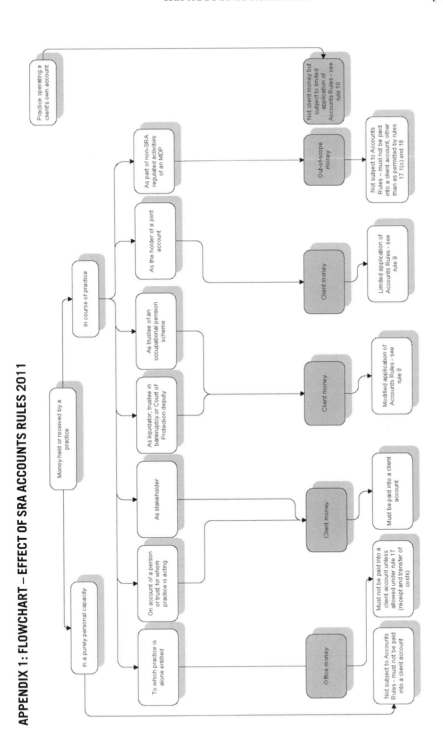

Accounts Rules

APPENDIX 2: SPECIAL SITUATIONS – WHAT APPLIES

	Is it client money?	Subject to reconciliations?	Keep books?	Retain statements?	Subject to accountant's report?	Produce records to SRA?	Interest?	Retain records generally?	Central records?	Subject to reporting accountant's comparisons?
1 R.15.1(a) a/cs in practice name (not client a/c)	Yes	Yes	Yes – r.29.1(a) and 29.2	Yes – r.29.17	Yes	Yes	Yes – r.22	Yes – r.29.17	Statements or register – r.29.19, bills – r.29.15	Yes – r.39.1(f)
2 R.15.1(b) a/cs in name of client – not operated by practice	No	No	No – record receipt and payment only	No	No	No	No – all interest earned for client – r.22, guidance note (i)(i)	No – except record of receipt and payment	Bills – r.29.15	No
3 R.15.1(b) a/cs in name of client – operated by practice	No	No	No – record receipt and payment only	Yes – r.30	Limited – r.39.1(n)	Yes – r.10	No – all interest earned for client – r.22, guidance note (i)(i)	No – except record of receipt and payment	Statements – r.30, Bills – r.29.15	No

	Is it client money?	Subject to reconciliations?	Keep books?	Retain statements?	Subject to accountant's report?	Produce records to SRA?	Interest?	Retain records generally?	Central records?	Subject to reporting accountant's comparisons?
4	Liquidators, trustees in bankruptcy and Court of Protection deputies	Yes – r.8	No – r.8	Modified – statutory records – r.8	Yes – r.8 and r.29.17(c)	Limited – r.39.1(l)	Yes – r.8	No – r.8 – comply with statutory rules (but see r.8.4 and r.22, guidance note (iv)(a))	Yes – modified r.29.17(c)	Yes – r.29.20 Bills – r.29.15	No – r.8
5	Trustees of occupational pension schemes	Yes – r.8	No – r.8	Modified – statutory records – r.8	Yes – r.8 and r.29.17(c)	Limited – r.39.1(l)	Yes – r.8	No – r.8 – comply with statutory rules (but see r.8.4 and r.22, guidance note (iv)(a))	Yes – modified r.29.17(c)	Yes – r.29.20 Bills – r.29.15	No – r.8

Accounts Rules

	Is it client money?	Subject to reconciliations?	Keep books?	Retain statements?	Subject to accountant's report?	Produce records to SRA?	Interest?	Retain records generally?	Central records?	Subject to reporting accountant's comparisons?
6	Joint accounts – r.9	Yes – r.9	No – r.9	No – r.9	Yes – r.9 and 29.17(b)(ii)	Limited – r.39.1(m)	Yes – r.9	No. For joint a/c with client, all interest to client (r.22, guidance note (v)(a)); for joint a/c with another practice or other third party, depends on agreement	No – r.9	Statements – r.29.21 Bills – r.29.15	No – r.9
7	Acting under power of attorney	Yes	Yes	Yes	Yes	Yes	Yes	Yes	Yes	Bills – r.29.15	Yes

	Is it client money?	Subject to reconciliations?	Keep books?	Retain statements?	Subject to accountant's report?	Produce records to SRA?	Interest?	Retain records generally?	Central records?	Subject to reporting accountant's comparisons?
8 Operating client's own a/c e.g. under power of attorney – r.10	No	No	No	Yes – r.30	Limited – r.39.1(n)	Yes – r.10	No – all interest earned for client (r.22, guidance note (i)(i))	No – r.10	Statements – r.30 Bills – r.29.15	No
9 Exempt persons under r.5	No	No	No	No	No	No	No	No	No	No
10 Non-SRA regulated activities of an MDP	No – out-of-scope money – r.12	No	No – but see guidance note (xi) to r.29	No	No	Yes – r.31 – only to extent needed to check rule compliance	No	No – but see guidance note (xi) to r.29	No	No

Accounts Rules

APPENDIX 3: SRA GUIDELINES – ACCOUNTING PROCEDURES AND SYSTEMS

1.   Introduction

1.1   These guidelines, published under rule 26 of the SRA Accounts Rules 2011, are intended to be a benchmark or broad statement of good practice requirements which should be present in an effective regime for the proper control of client money. They should therefore be of positive assistance to firms in establishing or reviewing appropriate procedures and systems. They do not override, or detract from the need to comply fully with, the Accounts Rules.

1.2   References to managers or firms in the guidelines are intended to include sole practitioners, recognised bodies and licensed bodies, and the managers of those bodies.

2.   General

2.1   Compliance with the Accounts Rules is the equal responsibility of all managers in a firm. This responsibility also extends to the Compliance Officer for Finance and Administration, whether or not a manager (see rule 6). They should establish policies and systems to ensure that the firm complies fully with the rules, including procedures for verifying that the controls are operating effectively. Responsibility for day to day supervision may be delegated to one or more managers to enable effective control to be exercised. Delegation of total responsibility to a cashier or book-keeper is not acceptable.

2.2   The firm should hold a copy of the current version of the Accounts Rules and/or have ready access to the current on-line version. The person who maintains the books of account must have a full knowledge of the requirements of the rules and the accounting requirements of firms.

2.3   Proper books of account should be maintained on the double-entry principle. They should be legible, up to date and contain narratives with the entries which identify and/or provide adequate information about the transaction. Entries should be made in chronological order and the current balance should be shown on client ledger accounts, or be readily ascertainable, in accordance with rule 29.9.

2.4   Ledger accounts for clients, other persons or trusts should include the name of the client or other person or trust and contain a heading which provides a description of the matter or transaction.

2.5   Manual systems for recording client money are capable of complying with these guidelines. A computer system, with suitable support procedures will, however, provide an efficient means of producing the accounts and associated control information.

2.6   When introducing new systems, care must be taken to ensure:

(1)   that balances transferred from the books of account of the old system are reconciled with the opening balances held on the new system before day to day operation commences;

(2) that the new system operates correctly before the old system is abandoned. This may require a period of parallel running of the old and new systems and the satisfactory reconciliation of the two sets of records before the old system ceases.

2.7   The firm should ensure that office account entries in relation to each client or trust matter are maintained up to date as well as the client account entries. Credit balances on office account in respect of client or trust matters should be fully investigated.

2.8   The firm should establish policies and operate systems for the payment of fair and reasonable interest to clients in accordance with rules 22 and 23.

3.   Receipt of client money

3.1   The firm should have procedures for identifying client money, including cash, when received in the firm, and for promptly recording the receipt of the money either in the books of account or a register for later posting to the client cash book and ledger accounts. The procedures should cover money received through the post, electronically or direct by fee earners or other personnel. They should also cover the safekeeping of money prior to payment to bank.

3.2   The firm should have a system which ensures that client money is paid promptly into a client account.

3.3   The firm should have a system for identifying money which should not be in a client account and for transferring it without delay.

3.4   The firm should determine a policy and operate a system for dealing with money which is a mixture of office money and client money, or client money and out-of-scope money, or client money, out-of-scope money and office money, in compliance with rules 17–19.

4.   Payments from client account

4.1   The firm should have clear procedures for ensuring that all withdrawals from client accounts are properly authorised. In particular, suitable persons should be named for the following purposes:

(1) authorisation of internal payment vouchers;

(2) signing client account cheques;

(3) authorising telegraphic or electronic transfers.

No other personnel should be allowed to authorise or sign the documents.

4.2   The firm should establish clear procedures and systems for ensuring that persons permitted to authorise the withdrawal of client money from a client account have an appropriate understanding of the requirements of the rules, including rules 20 and 21 which set out when and how a withdrawal from client account may properly be made.

4.3   Persons nominated for the purpose of authorising internal payment vouchers should, for each payment, ensure there is supporting evidence showing clearly the reason for the payment, and the date of it. Similarly, persons signing cheques and authorising transfers should ensure there is a suitable voucher or other supporting evidence to support the payment.

4.4   The firm should have clear systems and procedures for authorising withdrawals from client accounts by electronic means, with appropriate safeguards and controls to ensure that all such withdrawals are properly authorised.

4.5   The firm should have a system for checking the balances on client ledger accounts to ensure no debit balances occur. Where payments are to be made other than out of cleared funds, clear policies and procedures must be in place to ensure that adequate risk assessment is applied.

N.B. If incoming payments are ultimately dishonoured, a debit balance will arise, in breach of the rules, and full replacement of the shortfall will be required under rule 7. See also rule 20, guidance notes (iii)(a) and (iv)(a).

4.6   The firm should establish systems for the transfer of costs from client account to office account in accordance with rule 17.2 and 17.3. Normally transfers should be made only on the basis of rendering a bill or written notification. The payment from the client account should be by way of a cheque or transfer in favour of the firm or sole principal – see rule 21.4.

4.7   The firm should establish policies and operate systems to control and record accurately any transfers between clients of the firm. Where these arise as a result of loans between clients, the written authority of both the lender and borrower must be obtained in accordance with rule 27.2.

4.8   The firm should establish policies and operate systems for the timely closure of files, and the prompt accounting for surplus balances in accordance with rule 14.3.

4.9   The firm should establish systems in accordance with rule 14.4 to keep clients (or other people on whose behalf money is held) regularly informed when funds are retained for a specified reason at the end of a matter or the substantial conclusion of a matter.

5.   Overall control of client accounts

5.1   The firm should maintain control of all its bank and building society accounts opened for the purpose of holding client money. In the case of a joint account, a suitable degree of control should be exercised.

5.2   Central records or central registers must be kept in respect of:

(1)   accounts held for client money, which are not client accounts (rules 15.1(a), 16.1(d) and 29.19);

(2) practice as a liquidator, trustee in bankruptcy, Court of Protection deputy or trustee of an occupational pension scheme (rules 8 and 29.20);

(3) joint accounts (rules 9 and 29.21);

(4) dividend payments received by an executor, trustee or nominee company as nominee (rules 28.2 and 29.23); and

(5) clients' own accounts (rules 10, 15.1(b) and 30.3).

5.3 In addition, there should be a master list of all:

- general client accounts;

- separate designated client accounts;

- accounts held in respect of 5.2 above; and

- office accounts.

The master list should show the current status of each account; e.g. currently in operation or closed with date of closure.

5.4 The firm should operate a system to ensure that accurate reconciliations of the client accounts are carried out at least every five weeks. In particular it should ensure that:

(1) a full list of client ledger balances is produced. Any debit balances should be listed, fully investigated and rectified immediately. The total of any debit balances cannot be "netted off" against the total of credit balances;

(2) a full list of unpresented cheques is produced;

(3) a list of outstanding lodgements is produced;

(4) formal statements are produced reconciling the client account cash book balances, aggregate client ledger balances and the client bank accounts. All unresolved differences must be investigated and, where appropriate, corrective action taken;

(5) a manager or the Compliance Officer for Finance and Administration checks the reconciliation statement and any corrective action, and ensures that enquiries are made into any unusual or apparently unsatisfactory items or still unresolved matters.

5.5 The firm should have clear policies, systems and procedures to control access to computerised client accounts by determining the personnel who should have "write to" and "read only" access. Passwords should be held confidentially by designated personnel and changed regularly to maintain security. Access to the system should not unreasonably be restricted to a single person nor should more people than necessary be given access.

5.6 The firm should establish policies and systems for the retention of the accounting records to ensure:

- books of account, reconciliations, bills, bank statements and passbooks are kept for at least six years;

- paid cheques, digital images of paid cheques and other authorities for the withdrawal of money from a client account are kept for at least two years;

- other vouchers and internal expenditure authorisation documents relating directly to entries in the client account books are kept for at least two years.

5.7   The firm should ensure that unused client account cheques are stored securely to prevent unauthorised access. Blank cheques should not be pre-signed. Any cancelled cheques should be retained.

APPENDIX 4: REPORTING ACCOUNTANT'S CHECKLIST

[Any checks made in respect of the period [   ] to 5 October 2011 relate to compliance with the Solicitors' Accounts Rules 1998.]

The following items have been tested to satisfy the examination requirements under rules 38-40, with the results as indicated. Where the position has been found to be unsatisfactory as a result of these tests, further details have been reported in section 6 of this checklist or reported by separate appendix.

Name of practice

Results of test checks:

1. For all client money	Were any breaches discovered? (Tick the appropriate column.)		If "yes" should breaches be noted in the accountant's report?		Cross reference to audit file documentation.
(a) Book-keeping system for every office:	Yes	No	Yes	No	
(i) The accounting records satisfactorily distinguish client money from all other money dealt with by the firm.					
(ii) A separate ledger account is maintained for each client and trust (excepting section (I) below) and the particulars of all client money received, held or paid on account of each client and trust, including funds held on separate designated deposits, or elsewhere, are recorded.					
(iii) The client ledgers for clients and trusts show a current balance at all times, or the current balance is readily ascertainable.					
(iv) A record of all bills of costs and written notifications has been maintained, either in the form of a central record or a file of copies of such bills.					
(b) Postings to ledger accounts and casts:	Yes	No	Yes	No	
(i) Postings to ledger accounts for clients and trusts from records of receipts and payments are correct.					
(ii) Casts of ledger accounts for clients and trusts and receipts and payments records are correct.					
(iii) Postings have been recorded in chronological sequence with the date being that of the initiation of the transaction.					
(c) Receipts and payments of client money:	Yes	No	Yes	No	
(i) Sample receipts and payments of client money as shown in bank and building society statements have been compared with the firm's records of receipts and payments of client money, and are correct.					

Accounts Rules

For alternative formats, email info.services@sra.org.uk or telephone 0870 606 2555.

1. continued…..		Were any breaches discovered? (Tick the appropriate column.)		If "yes" should breaches be noted in the accountant¡'s report?		Cross reference to audit file documentation.
(ii)	Sample paid cheques, or digital images of the front and back of sample paid cheques, have been obtained and details agreed to receipts and payment records.					
(d)	**System of recording costs and making transfers:**	Yes	No	Yes	No	
(i)	The firm's system of recording costs has been ascertained and is suitable.					
(ii)	Costs have been drawn only where required for or towards payment of the firm's costs where there has been sent to the client a bill of costs or other written notification of the amount of the costs.					
(e)	**Examination of documents for verification of transactions and entries in accounting records:**	Yes	No	Yes	No	
(i)	Make a test examination of a number of client and trust files.					
(ii)	All client and trust files requested for examination were made available.					
(iii)	The financial transactions as detailed on client and trust files and other documentation (including transfers from one ledger account to another) were valid and appropriately authorised in accordance with Parts 1 and 2 of the SRA Accounts Rules 2011 (AR).					
(iv)	The financial transactions evidenced by documents on the client and trust files were correctly recorded in the books of account in a manner complying with Part 4 AR.					
(f)	**Extraction of client ledger balances for clients and trusts:**	Yes	No	Yes	No	
(i)	The extraction of client ledger balances for clients and trusts has been checked for no fewer than two separate dates in the period subject to this report.					
(ii)	The total liabilities to clients and trusts as shown by such ledger accounts has been compared to the cash account balance(s) at each of the separate dates selected in (f)(i) above and agreed.					
(iii)	The cash account balance(s) at each of the dates selected has/have been reconciled to the balance(s) in client bank account and elsewhere as confirmed directly by the relevant banks and building societies.					
(g)	**Reconciliations:**	Yes	No	Yes	No	
(i)	During the accounting year under review, reconciliations have been carried out at least every five weeks.					
(ii)	Each reconciliation is in the form of a statement set out in a logical format which is likely to reveal any discrepancies.					
(iii)	Reconciliation statements have been retained.					
(iv)	On entries in an appropriate sample of reconciliation statements:	Yes	No	Yes	No	
	(A) All accounts containing client money have been included.					
	(B) All ledger account balances for clients and trusts as at the reconciliation date have been listed and totalled.					
	(C) No debit balances on ledger accounts for clients and trusts have been included in the total.					

1. continued.......		Were any breaches discovered? (Tick the appropriate column.)		If "yes" should breaches be noted in the accountant's report?		Cross reference to audit file documentation.
	(D) The cash account balance(s) for clients and trusts is/are correctly calculated by the accurate and up to date recording of transactions.					
	(E) The client bank account totals for clients and trusts are complete and correct being calculated by:					
	the closing balance *plus* an accurate and complete list of outstanding lodgements *less* an accurate and complete list of unpresented cheques.					
(v)	Each reconciliation selected under paragraph (iv) above has been achieved by the comparison and agreement *without adjusting or balancing entries* of:					
	total of ledger balances for clients and trusts;					
	total of cash account balances for clients and trusts;					
	total of client bank accounts.					
(vi)	In the event of debit balances existing on ledger accounts for clients and trusts, the firm has investigated promptly and corrected the position satisfactorily.					
(vii)	In the event of the reconciliations selected under paragraph (iv) above not being in agreement, the differences have been investigated and corrected promptly.					
(h)	**Payments of client money:**	Yes	No	Yes	No	
	Make a test examination of the ledger accounts for clients and trusts in order to ascertain whether payments have been made on any individual account in excess of money held on behalf of that client or trust.					
(i)	**Office accounts - client money:**	Yes	No	Yes	No	
(i)	Check such office ledger and cash account and bank and building society statements as the firm maintains with a view to ascertaining whether any client money has not been paid into a client account.					
(ii)	Investigate office ledger credit balances and ensure that such balances do not include client money incorrectly held in office account.					
(j)	**Client money not held in client account:**	Yes	No	Yes	No	
(i)	Have sums not held on client account been identified?					
(ii)	Has the reason for holding such sums outside client account been established?					
(iii)	Has a written client agreement been made if appropriate?					
(iv)	Are central records or a central register kept for client money held outside client account on the client's instructions?					
(k)	**Rule 27 - inter-client transfers:**	Yes	No	Yes	No	
	Make test checks of inter-client transfers to ensure that rule 27 has been complied with.					
(l)	**Rule 29.10 - acting for borrower and lender:**	Yes	No	Yes	No	
	Make a test examination of the client ledger accounts in order to ascertain whether rule 29.10 AR has been complied with, where the firm acts for both borrower and lender in a conveyancing transaction.					
(m)	**Rule 29.23 – executor, trustee or nominee companies:**	Yes	No	Yes	No	
	Is a central book of dividend instruction letters kept?					

Accounts Rules

1. continued.......	Were any breaches discovered? (Tick the appropriate column.)		If "yes" should breaches be noted in the accountant;'s report?		Cross reference to audit file documentation.
(n)	**Information and explanations:**	Yes	No	Yes	No	
	All information and explanations required have been received and satisfactorily cleared.					

2.	Liquidators, trustees in bankruptcy, Court of Protection deputies and trustees of occupational pension schemes (rule 8)	Were any breaches discovered? (Tick the appropriate column.)		If 'yes' should breaches be noted in the accountant's report?		Cross reference to audit file documentation
		Yes	No	Yes	No	
(a)	A record of all bills of costs and written notifications has been maintained, either in the form of a central record or a file of copies of such bills or notifications.					
(b)	Records kept under rule 8 including any statements, passbooks and other accounting records originating outside the firm's office have been retained.					
(c)	Records kept under rule 8 are kept together centrally, or a central register is kept of the appointments.					

3.	Joint accounts (rule 9)	Were any breaches discovered? (Tick the appropriate column.)		If 'yes' should breaches be noted in the accountant's report?		Cross reference to audit file documentation
		Yes	No	Yes	No	
(a)	A record of all bills of costs and written notifications has been maintained, either in the form of a central record or a file of copies of such bills or notifications.					
(b)	Statements and passbooks and/or duplicate statements or copies of passbook entries have been retained.					
(c)	Statements, passbooks, duplicate statements and copies of passbook entries are kept together centrally, or a central register of all joint accounts is kept.					

4.	Clients' own accounts (rule 10)	Were any breaches discovered? (Tick the appropriate column.)		If 'yes' should breaches be noted in the accountant's report?		Cross reference to audit file documentation
		Yes	No	Yes	No	
(a)	Statements and passbooks and/or duplicate statements, copies of passbook entries and cheque details have been retained					
(b)	Statements and passbooks and/or duplicate statements, copies of passbook entries and cheque details are kept together centrally, or a central register of clients' own accounts is kept.					

5. SRA guidelines - accounting procedures and systems	Yes	No
Discovery of substantial departures from the guidelines? *If "yes" please give details below.*		

6. Please give further details of unsatisfactory items below. (Please attach additional schedules as required.)

Signature	Date
Reporting Accountant	Print Name

Accounts Rules

APPENDIX 5: ACCOUNTANT'S REPORT FORM

AR1

Accountant's Report Form

An annual accountant's report is required under rule 32 of the SRA Accounts Rules 2011 (the Rules). For further information on the Rules and for clarification on whether or not the requirement to deliver an accountant's report applies to you, see our website at http://www.sra.org.uk/solicitors/handbook/accountsrules/content page.

The accountant who prepares the report must be qualified under rule 34 of the Rules and is required to report on compliance with Parts 1, 2 and 4 of the Rules.

When a practice closes but the ceased practice continues to hold or receive client money during the process of dealing with outstanding costs and unattributable or unreturnable funds, the Rules, including the obligation to deliver accountant's reports, will continue to apply.

When a practice ceases to hold and/or receive client money (and/or to operate any client's own account as signatory), either on closure of the practice or for any other reason, the practice must deliver a final report within six months of ceasing to hold and/or receive client money (and/or to operate any client's own account as signatory), unless the SRA requires earlier delivery.

If you need any assistance completing this form please telephone the Contact Centre on 0370 606 2555 or email at contactcentre@sra.org.uk. Our lines are open from 08.00 to 18.00 Monday, Wednesday, Thursday, Friday and 09.30 to 18.00 Tuesday. Please note calls may be monitored/recorded for training purposes.

If you are calling from overseas please use +44 (0) 121 329 6800. Note that reports in respect of practice from an office outside England and Wales are submitted under Part 7 of the Rules. Specimen form **AR2** may be used for such reports.

Section one: Firm details

Insert here all names used by the firm or in-house practice from the offices covered by this report. This must include the registered name of a recognised body/licensed body which is an LLP or company, and the name under which a partnership or sole practitioner is recognised. It is assumed that all addresses used by the practice during the accounting period are covered by this report , except offices outside England and Wales (Refer to Part 7 of the Rules). All address(es) of the practice during the reporting period must be covered by an accountant's report.

Firm name(s) during the reporting period		Firm SRA no	
Report Period from		to	

Firm COFA(s) (if more than one) during the reporting period with dates of appointment		COFA's SRA no	
Dates of appointment (where appropriate)		to	

Is this a cease to hold report?	Yes ☐	No ☐

1

Have any consultants or employees held or received client money, or operated a client's own account as signatory, during the report period	Yes ☐	No ☐

If **'yes'** please set out the details on a separate sheet of paper if necessary

Section 2: Comparison dates

The results of the comparisons required under rule 39.1(f) of the SRA Accounts Rules 2011, at the dates selected by me/us were:

(a)   at [_____] *(insert date 1)*

     (i)   Liabilities to clients and trusts (and other persons for whom client money is held) as shown by ledger accounts for client and trust matters.   £ [_____]

     (ii)   Cash held in client account, and client money held in any account other than a client account, after allowances for lodgments cleared after date and for outstanding cheques.   £ [_____]

     (iii)   Difference between (i) and (ii) (if any).   £ [_____]

(b)   at [_____] *(insert date 2)*

     (i)   Liabilities to clients and trusts (and other persons for whom client money is held) as shown by ledger accounts for client and trust matters.   £ [_____]

     (ii)   Cash held in client account, and client money held in any account other than a client account, after allowances for lodgments cleared after date and for outstanding cheques.   £ [_____]

     (iii)   Difference between (i) and (ii) (if any).   £ [_____]

Notes:

The figure to be shown in 2(a)(i) and 2(b)(i) above is the total of credit balances, without adjustment for debit balances (unless capable of proper set off, i.e. being in respect of the same client), or for receipts and payments not capable of allocation to individual ledger accounts.

An explanation must be given for any significant difference shown at 2(a)(iii) or 2(b)(iii) - see rule 44 of the SRA Accounts Rules 2011. If appropriate, it would be helpful if the explanation is given here:

[_____]

Accounts Rules

2

Section 3: Qualified report

Have you found it necessary to make this report 'Qualified'?	No	☐	If 'No' proceed to section 5
	Yes	☐	If 'Yes' please complete the relevant boxes

(a) Please indicate in the space provided any matters (other than trivial breaches) in respect of which it appears to you that there has been a failure to comply with the provisions of Parts 1, 2 and 4 of the SRA Accounts Rules 2011 and, in the case of private practice only, any part of the period covered by this report for which the practice does not appear to have been covered in respect of its offices in England and Wales by the insurance/indemnity documents referred to in rule 39.1(p) of the SRA Accounts Rules 2011 *(continue on an additional sheet if necessary)*:

(b) Please indicate in the space provided any matters in respect of which you have been unable to satisfy yourself and the reasons for that inability, e.g. because a client's file is not available *(continue on an additional sheet if necessary)*.

Section 4: Accountant's details

The reporting accountant must be qualified in accordance with rule 34 of the SRA Accounts Rules 2011.

Name of accountant		Professional body	
		Accountant membership/ registration number	
Recognised Supervisory Body under which individual/firm is a registered auditor		Reference number of individual/firm audit registration(s)	
Firm name			
Firm address			
Email address			

3

Section 5: Declaration

1. In compliance with Part 6 of the SRA Accounts Rules 2011, I/we have examined to the extent required by rule 39 of those rules, the accounting records, files and other documents produced to me/us in respect of the above practice.

2. In so far as an opinion can be based on this limited examination, I am/we are satisfied that during the above mentioned period the practice has complied with the provisions of Parts 1, 2 and 4 of the SRA Accounts Rules 2011 except so far as concerns:

    (i)   certain trivial breaches due to clerical errors or mistakes in book-keeping, all of which were rectified on discovery and none of which, I am/we are satisfied, resulted in any loss to any client or trust; and/or

    (ii) any matters detailed in section 3 of this report.

3. In the case of private practice only, I/we certify that, in so far as can be ascertained from a limited examination of the insurance/indemnity documents produced to me/us, the practice was covered in respect of its offices in England and Wales for the period covered by this report by the insurance/indemnity documents referred to in rule 39.1(p) of the SRA Accounts Rules 2011, except as stated in section 3 of this report.

I/we have relied on the exception contained in rule 39.2 of the SRA Accounts Rules 2011.　　Yes ☐　　No ☐

Rule 39.2 of the SRA Accounts Rules 2011 states: "For the purposes of rule 39.1(f) above [extraction of balances] if you use a computerised or mechanised system of accounting which automatically produces an extraction of all client ledger balances, the accountant need not check all client ledger balances extracted on the list produced by the computer or machine against the individual records of client ledger accounts, provided the accountant:

    (a)   confirms that a satisfactory system of control is in operation and the accounting records are in balance;

    (b)   carries out a test check of the extraction against the individual records; and

    (c)   states in the report that he or she has relied on this exception."

In carrying out work in preparation of this report, I/we have discovered the following substantial departures from the SRA's current Guidelines for Accounting Procedures and Systems (*continue on an additional sheet if necessary*):

4

4. I/we have completed and signed the 'Reporting accountant's checklist' and retained a copy. The original checklist has been sent to the firm's current COFA as set out in Section 1 of this report .

5. I/we confirm that there are no circumstances which might affect my independence in preparing this report.

6. A copy of this report has been sent to the firm's current COFA as set out in Section 1 of this report

Date	
Signature	
Name (Block Capitals)	

Please return this form via one of the options below:

Email: SRAAccountantsReports@sra.org.uk

Post: Authorisation – Accountant's Reports
        Solicitors Regulation Authority
        The Cube
        199 Wharfside Street
        Birmingham
        B1 1RN

DX: DX 720293 Birmingham 47

The reporting accountant's checklist should be retained by the practice which is the subject of the report for at least three years, and not submitted to the Solicitors Regulation Authority with this report.

5

[E] Authorisation and Practising Requirements

[E.0] Introduction to Authorisation and Practising Requirements

This section of the Handbook contains the following sets of rules:

- SRA Practice Framework Rules;

- SRA Authorisation Rules for Legal Services Bodies and Licensable Bodies;

- SRA Practising Regulations;

- Solicitors Keeping of the Roll Regulations;

- SRA Training Regulations 2014 – Qualification and Training Provider Regulations;

- SRA Training Regulations 2011 Part 3 – CPD Regulations;

- SRA Admission Regulations;

- SRA Qualified Lawyers Transfer Scheme Regulations;

- SRA Higher Rights of Audience Regulations;

- SRA Quality Assurance Scheme for Advocates (Crime) Regulations; and

- SRA Suitability Test.

These rules must be read in conjunction with the Principles. The Principles underpin all aspects of practice, including applications for authorisation or approval by firms and individuals and achievement of training requirements.

The desired outcomes that apply to authorisation and training are that:

- clients and the general public remain confident that legal services provided by our regulated community will be delivered to the required standard and in a principled manner;

- firms and individuals provide the SRA with sufficient information to enable the SRA to make appropriate judgements concerning whether to authorise, or continue to authorise, any firm or person;

- only those individuals and firms who/that meet the SRA's criteria for authorisation (including the requirements to be suitable and capable of providing legal services to the required standard) are authorised;

- firms are managed in such a way, and with appropriate systems and controls, so as to protect the public and safeguard the reputation of the legal profession;

- solicitors, regardless of the route by which they qualify, have been educated and trained to a standard that clients, the public, the profession and the judiciary properly expect;

- providers of training are authorised and monitored to an appropriate standard;

- solicitors have demonstrated their competence to exercise rights of audience in the higher courts;

- solicitors have achieved the standard of competence required of advocates conducting criminal advocacy;

- solicitors demonstrate this competence through independent assessment;

- solicitors act so that clients, the judiciary and the wider public, have confidence that this has been demonstrated.

SRA Practice Framework Rules 2011

Rules dated 17 June 2011 commencing on 6 October 2011

made by the Solicitors Regulation Authority Board, under sections 31, 79 and 80 of the Solicitors Act 1974, sections 9 and 9A of the Administration of Justice Act 1985 and section 83 and Schedule 11 to the Legal Services Act 2007, with the approval of the Legal Services Board under paragraph 19 of Schedule 4 to the Legal Services Act 2007.

INTRODUCTION

Part 1 of these rules sets out the types of business through which solicitors, RELs, RFLs and authorised bodies may practise. It restricts the types of business available in order to reflect statutory provisions and to ensure that clients and the public have the protections provided for by statute.

Part 2 permits authorised bodies, solicitors, RELs and RFLs to carry out certain types of work, including immigration work.

Part 3 governs the formation and practice requirements which must be satisfied by bodies to be eligible for authorisation by the SRA, and is based on the requirements of sections 9 and 9A of the AJA and section 72 of the LSA.

Part 4 sets out certain requirements relating to compliance with these rules and the SRA's regulatory arrangements.

PART 1: FRAMEWORK OF PRACTICE

Rule 1: Solicitors

Practice from an office in England and Wales

1.1   You may *practise* as a *solicitor* from an office in England and Wales in the following ways only:

(a)   as a *recognised sole practitioner* or the *employee* of a *recognised sole practitioner*;

(b)   as a *solicitor* exempted under Rule 10.2 from the obligation to be a *recognised sole practitioner*;

(c)   as a *manager, employee, member* or *interest holder* of an *authorised body* provided that all work you do is:

(i)   of a sort the body is authorised by the *SRA* to carry out; or

(ii)   done for the body itself, or falls within Rule 4.1 to 4.11, and where this sub-paragraph applies, references in Rule 4 to *"employer"* shall be construed as referring to that body, accordingly;

(d) as a *manager, employee, member* or *interest holder* of an *authorised non-SRA firm*, provided that all work you do is:

    (i)   *reserved legal activity* of a sort the firm is authorised by the firm's *approved regulator* to carry out or any other activity that is not precluded by the terms of your authorisation from the firm's *approved regulator*; or

    (ii)   done for the firm itself, or falls within Rule 4.1 to 4.11, and where this sub-paragraph applies, references in Rule 4 to *"employer"* shall be construed as referring to that firm, accordingly;

(e) as the *employee* of another *person*, business or organisation, provided that you undertake work only for your *employer*, or as permitted by Rule 4 (In-house practice).

Practice from an office outside England and Wales

1.2   You may *practise* as a *solicitor* from an office outside England and Wales in the following ways only:

(a) as a *sole practitioner* (including a *recognised sole practitioner*);

(b) as the *employee* of a sole *principal* who is a *lawyer*;

(c) as a *manager, employee, member* or *interest holder* of an *authorised body* or of an *authorised non-SRA firm*, provided that if any of the body's *managers* or *interest holders* are non-lawyers and the office is in an *Establishment Directive state* other than the UK, the rules for local *lawyers* would permit a local *lawyer* to practise through a business of that composition and structure;

(d) as an *employee* of a business which is not required to be an *authorised body*, provided that it meets all the following conditions:

    (i)   the business carries on the provision of legal advice or assistance, or representation in connection with the application of the law or resolution of legal disputes;

    (ii)   a controlling majority of the *managers* and the *interest holders* are *lawyers* practising as such and/or *bodies corporate* in which *lawyers* practising as such constitute a controlling majority of the *managers* and *interest holders*;

    (iii)   if any of the business's *managers* or *interest holders* are non-lawyers and any *manager* or *interest holder* is subject to the rules for local *lawyers*, the composition and structure of the business complies with those rules; and

    (iv)   if any of the business's *managers* or *interest holders* are non-lawyers and the office is in an *Establishment Directive state*, the rules for local *lawyers* would permit a local *lawyer* to practise through a business of that composition and structure;

(e) as *manager, member* or *interest holder* of a business which is not required to be an *authorised body*, provided that it has no office in England and Wales, and that it meets all the conditions set out in sub-paragraph (d)(i) to (iv) above;

(f) as the *employee* of another *person*, business or organisation, provided that you undertake work only for your *employer*, or as permitted by Rule 4.22 to 4.25 (In-house practice overseas);

(g) as a *manager, employee, member* or *interest holder* of an *overseas practice*.

Guidance notes

(i) See also Rules 10 (Sole practitioners), 13 (Eligibility criteria and fundamental requirements for recognised bodies), 14 (Eligibility criteria and fundamental requirements for licensed bodies), 15 (Formation, registered office and practising address), 16 (Composition of an authorised body) and 17 (Authorised bodies which are companies) below, Chapter 13 of the SRA Code of Conduct (Application and waivers provisions) and the SRA Practising Regulations.

(ii) See Rule 4.3 below and the definition of "in-house practice" in the Glossary, in relation to in-house work that you carry out for clients which is outside of your firm's authorisation.

(iii) A recognised body which is a company may not have a corporate director (this also applies to a licensed body). However, when permitted, a corporate body owner and/or manager of a recognised body will need to be a legally qualified body (see the Glossary).

(iv) The rules do not prevent a solicitor establishing, for example, their own company for tax purposes (which is itself a recognised body) so that that company can be a corporate manager of another firm through which the solicitor practises.

Rule 2: RELs

Practice from an office in England and Wales

2.1 You may *practise* as an *REL* from an office in England and Wales in the following ways only:

(a) as a *recognised sole practitioner* or the *employee* of a *recognised sole practitioner*;

(b) as an *REL* exempted under Rule 10.2 from the obligation to be a *recognised sole practitioner*;

(c) as a *manager, employee, member* or *interest holder* of an *authorised body*, provided that all work you do is:

      (i)   of a sort the firm is authorised by the *SRA* to carry out; or

      (ii) done for the body itself, or falls within Rule 4.1 to 4.11, and where this sub-paragraph applies, references in Rule 4 to *"employer"* shall be construed as referring to that body, accordingly;

(d) as a *manager, employee, member* or *interest holder* of an *authorised non-SRA firm*, provided that all work you do is:

      (i)   *reserved legal activity* of a sort the firm is authorised by the firm's *approved regulator* to carry out or any other activity that is not precluded by the terms of your authorisation from the firm's *approved regulator*; or

      (ii) done for the firm itself, or falls within Rule 4.1 to 4.11, and where this sub-paragraph applies, references in Rule 4 to *"employer"* shall be construed as referring to that firm, accordingly;

(e) as the *employee* of another *person*, business or organisation, provided that you undertake work only for your *employer*, or as permitted by Rule 4 (In-house practice).

Practice from an office in Scotland or Northern Ireland

2.2 You may *practise* as an *REL* from an office in Scotland or Northern Ireland in the following ways only:

(a) as a *sole practitioner* (including a *recognised sole practitioner*);

(b) as the *employee* of a sole *principal* who is a *lawyer*;

(c) as a *manager, employee, member* or *interest holder* of an *authorised body* or of an *authorised non-SRA firm*;

(d) as an *employee* of a business which is not required to be an *authorised body*, provided that it meets all the following conditions:

      (i)   the business carries on the provision of legal advice or assistance, or representation in connection with the application of the law or resolution of legal disputes;

      (ii) a controlling majority of the *managers* and the *interest holders* are *lawyers* practising as such and/or *bodies corporate* in which *lawyers* practising as such constitute a controlling majority of the *managers* and *interest holders*; and

      (iii) if any of the business's *managers* or *interest holders* are non-lawyers, the professional rules governing a solicitor of that jurisdiction would allow such a solicitor to practise through a business of that composition and structure;

(e) as *manager, member* or *interest holder* of a business which is not required to be an *authorised body*, provided that it has no office in England and Wales and that it meets all the conditions set out in sub-paragraph (d)(i) to (iii) above;

(f) as the *employee* of another *person*, business or organisation, provided that you undertake work only for your *employer*, or as permitted by Rule 4.22 to 4.25 (In-house practice overseas);

(g) as a *manager, employee, member* or *interest holder* of an *overseas practice.*

Guidance notes

(i) The overseas provisions for an REL are the same as those for a solicitor practising overseas except that they apply only in Scotland and Northern Ireland. RELs are not subject to Rule 2 in relation to practice from an office outside the UK.

(ii) See Rule 4.3 and the definition of "in-house practice" in the Glossary, in relation to in-house work that you carry out for clients which is outside of your firm's authorisation.

(iii) A recognised body which is a company may not have a corporate director (this also applies to a licensed body). However, when permitted, a corporate body owner and/or manager of a recognised body will need to be a legally qualified body (see the Glossary).

(iv) The rules do not prevent an REL establishing, for example, their own company for tax purposes (which is itself a recognised body) so that that company can be a corporate manager of another firm through which the REL practises.

Rule 3: RFLs

Practice in the capacity of an RFL

3.1 Your *practice* as a *foreign lawyer* in the capacity of an *RFL* is confined to *practice* as:

(a) the *employee* of a *recognised sole practitioner*;

(b) a *manager, employee, member* or *interest holder* of an *authorised body*, provided that all work you do is:

    (i) of a sort the body is authorised by the *SRA* to carry out; or

    (ii) done for the body itself, or falls within Rule 4.1 to 4.11, and where this sub-paragraph applies, references in Rule 4 to "*employer*" shall be construed as referring to that body, accordingly;

(c) a *manager, employee, member* or *interest holder* of an *authorised non-SRA firm*, provided that all work you do is:

    (i) *reserved legal activity* of a sort the firm is authorised by the firm's

Authorisation and
Practising Requirements

approved regulator to carry out or any other activity that is not precluded by the terms of your authorisation from the firm's *approved regulator*; or

(ii)   done for the firm itself, or falls within Rule 4.1 to 4.11, and where this sub-paragraph applies, references in Rule 4 to "*employer*" shall be construed as referring to that firm, accordingly.

Practice in another capacity than as an RFL

3.2   If you provide services as a *foreign lawyer* in any of the following ways in England and Wales or elsewhere, you will not be *practising* in the capacity of an *RFL* and you must not be held out or described in that context as an *RFL*, or as regulated by or registered with the *Society* or the *SRA*:

(a)   as a sole *principal*; or

(b)   as a *manager, member* or *interest holder* of any business or organisation other than an *authorised body* or an *authorised non-SRA firm*; or

(c)   as a *manager, member* or *interest holder* of a *body corporate* which is a *manager, member* or *interest holder* of any business or organisation other than an *authorised body* or an *authorised non-SRA firm*; or

(d)   as the *employee* of any business or organisation other than a *recognised sole practitioner*, an *authorised body* or an *authorised non-SRA firm*.

3.3   If you have a *practice* under Rule 3.1 above, and another business under Rule 3.2 above, the latter is a *separate business* for the purpose of these rules and you must therefore comply with Chapter 12 (Separate businesses) of the *SRA Code of Conduct*.

Scope of practice

3.4   Whether or not you are *practising* in the capacity of an *RFL* you must not:

(a)   be held out in any way which suggests that you are, or are entitled to *practise* as, a *lawyer of England and Wales*;

(b)   undertake the following *reserved work* in England and Wales:

(i)   advocacy in open *court*;

(ii)   the conduct of *court* litigation;

(iii)   the administration of oaths and statutory declarations;

(c)   undertake advocacy in chambers in England and Wales, except under instructions given by a person qualified to supervise that *reserved work*;

(d)   undertake the following *reserved work* in England and Wales, except at the direction and under the supervision of a person qualified to supervise that *reserved work*:

(i)   the preparation of *court* documents;

    (ii)   the preparation of instruments and the lodging of documents relating to the transfer or charge of land;

    (iii) the preparation of papers on which to found or oppose a grant of probate or a grant of letters of administration;

    (iv) the preparation of trust deeds disposing of capital, unless you also are eligible to act as a *lawyer of England and Wales*;

(e) If you are not *practising* in the capacity of an *RFL* you must not carry out *immigration work* in the *UK* unless you are entitled to do so by virtue of being a qualified person within the meaning of section 84 of the Immigration and Asylum Act 1999, whether this is as a result of being entitled to do the work in your own right, doing so under supervision, or otherwise.

Guidance notes

(i)   A foreign lawyer must be registered with the SRA as an RFL to be a manager, member or interest holder of a recognised body, with the following exceptions:

(a) a foreign lawyer who is also qualified as a lawyer of England and Wales does not have to be an RFL;

(b) a member of an Establishment Directive profession – except that if the lawyer is not a national of an Establishment Directive state and will be based, or partly based, in England and Wales, he or she does have to be an RFL in order to be a manager, member or interest holder of a recognised body. See our website for additional guidance on RFLs and multi-national practice [**www.sra.org.uk/solicitors/code-of-conduct/guidance.page**].

(ii)   There is no requirement to register as an RFL in order to be employed by a recognised body or sole practitioner or to be a manager or interest holder of, or employed by, a licensed body but, if you are registered as an RFL, you will be subject to SRA regulation in this capacity when working for an SRA firm or an authorised non-SRA firm.

(iii)   An RFL is subject to the same restrictions as a solicitor or REL in relation to practice from an office in England and Wales with two exceptions. Your registration as an RFL does not entitle you to practise:

(a) as an RFL sole practitioner; or

(b) as an in-house RFL (subject to note (iv) below).

(iv)   Registration as an RFL is portable to the extent that it will enable you to be a manager, employee, member or interest holder of an authorised non-SRA firm, although your ability to work within such a firm will depend on the framework of practice requirements of the relevant approved regulator. You will be able to undertake work authorised by the firm's approved regulator (subject to any statutory limitations or requirements). Additionally you will be able to function as an in-house lawyer under Rule 4, doing other work for the employer, related bodies, work colleagues and pro bono clients under the SRA's rules.

Authorisation and Practising Requirements

(v)   Your registration as an RFL will not be relevant in the role of interest holder or employee of a business in England and Wales which is not regulated by the SRA or one of the other approved regulators. The SRA does not regulate any practice you might have outside the framework established under the LSA, so there must be no implication in such a context that you are an RFL, or that you or the business are regulated by or registered with the SRA or the Society.

(vi)   Where, in order to satisfy statutory requirements, there is a need for an RFL doing reserved work to be supervised or directed by someone in the firm, this can only be undertaken by a person of equivalent or higher status.

(vii)   See the application provisions in 4.2 of the SRA Principles. Also see the provisions relating to practice from an office outside England and Wales in Chapter 13 of the SRA Code of Conduct.

(viii)   See Rule 4.3 and the definition of "in-house practice" in the Glossary, in relation to in-house work that you carry out for clients which is outside of your firm's authorisation.

(ix)   A recognised body which is a company may not have a corporate director (this also applies to a licensed body). However, when permitted, a corporate body owner and/or manager of a recognised body will need to be a legally qualified body (see the Glossary).

Rule 4: In-house practice

4.1   If you are a *solicitor*, *REL* or *RFL* conducting *in-house practice*:

    (a)   you must not act for *clients* other than your *employer* except in the circumstances in 4.4 to 4.26 (all of which are subject to 4.1(b) and 4.2) and where you are able to act without compromising the *Principles* or your obligations under the *SRA Code of Conduct*;

    (b)   nothing in this rule permits any *person* to conduct *reserved legal activities* in circumstances where to do so would require authorisation under the *LSA* and you must satisfy yourself that any such authorisation is in place before conducting any such activity.

4.1A   If your *in-house practice* comprises:

    (a)   employment in a body within England and Wales, rules 4.2 to 4.18 and 4.26 apply to you;

    (b)   employment in a foreign law firm which is not an *overseas practice*, rules 4.19 to 4.21 apply to you; and

    (c)   employment in a body overseas, including where you are *practising overseas*, rules 4.22 to 4.25 apply to you.

4.2   Indemnity

(a) In order to act for a *client* other than your *employer* under Rule 4.10, 4.14, 4.16 and 4.19, you must have professional indemnity insurance cover.

(b) In all other cases you must consider whether your *employer* has appropriate indemnity insurance or funds to meet any award made as a result of a claim in professional negligence against you, for which your *employer* might be vicariously liable. If not, you must inform the *client* in writing that you are not covered by the compulsory insurance scheme.

4.3   If you are a *solicitor*, *REL* or *RFL* in a *licensed body* or an *authorised non-SRA firm*, you must comply with this rule as if you were an *in-house solicitor* or *REL* when, as a *manager* or *employee*, you do work of a type which is outside the scope of the firm's authorisation in accordance with Rules 1, 2 or 3, either for the firm itself or within 4.4 to 4.6 (Work colleagues), 4.7 to 4.9 (Related bodies) or 4.10 to 4.11 (Pro bono work).

Work colleagues

4.4   Subject to Rule 4.5 below, you may act for a *person* who is, or was formerly:

(a) an *employee*, a *manager*, the company secretary, a board member or a trustee of your *employer*;

(b) an *employee*, a *manager*, the company secretary, a board member or a trustee of a *related body* of your *employer*; or

(c) a contributor to a programme or periodical publication, broadcast or published by your *employer* or by a *related body*, but only where the contributor is a defendant or potential defendant in a defamation case.

4.5   You may act under Rule 4.4 above only if:

(a) the matter relates to and arises out of the work of the *employee*, *manager*, company secretary, board member, trustee or contributor in that capacity;

(b) the matter does not relate to a claim arising as a result of a personal injury to the *employee*, *manager*, company secretary, board member, trustee or contributor;

(c) you are satisfied that the *employee*, *manager*, company secretary, board member, trustee or contributor does not wish to instruct some other *lawyer*; and

(d) no charge is made for your work unless those costs are recoverable from another source.

4.6   Where acting in a conveyancing transaction under Rule 4.4(a) or (b) above you may also act for a joint owner or joint buyer of the property and for a mortgagee.

Related bodies

4.7   You may act for:

(a) your *employer's* holding, associated or subsidiary company;

(b) a *partnership*, syndicate, LLP or company by way of joint venture in which your *employer* and others have an interest;

(c) a trade association of which your *employer* is a member; or

(d) a club, association, pension fund or other scheme operated for the benefit of *employees* of your *employer*.

4.8 If you are employed in local government, Rule 4.7(a) and (b) above do not apply.

4.9 For the purpose of Rule 4.10 to 4.14 references to your *employer* include *related bodies* of the *employer*, and "employment" and "employed" must be construed accordingly.

Pro bono work

4.10 You may, in the course of your *practice*, conduct work on a pro bono basis for a *client* other than your *employer* provided:

(a) the work is covered by an indemnity reasonably equivalent to that required under the SRA Indemnity Insurance Rules;

(b) either:

(i) no fees are charged; or

(ii) a conditional fee agreement is used and the only fees charged are those which you receive by way of costs from your *client's* opponent or other third party and all of which you pay to a *charity* under a fee sharing agreement; and

(c) you do not undertake any *reserved legal activities*, unless the provision of relevant services to the public or a section of the public (with or without a view to profit) is not part of your employer's business.

4.11 Rule 4.10 above does not permit you to conduct work on a pro bono basis in conjunction with services provided by your *employer* under Rule 4.12 (Associations), Rule 4.13 (Insurers), Rule 4.14 (Commercial legal advice services) or Rule 4.19 to 4.21 (Foreign law firms).

Associations

4.12 If you are employed by an association you may act for a member of that association provided:

(a) the membership of the association is limited to *persons* engaged or concerned in a particular trade, occupation or specialist activity or otherwise having a community of interest, such interest being a specialist interest;

(b) the association is one formed bona fide for the benefit of its members and not formed directly or indirectly for your benefit or primarily for securing assistance in legal proceedings;

(c) there is no charge to the member in non-contentious matters, and in contentious matters the association indemnifies the member in relation to your costs and disbursements insofar as they are not recoverable from any other source; and

(d) you act only in matters that relate to or arise out of the particular trade, occupation or specialist activity of the association or otherwise relate to the specialist community of interest, for which the association is formed.

Insurers

4.13   If you are employed by an insurer subrogated to the rights of an insured in respect of any matter you may act on behalf of the insurer in relation to that matter in the name of the insured, and also:

(a) act on behalf of the insured in relation to uninsured losses in respect of the matter;

(b) act in proceedings both for the insured and for a defendant covered by another insurer where the insurers have agreed an apportionment of liability; and/or

(c) act in the matter on behalf of the *employer* and another insurer in the joint prosecution of a claim.

Commercial legal advice services

4.14   If you are employed by a commercial organisation providing a telephone legal advice service you may advise *persons* making enquiries of that organisation, provided:

(a) the advice comprises telephone advice only, together with a follow up letter to the enquirer when necessary;

(b) you are satisfied that there is indemnity cover reasonably equivalent to that required under the SRA Indemnity Insurance Rules; and

(c) you do not undertake any *reserved legal activities*.

Local government

4.15   If you are employed in local government you may act:

(a) for another organisation or *person* to which or to whom the *employer* is statutorily empowered to provide legal services, subject to the conditions in (b) to (g) below;

(b) for a member or former member of the local authority, provided that:

(i) the matter relates to or arises out of the work of the member in that capacity;

(ii)   the matter does not relate to a claim arising as a result of a personal injury to the member;

(iii) you are satisfied that the member does not wish to instruct some other *lawyer*; and

(iv)   no charge is made for your work unless those costs are recoverable from some other source;

(c)   for a *company* limited by shares or guarantee of which:

(i)   the *employer* or nominee of the *employer* is a shareholder or guarantor; or

(ii)   you are, or an officer of the *employer* is, appointed by the *employer* as an officer of the *company*,

provided the *employer* is acting in pursuance of its statutory powers;

(d)   for lenders in connection with new mortgages arising from the redemption of mortgages to the local authority, provided:

(i)   neither you nor any other *employee* acts on behalf of the borrowers; and

(ii)   the borrowers are given the opportunity to be independently advised by a qualified conveyancer of their choice;

(e)   for a *charity* or voluntary organisation whose objects relate wholly or partly to the *employer's* area;

(f)   for a patient who is the subject of a Court of Protection Order where you are acting for a work colleague (under Rule 4.4 to 4.6 above) who is appointed as deputy for the patient; or

(g)   for a child or young person subject to a Care Order in favour of the *employer* on an application to the Criminal Injuries Compensation Authority.

Law Centres, charities and other non-commercial advice services

4.16   If you are employed by a law centre or advice service operated by a charitable or similar non-commercial organisation you may give advice to and otherwise act for members of the public, provided:

(a)   no funding agent has majority representation on the body responsible for the management of the service, and that body remains independent of central and local government;

(b)   all fees you earn and costs you recover are paid to the organisation for furthering the provision of the organisation's services;

(c)   the organisation is not described as a law centre unless it is a member of the Law Centres Federation; and

(d) the organisation has indemnity cover in relation to the *legal activities* carried out by you, reasonably equivalent to that required under the SRA Indemnity Insurance Rules.

4.17 Rule 4.16 above does not apply to an association formed for the benefit of its members.

The Crown, non-departmental public bodies and the Legal Aid Agency

4.18 If you are employed by the Crown, a non-departmental public body or the Legal Aid Agency (or any body established or maintained by the Legal Aid Agency), you may give legal advice to, and act for, *persons* other than your *employer* if in doing so you are carrying out the lawful functions of your *employer*.

Foreign law firms

4.19 You may provide legal services to your *employer's clients*, subject to the conditions set out in Rule 4.20 below, if you are a *solicitor* or an *REL* employed by:

(a) a practising *lawyer* of another jurisdiction who:

    (i) is not struck off or suspended from the *register of foreign lawyers* or the *register of European lawyers*; and

    (ii) is not *practising* in that context as a *solicitor* or as an *REL*; or

(b) a business whose *managers* and *interest holders* are all practising through that business as *lawyers* of jurisdictions other than England and Wales, and do not include any person who:

    (i) is struck off or suspended from the *register of foreign lawyers* or the *register of European lawyers*; or

    (ii) is *practising* through or in the context of that business as a *solicitor* or as an *REL*.

4.20 You must meet the following conditions if acting, under Rule 4.19 above, for anyone other than your *employer*.

(a) Even if you are qualified to do such work for your *employer*, you must not do, or supervise or assume responsibility for doing any of the following:

    (i) drawing or preparing any instrument or papers comprising *reserved legal activities* under section 12(1)(c) or (d) of the *LSA*;

    (ii) exercising any right of audience, or right to conduct litigation (including making any application or lodging any document relating to litigation), before a *court* or immigration tribunal; or

    (iii) providing any immigration advice or immigration services, unless the *employer*, or a senior fellow *employee*, is registered with the Immigration Services Commissioner.

Authorisation and Practising Requirements

(b) You must ensure that the work you do is covered by professional indemnity insurance reasonably equivalent to that required under the SRA Indemnity Insurance Rules.

(c) You must:

   (i) inform your *client* that your *employer* is not regulated by the *SRA* and that the *SRA's* compulsory insurance scheme does not apply, and either give or confirm this information in writing, if you are a *solicitor*, and you are held out to a *client* as a *solicitor* (or as an English or Welsh *lawyer*) in connection with work you are doing for that *client*; and

   (ii) ensure that if you are identified on the notepaper as a *solicitor* (or as an English or Welsh *lawyer*) the notepaper also states that your *employer* is not regulated by the *SRA*.

4.21   Rule 4.20(c) above should also be read as referring to an *REL* being held out or identified as a *lawyer*, or under the *REL's* title from their home state.

In-house practice overseas

4.22   Rules 4.10 and 4.11 (Pro bono work) apply to your *in-house practice* where you are employed in a body outside England and Wales.

4.23   The other provisions of Rule 4 (In-house practice) do not apply to your *in-house practice* where you are employed in a body outside England and Wales, but you must comply with Rules 4.24 and 4.25 below.

4.24   Subject to 4.25 below, you may act as an *in-house lawyer*, but only for:

(a) your *employer*;

(b) a company or organisation controlled by your *employer* or in which your *employer* has a substantial measure of control;

(c) a company in the same group as your *employer*;

(d) a company which controls your *employer*; or

(e) an *employee* (including a *director* or a company secretary) of a company or organisation under (a) to (d) above, provided that the matter relates to or arises out of the work of that company or organisation, does not relate to a claim arising as a result of a personal injury to the *employee*, and no charge is made for your work unless those costs are recoverable from another source.

4.25   If you are a *solicitor* registered in another state under the *Establishment Directive* with the professional body for a local legal profession you may *practise in-house* to the extent that a member of that legal profession is permitted to do so.

Regulatory bodies

4.26   If you are employed by a regulatory body you may in carrying out the function of the *employer* give legal advice to other *persons* and, where those functions are statutory, may act generally for such *persons*.

Guidance notes

(i)   This rule applies to you if you are a solicitor or REL (or in limited circumstances an RFL) working in in-house practice, which is generally when you are working otherwise than through a regulated legal practice such as an authorised body or an authorised non-SRA firm. However, these provisions also apply to you if you are a solicitor, REL or RFL when working in a licensed body or an authorised non-SRA firm but are doing work, for example, for the firm itself which is outside the scope of the firm's own authorisation.

(ii)   The general principle, subject to limited exceptions, is that your employer itself will need to be authorised if, in your capacity as an employee and as part of your employer's business, you wish to provide reserved legal services to the public (see LSA, section 15(4)). The provisions of 4.4 to 4.26, regarding acting in an in-house capacity for clients other than your employer, are subject to the provisions of the LSA which may nonetheless require your employer to obtain authorisation, for example members of an association may be "the public or a section of the public" for the purposes of the LSA. Such issues should be kept under review as your position may change e.g. your employer's business may develop in such a way that it requires authorisation.

(iii)   If you are a solicitor working in-house (whether in or outside England and Wales) you must comply with Rule 9 (Practising certificates). For further guidance on the need for a practising certificate see our website. Examples of situations where you will be practising as a solicitor, and will therefore need a practising certificate, include:

(a)   you are employed as a solicitor;

(b)   you are held out, on stationery or otherwise, as a solicitor for your employer;

(c)   you administer oaths;

(d)   you appear before a court or tribunal in reliance upon your qualification as a solicitor;

(e)   you instruct counsel;

(f)   you undertake work which is prohibited to unqualified persons under the provisions of Part 3 of the LSA, unless you are supervised by, and acting in the name of, a solicitor with a practising certificate or another qualified person;

(g)   your only qualification as a lawyer is that you are a solicitor, and:

(A)   you are employed or held out as a lawyer;

(B)   you undertake work in another jurisdiction which is reserved to lawyers;

(C)   you are registered in a state other than the UK under the Establishment Directive; or

(D)   you are a registered foreign legal consultant in another jurisdiction.

(iv)   In England and Wales a number of statutory exceptions apply to qualify (ii). Certain in-house government solicitors are allowed to practise as solicitors without practising certificates. Some reserved work can be undertaken by non-solicitors working for local government, and therefore by non-practising solicitors working for local government. See also Rules 9, 10 and 11.

(v)   A solicitor acting only as a justices' clerk in England and Wales is not practising as a solicitor and can instruct counsel without a practising certificate.

(vi)   If you are an in-house solicitor the address of your employer's legal department is the place (or one of the places) where you practise and must therefore be notified to the SRA.

(vii)   If you handle client money, the SRA Accounts Rules will apply to you unless you are exempted under Rule 5 of those rules.

(viii)   If you are working in-house as the senior legal adviser of a company or a local authority you should have direct access to the board or to the council and its committees, and should try to ensure that your terms of employment provide for such access. "Direct access" does not mean that all instructions and advice must pass directly to and from the council, committee or board, but you must have direct access where necessary.

(ix)   An in-house solicitor may act for work colleagues, subject to certain safeguards, provided the matter relates to and arises out of the person's work for the employer. This will cover matters that relate directly to the fellow employee's work but would not, for example, permit reserved legal services to be offered as a benefit under an employment package. Those working in-house will need to consider whether they are allowed to act on a case by case basis and, in particular, the extent to which there is a direct relationship between the work colleague's employment and the reserved legal activity.

(x)   The ability of in-house solicitors to act for clients on a pro bono basis is limited by the LSA, which requires that, in general, the provision of reserved legal services to the public is carried out through an authorised body. There is no such limitation under the LSA in respect of unreserved services, such as providing legal advice. Rule 4.10 sets out the parameters within which in-house solicitors may provide reserved services on a pro bono basis, reflecting the position under the LSA. To determine whether you can undertake reserved legal activities within 4.10, one question will be whether the activities to be undertaken can be regarded as part of the business of the employer. Relevant factors are likely to be:

(a) relevancy of such work to the employer's business;

(b) whether the work is required of the employee by the employer;

(c) how often such work is carried out;

(d) where such work is carried out;

(e) when such work is carried out;

(f) whether such work is explicitly carried out on the employer's behalf;

(g) who provides the necessary professional indemnity insurance;

(h) the extent to which the employer relies on or publicises such work;

(i) whether the employer provides management, training or supervision in relation to such work;

(j) whether the employer specifically rewards the employee in any way in relation to such work;

(k) how many employees carry out the work, and the overall proportion of their time spent on such work;

(l) the extent to which such work complements or enhances the employer's business.

All the circumstances, and the context, will be critical to your decision about whether you may act, for example the work will not necessarily be part of the employer's business merely because it is carried out in office hours, or at the employer's premises.

There will be some situations which are likely to be easier to judge. If there is a clear relationship with the employer's business, acting will not be permissible. For example, you are likely to be prevented from acting:

(A) where the employer describes its business as including the provision of pro bono services;

(B) where the work may boost the employer's business by providing extra business opportunities or creating contacts.

(xi) If you are employed as a solicitor or REL by an insurer which runs a commercial legal telephone advice service, the restrictions in Rule 4.14 will not apply to prevent you acting for an insured in accordance with Rule 4.13.

(xii) If you are employed as a solicitor or REL by a law centre or advice service operated by a charitable or similar non-commercial organisation, you can advise and act for members of the public provided you comply with Rule 4.16 and 4.17. A solicitor or REL who works as a volunteer for such an advice service must comply with the SRA Indemnity Insurance Rules unless exempted by a waiver. If your employer obtains authorisation as a licensed body you will not need to rely on the exceptions in Rule 4.

(xiii)   As the in-house employee of a foreign law firm under Rule 4.19 and 4.20 you may not do reserved work for clients or (unless your employer is separately authorised) immigration work. You must also comply with special requirements as to insurance and "health warnings". Note also, that if you are employed by a foreign law firm and a principal, interest holder or director of the firm is a solicitor, Rule 4.19 and 4.20 will not apply unless the solicitor is dually qualified and is practising only as a lawyer of another jurisdiction in the context of that business.

(xiv)   By contrast, employment overseas by a foreign law firm will not usually fall within the definition of in-house practice in [...] the Glossary if your employer is a lawyer or a law firm.

(xv)   If you are a solicitor, REL or RFL practising as a manager, employee, member or interest holder of an authorised non-SRA firm, neither Rule 4, nor the bulk of the SRA Code of Conduct, nor the SRA Accounts Rules, will be relevant to you when you do work of a type that is within the scope of the firm's authorisation. See Chapter 13 of the SRA Code of Conduct (Application and waivers provisions).

(xvi)   If you are a solicitor, REL or RFL practising as a manager, employee, member or interest holder of an authorised non-SRA firm, you must comply with Rule 4, with the SRA Code of Conduct, and with the SRA Accounts Rules, as if you were an in-house solicitor or REL when you do work of a type which is outside the scope of the firm's authorisation – see Rule 4.3 and the definition of "in-house practice" in the Glossary.

(xvii)   Note that if you are a solicitor, REL or RFL and you are a manager, member or interest holder of an authorised non-SRA firm, or employed in such a firm in connection with the provision of any legal services, it must be:

(a)   in your capacity as a solicitor, REL or RFL, or

(b)   in the capacity of an individual authorised by an approved regulator other than the SRA, if you are so authorised, or

(c)   in both such capacities;

except that if you are a solicitor who is a director of an authorised non-SRA firm or employed in such a firm in connection with the provision of any legal services, you must be practising in your capacity as a solicitor, even if also in some other capacity. See Rule 11.2 and 11.3, as well as section 1A(d) of the SA.

Rule 5: Authorised bodies

Practice from an office in England and Wales

5.1   An *authorised body* may *practise* from an office in England and Wales in the following ways only:

(a)   as a stand-alone *firm*;

(b)   as a *manager*, *member* or *interest holder* of another *authorised body*;

(c)   as a *manager*, *member* or *interest holder* of an *authorised non-SRA firm*, in which case you must comply with any terms and requirements imposed on that firm's authorisation; or

(d)   as an executor, trustee or nominee *company*, or a *company* providing company secretarial services, wholly owned and operated by another *authorised body* or by a *recognised sole practitioner*.

Practice from an office outside England and Wales

5.2   An *authorised body* may *practise* from an office outside England and Wales in the following ways only:

(a)   as a stand-alone *firm*, provided that if any of the body's *managers* or *interest holders* are non-lawyers and the office is in an *Establishment Directive state* other than the *UK*, the rules for local *lawyers* would permit a local *lawyer* to practise through a business of that composition and structure;

(b)   as a *manager*, *member* or *interest holder* of a business which has no office in England and Wales and meets all the following conditions:

(i)   the business carries on the provision of legal advice or assistance, or representation in connection with the application of the law or resolution of legal disputes;

(ii)   a controlling majority of the *managers* and the *interest holders* are *lawyers* practising as such and/or *bodies corporate* in which *lawyers* practising as such constitute a controlling majority of the *managers* and *interest holders*;

(iii)   if any of the business's *managers* or *interest holders* are non-lawyers and any *manager* or *interest holder* is subject to the rules for local *lawyers*, the composition and structure of the business complies with those rules; and

(iv)   if any of the business's *managers* or *interest holders* are non-lawyers and the office is in an *Establishment Directive state* other than the *UK*, the rules for local *lawyers* would permit a local *lawyer* to practise through a business of that composition and structure;

(c)   as an executor, trustee or nominee *company*, or a *company* providing company secretarial services, wholly owned and operated by another *authorised body* or by a *recognised sole practitioner*.

5.3   Nothing in rule 5.2 above prevents an *authorised body* from practising through an *overseas practice* for which it is the *responsible authorised body*.

Guidance notes

(i)   See Part 3 of these rules for the formation and eligibility criteria for recognised bodies and licensed bodies.

(ii)   Authorised bodies can have a complex structure, involving multi-layered ownership. But note that a partnership cannot be a partner in another partnership which is an authorised body because a partnership does not have separate legal identity (although, as an exception, an overseas partnership with separate legal identity could be a partner in a partnership which is an authorised body).

(iii)   The rules do not prevent an authorised body being a manager, member or interest holder of a recognised body or an authorised non-SRA firm which has an office outside England and Wales.

(iv)   An authorised body may practise through one or more overseas practices, which do not themselves require authorisation by the SRA. However, when considering whether authorisation is required for offices overseas, authorised bodies should consider the activities to be carried on from those offices, and note that rule 8.4 of the SRA Authorisation Rules provides that an authorised body may not carry on an activity unless through a body and individual who is authorised to carry on that activity.

Rule 6: Managers and employees authorised by another approved regulator

6.1   If you are a *manager* or *employee* of an *authorised body* or an *employee* of a *recognised sole practitioner* and you are not a *solicitor* but you are authorised by an *approved regulator* other than the *SRA*, you must not:

(a)   be held out in any way which suggests that you are, or are entitled to *practise* as, a *solicitor*;

(b)   undertake the following *reserved work* in England and Wales, unless authorised by your *approved regulator* to do so:

(i)   advocacy in open *court*;

(ii)   the conduct of *court* litigation;

(iii)   the administration of oaths and statutory declarations;

(c)   undertake advocacy in chambers in England and Wales, unless authorised by your *approved regulator* or acting under instructions given by a person qualified to supervise that *reserved work*;

(d)   undertake the following *reserved work* in England and Wales, unless authorised by your *approved regulator* or acting under the supervision of a person qualified to supervise that *reserved work*:

(i)   the preparation of *court* documents;

(ii)   the preparation of instruments and the lodging of documents relating to the transfer or charge of land;

(iii) the preparation of papers on which to found or oppose a grant of probate or a grant of letters of administration;

(iv) the preparation of trust deeds disposing of capital.

Guidance notes

(i) Rule 16 permits lawyers and firms authorised by another approved regulator to be interest holders and managers of an authorised body.

(ii) An individual authorised by another approved regulator cannot practise as a sole practitioner regulated by the SRA as the SRA can only authorise and regulate sole solicitors and RELs.

(iii) Where, in order to satisfy statutory requirements, there is a need for an individual doing reserved work to be supervised or directed by someone in the firm, this can only be undertaken by a person of equivalent or higher status.

(iv) A lawyer of England and Wales who is an individual authorised by another approved regulator is subject to the SRA's regulatory arrangements in relation to practice outside England and Wales if he or she is a manager of an authorised body.

Rule 7: Managers and employees who are not lawyers

7.1 If you are a *manager* or *employee* of an *authorised body* or an *employee* of a *recognised sole practitioner* and you are not a *lawyer of England and Wales*, an *RFL* or a *lawyer* of an *Establishment Directive profession*, you must not:

(a) be held out in any way which suggests that you are, or are entitled to *practise* as, a *lawyer of England and Wales*;

(b) undertake the following *reserved work* in England and Wales:

   (i) advocacy in open *court*;

   (ii) the conduct of *court* litigation;

   (iii) the administration of oaths and statutory declarations;

(c) undertake advocacy in chambers in England and Wales, except under instructions given by a person qualified to supervise that *reserved work*;

(d) undertake the following *reserved work* in England and Wales, except at the direction and under the supervision of a person qualified to supervise that *reserved work*:

   (i) the preparation of *court* documents;

   (ii) the preparation of instruments and the lodging of documents relating to the transfer or charge of land;

   (iii) the preparation of papers on which to found or oppose a grant of probate or a grant of letters of administration;

   (iv) the preparation of trust deeds disposing of capital.

Authorisation and Practising Requirements

Guidance note

(i)   A non-lawyer manager is subject to the SRA's regulatory arrangements in relation to legal practice outside England and Wales if he or she is a manager of an authorised body.

PART 2: RIGHTS OF PRACTICE

Rule 8: Reserved work and immigration work

Solicitors

8.1   As a *solicitor*, provided that you comply with Rule 9.1, you are authorised by the *SRA*:

(a)   to undertake the following *reserved work*:

  (i)   the exercise of any right of audience which *solicitors* had immediately before 7 December 1989;

  (ii)   the exercise of any additional right of audience if you have a relevant higher courts advocacy qualification awarded by the *SRA* or another *approved regulator*;

  (iii)   the conduct of, and the preparation of documents in, *court* and immigration tribunal proceedings;

  (iv)   the preparation of instruments and the lodging of documents relating to the transfer or charge of land;

  (v)   the preparation of trust deeds disposing of capital;

  (vi)   the preparation of papers on which to found or oppose a grant of probate or a grant of letters of administration;

  (vii)   the administration of oaths and statutory declarations; and

(b)   to undertake *immigration work* not included under (a) above.

RELs

8.2   As an *REL*, you are authorised by the *SRA*:

(a)   to undertake the following *reserved work*:

  (i)   the exercise of any right of audience which *solicitors* had immediately before 7 December 1989;

  (ii)   the exercise of any additional right of audience provided that you have a relevant higher courts advocacy qualification awarded by the *SRA* or another *approved regulator*;

  (iii)   the conduct of, and the preparation of documents in, *court* and immigration tribunal proceedings;

(iv) the preparation of instruments and the lodging of documents relating to the transfer or charge of land, provided you are a member of a profession listed under regulation 12 of the European Communities (Lawyer's Practice) Regulations 2000;

(v) the preparation of trust deeds disposing of capital;

(vi) the preparation of papers on which to found or oppose a grant of probate or a grant of letters of administration, provided you are a member of a profession listed under regulation 13 of the European Communities (Lawyer's Practice) Regulations 2000;

(vii) the administration of oaths and statutory declarations; and

(b) to undertake *immigration work* not included under (a) above.

8.3 When as an *REL* you exercise a right of audience before a *court* under 8.2(a)(i) or (ii), conduct *court* litigation under 8.2(a)(iii) or prepare *court* documents under 8.2(a)(iii) you must act in conjunction with a *solicitor* or barrister authorised to do that work.

RFLs

8.4 As an *RFL* working within Rule 3 you are authorised by the *SRA*:

(a) to undertake the following *reserved work*:

(i) advocacy before immigration tribunals; and

(ii) the conduct of, and the preparation of documents in, immigration tribunal proceedings; and

(b) to undertake immigration services which are not *reserved work* and are not included under (a) above, and to provide immigration advice.

Recognised bodies

8.5 Recognised bodies

(a) A *recognised body* is authorised by the *SRA* to undertake the following *reserved work*:

(i) advocacy before a *court* or immigration tribunal provided the *manager* or *employee* exercising the right of audience is authorised by the *SRA*, or otherwise entitled, to do so;

(ii) the conduct of proceedings in a *court* or immigration tribunal;

(iii) the preparation of documents in proceedings before a *court* or immigration tribunal;

(iv) the preparation of instruments and the lodging of documents relating to the transfer or charge of land, provided the body has a *manager* who is:

Authorisation and Practising Requirements

        (A)   an individual who is authorised to do that work, or

        (B)   a *body corporate* which has a *manager* who is authorised to do that work;

    (v)   the preparation of trust deeds disposing of capital;

    (vi)   the preparation of papers on which to found or oppose a grant of probate or a grant of letters of administration, provided the body has a *manager* who is an individual authorised to do that work, or a *body corporate* with a *manager* who is authorised to do that work; and

    (vii)   the administration of oaths and statutory declarations.

  (b)   A *recognised body* is authorised to undertake immigration services which are not within (a) above, and to provide immigration advice.

Licensed bodies

8.6   A *licensed body* is authorised by the *SRA* to undertake the *reserved legal activities* and *immigration work* specified in the authorisation granted to the body under Rule 6 of the *SRA Authorisation Rules*.

Sole practitioner firms

8.7   Sole practitioner firms

  (a)   A *recognised sole practitioner* who is a *solicitor* is authorised by the *SRA*:

    (i)   to provide any *reserved work* which the *solicitor* is authorised to provide under Rule 8.1 above, and any other advocacy service through an *employee* of the *sole practitioner's firm* exercising a right of audience as authorised by the *SRA*, or otherwise entitled, to do; and

    (ii)   to undertake immigration services which are not within (i) above, and provide immigration advice.

  (b)   A *recognised sole practitioner* who is an *REL* is authorised by the *SRA*:

    (i)   to provide any *reserved work* which the *REL* is authorised to provide under Rule 8.2 above, and any other advocacy service through an *employee* of the *sole practitioner's firm* exercising a right of audience as authorised by the *SRA*, or otherwise entitled, to do; and

    (ii)   to undertake *immigration work* which is not within (i) above.

Guidance notes

(i)   Reserved work is work that is defined in Schedule 2 to the LSA as a "reserved legal activity". Certain categories of reserved work (rights of audience in chambers, reserved instrument activities and probate activities) can be done by an unqualified person under the supervision of a manager or fellow employee qualified to do that work – see Schedule 3 to the LSA.

(ii) Immigration work (immigration advice and immigration services) is restricted to certain persons under the Immigration and Asylum Act 1999. Immigration services relating to courts or immigration tribunals are reserved work – advocacy, the conduct of cases, and the preparation of papers. The court work is subject to the normal restriction on court work. Immigration Tribunal work can be done by RFLs who are practising as such. Other immigration work is not reserved work, but can only be done by an authorised person such as a solicitor, a barrister, a legal executive, a member of an Establishment Directive profession, or an RFL practising as such, or under the supervision of an authorised person, or under an exemption given by the Office of the Immigration Services Commissioner.

(iii) The Financial Services and Markets Act 2000 reserves the provision of "regulated activities" to persons authorised by the Financial Conduct Authority (FCA). Certain "regulated activities", ancillary to the provision of a professional service, are exempt from regulation by the FCA when carried out by firms authorised by the SRA – see the SRA Financial Services (Scope) Rules. For the definition of "regulated activity" see the activities specified in the Financial Services and Markets Act 2000 (Regulated Activities) Order 2001 (SI 2001/544).

(iv) From 31 March 2012 or the date on which an order made pursuant to section 69 of the LSA relating to the status of sole practitioners comes into force, whichever is the later, a sole practitioner's firm will be regulated as a type of authorised body and will be authorised under the SRA Authorisation Rules.

(v) The SRA does not authorise notarial activities. This does not prevent individuals, in an SRA authorised firm, providing notarial services where personally authorised to do so by the Master of the Faculties within paragraph 7 of Schedule 2 to the LSA.

(vi) See also Rule 8.4 of the SRA Authorisation Rules which provides that an authorised body may not carry on an activity unless through a body and individual who is authorised to carry on that activity.

(vii) In the case of solicitors and RELs who undertake criminal advocacy, see also the SRA QASA Regulations.

Rule 9: Practising certificates

9.1   If you are *practising* as a *solicitor* (including *in-house*), whether in England and Wales or overseas, you must:

(a)   have in force a practising certificate issued by the *SRA*; or

(b)   be exempt under section 88 of the *SA* from holding a practising certificate.

9.2   You will be *practising* as a *solicitor* if you are involved in legal practice and:

(a)   your involvement in the firm or the work depends on your being a *solicitor*;

(b)   you are held out explicitly or implicitly as a *practising solicitor*;

(c)   you are employed explicitly or implicitly as a *solicitor*; or

(d)   you are deemed by section 1A of the *SA* to be acting as a *solicitor*.

9.3   In 9.2 above "legal practice" includes not only the provision of legal advice or assistance, or representation in connection with the application of the law or resolution of legal disputes, but also the provision of other services such as are provided by *solicitors*.

9.4   If you are a *solicitor* who was formerly an *REL*, and you are *practising* from an office in the *UK* as a *lawyer* of an *Establishment Directive profession*, you must have in force a practising certificate issued by the *SRA*, even if you are not *practising* as a *solicitor*.

Guidance notes

(i)   Rule 9 includes, in rule form, the requirements of sections 1 and 1A of the SA. The issuing of practising certificates under that Act is the responsibility of the SRA. For further guidance on the need for a practising certificate see our website.

(ii)   If you practise as a solicitor, whether in a firm or in-house, without having a practising certificate, you will commit a criminal offence, as well as a breach of the rules, unless you are entitled to rely on the exemption in section 88 of the SA.

Rule 10: Sole practitioners

10.1   If you are a *solicitor* or *REL* you must not *practise* as a *sole practitioner* unless:

(a)   the *SRA* has first authorised you as a *recognised sole practitioner* by endorsing your practising certificate or certificate of registration to that effect;

(b)   your *practice* falls within 10.2 below and you are therefore exempt from the obligation to be a *recognised sole practitioner*; or

(c)   you are authorised to *practise* as a *sole practitioner* by an *approved regulator* other than the *SRA*.

10.2   For the purpose of 10.1(b) above you are exempt from the obligation to be a *recognised sole practitioner* if:

(a)   your *practice* is conducted entirely from an office or offices outside England and Wales;

(b)   your *practice* consists entirely of work as a temporary or permanent *employee* and any *firm* which employs you takes full responsibility for you as an *employee*; or

(c)   your *practice* consists entirely of:

(i)   providing professional services without remuneration for friends, relatives, companies wholly owned by you or your family, or registered *charities*; and/or

    (ii)   administering oaths and statutory declarations; and/or

    (iii)   activities which could constitute *practice* but are done in the course of discharging the functions of any of the offices or appointments listed in paragraph (i)(E) of the definition of *private practice*.

Guidance note

(i)   Until 31 March 2012 or the date on which an order made pursuant to section 69 of the LSA relating to the status of sole practitioners comes into force, whichever is the later, see regulation 4 of the SRA Practising Regulations. After that, see the SRA Authorisation Rules.

Rule 11: Participation in legal practice

11.1   If you are a *solicitor*, *REL* or *RFL* and you are:

    (a)   a *manager, member* or *interest holder* of:

        (i)   a *recognised body*; or

        (ii)   a *body corporate* which is a *European corporate practice* and is a *manager* of a *recognised body*; or

    (b)   a *manager, member* or *owner* of:

        (i)   a *licensed body*; or

        (ii)   a *body corporate* which is a *European corporate practice* and is a *manager* of a *licensed body*;

it must be in your capacity as a *solicitor*, *REL* or *RFL* (whether or not you are held out as such);

    (c)   employed in connection with the provision of legal services in England and Wales, by:

        (i)   a *recognised sole practitioner*; or

        (ii)   an *authorised body*;

it must be in your capacity as a *solicitor*, in accordance with section 1A of the *SA*, an *REL* or an *RFL* (whether or not you are held out as such);

    (d)   *Practising* in accordance with (a), (b) or (c) above does not prevent you from *practising* also as an individual authorised by an *approved regulator* other than the *SRA* or providing services as a member of a non-lawyer profession.

11.2   Subject to 11.3 below, if you are a *solicitor*, *REL* or *RFL* and you are:

    (a)   a *manager, member* or *interest holder* of:

        (i)   an *authorised non-SRA firm* which is not licensed under Part 5 of the *LSA*; or

        (ii)   a *body corporate* which is a *manager* of such an *authorised non-SRA firm*;

Authorisation and
Practising Requirements

(b)   a *manager*, *member* or *owner* of an *authorised non-SRA firm* which is licensed under Part 5 of the *LSA*; or

(c)   an *employee* who is employed in connection with the provision of legal services in England and Wales, by an *authorised non-SRA firm*;

it must be in your capacity as a *solicitor*, *REL* or *RFL* or as an individual authorised by an *approved regulator* other than the *SRA* (whether or not you are held out as such) but this does not prevent you from *practising* in both capacities or providing services as a member of a non-lawyer profession in addition to *practising* as a *lawyer*.

11.3   If you are a *solicitor* who is employed by, or is a *director* of, an *authorised non-SRA firm*, section 1A of the *SA* will require you to *practise* through that firm in the capacity of *solicitor*, even if also *practising* in some other capacity.

11.4   No *solicitor* or *REL*, while a prisoner in any prison, may commence, prosecute or defend any action, suit or other contentious proceedings, or appear as an advocate in any such proceedings, unless he or she does so as a litigant in person and not as a *solicitor* or *REL*.

Guidance note

(i)   A solicitor, REL or RFL is required to be involved in a recognised body in that capacity even if they merely have a small interest in the firm. There is greater flexibility in licensed bodies where a solicitor, REL or RFL is permitted to have a small share in a licensed body without being treated as practising merely because of that involvement. For example, a solicitor could have a small interest in a licensed body through a pension fund even though not practising.

Rule 12: Persons who must be "qualified to supervise"

12.1   The following persons must be "*qualified to supervise*":

(a)   a *recognised sole practitioner*;

(b)   one of the *lawyer managers* of an *authorised body* or of a *body corporate* which is a *legally qualified body* and which is a *manager* of the *authorised body*;

(c)   one of the *solicitors* or *RELs* employed by a law centre in England and Wales, unless the law centre is licensed under Part 5 of the *LSA* in which case the provisions in Rule 12.1(b) will apply; or

(d)   one *in-house solicitor* or *in-house REL* in any department in England and Wales where *solicitors* and/or *RELs*, as part of their employment:

(i)   do publicly funded work; or

(ii)   do or supervise advocacy or the conduct of proceedings for members of the public before a *court* or immigration tribunal.

12.2   To be "*qualified to supervise*" for the purpose of 12.1 a person must:

(a) have completed the training specified from time to time by the *SRA* for this purpose; and

(b) be a practising *lawyer*, and have been entitled to practise as a *lawyer* for at least 36 months within the last ten years; and

must be able to demonstrate this if asked by the *SRA*.

12.3   The following persons must ensure that their firm has at least one *manager* who is practising as a *lawyer* and has been entitled to practise as a *lawyer* for a minimum of 36 months within the last 10 years:

(a) a *solicitor manager* of a firm which is not an *authorised body* and which is practising from an office outside England and Wales, and *solicitors* control the firm, either directly as *partners*, *members* or *interest holders*, or indirectly by their ownership of *bodies corporate* which are *partners*, *members* or *interest holders*; and

(b) a *solicitor* or *REL manager* of a firm which is not an *authorised body* and which is practising from an office in Scotland or Northern Ireland, and *solicitors* and/or *RELs* control the firm, either directly as *partners*, *members* or *interest holders*, or indirectly by their ownership of *bodies corporate* which are *partners*, *members* or *interest holders*.

12.4   You must not set up as a *solicitor sole practitioner* outside England and Wales, or as an *REL sole practitioner* in Scotland or Northern Ireland, unless you have been entitled to *practise* as a *lawyer* for a minimum of 36 months within the last 10 years.

Guidance notes

(i)   The person "qualified to supervise" under Rule 12.2 does not have to be personally entitled by law to supervise all work undertaken by the firm. Responsibility for the overall supervision framework, including compliance with legal supervisory requirements, rests with the authorised body and its managers, or the recognised sole practitioner.

(ii)   In satisfying the requirement for 36 months entitlement to practise you can for example rely on a period as a lawyer of another jurisdiction. In calculating the 36 months, any period of entitlement to practise as a lawyer of another jurisdiction can be taken into account in addition to your time entitled to practise as a solicitor.

(iii)   Waivers may be granted in individual cases. See Rule 21.

(iv)   The training presently specified by the SRA is attendance at or participation in any course(s), or programme(s) of learning, on management skills involving attendance or participation for a minimum of 12 hours. The courses or programmes do not have to be CPD accredited in order to satisfy the requirement. It is not normally necessary to check with the SRA before undertaking a course or programme unless the course is unusual and outside the mainstream of management training. Advice may be sought from the Professional Ethics Guidance Team.

Authorisation and Practising Requirements

(v)   Controlling the firm in Rule 12.3 means constituting the largest (or equal largest) share of control of the firm either as individual managers or by their share in the control of bodies which are managers.

PART 3: FORMATION AND ELIGIBILITY CRITERIA FOR RECOGNISED BODIES AND LICENSED BODIES

Rule 13: Eligibility criteria and fundamental requirements for recognised bodies

13.1   To be eligible to be a *recognised body*, a body must be a *legal services body* namely a *partnership*, *company* or *LLP* of which:

(a)   at least one *manager* is:

   (i)   a *solicitor* with a current practising certificate, or

   (ii)   an *REL*, or

   (iii)   (in the case of a *partnership* or *LLP*) a *body corporate* which is a *legally qualified body* with at least one *manager* who is a *solicitor* with a current practising certificate or an *REL*; and

(b)   all of the *managers* and *interest holders* are *lawyers* and *legally qualified bodies*.

Services requirement

13.2   The business of a *recognised body* may consist only of the provision of:

(a)   professional services of the sort provided by individuals *practising* as *solicitors* and/or *lawyers* of other jurisdictions; and

(b)   professional services of the sort provided by notaries public, but only if a notary public is a *manager* or *employee* of a *recognised body*,

but this does not prevent a *recognised body* providing services within Chapter 12 (Separate businesses) of the *SRA Code of Conduct*, or holding an interest in a *company* which is a *separate business*.

Guidance notes

(i)   Although most organisations which involve non-lawyers as managers or interest holders must be licensed bodies, there is a limited exception under section 72(2) of the LSA which permits a small degree of non-lawyer involvement in recognised bodies. Where one or more bodies are involved in a firm as a manager or owner/interest holder, and in those bodies non-authorised persons have only a de minimis (less than 10%) control by way of voting rights, then the firm will remain a legal services body requiring recognition under the AJA. Where the control is 10% or more, the firm will be a licensable body.

(ii)   The services requirement in 13.2 should be read in conjunction with Chapter 12 of the SRA Code of Conduct. Certain services which could be offered through a "permitted separate business" (see Chapter 12) can also be provided in conjunction with a firm or in-house practice whilst still complying with the services requirement in 13.2. These services, which extend or fall outside the scope of the professional services mentioned in 13.2, are:

(a) education and training activities; and

(b) authorship, journalism and publishing.

Rule 14: Eligibility criteria and fundamental requirements for licensed bodies

14.1   To be eligible to be a *licensed body*, a body must comply with the *lawyer manager* requirement set out in Rule 14.2 below and be a "licensable body", as defined under section 72 of the *LSA*, and as set out in Rule 14.3 to 14.6 below.

14.2   At all times at least one *manager* of a *licensed body* must be an individual who is:

(a) a *solicitor* with a current practising certificate;

(b) an *REL*;

(c) a *lawyer of England and Wales* and who is authorised by an *approved regulator* other than the *SRA*; or

(d) registered with the *BSB* under regulation 17 of the European Communities (Lawyer's Practice) Regulations 2000 (SI 2000/1119).

14.3   A body ("B") is a *licensable body* if a *non-authorised person*:

(a) is a *manager* of B, or

(b) is an *interest holder* of B.

14.4   A body ("B") is also a *licensable body* if:

(a) another body ("A") is a *manager* of B, or is an *interest holder* of B, and

(b) *non-authorised persons* are entitled to exercise, or control the exercise of, at least 10% of the *voting rights* in A.

14.5   A body may be a *licensable body* by virtue of both 14.3 and 14.4.

14.6   For the purposes of this rule, a *non-authorised person* has an indirect interest in a *licensable body* if the body is a *licensable body* by virtue of 14.4 and the *non-authorised person* is entitled to exercise, or control the exercise of, *voting rights* in A.

Rule 15: Formation, registered office and practising address

15.1   An *authorised body* which is a *partnership* may be formed under the law of any country and may be a legal *person*.

15.2   An *authorised body* which is an *LLP* must be incorporated and registered in England and Wales, Scotland or Northern Ireland under the Limited Liability Partnerships Act 2000.

15.3   An *authorised body* which is a *company* must be:

(a)   incorporated and registered in England and Wales, Scotland or Northern Ireland under Parts 1 and 2 of the Companies Act 2006;

(b)   incorporated in an *Establishment Directive state* and registered as an overseas company under Part 34 of the Companies Act 2006; or

(c)   incorporated and registered in an *Establishment Directive state* as a *societas Europaea*.

15.4   An *authorised body* must have at least one *practising address* in England and Wales.

15.5   An *authorised body* must have its registered office at a *practising address* in England and Wales if the *authorised body* is registered in England and Wales:

(a)   under Parts 1 and 2 of the Companies Act 2006;

(b)   under the Limited Liability Partnerships Act 2000; or

(c)   as a *societas Europaea*.

Guidance note:

(i)   See also the reporting requirements relating to the practising address and registered addresses of your overseas practices set out in:

(a)   Rule 4.4 of the SRA Authorisation Rules;

(b)   Rule 18.2 of the SRA Practice Framework Rules; and

(c)   Rule 3.2 of the SRA Overseas Rules.

Rule 16: Composition of an authorised body

16.1   Provided that the requirements for all *authorised bodies* set out in Rule 13 or Rule 14, as appropriate, are met, an *authorised body* may have all or any of the following as a *partner* (if it is a *partnership*), a *member* (if it is an *LLP*), or a *director*, *member* or *shareowner* (if it is a *company*):

(a)   a *lawyer of England and Wales* (including a *solicitor* with a current practising certificate);

(b)   an *REL*;

(c)   an *RFL*;

(d)   an *EEL*;

(e)   in the case of a *partnership* or an *LLP*, a *body corporate* which is a *legally qualified body*;

(f)   in the case of a *company*, a *legally qualified body*, save that only an individual may be a *director* of a *recognised body* which is a *company*;

provided that, where necessary, they comply with the approval requirements in Part 4 of the *SRA Authorisation Rules*.

16.2   If the *authorised body* is a *licensed body*, then the list of permitted *partners*, *members* of an *LLP* or, in the case of a *company*, *directors*, registered *members* or *shareowners* at 16.1(a) to (f) shall include:

(a)   a *licensed body* or another body licensed under Part 5 of the *LSA* by an *approved regulator* other than the *SRA*; and

(b)   any other individual or *body corporate*;

subject to any necessary approval as a *manager* or *owner* under Part 4 (Approval of managers, owners and compliance officers) of the *SRA Authorisation Rules*, save that only an individual may be a *director* of a *licensed body* which is a *company*.

16.3   An *authorised body* which is an *LLP* must have at least two *members*.

Guidance notes

(i)   See 22.3 below regarding the position of firms which have non-lawyer managers prior to 6 October 2011.

(ii)   Although a legal services body can have a variety of types of manager, only a solicitor or an REL may be a sole practitioner.

(iii)   Where, in line with Rule 16, a firm has persons other than solicitors as managers (in particular where European lawyers are involved), any list of the managers will need to:

(a)   identify any solicitor as a solicitor;

(b)   in the case of any lawyer or notary of an Establishment Directive state other than the UK:

(A)   identify the jurisdiction(s) – local or national as appropriate – under whose professional title the lawyer or notary is practising;

(B)   give the professional title(s), expressed in an official language of the Establishment Directive state(s) concerned; and

(C)   if the lawyer is an REL, refer to that lawyer's registration with the SRA;

(c)   indicate the professional qualification(s) of any other lawyer and the country or jurisdiction of qualification of any RFL not included in (b) above;

(d)   identify any individual non-lawyer as a non-lawyer; and

(e)   identify the nature of any body corporate, if this is not clear from its name.

In addition, whenever an REL (whether or not a manager) is named on letterhead used in England and Wales by any firm or in-house practice, the firm or the employer will need to follow the guidance in (iii)(b) above.

Authorisation and
Practising Requirements

Rule 17: Authorised bodies which are companies

Record of non-member shareowners

17.1 Keeping a record

(a) A *recognised body* which is a *company* with shares must keep a record of any non-*member interest holders*, and retain the record for at least three years after their interest ceases;

(b) A *licensed body* which is a *company* with shares must keep a record of any non-*member owners*, and retain the record for at least three years after their ownership ceases.

17.2 A *member* who holds a share as nominee for a non-*member shareowner* in an *authorised body* must keep the *authorised body* informed of all facts necessary to keep an accurate and up-to-date record in accordance with Rule 17.1.

Rule 18: Information and documentation

18.1 An *authorised body* must supply any information and documentation relating to its composition and structure or to any of its *managers, employees, members* or *shareowners*, as and when requested to do so by the *SRA*.

18.2 Notwithstanding any requirement to obtain approval of a *manager, owner, COLP* or *COFA* under Part 4 of the *SRA Authorisation Rules*, an *authorised body* must notify the *SRA* within seven days of any change to its:

(a) name;

(b) registered office and/or any of its *practising addresses*;

(c) *managers*;

(d) *interest holders*, if it is a *recognised body*, and in the case of a *recognised body* which is a *company*, this includes *members* and *shareowners*;

(e) *owners*, if it is a *licensed body*, and in the case of a *licensed body* which is a *company*, this includes *members* and *shareowners*;

(f) *COLP*;

(g) *COFA*; or

(h) *overseas practices*, including any contact details and practising/registered addresses of its *overseas practices*.

18.3 An *authorised body* must notify the *SRA* within seven days if it is an unlimited *company* and it is re-registered as limited under the *Companies Acts*.

18.4 If a *relevant insolvency event* occurs in relation to an *authorised body* its *managers*, or in the case of an *authorised body* which is an overseas company, its *directors*, must notify the *SRA* within seven days.

Guidance notes

(i)   There are other SRA reporting and information requirements that apply to individuals or firms. See for example:

(a)   Rules 3, 8.7, 8.8, 8.9 and 8.10 and 18, 23, 24 and 25 of the SRA Authorisation Rules

(b)   Rule 32 of the SRA Accounts Rules

(c)   Regulations 1.2, 4.3, 4.5, 4.8, 4.12, 4.13 and 15 of the SRA Practising Regulations

(d)   Chapter 10 of the SRA Code of Conduct

(e)   Rule 17.3 of the SRA Indemnity Insurance Rules 2013 or any subsequent rules thereto.

(ii)   In addition to the requirement to inform the SRA when certain persons leave the firm, there are the requirements in Rule 8 of the SRA Authorisation Rules for firms to seek approval, where necessary, before certain persons join the firm. This is more onerous than simply informing the SRA of changes that have taken place.

PART 4: COMPLIANCE WITH PRACTICE REQUIREMENTS

Rule 19: Compliance with practice requirements

19.1   An *authorised body* and its *managers* and *employees* must at all times ensure that they act in accordance with the requirements of the *SRA's regulatory arrangements* as they apply to them.

19.2   A *solicitor*, *REL* or *RFL* who is a *member* or *shareowner* of an *authorised body* which is a *company* must not cause, instigate or connive at any breach of the requirements imposed under the *SRA's regulatory arrangements* by the *authorised body* or any of its *managers* or *employees*.

19.3   An *employee* of an *authorised body* must not cause, instigate or connive at any breach of any requirements imposed under the *SRA's regulatory arrangements*.

19.4   The *partners* in an *authorised body* which is a *partnership* are responsible not only as *managers* but also, jointly and severally, as the *authorised body*.

Rule 20: Overseas practice

[Deleted]

Rule 21: Waivers

21.1   Subject to provisions relating to any statutory obligations or the *SRA's regulatory arrangements* affecting its ability to waive any requirements, the *SRA* Board shall

Authorisation and
Practising Requirements

have power to waive in writing the provisions of these rules for a particular purpose or purposes expressed in such waiver, and to attach conditions to or revoke such waiver, at its own discretion.

Guidance note

(i) An applicant for a waiver must satisfy the SRA that the circumstances are sufficiently exceptional to justify a departure from the requirements of the rule in question, bearing in mind its purpose. Applications should be made to the Professional Ethics Guidance Team.

Rule 22: Transitional provisions and grace period

22.1 From 31 March 2012 or the date on which an order made pursuant to section 69 of the *LSA* relating to the status of *sole practitioners* comes into force, whichever is the later, these rules shall have effect subject to the following amendments:

(a) Rules 1.1(a), 2.1(a), 3.1(a), 8.7, 11.1(c)(i) and 12.1(a) shall be omitted;

(b) In Rules 1.1(b) and 2.1(b) the words, "authorised as a *sole practitioner*" shall be substituted for the words "a *recognised sole practitioner*";

(c) In Rules 1.2(a) and 2.2(a) the words "as a *recognised body*" shall be substituted for the words "a *recognised sole practitioner*";

(d) In Rule 3.2(d) the words "a *recognised sole practitioner*," shall be omitted;

(e) In Rules 5.1(d) and 5.2(c) the words "or by a *recognised sole practitioner*" shall be omitted;

(f) In Rules 6.1 and 7.1 the words "or an *employee* of a *recognised sole practitioner*" shall be omitted;

(g) In Rule 10.1(a) the word "*recognised*" shall be omitted and the words "by endorsing your practising certificate or certificate of registration to that effect" shall be omitted;

(h) In Rules 10.1(b) and 10.2 the words "authorised as a" shall be substituted for the words "a *recognised*";

(i) In Rule 12.1(b), the words "a *lawyer manager*" shall be substituted for the words "one of the *lawyer managers*"; and

(j) Rule 13.1 shall have effect as if the words "*sole practitioner*," were inserted after the words "namely a".

22.2 Unless the context otherwise requires, references in these rules to:

(a) these rules, or a provision of these rules; and

(b) the *SRA Code of Conduct*, rules, regulations or *regulatory arrangements*, or a provision of the same,

include a reference to the equivalent rules, regulations or provisions previously in force.

22.3   A body that has, at the time these rules come into force, been recognised by the *SRA* under section 9 *AJA* and that does not comply with Rule 13.1(b) above shall continue to be treated as a *legal services body* for the purposes of these rules and the *SRA's regulatory arrangements* until:

(a)   such time as it ceases to comply with the management and control requirements set out in Rule 22.4 below; or

(b)   the end of the transitional period under Part 2 of Schedule 5 to the *LSA*, or such earlier time as the body may elect,

at which time it shall be a *licensed body* for the purposes of these rules and the *SRA's regulatory arrangements*.

22.4   The management and control requirements referred to in Rule 22.3 above are:

(a)   At least 75% of the body's *managers* must be:

(i)   individuals who are, and are entitled to *practise* as, *lawyers of England and Wales*, *lawyers* of *Establishment Directive professions* or *RFLs*; or

(ii)   *bodies corporate* which are legally qualified bodies;

although a legally qualified body cannot be a *director* of a body which is a *company*;

(b)   Individuals who are, and are entitled to *practise* as, *lawyers of England and Wales*, *lawyers* of *Establishment Directive professions* or *RFLs* must make up at least 75% of the ultimate beneficial ownership of the body; and

(c)   Individuals who are, and are entitled to *practise* as, *lawyers of England and Wales*, *lawyers* of *Establishment Directive professions* or *RFLs*, and/or legally qualified bodies, must:

(i)   exercise or control the exercise of at least 75% of the *voting rights* in the body; and

(ii)   if the body is a *company* with shares, hold (as registered *members* of the *company*) at least 75% of the shares.

(d)   Subject to Rule 13.1(b) above, every *interest holder* of the *recognised body*, and every *person* who exercises or controls the exercise of any *voting rights* in the body, must be:

(i)   an individual who is, and is entitled to *practise* as, a *lawyer of England and Wales*, a *lawyer* of an *Establishment Directive profession* or an *RFL*;

(ii)   a legally qualified body; or

(iii)   an individual who is approved under regulation 3 of the SRA Recognised Bodies Regulations 2009, regulation 5 of the SRA Recognised Bodies Regulations 2011 or Part 4 of the *SRA Authorisation Rules* and, subject to (e) below, is a *manager* of the body.

Authorisation and Practising Requirements

(e)   An individual who is not entitled under (d)(i) above may be an *interest holder* of a *recognised body* without being a *manager* of the body if:

   (i)   the *recognised body* is a *company* which is wholly or partly owned by a *partnership* or *LLP* which is a *legally qualified body*;

   (ii)   the individual is approved under regulation 3 of the SRA Recognised Bodies Regulations 2009, regulation 5 of the SRA Recognised Bodies Regulations 2011 or Part 4 of the *SRA Authorisation Rules* and is a *manager* of the *partnership* or *LLP*; and

   (iii) the individual is precluded under the *partnership* agreement or *members'* agreement from exercising or authorising any vote in relation to the *company*.

For the purposes of Rule 22.4 and for the purposes of section 9A(6)(h) and (6C) of the *AJA* "legally qualified body" means a body which would meet the services requirement in Rule 13.2 and is:

(A)   a *recognised body*;

(B)   an *authorised non-SRA firm* of which individuals who are, and are entitled to practise as, *lawyers of England and Wales, lawyers* of *Establishment Directive professions* or *RFLs* make up at least 75% of the ultimate beneficial ownership; or

(C)   a European corporate practice which is a *lawyers'* practice and is a body incorporated in an *Establishment Directive state*, or a *partnership* with separate legal identity formed under the law of an *Establishment Directive state*:

   (I)   which has an office in an *Establishment Directive state* but does not have an office in England and Wales;

   (II)   whose ultimate beneficial owners include at least one individual who is not a *lawyer of England and Wales* but is, and is entitled to practise as, a *lawyer* of an *Establishment Directive profession*;

   (III) whose *managers* include at least one such individual, or at least one body corporate whose *managers* include at least one such individual;

   (IV)   75% of whose ultimate beneficial ownership is in the hands of individuals who are, and are entitled to practise as, *lawyers* of *Establishment Directive professions, lawyers of England and Wales*, and/or *RFLs*; and

   (V)   75% of whose *managers* comprise such individuals, and/or bodies corporate 75% of whose *managers* comprise such individuals.

22.5   These rules shall not apply to *licensable bodies* until such time as the *Society* is designated as a *licensing authority* under Part 1 of Schedule 10 to the *LSA* and all definitions shall be construed accordingly.

22.6   In these rules references:

(a) in the preamble to the rules being made under section 83 and Schedule 11 to the Legal Services Act 2007;

(b) to *COLPs* and *COFAs*; and

(c) to the approval of *managers*, *owners*, *COLPs* and *COFAs*;

shall have no effect until such time as the *Society* is designated as a *licensing authority* under Part 1 of Schedule 10 to the *LSA*.

22.7   Until the 180th day after the date on which the *Society* is designated as a *licensing authority* under Part 1 of Schedule 10 to the *LSA*:

(a) [Deleted];

(b) Rule 4.13 (insurers) shall have no effect;

(c) Rule 13.06 (insurers) of the Solicitors' Code of Conduct 2007 shall continue to have effect; and

(d) references to Rule 4.13 shall be treated as references to Rule 13.06 of the Solicitors' Code of Conduct 2007.

PART 5: INTERPRETATION

Rule 23: Interpretation

23.1   The SRA Handbook Glossary 2012 shall apply and, unless the context otherwise requires:

(a) all italicised terms shall be defined; and

(b) all terms shall be interpreted,

in accordance with the *Glossary*.

Authorisation and
Practising Requirements

[E.2]   SRA Authorisation Rules for Legal Services Bodies and Licensable Bodies 2011

Rules dated 17 June 2011

commencing in respect of licensable bodies, on the designation of the Law Society as a licensing authority under Part 1 of Schedule 10 to the Legal Services Act 2007; and in respect of legal services bodies, on 31 March 2012

made by the Solicitors Regulation Authority Board, under sections 79 and 80 of the Solicitors Act 1974, sections 9 and 9A of the Administration of Justice Act 1985 and section 83 and Schedule 11 to the Legal Services Act 2007, with the approval of the Legal Services Board under paragraph 19 of Schedule 4 to the Legal Services Act 2007.

PART 1: INTERPRETATION AND APPLICATIONS

Rule 1: Interpretation

1.1   The SRA Handbook Glossary 2012 shall apply and, unless the context otherwise requires:

(a)   all italicised terms shall be defined; and

(b)   all terms shall be interpreted,

in accordance with the *Glossary*.

Guidance notes

(i)   The Glossary definition of "owner" relates to anyone holding a material interest, together with any person who is a partner in a partnership (including salaried partners) regardless of the extent of their interest.

(ii)   When assessing whether a person is an owner with a "material interest", the calculation of the person's interest takes into account not only that person's interest, but also the interests of any associates. "Associates" is defined for these purposes in accordance with paragraph 5 to Schedule 13 of the LSA and includes relationships where the Act assumes a likelihood of influence such as employer over employee.

Rule 2: Form, timing and fees for applications made under these rules

2.1   All applications under these rules must comprise:

(a)   the *prescribed* form, correctly completed;

(b)   the fee or fees for the application, as determined from time to time by the *SRA* Board;

(c)   such additional information, documents and references considered by the *SRA* to be necessary to enable it to discharge its functions under these rules, as may be specified by the *SRA*; and

(d)   any additional information and documentation which the *SRA* may reasonably require.

2.2   It is not necessary to submit all documents, information and payments simultaneously, but an application will only have been made once the *SRA* has received all of the documentation, information and payments comprising that application.

Guidance notes

(i)   Application forms and guidance notes can be found on the SRA website.

(ii)   All parts of the application form must be fully completed. Where forms are only partially complete or where supporting information or documents are still to be provided, the application will not be deemed to have been made and the decision period in Rule 5.2 will not start to run.

Rule 3: Application information and notification of any change following application

3.1   The *applicant body* must:

(a)   ensure that all information given in an application under these rules is correct and complete;

(b)   notify the *SRA* as soon as it becomes aware that any information provided in its application under these rules has changed.

Guidance notes

(i)   During the application process an applicant body must notify the SRA of any changes to details or information provided as part of the application including notifying new information that the applicant body would have been required to supply if it had been known at the time of the application. It is an offence under the LSA (see Schedule 13 paragraphs 10–12) not to inform the SRA if there is any change to:

(a)   the list of non-authorised persons who hold or are expected to hold a material interest in the applicant body, and

(b)   the extent or nature of those interests held or to be held.

(ii)   Authorised bodies are subject to similar notification requirements under Rule 8.7.

PART 2: AUTHORISATION APPLICATIONS AND DECISION PERIOD

Rule 4: Applications for authorisation

4.1   A *licensable body* or a *legal services body* may make an application for *authorisation* in accordance with these rules.

4.2   An application by a *licensable body* for *authorisation* must include a statement about what *reserved legal activities* the body seeks *authorisation* for.

4.3   Where an application by a *licensable body* for *authorisation* relates to more than one *reserved legal activity*, the *SRA* may grant the application in relation to all or any of them.

4.4   An application by a *licensable body* or *legal services body* for *authorisation* must notify the *SRA* of the practising address and, where different, the registered address, of any *overseas practices* for which it would, if authorised, be the *responsible authorised body*.

Rule 5: Decision period

5.1   The *SRA* must:

(a)   decide an *authorisation* application;

(b)   notify the *applicant body* of its decision;

(c)   if it decides to refuse the application, set out in the notice the reasons for the refusal;

before the end of the *decision period*.

5.2   The *decision period* is the period of 6 months beginning with the day on which the application is made to the *SRA* in accordance with these rules.

5.3   The *SRA* may, on one occasion, give the *applicant body* a notice (an "extension notice") extending the *decision period* by a period specified in the notice.

5.4   But:

(a)   an extension notice must only be given before the time when the *decision period* would end, but for the extension notice; and

(b)   the total *decision period* must not exceed 9 months.

5.5   An extension notice must set out the reasons for the extension.

Guidance notes

(i)   See Rule 2.2 above for when an application is made.

(ii)   The SRA will extend the period for making a decision if it considers this necessary for the proper consideration of the application (see paragraph 2 of Schedule 11 to the LSA).

(iii)   The means of notice or notification can include any form of written electronic communication normally used for business purposes, such as emails.

Rule 6: Determination of authorisation applications

6.1   The *SRA* will determine applications for *authorisation*, so far as is reasonably practicable, in a way:

(a)   which is compatible with the *regulatory objectives* including the objective of improving access to justice; and

(b)   which the *SRA* considers most appropriate for the purpose of meeting those objectives.

6.2   The *SRA* may only grant an application for *authorisation* if the conditions in (a) to (d) below are met:

(a)   if it is an application for recognition, the *applicant body* is a *legal services body*;

(b)   if it is an application for a licence, the *applicant body* is a *licensable body*;

(c)   if it is a *partnership*, the body has adopted a name under which it is to be registered, and which complies with Chapter 8 (Publicity) of the *SRA Code of Conduct*; and

(d)   the *SRA* is satisfied that upon *authorisation*, the body will be in compliance with the following rules:

(i)   SRA Indemnity Insurance Rules;

(ii)   *SRA Compensation Fund Rules*;

(iii) Rule 8.5 (compliance officers), including any necessary approval of a *candidate* under Part 4;

(iv)   Rule 8.6 (management and control) including any necessary approval of a *candidate* under Part 4; and

(v)   Rules 15 (Formation, registered office and practising address), 16 (Composition of an authorised body) and 12 (Persons who must be "qualified to supervise") of the *SRA Practice Framework Rules*.

6.3   Notwithstanding that the conditions in 6.2 are met, the *SRA* may refuse an application for *authorisation* if:

(a)   it is not satisfied that the *applicant body's managers* and *interest holders* are suitable, as a group, to operate or control a business providing regulated legal services;

(b) it is not satisfied that the *applicant body's* management or governance arrangements are adequate to safeguard the *regulatory objectives*;

(c) it is not satisfied that if the *authorisation* is granted, the *applicant body* will comply with the *SRA's regulatory arrangements* including these rules and any conditions imposed on the *authorisation*;

(d) the *applicant body* has provided inaccurate or misleading information in its application or in response to any requests by the *SRA* for information;

(e) the *applicant body* has failed to notify the *SRA* of any changes in the information provided in the application in accordance with Rule 3; or

(f) for any other reason, the *SRA* considers that it would be against the public interest or otherwise inconsistent with the *regulatory objectives* to grant *authorisation*.

6.4   In reaching a decision under this rule, the *SRA* will take into account all the circumstances which the *SRA* considers to be relevant including, for the avoidance of doubt,

(a) any relevant information regarding:

  (i)   a *manager*, *employee* or *interest holder* of the *applicant body*;

  (ii) any *persons* that such a *manager*, *employee* or *interest holder* is related to, affiliated with, or acts together with where the *SRA* has reason to believe that such *persons* may have an influence over the way in which the *manager*, *employee* or *interest holder* will exercise their role; and

(b) any failure or refusal to disclose, or attempts to conceal relevant information.

Guidance notes

(i)   In considering applications the SRA must comply with the regulatory objectives. Relevant information will therefore be construed widely and the SRA will take account of a broad range of factors. These will include not only issues relevant to the Part 4 approval process, but also factors such as the applicant body's business and governance proposals.

(ii)   Where information is provided in respect of an application, the SRA will consider this to be misleading if, despite the fact that the information is accurate, there is a material omission.

(iii)   View the forms, SRA Suitability Test and the decision making criteria.

PART 3: CONDITIONS OF AUTHORISATION

Rule 7: Terms and conditions of authorisation

7.1   The *authorisation* of a body under these rules entitles:

Authorisation and
Practising Requirements

(a) a *recognised body* to undertake the activities set out in Rule 8.5 (reserved work and immigration work: recognised bodies) of the *SRA Practice Framework Rules*; and

(b) a *licensed body* to undertake the *reserved legal activities* and *immigration work* specified in the licence.

7.2 Every *authorisation* is granted by the *SRA* subject to:

(a) the general conditions in Rule 8; and

(b) any further conditions imposed by the *SRA*, at the time of the grant of *authorisation* or at any time subsequently, in accordance with Rule 9.

Guidance notes

(i) If a licensed body carries out a range of legal and non-legal activities (a multi-disciplinary practice or "MDP") the SRA's jurisdiction will not generally extend to cover the "non-legal" activities of the licensed body (unless covered by a specific condition on the licence). Such non-legal activities may be regulated by another regulator, and some activities may not fall within the regulatory ambit of any regulator. The SRA's jurisdiction may also not extend to some non-reserved legal activities in accordance with the terms of the licence.

Rule 8: General conditions on authorisation

8.1   *Regulatory compliance*

(a) An *authorised body* and its *managers* must ensure that:

(i) any obligations imposed from time to time on the *authorised body*, its *managers*, *employees* or *interest holders* by or under the *SRA's regulatory arrangements* are complied with; and

(ii) any other statutory obligations imposed on the *authorised body*, its *managers*, *employees* or *interest holders*, in relation to the body's business of carrying on *authorised activities*, are complied with.

(b) Without prejudice to the generality of sub-rule (a) above, an *authorised body* and its *managers* must agree to be subject to the *SRA Disciplinary Procedure Rules* and in particular the power of the *SRA* to:

(i) impose a written rebuke and publish details of a written rebuke or a decision to impose a penalty, in accordance with Rule 3 of those rules; and

(ii) conduct an internal appeal of a decision in accordance with Rule 11 of those rules,

subject to any right of appeal or challenge under those rules or any other enactment in relation to any action taken by the *SRA* under those rules.

(c)   Nothing in Rule 8 or any other provision in the *SRA's regulatory arrangements* affects the generality of the condition in Rule 8.1.

8.2   *Suitable arrangements for compliance*

(a)   An *authorised body* must at all times have suitable arrangements in place to ensure that:

(i)   the body, its *managers* and *employees*, comply with the *SRA's* regulatory arrangements as they apply to them, as required under section 176 of the *LSA* and Rule 8.1 above; and

(ii)   the body and its *managers* and *employees*, who are *authorised persons*, maintain the *professional principles*.

(b)   A *licensed body* must at all times have suitable arrangements in place to ensure that, as required under section 90 of the *LSA*, the *employees* and *managers* and *interest holders* of that body who are *non-authorised persons* do nothing which causes or substantially contributes to a breach by the *licensed body* or its *employees* or *managers* of the *SRA's regulatory arrangements*.

8.3   *Payment of periodical fees*

(a)   Every *authorised body* must pay to the *SRA* the *prescribed* periodical fees applicable to that body by the *prescribed* date.

(b)   The *SRA* shall determine the amount of any fees required under these rules and the *SRA's* decision shall be final.

(c)   The *SRA* may prescribe from time to time a fee moderation process under which an *authorised body* may make an application, in accordance with sub-rules (d) to (l) below, for the *prescribed* periodical fees applicable to that body to be varied. A decision under this process shall be final.

(d)   The turnover of an *authorised body* for the purpose of determining the *prescribed* periodical fees applicable to that body is based on a historic turnover figure submitted to the *SRA*. Where in the 12 months following the submission of that figure an *authorised body* merges or splits, a notice of succession identifying all *authorised bodies, recognised bodies* and *recognised sole practitioners* affected by the merger or split and any resulting apportionment of the historic turnover figures for those *firms* will enable the *SRA* to ensure that the turnover figure on which the fee is based reflects the impact of the merger or split.

(e)   A turnover figure submitted to the *SRA* shall be calculated in accordance with the *SRA's prescribed* method of calculation.

(f)   An *authorised body* which has succeeded to the whole or a part of one or more *authorised bodies, recognised bodies* or *recognised sole practitioners* must within 28 days of the change taking place deliver to the *SRA* a notice of succession in the *prescribed* form.

(g)   For the purposes of Rule 8.3(f), "succeeded" includes any taking over of the whole or any part of an *authorised body, recognised body* or *recognised sole practitioner*, for value or otherwise.

(h)   An *authorised body* which:

  (i)   has split or ceded part of the *practice* to an *authorised body* and/or *recognised body* or *recognised sole practitioner*; and

  (ii)   wishes this change to be considered by the *SRA* when determining the *authorised body's* next *prescribed* periodical fees applicable to that body

must within 28 days of the change taking place deliver to the *SRA* a notice of succession in the *prescribed* form.

(i)   A notice of succession delivered under these rules must:

  (i)   identify all *authorised bodies, recognised bodies* and *recognised sole practitioners* affected by the succession; and

  (ii)   provide details of any resulting apportionment of the turnover figures for those *authorised bodies, recognised bodies* and *recognised sole practitioners*.

(j)   An *authorised body* delivering a notice of succession under these rules must seek the agreement of all affected *authorised bodies, recognised bodies* or *recognised sole practitioners* to the contents of the notice of succession.

(k)   Where a notice of succession is delivered to the *SRA* which has not been agreed by all affected *authorised bodies, recognised bodies* or *recognised sole practitioners*, the *authorised body* delivering the notice of succession shall be treated as having made an application for the *SRA* to apportion the turnover figures of the affected *authorised bodies, recognised bodies* or *recognised sole practitioners* for the purposes of determining the periodic fee or the fee for renewal of recognition.

(l)   Before apportioning the turnover figures under Rule 8.3(k), the *SRA* will contact any affected *authorised body, recognised body* or *recognised sole practitioner* identified in the notice of succession who has not agreed with the notice of succession and may require the production of additional information.

8.4   *Carrying on of activities*

(a)   An *authorised body* may not carry on an activity unless through a body and individual who is authorised to carry on that activity.

8.5 *Compliance officers*

(a)   An *authorised body* must have suitable arrangements in place to ensure that its *compliance officers* are able to discharge their duties in accordance with these rules.

(b)   Subject to Rule 8.5(h), an *authorised body* must at all times have an individual:

(i)   who is a *manager* or an *employee* of the *authorised body*;

(ii)   who is designated as its *COLP*;

(iii)   who is of sufficient seniority and in a position of sufficient responsibility to fulfil the role; and

(iv)   whose designation is approved by the *SRA*.

(c)   The *COLP* of an *authorised body* must:

(i)   take all reasonable steps to:

(A)   ensure compliance with the terms and conditions of the *authorised body's authorisation* except any obligations imposed under the *SRA Accounts Rules*;

(B)   ensure compliance with any statutory obligations of the body, its *managers*, *employees* or *interest holders* in relation to the body's carrying on of *authorised activities*; and

(C)   record any failure so to comply and make such records available to the *SRA* on request; and

(ii)   in the case of a *licensed body*, as soon as reasonably practicable, report to the *SRA* any failure so to comply, provided that:

(A)   in the case of non-material failures, these shall be taken to have been reported as soon as reasonably practicable if they are reported to the *SRA* together with such other information as the *SRA* may require in accordance with Rule 8.7(a); and

(B)   a failure may be material either taken on its own or as part of a pattern of failures so to comply.

(iii)   in the case of a *recognised body*, as soon as reasonably practicable, report to the *SRA* any material failure so to comply (a failure may be material either taken on its own or as part of a pattern of failure so to comply).

(d)   Subject to Rule 8.5(i), an *authorised body* must at all times have an individual:

(i)   who is a *manager* or an *employee* of the *authorised body*;

(ii)   who is designated as its *COFA*;

(iii)   who is of sufficient seniority and in a position of sufficient responsibility to fulfil the role; and

(iv)   whose designation is approved by the *SRA*.

(e)   The *COFA* of an *authorised body* must:

    (i)   take all reasonable steps to:

        (A)   ensure that the body and its *employees* and *managers* comply with any obligations imposed upon them under the *SRA Accounts Rules*;

        (B)   record any failure so to comply and make such records available to the *SRA* on request; and

    (ii)   in the case of a *licensed body*, as soon as reasonably practicable, report to the *SRA* any failure so to comply, provided that:

        (A)   in the case of non-material failures, these shall be taken to have been reported as soon as reasonably practicable if they are reported to the *SRA* together with such other information as the *SRA* may require in accordance with Rule 8.7(a); and

        (B)   a failure may be material either taken on its own or as part of a pattern of failures so to comply.

    (iii)   in the case of a *recognised body*, as soon as reasonably practicable, report to the *SRA* any material failure so to comply (a failure may be material either taken on its own or as part of a pattern of failure so to comply).

(f)   The *SRA* may approve an individual's designation as a *COLP* or *COFA* if it is satisfied, in accordance with Part 4, that the individual is a suitable person to carry out his or her duties.

(g)   A designation of an individual as a *COLP* or *COFA* has effect only while the individual:

    (i)   consents to the designation;

    (ii)   in the case of a *COLP*:

        (A)   is not *disqualified* from acting as a *HOLP*; and

        (B)   is:

            (I)   a *lawyer of England and Wales*;

            (II)   an *REL*; or

            (III) registered with the *BSB* under Regulation 17 of the European Communities (Lawyer's Practice) Regulations 2000 (SI 2000/1119);

        and is an *authorised person* in relation to one or more of the *reserved legal activities* which the body is authorised to carry on; and

    (iii)   in the case of a *COFA*, is not *disqualified* from acting as a *HOFA*.

(h)   An *authorised body* is not required to comply with Rule 8.5(b)(i) where the individual designated as its *COLP*:

(i) has been approved by the *SRA* as a *COLP* for a *related authorised body*; and

(ii) is a *manager* or *employee* of that *related authorised body*.

(i) An *authorised body* is not required to comply with Rule 8.5(d)(i) where the individual designated as its *COFA*:

(i) has been approved by the *SRA* as a *COFA* for a *related authorised body*; and

(ii) is a *manager* or *employee* of that *related authorised body*.

8.6 *Management and control*

(a) An *authorised body* must ensure that:

(i) any *manager* or *owner* of the *authorised body*; or

(ii) any *manager* of a *body corporate* which is a *manager* or *owner* of the *authorised body*;

has been approved by the *SRA* under Part 4.

(b) No *manager* of a *licensed body* may be a *person* who is *disqualified* from being a *manager*.

(c) An *authorised body* (or *manager* or *employee* of such a body) must not employ or remunerate a person:

(i) who is subject to an order under Section 43 of the *SA*, without the *SRA's* written permission;

(ii) whose name has been struck off the roll, who is suspended from *practising* as a *solicitor*, or whose practising certificate has been suspended whilst he/she is an undischarged bankrupt, without the *SRA's* written permission;

(iii) if there is a direction in force in respect of that person under section 47(2)(g) of the *SA* (Prohibition on restoration to the roll), without the *SRA's* written permission; or

(iv) who is *disqualified* from being an *employee*.

(d) No *licensed body* (or *manager* or *employee* of such a body) may, except in accordance with the *SRA's* written permission, permit an individual to be a *manager* or *owner* of the body if:

(i) that person's name has been struck off the roll;

(ii) he/she is suspended from *practising* as a *solicitor*;

(iii) his/her practising certificate has been suspended whilst he/she is an undischarged bankrupt;

(iv) there is a direction in force in respect of that person under section 47(2)(g) of the *SA* (Prohibition on restoration to the roll); or

(v)   there is an order in force in respect of that individual under section 43 of the *SA* (Control of solicitors' employees and consultants).

(e)   No *recognised body* (or *manager* or *employee* of such a body) may, except in accordance with the *SRA's* written permission, permit an individual to be a *manager* or *interest holder* of the body if:

(i)   that person's name has been struck off the roll;

(ii)   he/she is suspended from *practising* as a *solicitor*;

(iii)   his/her practising certificate has been suspended whilst he/she is an undischarged bankrupt;

(iv)   there is a direction in force in respect of that person under section 47(2)(g) of the *SA* (Prohibition on restoration to the roll); or

(v)   there is an order in force in respect of that person under section 43 of the *SA* (Control of solicitors' employees and consultants).

8.7   *Information requirements*

(a)   An *authorised body* must properly complete and provide to the *SRA* an information report on an annual basis or such other period as specified by the *SRA* in the *prescribed* form and by the *prescribed* date.

(b)   An *authorised body* must provide any necessary permissions for information to be given to the *SRA* so as to enable it to:

(i)   use and prepare a report on the documents produced under (a) above; and

(ii)   seek verification from *clients, employees, managers* or any other body including banks, building societies or other financial institutions.

(c)   An *authorised body* must notify the *SRA* as soon as it becomes aware of any changes to relevant information about itself, its *employees, managers,* or *interest holders* including any non-compliance with these rules and the conditions on the body's *authorisation.*

(d)   If an *authorised body* becomes aware or has information that reasonably suggests that it has or may have provided the *SRA* with information which was or may have been false, misleading, incomplete or inaccurate, or has or may have changed in a materially significant way, it must notify the *SRA* immediately.

8.8   *Additional conditions for partnerships*

(a)   If a *partner* in a *partnership* which is an *authorised body*:

(i)   is committed to prison in civil or criminal proceedings;

(ii)   becomes and continues to be unable to attend to the *practice* of the body because of incapacity caused by illness, accident or age;

    (iii) becomes and continues to be a *person who lacks capacity under Part 1 of the Mental Capacity Act 2005*;

    (iv) abandons the *practice* of the body; or

    (v) is made subject to a condition on his or her practising certificate, registration or equivalent authorisation by an *approved regulator* other than the *SRA* which would be breached by continuing as a *partner*;

and this results in there being only one active *partner*, that *partner* must inform the *SRA* within seven days of the relevant event.

8.9   *Additional conditions for recognised bodies*

(a)   An *interest holder* of a *recognised body* must not create any charge or other third party interest over his or her interest in the *recognised body* except a *member* or *shareowner* of a *company* may hold a share as nominee for a non-*member shareowner* who is able to hold an interest in the body in compliance with Rule 8.6.

(b)   If the only, or last remaining:

    (i) *solicitor* or *REL* whose role in a *recognised body* ensures compliance with the *lawyer manager* requirement under Rule 13.1(a) (relevant lawyer requirement) of the *SRA Practice Framework Rules*, or

    (ii) *lawyer of England and Wales*, *lawyer* of an *Establishment Directive profession* or *RFL* whose role in the body ensures compliance with Rule 13.1(b) (management and control requirement) of the *SRA Practice Framework Rules*,

is subject to any of the following events:

    (A) is committed to prison in civil or criminal proceedings;

    (B) becomes and continues to be unable to attend to the *practice* of the body because of incapacity caused by illness, accident or age;

    (C) becomes and continues to be a *person who lacks capacity under Part 1 of the Mental Capacity Act 2005*;

    (D) abandons the *practice* of the body; or

    (E) is made subject to a condition on his or her practising certificate or registration which would be breached by continuing to be a *manager* of the body;

the body must inform the *SRA* within seven days of the relevant event and must within 28 days of the relevant event either ensure that the body becomes a *legal services body* again without reference to that person, or cease to *practise*.

8.10   *Additional conditions for licensed bodies*

(a)   If the only, or last remaining, *manager* of a *licensed body* who is:

    (i) a *solicitor* with a current practising certificate;

Authorisation and Practising Requirements

(ii) an *REL*;

(iii) a *lawyer of England and Wales* and who is authorised by an *approved regulator* other than the *SRA*; or

(iv) registered with the *BSB* under regulation 17 of the European Communities (Lawyer's Practice) Regulations 2000 (SI 2000/1119)

is subject to any of the following events:

(A) is committed to prison in civil or criminal proceedings;

(B) becomes and continues to be unable to attend to the *practice* of the body because of incapacity caused by illness, accident or age;

(C) becomes and continues to be a person who lacks capacity under Part 1 of the Mental Capacity Act 2005;

(D) abandons the *practice* of the body; or

(E) is made subject to a condition on his/her practising certificate, registration or equivalent *authorisation* by an *approved regulator* other than the *SRA* which would be breached by continuing to be a *manager* of the body;

the body must inform the *SRA* within seven days of the relevant event and must within 28 days of the relevant event either ensure that the body becomes a *licensable body* again without reference to that person, or cease to *practise*.

8.11 *Condition relating to the cessation period for indemnity purposes*

(a) When an *authorised body* becomes subject to cover under the *cessation period*, it must immediately, and for the duration of the *cessation period*, desist from carrying out any *legal activities*, save that it may undertake work required to discharge its obligations within the scope of *existing instructions*, or which is necessary in connection with the discharge of such obligations.

Guidance notes

(i) Rule 8.1 is to be read in conjunction with the obligations under sections 90 and 176 of the LSA. These require individuals and bodies regulated by the SRA to comply with its regulatory arrangements (reflected in Rule 19.1 of the SRA Practice Framework Rules), and for non-authorised employees, managers and interest holders of licensed bodies not to do anything which causes or substantially contributes to a breach of that requirement. In addition, Rule 8.2 requires the body to have suitable arrangements in place to ensure compliance with these provisions.

(ii) The SRA's outcomes focused approach to regulation means that the SRA will take into account all of the circumstances relevant to any issue of compliance, whether in relation to the regulatory arrangements or in respect of statutory obligations on firms and those in them. This will include taking into account the evidence that firms and individuals can produce to demonstrate their efforts to ensure compliance (by themselves or others).

(iii)   Rule 8.2 deals with the need for firms to have suitable arrangements for compliance (see also Chapter 7 of the SRA Code of Conduct (Management of your business)). What needs to be covered by a firm's compliance plan will depend on factors such as the size and nature of the firm, its work and its areas of risk. Firms will need to analyse the effectiveness of their compliance arrangements before applying for authorisation and monitor effectiveness on an on-going basis once authorised. Common areas for consideration will include:

(a)   clearly defined governance arrangements providing a transparent framework for responsibilities within the firm;

(b)   appropriate accounting procedures;

(c)   a system for ensuring that only the appropriate people authorise payments from client account;

(d)   a system for ensuring that undertakings are given only when intended, and compliance with them is monitored and enforced;

(e)   appropriate checks on new staff or contractors;

(f)   a system for ensuring that basic regulatory deadlines are not missed e.g. obtaining or delivery of the firm's accountant's report (in accordance with rule 32 of the SRA Accounts Rules 2011), arranging indemnity cover, renewal of practising certificates and registrations, renewal of all lawyers' licences to practise and provision of regulatory information;

(g)   a system for monitoring, reviewing and managing risks;

(h)   ensuring that issues of conduct are given appropriate weight in decisions the firm takes, whether on client matters or firm-based issues such as funding;

(i)   file reviews;

(j)   appropriate systems for supporting the development and training of staff;

(k)   obtaining the necessary approvals of managers, owners and COLP/COFA;

(l)   arrangements to ensure that any duties to clients and others are fully met even when staff are absent.

(iv)   Rule 8.4 confirms the legal position that for a firm to provide services to clients, the services/activities must be covered by the terms of its authorisation and, where it is a reserved legal activity such as litigation, the firm must have a manager or an employee who is authorised to do that work. For example, a firm cannot provide litigation services, even if its licence permits it to, if its only lawyer is a licensed conveyancer. In situations where a firm loses a lawyer who is responsible for supervising the work of non-lawyers, the firm will need to consider whether the reserved legal work can still be carried out until the situation is remedied.

(v)   Rule 8.5 requires all authorised bodies to have a COLP and a COFA. For COLPs and COFAs of licensed bodies, compliance with their obligations under

Authorisation and Practising Requirements

Rule 8.5 will assist in complying with their duties as Head of Legal Practice and Head of Finance and Administration under sections 91 and 92 respectively of the LSA.

(vi)   The roles of COLP and COFA are a fundamental part of a firm's compliance and governance arrangements. COLPs' and COFAs' ability to take the steps they need to ensure compliance is dependent on the firm having suitable arrangements in place under Rule 8.2. The firm must therefore ensure that any person designated as its COLP or COFA is of sufficient seniority, in a position of sufficient power and responsibility and has clear reporting lines to enable them to have access to all management systems and arrangements and all other relevant information including client files and business information. The existence of compliance officers in a firm and the requirements on them to ensure that the firm, as well as its managers and employees, are complying with the regulatory arrangements (COLP) and the SRA Accounts Rules (COFA) is not a substitute for the firm's and managers' responsibilities and their obligations to comply with Rule 8.1 (Regulatory compliance). Firms and managers need to take care not to obstruct, whether intentionally or unwittingly, a COLP or COFA in fulfilling their role.

(vii)   COLPs and COFAs are responsible for ensuring that the firm has systems and controls in place to enable the firm, as well as its managers and employees and anyone who owns any interest in the firm, to comply with the requirements on them. The firm and its managers are not absolved from any of their own obligations and remain fully responsible for compliance (see Rule 8.1).

(viii)   Those designated as COLP will need to be in a position to be able to discharge the role. They will need to consider whether they are in a position to, for example:

(a)   take all reasonable steps to ensure compliance with the terms of the firm's authorisation; compliance with the SRA's regulatory arrangements by the firm, its employees and managers; and with relevant statutory obligations e.g.

(A)   that non-authorised persons comply with the duty imposed by section 90 of the LSA (duty not to do anything which causes or substantially contributes to a breach of the SRA's regulatory arrangements by an authorised body or its employee or manager);

(B)   that authorised persons and other managers and employees comply with the duty imposed by section 176 of the LSA (duty to comply with the SRA's regulatory arrangements);

(C)   under the LSA, AJA and the SA in respect of practice matters;

(b)   in the case of a licensed body, as soon as reasonably practicable, report to the SRA any failure to comply. Where such failure is material, either on its own or because it forms part of a pattern, the immediacy of the report will depend on the circumstances and seriousness of the breach. Where such failure is neither material of itself nor because it forms part of a pattern of non-compliance, the report need not be made until the annual information report under Rule 8.7.

(c) in the case of a recognised body, as soon as reasonably practicable, report to the SRA any material failure to comply, whether such failure is material either on its own or because it forms part of a pattern of non-compliance. The immediacy of the report will depend on the circumstances and seriousness of the breach.

(ix) Those designated as COFA will need to be in a position to be able to discharge the role. They will need to consider whether they are in a position to, for example:

(a) ensure that they have access to all accounting records;

(b) carry out regular checks on the accounting systems;

(c) carry out file and ledger reviews;

(d) ensure that the reporting accountant has prompt access to all the information needed to complete the accountant's report;

(e) take steps to ensure that breaches of the SRA Accounts Rules are remedied promptly;

(f) monitor, review and manage risks to compliance with the SRA Accounts Rules;

(g) in the case of a licensed body, as soon as reasonably practicable report to the SRA any failure to comply with the SRA Accounts Rules. Where such failure is material, either on its own or because it forms part of a pattern, the immediacy of the report will depend on the circumstances and seriousness of the breach. The report need not be made until the annual information report under Rule 8.7 where such failure is neither material of itself nor because it forms part of a pattern of non-compliance.

(h) in the case of a recognised body, as soon as reasonably practicable, report to the SRA any material failure to comply with the SRA Accounts Rules, whether such failure is material either on its own or because it forms part of a pattern of non-compliance. The immediacy of the report will depend on the circumstances and seriousness of the breach.

(x) In considering whether a failure is "material", the COLP or COFA, as appropriate, will need to take account of various factors, such as:

(a) the detriment, or risk of detriment, to clients;

(b) the extent of any risk of loss of confidence in the firm or in the provision of legal services;

(c) the scale of the issue;

(d) the overall impact on the firm, its clients and third parties.

In addition, the COLP/COFA will need to keep appropriate records of failures in compliance to:

     (e)   monitor overall compliance with obligations;

     (f)   assess the effectiveness of the firm's systems;

     (g) be able to decide when the need has arisen to report breaches which are material because they form a pattern.

(xi) In developing their governance and administrative arrangements firms will need to consider how they approach unexpected risks such as the absence of key staff, including COLP and COFA, and whether the nature of the absence will trigger the need to notify the SRA (see Rule 8.7) and to obtain approval for a replacement.

(xii) The core statutory obligations of a recognised body are contained in the AJA and the SA and those for licensed bodies are contained in sections 90 and 176 of the LSA. An important aspect of the roles of COLP and COFA is the need to report breaches to the SRA. Although it will commonly be appropriate for the firm to take steps to remedy breaches immediately, this does not obviate the need for compliance officers to record the breach and make a report in compliance with Rule 8.5 where appropriate.

(xiii) Approval (see Rules 8.5 and 8.6) relates only to the role for which it is granted. Any change from one role that requires approval to another, will require a further approval. Firms need to ensure that they notify the SRA of any changes and, where necessary, apply for appropriate approval, for example where an employee develops into the role of manager, or an owner's participation amounts to being a manager.

(xiv) The scope of the duty in Rule 8.6(c) is beyond the strict employer-servant relationship (contract of service) and includes a relationship founded on a contract for services or indirect arrangements which are intended to have the effect of frustrating this rule.

(xv) Rule 8.7 imposes information requirements on authorised bodies. As well as the annual information report, firms must update the SRA by giving details of general changes that occur in respect of the firm. For example, if any of the circumstances referred to in Rule 8.8 occur in relation to any manager or person who has a significant role or responsibility in the firm, the SRA should be notified. Reporting and information requirements that apply to individuals or firms include:

     (a) SRA requirements

        (A) Rules 3, 8.7, 8.8, 8.9 and 8.10 and 18, 23, 24 and 25 of these rules;

        (B) Rule 18 of the SRA Practice Framework Rules;

        (C) Rule 32 of the SRA Accounts Rules;

        (D) Regulations 1.2, 4.3, 4.5, 4.8, 4.12 and 15 of the SRA Practising Regulations;

        (E) Chapter 10 of the Code of Conduct;

(F) Rule 17.3 of the SRA Indemnity Insurance Rules 2013 or any subsequent rules thereto;

(G) Rule 3.2 of the SRA Overseas Rules (and, to note in particular the obligation to notify the SRA where partners, managers, members, solicitor employees or other professionally qualified staff of an overseas practice are subject to a criminal conviction or disciplinary finding, and if the practice itself is in serious financial difficulty).

(b) Statutory requirements

(A) Section 84 of the SA (notification of a solicitor's place of business);

(B) Paragraph 21 of Schedule 13 to the LSA (non-authorised persons proposing to acquire an interest in a licensed body have continuing notification requirements. Note, it is an offence to fail to comply with the section 21 notification requirements).

(xvi) The purpose of Rule 8.9(a) is to ensure that control of a recognised body remains solely in the hands of persons who are eligible to be members, and that there is no breach of the management and control condition.

Rule 9: Further conditions

9.1 The *SRA* may at any time impose one or more further conditions on an *authorisation* if it considers:

(a) that:

(i) the condition would limit, restrict, halt or prevent an activity or activities on the part of the body, or of a *manager*, *employee*, or *interest holder* of the body, which is putting or is likely to put at risk the interests of *clients*, third parties or the public;

(ii) the condition would prevent or limit the activities of a *manager* or *employee* of the body who is considered unsuitable to undertake a particular activity, either at all or save as specified in the condition;

(iii) the condition would limit, halt or prevent a risk to *clients*, third parties or the public arising from a business agreement or association which the body has or is likely to enter into, or a business practice which the body has or is likely to adopt;

(iv) a *relevant insolvency event* has occurred in relation to the body but the *SRA* does not propose at that time to suspend or revoke the *authorisation* under Rule 22;

(v) the condition is necessary to facilitate effective monitoring by the *SRA* of compliance with its *regulatory arrangements* on the part of the body, its *managers*, *employees* or *interest holders*;

(vi) the *SRA* considers that imposing the condition will require the body concerned to take specified steps conducive to the proper, effective or efficient carrying on of a *legal activity* by that body; or

Authorisation and
Practising Requirements

(vii) the *SRA* considers that imposing a condition is necessary in order to ensure compliance with the *regulatory objectives*;

and

(b) that it is in the public interest to impose the condition.

9.2   A condition imposed under Rule 9.1 takes effect from the date on which the condition is imposed unless otherwise specified by the *SRA*.

Guidance note

(i)   Rule 9.1 permits the SRA to impose conditions "at any time", if certain criteria are met. This includes on the approval of a person under Part 4 of these rules or at the time of modification of the terms of an authorisation under Rule 10.

(ii)   The SRA may impose conditions on an authorised body in response to concerns about an overseas practice, in respect of the body's conduct as a responsible authorised body. This might include, for example, where the overseas practice is providing reserved legal activities when it is not authorised to do so and this is within the knowledge of the authorised body.

Rule 10: Modification of terms and conditions of an authorisation

10.1   The *SRA* may at any time, modify:

(a) any terms that specify the *reserved legal activities* that an *authorised body* is entitled to carry on by virtue of the *authorisation*:

(i)   on the application of the *authorised body*; or

(ii)   if the *SRA* considers it appropriate to do so, without such an application being made; and

having regard to the *regulatory objectives*;

(b) any further conditions of an *authorisation*, imposed under Rule 9:

(i)   on the application of the *authorised body*; or

(ii)   if the *SRA* considers it appropriate to do so, without such an application being made; and

having regard to the criteria in Rule 9.

Guidance notes

(i)   The certificate of authorisation of a licensed body will set out the reserved activities that the body is entitled to carry out. A licensed body may apply to change the categories of those activities at any time, or the SRA may do so (see also Rule 10), for example if the body no longer carries out that type of work or if there is an identified risk to the public in the body continuing to provide certain services (see section 86 of the LSA). Firms are also able to apply for a waiver of these rules, including the general conditions in Rule 8 (except Rule 8.1), under Rule 12 (Waivers).

(ii)   Authorised bodies are authorised to carry out non-reserved legal activities as well as the reserved activities for which they are authorised.

(iii)   Multi-disciplinary practices which provide a range of different services, some only of which are regulated by the SRA, will need to ensure that it is clear, both within and outside the firm, through which part of the business (and therefore under which regulatory system) non-legal services are provided. (See Chapter 8 of the SRA Code of Conduct.)

Rule 11: Regulatory conflict

11.1   If a conflict arises between:

   (a)   a requirement imposed:

      (i)   on an *authorised body* or on an *employee* or *manager* of the body by the *SRA* as the regulator of that body, and

      (ii)   on an individual *manager* or *employee* of that body by another *approved regulator*;

      then the requirement imposed by the *SRA* prevails over the requirement imposed by the other *approved regulator*;

   (b)   a requirement imposed:

      (i)   on an *authorised non-SRA firm* or on an *employee* or *manager* of the firm by another *approved regulator* as the regulator of that firm, and

      (ii)   on an individual *manager* or *employee* of that firm by the *SRA*;

      then the requirement imposed by the other *approved regulator* prevails over the requirement imposed by the *SRA*.

Rule 12: Waivers

12.1   Subject to Rule 12.2 below and to provisions in any enactments or the *SRA's regulatory arrangements* affecting its ability to waive any requirements, the *SRA* shall have power to waive in writing the provisions of these rules for a particular purpose or purposes expressed in such waiver, and to attach conditions to or revoke such waiver, at its own discretion.

12.2   The *SRA* shall not have power to waive any of the provisions of Rule 8.1 with respect to any *authorised bodies*.

12.3   The *SRA* shall not have power to grant a waiver under Rule 12 in respect of the *reserved legal activities* that an *authorised body* is entitled to carry on or any conditions of *authorisation* imposed under Rule 9.

Authorisation and
Practising Requirements

Guidance notes

(i)   A waiver cannot be granted where to do so would run counter to the overall purpose of the rule. In addition, many of the requirements set out in various Acts such as the LSA and AJA are mandatory provisions which, in spite of Rule 12, the SRA does not have the power to waive. The following are examples from the LSA:

   (a) **Management**

   (A)   Schedule 11 paragraph 11–14 – the rules must include that a licensed body must at all times have an individual designated as Head of Legal Practice and one designated as Head of Finance and Administration (in these rules referred to as COLP and COFA). This designation must be approved by the SRA, which must be satisfied that the designated individuals are suitable to carry out the duties. Rule 8.5 reflects this and therefore cannot be waived;

   (B)   Schedule 11 paragraph 17 – rules must provide that the licensed body must at all times have suitable arrangements in place to ensure that it, its managers and employees comply with the regulatory arrangements, and that any employees carrying out legal activities will maintain the professional principles. Rule 8.1 reflects this and therefore cannot be waived.

   (b) **Duration, suspension, modification and revocation of licence**

   (A)   Schedule 11 paragraph 26(1) – rules must provide criteria for the SRA to use in deciding whether to suspend, revoke or end the suspension of a licence. Rule 22 reflects this and therefore cannot be waived.

(ii)   A waiver of these rules "in writing" includes any form of written electronic communication normally used for business purposes, such as emails.

PART 4: APPROVAL OF MANAGERS, OWNERS AND COMPLIANCE OFFICERS

Rule 13: Application for approval

13.1   This Part governs the *SRA's* determination of applications for:

   (a) approval of an *authorised body's managers* and *owners* pursuant to Rule 8.6(a); and

   (b) approval of an *authorised body's compliance officers*, pursuant to Rule 8.5(b) and (d).

13.2   The *SRA* will deem a *person* to be approved as suitable to be a *manager* or *owner* of an *authorised body* under this Part if:

   (a) that *person* is:

   (i)   a *solicitor* who holds a current practising certificate;

   (ii)   an *authorised body*;

    (iii) an *REL*; or

    (iv) an *RFL*;

(b) there is no condition on the *person's* practising certificate, registration or *authorisation* as appropriate, preventing or restricting them from being a *manager*, *owner* or *interest holder* of an *authorised body* or being a *sole practitioner*;

(c) the *SRA* is notified on the *prescribed* form at least seven days in advance of the *person* becoming a *manager* or *owner* of the *authorised body*; and

(d) the *SRA* has not withdrawn its approval of that *person* to be a *manager* or *owner* under Rule 17.

Rule 14: Approval process and production of information or documentation

14.1   An application for approval of a *manager*, *owner* or *compliance officer* may be made by an *applicant body* or an *authorised body* and must include evidence to satisfy the *SRA* that the *candidate* is suitable to be a *manager*, *owner* or *compliance officer* of the body, as appropriate.

14.2   The *applicant body* or *authorised body*, as appropriate, must:

(a) co-operate, and secure the co-operation of the *candidate*, to assist the *SRA* to obtain all information and documentation the *SRA* requires in order to determine the application;

(b) obtain all other information and documentation in relation to the *candidate* which the *prescribed* form requires the body to obtain and keep; and

(c) keep all information and documentation under (b) above for a period of not less than 6 years after the *person* concerned has ceased to be a *manager*, *owner* or *compliance officer* of the body.

14.3   The *candidate* must declare in the application that the information supplied about them is correct and complete.

14.4   The *SRA's* decision to approve or refuse approval must be notified in writing to the *applicant body* or *authorised body* as appropriate, and separately to the *candidate*, as soon as possible.

14.5   The *SRA* may, at the time of granting its approval or at any time subsequently:

(a) approve the holding of a *material interest* in a *licensed body* subject to conditions in accordance with paragraphs 17, 28 or 33 of Schedule 13 to the *LSA*; and

(b) make its approval of a *person* to be an *owner*, *manager* or *compliance officer* of an *authorised body* subject to such conditions on the body's *authorisation* as it considers appropriate having regard to the criteria in Rule 9.

Authorisation and Practising Requirements

14.6   If the *SRA* proposes to object to a *candidate* becoming an *owner* of an *applicant body* or *authorised body*, or to approve such a *person* becoming an *owner* subject to conditions imposed under Rule 14.5(a) or (b), the *SRA* must:

    (a)   give the *candidate* and the body a warning notice which:

        (i)   specifies the *SRA's* intention to object or to impose conditions; and

        (ii)   states that any representations must be made to the *SRA* within the period of 28 days from the date of the notice; and

    (b)   consider any representations made to the *SRA* by the body and/or the *candidate* within the 28 day period in (a)(ii) above.

14.7   The *SRA* may issue a conditional approval or objection without a warning notice under Rule 14.6 if the application for approval has been made after the grant of *authorisation* and the *SRA* considers it necessary or desirable to dispense with the warning notice for the purpose of protecting any of the *regulatory objectives*.

14.8   The *SRA* may at any time require the production of information or documentation from:

    (a)   a *person* who has been approved as an *owner*, *manager* or *compliance officer* under this Part (including a deemed approval under Rule 13.2);

    (b)   an *authorised body* of which that *person* is a *manager*, *owner* or *compliance officer*; or

    (c)   the body which originally obtained approval for that *person* and holds information and documentation under Rule 14.2(c);

in order to satisfy the *SRA* that the *person* met, meets, or continues to meet the criteria for approval.

Guidance notes

(i)   See also the guidance notes to Rule 1 regarding ownership and material interest.

(ii)   The SRA's notification "in writing" includes any form of written electronic communication normally used for business purposes, such as emails.

(iii)   See also Regulation 7 of the SRA Practising Regulations under which the SRA has the power to impose conditions on a practising certificate or registration which restrict an individual's ability to be involved in an authorised body.

(iv)   Specific provisions exist in the LSA about imposing conditions on the approval of owners of a licensed body:

    (a)   For the approval of ownership on an application for a licence, see paragraph 17 of Schedule 13 to the LSA. For the approval of ownership on a change of interests after a licence is issued, see paragraph 28 of that Schedule. These give the SRA the power to approve an owner's or a prospective owner's holding subject to conditions where the Rule 15 criteria are not met in relation to that investment, but only if the SRA considers that, if the conditions are complied with, it will be appropriate for the owner to hold the interest.

(b) For the imposition of conditions (or further conditions) on an existing ownership interest, see paragraph 33 of Schedule 13 to the LSA. This gives the SRA the power to impose conditions (or further conditions) on a person's holding of an interest, if the SRA is not satisfied that the Rule 15 criteria are met, or if the SRA is satisfied that a condition imposed under paragraphs 17, 28 or 33 of Schedule 13 (see above) on the person's holding of that interest has not been, or is not being, complied with. The SRA may only use the paragraph 33 power if it considers that, if the conditions are complied with, it will be appropriate for the owner to hold the interest without the approval requirements being met.

Rule 15: Criteria for approval

15.1 When considering whether a *candidate* should be approved to be a *manager*, *owner* or *compliance officer* of the body, as appropriate, the *SRA* will take into account the criteria set out in the *SRA Suitability Test* and any other relevant information.

Guidance notes

(i) As well as evidence about the candidate, the Suitability Test takes into account evidence about the honesty and integrity of a person that the candidate is related to, affiliated with, or acts together with where the SRA has reason to believe that that person may have an influence over the way in which the candidate will exercise their role.

(ii) Under paragraphs 19 and 20 of Schedule 13 to the LSA the SRA has the power, when dealing with an application for a licence, to object to the holding of an interest if it is not satisfied that the Rule 15 criteria are met in relation to that holding. The mechanism for objecting is set out in those paragraphs.

Rule 16: Effect of approval

16.1 Approval takes effect from the date of the decision unless otherwise stated and remains effective only if the *candidate* takes up the position for which he or she has been approved within the period specified in the notice of approval.

16.2 Subject to Rule 16.1, approval continues until:

(a) it is withdrawn by the *SRA*; or

(b) the approved *person* ceases to be a *manager*, *interest holder*, *COLP* or *COFA* of the *authorised body*, as appropriate.

Guidance note

(i)   The period specified in the notice of approval in Rule 16.1 will normally be 90 days although may be varied in individual cases.

Rule 17: Withdrawal of approval

17.1   Where the *SRA* has granted an approval of a *person* to be a *manager*, *owner* or *compliance officer* of a body (including a deemed approval under Rule 13.2), it may subsequently withdraw that approval if:

   (a)   it is not satisfied that an approved *person* met or meets the criteria for approval in Rule 15;

   (b)   it is satisfied that a condition imposed on the body's *authorisation* under Rule 14.5 has not been, or is not being complied with;

   (c)   it is satisfied that the approved *person* has breached a duty or obligation imposed upon them in or under the *SRA's regulatory arrangements* or any enactments; or

   (d)   information or documentation is not promptly supplied in response to a request made under Rule 14.8.

17.2   Where withdrawal of approval relates to a *director* of a *company*, the *SRA* may set separate dates for that individual ceasing to be a *director* and disposing of his or her shares.

Rule 18: Temporary emergency approvals for compliance officers

18.1   If an *authorised body* ceases to have a *COLP* or *COFA* whose designation has been approved by the *SRA*, the *authorised body* must immediately and in any event within seven days:

   (a)   notify the *SRA*;

   (b)   designate another *manager* or *employee* to replace its previous *COLP* or *COFA*, as appropriate; and

   (c)   make an application to the *SRA* for temporary approval of the new *COLP* or *COFA*, as appropriate.

18.2   The *SRA* may grant a temporary approval under this rule if:

   (a)   it is satisfied that the *authorised body* could not reasonably have commenced an application for approval of designation in advance of the non-compliance; and

   (b)   on the face of the application and any other information immediately before the *SRA*, there is no evidence suggesting that the new *compliance officer* is not suitable to carry out the duties imposed on them under these rules.

18.3   Temporary approval under this rule:

(a)   may be granted initially for 28 days;

(b)   may be granted to have effect from the date the body ceases to have a *COLP* or *COFA* whose designation has been approved;

(c)   may be extended in response to a reasonable request by the *authorised body*;

(d)   must be extended pending determination of a substantive application for approval commenced in accordance with Rule 18.4;

(e)   may be granted or extended subject to such conditions on the *authorised body's authorisation* as the *SRA* thinks fit, having regard to the criteria in Rule 9;

(f)   has effect only while the criteria in Rule 8.5(g) are met;

(g)   if granted, cannot prejudice the discretion of the *SRA* to refuse a substantive application for approval of designation or to impose any conditions on that approval; and

(h)   in exceptional circumstances, and for reasonable cause, may be withdrawn at any time.

18.4   If granted temporary approval under Rule 18.3 above for its designation of a new *COLP* or *COFA*, the *authorised body* must:

(a)   designate a permanent *COLP* or *COFA*, as appropriate; and

(b)   submit a substantive application for approval of that designation under Rule 13;

before the expiry of the temporary approval or any extension of that approval by the *SRA*.

PART 5: NOTIFICATION, EFFECT AND DURATION OF AUTHORISATION

Rule 19: Notification of decisions

19.1   The *SRA* must notify its decision and reasons in writing when it:

(a)   refuses an application made under these rules;

(b)   grants an application subject to a condition;

(c)   refuses a permission required under a condition on a body's *authorisation*; or

(d)   withdraws its approval of a *candidate* under Rules 17 and 18.

19.2   The notification in Rule 19.1 must be given:

(a)   to the *applicant body* or *authorised body* as appropriate; and

(b)   where appropriate, to the *candidate* concerned.

19.3   The *SRA* must give 28 days written notice, with reasons:

Authorisation and
Practising Requirements

(a)   to the *authorised body* concerned, when the *SRA* decides to impose a condition on an *authorised body's authorisation* at any time after the grant of the *authorisation*;

(b)   to the body and the individual concerned, when the *SRA* decides to withdraw an approval under Rules 17 and 18;

19.4   The *SRA* may shorten or dispense with the 28 day period under Rule 19.3(a) if it is satisfied that it is in the public interest to do so.

Guidance note

(i)   The SRA's notification "in writing" may be by any form of written electronic communication normally used for business purposes, such as emails.

Rule 20: Notifying third parties of decisions

20.1   The *SRA* may, if it considers it in the public interest to do so, publish and notify any *persons* of a decision concerning a body or an individual made under these rules, including but not limited to:

(a)   an *authorised person* of which the body or individual concerned is a current, past or prospective *manager*, *employee* or *interest holder*;

(b)   any *approved regulator*;

(c)   any statutory regulator;

(d)   the Legal Services Board;

(e)   the *Legal Ombudsman*;

(f)   the regulatory body for any profession of which the individual concerned is a member or which regulates the body concerned;

(g)   any law enforcement agency.

Rule 21: Effect and validity of authorisation

21.1   A grant of *authorisation* takes effect from the date of the decision unless otherwise stated, except in the case of a *licensed body* when *authorisation* takes effect from the date on which the licence is issued.

21.2   *Authorisation* continues in force unless it ceases to have effect in accordance with Rule 21.3.

21.3   An *authorised body's authorisation* ceases to have effect so that the body is no longer authorised by the *SRA* under these rules:

(a)   from the time that the *authorisation* is revoked under Rule 22;

(b)   at any time during which the *authorisation* is suspended;

(c)   subject to Part 6, if the body is wound up or for any other reason ceases to exist; or

(d) if in relation to a *licensed body*, the body is issued with a licence by another *approved regulator*.

Rule 22: Revocation and suspension of authorisation

22.1 Subject to Rule 23, the *SRA* may revoke or suspend a body's *authorisation*, where:

(a) in the case of an *authorised body*:

(i) *authorisation* was granted as a result of error, misleading or inaccurate information, or fraud;

(ii) the body is or becomes ineligible to be authorised in accordance with the criteria set out in Rule 6;

(iii) the *SRA* is satisfied that the body has no intention of carrying on the *legal activities* for which it has been authorised under these rules;

(iv) the body has failed to provide any information required by the *SRA* under these rules;

(v) the body has failed to pay any *prescribed* fee payable by the *firm* to the *SRA*;

(vi) a *relevant insolvency event* has occurred in relation to the body;

(vii) the body makes an application to the *SRA* for its *authorisation* to be revoked or suspended;

(viii) the *SRA* has decided to exercise its intervention powers under section 102 of and Schedule 14 to the *LSA*, Parts I and II of Schedule 1 to the *SA*, paragraph 5 of Schedule 14 to the Courts and Legal Services Act 1990 and Part II of Schedule 1 to the *SA* or paragraph 32 of Schedule 2 to the *AJA* and Part II of Schedule 1 to the *SA*, as appropriate;

(ix) the body, or an *owner*, *interest holder*, *manager* or *employee* of the body fails to comply with the duties imposed by or under these rules or under any statutory obligations in relation to the body's business of carrying on *authorised activities* including payment of any fine or other financial penalty imposed on the body by the *SRA*, the *Tribunal*, the High Court or the *appellate body*;

(x) where:

(A) in the case of a *licensed body*, the body fails to comply with Rule 8.6(b) (prohibition on *disqualified managers*); or

(B) in the case of an *authorised body*, the body fails to comply with Rule 8.6(c) (employment or remuneration of certain individuals);

and the *manager* or *employee* concerned was *disqualified* as a result of breach of the duties imposed upon the *manager* or *employee* by sections 176 or 90 of the *LSA*;

(xi) the body does not comply with Rule 8.5 (compliance officers);

(xii) the body fails to comply with Rule 8.6 (management and control);

(xiii) for any other reason it is in the public interest; or

(xiv) the body, where it is a *responsible authorised body*, has failed to comply with any obligations under the SRA's *regulatory arrangements* in respect of its *overseas practices*.

(b) in the case of a *licensed body*

a *non-authorised person holds an interest* in the *licensed body*:

(i)   as a result of the *person* taking a step in circumstances where that constitutes an offence under paragraph 24(1) of Schedule 13 to the *LSA* (whether or not the *person* is charged with or convicted of an offence under that paragraph),

(ii) in breach of conditions imposed under paragraphs 17, 28 or 33 of that Schedule, or

(iii) the *person's* holding of which is subject to an objection by the *SRA* under paragraph 31 or 36 of that Schedule.

22.2   The *SRA* must not revoke or suspend an *authorisation* under this rule:

(a)   unless it has first provided the *authorised body* with an opportunity to provide representations to it regarding the issues giving rise to the proposed revocation or suspension;

(b)   unless it has first given the *authorised body* notice of its intention to revoke or suspend the *authorisation*; and

(c)   before the end of the period of 28 days beginning with the day on which the notice in (b) above is given to the body or any longer period specified in the notice.

Guidance notes

(i)   Rule 22.1(a)(x) refers to sections 90 and 176 of the LSA. Section 90 sets out the duty of non-authorised persons, as defined by the LSA, not to do anything which causes or substantially contributes to a breach by a licensed body, or by a manager or an employee of the licensed body who is an authorised person, of the duties imposed on them by section 176. Section 176 imposes the statutory duty on a regulated person to comply with the SRA's regulatory arrangements when practising through an SRA firm. Regulated person includes the firm itself as well as the managers and employees of the firm.

(ii) Rule 22.1(b)(i) refers to the offence under paragraph 24(1) of Schedule 13 to the LSA. This is the offence of a non-authorised person who is required to notify the licensed body and the SRA of a proposal to take a step leading to acquiring a restricted interest in a licensed body taking the step prior to the SRA's approval. Rule 22.1(b)(ii) refers to breaches of the specific provisions about imposing conditions on approval of owners – see guidance note (ii) to Rule 15 above. Rule

22.1(b)(iii) refers to paragraphs 31 (the SRA having an objection to a notifiable interest) and 36 (the SRA having an objection to an existing restricted interest) of Schedule 13 to the LSA.

(iii) In addition to the power to revoke or suspend authorisation, there are statutory divestiture procedures available to the SRA in respect of owners of licensed bodies. These are set out in Part 5 of Schedule 13 to the LSA. See also the guidance notes to Rule 15 for more information about other statutory powers relating to owners of licensed bodies.

(iv) Revocation and suspension of authorisation is a discretionary power of the SRA. The SRA is unlikely to revoke or suspend authorisation if doing so at that time would present any risk to clients, the public, the protection of public money or to any SRA investigation.

Rule 23: Unforeseen temporary breach of certain conditions and eligibility criteria

23.1   Unforeseen breach of eligibility criteria

(a)   If due to an event which could not reasonably have been foreseen, a *licensed body* is no longer a *licensable body*:

   (i)   because the body no longer has at least one *manager* who is an individual and who is an *authorised person* (other than an *RFL* or an *EEL* who is not registered with the *BSB* under Regulation 17 of the European Communities (Lawyer's Practice) Regulations 2000 (SI 2000/1119)) in relation to a licensed activity; or

   (ii)   because:

      (A)   the body no longer has a *manager* or *interest holder* who is a *non-authorised person*; and

      (B)   *non-authorised persons* are no longer entitled to exercise, or control the exercise of, at least 10% of the *voting rights* in any body which is a *manager* or *interest holder* of the *licensed body*;

   but the *SRA* is informed of that fact within seven days of the event first occurring and the body becomes a *licensable body* again within 28 days of the event first occurring, then the *licensable body* will be deemed to have remained a *licensable body* and to that extent will not be liable to have its *authorisation* revoked or suspended under Rule 22.

(b)   If due to an event which could not reasonably have been foreseen, a *recognised body* is no longer a *legal services body* because the body no longer has at least one *manager* who is:

   (i)   a *solicitor*;

   (ii)   an *REL*; or

   (iii)   a *legally qualified body* with at least one *manager* who is a *solicitor* or an *REL*;

Authorisation and Practising Requirements

but the *SRA* is informed of the fact within seven days of the event first occurring and the body becomes a *legal services body* again within 28 days of the event first occurring, then the *recognised body* will be deemed to have remained a *legal services body* and to that extent will not be liable to have its *authorisation* revoked or suspended under Rule 22.

23.2   An *LLP* having fewer than two *members*

(a)   If an event which could not reasonably have been foreseen results in an *LLP* having fewer than two *members*, and therefore being in breach of Rule 16.3 (requirement to have at least two *members*) of the *SRA Practice Framework Rules*, but within six months the situation is remedied, and provided the *LLP* has remained in a position to comply with the remainder of the *SRA's regulatory arrangements* including these rules and any conditions imposed on its *authorisation*, the *LLP* will be deemed to have remained in compliance with Rule 16.3 of the *SRA Practice Framework Rules* and to that extent will not be liable to have its *authorisation* revoked under Rule 22.

23.3   Death of *member* or *shareowner* of a *company*

(a)   If an *authorised body* is a *company* with shares and a *member* or *shareowner* dies who had been approved under Part 4 to be a *member* or *shareowner* of the body at the date of death, then, whether or not the personal representatives have been approved under Part 4, the personal representatives may replace the deceased *member* or *shareowner* in their capacity as personal representatives, provided that:

(i)   no vote may be exercised by or on behalf of a personal representative (and no such vote may be accepted) unless all the personal representatives have been approved under Part 4 to be *members* or *shareowners*;

(ii)   no personal representative may hold or own a share in that capacity for longer than 12 months from the date of death;

(iii) within 12 months of the death the *authorised body* must cancel or acquire the shares or ensure that they are held and owned by *persons* who can *hold the interest* in the body in compliance with Rule 8.6 (management and control), but without this resulting in *RFLs* being the only *shareowners* of a *recognised body*; and

(iv)   no vote may be exercised by or on behalf of any personal representative (and no such vote may be accepted) after the 12 month period has expired.

(b)   If, following the death of a *member* or *shareowner*, a *company* meets the requirements of (a) above, the *company* will be deemed to have remained in compliance with Rule 8.6 (management and control), and to that extent will not be liable to have its *authorisation* revoked under Rule 22.

23.4   *Member* or *shareowner* ceasing to be approved

(a)   If an *authorised body* is a *company* with shares and a *member* or *shareowner* ceases to be approved under Part 4 to be a *member* or *shareowner* of the body, or ceases to exist as a *body corporate*, then provided that:

(i) no vote is exercised or accepted on the shares held by or on behalf of that *member* or *shareowner*;

(ii) a trustee in bankruptcy or liquidator (whether approved under Part 4 or not) replaces that *member* or *shareowner* in the capacity of trustee or liquidator for a period not exceeding six months from the date the *member* or *shareowner* ceased to be approved; and

(iii) the *company* cancels or acquires the shares within six months, or within that time ensures that the shares are held and owned by *persons* in compliance with Rule 8.6, but without this resulting in the body ceasing to be a *licensable body* (in the case of a *licensed body*), or ceasing to be a *legal services body* (in the case of a *recognised body*);

the *company* will be deemed to have remained in compliance with Rule 8.6 (management and control), and to that extent will not be liable to have its *authorisation* revoked under Rule 22.

23.5 *Member* or *shareowner* becoming insolvent but remaining compliant

(a) If an *authorised body* is a *company* with shares and a *member* or *shareowner* becomes insolvent but continues to *hold an interest* in the body in compliance with Rule 8.6, then the trustee in bankruptcy or liquidator (whether approved under Part 4 or not) may replace the insolvent *member* or *shareowner* in the capacity of trustee in bankruptcy or liquidator, provided that:

(i) no vote may be exercised by or on behalf of a trustee in bankruptcy or liquidator (and no such vote may be accepted) unless the trustee or liquidator can *hold the interest* in the *company* in compliance with Rule 8.6;

(ii) no trustee in bankruptcy or liquidator may hold or own a share in that capacity for longer than six months from the date of the insolvency;

(iii) within six months of the insolvency the *company* must cancel or acquire the shares or ensure that they are held and owned by *persons* who can *hold an interest* in the *company* in compliance with Rule 8.6, but without this resulting in the body ceasing to be a *licensable body* (in the case of a *licensed body*), or ceasing to be a *legal services body* (in the case of a *recognised body*); and

(iv) no vote may be exercised by or on behalf of any trustee in bankruptcy or liquidator (and no such vote may be accepted) after the six month period has expired.

(b) If (a) above applies and a *company* meets its requirements, the *company* will be deemed to have remained in compliance with Rule 8.6 (management and control), and to that extent will not be liable to have its *authorisation* revoked under Rule 22.

Authorisation and
Practising Requirements

23.6   Court of Protection deputy

(a) A *Court of Protection deputy* appointed under section 19 of the Mental Capacity Act 2005 may be a *member* or *shareowner* in that capacity of an *authorised body*, without breaching Rule 8.6 (management and control), provided that:

(i)   the person in respect of whom the deputy has been appointed *holds the interest* in compliance with Rule 8.6; and

(ii)   if the deputy is not a *member* or *shareowner* in compliance with Rule 8.6, no vote is exercised or accepted on the shares.

(b) If (a) above applies and a *company* meets its requirements, the *company* will be deemed to have remained in compliance with Rule 8.6, and to that extent will not be liable to have its *authorisation* revoked under Rule 22.

Guidance notes

(i)   The provisions in Rule 23 allow firms time to rectify the position where unexpected changes occur. The effect of the provisions is to allow firms a period to avoid being in breach of SRA rules. Recognised bodies need also to consider the time limit of 90 days to obtain a licence which is imposed by section 18(3) of the LSA on such existing bodies that become licensable. Likewise, licensed bodies need to consider the time limit of 90 days to obtain a certificate of recognition which is imposed by section 18(6) of the LSA on existing licensed bodies that cease to be licensable.

(ii)   If the changes in 23.2, 23.3, 23.4, 23.5 and 23.6 occur, firms will need to notify the SRA under Rule 8.7 and under Rule 18.2 of the SRA Practice Framework Rules.

PART 6: CHANGES IN PARTNERSHIPS

Rule 24: Change to the composition of a partnership

24.1   *Authorisation* of a *partnership* may continue despite a change in its composition, subject to Rules 24.2, 24.3, 24.4 and 25.

24.2   If there is a change to an *authorised body*, which is a *partnership*, which results in there being:

(a) no remaining *partner* who was a *partner* before the change the *authorised body* must cease to *practise* from the date of the change; the 28 day period under Rule 23.1 does not apply;

(b) only one remaining *principal* who needs to be authorised as a *sole practitioner* but could not reasonably have commenced an application in advance of the change:

(i)   the *firm* may continue to *practise* provided that the remaining *principal*:

        (A) is a *solicitor* or *REL*;

        (B) notifies the *SRA* within seven days;

        (C) is granted temporary emergency recognition under Regulation 4 of the *SRA Practising Regulations*;

    (ii) during the initial 28 day period, or such extended period as the *SRA* may allow, under any such temporary emergency recognition, the remaining *principal* must:

        (A) cease to *practise*, and notify the *SRA*; or

        (B) commence a substantive application for *authorisation* as a *recognised sole practitioner* under the *SRA Practising Regulations*, or if the remaining *principal* has taken on a new *partner*, as an *authorised body*;

(c) an *authorised body* which will continue but one or more of the former *partners* intend to carry on as a separate *firm*, which must be authorised as an *authorised body*, a *recognised body* or a *recognised sole practitioner*, but the *principal(s)* in the new firm could not reasonably have commenced an application for *authorisation* in advance of the change:

    (i) the new *firm* may *practise* from the date of the change provided that the new *firm*:

        (A) is a *partnership* which complies with Part 3 of the *SRA Practice Framework Rules* in its formation, composition and structure, or is a *solicitor* or *REL sole practitioner*;

        (B) complies with the SRA Indemnity Insurance Rules;

        (C) notifies the *SRA* within seven days; and

        (D) is granted temporary emergency *authorisation* under Rule 25 below or temporary emergency recognition under Regulation 7 of the SRA Recognised Bodies Regulations 2011 or Regulation 4 of the *SRA Practising Regulations*;

    (ii) during the initial 28 day period, or such extended period as the *SRA* may allow, the new *firm* must:

        (A) cease to *practise*, and notify the *SRA*; or

        (B) commence a substantive application for *authorisation*;

(d) a failure by:

    (i) a *recognised body* to comply with Rules 13.1 and 16.1 of the *SRA Practice Framework Rules*; or

    (ii) a *licensed body* to comply with Rules 14 and 16 of the *SRA Practice Framework Rules*,

the *firm* must cease to *practise*.

24.3   Following a *partnership* change under Rule 24.2(c), the *SRA* will if necessary decide which of the groups of former *partners* will continue to be covered by the existing *authorisation* and which must apply for a new *authorisation*, and may apportion *authorisation* fees and Compensation Fund contributions between the groups.

24.4   Any decision made under Rule 24.3 will be without prejudice to the outcome of any legal dispute between the former *partners*.

Rule 25: Temporary emergency authorisation

25.1   If a *partnership* split brings into being a new *partnership* which is not an *authorised body*:

(a)   the *SRA* must be notified within seven days; and

(b)   temporary emergency *authorisation* may be granted, subject to Rule 25.2 to 25.4 below, so as to enable the *partners* in the new *partnership* to *practise* through the new *firm* for a limited period without breach of these rules and the *SRA Practice Framework Rules*.

25.2   An application for temporary emergency *authorisation* must be made on the *prescribed* form within seven days of the *partnership* split, and must be accompanied by all information and documentation the *SRA* may reasonably require.

25.3   The *SRA* may grant an application for temporary emergency *authorisation* if the following conditions are met.

(a)   The *SRA* must be satisfied that the *partners* could not reasonably have commenced an application for *authorisation* in advance of the change.

(b)   In the case of a *licensable body*, the *partnership* must comply with Rule 14 (Eligibility criteria and fundamental requirements for licensed bodies) of the *SRA Practice Framework Rules*.

(c)   In the case of a *legal services body*, the *partnership* must comply with Rule 13 (Eligibility criteria and fundamental requirements for recognised bodies) of the *SRA Practice Framework Rules*.

(d)   The *partnership* must comply with Rules 12 (Persons who must be "qualified to supervise"), 15 (Formation, registered office and practising address) and 16 (Composition of an authorised body) of the *SRA Practice Framework Rules*.

(e)   The *partnership* must comply with the SRA Indemnity Insurance Rules, and must have adopted a name under which the *firm* is to be registered and which complies with Chapter 8 (Publicity) of the *SRA Code of Conduct*.

25.4   Temporary emergency *authorisation*:

(a)   may be granted initially for 28 days;

(b) may be granted to have effect from the date of the *partnership* split or any other appropriate subsequent date;

(c) may be extended in response to a reasonable request by the *applicant body*;

(d) must be extended (subject to (h) below) pending determination of a substantive application for *authorisation* commenced during the currency of a temporary emergency *authorisation*;

(e) is granted or extended subject to the general conditions in Rule 8, unless otherwise specified by the *SRA*, and may be granted or extended subject to such other conditions as the *SRA* sees fit to impose having regard to the criteria in Rule 9;

(f) is to be treated as a new *authorisation* for the purpose of these rules;

(g) if granted, cannot prejudice the discretion of the *SRA* to refuse a substantive application for *authorisation* of the body under Part 2 or to impose any conditions on any such *authorisation*; and

(h) in exceptional circumstances, and for reasonable cause, may be revoked at any time.

PART 7: SPECIAL BODIES, TRANSITIONAL PROVISIONS AND PASSPORTING

Rule 26: Special kinds of licensable bodies

26.1   The *SRA* does not accept applications for any order to be made by it under section 106 of the *LSA* from any *licensable body*.

Guidance note

(i)   The LSA provides the special kind of licensable bodies mentioned in section 23 with a grace period during which they are not required to apply for authorisation as a licensed body. However, during the grace period, such bodies may apply for authorisation under these rules but will not be able to request special treatment under section 106 until this section is commenced.

Rule 27: Commencement, transitional provisions and repeals

27.1   These rules shall come into force:

(a) on the designation of the *Society* as a *licensing authority* under Part 1 of Schedule 10 to the *LSA*, in respect of *licensable bodies*;

(b) on 31 March 2012 ("the relevant date"), in respect of *legal services bodies*, and the SRA Recognised Bodies Regulations 2011 (in Rule 27.1 referred to as "the Regulations") shall be repealed, save that:

   (i)   applications for initial recognition made under Regulation 2.1 of the Regulations but not decided on the relevant date shall be considered and decided in accordance with the Regulations;

   (ii)   applications for approval of an individual as suitable to be a *manager* made under Regulation 5 of the Regulations but not decided on the relevant date shall be considered and decided in accordance with the Regulations;

(iii) applications for temporary emergency recognition made under Regulation 7.5 of the Regulations, or requests for extension of temporary emergency recognition made under Regulation 7.8(c) of the Regulations, but not decided on the relevant date shall be considered and decided in accordance with the Regulations;

(iv) where a *person* has invoked the internal appeal procedure under Regulation 9 of the Regulations, but the appeal has not been concluded by the relevant date, then the appeal shall be considered and determined in accordance with the Regulations; and

(v) where directions have been issued in respect of a reconsideration under Regulation 18 of the Regulations, the reconsideration shall proceed in accordance with the Regulations,

and for the avoidance of doubt, on the relevant date:

(A) where a notice of succession has been delivered to the *SRA* under Regulation 3.1 or 3.3 of the Regulations in respect of which the *SRA* has made no fee determination, the *SRA* will proceed to consider the matter in accordance with Rule 8.3(d) to (k) above;

(B) where condition(s) have been imposed on a *recognised body's* recognition under Regulation 6 of the Regulations, such condition(s) shall continue to apply as if they had been imposed under Rule 9 above; and

(c) From 31 March 2012 or the date on which an order made pursuant to section 69 of the *LSA* relating to the status of *sole practitioners* comes into force, whichever is the later, ("the relevant date" for the purposes of sub-rules (c) and (d)) the *SRA Practising Regulations* (in Rule 27.1 referred to as "the Practising Regulations") shall have effect with the following amendments:

(i) Regulations 1.6, 4, 5, 8.2(b), 8.3(c), 8.3(d), 8.4(d), 8.4(j), 8.4(l), 9.1(d), 9.2(d), 10.1(d), 10.2(b), 11.2(g), 12.2(h), 14.1(d) and 19.5 shall be repealed;

(ii) in Regulation 8.3 the words "who is the subject of any decision in (a)-(d) below and/or the person who is the subject of a decision in (c) or (d) below" shall be omitted;

(iii) in Regulation 8.4(e), "13ZA(6)," shall be omitted;

(iv) in Regulation 8.5(a)(ii) the words "including, where applicable, the renewal of an existing authorisation as a *recognised sole practitioner* endorsed on the practising certificate or registration," shall be omitted;

(v) in Regulation 10.2(c) the word "or" shall be substituted for the "," between "practising certificate" and "registration" and the words ", or authorisation as a *recognised sole practitioner*" shall be omitted;

(vi) in Regulation 10.3(a) the word "or" shall be substituted for the ","
between "practising certificate" and "registration" and for the ","
between "practising certificate" and "renew a registration", and the
words ", or authorisation as a *recognised sole practitioner*" and the
words "or renew an authorisation" shall be omitted;

(vii) in Regulation 11.2(k) the words "or suspension of the *solicitor* from
practice as a *sole practitioner*, or suspension of the *solicitor's authorisation* as a *recognised sole practitioner*," shall be omitted;

(viii) in Regulation 12.2(k) the words "or suspension of the *lawyer* from
practice as a *sole practitioner*, or suspension of the *lawyer's* authorisation as a *recognised sole practitioner*," shall be omitted;

(ix) in Regulation 13.2(h) and 16.1(b) the words "*recognised sole practitioner*," shall be omitted;

(d) Notwithstanding the provisions of sub-rule (c) above:

(i) applications for authorisation as a *recognised sole practitioner* made
under Regulation 4.1 of the Practising Regulations but not decided on
the relevant date shall be considered and decided in accordance with
the Practising Regulations;

(ii) applications for temporary emergency recognition made under Regulation 4.4(a) or for recognition made under Regulation 4.5(b) of the
Practising Regulations, or requests for extension of temporary emergency recognition made under Regulation 4.4(c)(iii) of the Practising
Regulations, but not decided on the relevant date shall be considered
and decided in accordance with the Practising Regulations;

(iii) applications for approval of a person's designation as a *COLP* or
COFA made under Regulation 4.9 of the Practising Regulations but
not decided on the relevant date shall be considered and decided in
accordance with the Practising Regulations;

and, for the avoidance of doubt, where on the relevant date, a notice of
succession has been delivered to the *SRA* under Regulation 5.1 or 5.3 of the
Practising Regulations in respect of which the *SRA* has made no fee determination, the *SRA* will proceed to consider the matter in accordance with Rule
8.3(d) to (l) above.

27.2 From 31 March 2012 these rules shall have effect subject to the following
amendments:

(a) in Rule 8.3(d), 8.3(i)(i) and 8.3(i)(ii) the words ", *recognised bodies*" shall be
omitted;

(b) in Rule 8.3(f), 8.3(j) and 8.3(k) the words ", *recognised bodies*" shall be
omitted;

(c) in Rule 8.3(g) and 8.3(l), the words ", *recognised body*" shall be omitted;

(d) in Rule 8.3(h)(i), the words "*recognised body* or" shall be omitted;

(e) in Rule 24.2(c), the words ", a *recognised body*" shall be omitted; and

(f) in Rule 24.2(c)(i)(D), the words "Regulation 7 of the SRA Recognised Bodies Regulations 2011 or" shall be omitted.

27.3   From 31 March 2012 or the date on which an order made pursuant to section 69 of the Legal Services Act relating to the status of *sole practitioners* comes into force, whichever is the later, these rules shall have effect subject to the following amendments:

(a) in Rule 6.3(a) the words ", as a group, are, or the *sole practitioner* is, suitable" shall be substituted for the words "are suitable, as a group";

(b) in Rule 8.3(d), 8.3(i)(i) and 8.3(i)(ii) the words "and *recognised sole practitioners*" shall be omitted;

(c) in Rule 8.3(f), 8.3(j) and 8.3(k) the words "or *recognised sole practitioners*" shall be omitted;

(d) in Rule 8.3(g) and 8.3(l), the words "or *recognised sole practitioner*" shall be omitted;

(e) in Rule 8.3(h)(i), the words "and/or *recognised sole practitioner*" shall be omitted;

(f) Rule 24.2(b) shall be omitted;

(g) in Rule 24.2(c), the words "or a *recognised sole practitioner*" shall be omitted;

(h) in Rule 24.2(c)(i)(D), the words "or temporary emergency recognition under Regulation 4 of the *SRA Practising Regulations*" shall be omitted;

(i) Rule 25.1 shall have effect as if the words "or a new *sole practitioner firm*" were inserted after the word "*partnership*";

(j) Rule 25.1(b) shall have effect as if the words ", or the new sole *principal*," were inserted after the words "the new *partnership*";

(k) Rule 25.3(a) shall have effect as if the words "or sole *principal*" were inserted after the word "*partners*";

(l) Rule 25.3(c), 25.3(d) and 25.3(e) shall have effect as if the words "or sole *principal*" were inserted after the word "*partnership*"; and

(m) Rule 25 shall have effect as if the following provisions were inserted:

25.5 Sole practitioners

(a) If a *sole practitioner* dies:

(i) the *SRA* must be notified within seven days;

(ii) within 28 days of the death an emergency application may be made, on the *prescribed* form, for recognition as a *recognised body* in the capacity of personal representative, practice manager or *employee* by a *solicitor* or an *REL* who is:

        (A)   the *sole practitioner's* executor;

        (B)   practice manager appointed by the *sole practitioner's* personal representatives; or

        (C)   an *employee* of the *firm*.

    (b)   If the application for recognition in the capacity of personal representative, practice manager or *employee* is granted:

        (i)   recognition will be deemed to run from the date of death;

        (ii) recognition will cease to have effect on the winding up of the estate or 12 months from the date of death, whichever is the earlier.

27.4   From 31 March 2012, a *legal services body* which does not comply with Rule 8.5 above may be treated as an *authorised body* for the purposes of these rules and the *SRA's regulatory arrangements*, until 31 December 2012, at which time a *legal services body* shall be required to comply with Rule 8.5 in order to be authorised under these rules.

27.5   Unless the context otherwise requires, references in these rules to:

    (a)   these rules, or a provision of these rules; and

    (b)   the *SRA Code of Conduct*, rules, regulations or *regulatory arrangements*, or a provision of the same,

include a reference to the equivalent rules, regulations or provisions previously in force.

Rule 28: Transition of recognised bodies and sole practitioners

28.1   From 31 March 2012:

    (a)   the recognition of a body recognised under section 9 of the *AJA*, shall have effect as if it were *authorisation* granted under these rules; and

    (b)   all *managers* and *owners* of bodies falling within sub-rule (a) shall be deemed to have been approved under Part 4 of these rules, as applicable, including those approved under Rule 27.1(b)(ii) above.

28.2   From 31 March 2012 or the date on which an order made pursuant to section 69 of the Legal Services Act relating to the status of *sole practitioners* comes into force, whichever is the later, these rules shall have effect subject to the following amendments:

    (a)   a sole *solicitor* or *REL* who has been recognised as a *sole practitioner* by way of an endorsement under section 1B of the *SA* shall be deemed to have been recognised as a *legal services body* under section 9 of the *AJA*;

    (b)   all sole *solicitors* and *RELs* falling within sub-rule (a) shall be deemed to have been approved as *managers* and *owners* under Part 4 of these rules; and

    (c)   all *COLPs* and *COFAs* approved as such under the *SRA Practising Regulations* shall be deemed to have been approved as such under Part 4 of these rules, as applicable.

Authorisation and Practising Requirements

PART 8: RECONSIDERATION AND APPEALS

Rule 29: Reconsideration

29.1   The *SRA* may reconsider a decision made under these rules when it appears that the decision maker:

(a)   was not provided with material evidence that was available to the *SRA*;

(b)   was materially misled;

(c)   failed to take proper account of material facts or evidence;

(d)   took into account immaterial facts or evidence;

(e)   made a material error of law;

(f)   made a decision which was otherwise irrational or procedurally unfair;

(g)   made a decision which was otherwise ultra vires; or

(h)   failed to give sufficient reasons.

29.2   A decision may be reconsidered under Rule 29.1 only on the initiative of the *SRA*.

29.3   The *SRA*, when considering the exercise of its powers under this rule, may also give directions for:

(a)   further investigations to be undertaken;

(b)   further information or explanation to be obtained from any *person*; and

(c)   the reconsideration to be undertaken by the original decision maker or by a different decision maker or panel.

Rule 30: Appeals by legal services bodies

30.1   A *legal services body* which is the subject of any decision in (a)–(b) below may invoke the *SRA's* own appeals procedure:

(a)   against the *SRA's* decision to modify or refuse an application for modification of the terms and conditions of an *authorisation* under Rule 10;

(b)   before exercising its right of appeal to the High Court:

(i)   against refusal of *authorisation*, under paragraph 2(1)(a) of Schedule 2 to the *AJA*;

(ii)   against the imposition of a condition on its *authorisation*, under paragraph 2(1)(b) or (c) of that Schedule; or

(iii)   against refusal by the *SRA* to approve a step which, under a condition on the body's *authorisation*, requires such prior approval, under paragraph 2(2) of that Schedule.

30.2   A *legal services body* which is the subject of any decision in (a)–(c) below and/or the *person* who is the subject of any decision in (a)–(c) below, may invoke the *SRA's* own appeals procedure against the *SRA's* decision:

(a)   not to approve the *person* to be a *manager, owner* or *compliance officer* of a *legal services body* under Rules 8.5(b) or (d) or 8.6(a);

(b)   to approve the *person* to be a *manager, owner* or *compliance officer* of a *legal services body* under Rules 8.5(b) or (d) or 8.6(a) subject to conditions on the body's *authorisation*; or

(c)   to withdraw its approval of the *person* to be a *manager, owner* or *compliance officer* of the body under Rule 17 or Rule 18.

30.3   A *legal services body* may appeal to the High Court against the *SRA's* decision to suspend or revoke the body's *authorisation*, but must first invoke the *SRA's* own appeals procedure.

30.4   A *legal services body*, treated as such in accordance with Rule 22.3 of the *SRA Practice Framework Rules*, which is the subject of any decision in (a)–(b) below and/or the *person* who is the subject of any decision in (a)–(b) below, may appeal to the High Court against the *SRA's* decision:

(a)   not to approve the individual as suitable to be a non-lawyer *manager* of the body under Rule 8.6(a); and

(b)   to withdraw its approval of the individual as suitable to be a non-lawyer *manager* of the body under Rule 17;

but must first invoke the *SRA's* own appeals procedure, and for the purposes of 30.4 and 30.6(c) "non-lawyer" means an individual who is not listed in Rule 22.4(d)(i) of the *SRA Practice Framework Rules*.

30.5   Deemed refusal

(a)   An application by a *legal services body* for *authorisation* under Rule 4 is deemed, for the purpose of any appeal under Rule 30.1(b) above, to be refused on the day of the expiry of the *decision period*, if by the end of that day the *SRA* has not notified the *applicant body* of its decision.

(b)   An application for approval of a *person* under Part 4 is deemed, for the purpose of any appeal under Rule 30.4(a) above, to be refused on the day of the expiry of the *decision period*, if by the end of that day the *SRA* has not notified the *applicant body* or *authorised body* as appropriate, and the *person* who is the subject of the approval, of its decision.

30.6   If an appeal is made to the High Court in relation to a decision made in respect of a *legal services body* to:

(a)   impose conditions on an *authorisation* under Rule 9;

(b)   modify terms and conditions of an *authorisation* under Rule 10;

(c)   withdraw approval of a non-lawyer *manager* under 30.4; or

(d)   revoke or suspend a body's *authorisation*;

the appellant may apply to the High Court for a stay of the decision pending the determination or discontinuance of the appeal, and if the High Court imposes an order for a stay in relation to a decision, the *SRA* shall stay the decision accordingly.

Guidance note

(i)   Rule 30.5 allows an applicant body or authorised body to regard their application as refused on certain dates to allow an appeal to be commenced. However, this is only for the purpose of ensuring the body has appeal rights and despite the deemed refusal the SRA may still determine the application.

Rule 31: Appeals by licensable bodies

31.1   A *licensable body* which is the subject of any decision in (a)–(b) below may appeal to the *appellate body* against:

(a)   the *SRA's* decision to:

(i)   refuse an application for *authorisation*;

(ii)   impose a condition on an *authorisation*;

(iii)   revoke or suspend a body's *authorisation*;

(iv)   refuse to approve a step which, under a condition on the body's *authorisation*, requires such prior approval;

(v)   modify or refuse an application for modification of the terms and conditions of an *authorisation* under Rule 10; or

(b)   the *SRA's* failure to make a decision within the *decision period*;

but must first invoke the *SRA's* own appeal procedure.

31.2   A *licensable body* which makes the application for approval pursuant to Rule 8.5 or 8.6 and/or the *person* who is the subject of the application for approval may appeal to the *appellate body* against the *SRA's* decision:

(a)   not to approve the *person* to be a *manager* or *compliance officer* of the body under Rules 8.5(b) or (d) or 8.6(a);

(b)   to approve the *person* to be a *manager* or *compliance officer* of the body under Rules 8.5(b) or (d) or 8.6(a) subject to conditions on the body's *authorisation*; or

(c)   to withdraw its approval of the *person* to be a *manager* or *compliance officer* of the body under Rule 17 or 18;

but must first invoke the *SRA's* own appeals procedure.

31.3   Any *person* who is the subject of any decision in (a)–(c) below may invoke the *SRA's* own appeals procedure, before exercising their right of appeal to the *appellate body*:

(a) against the *SRA's* imposition of a financial penalty, under section 96 of the *LSA*;

(b) against the *SRA's* imposition of conditions on an *authorisation* in connection with its approval of a *person* being an *owner* of a *licensed body*, under paragraphs 18, 29 or 34 of Schedule 13 to the *LSA*; or

(c) against the *SRA's* decision not to approve, or its decision to withdraw its approval of, a *person* being an *owner* of a *licensed body*, under paragraphs 20, 32 or 37 of Schedule 13 to the *LSA*.

31.4   If an appeal is made to the *appellate body* in relation to a decision in respect of a *licensable body* to:

(a) impose conditions on an *authorisation* under Rule 9;

(b) modify terms and conditions of an *authorisation* under Rule 10;

(c) withdraw approval of an *owner*, *manager*, COLP or COFA;

(d) revoke or suspend a body's *authorisation*; or

(e) impose conditions on the holding of an interest under paragraph 28 or 33 of Schedule 13 of the *LSA*;

the appellant may apply to the *appellate body* for a stay of the decision pending the determination or discontinuance of the appeal, and if the *appellate body* imposes an order for a stay in relation to a decision, the *SRA* shall stay the decision accordingly.

Rule 32: Appeals – general provisions

32.1   Appeals under the *SRA's* own appeals procedure in respect of a decision made under these rules must be made within 28 days of:

(a) notification of the *SRA's* decision and reasons;

(b) deemed refusal under Rule 30.5 above; or

(c) expiry of the *decision period* or extension notice under Rule 5;

as applicable.

32.2   Unless otherwise provided in rules of the High Court or the Legal Services Board or in the relevant decision, an appeal to the High Court or *appellate body* in respect of a decision made under these rules must be made:

(a) within the period of 28 days from the date on which the notice of the decision that is subject to appeal is given to the appellant;

(b) within the period of 28 days from the date on which the notice of the refusal of an appeal under the *SRA's* own appeals procedure is given; or

(c) within the period of 28 days from the date on which the notice of the decision to impose a condition under the *SRA's* own appeals procedure is given;

as appropriate.

Authorisation and
Practising Requirements

32.3   An appeal under the *SRA's* own appeals procedure under Rules 30.2(a), 30.4(a) or 31.2(a), or against the *SRA's* decision to refuse an approval under Rule 31.3(c), shall be treated as an application for the purpose of these rules.

32.4   If an appeal is made under:

(a)   Rules 30.2(c), 30.4(b), 31.2(c) or 31.3(c), against the *SRA's* decision to withdraw an approval; or

(b)   Rules 30.3 or 31.1(a)(iii), against the *SRA's* decision to revoke or suspend an *authorisation* under Rule 22;

before the decision takes effect, the decision shall not take effect pending the determination or discontinuance of the appeal, unless in the opinion of the *SRA* the proceedings on that appeal have been unduly protracted by the appellant or are unlikely to be successful.

32.5   Any decision referred to in Rule 30.6 and 31.4 which is made by the *SRA* may include a direction that the condition, modification, withdrawal, revocation or suspension shall not take effect until the determination or discontinuance of any appeal.

PART 9: REGISTER AND CERTIFICATE OF AUTHORISATION

Rule 33: Name of an authorised body

33.1   A *body corporate* will be authorised under its corporate name.

33.2   A *partnership* must elect to have a name under which it is to be authorised.

Rule 34: The register of authorised bodies

34.1   The *SRA* must keep a register of all *authorised bodies* authorised by the *SRA*, which may be kept in electronic form.

34.2   The register must contain, for each *authorised body*:

(a)   The:

(i)   name and number under which the body is authorised;

(ii)   any previous name(s) under which the body has been authorised by the SRA;

(iii)   date from which the *authorisation* has effect; and

(iv)   details of the *reserved legal activities* that the body is authorised to undertake.

(b)   whether the *authorised body* is a *recognised body* or a *licensed body*;

(c)   any other *practising* styles used by the body;

(d)   the *authorised body's* registered office and registered number, if it is an *LLP* or *company* and, if it is a *charity*, its *charity* number;

(e) the *authorised body's* main *practising address* in England and Wales;

(f) all the *authorised body's* other *practising addresses* and the addresses of its *overseas practices*;

(g) whether the *authorised body* is a *partnership*, an *LLP* or a *company*;

(h) if the *authorised body* is a *company* its registered office address and, whether it is:

    (i) a *company* limited by shares;

    (ii) a *company* limited by guarantee;

    (iii) an unlimited *company*;

    (iv) an overseas *company* registered in England and Wales;

    (v) an overseas *company* registered in Scotland;

    (vi) an overseas *company* registered in Northern Ireland; or

    (vii) a *societas Europaea*;

(i) a list of the *authorised body's managers*, and in respect of each *manager*, whether that *manager* is:

    (i) a *lawyer of England and Wales*, and if so the nature of his or her qualification;

    (ii) an *REL*, and if so his or her professional title and jurisdiction of qualification;

    (iii) an *EEL* registered with the *BSB*, and if so his or her professional title and jurisdiction of qualification;

    (iv) an *EEL* based entirely at an office or offices outside England and Wales, and if so his or her professional title and jurisdiction of qualification;

    (v) an *RFL*, and if so his or her professional title and jurisdiction of qualification;

    (vi) any other individual approved under Part 4;

    (vii) a *company* approved under Part 4, and if so whether it is a *licensed body*, a *recognised body*, a *European corporate practice* or an *authorised non-SRA firm*;

    (viii) an *LLP* approved under Part 4, and if so whether it is a *licensed body*, a *recognised body*, a *European corporate practice* or an *authorised non-SRA firm*; or

    (ix) a *partnership* with separate legal personality approved under Part 4, and if so whether it is a *licensed body*, a *recognised body*, a *European corporate practice* or an *authorised non-SRA firm*;

(j) the name of the individual who is the *firm's COLP*, and the name of the *approved regulator* which authorises that individual as an *authorised person*;

(k) the name of the individual who is the *firm's COFA*;

(l) any condition to which the body's *authorisation* is subject;

(m) if the *authorised body's authorisation* is for the time being suspended or revoked, a note to state that fact and the date on which the suspension or revocation took place;

(n) in the case of a *licensed body*, any enforcement action or sanction on the body, any *owner* or employee of the body, excluding administrative fines; and

(o) any other information considered necessary by the *SRA* for carrying out its statutory functions in the public interest, as may from time to time be *prescribed*.

34.3   Public information

(a) Entries in the register must be available for inspection by any member of the public except that the *SRA* may withhold a *recognised body's* address in exceptional circumstances where the *SRA* considers that to do so would be in the public interest.

(b) The date on which, and the circumstances in which, an *authorised body's authorisation* expired or was revoked must be made available to a member of the public on request.

Rule 35: Certificates of authorisation

35.1   When a body is granted an *authorisation*, the *SRA* must issue a *certificate of authorisation*.

35.2   Each *certificate of authorisation* must state, in respect of the *authorised body*:

(a) whether it is a licence or a certificate of recognition;

(b) the name and number under which the body is authorised;

(c) its registered office, if it is an *LLP* or *company*;

(d) its main *practising address* in England and Wales;

(e) whether it is a *partnership*, an *LLP* or a *company*; and

(f) if it is a *company*, whether it is:

     (i) a *company* limited by shares;

     (ii) a *company* limited by guarantee;

     (iii) an unlimited *company*;

     (iv) an overseas *company* registered in England and Wales;

      (v)   an overseas *company* registered in Scotland;

      (vi) an overseas *company* registered in Northern Ireland; or

      (vii) a *societas Europaea*;

(g) the date from which *authorisation* is granted; and

(h) the terms and conditions to which the body's *authorisation* is subject.

Regulations and rules about:

- applications for practising certificates by solicitors and for registration by European lawyers and foreign lawyers;

- applications for authorisation to practise as sole practitioners (until superseded by provisions in the SRA Authorisation Rules), by solicitors and registered European lawyers;

- applications for renewal of practising certificates and registration;

- the issue of practising certificates to solicitors and the issue of certificates of registration to European lawyers and foreign lawyers; and

- the keeping of the register of solicitors who hold practising certificates, the register of European lawyers and the register of foreign lawyers,

dated 17 June 2011 commencing on 6 October 2011

made by the Solicitors Regulation Authority Board under sections 13, 13ZA, 31, 79 and 80 of the Solicitors Act 1974 and paragraphs 2 and 3 of Schedule 14 to the Courts and Legal Services Act 1990

with the approval of the Legal Services Board under paragraph 19 of Schedule 4 to the Legal Services Act 2007.

PART 1: APPLICATIONS, CONDITIONS AND APPEALS

Regulation 1: General requirements for applications under these regulations

1.1 An application under these regulations must comprise:

(a) the *prescribed* form, correctly completed;

(b) the *prescribed* fee or fees;

(c) if the application is for a practising certificate, for replacement of a practising certificate, for registration or for renewal of registration, any *prescribed* contribution to the Solicitors' Compensation Fund;

(d) such additional information, documents and references as may be specified by the *SRA*; and

(e) any additional information and documentation which the *SRA* may reasonably require.

It is not necessary to submit all documents, information and payments simultaneously, but an application will only have been made once the *SRA* has received all of the documentation, information and payments comprising that application.

1.2   Every applicant must:

    (a) ensure that all details relating to him or her given on any form *prescribed* under these regulations are correct and complete;

    (b) notify the *SRA* as soon as he or she becomes aware that any information provided in an application under these regulations has changed.

1.3   Every form submitted under these regulations must be personally signed by the applicant unless:

    (a) a *solicitor* or *REL* has been given written permission by the *SRA*, in exceptional circumstances, to sign on the applicant's behalf; or

    (b) the application is made wholly or partly on a *prescribed* form which is designed to be completed and signed on behalf of a number of applicants in one *firm* or organisation. In that case, the form must be signed by a *solicitor* or *REL* who:

        (i)   is authorised to sign the form by the *firm* or organisation;

        (ii) has the consent of all the persons named in the form to sign the form on their behalf; and

        (iii) has taken reasonable steps to ensure that all details given on the form are correct and complete.

1.4   The *SRA* must notify its decision and reasons in writing to the applicant when it:

    (a) refuses an application;

    (b) grants an application subject to a condition; or

    (c) refuses a permission required under a condition on a practising certificate or registration.

1.5   The *SRA* shall determine the amount of any fees required under these regulations and the *SRA's* decision shall be final.

1.6   The *SRA* may prescribe from time to time a fee moderation process under which a *recognised sole practitioner* may make an application for the fee for renewal of authorisation as a *recognised sole practitioner* to be varied. A decision under this process shall be final.

Guidance notes

(i)   Please refer to the forms and notes.

(ii)   "In writing" includes any form of written electronic communication normally used for business purposes, such as emails.

(iii)   Fees prescribed for the purposes of these regulations are prescribed:

(a) under section 11 of the SA for a practising certificate or registration in the register of European lawyers;

(b) under section 13ZB of the SA for authorisation as a sole practitioner; or

(c) under paragraph 2 of Schedule 14 to the Courts and Legal Services Act 1990 or section 11 of the SA for registration in the register of foreign lawyers.

Regulation 2: Applications for practising certificates and registration

2.1   The following applications may be made under regulation 2:

(a) unless regulation 3 applies, initial applications for practising certificates and applications for replacement of practising certificates under section 9 of the *SA*;

(b) unless regulation 3 applies, initial applications for registration in the *register of European lawyers* and applications for renewal of registration in the *register of European lawyers* under regulation 17 of the European Communities (Lawyer's Practice) Regulations 2000; and

(c) initial applications for registration in the *register of foreign lawyers* and applications for renewal of registration in the *register of foreign lawyers* under section 89 of the Courts and Legal Services Act 1990.

2.2   Where application is made under regulation 2 for a practising certificate or for replacement of a practising certificate the *SRA* must grant the application if:

(a) the applicant's name is on the roll of *solicitors*;

(b) the applicant is not suspended from *practice* as a *solicitor*;

(c) the applicant has supplied satisfactory evidence that he or she will comply with or be exempt from the SRA Indemnity Insurance Rules; and

(d) the application is made in accordance with these regulations,

and the *SRA* must not grant the application unless conditions (a) to (c) are met.

2.3   Applications for initial registration or for renewal of registration in the *register of European lawyers*

(a) Where application is made under regulation 2 for initial registration or for renewal of registration in the *register of European lawyers* the *SRA* must grant the application if:

(i) the applicant is not (subject to (c) below) a solicitor, barrister or advocate of any of the *UK* jurisdictions, a barrister of the Irish Republic, or registered under the *Establishment Directive* with the *BSB*, the Faculty of Advocates or the Bar Council of Northern Ireland;

(ii) the applicant is a member, and entitled to practise as such, of an *Establishment Directive profession*;

Authorisation and
Practising Requirements

(iii)   the applicant is a national of an *Establishment Directive* state;

(iv)   the applicant applies with the intention of *practising* on a permanent basis in the *UK* and is legally entitled to do so;

(v)   the applicant is not struck off the register, suspended from the register, or subject to a direction of the *Tribunal* prohibiting his or her restoration to the register;

(vi)   the applicant has supplied satisfactory evidence that he or she will comply with or be exempt from the SRA Indemnity Insurance Rules; and

(vii)   the application is made in accordance with these regulations,

except that if the *SRA* has reasonable cause to believe that the applicant is not a fit and proper person to *practise* in the *UK* it may refuse an application for initial registration.

(b)   The *SRA* must not grant the application unless the conditions in (a)(i) to (vi) are met.

(c)   The provisions of (a)(i) above will not apply to prevent the renewal of the registration of a European *lawyer* who has become a solicitor of Scotland or Northern Ireland at a time when he or she was registered both with the *SRA* and with the Law Society of Scotland and/or the Law Society of Northern Ireland.

2.4   Where application is made under regulation 2 for initial registration or for renewal of registration in the *register of foreign lawyers*, the following provisions apply.

(a)   The *SRA* may grant the application (subject to such conditions as it may think fit) if:

(i)   the applicant is not a *solicitor*, *REL* or barrister;

(ii)   the applicant is a member, and entitled to practise as such, of a legal profession which is regulated within a jurisdiction outside England and Wales and is approved by the *SRA* in accordance with paragraph 2(2) of Schedule 14 to the Courts and Legal Services Act 1990;

(iii)   the applicant is not struck off the register, subject to an order of the *Tribunal* suspending his or her registration or subject to a direction of the *Tribunal* prohibiting his or her restoration to the register; and

(iv)   the application is made in accordance with these regulations.

(b)   The *SRA* may (without prejudice to its general discretion under paragraph 2 of Schedule 14 to the Courts and Legal Services Act 1990) reject the application if:

(i)   the *SRA* is not satisfied that the applicant is eligible for registration;

(ii)   the applicant is prohibited by the rules of his or her profession from *practising* as a *manager* of a *recognised body*;

      (iii) the *SRA* is not satisfied that the applicant will be in compliance with the SRA Indemnity Insurance Rules;

      (iv) the *SRA* is not satisfied that the applicant intends to *practise* in the capacity of an *RFL* in accordance with Rule 3 of the *SRA Practice Framework Rules*; or

      (v) the *SRA* is not satisfied that the applicant is a fit and proper person to *practise* as an *RFL*.

(c) A person who has been reinstated to the register under paragraph 12 of Schedule 14 to the Courts and Legal Services Act 1990 is to be treated as entitled to practise as a member of his or her home legal profession.

2.5 The granting of a practising certificate or registration free of conditions under regulation 2 does not prevent the *SRA* subsequently imposing a condition in accordance with regulation 7.

Regulation 3: Application following certain events

3.1 Regulation 3 applies to an initial application for a practising certificate, an application for replacement of a practising certificate, an initial application for registration in the *register of European lawyers* and an application for renewal of registration in the *register of European lawyers*, in any of the following circumstances, subject to the exceptions set out in 3.3 below, relating for example to a previously declared event.

(a) The applicant has been:

      (i) reprimanded, made the subject of disciplinary sanction or made the subject of an order under section 43 of the *SA*, ordered to pay costs or made the subject of a recommendation to the *Society* or the *SRA* to consider imposing a condition, by the *Tribunal*, or struck off or suspended by the *court*;

      (ii) made the subject of an order under section 43 of the *SA* by the *Society* or the *SRA* or rebuked or fined under section 44D of that Act by the *SRA*;

      (iii) made the subject of an intervention by the *Society*, the *SRA* or by any other *approved regulator*, or been:

          (A) a *manager*, *interest holder* or *compliance officer*, of a *recognised body*;

          (B) a *compliance officer* of a *sole practitioner firm*;

          (C) a *manager*, *owner* or *compliance officer* of a *licensed body*;

          (D) a *manager* or *interest holder* of an *authorised non-SRA firm* which is not licensed under Part 5 of the *LSA*; or

          (E) a *manager*, *material interest* holder, *HOLP* or *HOFA* of an *authorised non-SRA firm* licensed under Part 5 of the *LSA*;

Authorisation and Practising Requirements

which has been the subject of an intervention by the *Society*, the *SRA* or by any other *approved regulator*;

(iv) made the subject of a disciplinary sanction by, or refused registration with or authorisation by, another *approved regulator*, professional or regulatory tribunal, or regulatory authority, whether in England and Wales or elsewhere;

(v) *disqualified* from acting as a *HOLP* or a *HOFA* or from being a *manager* of, or being employed by, a *licensed body* or an *authorised non-SRA firm*;

(vi) refused authorisation as a *recognised sole practitioner* or approval as a *compliance officer* of such a *firm* or had such authorisation revoked under regulation 10.2(b)(i), (iii), (iv) or (vi);

(vii) refused approval to be a *manager*, *owner* or *compliance officer* of an *authorised body* or had such approval withdrawn;

(viii) refused approval to be a *manager*, *material interest* holder, *HOLP* or *HOFA* of an *authorised non-SRA firm* or had such approval withdrawn;

(ix) a *manager*, *owner* or *compliance officer* of an *authorised body* the authorisation of which has been suspended or revoked by the *SRA* under Rule 22 of the *SRA Authorisation Rules*, except under 22.1(a)(vii);

(x) a *manager*, *material interest* holder, *HOLP* or *HOFA* of an *authorised non-SRA firm* the authorisation of which has been suspended or revoked by another *approved regulator*; or

(xi) made subject to a *revocation* of his or her practising certificate or registration under regulation 10.2(a)(i) or (v) or of his or her authorisation as a *recognised sole practitioner* under regulation 10.2(b)(i), (iv) or (vi).

(b) The *SRA* (or previously the *Society*) has requested an explanation from the applicant in respect of a matter relating to the applicant's conduct and has notified the applicant in writing that it does not regard the applicant's response, or lack of response, as satisfactory.

(c) The applicant has failed to obtain or deliver within the period allowed an accountant's report required by rules made under section 34 of the *SA*.

(d) The applicant's practising certificate or registration has been suspended and the suspension:

(i) has come to an end;

(ii) was continuing when the applicant's last practising certificate or previous registration expired or was revoked; or

(iii) is continuing.

(e) The applicant has been suspended from *practice* (or suspended from the register, if the applicant is a European *lawyer*), and the suspension has come to an end.

(f) The applicant's last practising certificate or previous registration expired or was revoked whilst subject to a condition.

(g) The applicant's practising certificate or registration is currently subject to a condition.

(h) The applicant's right to practise as a *lawyer* of another jurisdiction or as a *lawyer of England and Wales* (other than as a *solicitor*) is subject to a condition or restriction.

(i) The applicant has been restored to the roll or register, having previously been struck off.

(j) The applicant is an undischarged bankrupt.

(k) The applicant:

    (i) has been adjudged bankrupt and discharged;

    (ii) has entered into an individual voluntary arrangement or a partnership voluntary arrangement under the Insolvency Act 1986;

    (iii) has at any time during the last 36 months of trading of a *recognised body*, a *licensed body* or an *authorised non-SRA firm* which has entered into a voluntary arrangement under the Insolvency Act 1986, been a *manager* of that *recognised body*, *licensed body* or *authorised non-SRA firm*;

    (iv) has at any time during the last 36 months of trading of a *company* or of an *LLP* which has been the subject of a winding up order, an administration order or administrative receivership; or has entered into a voluntary arrangement under the Insolvency Act 1986; or has been voluntarily wound up in circumstances of insolvency, been a *director* of that company or a *member* of that LLP.

(l) The applicant lacks capacity (within the meaning of the Mental Capacity Act 2005) and powers under sections 15 to 20 or section 48 of that Act are exercisable in relation to the applicant.

(m) The applicant has been committed to prison in civil or criminal proceedings and:

    (i) has been released; or

    (ii) has not been released.

(n) The applicant has been made subject to a judgment which involves the payment of money, other than one:

    (i) which is limited to the payment of costs; or

Authorisation and Practising Requirements

(ii) in respect of which the applicant is entitled to indemnity or relief from another person as to the whole sum; or

(iii) which the applicant has paid, and supplied evidence of payment to the *SRA* (or previously to the *Society*).

(o) The applicant is currently charged with an indictable offence.

(p) The applicant has been convicted of an indictable offence or any offence under the *SA*, the Financial Services and Markets Act 2000, the Immigration and Asylum Act 1999 or the Compensation Act 2006.

(q) The applicant has been disqualified from being a *company director*.

(r) The applicant is disqualified from being a *charity* trustee or trustee for a *charity* under section 178(1)(D) or (E) of the Charities Act 2011.

(s) The applicant has been the subject in another jurisdiction of any circumstance equivalent to those listed in (j) to (r).

3.2 If regulation 3 applies, the *SRA*:

(a) has no discretion under regulation 3 to grant the application if the applicant does not meet the conditions in regulation 2.2(a) to (c) or 2.3(a)(i) to (vi);

(b) has discretion to impose a condition or conditions in accordance with regulation 7; and

(c) has discretion to refuse the application.

3.3 The provisions of 3.1 and 3.2 above are subject to the following exceptions.

(a) Regulation 3 does not apply by virtue of 3.1(a), (b), (c), (d)(i), (e), (j), (k), (m)(i), (n), (o), (p), (q), (r) or (s) if the applicant has previously applied for and obtained a practising certificate or registration, provided that:

(i) the applicant's practising certificate or registration is not subject to a condition relating to any of those provisions;

(ii) the *SRA* (or previously the *Society*) was aware, when granting that application, of all the relevant facts; and

(iii) no new circumstances have arisen which would bring the application within any of those provisions.

(b) If regulation 3 applies only by virtue of 3.1(j), (m), (n) or (p) and an appeal has been made to the appropriate *court* against the order or judgment in question, the following provisions apply.

(i) The application must not be refused before the determination of that appeal, unless in the opinion of the *SRA* the proceedings on that appeal have been unduly protracted by the appellant or are unlikely to be successful.

(ii) The *SRA* may in the meantime postpone a decision on the application and may impose a condition on the applicant's practising certificate or registration.

(c) If regulation 3 applies only by virtue of 3.1(o), the application may not be refused unless the applicant is convicted, but the *SRA* may postpone a decision on the application and may impose a condition on the applicant's practising certificate or registration.

Guidance notes

(i) "In writing" includes any form of written electronic communication normally used for business purposes, such as emails.

(ii) Exceptions to the application of Regulation 3 are set out at 3.3. An applicant is not, for example, subject to Regulation 3 in respect of a previously declared event where the SRA was aware of all the relevant facts and issued a practising certificate or registered the applicant as a European lawyer free from conditions, and where no new circumstances have arisen to bring the application within Regulation 3.

Regulation 4: Requirements for sole practitioners

4.1 An application may be made under regulation 4 by a *solicitor* or European *lawyer*:

(a) for initial authorisation as a *recognised sole practitioner*:

(i) when making an initial application for a practising certificate or for registration in the *register of European lawyers*;

(ii) when applying for replacement of a practising certificate or for renewal of registration in the *register of European lawyers*; or

(iii) at any time during the currency of a *solicitor's* practising certificate or an *REL's* registration; or

(b) for renewal of an existing authorisation as a *recognised sole practitioner* when applying for replacement of a practising certificate or for renewal of registration in the *register of European lawyers*.

4.2 When the *SRA* may grant an application

(a) The *SRA* may grant an application under regulation 4 if the applicant:

(i) will be *practising* as a *sole practitioner from an office* in England and Wales;

(ii) is not, and is not about to be made, subject to a condition on his or her practising certificate or registration which would prohibit *practice* as a *sole practitioner*;

(iii) has adopted a name under which his or her *firm* is to be recognised, and which will comply with Chapter 8 of the *SRA Code of Conduct* (Publicity);

Authorisation and Practising Requirements

(iv) will comply with (or has a waiver of) Rule 12 of the *SRA Practice Framework Rules* (Persons who must be qualified to supervise);

(v) will comply with the SRA Indemnity Insurance Rules in respect of his or her *firm*; and

(vi) will comply with regulation 4.8 (Compliance officers).

(b) The *SRA* may refuse an application under regulation 4 if it is not satisfied that the applicant is suitable to run and manage a business providing regulated legal services or if for any other reason the *SRA* reasonably considers that it would be against the public interest to grant recognition.

(c) In reaching a decision on an application under regulation 4 the *SRA* may take into account:

(i) any event listed in regulation 3.1 applying to the applicant;

(ii) any other conduct on the part of the applicant which calls into question his or her honesty, integrity or respect for law;

(iii) failure or refusal to disclose, or an attempt to conceal, any matter within (i) or (ii) above in relation to the application; or

(iv) that the *SRA* is not satisfied that the applicant has sufficient skills or knowledge in relation to the running and management of a business which provides regulated legal services.

(d) When granting an application under regulation 4 the *SRA* may impose a condition on the applicant's practising certificate or registration in accordance with regulation 7.

4.3   If a change to the composition of a *recognised body* or a *licensed body* which was a *partnership* results in a *solicitor* or *REL* becoming its sole *principal*:

(a) the *SRA* must be notified within seven days; and

(b) temporary emergency recognition may be granted, subject to 4.4 below, so as to enable that sole *principal* to continue in *practice* without breach of Rule 1 or Rule 2, as appropriate, of the *SRA Practice Framework Rules*.

4.4   Application for temporary emergency recognition

(a) An application for temporary emergency recognition must be made on the *prescribed* form within seven days of the change and accompanied by all information and documentation the *SRA* reasonably requires.

(b) The *SRA* may grant an application for temporary emergency recognition if the following conditions are met:

(i) the *SRA* must be satisfied that the applicant could not reasonably have commenced an application for recognition as a *sole practitioner* in advance of the change; and

(ii) the *sole practitioner*:

      (A) must be *practising from an office* in England and Wales;

      (B) is not, and is not about to be made, subject to a condition on his or her practising certificate or registration which would prohibit *practice* as a *sole practitioner*;

      (C) must have adopted a name under which the *firm* is to be recognised, and which complies with Chapter 8 of the *SRA Code of Conduct* (Publicity);

      (D) must comply with or have a waiver of Rule 12 of the *SRA Practice Framework Rules* (Persons who must be qualified to supervise);

      (E) must comply with the SRA Indemnity Insurance Rules in respect of his or her *firm*; and

      (F) will comply with regulation 4.8 (Compliance officers).

(c) Temporary emergency recognition:

    (i)   may be granted initially for 28 days;

    (ii)   may be granted to have effect from the date of the *partnership* split or any other appropriate subsequent date;

    (iii) may be extended for a further specified period or periods in response to a reasonable request by the applicant;

    (iv) must be extended (subject to (viii) below) pending determination of a substantive application for initial recognition commenced during the currency of a temporary emergency recognition;

    (v)   may be granted or extended subject to such conditions as the *SRA* thinks fit, in circumstances falling within regulation 7;

    (vi) is to be treated as initial recognition for the purpose of these regulations;

    (vii) if granted, cannot prejudice the discretion of the *SRA* to refuse a substantive application for recognition under this regulation (which is also, for the purpose of these regulations, to be treated as initial recognition); and

    (viii) in exceptional circumstances, and for reasonable cause, may be revoked at any time.

4.5 If a *recognised sole practitioner* dies:

(a) the *SRA* must be notified within seven days;

(b) within 28 days of the death an emergency application may be made, on the *prescribed* form, for recognition in the capacity of personal representative, practice manager or *employee* by a *solicitor* or an *REL* who is:

    (i)   the *sole practitioner's* executor;

Authorisation and Practising Requirements

(ii) a practice manager appointed by the *sole practitioner's* personal representatives;

(iii) an *employee* of the *firm*.

4.6   If the application for recognition in the capacity of personal representative, practice manager or *employee* is granted:

(a) recognition will be deemed to run from the date of death;

(b) recognition will not be renewed for any period after the winding up of the estate or 12 months from the date of death, whichever is the earlier.

4.7   Regulatory compliance and suitable arrangements for compliance

(a) A *recognised sole practitioner* must ensure that:

(i) any obligations imposed from time to time on the *firm* or its *employees* by or under the *SRA's regulatory arrangements* are complied with; and

(ii) any other statutory obligations imposed on the *firm* or its *employees*, in relation to the *firm's* carrying on of *authorised activities*, are complied with.

(b) A *recognised sole practitioner* must at all times have suitable arrangements in place to ensure that:

(i) the *firm* and its *employees* comply with the *SRA's regulatory arrangements* as they apply to them, as required under section 176 of the *LSA* and regulation 4.7(a); and

(ii) the *firm* and its *employees* who are *authorised persons* maintain the *professional principles*.

4.8   Compliance officers

(a) A *recognised sole practitioner* must have suitable arrangements in place to ensure that the *firm's compliance officers* are able to discharge their duties in accordance with these regulations.

(b) Subject to regulation 4.8(h) a *recognised sole practitioner's firm* must at all times have an individual:

(i) who is:

(A) the *sole practitioner*; or

(B) an *employee* of the *firm* of sufficient seniority and in a position of sufficient responsibility to fulfil the role;

(ii) who is designated as its *COLP*; and

(iii) whose designation is approved by the *SRA*.

(c) The *COLP* must:

(i) take all reasonable steps to:

(A) ensure compliance with the *SRA's regulatory arrangements* except any obligation imposed under the *SRA Accounts Rules*;

(B) ensure compliance with any statutory obligations of the *recognised sole practitioner* and any *employees* of the *firm*; and

(C) record any failure so to comply and make such records available to the *SRA* on request; and

(ii) as soon as reasonably practicable, report to the *SRA* any material failure so to comply (a failure may be material either taken on its own or as part of a pattern of failure so to comply).

(d) Subject to regulation 4.8(i) a *recognised sole practitioner's firm* must at all times have an individual:

(i) who is:

(A) the *sole practitioner*; or

(B) an *employee* of the *firm* of sufficient seniority and in a position of sufficient responsibility to fulfil the role;

(ii) who is designated as its *COFA*; and

(iii) whose designation is approved by the *SRA*.

(e) The *COFA* must:

(i) take all reasonable steps to:

(A) ensure compliance with any obligations imposed upon the *recognised sole practitioner* or any *employees* of the *firm* under the *SRA Accounts Rules*; and

(B) record any failure so to comply and make such records available to the *SRA* on request; and

(ii) as soon as reasonably practicable, report to the *SRA* any material failure so to comply (a failure may be material either taken on its own or as part of a pattern of failure so to comply).

(f) The *SRA* may approve an individual's designation as a *COLP* or *COFA* if it is satisfied that the individual is a suitable person to carry out his or her duties. When considering whether a candidate should be approved under regulation 4.9, the *SRA* will take into account the criteria set out in the *SRA Suitability Test* and any other relevant information.

(g) A designation of an individual as *COLP* or *COFA* has effect only while the individual:

(i) is authorised as a *recognised sole practitioner*, where the *compliance officer* is the *recognised sole practitioner*;

(ii) consents to the designation and continues to be an *employee* of the *firm*, where the *compliance officer* is an *employee*;

Authorisation and
Practising Requirements

(iii) in the case of a *COLP*:

    (A) is not *disqualified* from acting as a *HOLP*;

    (B) is:

       (I) a *lawyer of England and Wales*;

       (II) an *REL*; or

       (III) registered with the *BSB* under Regulation 17 of the European Communities (Lawyer's Practice) Regulations 2000 (SI 2000/1119);

and is an *authorised person* in relation to one or more of the *reserved legal activities* which the body is authorised to carry on; and

(iv) in the case of a *COFA*, is not *disqualified* from acting as a *HOFA*.

(h) A *recognised sole practitioner's firm* is not required to comply with regulation 4.8(b)(i) where the individual designated as its *COLP*:

    (i) has been approved by the *SRA* as a *COLP* for a *related authorised body*; and

    (ii) is a *manager* or *employee* of that *related authorised body*.

(i) A *recognised sole practitioner's firm* is not required to comply with regulation 4.8(d)(i) where the individual designated as its *COFA*:

    (i) has been approved by the *SRA* as a *COFA* for a *related authorised body*; and

    (ii) is a *manager* or *employee* of that *related authorised body*.

4.9   Approval of compliance officers

(a) An application for approval of a *compliance officer* may be made by a *recognised sole practitioner* or a *solicitor* or *REL* applying under regulation 4.1 to be a *recognised sole practitioner* (in regulation 4.9, the person applying for approval of a *compliance officer* is referred to as "the applicant").

(b) The application must include evidence to satisfy the *SRA* that the person to be approved (in regulations 4.8 to 4.10 referred to as "the candidate") is suitable to be a *compliance officer* of the *firm*.

(c) The applicant must:

    (i) secure the co-operation of a candidate who is an *employee*, to assist the *SRA* to obtain all information and documentation the *SRA* requires in order to determine the application for approval;

    (ii) obtain all other information and documentation in relation to the candidate which the *prescribed* form requires the applicant to obtain and keep; and

    (iii) keep all information and documentation under (ii) above for a period of not less than 6 years after the individual concerned has ceased to be a *compliance officer* of the *firm*.

(d) Where the candidate is an *employee*, he or she must declare in writing on the face of the application that the information supplied about them is correct and complete.

(e) The *SRA's* decision to approve or refuse approval must be notified in writing to the applicant and, where the candidate is an *employee*, separately to the candidate.

(f) In accordance with regulation 7, the *SRA* may at the time of granting its approval or at any time subsequently, make its approval of a person to be a *compliance officer* subject to such conditions as it considers appropriate on the practising certificate or registration of:

    (i)   the *recognised sole practitioner*; and

    (ii)   if applicable, the *compliance officer*.

4.10   Effect of approval of compliance officers

(a) Approval takes effect from the date of the decision unless otherwise stated, and remains effective only if the candidate takes up the position for which he or she has been approved within the period specified in the notice of approval.

(b) Subject to regulation 4.10(a), approval continues until:

    (i)   it is withdrawn by the *SRA*; or

    (ii)   the approved person ceases to be a *compliance officer* of the *firm*.

4.11   Withdrawal of approval of compliance officers

(a) Where the *SRA* has granted an approval under regulation 4.9, it may subsequently withdraw its approval of a person to be a *compliance officer* if:

    (i)   it is not satisfied that the person met or meets the criteria for approval;

    (ii)   it is satisfied that a condition imposed on the practising certificate or registration of the *recognised sole practitioner* or the *compliance officer* has not been, or is not being, complied with;

    (iii) it is satisfied that the person has breached a duty or obligation imposed upon them in or under the *SRA's regulatory arrangements* or any enactments; or

    (iv) information or documentation is not promptly supplied in response to a request made under regulation 4.13(d).

4.12   Temporary emergency approvals for compliance officers

(a) If the *firm* ceases to have a *COLP* or *COFA* whose designation has been

Authorisation and
Practising Requirements

approved by the *SRA*, the *recognised sole practitioner* must immediately and in any event within seven days:

(i)   notify the *SRA*;

(ii) designate another individual to replace the *firm's* previous *COLP* or *COFA*, as appropriate; and

(iii) make an application to the *SRA* for temporary approval of the new *COLP* or *COFA*, as appropriate.

(b) The *SRA* may grant a temporary approval under this regulation if:

(i)   it is satisfied that the *recognised sole practitioner* could not reasonably have commenced an application for approval of designation in advance of the non-compliance; and

(ii) on the face of the application and any other information immediately before the *SRA*, there is no evidence suggesting that the new *compliance officer* is not suitable to carry out the duties imposed on them under these regulations.

(c) Temporary approval under this regulation:

(i)   may be granted initially for 28 days;

(ii) may be granted to have effect from the date the *firm* ceases to have a *COLP* or *COFA* whose designation has been approved;

(iii) may be extended in response to a reasonable request by the *recognised sole practitioner*;

(iv) must be extended pending determination of a substantive application for approval commenced in accordance with regulation 4.9;

(v)   may be granted or extended subject to such conditions as it considers appropriate on the practising certificate or registration of:

(A) the *recognised sole practitioner*; and

(B) if applicable, the *compliance officer*;

(vi) has effect only while the criteria in regulation 4.8(g) are met;

(vii) if granted, cannot prejudice the discretion of the *SRA* to refuse a substantive application for approval of designation or to impose any conditions on that approval; and

(viii) in exceptional circumstances, and for reasonable cause, may be withdrawn at any time.

(d) If granted temporary approval under regulation 4.12(c) above for the designation of a new *COLP* or *COFA*, the *recognised sole practitioner* must:

(i)   designate a permanent *COLP* or *COFA*, as appropriate; and

(ii) submit a substantive application for approval of that designation under regulation 4.9;

before the expiry of the temporary approval or any extension of that approval by the *SRA*.

4.13 Information requirements

(a) A *recognised sole practitioner* must properly complete and provide to the *SRA* an information report on an annual basis or such other period as specified by the *SRA* in the *prescribed* form and by the *prescribed* date.

(b) A *recognised sole practitioner* must provide any necessary permissions for information to be given to the *SRA* so as to enable it to:

(i) use and prepare a report on the documents produced under (a) above; and

(ii) seek verification from *clients*, *employees* or any other body including banks, building societies or other financial institutions.

(c) A *recognised sole practitioner* must notify the *SRA* as soon as he or she:

(i) becomes aware of any changes to relevant information about himself or herself, the *firm* or any *employees* of the *firm* including any non-compliance with these regulations and any conditions on the *recognised sole practitioner's* practising certificate or registration; or

(ii) becomes aware of or has information that reasonably suggests that he or she has or may have provided the *SRA* with information which was or may have been false, misleading, incomplete or inaccurate, or has or may have changed in a materially significant way.

(d) The *SRA* may at any time require the production of information or documentation from a *recognised sole practitioner* or a person approved as a *compliance officer* of the *firm* in order to satisfy the *SRA* that that person met, meets, or continues to meet the criteria for approval as suitable to be a *compliance officer*.

4.14 Waivers

(a) Subject to provisions in any statutory obligations or the *SRA's regulatory arrangements* affecting its ability to waive any requirements, the *SRA* shall have power to waive in writing the provisions of regulations 4.8, 4.9, 4.12 and 4.13 for a particular purpose or purposes expressed in such waiver, and to attach conditions to or revoke such waiver, at its own discretion.

4.15 Condition relating to the cessation period for indemnity purposes

(a) When a *recognised sole practitioner's firm* becomes subject to cover under the *cessation period*, it must immediately, and for the duration of the *cessation period*, desist from carrying out any *legal activities*, save that it may undertake work required to discharge its obligations within the scope of *existing instructions*, or which is necessary in connection with the discharge of such obligations.

Guidance notes

(i)   The approval process for authorisation under regulation 4 will cease when recognised sole practitioners are passported to become recognised bodies and are transitioned to be regulated under the SRA Authorisation Rules. The SRA will establish a process for those practising as recognised sole practitioners at that time to be deemed approved as managers and owners for the purpose of Rule 8.6 of the SRA Authorisation Rules.

(ii)   The SRA's outcomes focused approach to regulation means that the SRA will take into account all of the circumstances relevant to any issue of compliance, whether in relation to the regulatory arrangements or in respect of statutory obligations on firms and those in them. This will include taking into account the evidence that firms and individuals can produce to demonstrate their efforts to ensure compliance (by themselves or others).

(iii)   Regulation 4.7(b) deals with the need for recognised sole practitioners to have suitable arrangements for compliance (see also Chapter 7 of the SRA Code of Conduct (Management of your business)). What needs to be covered by a firm's compliance plan will depend on factors such as the size and nature of the firm, its work and its areas of risk. Solicitors and RELs will need to analyse the effectiveness of their proposed compliance arrangements before applying for authorisation as a sole practitioner and monitor effectiveness on an on-going basis once authorised. Common areas for consideration will include:

(a)   clearly defined governance arrangements providing a transparent framework for responsibilities within the firm;

(b)   appropriate accounting procedures;

(c)   a system for ensuring that only the appropriate people authorise payments from client account;

(d)   a system for ensuring that undertakings are given only when intended, and compliance with them is monitored and enforced;

(e)   appropriate checks on new staff or contractors;

(f)   a system for ensuring that basic regulatory deadlines are not missed e.g. obtaining or delivery of the firm's accountant's report (in accordance with rule 32 of the SRA Accounts Rules 2011), arranging indemnity cover, renewal of practising certificates and registrations, renewal of all lawyers' licences to practise and provision of regulatory information;

(g)   a system for monitoring, reviewing and managing risks;

(h)   ensuring that issues of conduct are given appropriate weight in decisions the firm takes, whether on client matters or firm-based issues such as funding;

(i)   file reviews;

(j)   appropriate systems for supporting the development and training of staff;

(k)   obtaining the necessary approvals of COLP/COFA;

(l)   arrangements to ensure that any duties to clients and others are fully met even when staff are absent.

(iv)   The roles of COLP and COFA are a fundamental part of a firm's compliance and governance arrangements. COLPs' and COFAs' ability to take the steps they need to ensure compliance is dependent on the firm having suitable arrangements in place under regulation 4.7. So, for example, the recognised sole practitioner must therefore ensure that any employee designated as the firm's COLP or COFA is of sufficient seniority, in a position of sufficient power and responsibility and has clear reporting lines to enable them to have access to all management systems and arrangements and all other relevant information including client files and business information. The existence of compliance officers in a firm who are employees and the requirements on them to ensure that the firm, as well as its employees, are complying with the regulatory arrangements (COLP) and the SRA Accounts Rules (COFA) is not a substitute for the recognised sole practitioner's responsibilities and their obligations to comply with regulation 4.7 (Regulatory compliance and suitable arrangements for compliance). Recognised sole practitioners need to take care not to obstruct, whether intentionally or unwittingly, a COLP or COFA employee in fulfilling their role.

(v)   COLPs and COFAs are responsible for ensuring that the firm has systems and controls in place to enable the firm, as well as its employees, to comply with the requirements on them. Recognised sole practitioners are not absolved from any of their own obligations and remain fully responsible for compliance (see regulation 4.7).

(vi)   Those designated as COLP will need to be in a position to be able to discharge the role. They will need to consider whether they are in a position to, for example:

(a)   take all reasonable steps to ensure compliance with the SRA's regulatory arrangements by the firm and its employees; and with relevant statutory obligations e.g.

(A)   that authorised persons and other employees comply with the duty imposed by section 176 of the LSA (duty to comply with the SRA's regulatory arrangements);

(B)   under the LSA and the SA in respect of practice matters;

(b)   as soon as reasonably practicable, report to the SRA any material failure to comply, whether such failure is material either on its own or because it forms part of a pattern of non-compliance. The immediacy of the report will depend on the circumstances and seriousness of the breach.

(vii)   Those designated as COFA will need to be in a position to be able to discharge the role. They will need to consider whether they are in a position to, for example:

(a)   ensure that they have access to all accounting records;

(b) carry out regular checks on the accounting systems;

(c) carry out file and ledger reviews;

(d) ensure that the reporting accountant has prompt access to all the information needed to complete the accountant's report;

(e) take steps to ensure that breaches of the SRA Accounts Rules are remedied promptly;

(f) monitor, review and manage risks to compliance with the SRA Accounts Rules;

(g) as soon as reasonably practicable, report to the SRA any material failure to comply with the SRA Accounts Rules, whether such failure is material either on its own or because it forms part of a pattern of non-compliance. The immediacy of the report will depend on the circumstances and seriousness of the breach.

(viii) In considering whether a failure is "material", the COLP or COFA, as appropriate, will need to take account of various factors, such as:

(a) the detriment, or risk of detriment, to clients;

(b) the extent of any risk of loss of confidence in the firm or in the provision of legal services;

(c) the scale of the issue;

(d) the overall impact on the firm, its clients and third parties.

In addition, the COLP/COFA will need to keep appropriate records of failures in compliance to:

(e) monitor overall compliance with obligations;

(f) assess the effectiveness of the firm's systems;

(g) be able to decide when the need has arisen to report breaches which are material because they form a pattern.

(ix) In developing their governance and administrative arrangements recognised sole practitioners will need to consider how they approach unexpected risks such as the absence of key staff, including COLP and COFA, and whether the nature of the absence will trigger the need to notify the SRA (see regulation 4.12) and to obtain approval for a replacement.

(x) Approval of compliance officers under regulation 4.9 relates only to the role for which it is granted. Any change from one role that requires approval to another, will require a further approval and firms need to ensure that they notify the SRA of any changes and apply for fresh approvals, as necessary.

(xi) The period specified in the notice of approval in regulation 4.10(a) will normally be 90 days although may be varied in individual cases.

(xii) Regulation 4.13 imposes information requirements on recognised sole practitioners. As well as the annual information report, firms must update the SRA by giving details of general changes that occur in respect of the firm. Other reporting and information requirements that apply to individuals or firms include:

(a) SRA requirements

(A) Regulations 1.2, 4.3, 4.5, 4.8, 4.12 and 15 of these regulations;

(B) Rule 18 of the SRA Practice Framework Rules;

(C) Rule 32 of the SRA Accounts Rules;

(D) Chapter 10 of the Code of Conduct;

(E) Rule 17.3 of the SRA Indemnity Insurance Rules 2013 or any subsequent rules thereto;

(F) Rule 3 of the SRA Overseas Rules.

(b) Statutory requirements

(A) Section 84 of the SA (notification of a solicitor's place of business).

Regulation 5: Fee determinations for acquisitions, mergers and splits

The turnover of a *recognised sole practitioner* for the purpose of determining the fee for renewal of authorisation as a *recognised sole practitioner* is based on a historic turnover figure submitted to the *SRA*. Where in the 12 months following the submission of that figure a *recognised sole practitioner* merges or splits, a notice of succession identifying all *recognised bodies*, *licensed bodies* and *recognised sole practitioners* affected by the merger or split and any resulting apportionment of historic turnover figures for those *firms* will enable the *SRA* to ensure that the turnover figure on which the fee is based reflects the impact of the merger or split.

5.1 A *recognised sole practitioner* who has succeeded to the whole or a part of one or more *recognised bodies*, *licensed bodies* or *recognised sole practitioners* must within 28 days of the change taking place deliver to the *SRA* a notice of succession in the *prescribed* form.

5.2 For the purposes of regulation 5.1, "succeeded" includes any taking over of the whole or any part of a *recognised body*, *licensed body* or *recognised sole practitioner*, for value or otherwise.

5.3 A *recognised sole practitioner* who:

(a) has split or ceded part of the *practice* to a *recognised body*, *licensed body* or *recognised sole practitioner*; and

(b) wishes this change to be considered by the *SRA* when determining the *recognised sole practitioner's* next fee for renewal of authorisation as a *recognised sole practitioner* must within 28 days of the change taking place deliver to the *SRA* a notice of succession in the *prescribed* form.

5.4   A notice of succession delivered under these regulations must:

(a)   identify all *recognised bodies, licensed bodies* and *recognised sole practitioners* affected by the succession; and

(b)   provide details of any resulting apportionment of the turnover figures for those *recognised bodies, licensed bodies* and *recognised sole practitioners*.

5.5   A *recognised sole practitioner* delivering a notice of succession under these regulations must seek the agreement of all affected *recognised bodies, licensed bodies* or *recognised sole practitioners* to the contents of the notice of succession.

5.6   Where a notice of succession is delivered to the *SRA* which has not been agreed by all affected *recognised bodies, licensed bodies* or *recognised sole practitioners*, the *recognised sole practitioner* delivering the notice of succession shall be treated as having made an application for the *SRA* to apportion the turnover figures of the affected *recognised bodies, licensed bodies* or *recognised sole practitioners* for the purposes of determining the fee for renewal of recognition.

5.7   Before apportioning the turnover figures under regulation 5.6, the *SRA* will contact any affected *recognised body, licensed body* or *recognised sole practitioner* identified in the notice of succession who has not agreed with the notice of succession and may require the production of additional information.

5.8   A turnover figure submitted to the *SRA* under this regulation shall be calculated in accordance with the *SRA's prescribed* method of calculation.

Guidance note

(i)   Regulation 5 will be repealed when Rule 8.3 of the SRA Authorisation Rules (which contains equivalent provisions) comes into force for sole practitioners.

Regulation 6: Applications for reinstatement

6.1   The following applications are to be treated as made under these regulations:

(a)   an application for reinstatement of a suspended practising certificate or suspended registration in the *register of European lawyers* under section 16(3) of the *SA*; and

(b)   an application for reinstatement of a suspended registration in the *register of foreign lawyers* under paragraph 12(2) of Schedule 14 to the Courts and Legal Services Act 1990 or under section 16(3)(b) of the *SA*.

Regulation 7: Conditions

7.1   The *SRA* may impose one or more conditions on a practising certificate or on the registration of a European *lawyer* when granting an application under regulation 3 to 6, or at any time during the practising year, for the following purposes.

(a)   The *SRA* considers the individual concerned unsuitable to undertake certain activities in relation to a legal *practice*, either at all or save as specified in the condition, and that imposing the condition will, in the public interest, limit, restrict, halt or prevent the involvement of the individual concerned in those activities.

(b)   The *SRA* considers that the individual concerned is putting or is likely to put at risk the interests of *clients*, third parties or the public by taking certain steps in relation to a legal *practice*, and that imposing the condition will, in the public interest, limit, restrict, halt or prevent the taking of such steps by the individual concerned.

(c)   The *SRA* considers the individual concerned unsuitable to engage in certain business agreements, business associations or *practising* arrangements and that imposing a condition requiring the applicant to obtain the *SRA's* written approval before taking certain steps will, in the public interest, limit, halt or prevent a risk to *clients*, third parties or the public.

(d)   The *SRA* considers that imposing the condition will, in the public interest, require the individual concerned to take specified steps conducive to the carrying on of efficient *practice* by the individual concerned.

(e)   The *SRA* considers that imposing the condition will, in the public interest, facilitate closer monitoring by the *SRA* of compliance by the individual concerned with rules and regulations.

(f)   The *SRA* considers that it would be in the public interest to impose the condition in any other case during the currency of a practising certificate or registration.

7.2   Without prejudice to the powers of the *SRA* under paragraph 2A, 12 or 13 of Schedule 14 to the Courts and Legal Services Act 1990, the *SRA* may when granting an application under regulation 2.1(c) or at any time during the currency of a registration, impose such conditions on a *foreign lawyer's* registration as it sees fit:

(a)   if any event listed in regulation 3.1 applies to the individual concerned;

(b)   for a purpose within regulation 7.1(a) to (f); or

(c)   where the *SRA* considers in any other case that imposing the condition would be in the public interest.

7.3   When the *SRA* decides, on an initial application for a practising certificate or registration or on an application for replacement of a practising certificate or renewal of registration, to grant the application subject to a condition:

**Authorisation and
Practising Requirements**

(a) the *SRA* may postpone the issue of the certificate or the registration pending determination or discontinuance of any appeal; but

(b) the postponement may be rescinded if in the *SRA's* opinion proceedings on appeal have been unduly protracted by an appellant or are unlikely to be successful.

7.4   Notice and effective date of conditions

(a) The *SRA* must, subject to (b) below, give 28 days written notice, with reasons, to the individual concerned, when the *SRA* decides to impose a condition on a practising certificate or registration, except when conditions are imposed in the following applications:

   (i)   initial application for a practising certificate;

   (ii) initial application for registration in the *register of European lawyers* or in the *register of foreign lawyers*;

   (iii) application for replacement of a practising certificate;

   (iv) application for renewal of registration in the *register of European lawyers* or in the *register of foreign lawyers*;

   (v)   application for reinstatement under regulation 6.

(b) The *SRA* may shorten or dispense with the 28 day period under (a) if it is satisfied on reasonable grounds that it is in the public interest to do so.

(c) A condition is effective from the date on which the condition is imposed unless a later date is specified in the condition.

Regulation 8: Appeals

8.1   The rights of appeal conferred by regulation 8 supplement the statutory rights of appeal referred to in 8.4.

8.2   A person who is the subject of any of the following decisions has a right of appeal to the High Court against:

(a) *revocation*, under regulation 10.2(a)(i), (iii), (iv) or (v), of a *solicitor's* practising certificate;

(b) *revocation*, under regulation 10.2(b), of a *solicitor's* or European *lawyer's* authorisation as a *recognised sole practitioner*.

8.3   A *solicitor, REL* or *RFL* who is the subject of any decision in (a)-(d) below and/or the person who is the subject of a decision in (c) or (d) below may appeal under the *SRA's* own appeals procedure against:

(a) refusal to revoke a practising certificate or registration under regulation 10.2(c);

(b) refusal to withhold a *solicitor's*, European *lawyer's* or *foreign lawyer's* place of business from the relevant register under regulation 11, 12 or 13;

(c) refusal to approve a person as suitable to be a *compliance officer* under regulation 4.9;

(d) withdrawal of approval of a person as suitable to be a *compliance officer* under regulation 4.11.

8.4   A *solicitor*, European *lawyer* or *foreign lawyer* may invoke the *SRA's* own appeals procedure before exercising a right of appeal to the High Court:

(a) under section 13(1) of the *SA*, against refusal to issue or replace a practising certificate or refusal to renew registration in the *register of European lawyers*;

(b) under regulation 20 of the European Communities (Lawyer's Practice) Regulations 2000 (S.I. 2000/1119), against refusal to grant initial registration in the *register of European lawyers*;

(c) under paragraph 14 of Schedule 14 to the Courts and Legal Services Act 1990, against refusal to grant or renew registration in the *register of foreign lawyers*, or against a decision of the *SRA* to revoke his or her registration;

(d) under section 13(1) or 13ZA(6) of the *SA* or regulation 20 of the European Communities (Lawyer's Practice) Regulations 2000, against refusal to grant or renew authorisation of a *solicitor* or *REL* as a *recognised sole practitioner*;

(e) under section 13(1), 13ZA(6), 13A(6) or 16(5) of the *SA*, regulation 20 of the European Communities (Lawyer's Practice) Regulations 2000 or paragraph 14 of Schedule 14 to the Courts and Legal Services Act 1990, against the imposition of a condition on a practising certificate or the registration of a European *lawyer* or *foreign lawyer*;

(f) under section 13(2) or 13A(9) of the *SA*, against refusal of permission to take a step for which the *SRA's* permission is required under a condition on a practising certificate or the registration of a European *lawyer* or *foreign lawyer*;

(g) under section 13B(7) of the *SA*, against suspension of a practising certificate or suspension of registration in the *register of foreign lawyers*;

(h) under regulation 20 of the European Communities (Lawyer's Practice) Regulations 2000, against suspension of registration in the *register of European lawyers*;

(i) under section 13B(7) of the *SA*, against extension of suspension of a practising certificate or suspension of the registration of a European *lawyer* or *foreign lawyer*;

(j) under section 13B(7) of the *SA*, against suspension of authorisation of a *solicitor* or *REL* as a *recognised sole practitioner*;

(k) under section 16(5) of the *SA* or paragraph 14 of Schedule 14 to the Courts and Legal Services Act 1990, against refusal to reinstate a suspended practising certificate or the suspended registration of a European *lawyer* or *foreign lawyer*;

(l) under section 16(5) of the *SA*, against refusal to reinstate a suspended authorisation as a *recognised sole practitioner*;

(m) under regulation 20 of the European Communities (Lawyer's Practice) Regulations 2000 against *revocation* of registration in the *register of European lawyers*;

(n) under regulations 19 and 20 of the European Communities (Lawyer's Practice) Regulations 2000 against failure to determine, within four months, an application for initial registration in the *register of European lawyers*;

(o) under paragraph 14 of Schedule 14 to the Courts and Legal Services Act 1990, against failure to determine, within a reasonable time, an application for registration, renewal of registration or reinstatement of a suspended registration in the *register of foreign lawyers*;

(p) against a decision mentioned in regulation 8.2(a) or (b).

8.5 Deemed refusal

(a) If an application is made in accordance with regulation 1.1, and the *SRA* has not notified the applicant of its decision:

   (i) by the end of the 90th day, in the case of any application except an application for renewal of a practising certificate or registration which is made under regulation 3; or

   (ii) by the end of the 180th day, in the case of an application for renewal of a practising certificate or registration including, where applicable, the renewal of an existing authorisation as a *recognised sole practitioner* endorsed on the practising certificate or registration, which is made under regulation 3,

   the application is to be treated as having been refused and the refusal having been duly notified to the applicant on that day for the purpose of an appeal. For the avoidance of doubt, the fact that an application is treated as refused under regulation 8.5 does not prevent the application being granted or refused with reasons after expiry of the time limits above.

(b) The provisions of (a) above do not apply to an application from which an appeal lies under 8.4(n) or (o).

8.6 Appeal time limits

(a) Appeals under the *SRA's* own appeals procedure must be commenced within 28 days of notification of the relevant decision.

(b) Unless otherwise provided in the relevant statute, regulations or rules of Court or in the relevant decision, an appeal to the High Court must be commenced:

   (i) within the period of 28 days from the *date of notification* of the decision that is subject to appeal;

(ii) within a period of 28 days from the *date of notification* of the refusal of an appeal under the *SRA's* own appeals procedure; or

(iii) within a period of 28 days from the *date of notification* of the decision to impose a condition under the *SRA's* own appeals procedure,

as appropriate.

PART 2: DURATION, EXPIRY AND REVOCATION OF PRACTISING CERTIFICATES AND REGISTRATIONS

Regulation 9: Commencement, replacement and renewal dates

9.1 Commencement

(a) The commencement date for a practising certificate is the day on which it is entered in the register of holders of practising certificates as having commenced.

(b) The commencement date for registration in the *register of European lawyers* is the day on which the *lawyer's* name is entered in the register as having commenced.

(c) The commencement date for registration in the *register of foreign lawyers* is the day on which the *lawyer's* name is entered in the register as having commenced.

(d) The commencement date for authorisation as a *recognised sole practitioner* is the day on which the authorisation is entered in the register of holders of practising certificates or the *register of European lawyers* as having commenced.

9.2 Replacement and renewal

(a) The replacement date for a practising certificate is the 31 October following the issue of the certificate.

(b) The renewal date for registration in the *register of European lawyers* is the first 31 October following initial registration, and 31 October in each successive year.

(c) The renewal date for registration in the *register of foreign lawyers* is the first 31 October following initial registration, and 31 October in each successive year.

(d) The renewal date for authorisation as a *recognised sole practitioner* is the first 31 October following the initial authorisation, and 31 October in each successive year.

Guidance note

(i) When recognised sole practitioners are passported to become recognised bodies and transitioned to be regulated under the SRA Authorisation Rules, their recognition will become a lifetime recognition and annual renewal of recognition will not be necessary. Other requirements will apply annually to the firm, including Rule 8.3 (Payment of periodical fees) and 8.7 (Information requirements) of the SRA Authorisation Rules rather than those in regulation 4 above.

Regulation 10: Expiry and revocation

10.1   Expiry

  (a)   A practising certificate expires:

   (i)   when a replacement certificate is issued;

   (ii)   on the death of the *solicitor*;

   (iii)   if the *solicitor* is removed from or struck off the roll;

   (iv)   in the case of a practising certificate which is suspended, on its replacement date, or if its replacement date has passed, 14 days after the suspension took effect.

  (b)   The registration of an *REL* expires:

   (i)   if the *lawyer* becomes a *solicitor*, barrister or advocate of any of the *UK* jurisdictions or a barrister of the Irish Republic;

   (ii)   if the *lawyer* ceases to be a member, and entitled to practise as such, of an *Establishment Directive profession*;

   (iii)   if the *lawyer* ceases to be a national of an *Establishment Directive state*;

   (iv)   on the death of the *lawyer*;

   (v)   if the *lawyer* is removed from or struck off the register; or

   (vi)   in the case of a registration which is suspended, on its renewal date, or if its renewal date has passed, 14 days after the suspension took effect,

  except that the registration of a European *lawyer* will not expire by virtue of the *lawyer* becoming a solicitor of Scotland or Northern Ireland at a time when he or she is registered both with the *SRA* and with the Law Society of Scotland and/or the Law Society of Northern Ireland.

  (c)   The registration of an *RFL* expires:

   (i)   if the *lawyer* becomes a *solicitor*, *REL* or barrister;

   (ii)   if the *lawyer* ceases to be a member, and entitled to practise as such, of a legal profession which is regulated within a jurisdiction outside England and Wales and is approved by the *SRA* in accordance with paragraph 2(2) of Schedule 14 to the Courts and Legal Services Act 1990;

   (iii)   on the death of the *lawyer*;

   (iv)   if the *lawyer* is removed from or struck off the register; or

   (v)   in the case of a registration which is suspended, on its renewal date or if its renewal date has passed, 14 days after the suspension took effect.

(d) Authorisation as a *recognised sole practitioner* expires on:

(i) the expiry or *revocation* of the *solicitor's* practising certificate or the European *lawyer's* registration;

(ii) the imposition of a condition on the *solicitor's* practising certificate or the European *lawyer's* registration which prohibits *practice* as a *sole practitioner*; or

(iii) the date on which *recognised sole practitioners* are passported to become *recognised bodies* under Rule 28.2 of the *SRA Authorisation Rules.*

10.2 Revocation

(a) The *SRA* may revoke a practising certificate, registration in the *register of European lawyers* or registration in the *register of foreign lawyers*:

(i) at any time, if the *SRA* is satisfied that the practising certificate or registration was granted as a result of error or fraud;

(ii) on a date chosen by the *SRA*, if the replacement or renewal date has passed and the *SRA* has not received an application for replacement of the practising certificate or renewal of the registration made in accordance with regulation 1;

(iii) at any time, if the *SRA* is satisfied, in the case of an *REL*, that the *lawyer* has no intention of *practising* on a permanent basis in the *UK*;

(iv) at any time, if the *SRA* is satisfied, in the case of an *RFL*, that the *lawyer* has no intention of *practising* in the capacity of an *RFL* in accordance with Rule 3 of the *SRA Practice Framework Rules*; or

(v) on refusing, under regulation 2 or 3, to replace a practising certificate or to renew a registration.

(b) The *SRA* may revoke authorisation as a *recognised sole practitioner* at any time if:

(i) the authorisation as a *recognised sole practitioner* was granted as a result of error or fraud;

(ii) the *solicitor* or *REL* is not *practising from an office* in England and Wales;

(iii) the *SRA* is not satisfied that the *recognised sole practitioner* continues to meet the criteria for authorisation as a *recognised sole practitioner*;

(iv) the *recognised sole practitioner* or any *employee* of the *firm* fails to comply with the duties imposed under the *SRA's regulatory arrangements* or any statutory obligations, including failure to pay any fine or other financial penalty imposed by the *SRA*, the *Tribunal* or the High Court;

    (v)   the *recognised sole practitioner* has a temporary emergency recognition but has not within the initial 28 day period or any extension of that period commenced a substantive application for recognition; or

    (vi)   the *SRA* has decided under regulation 4 not to renew authorisation as a *recognised sole practitioner*.

(c)   The *SRA* may revoke a practising certificate, registration, or authorisation as a *recognised sole practitioner* on the application of the person concerned but:

    (i)   there is no discretion to refund any part of the fee paid for that practising year; and

    (ii)   the *SRA* may refuse the application if there is an outstanding complaint against the applicant or for any other reason relating to the public interest.

10.3   Notice of revocation

(a)   When the *SRA* decides to revoke a practising certificate, registration, or authorisation as a *recognised sole practitioner* under 10.2(a)(i), (iii), (iv) or (v) or 10.2(b) it must give the person concerned 28 days notice, with reasons. The notice may be given together with notification of refusal of an application to replace a practising certificate, renew a registration or renew an authorisation.

(b)   *Revocation* takes effect on expiry of the notice under (a), or on such later date as may be stated in the notice, except that if an appeal is made during the period of notice the *revocation* does not take effect until determination or discontinuance of any appeal, whether under the *SRA's* own procedure, or to the High Court under statutory provisions, or to the High Court under regulation 8.6(b).

Guidance note

(i)   The authorisation of solicitors and RELs as recognised sole practitioners will cease when they are passported to become recognised bodies with recognition under the SRA Authorisation Rules. See also the guidance note to regulation 9.

PART 3: THE REGISTERS, PRACTISING CERTIFICATES AND CERTIFICATES OF REGISTRATION

Regulation 11: The register of holders of practising certificates

11.1   The *SRA* must keep a register of *solicitors* who hold practising certificates, which may be kept in electronic form.

11.2   The register must contain, in respect of each *solicitor* who holds a practising certificate, the following information:

(a)   full name as shown on the roll;

(b)   date of birth;

(c) registration number;

(d) any other legal profession of which the *solicitor* is a member and whether the *solicitor* is entitled to practise as a member of that profession;

(e) date of admission as a *solicitor*;

(f) the commencement and replacement dates for the *solicitor's* current practising certificate;

(g) whether the *solicitor* is a *recognised sole practitioner*, and if so:

  (i) the registered name of the *solicitor's* sole *practice*; and

  (ii) any other *practising* styles used by the *solicitor* as a *sole practitioner*;

(h) the *solicitor's* place or places of business, except in the case of a non-*practising solicitor*;

(i) an address for correspondence in the case of a non-*practising solicitor*;

(j) any condition to which the *solicitor's* practising certificate is subject;

(k) a note about any suspension of the *solicitor* from *practice*, or suspension of the *solicitor's* practising certificate, or suspension of the *solicitor* from *practice* as a *sole practitioner*, or suspension of the *solicitor's* authorisation as a *recognised sole practitioner*, or the termination of any such suspension;

(l) a note of any order of the *Tribunal* under section 47 of the *SA* in respect of the *solicitor* (or former *solicitor*), and a note of any order of the High Court or the Court of Appeal striking the *solicitor* off the roll; and

(m) any other reasonable information, necessary for carrying out the *SRA's* statutory objectives, from time to time prescribed by the *SRA*.

11.3   Public information

(a) Entries in the register under 11.2(a), (c) to (h) and (j) to (m) must be available for inspection by any member of the public, except that the *SRA* may in exceptional circumstances and if it considers that to do so would be in the public interest, withhold:

  (i) the address of any or all a *solicitor's* places of business; or

  (ii) all information about a condition to which a *solicitor's* practising certificate is subject, or details of the condition.

(b) The date on which a *solicitor's* practising certificate or authorisation as a *recognised sole practitioner* expired or was revoked must be made available to a member of the public on request.

Guidance note

(i) Because sole practitioners are not authorised by means of endorsement on their practising certificate after 31 March 2012 or the date on which an order made pursuant to section 69 of the LSA relating to the status of sole practitioners comes into force, whichever is the later, the register shows only suspensions of authorisation as a recognised sole practitioner occurring up to that date. For information on sole practitioner firms after that please refer to the register of authorised bodies (see Rule 34 of the SRA Authorisation Rules).

Regulation 12: The register of European lawyers

12.1   The *SRA* must keep a *register of European lawyers*, which may be kept in electronic form.

12.2   The register must contain, in respect of each *REL*, the following information:

(a)   full name;

(b)   date of birth;

(c)   registration number;

(d)   in relation to each *Establishment Directive profession* of which the *lawyer* is a member:

(i)   the professional title;

(ii)   the professional body; and

(iii) whether the *lawyer* is entitled to practise as a member of that profession;

(e)   any other legal profession of which the *lawyer* is a member and whether the *lawyer* is entitled to practise as a member of that profession;

(f)   the date of initial registration;

(g)   the commencement and renewal dates for the current period of registration;

(h)   whether the *lawyer* is a *recognised sole practitioner*, and if so:

(i)   the registered name of the *lawyer's* sole *practice*; and

(ii)   any other *practising* styles used by the *lawyer* as a *sole practitioner* in the *UK*;

(i)   the *lawyer's* place or places of business in the *UK*;

(j)   any condition to which the *lawyer's* registration is subject;

(k)   a note about any suspension of the *lawyer's* registration, or suspension of the *lawyer* from *practice* as a *sole practitioner*, or suspension of the *lawyer's* authorisation as a *recognised sole practitioner*, or the termination of any such suspension;

(l)   a note of any order of the *Tribunal* under section 47 of the *SA* in respect of the *lawyer*, and a note of any order of the High Court or the Court of Appeal striking the *lawyer* off the register; and

(m) any other reasonable information, necessary for carrying out the *SRA's* statutory objectives, from time to time prescribed by the *SRA*.

12.3   Public information

(a)   Entries in the register under 12.2(a) and (c) to (m) must be available for inspection by any member of the public, except that the *SRA* may in exceptional circumstances and if it considers that to do so would be in the public interest, withhold:

(i)   the address of any or all an *REL's* places of business; or

(ii)   all information about a condition to which an *REL's* registration is subject or details of the condition.

(b)   The date on which an *REL's* registration or authorisation as a *recognised sole practitioner* expired or was revoked must be made available to a member of the public on request.

12.4   An *REL* whose name has changed may apply to the *SRA* to change his or her name on the register.

Guidance note

(i)   Because sole practitioners are not authorised by means of endorsement on their registration after 31 March 2012 or the date on which an order made pursuant to section 69 of the LSA relating to the status of sole practitioners comes into force, whichever is the later, the register shows only suspensions of authorisation as a recognised sole practitioner occurring up to that date. For information on sole practitioner firms after that please refer to the register of authorised bodies (see Rule 34 of the SRA Authorisation Rules).

Regulation 13: The register of foreign lawyers

13.1   The *SRA* must keep a *register of foreign lawyers*, which may be kept in electronic form.

13.2   The register must contain, in respect of each *RFL*, the following information:

(a)   full name;

(b)   date of birth;

(c)   registration number;

(d)   in relation to each legal profession of which the *lawyer* is a member:

(i)   the professional title;

(ii)   the professional body; and

(iii)   whether the *lawyer* is entitled to practise as a member of that profession;

(e)   the date of initial registration;

(f)   the commencement and renewal dates for the current period of registration;

(g)   the registered name and place or places of business of:

(i) any *recognised body*, or *authorised non-SRA firm* which is not licensed under Part 5 of the *LSA*, of which the *lawyer* is a *manager* or *interest holder*;

(ii) any *licensed body* of which the *lawyer* is a *manager* or *owner*; or

(iii) any *authorised non-SRA firm* licensed under Part 5 of the *LSA* of which the *lawyer* is a *manager* or a *material interest* holder;

(h) the registered name of any *recognised sole practitioner*, *recognised body*, *licensed body* or *authorised non-SRA firm* who or which is the *lawyer's employer*, and the address of the *lawyer's* place of employment;

(i) any condition to which the *lawyer's* registration is subject;

(j) a note about any suspension of the *lawyer's* registration, or the termination of such suspension;

(k) a note of any order of the *Tribunal* in respect of the *lawyer*; and

(l) any other reasonable information, necessary for carrying out the *SRA's* statutory objectives, from time to time prescribed by the *SRA*.

13.3   Public information

(a) Entries in the register under 13.2(a) and (c) to (l) must be available for inspection by any member of the public, except that the *SRA* may in exceptional circumstances and if it considers that to do so would be in the public interest, withhold:

(i) the address of any or all an *RFL's* places of business; or

(ii) all information about a condition to which an *RFL's* registration is subject or details of the condition.

(b) The date on which an *RFL's* registration expired or was revoked must be made available to a member of the public on request.

13.4   An *RFL* whose name has changed may apply to the *SRA* to change his or her name on the register.

Regulation 14: Practising certificates and certificates of registration

14.1   Each practising certificate and each certificate of registration must specify:

(a) the individual's full name;

(b) its commencement date;

(c) its replacement date;

(d) in the case of a *solicitor* or *REL* who is authorised as a *recognised sole practitioner*, a statement to that effect; and

(e) any condition to which the practising certificate or registration is subject, to the extent that it is public information under regulation 11, 12 or 13.

14.2   Every practising certificate or certificate of registration must be delivered to the applicant at the applicant's principal place of business or to such other address as may be specified by or on behalf of the applicant in writing, and may be delivered by post or electronically.

PART 4: INFORMATION REQUIREMENTS, NOTIFYING THIRD PARTIES AND REVIEW OF DECISIONS

Regulation 15: Information requirements

15.1   In addition to any requirements under section 84 of the *SA* or any other rules applicable by virtue of that Act, a *solicitor*, *REL* or *RFL* must inform the *SRA* within seven days if he or she:

(a)   is committed to prison in civil or criminal proceedings;

(b)   is charged with or convicted of an indictable offence;

(c)   is made the subject of bankruptcy proceedings;

(d)   makes a proposal for an individual voluntary arrangement or is a *manager* of a *firm* which makes a proposal for a company voluntary arrangement or a partnership voluntary arrangement under the Insolvency Act 1986;

(e)   is admitted as:

　　(i)   a member of a legal profession of a jurisdiction other than England and Wales;

　　(ii)   a *lawyer of England and Wales* other than a *solicitor*;

(f)   is made subject to disciplinary proceedings as:

　　(i)   a member of a legal profession of a jurisdiction other than England and Wales; or

　　(ii)   a *lawyer of England and Wales* other than a *solicitor*;

(g)   becomes:

　　(i)   a *manager* of or acquires any interest in a *recognised body*, or in an *authorised non-SRA firm* which is not licensed under Part 5 of the *LSA*;

　　(ii)   a *manager* or *owner* of a *licensed body*; or

　　(iii)   a *manager* of or acquires a *material interest* in an *authorised non-SRA firm* licensed under Part 5 of the *LSA*;

(h)   sets up a sole *practice* as:

　　(i)   a member of a legal profession of a jurisdiction other than England and Wales; or

　　(ii)   a *lawyer of England and Wales* other than a *solicitor*;

(i)   changes his or her name as shown on the register of holders of practising certificates, the *register of European lawyers* or the *register of foreign lawyers*, and must at the same time provide details of his or her new name.

15.2   A *solicitor*, *REL* or *RFL* who ceases to *practise* must inform the *SRA* within seven days and supply the *SRA* with a contact address.

Regulation 16: Notifying third parties of decisions

16.1   The *SRA* may, if it considers it in the public interest to do so, notify any or all of the following *persons* of a decision made under these regulations:

(a)   a *recognised body*, *licensed body* or an *authorised non-SRA firm* of which the *solicitor*, *REL* or *RFL* concerned is a *manager*, or in which he or she has any interest;

(b)   a *recognised sole practitioner*, *recognised body*, *licensed body* or *authorised non-SRA firm* of which the *solicitor*, *REL* or *RFL* concerned is an *employee*;

(c)   any *approved regulator*;

(d)   the Legal Services Board;

(e)   the *Legal Ombudsman*;

(f)   the regulatory body for any profession of which the *solicitor*, *REL* or *RFL* concerned is a member;

(g)   any law enforcement agency.

Regulation 17: Reconsideration

17.1   The *SRA* may reconsider or rescind a decision made under these regulations when it appears that the decision maker:

(a)   was not provided with material evidence that was available to the *SRA*;

(b)   was materially misled;

(c)   failed to take proper account of material facts or evidence;

(d)   took into account immaterial facts or evidence;

(e)   made a material error of law;

(f)   made a decision which was otherwise irrational or procedurally unfair;

(g)   made a decision which was otherwise ultra vires; or

(h)   failed to give sufficient reasons.

17.2   A decision may be reconsidered under 17.1 only on the initiative of the *SRA*.

17.3   The *SRA* may also give directions:

(a)   for further investigations to be undertaken;

(b)   for further information or explanation to be obtained; and

(c) for the reconsideration to be undertaken by the original decision maker or by a different decision maker or panel.

PART 5: INTERPRETATION AND TRANSITIONAL PROVISIONS

Regulation 18: Interpretation

18.1 The SRA Handbook Glossary 2012 shall apply and, unless the context otherwise requires:

(a) all italicised terms shall be defined; and

(b) all terms shall be interpreted,

in accordance with the *Glossary*.

Regulation 19: Transitional provisions

19.1 In these regulations references to *licensed bodies* shall have no effect until such time as the *Society* is designated as a *licensing authority* under Part 1 of Schedule 10 to the *LSA* and all definitions shall be construed accordingly.

19.2 Regulation 10.1(d)(iii) shall have no effect until such time as the *Society* is designated as a *licensing authority* under Part 1 of Schedule 10 to the *LSA*.

19.3 Until such time as the *Society* is designated as a *licensing authority* under Part 1 of Schedule 10 to the *LSA*, references in Regulation 3.1(a) to compliance officers of a *licensed body* (3.1(a)(iii)) or of an *authorised body* (3.1(a)(vii) and (viii)) shall have no effect.

19.4 Until such time as the *Society* is designated as a *licensing authority* under Part 1 of Schedule 10 to the *LSA* the reference in Regulation 3.1(a)(viii) to revocation or suspension under the *SRA Authorisation Rules* shall have no effect.

19.5 From 31 March 2012, a *recognised sole practitioner* who does not comply with regulation 4.8 above may be treated as being in compliance for the purposes of that regulation and the *SRA's regulatory arrangements*, until 31 December 2012, at which time the *recognised sole practitioner* shall be required to comply with regulation 4.8.

Authorisation and Practising Requirements

[E.4] Solicitors Keeping of the Roll Regulations 2011

These regulations, dated 17 June 2011, commencing on 6 October 2011, made by the Solicitors Regulation Authority Board, under sections 28, 79 and 80 of the Solicitors Act, with the approval of the Legal Services Board under paragraph 19 of Schedule 4 to the Legal Services Act 2007.

PART 1: THE ROLL AND INFORMATION

Regulation 1: The roll

1.1   The *SRA* shall continue to keep a list of all *solicitors* of the Senior Courts of England and Wales, called "the roll".

Regulation 2: Mode of keeping the roll

2.1   The roll will be kept in electronic form.

Regulation 3: Content of the roll

3.1   In respect of entries made or altered as from 6 October 2011, the roll must contain, in respect of each *solicitor*, the following information:

(a)   full name, including title;

(b)   date of birth;

(c)   registration number;

(d)   date of admission;

(e)   principal place of business in the case of a *practising solicitor*;

(f)   address for correspondence in the case of a non-practising *solicitor*;

(g)   a note about any suspension of the *solicitor* from *practice*, or suspension of the *solicitor's* practising certificate, or suspension of the *solicitor* from *practice* as a *sole practitioner*, or suspension of the *solicitor's* authorisation as a *recognised sole practitioner*, or the termination of any such suspension;

(h)   a note of any order of the *Tribunal* under section 47 of the *SA* in respect of the *solicitor* (or former *solicitor*), and a note of any order of the High Court or the Court of Appeal striking the *solicitor* off the roll; and

(i)   any other reasonable information, necessary for carrying out the *SRA's* statutory objectives, from time to time prescribed by the *SRA*.

Guidance note

(i)   Because sole practitioners are not authorised by means of endorsement on their practising certificate after 31 March 2012 or the date on which an order made pursuant to section 69 of the Legal Services Act 2007 relating to the status of sole practitioners comes into force, whichever is the later, the roll shows only suspensions of authorisation occurring up to that date. For information on sole practitioner firms after that please refer to the register of authorised bodies (see rule 34 of the SRA Authorisation Rules).

Regulation 4: Public access to information

4.1   Entries on the roll under regulation 3.1(a), (c), (d), (e), (g) and (h) must be available for inspection by any member of the public during office hours without charge, except that the *SRA* may in exceptional circumstances, and if it considers that to do so would be in the public interest, withhold the address of a *solicitor's* principal place of business.

4.2   The date on which a *solicitor's* name was

(a)   removed from or

(b)   struck off

the roll must be made available to a member of the public on request.

Regulation 5: Address for correspondence

5.1   When the *SRA* writes to any person under these regulations it shall write either by letter or email to the *solicitor's* last notified address or to the *solicitor's* last notified email address.

Regulation 6: Enquiry

6.1   The *SRA* shall at such times it decides appropriate ask every *solicitor* without a practising certificate whether the *solicitor* wishes his or her name to remain on the roll.

PART 2: REMOVAL, RESTORATION AND CHANGE OF NAME

Regulation 7: Removal from the roll

7.1   The *SRA* may remove from the roll the name of any *solicitor* who:

(a)   replies, following an enquiry under regulation 6, that he or she does not wish to remain on the roll; or

(b)   fails to reply within eight weeks to an enquiry under regulation 6; or

(c)   fails, within eight weeks of an enquiry under regulation 6, to pay the fee prescribed by regulation 15.1 for remaining on the roll; or

(d)   applies to have his or her name removed from the roll; or

(e)   has died.

Regulation 8: Application for restoration to the roll

8.1   A person whose name has been removed from the roll may apply to the *SRA* for his or her name to be restored to the roll.

8.2   This regulation does not apply if:

(a)   the *Tribunal* has made an order prohibiting the restoration of the person's name to the roll except by order of the *Tribunal*; or

(b)   the person's name has been struck off the roll.

8.3   The *SRA* shall not restore a person's name to the roll unless satisfied as to that person's character and suitability to be a *solicitor*.

Guidance note

(i)   The SRA will satisfy itself as to a person's character and suitability in a number of ways. These may include, but are not limited to, CRB disclosures and Police National Computer checks, as well as self-disclosure, in accordance with the Suitability Test. This will be in addition to taking into account the factors set out in regulations 10 and 11.

Regulation 9: Application for change of name on the roll

9.1   A *solicitor* whose name has changed may apply to the *SRA* to change his or her name on the roll.

Regulation 10: Outstanding complaints

10.1   The *SRA* may refuse to remove from or restore to the roll the name of a *solicitor* or former *solicitor* against whom there is an outstanding complaint.

Regulation 11: Disciplinary proceedings

11.1   The *SRA* shall not remove from or restore to the roll the name of any *solicitor* or former *solicitor* against whom disciplinary proceedings are pending before the Senior Courts or the *Tribunal*.

Regulation 12: Notice of intention to remove name

12.1   Where regulation 7.1(b) or (c) applies, the *SRA* shall not remove a *solicitor's* name from the roll until it has notified the *solicitor* in writing that it intends to remove his or her name.

Regulation 13: Letter of confirmation or notice of refusal

13.1   The *SRA* shall write to a *solicitor* or former *solicitor*:

(a)   confirming that his or her name on the roll has been removed from, restored to or changed on the roll; or

(b) giving notice that the *SRA* has refused to remove from, restore to or change his or her name on the roll.

PART 3: FORMS, FEES AND APPEALS

Regulation 14: Forms

14.1   The *SRA* may prescribe forms for replies or applications to the *SRA* and in the case of an application under regulation 9 may require such evidence as it sees fit.

Regulation 15: Fees

15.1   Subject to regulation 15.2 any reply, following an enquiry under regulation 6, that a *solicitor* wishes to remain on the roll must be accompanied by a fee of £20.

15.2   No fee is payable under regulation 6 by any *solicitor* whose name has been on the roll for 50 years or more or for such shorter *prescribed* period.

15.3   Any application under regulation 8 for restoration of a person's name to the roll shall be accompanied by the *prescribed* fee.

Regulation 16: Appeals

16.1   Any person who is aggrieved because:

(a) the *SRA* has removed his or her name from the roll;

(b) the *SRA* refused to remove his or her name from the roll; or

(c) the *SRA* refused to change his or her name on the roll

may appeal to the High Court under this regulation.

16.2   Any person aggrieved by the *SRA's* refusal to restore his or her name to the roll under regulation 8 may appeal to the High Court under section 8(4) of the *SA*.

16.3   A person must invoke the *SRA's* own appeals procedure before appealing to the High Court under this regulation, and may invoke the *SRA's* own appeals procedure before appealing to the High Court under section 8(4) of the *SA*.

16.4   Appeals under the *SRA's* own appeals procedure must be commenced within 28 days of notification of the *SRA's* initial decision.

16.5   Unless otherwise provided in the relevant statute, regulations or rules of Court or in the relevant decision, an appeal to the High Court must be commenced within 28 days of the *date of notification* of the relevant decision, whether that is the *SRA's* initial decision or a decision under the *SRA's* own appeals procedure.

16.6   Under sections 8(4B) and 28(3F) of the *SA* the decision of the High Court is final.

PART 4: INTERPRETATION AND TRANSITIONAL ARRANGEMENTS

Regulation 17: Interpretation

17.1   The SRA Handbook Glossary 2012 shall apply and, unless the context otherwise requires:

   (a)   all italicised terms shall be defined; and

   (b)   all terms shall be interpreted,

in accordance with the *Glossary*.

Regulation 18: Transitional provision

18.1   From 31 March 2012 or the date on which an order made pursuant to section 69 of the *LSA* relating to the status of *sole practitioners* comes into force, whichever is the later, in regulation 3.1(g) the words "or suspension of the *solicitor* from *practice* as a *sole practitioner*, or suspension of the *solicitor's* authorisation as a *recognised sole practitioner*," shall be omitted.

INTRODUCTION TO THE TRAINING REGULATIONS 2014 – QUALIFICATION AND PROVIDER REGULATIONS

Preamble

Authority: Made on the 6 June 2014 by the Solicitors Regulation Authority Board under section 2, 28, 79, and 80 of the Solicitors Act 1974, with the approval of the Legal Services Board under paragraph 19 of Schedule 4 to the Legal Services Act 2007.

Date: The regulations came into force on 1 July 2014.

Replacing: The SRA Training Regulations 2011 Part 1 – Qualification Regulations, the SRA Training Regulations Part 2 – Training Provider Regulations 2011 and the Monitoring of Courses Regulations 1991.

Regulating: Any individual seeking to be admitted as a solicitor and any organisation providing, or intending to provide, recognised training or the QLD, CPE, Exempting Law Degree, LPC or PSC. These regulations do not apply to those seeking admission under the SRA Qualified Lawyer Transfer Scheme Regulations 2011.

Overview

Outcomes-focused regulation concentrates on providing positive outcomes, which when achieved, will benefit and protect *clients* and the public. These regulations, together with the *SRA Training Regulations* 2011 Part 3 – Continuing Professional Development Regulations, form the *SRA Training Regulations*, which set out the outcomes-focused requirements governing the education and training for people seeking to be admitted as *solicitors* and those providing training.

Education and training underpins the regulation of *solicitors* – it ensures the creation of competent and ethical practitioners. *We* regulate and set requirements for all stages of pre-qualification training in order to ensure that individuals have achieved the required level of competency before admission as a *solicitor*.

The Principles

The regulations form part of the Handbook, in which the 10 mandatory *Principles* are all-pervasive. They apply to all those *we* regulate and to all aspects of practice. Outcomes relevant to education and training are listed beneath the *Principles*.

You must:

1. uphold the rule of law and the proper administration of justice;

2. act with integrity;

3. not allow *your* independence to be compromised;

4. act in the best interests of each *client*;

5. provide a proper standard of service to *your clients*;

6. behave in a way that maintains the trust the public places in *you* and in the provision of legal services;

7. comply with *your* legal and regulatory obligations and deal with *your* regulators and ombudsmen in an open, timely and co-operative manner;

8. run *your* business or carry out *your* role in the business effectively and in accordance with proper governance and sound financial risk management principles;

9. run *your* business or carry out *your* role in the business in a way that encourages equality of opportunity and respect for diversity; and

10. protect *client money* and *assets*.

Outcomes

The outcomes which apply to these regulations are that, if *you* qualify as a *solicitor*, *you*:

O(TR1) will have achieved and demonstrated a standard of competence appropriate to the work *you* are carrying out;

O(TR2) will have had such competence objectively assessed where appropriate;

O(TR3) will have undertaken the appropriate practical training and workplace experience;

O(TR4) are of proper *character and suitability*;

O(TR5) will have achieved an appropriate standard of written and spoken English; and

O(TR6) act so that *clients*, and the wider public, have confidence that outcomes TR1–TR5 have been met.

You must achieve, and where relevant continue to meet, these outcomes.

These outcomes, and the regulations that flow from them, apply to *unadmitted persons* – i.e. those who are intending to become *solicitors* under these regulations – and to *approved education providers*, *authorised education providers* and *authorised training providers*. They do not apply to individuals who are entitled to seek admission through the *QLTSR*.

PART 1: INTERPRETATION

Regulation 1: Interpretation and definitions

1.1   The SRA Handbook Glossary 2012 shall apply to these regulations and, unless the context otherwise requires:

(a)   all italicised terms shall be defined; and

(b)   all terms shall be interpreted;

in accordance with the *Glossary*.

PART 2: EDUCATION AND TRAINING REQUIREMENTS

Regulation 2: Admission as a solicitor

2.1   *We* will admit *you* as a *solicitor* if:

(a)   *you* have completed the *academic stage*;

(b)   *you* have completed the *vocational stage*;

(c)   *you* have complied with the *SRA Admission Regulations*; and

(d)   *we* are satisfied as to *your character and suitability* to be a *solicitor* in accordance with Part 1 of the *SRA Suitability Test*.

2.2   *We* may admit *you* as a *solicitor* if *you* have completed all or any part of 2.1(a) or (b) by *equivalent means*.

2.3   Where 2.2 applies *you* must apply to *us* in writing in the *prescribed* form and support *your* application with such evidence as *we* consider necessary.

2.4   If *you* are subject to the *QLTSR* those regulations apply to *your* admission as a *solicitor* and *you* are not subject to these regulations.

Regulation 3: Eligibility to undertake the academic stage and vocational stage

3.1   *Your* eligibility to commence the *academic stage* will be determined according to the requirements, approved by *us*, of the *approved education provider*.

3.2   *Your* eligibility to commence the *LPC* will be determined according to the requirements, approved by *us*, of the *authorised education provider*.

Regulation 4: Vocational stage

4.1   To complete the *vocational stage you* must:

(a)   complete the *LPC* with an *authorised education provider*;

Authorisation and
Practising Requirements

(b)   complete a *period of recognised training* with an *authorised training provider*; and

(c)   complete the *Professional Skills Course* with an *authorised education provider*;

unless *we* are satisfied that *you* have completed all or any part of the *academic stage* or the *vocational stage* by *equivalent means*.

Regulation 5: Recognised training

5.1   Subject to regulation 2.2, *you* must complete a *period of recognised training* before *we* admit *you* as a *solicitor*.

5.2   The *recognised training* is required to enable *you* to meet the *Practice Skills Standards* and comply with the *Principles* and shall normally be not less than two years if undertaken *full time* or pro-rata if *part time*.

5.3   *You* must maintain a *record of training* in accordance with regulation 14.

5.4   If at any time *we* are not satisfied that *you* have received or are receiving *adequate training*, *we* may:

(a)   refuse to recognise all or any part of the training undertaken;

(b)   require *you* to undertake further training; or

(c)   impose any condition or take any other action that *we* consider necessary.

5.5   *Your training principal* must certify to *us* in the *prescribed* form that *you* have completed the *recognised training* required by regulation 5.

5.6   *We* may recognise a period or periods of training which meet *our* published requirements for *recognised training* where appropriate to do so, including where a *training principal* for any reason has not certified completion of *recognised training* under regulation 5.5.

Regulation 6: Character and suitability

6.1   *You* must disclose any issue to *us* which may cause *you* not to meet the outcomes of the *SRA Suitability Test*:

(a)   before *you* commence any *period of recognised training*, or;

(b)   if the issue occurs after commencement, during any *period of recognised training*.

6.2   *You* may ask *us* to assess any issue which may cause *you* not to meet the outcomes of the *SRA Suitability Test* before commencement of the *LPC*.

6.3   If *you* have either disclosed an issue as required by regulation 6.1, or asked *us* to assess an issue under regulation 6.2, which may cause *you* not to meet the outcomes of the *SRA Suitability Test*, *you* are not eligible to commence *recognised training* until *we* have determined that *you* satisfy the outcomes of the *SRA Suitability Test*.

6.4   If *you* fail to meet the requirements of regulation 6.1 *we* may refuse to *recognise training* undertaken during this period and treat *your* failure to notify *us* as prima facie evidence of dishonest behaviour.

6.5   *We* may determine on the grounds of *your character and suitability* to be a *solicitor* that *you* are not eligible to commence or continue *recognised training*. *You* may make up to three further applications for eligibility to commence *recognised training* where there has been a material change in circumstances after intervals of not less than 12 months from the final determination of *your* previous application.

6.6   By making a request for assessment of a *character and suitability* issue under regulation 6.1 or 6.2 *you* become subject to these regulations.

6.7   *You* must disclose any new *character and suitability* issue to *us* at any time:

(a)   following a request for assessment of a *character and suitability* issue under regulation 6.1 or 6.2 but before *we* have reached a decision; or

(b)   after commencing a *period of recognised training*.

6.8   If during a *period of recognised training you* disclose a *character and suitability* issue under regulation 6.1 and/or 6.6 to *us*, or *we* discover a *character and suitability* issue, which may require assessment under the *SRA Suitability Test*, *we* may:

(a)   permit *you* to continue *recognised training*;

(b)   require *you* to suspend *your recognised training* pending *our* assessment of the issue;

(c)   not recognise part or all of that training if *we* decide that *you* do not have the required *character and suitability*, or;

(d)   apply such conditions to *your* training as *we* consider appropriate.

Regulation 7: Exemptions from the academic stage

7.1   *You* may be entitled to credit for prior certified or experiential learning which may entitle *you* to exemption from assessment in some subjects required by the *Joint Statement*. Applications for credit for prior learning shall be made to the *approved education provider* in accordance with its policies and procedures for accreditation of prior learning.

PART 3: APPROVED EDUCATION PROVIDERS AND AUTHORISED EDUCATION PROVIDERS REQUIREMENTS

Regulation 8: Approved education providers

8.1   Only an *approved education provider* may provide and assess:

    (a)   a *QLD*;

    (b)   a *CPE*; or

    (c)   an *Exempting Law Degree*.

8.2   An organisation may apply to *us* in the *prescribed* form to be an *approved education provider*.

Regulation 9: Authorised education providers

9.1   Only an *authorised education provider* may provide and assess the *LPC* and/or the *PSC*.

9.2   *We* may grant any approval or authorisation under regulation 8.2 and 9.1 respectively, subject to conditions and for such period, as *we* consider appropriate.

9.3   *We* may from time to time monitor the relevant programmes of study provided by an *approved education provider* and *authorised education provider*, including visiting the provider's premises.

PART 4: AUTHORISED TRAINING PROVIDERS REQUIREMENTS

Regulation 10: Authorised training providers

10.1   Only an *authorised training provider* may provide *recognised training* to *trainee solicitors*.

10.2   To provide *recognised training* an *authorised training provider* must:

    (a)   meet the requirements for authorisation set out in regulation 11;

    (b)   have a *training principal* who meets the requirements of regulation 13, and notify *us* in the *prescribed* form;

    (c)   meet the requirements for *recognised training* set out in regulation 12;

    (d)   notify *us* in the *prescribed* form of any individual who will commence a *period of recognised training* with the *authorised training provider*;

    (e)   pay the fees and expenses for their *trainees'* first attempt at the *PSC*, and

    (f)   pay their *trainees*:

        (i)   until 31 July 2014, at least the minimum salary prescribed by *us*;

        (ii)   from 1 August 2014, at least the single hourly rate of the national minimum wage specified in regulation 11 of the National Minimum Wage Regulations 1999.

Regulation 11: Requirements for authorisation as a training provider

11.1   To become an *authorised training provider*, an organisation must make an application in the *prescribed* form.

11.2   An application submitted under regulation 11.1 should declare that the organisation is able to provide training:

(a)   and experience in at least three distinct areas of English and Welsh law and practice;

(b)   to enable a *trainee* to develop the skills needed to meet the *Practice Skills Standards* and comply with the *Principles*;

(c)   which is appropriately supervised; and

(d)   which meets the requirements of regulation 12.

11.3   *We* may refuse to authorise any organisation or may grant authorisation with or without conditions and for such period as *we* consider appropriate.

Regulation 12: Requirements of recognised training

12.1   An *authorised training provider* must provide a *trainee* with training which:

(a)   is supervised by *solicitors* and other individuals who have the necessary skills and experience to provide effective supervision, to ensure that the *trainee* has relevant learning and development opportunities and personal support to enable the *trainee* to meet the *Practice Skills Standards*;

(b)   provides practical experience in at least three distinct areas of English and Welsh law and practice;

(c)   provides appropriate training to ensure that the *trainee* knows the requirements of the *Principles* and is able to comply with them; and

(d)   includes regular review and appraisal of the *trainee's* performance and development in respect of the *Practice Skills Standards* and the *Principles*, and the *trainee's record of training*.

12.2   If an *authorised training provider* is not able to provide training in all areas of the *Practice Skills Standards* or in at least three distinct areas of English and Welsh law and practice, the requirements of regulations 12.1(a) and 12.1(b) may be satisfied by a *secondment* of the *trainee*.

12.3   An *authorised training provider* may recognise previous *relevant work-based experience* undertaken by the trainee as satisfying up to six months of the required *period of recognised training*.

12.4   An *authorised training provider* must notify *us* in the *prescribed* form of any change in the *training principal*.

12.5   An *authorised training provider* must certify to *us* in the form *we* prescribe that the *trainee*:

(a)   is of the proper *character and suitability* to be admitted as a *solicitor*, and;

(b)   has completed the *recognised training* required by regulation 5.

Authorisation and
Practising Requirements

Regulation 13: Training principal

13.1   A *training principal* must:

(a)   hold a current practising certificate or be a practising *barrister*;

(b)   be competent to meet the requirements of these regulations;

(c)   ensure that the training provided meets the requirements of regulation 12;

(d)   ensure that the *trainee* maintains a *record of training* which will meet the requirements of regulation 14; and

(e)   ensure that any person involved in the training and supervision of a *trainee* has adequate legal knowledge and experience in the practice area they are supervising and the skills to provide effective supervision.

Regulation 14: Record of training

14.1   The *trainee* must maintain a *record of training* which:

(a)   contains details of the work performed;

(b)   records how the *trainee* has acquired, applied and developed their skills by reference to the *Practice Skills Standards* and the *Principles*;

(c)   records the *trainee's* reflections on his or her performance and development plans; and

(d)   is verified by the individual(s) supervising the *trainee*.

Regulation 15: Monitoring of recognised training

15.1   *We* may monitor the training provided by an *authorised training provider*. Monitoring may include a visit to the *authorised training provider*.

Regulation 16: Revocation of authorised training status and refusal to recognise training

16.1   *We* may revoke *authorised training provider* status or grant continued authorisation subject to conditions where the *authorised training provider* has not complied with these regulations or *our* requirements.

16.2   Where the *authorised training provider* or the *trainee* has not complied with these regulations or *our* requirements, *we* may refuse to recognise any training received by the *trainee* as a *period of recognised training*.

PART 5: RIGHT OF REVIEW AND WAIVERS

Regulation 17: Right of review

17.1   If *we* have:

(a)   refused to grant *approved education provider* status, or granted approval or authorisation subject to conditions under regulation 8;

(b) refused to grant *authorised education provider* status, or granted approval or authorisation subject to conditions under regulation 9;

(c) refused to grant *authorised training provider* status or granted authorisation subject to conditions under regulation 11;

(d) revoked *authorised training provider* status or imposed conditions under regulation 16.1;

(e) refused to recognise a period of training under regulations 5.5 or 16.2; or

(f) determined that an individual is not eligible to commence or continue *recognised training* under regulation 6.4;

the applicant may apply to *us* in writing for a review of the decision within one month of receiving notification of it.

17.2   Where *we* have determined that an individual is not eligible to commence or continue *recognised training* and have subsequently upheld that decision following a review under regulation 17.1, that individual has a right of appeal under regulation 2.1 of the *SRA Admission Regulations*.

17.3   If an organisation is seeking a review of *our* decision relating to its status as an *authorised training provider*, the organisation must not permit a new *trainee* to commence a proposed *period of recognised training* until the outcome of the review is determined. For *trainees* already in periods of *recognised training*, *we* reserve the right to recognise or refuse to recognise part or all of their training in accordance with regulation 5.4.

Regulation 18: Waiver of regulations

18.1   In any particular case *we* may waive in writing any of these regulations, in accordance with the requirements of *our* waivers policy.

PART 6: FORMS AND FEES

Regulation 19: Forms and fees

19.1   Any application made to *us* or notice or certification given to *us* under these regulations must be in the *prescribed* form and accompanied by the *prescribed* fee.

19.2   *We* may require an applicant to support any application under these regulations by such evidence as *we* consider necessary.

PART 7: COMMENCEMENT, REPEAL AND TRANSITIONAL PROVISIONS

Regulation 20: Commencement and repeal provisions

20.1   These regulations come into force on 1 July 2014 or the date of approval of the Legal Services Board, whichever is the later.

Authorisation and Practising Requirements

20.2   The SRA Training Regulations 2011 Part 1 – Qualification Regulations, the SRA Training Regulations 2011 Part 2 – Training Provider Regulations, and the Monitoring of Courses Regulations 1991 are repealed on 30 June 2014.

Regulation 21: Transition from previous regulations

21.1   If your organisation was authorised or recognised under the SRA Training Regulations 2011 and/or the Monitoring of Courses Regulations 1991 your authorisations continue under these, the 2014 regulations. This means:

(a) *QLD* , *CPE* and *Exempting Law Degree* providers are authorised and regulated as *approved education providers*;

(b) *LPC* and *PSC* providers are authorised and regulated as *authorised education providers*;

(c) training establishments and training contract consortia are authorised and regulated as *authorised training providers*.

21.2   Any applications submitted under the Monitoring of Courses Regulations 1991 before 1 July 2014 that have not yet been decided upon by that date will be considered and decided upon under these, the 2014 regulations.

21.3   A training contract entered into on or before 30 June 2014 will continue to governed by the SRA Training Regulations 2011, unless the parties agree by mutual consent to adopt these, the 2014 regulations and they notify their agreement to *us* in the *prescribed* form.

INTRODUCTION TO THE TRAINING REGULATIONS PART 3 – CPD REGULATIONS

Preamble

Authority: Made on 17 June 2011 by the Solicitors Regulation Authority Board under sections 2, 28, 79 and 80 of the Solicitors Act 1974, with the approval of the Legal Services Board under paragraph 19 of Schedule 4 to the Legal Services Act 2007

Date: These regulations came into force on 6 October 2011

Replacing: The Solicitors' Training Regulations 2009

Regulating: Solicitors and RELs and their post-qualification, or post registration, education and training requirements.

Overview

Outcomes-focused regulation concentrates on providing positive outcomes which when achieved will benefit and protect *clients* and the public.

These regulations govern the ongoing training of those practising as *solicitors* and *RELs*.

Education and training performs the underpinning, fundamental role in regulating *solicitors* – the creation and maintenance of competent and ethical practitioners. *We* regulate post-qualification training in order to give *solicitors* and *RELs* the tools they need to adhere to the *Principles*.

The Principles

These regulations form part of the Handbook, in which the 10 mandatory *Principles* are all-pervasive. They apply to all those *we* regulate and underpin all aspects of *practice*. Outcomes relevant to education and training are listed beneath the *Principles*.

You must:

1. uphold the rule of law and the proper administration of justice;

2. act with integrity;

3. not allow *your* independence to be compromised;

4. act in the best interests of each *client*;

5. provide a proper standard of service to *your clients*;

6. behave in a way that maintains the trust the public places in *you* and in the provision of legal services;

7. comply with *your* legal and regulatory obligations and deal with *your* regulators and ombudsmen in an open, timely and co-operative manner;

8. run *your* business or carry out *your* role in the business effectively and in accordance with proper governance and sound financial and risk management principles;

9. run *your* business or carry out *your* role in the business in a way that encourages equality of opportunity and respect for diversity; and

10. protect *client money* and *assets*.

Outcome

The outcome which applies to these regulations is that:

O(TR1) *you* maintain competence through relevant ongoing training.

This outcome, and the regulations that flow from it, applies to *solicitors* admitted in England and Wales and *RELs*.

PART 1: INTERPRETATION

Regulation 1: Interpretation and definitions

1.1 The SRA Handbook Glossary 2012 shall apply and, unless the context otherwise requires:

    (a) all italicised terms shall be defined; and

    (b) all terms within these regulations shall be interpreted;

in accordance with the *Glossary*.

Regulation 2: Application of these regulations

2.1 These regulations apply to *your* obligations regarding *CPD*.

2.2 All *solicitors* and *RELs* are required to undertake *CPD*. Non-compliance could lead to disciplinary procedures and/or delays in the issue of *your* practising certificate.

2.3 These regulations do not apply to *RFLs*.

PART 2: BASIC REQUIREMENT

Regulation 3: Basic CPD requirement

3.1 *You* must undertake 16 hours of *CPD* during each complete *CPD year* in legal *practice* or employment in England and Wales.

3.2   If *you* work *part-time* the requirements are reduced, in accordance with regulation 7.

Guidance note:

(i)   Any hours accrued over and above the 16 hours per year minimum cannot be carried over to the next *CPD year*.

(ii)   Separate legislation may detail further *CPD* requirements. For example, the SRA Higher Rights of Audience Regulations require five hours of the annual *CPD* requirement to be undertaken relating to the provision of advocacy services in the higher courts in each of the first five *CPD years* following the grant of the higher rights qualification.

PART 3: REQUIREMENTS FOR NEW SOLICITORS/RELS

Regulation 4: CPD requirement during the first three years of admission

4.1   If *you* are a *solicitor*, in the first three *CPD years* following admission *you* must attend the SRA Management Course Stage 1.

4.2   A minimum of three topics must be covered on the SRA Management Course Stage 1 from the list below:

(a)   Managing finance;

(b)   Managing the *firm*;

(c)   Managing *client* relationships;

(d)   Managing information;

(e)   Managing people.

4.3   If *you* are an *REL*, *you* are not required to attend the SRA Management Course Stage 1.

4.4   *You* can make a written request to *us* for exemption from the SRA Management Course Stage 1 if *you* have, within the last five years:

(a)   gained significant experience of a *solicitor's practice* and of management issues as they arise in *practice* (and can provide examples of experience gained in at least three of the five topic areas of the course); or

(b)   attended a similar course, covering the same ground.

4.5   If *you* qualified by undertaking the *QLTT you* are also required to attend the Financial and Business Skills (but not required to attempt or pass the examination) and the Client Care and Professional Standards modules of the *PSC* during *your* first *CPD year*.

4.6   *You* are exempt from the requirement in regulation 4.5 to attend the two *PSC* modules if *you*:

(a)   undertook the *LPC* and *PSC* prior to admission;

(b)   sat the Professional Conduct and Accounts heads of the *QLTT*; or

(c)   are transferring from Scotland via the *QLTT*.

4.7   Regulations 4.5 and 4.6 do not apply to those qualifying via the *QLTSR*.

Guidance note:

(i)   The SRA Management Course Stage 1 is a course that requires at least seven hours' attendance. It can be completed in a single day or be undertaken on a modular basis, but it has to be completed in full before claiming *CPD* hours.

(ii)   In addition to the compulsory SRA Management Course Stage 1, there is an optional five hour course, the SRA Management Course Stage 2.

(iii)   Full guidance on both courses is available.

Regulation 5: CPD requirement during the first months after admission

5.1   *You* must undertake one hour of *CPD* for each whole month in legal *practice* or employment between *your* admission and the start of the next full *CPD year*.

Regulation 6: CPD requirement during the first months after registration with the SRA pursuant to the Establishment Directive

6.1   If *you* are an *REL*, *you* must undertake one hour of *CPD* for each whole month in legal *practice* or employment between the date of initial registration and the start of the next full *CPD year*.

Guidance note:

(i)   If *your* admission date or date of initial registration is 1 November, *you* will automatically enter into *your* first full *CPD year* and be required to complete 16 hours of *CPD*. This also applies in those years where 1 November falls at the weekend and *you* are admitted or initially registered the following week.

Regulation 7: Part-time employment

7.1   Notwithstanding regulations 7.2 and 7.3 and regulation 16, if *you* work *part-time* in legal *practice* or employment, *your* CPD requirements are reduced such that *you* must complete one hour of *CPD* each year for every two hours worked per week.

7.2   If *you* work *part-time* in a newly admitted or newly registered period, regulations 5 and 6 apply to the period worked between *your* admission or registration and the start of the next full *CPD year*.

7.3   If *you* work an average of fewer than two hours per week, *you* are permitted to suspend the *CPD* requirements.

7.4   Details of *part-time* working hours, with starting and finishing dates, should be entered in *your CPD training record*.

Guidance note:

(i)   For example, a *solicitor* working 10 hours per week must complete five hours of *CPD* each year.

(ii)   It may be necessary for *you* to keep a record of hours worked to enable *you* to calculate the average number of hours worked per week over the course of a year.

(iii)   If *you* work a variable number of hours each week *you* should calculate the average number of hours worked per week during the *CPD year*, and then halve this amount to calculate *your CPD* requirement for the year.

(iv)   For example, a *solicitor* who works an average of seven hours per week has an annual *CPD* requirement of three and a half hours.

(v)   Part hours worked should be rounded to the nearest whole hour.

PART 4: ACTIVITIES

Regulation 8: CPD activities

8.1   At least 25 per cent of the *CPD* requirement must be met by *participation* in accredited courses.

8.2   The remaining 75 per cent of the *CPD* requirement may be met by further accredited courses or a wide range of other activities.

8.3   The *CPD* activity should be at an appropriate level and contribute to *your* general professional skill and knowledge, in order to count towards meeting *your CPD* requirements.

8.4   Attendance at a course means attendance at the complete course. Part attendance will not count at all towards *your CPD* requirement.

8.5   The responsibility for meeting the *CPD* requirements falls on *you*, not *your* employer.

Guidance note to 8.1:

(i)   For the purposes of the above regulation, an accredited course means a structured training session, delivered face-to-face or by distance learning, of one hour or more which has written aims and objectives, and is approved specifically for the purpose of compliance with *our CPD* requirements. Examples include:

Authorisation and Practising Requirements

(a) face-to-face sessions including those delivered by an *authorised distance learning provider*;

(b) a course wholly provided by distance learning which involves assessment by dissertation and written examination;

(c) structured coaching sessions, delivered face-to-face, of one hour or more which have written aims and objectives, are documented showing an outcome and are provided by an organisation authorised by *us*;

(d) structured mentoring sessions involving professional development, delivered face-to-face, of one hour or more which have written aims and objectives, are documented showing an outcome and are provided by an organisation authorised by *us*; or

(e) webinars, i.e. courses broadcast via a website in real time where participants have contact with the speaker(s) and can ask questions and receive answers, and which are provided by an organisation authorised by *us*.

Guidance note to 8.2:

(i) For the purposes of regulation 8.2, the following will be deemed to be activities:

(a) participation in non-accredited courses;

    (A) preparing, delivering and/or attending courses, which are of particular relevance and benefit to an individual's area of work which last more than 30 minutes;

    (B) actual time may be claimed.

(b) coaching and mentoring sessions of less than one hour;

    (A) structured coaching sessions and structured mentoring sessions involving professional development, delivered face-to-face lasting between 30 minutes and one hour which have written aims and objectives, are documented showing an outcome and are provided by an organisation authorised by *us*;

    (B) actual time may be claimed.

(c) coaching and mentoring sessions delivered from a distance;

    (A) structured coaching sessions or structured mentoring sessions involving professional development, delivered from a distance (e.g. by webinars) of 30 minutes or more which have written aims and objectives, are documented showing an outcome and are provided by an organisation authorised by *us*;

    (B) actual time may be claimed.

(d) writing on law or *practice*;

    (A) for example law books, journals, publications for *clients*, *client's* own publications, newspapers and magazines (whether legal publications or not), on the Internet;

    (B)   topics may include, for example, law *practice*, issues arising from transactions, *clients*, markets, industries, products;

    (C)   actual time may be claimed.

(e) work shadowing;

    (A)   participation in structured work shadowing schemes with clear aims and objectives and requiring feedback or reflection on the activity;

    (B)   actual time may be claimed.

(f) research;

    (A)   research which relates to legal topics or has relevance to the *practice/organisation* which results in some form of written document, precedent, memorandum, questionnaire/survey etc;

    (B)   actual time may be claimed.

(g) production of a dissertation;

    (A)   study for or production of a dissertation counting towards a qualification recognised by *us*;

    (B)   actual time may be claimed.

(h) watching DVDs, webinars, webcasts, podcasts, television broadcasts or videotapes and/or listening to audio podcasts, radio broadcasts or audio tapes offered by *authorised CPD course providers* or *authorised distance learning providers*;

    (A)   actual time may be claimed.

(i) distance learning courses where there is provision for the answering of enquiries or for discussion;

    (A)   actual time may be claimed.

(j) preparation and delivery of training courses forming part of the process of qualification or post admission training;

    (A)   actual time may be claimed.

(k) work towards the Qualification Credit Framework (QCF) awards relating to assessment, verification and/or quality assurance of competence-based assessment models (such as, for example, National Vocational Qualifications);

    (A)   actual time spent building a portfolio of evidence and/or attending lectures, workshops, etc may be claimed.

(l) participating in the development of specialist areas of law and *practice* by attending meetings of specialist committees and/or working parties of relevant professional or other competent bodies charged with such work;

Authorisation and
Practising Requirements

    (A)   actual time spent at meetings may be claimed.

  (m) work towards the achievement of an National Vocational Qualifications in any business-related area and at any level;

    (A)   actual time spent building a portfolio of evidence and/or attending lectures, workshops, etc may be claimed.

  (n) study towards professional qualifications;

    (A)   examination must be taken to claim time for study and examination itself;

  (o) actual time spent in study and examination may be claimed.

Regulation 9: Requirements for solicitors who have been RELs

9.1   If *you* are an *REL* and become admitted as a *solicitor* in England and Wales, regulations 3 and 5 shall apply as if *you* were a *solicitor* admitted on the date of initial registration and regulations 6 and 11 shall not apply.

9.2   Nothing in these regulations shall be taken as requiring *you* to meet the requirements of regulation 4 if *you* are a *solicitor* who has previously been an *REL*.

PART 5: RECORDS

Regulation 10: Obligation to keep a CPD training record

10.1   *You* must keep a record of all *CPD* undertaken to comply with these regulations.

10.2   For any courses attended, *you* must enter the number of hours' credit allocated and the *authorised CPD course providers* reference, together with the date and course title, into *your CPD training record*.

10.3   *We* may request to see a copy of *your CPD training record* at any time, and if *we* do so *you* must produce *your* record upon demand.

10.4   *You* should keep *your CPD training record* on file for a period of at least six years.

10.5   *You* should enter the start and finish dates of any period of suspension, and the reasons for suspending, in *your CPD training record*.

Guidance note:

(i)   Details of other activities and the number of hours undertaken should be entered on *your CPD training record*. It is advisable to enter all development activities even if *you* are unsure whether they can be claimed for *CPD* credit.

PART 6: PRE-QUALIFICATION TRAINING

Regulation 11: CPD undertaken before admission

11.1   *You* are only entitled to count *CPD* undertaken between the expiry of *your* training contract and the day of admission for the purposes of regulation 5, if at the time of undertaking it:

    (a)   an application for admission has been lodged with *us*, and

    (b)   a *CPD training record* has been kept in accordance with regulation 10.

PART 7: SUSPENSION OF REQUIREMENTS

Regulation 12: Suspension of CPD requirement

12.1   If *you* do not work for any period in legal *practice* or employment in England and Wales, the application of these regulations may be suspended for that period.

12.2   *You* may suspend *your CPD* requirements in the following circumstances:

    (a)   *you* are not working in legal *practice* or employment;

    (b)   *you* are retired from *practice* as a *solicitor* or *REL*;

    (c)   *you* are working, on average, less than two hours a week in legal *practice* or employment.

12.3   Any training undertaken during the suspension will not count towards *your CPD* requirement upon *your* return to legal *practice* or employment.

12.4   It is not necessary to notify *us* of the intention to suspend the *CPD* requirements.

Guidance note to 12.2:

(i)   This would apply where *you* are in a role in which *you* are not required to give legal advice to:

    (a)   a member of the public;

    (b)   a company;

    (c)   an internal department;

    (d)   an officer or member of staff, or representative of *your* organisation.

(ii)   This applies regardless of whether the employment is paid or voluntary and whether or not a practising certificate is held.

(iii)   This also covers time when *you* are out of legal *practice* or employment, whether or not *you* hold a current practising certificate, due to unemployment, maternity/paternity leave, long-term illness and/or working abroad.

Authorisation and Practising Requirements

(iv)   If *you* are a retired *solicitor you* are eligible to suspend the *CPD* requirements, provided *you* do not *practise* or undertake legal work of any description, whether paid or unpaid. If *you* are a retired *solicitor* acting as a consultant, or who undertakes pro-bono or voluntary work of a legal nature *you* are not entitled to suspend the *CPD* requirements.

Guidance note to 12.4:

(i)   It is for *you* to decide whether or not *you* want to suspend *your CPD* requirements. Consideration of the following may be of assistance:

- (a)   the length of time *you* will be out of *practice* or legal employment;

- (b)   the amount of credit already accrued during the *CPD year* or first three years after admission in which the suspension would begin;

- (c)   the availability of courses/access to training while out of *practice*;

- (d)   *your* financial circumstances and whether *you* would be required to fund the training *yourself*.

PART 8: RETURNING TO PRACTICE

Regulation 13: CPD requirements upon return to full-time or part-time legal practice or employment following a suspension during the newly admitted or registered period

13.1   Upon *your* return to full-time or *part-time* legal *practice* or employment, *your* CPD requirements will be dependent upon the length of time *you* have worked from the date of *your* admission to the roll or registration with *us*.

13.2   If *you* have:

- (a)   suspended the requirements in the newly admitted or newly registered period; and

- (b)   not worked at all from the date of admission or registration;

you must undertake one hour of *CPD* for each complete month from the date of *your* return, up to the end of the *CPD year*.

13.3   If *you*:

- (a)   suspended the requirements in the newly admitted or newly registered period; but

- (b)   worked following the date of *your* admission or registration;

you must undertake one hour for each month before and after the suspension if returning before the end of the *CPD year*.

13.4   If *you* have not completed all of *your CPD* requirement for the period before the suspension began *you* should make up any shortfall and undertake the requisite number of hours when *you* return to work. *We* may grant an extension of time if necessary.

Guidance note to 13.2:

(i)   If *you* have not worked at all from the date of *your* admission to the roll, or of registration with *us*, *you* will be treated as newly admitted on *your* return regardless of the length of the suspension.

(ii)   The newly admitted or registered period covers the first 12 months following the date of *your* admission or registration.

Guidance note to 13.3:

(i)   If *you* have completed all of *your CPD* requirement for the period before the suspension began *you* may, upon returning to work, choose one of the following options:

(a)   if *you* return on or before 1 May, undertake two hours for every complete month up to the end of the *CPD year*, up to a maximum of 16 hours, attending if *you* feel necessary due to the length of the suspension, the Financial and Business Skills (but *you* would not be required to attempt or pass the examination) and Client Care and Professional Standards modules of the *PSC*; or

(b)   if *you* return after 1 May, undertake at least 12 hours, attending, if *you* feel necessary due to the length of the suspension, the Financial and Business Skills (but *you* would not be required to attempt or pass the examination) and Client Care and Professional Standards modules of the *PSC*.

(ii)   Either option would count as completion of the first *CPD year*.

Guidance note to 13.4:

(i)   In determining whether *you* have completed *your* requirements *you* may count the following circumstances as a complete *CPD year*:

(a)   accrual of at least 12 hours of *CPD* and attendance, where appropriate, at a compulsory course or the Financial and Business Skills (but not the examination) and Client Care and Professional Standards modules of the *PSC*, whichever was applicable at the time before the suspension began;

(b)   accrual of at least 12 hours of *CPD* and attendance, where appropriate, at a compulsory course or the Financial and Business Skills (but not the examination) and Client Care and Professional Standards modules of the *PSC* between the date of *your* return and the end of the *CPD year*; or

(c)   accrual of a total of 12 hours during the period before the suspension began added to the amount required from the date of *your* return to the end of the *CPD year*, plus, where appropriate attendance at a compulsory course or the Financial and Business Skills (but not the examination) and Client Care and Professional Standards modules of the *PSC*.

Authorisation and
Practising Requirements

Regulation 14: CPD requirements upon return to full-time legal practice or employment following a suspension at any time from the end of your first CPD year or onwards

14.1   If *you* have suspended the requirements at any time from the end of *your* first *CPD year* or onwards, and return to work full-time *you* will be required to complete two hours of *CPD* for every complete month from the date of *your* return until the end of that *CPD year*, up to a required maximum of 16 hours.

Guidance note:

(i)   The table below can be used to calculate *your CPD* requirement for the remainder of the *CPD year*.

(ii)   If *you* return to work on for example 5 December, *your CPD* requirements will start from 1 January, the first full month following *your* return. If *you* return to work between 2 October and 31 October, *your CPD* requirements will start at the commencement of the new *CPD year*.

Return date	CPD hours
1 November	16
1 December	16
1 January	16
1 February	16
1 March	16
1 April	14
1 May	12
1 June	10
1 July	8
1 August	6
1 September	4
1 October	2
2 October – 31 October	0

Regulation 15: CPD requirements upon return to part-time legal practice or employment following a suspension at any time from the end of your first CPD year or onwards

15.1   If *you* have suspended the requirements at any time from the end of *your* first *CPD year* or onwards, and *you* return to work *part-time*, *you* will be required to complete one hour of *CPD* per year, for every two hours worked weekly.

15.2   If *you* return to *part-time* legal *practice* or employment after 1 March *you* should calculate *your* annual *CPD* requirement based on the number of hours worked per week, and undertake one-eighth of the annual requirement for each complete month from the date of *your* return to the end of that *CPD year*.

Guidance note:

For example,

(i) if *you* work 20 hours a week *you* are required to undertake 10 hours of *CPD* per *CPD year*.

(ii) if *you* return to work on 1 April, and *you* are working 20 hours a week, *you* would be required to undertake eight and three quarter hours of *CPD* up until the end of the *CPD year*.

PART 9: APPLICATIONS AND WAIVERS

Regulation 16: CPD questions on the practising certificate application form

16.1   *You* will be required to confirm whether or not *you* have complied with the *CPD* requirements during the past full *CPD year* when applying for *your* practising certificate.

Guidance note:

(i) When applying for a practising certificate in 2011 for example, the question relates to *your CPD* position as at 31 October 2010. If *you* are making an application for the first time and have not completed a full *CPD year*, the "not applicable" box on the form should be ticked. Likewise, if *you* are subject to the requirement but were out of *practice* during the year, and have suspended the requirements, *you* should tick the "not applicable" box on the form.

Regulation 17: Waivers of CPD monitoring requirements

17.1   There are no exemptions from the *CPD* scheme but general waivers apply in relation to *CPD* monitoring as follows:

(a) *firms* and organisations with Lexcel/Investors in People accreditation have a waiver from the routine monitoring of in-house *CPD* courses and the requirements to submit details of courses, course tutors and/or discussion group leaders;

(b) *solicitors/RELs* in *firms* and organisations with Lexcel/Investors in People accreditation have a waiver from routine monitoring of *CPD training records*, and the requirement to satisfy a minimum of 25 per cent of the *CPD* requirement by *participation* in accredited courses;

(c) *solicitors/RELs* in *firms* holding a Legal Aid franchise have a waiver from routine monitoring of *CPD training records*;

(d) *solicitors/RELs* in *firms* and organisations holding ISO 9000 accreditation have a waiver from routine monitoring of *CPD training records*;

(e) *solicitors/RELs* in *firms* and organisations which are authorised in-house *CPD* providers may have a waiver from the requirement to satisfy 25 per cent of their *CPD* requirement by *participation* in accredited courses, if *you* develop a training plan which is acceptable to the *firm*.

17.2   Even where any of the above waivers are applicable to *you* or *your firm*, the number of *CPD* hours to be completed will not be affected, and *you* are still required to maintain *your* personal *CPD training record* to assist *you* with planning *your CPD* activity.

17.3   In any particular case *we* have the power to waive in writing any of the provisions of these regulations and to revoke such waivers.

SRA Admission Regulations 2011

INTRODUCTION TO THE ADMISSION REGULATIONS

Preamble

Authority: Made on 17 June 2011 by the Solicitors Regulation Authority Board under sections 28, 79 and 80 of the Solicitors Act 1974 with the approval of the Legal Services Board under paragraph 19 of Schedule 4 to the Legal Services Act 2007

Date: These regulations came into force on 6 October 2011

Replacing: The Solicitors' Admission Regulations 2009

Regulating: Those individuals seeking admission to the roll of solicitors in England and Wales

Regulating: appeals from SRA decisions relating to admission as a solicitor.

Overview

Outcomes-focused regulation concentrates on providing positive outcomes which when achieved will benefit and protect *clients* and the public. These regulations set out the outcomes-focused requirements governing the process for admitting people to the roll of *solicitors*. They also cover appeals against *SRA* decisions taken under the *SRA Training Regulations* and the *SRA* Qualified Lawyers Transfer Scheme Regulations.

Education and training underpins the regulation of *solicitors* – it ensures the creation of competent and ethical practitioners. *We* regulate and set requirements for all stages of pre-qualification training in order to give *solicitors* the tools they need to adhere to the *Principles*.

The Principles

These regulations form part of the Handbook, in which the 10 mandatory *Principles* are all-pervasive. They apply to all those *we* regulate and underpin all aspects of practice. Outcomes relevant to education and training are listed beneath the *Principles*.

You must:

1. uphold the rule of law and the proper administration of justice;

2. act with integrity;

3. not allow *your* independence to be compromised;

4. act in the best interests of each *client*;

5. provide a proper standard of service to *your clients*;

6.   behave in a way that maintains the trust the public places in *you* and in the provision of legal services;

7.   comply with *your* legal and regulatory obligations and deal with *your* regulators and ombudsmen in an open, timely and co-operative manner;

8.   run *your* business or carry out *your* role in the business effectively and in accordance with proper governance and sound financial and risk management principles;

9.   run *your* business or carry out *your* role in the business in a way that encourages equality of opportunity and respect for diversity; and

10.   protect *client money* and *assets*.

Outcomes

The outcomes which apply to these regulations are that if *you* are an individual seeking admission to the roll of *solicitors*:

O(AR1)   *you* have complied with all relevant training and/or assessment requirements; and

O(AR2)   *you* have recourse to appeal decisions taken by *us* in relation to qualification as a *solicitor*.

These outcomes, and the regulations that flow from them, apply to all individuals seeking admission to the roll of *solicitors* in England and Wales – i.e. *unadmitted persons*, *trainee solicitors*, and qualified lawyers from another jurisdiction seeking qualification via transfer.

PART 1: INTERPRETATION

Regulation 1: Interpretation and definitions

1.1   The SRA Handbook Glossary 2012 shall apply and, unless the context otherwise requires:

(a)   all italicised terms shall be defined; and

(b)   all terms shall be interpreted;

in accordance with the *Glossary*.

1.2   On any appeal to the High Court under these regulations:

(a)   section 28(3E) of the *SA* provides that the High Court may make such order as it thinks fit as to payment of costs, and

(b)   section 28(3F) of the *SA* provides that the decision of the High Court shall be final.

PART 2: APPEALS

Regulation 2: Appeals against our decisions on eligibility to commence recognised training and certificates of eligibility for overseas lawyers

2.1   If *you* are an applicant for assessment of a *character and suitability* issue under regulation 6 of the *SRA Training Regulations* – Qualification and Provider Regulations, whose application has been refused under regulation 6.4 of those regulations, *you* may appeal to the High Court under this regulation against *our* decision on a review of the application under regulation 17.1 of the *SRA Training Regulations* – Qualification and Provider Regulations.

2.2   If *you* are seeking to establish eligibility under regulation 4 of the *QLTR* or regulation 2 of the *QLTSR* other than pursuant to Directive 2005/36/EC or the *Establishment Directive*, *you* may appeal to the High Court under this regulation against *our* decision on a review under regulation 16(1) of the *QLTR*, or, where appropriate, regulation 6.1 of the *QLTSR*, where *we* have:

(a)   refused *your* initial application on the ground that *you* are not suitable to be admitted as a *solicitor*; and

(b)   refused to reverse that decision on the review.

2.3   If *you* are seeking to establish eligibility pursuant to Directive 2005/36/EC or the *Establishment Directive*, *you* have rights of appeal under regulation 36 of the European Communities (Recognition of Professional Qualifications) Regulations 2007 or regulation 35 of the European Communities (Lawyer's Practice) Regulations 2000 respectively – see 16(3) and (4) of the *QLTR* or, where appropriate, regulations 6.3 and 6.4 of the *QLTSR*.

2.4   An appeal under regulation 2.1 or 2.2 above must be brought within three months of *you* receiving notification of *our* decision.

2.5   On an appeal under regulation 2.1 or 2.2 above, the High Court may:

(a)   affirm *our* decision;

(b)   direct *us* to grant eligibility to commence or continue a period of *recognised training*, or to issue a *certificate of eligibility*, as the case may be; or

(c)   make such recommendations to *us* as the High Court thinks fit.

Regulation 3: Appeals against our decisions arising from character and suitability issues

3.1   If *you* are an *unadmitted person*, *you* may appeal to the High Court under this regulation against *our* decision:

(a)   on an application under regulation 17.1 of the *SRA Training Regulations* Qualification and Provider Regulations for review of a refusal to recognise a period of training or eligibility to commence or continue *recognised training*;

Authorisation and Practising Requirements

(b) if *you* have been certified eligible under regulation 4 of the *QLTR* or regulation 2 of the *QLTSR* other than pursuant to Directive 2005/36/EC, on an application under regulation 17(2) of the *QLTR*, or regulation 7.2 of the *QLTSR*, for review of the imposition of a prohibition or sanction;

(c) on an application under regulation 17(5) of the *QLTR*, or regulation 7.5 of the *QLTSR*, for removal of a prohibition or sanction.

3.2   If *you* are an *unadmitted person* who has been certified eligible pursuant to Directive 2005/36/EC, *you* have rights of appeal under regulation 36 of the European Communities (Recognition of Professional Qualifications) Regulations 2007 against:

(a) prohibition of an attempt at the *QLTT*, or any attempt at any or all of the assessments under *QLTSR*; or

(b) refusal to lift that prohibition on an application for review;

(c) see regulation 17(4) of the *QLTR* or 7.4 of the *QLTSR*.

3.3   An appeal under:

(a) regulation 3.1(a) or (b) above must be brought within three months of *you* receiving notification of *our* decision on the review;

(b) regulation 3.1(c) above must be brought within three months of *you* receiving notification of *our* decision on the application for removal of the prohibition or sanction.

3.4   On any appeal under regulation 3.1 above, the High Court may:

(a) affirm *our* decision;

(b) direct *us* to grant eligibility to commence a period of *recognised training*, or to issue a *certificate of eligibility*, as the case may be; or

(c) make such recommendations to *us* as the High Court thinks fit.

PART 3: APPLICATIONS FOR ADMISSION

Regulation 4: When you can make an application for admission

4.1   *Your application for admission* may be made at any time after *you* have complied with the *SRA Training Regulations*, the *QLTR* or the *QLTSR*.

Regulation 5: Form and fees

5.1   *Your application for admission* must be made to *us* in such form and be accompanied by such fee and documents as *we* may from time to time prescribe.

Regulation 6: Our decisions

6.1   If *we*:

(a) are satisfied that *you* have complied with the *SRA Training Regulations*, the *QLTR* or the *QLTSR*; and

(b) are satisfied as to *your character and suitability* to be a *solicitor*;

we shall issue *you* with a *certificate of satisfaction* in accordance with section 3(1) of the Solicitors Act 1974.

Guidance note

(i)   *We* will satisfy *ourselves* as to *your character and suitability* in a number of ways. These will include, but are not limited to, Disclosure and Barring Service disclosures as well as self-disclosure in accordance with the *SRA Suitability Test*.

6.2   In any case where *we* refuse to issue a *certificate of satisfaction* under regulation 6.1 *we* shall notify *you* to this effect stating the grounds for refusal within one month of *you* complying with all reasonable requirements *we* make in respect of the application.

6.3   If *we* refuse to issue a *certificate of satisfaction* for either reason given in regulation 6.1(a) or (b), *you* may apply to *us* in writing for a review of the decision within one month of receiving notification of the refusal.

6.4   Once the deadline in regulation 6.2 has passed without *us* issuing a *certificate of satisfaction* or notifying *you* of refusal, the application is deemed, for the purpose of any appeal, to have been refused and refusal notified to *you* on that date.

6.5   Where *we* refuse or fail to issue a *certificate of satisfaction* under regulation 6.1, except where *you* have established eligibility under regulation 4 of the *QLTR*, or regulation 2 of the *QLTSR* pursuant to Directive 2005/36/EC or the *Establishment Directive*, and *we* have upheld that refusal or deemed refusal following a review under regulation 6.3, *you* may appeal under this regulation to the High Court, which may:

(a)   affirm *our* decision;

(b)   direct *us* to issue a *certificate of satisfaction* to *you*; or

(c)   make such recommendations to *us* as the High Court thinks fit.

6.6   If *you* have established eligibility pursuant to:

(a)   Directive 2005/36/EC, *you* have the right to appeal to the High Court under regulation 36 of the European Communities (Recognition of Professional Qualifications) Regulations 2007; or

(b)   the *Establishment Directive*, *you* have the right to appeal to the High Court under regulation 35 of the European Communities (Lawyer's Practice) Regulations 2000;

within three months of receiving notification or deemed notification of *our* refusal, against refusal or deemed refusal of a *certificate of satisfaction*.

Authorisation and
Practising Requirements

Regulation 7: Admission following issue of certificate of satisfaction

7.1   Where a *certificate of satisfaction* has been issued under regulation 6.1, *you* shall be admitted as a *solicitor* within a reasonable period on a day *we* determine, unless cause to the contrary in writing is shown to *our* satisfaction.

Regulation 8: Cause for preventing admission following issue of a certificate of satisfaction, and review of such a decision

8.1   If, after *we* issue a *certificate of satisfaction* but before *your* admission, cause is shown in writing to *our* satisfaction that *you* should not be admitted, *we* shall not admit *you* as a *solicitor* and *we* shall notify *you* of *our* decision in writing.

8.2   *You* may within one month of receiving notification of *our* decision, ask for the matter to be reviewed.

8.3   In such a case, except where *you* have established eligibility under regulation 4 of the *QLTR* or regulation 2 of the *QLTSR*, pursuant to Directive 2005/36/EC or the *Establishment Directive*, *you* may appeal under this regulation to the High Court, which may:

(a)   affirm *our* decision;

(b)   direct *us* to admit *you* as a *solicitor*; or

(c)   make such recommendations to *us* as the High Court thinks fit.

8.4   If *you* have been certified eligible pursuant to Directive 2005/36/EC *you* have the right, within three months of receiving notification of *our* decision, to appeal to the High Court under regulation 36 of the European Communities (Recognition of Professional Qualifications) Regulations 2007 against:

(a)   *our* decision under regulation 8.1 above not to admit *you* as a *solicitor*; or

(b)   *our* refusal to reverse that decision on a review under regulation 8.2 above.

8.5   If *you* have been certified eligible pursuant to the *Establishment Directive*, *you* have the right, within three months of receiving notification of *our* decision, to appeal to the High Court under regulation 35 of the European Communities (Lawyer's Practice) Regulations 2000 against:

(a)   *our* decision under regulation 8.1 above not to admit *you* as a *solicitor*; or

(b)   *our* refusal to reverse that decision on a review under regulation 8.2 above.

8.6   An appeal under regulation 8.3 above must be brought within three months of the applicant receiving notification of *our* decision on the review.

8.7   *You* may make up to three applications to *us* to reverse *our* decision not to admit *you* as a *solicitor*, after intervals of not less than twelve months from the final determination as to the initial decision, or from the final determination of *your* previous application for review, as the case may be.

8.8   Within three months of receiving notification from *us* of *our* decision on an application to reverse the decision not to admit *you* as a *solicitor*, *you* may appeal under this regulation to the High Court, which may:

(a)   affirm *our* decision;

(b)   direct *us* to admit *you* as a *solicitor*; or

(c)   make such recommendations to *us* as the High Court thinks fit.

Regulation 9: Admission certificates

9.1   *We* shall prepare an admission certificate in respect of each person admitted. Every certificate shall be signed by the Chief Executive of the *SRA* or attested in such manner as the Chief Executive shall authorise.

[E.7] SRA Qualified Lawyers Transfer Scheme Regulations 2011

INTRODUCTION TO THE QUALIFIED LAWYERS TRANSFER SCHEME REGULATIONS

Preamble

Authority: Made on 17 June 2011 by the Solicitors Regulation Authority Board under sections 2 , 79 and 80 of the Solicitors Act 1974 with the approval of the Legal Services Board under paragraph 19 of Schedule 4 to the Legal Services Act 2007

Date: These regulations came into force on 6 October 2011

Replacing: The SRA Qualified Lawyers Transfer Scheme Regulations 2010

Regulating: Lawyers seeking to be admitted as solicitors via transfer from another jurisdiction or other UK qualified lawyer, and lawyers seeking admission by virtue of European Directives 2005/36/EC and 98/5/EC.

Overview

Outcomes-focused regulation concentrates on providing positive outcomes which when achieved will benefit and protect *clients* and the public. These regulations set out the outcomes-focused requirements governing the qualification process for lawyers seeking to be admitted as *solicitors* via transfer from another jurisdiction or *barristers*. They also set out the means by which certain lawyers can seek admission by virtue of European Directive 2005/36/EC and the *Establishment Directive*.

Education and training performs the underpinning, fundamental role in regulating *solicitors* – the creation of competent and ethical practitioners. *We* regulate the transfer process in order to give admitted *solicitors* the tools they need to adhere to the *Principles*.

The Principles

These regulations form part of the Handbook, in which the 10 mandatory *Principles* are all-pervasive. They apply to all those *we* regulate and underpin all aspects of practice. Outcomes relevant to lawyers transferring from another jurisdiction are listed beneath the *Principles*.

You must:

1. uphold the rule of law and the proper administration of justice;

2. act with integrity;

3. not allow *your* independence to be compromised;

Authorisation and Practising Requirements

4.   act in the best interests of each *client*;

5.   provide a proper standard of service to *your clients*;

6.   behave in a way that maintains the trust the public places in *you* and in the provision of legal services;

7.   comply with *your* legal and regulatory obligations and deal with *your* regulators and ombudsmen in an open, timely and co-operative manner;

8.   run *your* business or carry out *your* role in the business effectively and in accordance with proper governance and sound financial and risk management principles;

9.   run *your* business or carry out *your* role in the business in a way that encourages equality of opportunity and respect for diversity; and

10.   protect *client money* and *assets*.

Outcomes

The outcomes which apply to these regulations are that if *you* qualify as a *solicitor* by transfer from another jurisdiction, *you*:

O(QR1)   have achieved an appropriate standard of competence;

O(QR2)   undergo objective assessment to demonstrate this competence;

O(QR3)   are of proper *character and suitability*;

O(QR4)   have achieved an appropriate standard of written and spoken English;

O(QR5)   maintain competence through relevant ongoing training; and

O(QR6)   act so that *clients*, and the wider public, will have confidence that O(QR1) – O(QR5) have been demonstrated.

You must achieve, and where relevant continue to meet, these outcomes.

These outcomes, and the regulations that flow from them, apply to all those who are intending to become *solicitors* via transfer.

PART 1: INTERPRETATION AND ELIGIBILITY

Regulation 1: Interpretation and definitions

1.1   The SRA Handbook Glossary 2012 shall apply and, unless the context otherwise requires:

   (a)   all italicised terms shall be defined; and

   (b)   all terms shall be interpreted;

in accordance with the *Glossary*.

Regulation 2: Eligibility

2.1   Subject to regulations 2.2 and 2.4 below, if *you* seek to establish eligibility to apply for admission under these regulations, *you* must provide such evidence as *we* may require to show that *you*:

(a) are a *qualified lawyer* in a *recognised jurisdiction*;

(b) have followed the *full route to qualification* in the *recognised jurisdiction*;

(c) are *entitled to practise* as a *qualified lawyer* of the *recognised jurisdiction*;

(d) have satisfied any applicable English language requirements published by *us*; and

(e) are of the *character and suitability* to be admitted as a *solicitor*.

2.2   For the avoidance of doubt, any lawyer applying for admission pursuant to European Communities Directive 2005/36/EC or any legislation implementing that Directive in the *UK* is deemed to have satisfied 2.1(b) and (d) above.

2.3   *We* shall acknowledge receipt of *your* application under Directive 2005/36/EC within one month of receipt, and shall inform *you* if any document is missing.

2.4   Any lawyer applying for admission pursuant to the *Establishment Directive* or any legislation implementing that Directive in the *UK*, is deemed to have satisfied 2.1(b) and (d) above.

2.5   If *we* are satisfied that *you* are eligible, and *we* have determined that *you* must pass one or more of the *QLTS assessments*, *we* must issue a *QLTS certificate of eligibility* to that effect.

2.6   If *you* do not hold a *QLTS certificate of eligibility*, *you* may not register with the *assessment organisation* to take any of the *QLTS assessments*.

2.7   Where regulation 3.3 applies, if *we* are satisfied that *you* are eligible, and *we* have determined that *you* do not need to take any of the *QLTS assessments*, then *you* may proceed to admission.

2.8   A *QLTS certificate of eligibility* shall remain valid for a period of five years from the date of its issue. *You* cannot apply for a second or subsequent *QLTS certificate of eligibility* before the expiry of any existing certificate of eligibility.

2.9   These regulations apply to *qualified lawyers* seeking to be admitted as *solicitors* via transfer from another jurisdiction or *barristers*. Such individuals are not eligible to qualify under the *SRA Training Regulations*.

Authorisation and Practising Requirements

PART 2: ASSESSMENTS, RECOGNISED JURISDICTIONS AND QUALIFIED LAWYERS

Regulation 3: QLTS assessments

3.1   *We* shall:

(a)   publish guidelines and outcomes in relation to the *QLTS assessment*,

(b)   validate and authorise the provision of the *QLTS assessments* by the *assessment organisation*, and

(c)   monitor the provision of the *QLTS assessments* by the *assessment organisation*.

3.2   Subject to regulation 3.4 below, *international lawyers* must pass all the *QLTS assessments*.

3.3   If *you* are a lawyer applying for admission pursuant to European Communities Directive 2005/36/EC or any legislation implementing the Directive in the *UK*, or any *UK qualified lawyer*, *you* may be required to pass one or more *QLTS assessments*, as *we* shall determine.

3.4   Any applicant who has passed the *LPC* is eligible to apply for an exemption from Part 1 of the *QLTS assessments*.

Regulation 4: Review of lists of recognised jurisdictions and qualified lawyers

4.1   *We* will review the lists of *recognised jurisdictions* and *qualified lawyers* every five years or whenever written evidence is received which suggests the need for a jurisdiction or qualification to be reviewed.

4.2   For the avoidance of doubt, if *you* have not qualified in a *recognised jurisdiction* and/or are not a *qualified lawyer* for the purposes of these regulations, *you* have no right to appeal this designation by *us*.

Regulation 5: Lawyers seeking admission under the Establishment Directive

5.1   If *you* seek to establish eligibility pursuant to the *Establishment Directive* or any legislation implementing that Directive in the *UK*, *you* must prove to *us* that *you* have met the requirements of the *Establishment Directive* and implementing legislation and in particular that *you* have:

(a)   satisfied the nationality requirements set out in the legislation; and

(b)   satisfied *our* registration requirements; and either

(c)   effectively and regularly pursued for a period of at least three years a professional activity in the *UK* in the law of the *UK* including Community Law in accordance with article 10.1 of the *Establishment Directive*; or

(d)   effectively and regularly pursued a professional activity in the *UK* for a period of at least three years where your professional activity in the law of the

UK has been for a period of less than three years, under the conditions set out in article 10.3 of the *Establishment Directive*.

PART 3: APPEALS, AND SUITABILITY

Regulation 6: Review of decisions on eligibility

6.1   Subject to regulation 4.2, if *you* seek to establish eligibility under regulation 2 (including regulation 5) *you* may, within one month of receiving notification from *us* of:

(a)   any decision to refuse to issue a *QLTS certificate of eligibility*; or

(b)   (under regulation 3.3) any decision to require *you* to pass one or more of the *QLTS assessments*;

ask for the application to be reviewed.

6.2   Where *you* are seeking to establish eligibility (other than pursuant to Directive 2005/36/EC or the *Establishment Directive*) and *we* have:

(a)   refused the initial application on the ground that *you* are not suitable to be admitted as a *solicitor*; and

(b)   determined not to reverse that refusal on review;

you have the right, within three months of receiving notification or deemed notification from *us* of *our* decision on the review, to appeal to the High Court under regulation 3 of the *SRA Admission Regulations*.

6.3   Where *you* are seeking to establish eligibility pursuant to Directive 2005/36/EC and *we* make a decision in respect of that application *you* have the right, within four months of receiving notification or deemed notification of *our* decision, to appeal to the High Court under regulation 36 of the European Communities (Recognition of Professional Qualifications) Regulations 2007.

6.4   Where *you* are seeking to establish eligibility pursuant to the *Establishment Directive* and *we*:

(a)   fail to take a decision on the initial application and notify it to *you* within four months of receipt of all the relevant documents;

(b)   refuse the initial application; or

(c)   have determined not to reverse that refusal on a review;

you have the right, within three months of receiving notification or deemed notification of *our* decision, to appeal to the High Court under regulation 35 of the European Communities (Lawyer's Practice) Regulations 2000.

Guidance note

(i)   Deemed notification in regulation 6 is:

(a) the date on which the communication is delivered to or left at *your* last notified address or is sent electronically to *your* last notified email address or fax number;

(b) for recipients in the EEA or Switzerland, seven days after the communication has been sent by post or document exchange to *your* last notified contact address; or

(c) for recipients outside the EEA or Switzerland, 14 days after the communication has been sent by post or document exchange to *your* last notified contact address.

Regulation 7: Character and suitability of prospective solicitors

7.1   If *we* have granted *you* a *QLTS certificate of eligibility* under regulation 2, and at any time *we* are not satisfied as to *your character and suitability* to become a *solicitor*, *we* may on such terms as *we* determine prohibit any attempt at any or all of the *QLTS assessments*.

7.2   If *we* impose a prohibition under regulation 7.1, *you* may within one month of receiving notification or deemed notification from *us* of *our* decision, ask for the matter to be reviewed.

7.3   If *you* have been authorised to apply other than pursuant to Directive 2005/36/EC, *you* have the right to appeal to the High Court under regulation 3 of the *SRA Admission Regulations* within three months of receiving notification or deemed notification from *us* of *our* decision on a review under regulation 7.2.

7.4   If *you* have been authorised to apply pursuant to Directive 2005/36/EC, and *we*:

(a) prohibit any attempt at any or all of the *QLTS assessments* under regulation 7.1; or

(b) refuse to lift that prohibition on *your* application for review;

you have the right, within four months of receiving notification or deemed notification of *our* decision, to appeal to the High Court under regulation 36 of the European Communities (Recognition of Professional Qualifications) Regulations 2007.

7.5   *You* may make up to three applications to *us* to remove a prohibition after intervals of not less than 12 months from the final determination as to the imposition of the prohibition, or from the final determination of *your* previous application for review, as the case may be.

7.6   *You* have the right to appeal to the High Court under regulation 3 of the *SRA Admission Regulations* within three months of receiving notification or deemed notification from us of *our* decision on an application for the removal of a prohibition under 7.5.

Guidance note

(i)   For further information please consult the Suitability Test.

(ii)   For deemed notification guidance, please see the guidance note under regulation 6.

PART 4: FORMS, FEES AND ADMISSION

Regulation 8: Forms and fees

8.1   If *you* wish to sit the *QLTS assessments*, *you* must give notice to the *assessment organisation* in the prescribed form and pay the prescribed fee.

8.2   If *you* wish to make an application or give notice to *us* in accordance with these regulations, *you* must do so in the prescribed form and pay the prescribed fee.

8.3   If at the time of making *your* application or giving a notice, no form has been prescribed by *us* or the *assessment organisation*, the application or notice must be in writing, signed by *you* or the person giving it and provide such information as is necessary to enable *us* or the *assessment organisation* to deal with the application.

8.4   Whether or not the application is made or notice given on a prescribed form *we* may, in *our* absolute discretion, require *you*, or the person giving notice, to furnish such further information as *we* consider necessary.

8.5   *We* may require:

(a)   *your* application to be supported by such evidence as *we* consider necessary;

(b)   facts relevant to *your* application to be accompanied by statutory declaration; and

(c)   *your* attendance for an interview.

8.6   For the avoidance of doubt, *you* may not apply to *us* for a review of a decision by an *assessment organisation* where *you* have failed one or more *QLTS assessment(s)*.

Regulation 9: Admission as a solicitor

9.1   Admission as a *solicitor* takes place under Part 3 of the *SRA Admission Regulations*.

PART 5: TRANSITION FROM PREVIOUS REGULATIONS

Regulation 10: Commencement and repeal

10.1   The *QLTSR* 2010 came into force on 1 September 2010. On this date the *QLTR* 2009 ceased to have effect for new applications. The *QLTR* will continue in force for:

(a)   candidates holding valid *QLTR certificates of eligibility*; or

(b)   candidates who have submitted an application for a *QLTR certificate of eligibility* prior to 1 September 2010; and

(c)   those candidates that fall within regulation 11.3 below.

Regulation 11: Transitional arrangements

11.1   On 1 September 2010, *we* ceased to issue *QLTR certificates of eligibility* and instead began issuing *QLTS certificates of eligibility*.

11.2   The *QLTT* will continue to be available until the expiry of all *QLTR certificates of eligibility*.

11.3   If *you* have commenced the Bar Vocational Course after 1 August 2009 and before the commencement of these regulations on a part-time basis, your application for a *certificate of eligibility* shall be treated as if it were made under the *QLTR* provided that *you* have successfully completed the Bar Vocational Course:

(a)   prior to 31 August 2011; or

(b)   if *we*, in the exercise of *our* discretion, determine that *your* circumstances are exceptional, such later date as *we* determine shall apply.

SRA Higher Rights of Audience Regulations 2011

INTRODUCTION TO THE HIGHER RIGHTS OF AUDIENCE REGULATIONS

Preamble

Authority: Made on 17 June 2011 by the Solicitors Regulation Authority Board under sections 2, 79 and 80 of the Solicitors Act 1974 with the approval of the Legal Services Board under paragraph 19 of Schedule 4 to the Legal Services Act 2007

Date: These regulations came into force on 6 October 2011

Replacing: Solicitors' Higher Rights of Audience Regulations 2010

Regulating: The qualifications that solicitors and RELs require to exercise rights of audience in the higher courts in England and Wales.

Overview

Outcomes-focused regulation concentrates on providing positive outcomes which when achieved will benefit and protect *clients* and the public. These regulations aim to ensure that *solicitors* and *RELs* who want to exercise rights of audience in the *higher courts* of England and Wales are competent to do so.

Solicitors and *RELs* are granted rights of audience in all courts upon qualification/ registration but cannot exercise those rights in the *higher courts* until they have complied with additional requirements. *Solicitors* and *RELs* wishing to undertake *criminal advocacy* must comply with the *SRA QASA Regulations*. *We* are required to set the education and training requirements which *you* must comply with in order for these rights to be used. These regulations describe the qualifications available, where rights can be transferred, and set out the process for becoming eligible to exercise rights of audience in the *higher courts*.

The intention is to give the public confidence that *solicitor* higher court advocates have met appropriate standards and adhere to the relevant *Principles*.

The Principles

These regulations form part of the Handbook, in which the 10 mandatory *Principles* are all-pervasive. They apply to all those *we* regulate and underpin all aspects of practice. Outcomes relevant to these regulations are listed beneath the *Principles*.

You must:

1. uphold the rule of law and the proper administration of justice;

2. act with integrity;

3. not allow *your* independence to be compromised;

4. act in the best interests of each *client*;

5. provide a proper standard of service to *your clients*;

6. behave in a way that maintains the trust the public places in *you* and in the provision of legal services;

7. comply with *your* legal and regulatory obligations and deal with *your* regulators and ombudsmen in an open, timely and co-operative manner.

8. run *your* business or carry out *your* role in the business effectively and in accordance with proper governance and sound financial and risk management principles;

9. run *your* business or carry out *your* role in the business in a way that encourages equality of opportunity and respect for diversity; and

10. protect *client money* and *assets*.

Outcomes

The outcomes which apply to these regulations are that:

O(HR1) *you* have achieved the standard of competence required of *higher courts* advocates;

O(HR2) *you* demonstrate this competence through objective assessment;

O(HR3) *you* maintain competence through relevant ongoing training; and

O(HR4) *you* act so that *clients*, the judiciary and the wider public, have confidence that this has been demonstrated.

These outcomes, and the regulations that flow from them, apply to admitted *solicitors*, and *RELs*.

PART 1: INTERPRETATION

Regulation 1: Interpretation and definitions

1.1 The SRA Handbook Glossary 2012 shall apply and, unless the context otherwise requires:

(a) all italicised terms shall be defined; and

(b) all terms shall be interpreted;

in accordance with the *Glossary*.

PART 2: RIGHTS, AND QUALIFICATION

Regulation 2: Rights of audience

2.1   Subject to the provisions of these regulations, and in relation to *criminal advocacy* the *SRA QASA Regulations*, *you* may be authorised by *us* to exercise rights of audience in the *higher courts*.

2.2   *Solicitors* and *RELs* appearing in the Intellectual Property Enterprise Court (IPEC) do not need to hold a Higher Courts (Civil Advocacy) Qualification under these regulations.

> *Guidance note:*
>
> (i)   As a *solicitor* or *REL you* already have full rights of audience in Tribunals, Coroners Courts, Magistrates Courts, County Courts, the Family Court and European Courts. An application for civil higher rights of audience allows *you* to also appear in civil proceedings in the Crown Court, High Court, Court of Appeal and Supreme Court. *Solicitors* and *RELs* undertaking *criminal advocacy* must also comply with the *SRA QASA Regulations*.
>
> (ii)   The IPEC, a specialist court within the Chancery Division of the High Court, replaced the Patents County Court (PCC) in October 2013. Prior to this, *solicitors* and *RELs* appearing did not need a higher rights qualification to appear in the PCC. As the cases, rules and procedures are not materially different, and the costs and damages limits are the same, *we* do not require *solicitors* and *RELs* to possess the civil qualification in order to exercise their rights of audience in the IPEC.

Regulation 3: Qualifications to exercise extended rights of audience

3.1   If *you* meet the requirements of these regulations, *we* may grant one or both of the following qualifications:

(a)   Higher Courts (Civil Advocacy) Qualification which entitles the *solicitor* or *REL* to exercise rights of audience in all civil proceedings in the *higher courts*, including judicial review proceedings in any *court* arising from any criminal cause;

(b)   Higher Courts (Criminal Advocacy) Qualification which, subject to the *SRA QASA Regulations* in relation to *criminal advocacy*, entitles the *solicitor* or *REL* to exercise rights of audience in all criminal proceedings in the *higher courts* and judicial review proceedings in any *court* arising from any criminal cause.

3.2   If *you* have been granted a *higher courts* qualification by the Law Society or *us* under the *previous regulations*, *you* shall be deemed to have been granted the equivalent qualification or qualifications under regulation 3.1 above.

Authorisation and Practising Requirements

Guidance note

(i)   If *you* have been granted a *higher courts advocacy qualification* under previous regulations, *you* are not required to re-apply under these regulations.

(ii)   *You* may not undertake *criminal advocacy* unless *accredited* to do so in accordance with the *SRA QASA Regulations*.

Regulation 4: Qualifying to exercise extended rights of audience

4.1   When applying for a *higher courts advocacy qualification you* must demonstrate to *us* that *you* are competent to undertake advocacy in the proceedings in relation to which *you* have applied by:

(a)   successfully completing assessments prescribed by *us*;

(b)   being an *REL* and having undertaken any further step(s) as may be specified by *us* under regulation 5.2; or

(c)   being a lawyer to whom Directive 2005/36 applies and having undertaken any further step(s) as may be specified by *us* under regulation 5.2.

4.2   *We* will issue *standards* against which the competence of those applying for a *higher courts advocacy qualification* and exercising those rights of audience conferred by the qualification awarded will be assessed. The *standards* do not form part of these regulations and may be amended from time to time by *us*.

PART 3: RIGHTS FROM PREVIOUS PROFESSIONAL STATUS

Regulation 5: Qualification gained in a European jurisdiction

5.1   *You* may apply for a qualification to exercise rights of audience in the *higher courts* if *you* are an *REL* or a lawyer to whom Directive 2005/36 applies.

5.2   Each application will be considered by *us* on its merits and *we* may require *you* to undertake such steps as *we* may specify in order to gain the qualification.

Regulation 6: Conversion provisions for barristers

6.1   In accordance with paragraph 86 of Schedule 21 of the LSA, a *barrister* with existing higher rights of audience will automatically be awarded the *solicitors'* higher rights of audience when applying to the roll.

Guidance note

(i)   *You* will be required to declare when applying to be admitted to the roll that *you* were formerly a *barrister* with higher rights of audience and that *you* have no disciplinary proceedings in progress against *you*.

(ii) *You* may not undertake *criminal advocacy* unless *you* are *accredited* under the *SRA QASA Regulations*. If *you* have qualified as a *solicitor* under the *QLTSR* on the basis of being a *barrister you* will be entitled to bring *your QASA* accreditation level with *you*.

Regulation 7: Conversion provision for RELs

7.1   If *you* are an *REL* who is granted a qualification listed in regulation 3.1, *you* shall keep that qualification upon being admitted as a *solicitor*.

PART 4: ASSESSMENTS AND ONGOING TRAINING

Regulation 8: Assessments

8.1   *We* shall:

(a)   issue guidelines and *standards* for the provision of competence assessments in *higher courts* civil advocacy and *higher courts* criminal advocacy;

(b)   validate and authorise organisations to provide assessments; and

(c)   monitor the provision of assessments.

Guidance note

(i)   *You* are not required to undertake any training before taking the assessments, but *you* may decide that *you* need to undertake additional training, which will be offered by assessment organisations. Whether or not *you* require additional training is a decision for *you*.

(ii)   In satisfying the *standards*, *you* will need to comply with the relevant legislation and procedures in force at the time.

(iii)   *You* can apply for the qualification in either civil or criminal proceedings. Assessment providers will offer assessments that cover the generic standards in evidence, ethics, advocacy and equality and diversity as well as specific standards in either civil or criminal proceedings. If *you* wish to obtain the qualification in both proceedings *you* must take both assessments.

(iv)   A *trainee* may undertake the assessments but will not be permitted to exercise the rights until admission as a *solicitor*.

Regulation 9: Continuing professional development

9.1   If *you* have gained a *higher courts advocacy qualification* under regulation 3.1, *you* must undertake at least five hours of *CPD* relating to the provision of advocacy services in the *higher courts* in each of the first five *CPD years* following the grant of the qualification.

9.2   If *you* have gained a *higher courts advocacy qualification* under regulation 5.1 or are exercising any right of audience in the *higher courts* by virtue of any exemption *you* have under regulation 6, *you* must undertake at least five hours of *CPD* relating to the provision of advocacy services in the *higher courts* in each of the first five *CPD years* following the date of *your* first exercise of the right.

Guidance note

(i)   The requirements in regulation 9.1 and 9.2 are not an additional requirement to that required by the SRA Training Regulations Part 3 – CPD Regulations.

(ii)   This requirement commences the *CPD year* following the year in which the qualification is awarded or from the date *you* first undertake advocacy in the *higher courts* if qualifying via a comparable qualification. It is up to *you* to decide what *your* training needs are in relation to the advocacy services *you* provide. Therefore, the training may be advocacy training, training on new procedures or on substantive law if relevant to higher court practice.

PART 5: APPLICATIONS, REVIEWS AND TRANSITIONAL ARRANGEMENTS

Regulation 10: Applications and reviews

10.1   *You* shall make an application under these regulations in the manner prescribed by *us* and accompanied by the appropriate fee fixed from time to time.

10.2   *You* shall not apply for a *higher courts advocacy qualification* until one of the requirements of regulation 4 has been met.

10.3   When applying for a *higher courts advocacy qualification*, *you* may within 28 days of receiving notification of *our* decision ask for the decision to be reviewed.

10.4   *You* may not apply to *us* for a review of a decision by an assessment provider where *you* have failed an assessment.

Guidance note

(i)   An application for higher rights of audience should be made via *our* website – **www.sra.org.uk**.

Regulation 11: Transitional arrangements

11.1   If, at the time the Solicitors' Higher Rights of Audience Regulations 2010 came into force *you* had undertaken in part the requirements specified in regulation 5 of the Higher Courts Qualification Regulations 2000 (the development route) and have not been granted the Higher Courts (All Proceedings) Qualification, *you* may either:

(a)   within 24 months of the coming into force of the Solicitors' Higher Rights of Audience Regulations 2010, complete the requirements set out in regulations 5(1)(a) and 5(1)(b) of the Higher Courts Qualification Regulations 2000, which will be treated as meeting the requirements of regulation 4 of these regulations, and may be granted both the Higher Courts (Civil Advocacy) Qualification and the Higher Courts (Criminal Advocacy) Qualification; or

(b) apply for a *higher courts advocacy qualification* in accordance with these regulations.

11.2   If, at the time the Solicitors' Higher Rights of Audience Regulations 2010 came into force, *you* had applied to *us* under regulation 6 of the Higher Courts Qualification Regulations 2000 (the accreditation route) but have not been granted a higher courts advocacy qualification, *you* may either:

(a) within 24 months of the coming into force of the Solicitors' Higher Rights of Audience Regulations 2010 regulations complete the requirements set out in regulations 4(1)(b) and 6 of the Higher Courts Qualification Regulations 2000, which will be treated as meeting the requirements of regulation 4 of these regulations, and may be granted one of or both the Higher Courts (Civil Advocacy) Qualification and the Higher Courts (Criminal Advocacy) Qualification; or

(b) withdraw *your* application under the Higher Courts Qualification Regulations 2000 and apply for one of or both the Higher Courts (Civil Advocacy) Qualification and the Higher Courts (Criminal Advocacy) Qualification in accordance with these regulations.

11.3   *We* have the power to waive in writing any of the provisions of regulation 11 and to place conditions on and to revoke such waiver.

Authorisation and Practising Requirements

SRA Quality Assurance Scheme for Advocates (Crime) Regulations 2013

INTRODUCTION TO THE QUALITY ASSURANCE SCHEME FOR ADVOCATES (CRIME) REGULATIONS

Preamble

Authority: Made on 26 July 2013 by the Solicitors Regulation Authority Board under sections 2, 79 and 80 of the Solicitors Act 1974 with the approval of the Legal Services Board under paragraph 19 of Schedule 4 to the Legal Services Act 2007

Date: These regulations came into force on 30 September 2013

Replacing: SRA Quality Assurance Scheme for Advocates (Crime) Notification Regulations 2012

Regulating: The practice of criminal advocacy in England and Wales

Overview

Outcomes-focused regulation concentrates on providing positive outcomes which when achieved will benefit and protect *clients* and the public. These regulations aim to ensure that *solicitors* and *RELs* who want to conduct *criminal advocacy* in England and Wales are competent to do so.

Advocacy is part of an effective justice system. *Solicitors* and *RELs* are granted rights of audience in all courts upon qualification/registration but must, in those proceedings which fall under the definition of *criminal advocacy*, exercise those rights of audience only where accredited by the *SRA* under these regulations.

The *QASA*, to which these regulations give effect so far as *solicitors* and *RELs* are concerned, is designed so that all advocates in the criminal courts have undergone a process of *accreditation* to ensure they are only dealing with cases within their competence and that they are subject to assessment and independent monitoring of their performance against agreed criteria.

The intention is to give the public confidence that those conducting criminal advocacy have met appropriate standards and adhere to the relevant *Principles*.

The Principles

These regulations form part of the Handbook, in which the 10 mandatory *Principles* are all-pervasive. They apply to all those *we* regulate and underpin all aspects of practice. Outcomes relevant to these regulations are listed beneath the *Principles*.

You must:

1. uphold the rule of law and the proper administration of justice;

2. act with integrity;

3. not allow *your* independence to be compromised;

4. act in the best interests of each *client*;

5. provide a proper standard of service to *your clients*;

6. behave in a way that maintains the trust the public places in *you* and in the provision of legal services;

7. comply with *your* legal and regulatory obligations and deal with *your* regulators and ombudsmen in an open, timely and co-operative manner;

8. run *your* business or carry out *your* role in the business effectively and in accordance with proper governance and sound financial and risk management principles;

9. run *your* business or carry out *your* role in the business in a way that encourages equality of opportunity and respect for diversity; and

10. protect *client money* and *assets*.

Outcomes

The outcomes which apply to these regulations are that:

O(QS1)   *you* have achieved the standard of competence required of advocates conducting *criminal advocacy*;

O(QS2)   *you* demonstrate this competence through independent assessment;

O(QS3)   *you* act so that *clients*, the judiciary and the wider public, have confidence that this has been demonstrated.

PART 1: INTERPRETATION

Regulation 1: Interpretation and definitions

1.1   The SRA Handbook Glossary 2012 shall apply and, unless the context otherwise requires:

(a) all italicised terms shall be defined; and

(b) all terms shall be interpreted,

in accordance with the *Glossary*.

PART 2: QUALITY ASSURANCE SCHEME FOR ADVOCATES (CRIME) ("QASA")

Regulation 2: Scope of scheme

2.1   *You* may not undertake *criminal advocacy* unless *accredited* to do so in accordance with these regulations and the *QASA*.

2.2   *You* may be *accredited* under these regulations at a level ranging from 1 to 4 corresponding to the increasing seriousness and complexity of criminal cases falling within those levels as set out in the *QASA*.

2.3   *You* may only accept instructions to conduct *criminal advocacy* where *you* are satisfied they fall within or below the level at which *you* are *accredited*, unless *you* are satisfied that *you* are competent to accept instructions for a case at a higher level in light of the particular circumstances and in accordance with the guidance in the *QASA*.

Regulation 3: Accreditation requirement

3.1   *You* may only be *accredited* under these regulations if *you* are a *solicitor* holding a current practising certificate or an *REL*.

3.2   *You* may only be *accredited* under these regulations at levels 2, 3 or 4 if *you* have obtained the *higher courts advocacy qualification* for *criminal advocacy*.

Regulation 4: General provisions relating to applications made under these regulations

4.1   *You* may register, make an application or give a notification under these regulations by:

(a) completing the *prescribed* form;

(b) submitting such information as may be *prescribed*; and

(c) paying the *prescribed* fee, if any.

4.2   On receipt of an application under these regulations the *SRA* shall decide whether to grant or refuse the application, and shall notify *you* accordingly giving reasons for any decision to refuse the application.

4.3   Before reaching a decision on an application, the *SRA* may:

(a) require *you* to undertake such other steps as the *SRA* may specify in order for *you* to be accredited at one of the levels under the *QASA*.

(b) require from *you* or a third party, such additional information, documents or references as it considers appropriate.

Authorisation and
Practising Requirements

PART 3: ACCREDITATION FOR CURRENT PRACTITIONERS

Regulation 5: Application of Part 3

5.1   Part 3 of these regulations applies to you if you were admitted as a *solicitor* or became an *REL* before 1 September 2015.

Regulation 6: Accreditation at level 1

6.1   *You* may register with the *SRA* to conduct *criminal advocacy* at level 1 by submitting an application in the manner prescribed by the *SRA*.

6.2   After *you* have registered with the *SRA* under regulation 6.1, *you* will be granted *full accreditation* at level 1.

Regulation 7: Registration and Provisional accreditation at level 2, 3 or 4

7.1   *You* may register to conduct criminal advocacy at levels 2, 3 or 4 by submitting an application in the manner *prescribed* by the *SRA*.

7.2   After *you* have registered with the *SRA* under regulation 7.1, *you* will be granted *provisional accreditation* at *your* chosen level.

7.3   Subject to regulation 8.2 below, if *you* have been granted *provisional accreditation* at level 2, 3 or 4 *you* must apply to the *SRA* for *full accreditation* at *your* chosen level within 24 months of the date *you* were granted *provisional accreditation*.

7.4   If *you* do not apply for *full accreditation* or for an extension of time under regulation 18 within 24 months of the date *you* were granted *provisional accreditation*, *you* will not be *accredited* under these regulations.

Regulation 8: Full accreditation at level 2

8.1   Subject to regulation 8.2, if *you* do not intend to undertake trials, *you* may apply for *full accreditation* at level 2 by submitting an application in the manner *prescribed* by the *SRA* enclosing an assessment by an assessment organisation approved by the *SRA* demonstrating that *you* have met all the competencies as set out in the *QASA*.

> *Guidance note:*
>
> (i)   A list of approved assessment organisations is available via *our* website – www.sra.org.uk. The assessment shall be in the form approved by *us* for the purpose.

8.2   If *you* do not intend to undertake trials and *you* have obtained *your higher courts advocacy qualification* for *criminal advocacy* by assessment in accordance with the *SRA Higher Rights of Audience Regulations*, *you* will automatically be granted *full accreditation* and will not be required to apply for *re-accreditation* until:

(a)   2015, if *you* obtained *your higher courts advocacy qualification* for criminal advocacy in 2010; or

(b) 2016, if *you* obtained *your higher courts advocacy qualification* for criminal advocacy in 2011, 2012 or 2013.

8.3   If *you* intend to undertake trials *you* may apply for *full accreditation* at level 2 by submitting:

(a) an application in the manner *prescribed* by the *SRA*; and

(b) the prescribed number of *CAEFs* obtained in the *prescribed* manner in accordance with the *QASA* demonstrating that *you* have met the level 2 competencies set out in the *QASA* in level 2 trials.

Regulation 9: Full accreditation at Levels 3 and 4

9.1   *You* may apply for *full accreditation* at levels 3 or 4 by submitting:

(a) an application in the manner *prescribed* by the *SRA*;

(b) the *prescribed* number of *CAEFs* obtained in the *prescribed* manner in accordance with the *QASA* demonstrating that *you* have met the required competencies set out in the *QASA* in trials at that level.

Regulation 10: Level 2 advocates intending to undertake trials

10.1   If *you* are *provisionally accredited* in accordance with regulation 7 or *fully accredited* in accordance with regulation 8.1 or 8.2 at level 2 and intend to undertake trials, *you* must:

(a) notify the SRA of *your* intention to undertake level 2 trial work in the manner *prescribed* by the *SRA*; and

(b) within 24 months of the *SRA* accepting such notification submit the prescribed number of *CAEFs* obtained in the *prescribed* manner in accordance with the *QASA* demonstrating that *you* have met the level 2 competencies set out in the *QASA* in level 2 trials.

Regulation 11: Progression to level 3 or 4

11.1   If *you* are *fully accredited* in accordance with regulation 8.3 at level 2 or are *fully accredited* at level 3, and in either case *you* intend to progress to the level above, *you* must:

(a) notify the *SRA* of *your* intention to progress in the manner prescribed by the *SRA*; and

(b) within 12 months of the *SRA* accepting such notification submit the *prescribed* number of *CAEFs* obtained in the *prescribed* manner in accordance with the *QASA* demonstrating that *you* have met the required competencies set out in the *QASA* in trials at the level at which *you* are *fully accredited*.

Authorisation and Practising Requirements

11.2   After *you* have complied with the requirements of regulation 11.1 above, *you* may be *provisionally accredited* at the next level and *you* may apply for *full accreditation* under regulation 9 above within 12 months of the date *you* were granted *provisional accreditation*.

11.3   If *you* do not apply for *full accreditation* or for an extension of time under regulation 18 within 12 months of the date *you* were granted *provisional accreditation*, *you* will revert to the level at which *you* were *fully accredited*.

PART 4: ACCREDITATION FOR NEW PRACTITIONERS

Regulation 12: Application of Part 4

12.1   Part 4 of these regulations applies to *you* if *you* were admitted as a *solicitor* or became an *REL* after 1 September 2015.

Regulation 13: Accreditation at level 1

13.1   When *you* are either issued with *your* first practising certificate or become an *REL*, *you* will be granted *full accreditation* at level 1.

Regulation 14: Accreditation at level 2

14.1   If *you* obtain the *higher courts advocacy qualification* for *criminal advocacy* by assessment, *you* will be granted *full accreditation* at level 2.

14.2   If *you* intend to undertake trials at level 2, *you* must comply with regulation 10 above.

Regulation 15: Progression to level 3 or 4

15.1   If *you* are *fully accredited* in accordance with regulation 10 at level 2 or are *fully accredited* at level 3, and in either case *you* intend to progress to the level above, *you* must comply with regulation 11 above.

PART 5: PRACTITIONERS RETURNING TO QASA

Regulation 16: Procedure for returning to QASA

16.1   If *your accreditation* has lapsed, *you* may apply to re-enter *QASA* by complying with the procedures set out in Part 3 of these regulations.

16.2   If *your accreditation* has lapsed and *you* are applying for *accreditation* at level 1, *you* must submit evidence of assessed continuing professional development in the field of *criminal advocacy* in the period since *you* were first accredited at level 1 or since *your* most recent *re-accreditation*.

Guidance note:

(i) *You* may tell *us* that *you* no longer wish to conduct *criminal advocacy*, in which case *you* should write to notify *us* and *we* will stop corresponding with *you* about *accreditation* or *re-accreditation*.

PART 6: RE-ACCREDITATION, SPECIAL CIRCUMSTANCES AND APPEALS

Regulation 17: Re-accreditation

17.1   Subject to regulation 8.2 above, if *you* are *accredited* to conduct *criminal advocacy*, then *you* must apply for *re-accreditation* at *your* current level in the manner *prescribed* by the *SRA* within five years of the date *you* were first *accredited* or *your* most recent *re-accreditation* at that level.

17.2   The *SRA* may where it thinks appropriate ask *you* to apply for *re-accreditation* within a different period to that specified in regulation 17.1 above and *you* must comply with such a request.

17.3   *You* must supply appropriate evidence to support *your* application for *re-accreditation* demonstrating *your* competence to conduct *criminal advocacy* in accordance with the *QASA*.

17.4   If *you* fail to apply for *re-accreditation* within the period required by the *SRA* and have not been granted an extension of the period under regulation 18, *your* *accreditation* at *your* current level will lapse.

17.5   If *you* do not satisfy the requirements for *re-accreditation*, *your* *accreditation* at *your* current level will lapse and *you* will be *provisionally accredited* at the level below.

Regulation 18: Special circumstances

18.1   *You* may, on application to the *SRA*, apply for an extension of the period for *accreditation* or *re-accreditation*, which the *SRA* may grant. An extension of the period for *accreditation* or *re-accreditation* may be granted on such terms as the *SRA* sees fit.

18.2   *You* may, on providing the *SRA* with adequate reasons, apply for an independent assessment of *your* competence to conduct *criminal advocacy* at levels 2, 3 or 4 and submit such an assessment in place of one or more *CAEFs*.

18.3   An application under regulation 18.1 for an extension of the period for *accreditation* or *re-accreditation* must be made before the expiry of the date by which the relevant application for *accreditation* or *re-accreditation* must be made.

Regulation 19: Additional measures

19.1   The *SRA* may receive at any point during the currency of *your* *accreditation* *CAEFs* which raise a concern about *your* competence to conduct *criminal advocacy*. Where the *SRA* receives any such concern, either because *you* have provided such information or otherwise, the *SRA* may do one or more of the following:

(a) appoint an independent assessor to conduct an assessment of *your criminal advocacy*;

(b) require *you* to take specific steps;

(c) revoke *your accreditation* at *your* current level; or

(d) where such concerns amount to a breach of the *Principles*, refer *you* for consideration of disciplinary action.

Guidance note:

(i) *We* will inform *you* and provide *our* reasons for taking action in any case where regulation 19 is relied upon.

19.2   Where *you* have applied for *accreditation* or *re-accreditation* at level 1 and *your* application has been refused, *you* will not be entitled to accept any instructions to conduct *criminal advocacy* and the *SRA* may recommend *you* to take specific steps in accordance with regulation 19.1 before *you* reapply for *accreditation* or *re-accreditation* as appropriate.

19.3   Where the *SRA* has required *you* to take specific steps under regulation 19.1(b), the *SRA* shall assess the outcome of that action before deciding upon any pending application or further application that *you* may have submitted or any further action that the *SRA* intends to take.

Regulation 20: Appeals against decisions

20.1   *You* may within 28 days of receiving notification of the *SRA's* decision appeal against that decision.

20.2   *You* may not appeal to the *SRA* against a decision by an assessment organisation where you have failed an assessment.

20.3   *You* may not appeal to the *SRA* against an evaluation by an external assessor or a Judge.

PART 7: REPEAL, COMMENCEMENT AND TRANSITIONAL PROVISIONS

Regulation 21: Repeal, commencement and transitional provisions

21.1   The *SRA Quality Assurance Scheme for Advocates (Crime) Notification Regulations* shall cease to have effect on 30 September 2013.

21.2   These regulations come into force on 30 September 2013 but shall be implemented in phases in accordance with the table set out below.

Phase	Dates	Circuits
1	30 September 2013 – 30 May 2014	Midland
		Western
2	31 May – 3 October 2014	South Eastern
3	4 October – 31 December 2014	Northern
		North Eastern
		Wales and Chester

21.3   Subject to regulation 21.4, *you* must register under Part 3 of these regulations in accordance with the dates set out in the table above for the Circuit within which *your* practising address falls or, where different, the Circuit within which *you* undertake the majority of *your criminal advocacy*.

21.4   After the relevant dates for each Circuit, as set out in the table at regulation 21.2 above, *you* must be *accredited* in accordance with these regulations before *you* undertake any *criminal advocacy* in that Circuit.

INTRODUCTION TO THE SUITABILITY TEST

Preamble

Authority: Made on 17 June 2011 by the Solicitors Regulation Authority Board under sections 28, 79 and 80 of the Solicitors Act 1974 with the approval of the Legal Services Board under paragraph 19 of Schedule 4 to the Legal Services Act 2007

Date: These regulations came into force on 6 October 2011

Replacing: The SRA guidelines on the assessment of character and suitability

Applicability: Trainee solicitors under the SRA Training Regulations;

Qualified lawyers under the QLTSR;

Those seeking admission as solicitors under the Admission Regulations, fulfilling the duties under section 3 of the Solicitors Act 1974;

Those seeking to become authorised role holders in accordance with rules 8.5 and 8.6 of the SRA Authorisation Rules, and regulation 4.8 of the SRA Practising Regulations;

Those seeking restoration to the roll of solicitors under regulation 8 of the Solicitors Keeping of the Roll Regulations 2011.

Overview

Outcomes-focused regulation concentrates on providing positive outcomes which when achieved will benefit and protect *clients* and the public. *We* must ensure that any individual admitted as a *solicitor* has, and maintains, the level of honesty, integrity and the professionalism expected by the public and other stakeholders and professionals, and does not pose a risk to the public or the profession.

The Suitability Test will apply the same high standards to all those seeking admission or restoration to the roll as a *solicitor*, as well as legally qualified and non-legally qualified applicants for roles in authorised bodies as *authorised role holders*.

The test is the same for non-solicitors as they will be working within the profession and must meet the same high standards that the general public expect of *solicitors*. This document is intended to make it clear to *you* what this standard is in terms of *your* character, suitability, fitness and propriety.

No applicant has the automatic right of admission, restoration or authorisation and it will always be for *you* to discharge the burden of satisfying suitability under this test. Any application that requires *us* to be satisfied as to character, suitability, fitness and propriety will be determined by reference to this test.

The Principles

The Suitability Test forms part of the Handbook, in which the 10 mandatory *Principles* are all-pervasive. They apply to all those *we* regulate and underpin all aspects of practice.

You must:

1.   uphold the rule of law and the proper administration of justice;

2.   act with integrity;

3.   not allow *your* independence to be compromised;

4.   act in the best interests of each *client*;

5.   provide a proper standard of service to *your clients*;

6.   behave in a way that maintains the trust the public places in *you* and in the provision of legal services;

7.   comply with *your* legal and regulatory obligations and deal with *your* regulators and ombudsmen in an open, timely and co-operative manner;

8.   run *your* business or carry out *your* role in the business effectively and in accordance with proper governance and sound financial and risk management principles;

9.   run *your* business or carry out *your* role in the business in a way that encourages equality of opportunity and respect for diversity; and

10.   protect *client money* and *assets*.

Outcomes

The outcomes which apply to this test are as follows:

O(SB1)   if *you* are a *solicitor*, *you* are of the required standard of *character and suitability*;

O(SB2)   if *you* are an *authorised role holder*, *you* are fit and proper; and

O(SB3)   *you* act so that *clients*, and the wider public, have confidence that O(SB1) has been demonstrated.

The outcomes, and the criteria that flow from them, apply to all those who are intending to become *solicitors* – i.e. students, *trainee solicitors*, and qualified lawyers from other jurisdictions seeking qualification via transfer – at the point of applying for eligibility to commence *recognised training*, admission, and throughout the pre-qualification period. They also apply to *compliance officers*, *owners*, and/or *managers* at the point of and throughout their period of authorisation, and for former *solicitors* seeking restoration to the roll.

Interpretation and definitions

1   The SRA Handbook Glossary 2012 shall apply and, unless the context otherwise requires:

(a)   all italicised terms shall be defined; and

(b)   all terms shall be interpreted;

in accordance with the *Glossary*.

2   In this test, the reference in the preamble to those seeking to become *authorised role holders* in accordance with rules 8.5 and 8.6 of the *SRA Authorisation Rules*, fulfilling the duties under Sections 89, 90, 91 and 92 of the *LSA* shall have no effect until such time as the Society is designated as a licensing authority under Part 1 of Schedule 10 to the *LSA*.

3   This test shall not apply to licensed bodies until such time as the Society is designated as a licensing authority under Part 1 of Schedule 10 to the *LSA* and all definitions shall be construed accordingly.

4   Part 2 of this test shall have no effect until such time as the Society is designated as a licensing authority under Part 1 of Schedule 10 to the *LSA*.

PART 1: BASIC REQUIREMENTS

If *you* are applying for eligibility to commence or continue a period of *recognised training*, admission or restoration to the roll, *you* must comply with Part 1. If *you* are applying for authorisation as an *authorised role holder* then *you* must comply with Part 1 and Part 2.

When considering any application under this test, *we* will take the following actions:

1: Criminal offences

1.1   Unless there are exceptional circumstances, *we* will refuse *your* application if *you* have been convicted by a *court* of a criminal offence:

(a)   for which *you* received a custodial or suspended sentence;

(b)   involving dishonesty, fraud, perjury and/or bribery;

(c)   specifically in relation to which *you* have been included on the Violent and Sex Offender Register;

(d)   associated with obstructing the course of justice;

(e)   which demonstrated behaviour showing signs of *discrimination* towards others;

(f)   associated with terrorism;

(g) which was racially aggravated;

(h) which was motivated by any of the "protected" characteristics defined within the Equality Act 2010;

(i) which in *our* judgment is so serious as to prevent commencement or continuation of a period of *recognised training*, admission as a *solicitor*, or approval as an *authorised role holder*; and/or

(j) *you* have been convicted by a *court* of more than one criminal offence.

Guidance note

(i) The provisions in 1.1(a) will not be relevant to entities because *bodies corporate*, and other unincorporated bodies and bodies of persons, cannot themselves receive custodial sentences.

1.2 *We* are more likely than not to refuse *your* application if *you* have:

(a) been convicted by a *court* of a criminal offence not falling within 1.1 above but which has an impact on *your character and suitability*;

(b) been included on the Violent and Sex Offender Register but in relation to *your* inclusion on the Register, *you* have not been convicted by a *court* of a criminal offence; and/or

(c) accepted a caution for an offence involving dishonesty.

1.3 *We* may refuse *your* application if *you* have:

(a) received a local warning from the police;

(b) accepted a caution from the police for an offence not involving dishonesty;

(c) received a Penalty Notice for Disorder from the police;

(d) received a final warning or reprimand from the police (youths only); and/or

(e) received a referral order from the *courts* (youths only).

Guidance note

(i) Where a criminal conviction, warning, simple caution, Penalty Notice for Disorder and/or inclusion on the Violent and Sex Offender Register has been disclosed, *we* will not look behind the decision made by the police or the finding made by a *court*. However, *we* will take into account material such as sentencing remarks and any other independent information. See also Section 7 Evidence.

(ii) *You* should disclose details of any criminal charge(s) *you* may be facing. *We* will not determine *your* application until *you* can confirm that the charge(s) has/have either been dropped or the outcome of *your* case is known.

(iii)   Police can only issue a caution if there is evidence that *you* are guilty of an offence and if *you* admit that *you* committed the offence. Therefore, by accepting a caution, please bear in mind that *you* are making an admission of guilt.

(iv)   On Penalty Notices for Disorder no admission of guilt is required, and by paying the penalty, a recipient discharges liability for conviction for the offence – however, *you* should still disclose such matters as *we* will need to consider them.

(v)   Motoring offences that result in a criminal conviction must be disclosed. Motoring offences that do not result in a criminal conviction do not need to be disclosed.

2: Disclosure

2.1   All material information relating to *your* application must be disclosed. Failure to disclose material information will be treated as prima facie evidence of dishonest behaviour.

2.2   *You* must disclose any matters that have occurred in the *UK* and/or overseas.

Guidance note

(i)   *We* require all those seeking admission as *solicitors* to apply for a standard disclosure from the Disclosure and Barring Service.

(ii)   If *you* are seeking approval as an *authorised role holder*, *you* should bear in mind that Rule 14 of the *SRA Authorisation Rules* allows *us* to seek other information relating to *your* application and this would normally include Disclosure and Barring Service disclosure.

(iii)   It is therefore highly likely that matters will come to light.

3: Behaviour not compatible with that expected of a prospective solicitor or authorised role holder

3.1   Unless there are exceptional circumstances *we* will refuse *your* application if *you* have:

   (a)   been responsible for behaviour:

      (i)   which is dishonest;

      (ii)   which is violent;

      (iii)   where there is evidence of *discrimination* towards others;

   (b)   misused *your* position to obtain pecuniary advantage;

   (c)   misused *your* position of trust in relation to vulnerable people; and/or

   (d)   been responsible for other forms of behaviour which demonstrate that *you* cannot be relied upon to discharge *your* regulatory duties as a *solicitor* or *authorised role holder*.

Authorisation and
Practising Requirements

4: Assessment offences

4.1   Unless there are exceptional circumstances *we* will refuse *your* application if *you* have committed and/or have been adjudged by an education establishment to have committed a deliberate assessment offence which amounts to plagiarism or cheating to gain an advantage for *yourself* or others.

Guidance note

(i)   Exceptional circumstances may include where the finding does not amount to cheating or dishonesty, e.g. incorrect referencing, or failure to attribute correctly, in an essay or paper.

5: Financial evidence

5.1   Unless there are exceptional circumstances *we* will refuse *your* application if:

(a)   there is evidence that *you* cannot manage *your* finances properly and carefully;

(b)   there is evidence that *you* have deliberately sought to avoid responsibility for *your* debts; and/or

(c)   there is evidence of dishonesty in relation to the management of *your* finances.

5.2   If *you* have been declared bankrupt, entered into any individual voluntary arrangements (IVA) or have had a County Court Judgment issued against *you* it will raise a presumption that there has been evidence that *you* cannot manage *your* finances properly and carefully.

Guidance note

(i)   The following might help to establish confidence in *your* ability to run *your* business/carry out *your* role in the business effectively and in accordance with proper governance and sound financial and risk management principles:

(a)   the bankruptcy/IVA/County Court Judgment occurred many years ago and there is evidence of subsequent sound financial management and conduct to show that creditors have been repaid;

(b)   *you* were affected by exceptional circumstances beyond *your* control which *you* could not have reasonably foreseen.

6: Regulatory history

6.1   Unless there are exceptional circumstances *we* will refuse *your* application if *you*:

(a)   have been made the subject of a serious disciplinary finding, sanction or action by a regulatory body and/or any *court* or other body hearing appeals in relation to disciplinary or regulatory findings;

(b)   have failed to disclose information to a regulatory body when required to do so, or have provided false or misleading information;

(c)   have significantly breached the requirements of a regulatory body;

(d)   have been refused registration by a regulatory body; and/or

(e)   have failed to comply with the reasonable requests of a regulatory body.

6.2   *We* may refuse *your* application if *you* have been rebuked, reprimanded or received a warning about *your* conduct by a regulatory body, unless there are exceptional circumstances.

Guidance note

(i)   "Regulatory body" includes *us* and the Solicitors Disciplinary Tribunal, approved regulators under the Legal Services Act 2007, as well as any other body responsible for regulation of a profession.

(ii)   *You* should disclose details of any disciplinary proceeding(s) or investigation(s) *you* may be facing. *We* may not determine *your* application until *you* can confirm that the matter(s) has/have either been dropped or the outcome of *your* case is known.

7: Evidence

7.1   To help *us* consider an application where a disclosure has been made, *you* should include the following evidence, where relevant:

(a)   at least one independent report relating to the event(s), such as sentencing remarks following a criminal conviction;

(b)   references from at least two independent professional people (of which one should preferably be from an employer or tutor) who know *you* well and are familiar with the matters being considered;

(c)   evidence of any rehabilitation (e.g. probation reports, references from employers and/or tutors);

(d)   documentary evidence in support of *your* case and where possible, an independent corroboration of *your* account of the event(s);

(e)   *your* attitude towards the event(s);

(f)   the extent to which *you* were aware of the rules and procedures governing the reference of material, or the use of group work or collaborative material;

(g)   the extent to which *you* could reasonably have been expected to realise that the offence did not constitute legitimate academic practice;

(h)   credit check information (in the relevant circumstances); and/or

(i)   actions *you* have taken to clear any debts, satisfy any judgments and manage *your* finances.

Authorisation and Practising Requirements

7.2   The onus is on *you* to provide any evidence *you* consider necessary and/or appropriate. However, should *we* consider that *you* have provided insufficient evidence, *we* reserve the right to carry out *our* own investigation and/or refuse the application if further evidence is not forthcoming.

8: Rehabilitation

8.1   It is for *you* to demonstrate that *you* have undergone successful rehabilitation, where relevant. The individual circumstances *you* put forward must be weighed against the public interest and the need to safeguard members of the public and maintain the reputation of the profession. However, *we* will consider each application on its own merits.

8.2   If the Rehabilitation of Offenders Act 1974 (Exceptions) Order 1975 is applicable to *your* occupation, profession or role, *you* must declare all convictions and cautions, even if they are deemed to be spent in accordance with the Act, unless they are protected convictions or cautions.

8.3   In accordance with paragraph 2 above (disclosure), if *you* fall within the Rehabilitation of Offenders Act 1974 (Exceptions) Order 1975 and *you* fail to disclose information about convictions and/or cautions for criminal offences which are not protected convictions or cautions, whether they are spent or unspent, *we* will consider this as amounting to prima facie evidence of dishonest behaviour.

Guidance note

(i)   The provisions of the Rehabilitation of Offenders Act 1974 and the Rehabilitation of Offenders Act 1974 (Exceptions) Order 1975 will be taken into account by *us* in considering any application *you* make.

(ii)   This means that if *you* fall within the Rehabilitation of Offenders Act 1974 (Exceptions) Order 1975, the fact that the conviction is spent, and the time that has passed since the conviction was given, together with any other material circumstances will be taken into account by *us* when determining any application made by *you*.

(iii)   A period of rehabilitation, particularly after *we* have decided to refuse *your* application, will not in itself result in automatic admission/authorisation. *We* need *you* to show, through a period of good behaviour, that *you* have taken steps to rehabilitate *yourself* by *your* own volition.

(iv)   Amendments made to the Rehabilitation of Offenders Act 1974 (Exceptions) Order 1975 in May 2013 introduced "protected convictions" and "protected cautions". Questions *we* ask about convictions or cautions will, therefore, exclude protected convictions or cautions and failure to disclose will not be considered as prima facie evidence of dishonesty.

(v)   A caution is a "protected caution" if:

(a) it was given other than for an offence listed in article 2A(5) of the Exceptions Order, and;

(b) where the person was aged:

(A) 18 or over at the time the caution was given, six years or more have passed since the caution was given, or;

(B) under 18 at the time the caution was given, two years or more have passed since the caution was given.

(vi) A conviction is a "protected conviction" if:

(a) it was given other than for an offence listed in article 2A(5) of the Exceptions Order;

(b) a sentence other than custody or service detention was imposed;

(c) the person has not been convicted of any other offence at any time, and;

(d) where the person was aged:

(A) 18 or over at the time of the conviction, 11 years or more have passed since the date of conviction, or

(B) under 18 at the time of the conviction, five and a half years or more have passed since the date of conviction.

(vii) The DBS will filter any protected convictions and cautions, so they will not appear on standard disclosures.

(viii) The following individuals and roles are covered by the Exceptions Order and spent convictions and cautions, excluding protected convictions and cautions, must be disclosed:

(a) applicants seeking admission to the profession, i.e. applicants for eligibility to commence or continue a period of *recognised training*, *QLTS certificates of eligibility*, and admission;

(b) *non-lawyer managers* in existing Legal Disciplinary Practices;

(c) *non-lawyer owners* who hold a *material interest* in a *licensed body*; and

(d) *COLPs* and *COFAs* of *licensed bodies*.

(ix) The following individuals and roles are not covered by the Exceptions Order and spent convictions and cautions should not be disclosed:

(a) former *solicitors* seeking restoration to the roll;

(b) *owners* of *recognised bodies*;

(c) *COLPs* and *COFAs* of *recognised bodies*;

(d) *owners* of *licensed bodies* who do not require approval under Schedule 13 to the *LSA*; and

(e)   *managers* of *authorised bodies*.

PART 2: ADDITIONAL REQUIREMENTS TO BECOME AUTHORISED UNDER THE SRA AUTHORISATION RULES

9: All applicants must comply with Part 1

9.1   Under this test, when considering any application by an individual seeking to become an *authorised role holder*, all of the tests set out in Part 1 will apply in addition to this Part.

10: Additional requirements

10.1   Unless there are exceptional circumstances *we* may refuse *your* application if:

(a)   The applicant is disqualified from being a *charity* trustee or a trustee for a *charity* under section 178(1)(D) or (E) of the Charities Act 2011.

(b)   *you* have been removed and/or disqualified as a company director;

(c)   any body corporate of which *you* are/were a *manager* or *owner* has been the subject of a winding up order, an administrative order or an administrative receivership, or has otherwise been wound up or put into administration in circumstances of insolvency;

(d)   *you* have a previous conviction which is now spent for a criminal offence relating to bankruptcy, IVAs or other circumstances of insolvency;

(e)   *you* are a corporate person/entity subject to a relevant insolvency event defined in rule 1.2 of the *SRA Authorisation Rules*;

(f)   *you* are a corporate person/entity and other matters that call *your* fitness and propriety into question are disclosed or come to light;

(g)   *you* have committed an offence under the Companies Act 2006; and/or

(h)   *we* have evidence reflecting on the honesty and integrity of a person *you* are related to, affiliated with, or act together with where *we* have reason to believe that the person may have an influence over the way in which *you* will exercise *your authorised role*.

Guidance note

(i)   The provisions of the Rehabilitation of Offenders Act 1974 (as amended) and the Rehabilitation of Offenders Act 1974 (Exceptions) Order 1975 (as amended) do not apply to corporate persons/entities. Therefore, corporate convictions cannot become spent, so if *you* are a corporate person/entity *you* must disclose any and all matters in *your* application.

(ii)   Other matters under 10.1(f) include but are not limited to debts, corporate criminal matters, Companies Act transgressions such as late submission of accounts, and taking steps without submitting proper documents to Companies House.

(iii)   For the avoidance of doubt, the guidance notes to section 8.3 also apply to Part 2 of the Suitability Test.

[F] Client Protection

[F.0] Introduction to Client Protection

This section of the Handbook contains the following sets of rules:

- SRA Indemnity Insurance Rules;

- SRA Indemnity (Enactment) Rules;

- SRA Indemnity Rules;

- SRA Compensation Fund Rules; and

- SRA Intervention Powers (Statutory Trust) Rules.

The rules must be read in conjunction with the Principles. The Principles underpin all aspects of practice, including the maintenance of professional indemnity insurance and contributions to the Solicitors' Compensation Fund.

These rules provide vital financial protections for clients by requiring that:

- negligence claims against firms, their managers and their employees can be met;

- clients can be compensated if their money has been misappropriated; and

- money belonging to clients can be returned to them when the SRA intervenes in a firm.

The desired outcome to these rules is that clients are protected against negligence and dishonesty by firms and individuals through professional indemnity insurance and compensation arrangements.

Client Protection

[F.1] SRA Indemnity Insurance Rules 2013

The commentary provided with these Rules does not form part of the Rules, is provided for guidance only, and does not affect the meaning or interpretation of the Rules in any way.

PART 1: GENERAL

Rule 1: Authority and commencement

1.1   These Rules are made on 13 June 2013 by the Solicitors Regulation Authority Board under sections 31, 37, 79 and 80 of the Solicitors Act 1974, section 9 of the Administration of Justice Act 1985, and paragraph 19 of Schedule 11 to the Legal Services Act 2007, with the approval of the Legal Services Board under paragraph 19 of Schedule 4 to the Legal Services Act 2007.

1.2   These Rules come into force on 1 October 2013.

1.3   These Rules require *solicitors*, *RELs*, *RFLs*, *recognised bodies* and their *managers* and *licensed bodies* (in respect of their *regulated activities*) in *private practice* in England and Wales to take out and maintain professional indemnity insurance with *participating insurers* with effect from 1 October 2013.

Commentary:

These Rules apply to:

- solicitors
- RELs
- RFLs
- recognised bodies and their managers and
- licensed bodies in respect of their regulated activities (but not to any other activities that may be undertaken by the licensed body concerned)

carrying on private practice in England and Wales as a firm at any time after 1 October 2013. Refer to the interpretation provisions in Rule 3 and the SRA Handbook Glossary 2012 (the Glossary) and to the definitions in the Glossary for guidance on the exact meanings of these terms.

1.4   These Rules will apply to any *indemnity period* beginning on or after 1 October 2013.

Commentary:

Before 1 September 2000, firms were required to take out insurance with the Solicitors Indemnity Fund. Since 1 September 2000, firms have been required to take out insurance in accordance with the Solicitors' Indemnity Insurance Rules and SRA Indemnity Insurance Rules. From 1 October 2013, firms must take out insurance in accordance with these Rules with one or more participating insurers. Continuing arrangements dealing with past claims on the Solicitors Indemnity Fund are covered in the Solicitors' Indemnity Rules and the SRA Indemnity Rules.

1.5   The SRA Indemnity Insurance Rules 2012 shall not apply in respect of any *indemnity period* beginning on or after 1 October 2013 but they shall remain in force in respect of the *indemnity period* from 1 October 2012 to 30 September 2013 inclusive subject to the provisions of Rules 19.1(a), 19.1(b), 19.1(c) and 19.1(d) below.

Commentary:

You should refer to previous Solicitors' Indemnity Insurance Rules and SRA Indemnity Insurance Rules in relation to earlier indemnity periods since 1 September 2000. However, you should refer to Rules 19.1(a) to 19.1(d) in relation to time limits in respect of an application for a waiver of the provisions of the Solicitors' Indemnity Insurance Rules 2000 to 2010 and the SRA Indemnity Insurance Rules 2011 and 2012.

Rule 2: Citation

2.1   These Rules may be cited as the SRA Indemnity Insurance Rules 2013.

Rule 3: Definitions and interpretation

3.1   The SRA Handbook Glossary 2012 (the Glossary) shall apply and, unless the context otherwise requires:

(a)   all italicised terms shall be defined in accordance with the Glossary;

(b)   terms shall be interpreted in accordance with the Glossary;

(c)   a reference to a Rule is to a Rule forming part of these Rules;

(d)   these Rules will be governed by and interpreted in accordance with English law.

PART 2: RESPONSIBILITY AND MONITORING

Rule 4: Obligation to effect insurance

4.1   All *firms* carrying on a *practice* during any *indemnity period* beginning on or after 1 October 2013 must take out and maintain *qualifying insurance* under these Rules.

4.2   A *firm* must:

(a) obtain a *policy* of *qualifying insurance* prior to the expiry of the *policy period* that provides cover incepting on and with effect from the expiry of the *policy period*;

(b) if the *firm* has been unable to obtain a *policy* of *qualifying insurance* prior to the expiry of the *policy period* in accordance with Rule 4.2(a), obtain a *policy* of *qualifying insurance* during or prior to the expiry of the *extended indemnity period* that provides cover incepting on and with effect from the expiry of the *policy period*; and

(c) if the *firm* has been unable to obtain a *policy* of *qualifying insurance* prior to the expiry of the *extended indemnity period* in accordance with Rule 4.2(b), cease *practice* promptly, and by no later than the expiration of the *cessation period*, unless the *firm* obtains a *policy* of *qualifying insurance* during or prior to the expiry of the *cessation period* that provides cover incepting on and with effect from the expiry of the *policy period* and covers all activities in connection with *private legal practice* carried out by the *firm* including, without limitation, any carried out in breach of Rule 5.2.

4.3   A *solicitor* or *REL* is not required to take out and maintain *qualifying insurance* under these Rules in respect of work done as an employee or whilst otherwise directly engaged in the *practice* of another *firm* (including without limitation as an *appointed person*), where that *firm* is required by these Rules to take out and maintain *qualifying insurance*.

Commentary:

Under these Rules, firms have a continuing obligation to ensure that they have qualifying insurance in place at all times with effect from 1 October 2013. Refer to the definitions of practice, amongst others, to establish whether a firm falls within the scope of these Rules. Firms should also check that any insurance that they take out in order to comply with these Rules (as opposed to any "top-up" cover) is taken out with a participating insurer. A list of participating insurers appears on the website of the SRA at **www.sra.org.uk**, and is also available from the SRA. Contact details appear at the end of the introductory commentary.

Firms should note in particular that work carried out by an appointed person for that firm may be covered by the firm's policy, whether that person is engaged as an employee or on a contract for services.

If a firm, on or before the expiry of the policy period, fails to obtain a policy of qualifying insurance from a participating insurer commencing on the day following such expiration, the firm's participating insurer is required to extend cover under the existing policy for a further 30 days. If a firm fails to obtain an alternative policy of qualifying insurance during or prior to the expiration of the 30 day extended indemnity period it must cease practice within a further period of 60 days (known as the cessation period) unless the firm obtains a policy of qualifying insurance on or before the expiry of the cessation period which provides cover that incepts or is backdated to incept with effect on and from the expiry of the policy period. Any such policy of qualifying insurance must cover all activities carried out in connection with private legal practice by the firm, including any carried out during the cessation period in breach of Rule 5.2. During the cessation period, the firm (and its principals, employees, consultants and agents) may only engage in activities in connection with private legal practice on behalf of the firm to discharge its obligations within the scope of the existing instructions the firm held before the cessation period commenced or which are necessary in connection with the discharge of such obligations. Disciplinary action will be taken against those who accept new instructions and/or engage in other non-permitted legal activities during the cessation period. The firm's participating insurer is required to provide cover during the cessation period which, as a minimum, satisfies the MTC.

The SRA will work with the firm to ensure that it has ceased practice prior to the expiration of the 60 day cessation period. Firms must be aware that the participating insurer under the existing policy will not be required to provide any cover beyond this period except for run-off cover for a period of six years commencing on the expiry of the firm's final policy of qualifying insurance (excluding any extended indemnity period and cessation period (as may be applicable)).

Note that, under the MTC, a policy, once taken out, cannot be cancelled unless:

1. the firm merges with another firm and a policy of qualifying insurance is in place for the merged firm; or

2. it subsequently transpires that the firm was not in fact required to take out and maintain a policy under these Rules; or

3. the participating insurer which issues the policy becomes the subject of an insolvency event, and the firm has replaced the policy with another policy of qualifying insurance.

Most recognised bodies and licensed bodies (in respect of their regulated activities) are required to obtain cover complying with the MTC and with a sum insured of £3 million, rather than £2 million for other firms. The definition of "relevant recognised body" and "relevant licensed body" in these Rules indicates which recognised bodies and licensed bodies this requirement applies to.

4.4   The provisions of this Rule 4 shall be without prejudice to the ability of *firms* to include as insureds on a *policy* persons not required under these Rules to be insured.

Rule 5: Responsibility

5.1   Each *firm* carrying on a *practice* on or after 1 October 2013, and any person who is a *principal* of such a *firm*, must ensure that the *firm* has in place and maintains *qualifying insurance* at all times.

Commentary:

Note that the duty to ensure that qualifying insurance is in place rests not just on the firm as a whole, but also on every principal within that firm.

5.2   Each *firm* that has been unable to obtain a *policy* of *qualifying insurance* prior to the expiration of the *extended indemnity period*, and any *person* who is a *principal* of such a *firm*, must ensure that the *firm*, and each *principal* or *employee* of such *firm*, undertakes no activities in connection with *private legal practice* and accepts no instructions in respect of any such activities during the *cessation period* save to the extent that the activity in connection with *private legal practice* is undertaken to discharge its obligations within the scope of the *firm's existing instructions* or is necessary in connection with the discharge of such obligations.

Rule 6: Insolvency of participating insurer

6.1 If a *firm* is carrying on a *practice* which is being provided with *qualifying insurance* by a *participating insurer* (whether alone or together with other *participating insurers*) and that *participating insurer* is the subject of an *insolvency event* then, subject to any waiver under Rule 19.1, the *firm* and any person who is a *principal* of the *firm* must ensure that the *firm* has in place *qualifying insurance* with another *participating insurer* which must be arranged as soon as may be reasonably practicable and in any event within four weeks of such an *insolvency event*.

> *Commentary:*
>
> It is important to be aware that the arrangements for professional indemnity insurance put in place by the SRA do not seek to protect firms against the insolvency of a participating insurer. If an insolvency event occurs in respect of an insurer, that insurer will cease to be a participating insurer for the purposes of writing new policies and firms insured by that insurer must effect alternative insurance in accordance with these Rules. This is because, in such circumstances, the insurer may not be in a position to pay claims in full. Any firm which has qualifying insurance with a participating insurer which is the subject of an insolvency event is required therefore to obtain replacement cover as soon as possible, and in any event within four weeks of the insolvency event occurring. Having done so, a firm should cancel the policy with the insolvent insurer and, if entitled to do so, seek a return of the premium relating to the balance of the policy period from the insurer which has become the subject of the insolvency event.

Rule 7: Monitoring

7.1 The *Council* may require from a *firm* or any *principal* in a *firm* carrying on, or reasonably believed by the *Council* to be carrying on, a *practice* such information and evidence as it may reasonably require to satisfy itself that such a *firm* has in place *qualifying insurance*.

Rule 8: RELs

8.1 The special provisions contained in Appendix 3 to these Rules shall apply to a *firm* that has at least one *principal* who is a *REL*.

PART 3: THE ARP

Rule 9:

[Deleted]

Client Protection

Rule 10:

[Deleted]

Rule 11:

[Deleted]

Rule 12:

[Deleted]

Rule 13: Power to collect contribution from firms

13.1   Every *firm* and/or *principal* shall make contributions in such amounts, at such times and in such circumstances, as may be prescribed from time to time by the *SRA* in respect of the *ARP*, the cost of funding all or any part of the *ARP* or funding or providing any contribution, consideration, payment, undertaking, reimbursement, guarantee, surety or security in respect of the *ARP*, in each case, that the *SRA* agrees or determines is to be contributed or made available on behalf of *firms* and/or *principals* to or in consideration for *participating insurers* agreeing to underwrite the liabilities of the *ARP* in respect of the *indemnity period* commencing on 1 October 2012.

13.2   Any unpaid contribution under Rule 13.1 may be recovered as a debt due to the *Society*. The *SRA* may recover any unpaid contribution from a *licensed body*, and may require *licensed bodies* to make such further contributions as the *SRA* considers necessary in respect of the *ARP*, the cost of funding all or any part of the *ARP* or funding or providing any contribution, consideration, payment, undertaking, reimbursement, guarantee, surety or security in respect of the *ARP*, in each case, that the *SRA* agrees or determines is to be contributed or made available to or in consideration for *participating insurers* agreeing to underwrite the liabilities of the *ARP* in respect of the *indemnity period* commencing on 1 October 2012.

PART 4:

[Deleted]

Rule 14:

[Deleted]

Rule 15:

[Deleted]

PART 5: DISCIPLINARY OFFENCES AND REPORTING

Rule 16: Disciplinary consequences of failure to comply with these Rules

16.1   Without prejudice to any other disciplinary offence which may arise under these Rules, it shall be a disciplinary offence for any *firm* or any person who is at the relevant time a *principal* in a *firm* to

(a) be in *policy default*, and

(b) undertake any activities in connection with *private legal practice* in breach of Rule 5.2.

Rule 17: Use of information

17.1   Any *participating insurer* shall, in relation to any *firm* which applies to it for *qualifying insurance*, bring to the attention of the *Society* (including, in the case of the matters referred to in Rule 17.1(f), the Office for Legal Complaints (including the *Legal Ombudsman*)) at any time and without notice to the *firm* concerned:

(a) any failure on the part of the *firm* or any person who is a *principal* of that *firm* to pay any sum on or before the date specified in these Rules or to reimburse any amount falling within a *policy* excess which has been paid out by a *participating insurer* to a *claimant*;

(b) a material inaccuracy in any proposal form submitted by or on behalf of the *firm*;

(c) the fact that the *firm* has become or is believed to have become a *run-off firm*;

(d) any matter or circumstances that would entitle the *firm's participating insurer* to avoid or repudiate a *policy* but for the provisions of clause 4.1 of the *MTC* (and/or the corresponding of the *policy*);

(e) any dishonesty or fraud suspected by a *participating insurer* on the part of any *insured*; and

(f) any *claim* of inadequate professional services made against the *firm* or any *insured* of that *firm* of which it becomes aware.

Commentary:

All firms are deemed to have consented to their participating insurer bringing to the attention of the SRA any of the matters referred to Rule 17.1 that may be applicable to the firm. Any such information is subject to the confidentiality provisions of Rule 17.4.

17.2   The *Council* may require any *participating insurer* to bring to the attention of the *Society* any of the matters referred to in Rule 17.1 where it reasonably believes there are matters which ought to be brought to the attention of the *Society* in accordance with Rule 17.1.

17.3   Each *firm* shall notify the *Society* (or such *person* as the *Society* may notify to the *firm* from time to time) and its *participating insurer* in writing as soon as reasonably practicable and in no event later than five (5) business days after the date on which:

(a) the *firm* enters the *extended indemnity period* under its *policy*;

(b) the *firm* enters the *cessation period* under its *policy*; and

(c) the *firm* obtains a *policy* of *qualifying insurance* where the *firm* is in the *extended indemnity period* or the *cessation period*, and in such case the

Client Protection

notification shall include the name of the *participating insurer* who has issued the *policy* of *qualifying insurance* and the *policy* number.

17.4   In respect of any information that may be brought to the attention of the *Society* in accordance with Rules 17.1, 17.2 and 17.3:

(a)   the *Society* shall keep all such information confidential;

(b)   the *Society* shall not (except where and to the extent required by law or in the proper performance by the *Society* of its regulatory functions) at any time reveal any such information to any person other than a duly authorised employee of the *Society* or any of its subsidiaries; and

(c)   any privilege attaching to such information shall not be regarded as having been waived whether by virtue of such information having been provided to the *Society* or otherwise.

17.5   The provisions of Rule 17.4 shall not prevent the *Society* from:

(a)   making use of any information referred to in that Rule for the purpose of bringing disciplinary proceedings against any person; or

(b)   in relation to information about a *firm's policy* under Rule 18, disclosing that information, where and to the extent that the *Society* in its absolute discretion considers it appropriate, to any person entitled to such information, and to any other department or office of the *Society*, including without limitation to the Office for Legal Complaints (including the *Legal Ombudsman*).

17.6   The *Society* may, without limitation and in its absolute discretion, disclose and make available for public inspection the identity of a *firm's participating insurer*. Nothing in these Rules shall act to prohibit the *Society* from making such a disclosure nor give rise to any liability of the *Society*, for breach of any obligations of confidentiality or otherwise.

Rule 18: Details of participating insurer

18.1   If a *claimant* asserts a *claim* against a *firm* or any person insured under that *firm's policy*, and where such *claim* relates to any matter within the scope of cover of the *MTC* (whether or not such *claim* would or may be upheld), the *firm* and any person who is at the relevant time (or, in the case of a *firm* which has ceased *practice*, any person who was immediately before that *firm* ceased *practice*) a *principal* in that *firm* shall be required, upon being so requested by that *claimant*, by any person insured under that *firm's policy*, or by any other person with a legitimate interest, to provide to that person the following details in relation to that *firm's policy*:

(a)   the name of the *participating insurer(s)* who issued the *policy*; and

(b)   the *policy* number; and

(c)   the address and contact details of the *participating insurer(s)* for the purpose of making a *claim* under the *policy*;

in each case in respect of the *policy* which it is reasonably believed to be the relevant *policy* to respond to the *claim*, or, if applicable, the fact that the *firm* or person against whom the *claim* is asserted is covered by *supplementary run-off cover*.

Commentary:

A firm, and each principal in that firm, is required to provide details of that firm's policy of qualifying insurance to any person who asserts a claim against anyone insured under that firm's policy. Under Rule 17, the SRA has the power to disclose information regarding a firm's participating insurer where it considers it appropriate to do so.

PART 6: GENERAL POWERS OF THE COUNCIL

Rule 19: Waiver powers

19.1   The *Council* shall have power on such terms and conditions as it shall think fit to waive any Rule or part of any Rule in a particular case or cases including extending the time, either prospectively or retrospectively, for the doing of any act under any Rule.

(a)   Any application by any person for a waiver of any Rule or part of any Rule under the Solicitors' Indemnity Insurance Rules 2001 to 2010 or SRA Indemnity Insurance Rules 2011 to 2013 must be made in writing to the *Society* as soon as reasonably practicable.

(b)   No application by any person for a waiver of any Rule or part of any Rule under the Solicitors' Indemnity Insurance Rules 2000 may be considered unless it was made in writing to the *Society* as soon as reasonably practicable and in any event no later than 28 February 2002.

(c)   Any appeal against any decision made by the *Society* in respect of any application for a waiver of any Rule or part of any Rule under the Solicitors' Indemnity Insurance Rules 2000 to 2010 or SRA Indemnity Insurance Rules 2011 to 2013 must be made in writing to the *Society* within 21 days from the date of the decision.

(d)   An application for a waiver as contemplated by this Rule 19.1 or the making of an appeal against any decision made by the *Society* in respect of such application shall not relieve any person from any obligation under the Solicitors' Indemnity Insurance Rules 2000 to 2010 or SRA Indemnity Insurance Rules 2011 to 2013 pending the determination of any such application or appeal.

Commentary:

It is envisaged that Rules will be waived only in exceptional circumstances. Anyone who wishes to apply for a waiver, or to appeal against an initial decision, must do so in accordance with the time limits set out in this Rule. Contact details appear at the end of the introductory commentary. The Panel of Adjudicators Sub Committee has adopted a waiver policy, which is available on request. Unless and until any waiver is granted, the person concerned must comply with the requirements of

Client Protection

these Rules in full. A waiver may be granted subject to conditions, and may be revoked without notice.

19.2   The *Council* shall have power to treat any *firm* as complying with any Rule or Rules for the purposes of the *SA* notwithstanding that the *firm* has failed to comply with a Rule or Rules where such non-compliance is regarded by the *Council* in a particular case or cases as being insignificant.

19.3   For the purposes of the *SA* (including without limitation section 10 of that Act), any person who is in breach of any Rule or part of any Rule under the Solicitors' Indemnity Insurance Rules 2000 to 2010 or SRA Indemnity Insurance Rules 2011 to 2013 shall be deemed, for so long as he remains in breach, not to be complying with these Rules.

Commentary:

The effect of this general power is that, for example, a practising certificate may be issued to a person notwithstanding a technical and insignificant breach by that person or a firm of any provision of these Rules.

PART 7: OTHER OBLIGATIONS

Rule 20: Accountants' reports

20.1   Any accountant's report which a *solicitor*, *REL* or *RFL* who is a *principal* in a *practice* or a *recognised body* or a *licensed body* is required to deliver to the *Society* under section 34 of the *SA* or paragraph 8 of Schedule 14 to the Courts and Legal Services Act 1990 or under section 83(5)(h) of and paragraph 20 of Schedule 11 to the *LSA* containing such information as is prescribed by rule 35 of the Solicitors' Accounts Rules 1998 (as amended from time to time), or any rules (including, without limitation, the *SRA Accounts Rules*) which replace the Solicitors' Accounts Rules 1998 in whole or in part, must contain a statement certifying (if it is the case) for the whole period covered by the report (excluding any part of that period falling before 1 September 2000) that the *firm* has one or more certificates of *qualifying insurance* (or in respect of any period prior to 1 October 2013, that the *firm* has been issued with one or more policies by the *ARP manager*).

Commentary:

Firms are required to provide evidence to their accountants that a policy of qualifying insurance is in place. Each participating insurer is required under the participating insurer's agreement to provide a certificate of qualifying insurance to each firm within 20 working days of the start of the period covered by the policy. Producing the relevant certificate(s) to the reporting accountant will satisfy the requirement of this Rule.

APPENDIX 1 – SRA MINIMUM TERMS AND CONDITIONS OF PROFESSIONAL INDEMNITY INSURANCE

1   Scope of cover

1.1   *Civil liability*

The insurance must indemnify each *insured* against civil liability to the extent that it arises from *private legal practice* in connection with the *insured firm's practice*, provided that a *claim* in respect of such liability:

(a)   is first made against an *insured* during the *period of insurance*; or

(b)   is made against an *insured* during or after the *period of insurance* and arising from *circumstances* first notified to the *insurer* during the *period of insurance*.

1.2   *Defence costs*

The insurance must also indemnify the *insured* against *defence costs* in relation to:

(a)   any *claim* referred to in clause 1.1, 1.4 or 1.6; or

(b)   any *circumstances* first notified to the *insurer* during the *period of insurance*; or

(c)   any investigation or inquiry (save in respect of any disciplinary proceeding under the authority of the *Society* (including, without limitation, the *SRA* and the *Tribunal*)) during or after the *period of insurance* arising from any *claim* referred to in clause 1.1, 1.4 or 1.6 or from *circumstances* first notified to the *insurer* during the *period of insurance*.

1.3   *The insured*

For the purposes of the cover contemplated by clause 1.1, the *insured* must include:

(a)   the *insured firm*; and

(b)   each service, administration, trustee or nominee *company* owned as at the date of occurrence of relevant *circumstances* by the *insured firm* and/or the *principals* of the *insured firm*; and

(c)   each *principal*, each former *principal* and each *person* who becomes a *principal* during the *period of insurance* of the *insured firm* or a *company* referred to in paragraph (b); and

(d)   each *employee*, each former *employee* and each *person* who becomes during the *period of insurance* an *employee* of the *insured firm* or a *company* referred to in paragraph (b); and

(e)   the estate or legal personal representative of any deceased or legally incapacitated *person* referred to in paragraph (c) or (d).

Client Protection

1.4 *Prior practice*

The insurance must indemnify each *insured* against civil liability to the extent that it arises from *private legal practice* in connection with a *prior practice*, provided that a *claim* in respect of such liability is first made against an *insured*:

(a) during the *period of insurance*; or

(b) during or after the *period of insurance* and arising from *circumstances* first notified to the *insurer* during the *period of insurance*.

1.5 *The insured – prior practice*

For the purposes of the cover contemplated by clause 1.4, the *insured* must include:

(a) each *partnership*, *recognised body* or *licensed body* (in respect of its *regulated activities*) which, or *sole practitioner* who, carried on the *prior practice*; and

(b) each service, administration, trustee or nominee *company* owned as at the date of occurrence of relevant *circumstances* by the *partnership*, *recognised body* or *licensed body* (in respect of its *regulated activities*) which, or *sole practitioner* who, carried on the *prior practice* and/or the *principals* of such *partnership*, *recognised body* or *licensed body*; and

(c) each *principal* and former *principal* of each *partnership*, *recognised body* or *licensed body* (in respect of its *regulated activities*) referred to in paragraph (a) or *company* referred to in paragraph (b); and

(d) each *employee* and former *employee* of the *partnership*, *recognised body*, *licensed body* (in respect of its *regulated activities*) or *sole practitioner* referred to in paragraph (a) or *company* referred to in paragraph (b); and

(e) the estate or legal personal representative of any deceased or legally incapacitated *sole practitioner* referred to in paragraph (a) or *person* referred to in paragraph (c) or (d).

1.6 *Successor practice*

The insurance must indemnify each *insured* against civil liability to the extent that it arises from *private legal practice* in connection with a *successor practice* to the *insured firm's practice* (where succession is as a result of one or more separate mergers, acquisitions, absorptions or other transitions), provided that a *claim* in respect of such liability is first made against an *insured*:

(a) during the *period of insurance*; or

(b) during or after the *period of insurance* and arising from *circumstances* first notified to the *insurer* during the *period of insurance*

unless run-off cover is provided in accordance with clause 5.6.

1.7 *The insured – successor practice*

For the purposes of the cover contemplated by clause 1.6, the *insured* must include:

(a) each *partnership*, *recognised body* or *licensed body* (in respect of its *regulated activities*) which, or *sole practitioner* who, carries on the *successor practice* during the *period of insurance*; and

(b) each service, administration, trustee or nominee *company* owned as at the date of occurrence of relevant *circumstances* by the *partnership*, *recognised body* or *licensed body* (in respect of its *regulated activities*) which, or *sole practitioner* who, carries on the *successor practice* and/or the *principals* of such *partnership*, *recognised body* or *licensed body*; and

(c) each *principal*, each former *principal* and each *person* who becomes during the *period of insurance* a *principal* of any *partnership*, *recognised body* or *licensed body* (in respect of its *regulated activities*) referred to in paragraph (a) or *company* referred to in paragraph (b); and

(d) each *employee*, each former *employee* and each *person* who becomes during the *period of insurance* an *employee* of the *partnership*, *recognised body*, *licensed body* (in respect of its *regulated activities*) or *sole practitioner* referred to in paragraph (a) or *company* referred to in paragraph (b); and

(e) the estate or legal personal representative of any deceased or legally incapacitated *sole practitioner* referred to in paragraph (a) or *person* referred to in paragraph (c) or (d).

1.8 *Award by regulatory authority*

The insurance must indemnify each *insured* against any amount paid or payable in accordance with the recommendation of the Legal Services Ombudsman, the Office for Legal Complaints (including the *Legal Ombudsman* pursuant to section 137(2)(c) and section 137(4)(b) of the *LSA*) or any other regulatory authority to the same extent as it indemnifies the *insured* against civil liability provided that the *insurer* will have no liability in respect of any determination by the *Legal Ombudsman* pursuant to section 137(2)(b) of the *LSA* to refund any fees paid to the *insured*.

2 Limit of insurance cover

2.1 *Any one claim*

The *sum insured* for any one *claim* (exclusive of *defence costs*) must be, where the *insured firm* is a *relevant recognised body* or a *relevant licensed body* (in respect of its *regulated activities*), at least £3 million, and in all other cases, at least £2 million.

2.2 *No limit on defence costs*

There must be no monetary limit on the cover for *defence costs*.

2.3 *Proportionate limit on defence costs*

Notwithstanding clauses 2.1 and 2.2, the insurance may provide that liability for *defence costs* in relation to a *claim* which exceeds the *sum insured* is limited to the proportion that the *sum insured* bears to the total amount paid or payable to dispose of the *claim*.

Client Protection

2.4 No other limit

The insurance must not limit liability to any monetary amount (whether by way of an aggregate limit or otherwise) except as contemplated by clauses 2.1 and 2.3.

2.5 One claim

The insurance may provide that, when considering what may be regarded as one *claim* for the purposes of the limits contemplated by clauses 2.1 and 2.3:

  (a) all *claims* against any one or more *insured* arising from:

    (i) one act or omission;

    (ii) one series of related acts or omissions;

    (iii) the same act or omission in a series of related matters or transactions;

    (iv) similar acts or omissions in a series of related matters or transactions

    and

  (b) all *claims* against one or more *insured* arising from one matter or transaction

will be regarded as one *claim*.

2.6 Multiple underwriters

2.6.1 The insurance may be underwritten by more than one *insurer*, each of which must be a *participating insurer*, provided that the insurance may provide that the *insurer* shall be severally liable only for its respective proportion of liability in accordance with the terms of the insurance.

2.6.2 Where the insurance is underwritten jointly by more than one *insurer*:

  (a) the insurance must state which *participating insurer* shall be the lead *insurer*; and

  (b) in addition to any proportionate limit on *defence costs* in accordance with clause 2.3, the insurance may provide that each *insurer's* liability for *defence costs* is further limited to the extent or the proportion of that *insurer's* liability (if any) in relation to the relevant *claim*.

[Note: under clause 2.6 of the participating insurer's agreement, a policy may be issued on an excess of loss basis only in the layers set out in that clause.]

3 Excesses

3.1 The excess

The insurance may be subject to an *excess* of such monetary amount and on such terms as the *insurer* and the *insured firm* agree. Subject to clause 3.4, the *excess* may be "self-insured" or partly or wholly insured without regard to these *MTC*.

3.2   *No deductibles*

The insurance must provide that the *excess* does not reduce the limit of liability contemplated by clause 2.1.

3.3   *Excess not to apply to defence costs*

The *excess* must not apply to *defence costs*.

3.4   *Funding of the excess*

The insurance must provide that, if an *insured* fails to pay to a *claimant* any amount which is within the *excess* within 30 days of it becoming due for payment, the *claimant* may give notice of the *insured's* default to the *insurer*, whereupon the *insurer* is liable to remedy the default on the *insured's* behalf. The insurance may provide that any amount paid by the *insurer* to remedy such a default erodes the *sum insured*.

3.5   *One claim*

The insurance may provide for multiple *claims* to be treated as one *claim* for the purposes of an *excess* contemplated by clause 3.1 on such terms as the *insured firm* and the *insurer* agree.

3.6   *Excess layers*

In the case of insurance written on an excess of loss basis, there shall be no *excess* except in relation to the primary layer.

4   **Special conditions**

4.1   *No avoidance or repudiation*

The insurance must provide that the *insurer* is not entitled to avoid or repudiate the insurance on any grounds whatsoever including, without limitation, non-disclosure or misrepresentation, whether fraudulent or not.

4.2   *No adjustment or denial*

The insurance must provide that the *insurer* is not entitled to reduce or deny its liability under the insurance on any grounds whatsoever including, without limitation, any breach of any term or condition of the insurance, except to the extent that one of the exclusions contemplated by clause 6 applies.

4.3   *No cancellation*

The insurance must provide that it cannot be cancelled except (in the case of (a), (b) or (c) below) by the agreement of both the *insured firm* and the *insurer*, and in any event only in circumstances where:

   (a)   the *insured firm's practice* is merged into a *successor practice*, provided that there is insurance complying with these *MTC* in relation to that *successor practice*, in which case cancellation shall have effect no earlier than the date of such merger; or

Client Protection

(b) replacement insurance, complying with the minimum terms and conditions in effect at its commencement, commences, in which case cancellation shall have effect no earlier than the date on which such replacement insurance commences; or

(c) it subsequently transpires that the *insured firm* is not required under the *SIIR* to effect a *policy* of *qualifying insurance*, in which case cancellation shall have effect from the later of (a) the start of the relevant *policy period* and (b) the date on which the *insured firm* ceased to be required to effect a policy of *qualifying insurance*, or such later date as the *insured firm* and the *insurer* may agree.

Cancellation must not affect the rights and obligations of the parties accrued under the insurance prior to the date from which cancellation has effect.

4.4   No set-off

The insurance must provide that any amount payable by the *insurer* to indemnify an *insured* against civil liability to a *claimant* will be paid only to the *claimant*, or at the *claimant's* direction, and that the *insurer* is not entitled to set-off against any such amount any payment due to it by any *insured* including, without limitation, any payment of premium or to reimburse the *insurer*.

4.5   No "other insurance" provision

The insurance must not provide that the liability of the *insurer* is reduced or excluded by reason of the existence or availability of any other insurance other than: (i) as contemplated by clause 6.1; or (ii) where the *insured*, having entered the *extended indemnity period* or *cessation period*, obtains a *policy* of *qualifying insurance* that incepts from and with effect from the expiration of the *policy period*. For the avoidance of doubt and subject to the provisions of the *participating insurer's agreement*, this requirement is not intended to affect any right of the *insurer* to claim contribution from any other insurer which is also liable to indemnify any *insured*.

4.6   No retroactive date

The insurance must not exclude or limit the liability of the *insurer* in respect of *claims* arising from incidents, occurrences, facts, matters, acts and/or omissions which occurred prior to a specified date.

4.7   Successor practice – "double insurance"

The insurance may provide that, if the *insured firm's practice* is succeeded during the *period of insurance* and, as a result, a situation of "double insurance" exists between two or more insurers of the *successor practice*, contribution between insurers is to be determined in accordance with the relative numbers of *principals* of the owners of the constituent *practices* immediately prior to succession.

4.8   Advancement of defence costs

The insurance must provide that the *insurer* will meet *defence costs* as and when they are incurred, including *defence costs* incurred on behalf of an *insured* who is alleged to have committed or condoned dishonesty or a fraudulent act or omission, provided that the *insurer* is not liable for *defence costs* incurred on behalf of that *insured* after the earlier of:

    (a) that *insured* admitting to the *insurer* the commission or condoning of such dishonesty, act or omission; or

    (b) a court or other judicial body finding that that *insured* was in fact guilty of such dishonesty, act or omission.

4.9   *Resolution of disputes*

The insurance must provide that, if there is a dispute as to whether a *practice* is a *successor practice* for the purposes of clauses 1.4, 1.6 or 5.6, the *insured* and the *insurer* will take all reasonable steps (including, if appropriate, referring the dispute to arbitration) to resolve the dispute in conjunction with any related dispute between any other party which has insurance complying with these *MTC* and that party's insurer.

4.10   *Conduct of a claim pending dispute resolution*

The insurance must provide that, pending resolution of any coverage dispute and without prejudice to any issue in dispute, the *insurer* will, if so directed by the *Society*, conduct any *claim*, advance *defence costs* and, if appropriate, compromise and pay the *claim*. If the *Society* is satisfied that:

    (a) the party requesting the direction has taken all reasonable steps to resolve the dispute with the other party/ies; and

    (b) there is a reasonable prospect that the coverage dispute will be resolved or determined in the *insured's* favour; and

    (c) it is fair and equitable in all the circumstances for such direction to be given;

it may in its absolute discretion make such a direction.

4.11   *Minimum terms and conditions to prevail*

The insurance must provide that:

    (a) the insurance is to be construed or rectified so as to comply with the requirements of these *MTC*; and

    (b) any provision which is inconsistent with these *MTC* is to be severed or rectified to comply.

5   Extended indemnity period and run-off cover

5.1   *Extended indemnity period*

The insurance must provide cover for the duration of the *extended indemnity period* where an *insured firm* has not, prior to the expiration of the *policy period*, obtained insurance complying with the *MTC* and incepting on and with effect from the day immediately following the expiration of the *policy period*.

Client Protection

5.2   Cessation period

The insurance must provide cover for the duration of the *cessation period* where an *insured firm* has not, prior to the expiration of the *extended indemnity period*, obtained insurance complying with the *MTC* and incepting on and with effect from the day immediately following the expiration of the *policy period*.

5.3   Scope of cover during the extended indemnity period and the cessation period

The cover to be provided in respect of the *extended indemnity period* referred to in clause 5.1 and the *cessation period* referred to in clause 5.2 must indemnify each *insured* in accordance with clauses 1.1 to 1.8 (but may be subject to the limits, exclusions and conditions of the insurance which are in accordance with the *MTC*).

5.4   Run-off cover

The insurance must provide run-off cover:

    (a) subject to clause 5.4(b), in the event of a *cessation*. For these purposes, an *insured firm's practice* shall (without limitation) be regarded as ceasing if (and with effect from the date upon which) the *insured firm* becomes a *non-SRA firm*; and

    (b) with effect from the commencement of the *extended indemnity period* in the event that the *insured firm* has not, on or before the expiration of the *cessation period* referred to in clause 5.2, obtained insurance complying with the *MTC* and incepting on and with effect from the day immediately following the expiration of the *policy period*.

5.5   Scope of run-off cover

The run-off cover referred to in clause 5.4 must indemnify each *insured* in accordance with clauses 1.1 to 1.8 (but may be subject to the limits, exclusions and conditions of the insurance which are in accordance with the *MTC*) on the basis that the *period of insurance* extends for an additional six years (ending on the sixth anniversary of the date upon which, but for this requirement, it would have ended, and for the avoidance of doubt, includes the *extended indemnity period* and *cessation period*).

5.6   Succession

The insurance must provide that, if there is a *successor practice* to the ceased *practice*, the *insured firm* may elect before its *cessation*, whether it wishes the ceased *practice*:

    (a) to be insured under the run-off cover referred to in clause 5.4(a); or

    (b) provided that there is insurance complying with these *MTC* in relation to that *successor practice*, to be insured as a *prior practice* under such insurance.

If the *insured firm* fails to make an election and/or fails to pay any premium due under the terms of the *policy*, before its *cessation*, clause 5.6(b) above shall apply.

The insurance must also provide that where an *insured firm* makes an election pursuant to this clause 5.6, the *insurer* shall give notice to the *Society* in writing of the election not later than seven days following the receipt by the *insurer* of the *insured firm's* election and that election has become effective and the *insured firm* shall irrevocably consent to that notification.

5.7   *Suspended practices*

The insurance must provide that, where run-off cover has been activated in accordance with this clause 5, but where the *insured firm's practice* restarts, the *insurer* may (but shall not be obliged to) cancel such run-off cover, on such terms as may be agreed, provided that:

(a)   there is insurance complying with these *MTC* in relation to that *insured firm* in force on the date of cancellation;

(b)   the *participating insurer* providing such insurance confirms in writing to the *insured firm* and the *insurer* (if different) that:

(i)   it is providing insurance complying with these *MTC* in relation to that *insured firm* for the then current *indemnity period*; and

(ii)   it is doing so on the basis that the *insured firm's practice* is regarded as being a continuation of the *insured firm's practice* prior to *cessation* and that accordingly it is liable for *claims* against the *insured firm* arising from incidents, occurrences, facts, matters, acts and/or omissions which occurred prior to *cessation*.

6   Exclusions

The insurance must not exclude or limit the liability of the *insurer* except to the extent that any *claim* or related *defence costs* arise from the matters set out in this clause 6.

6.1   *Prior cover*

Any *claim* in respect of which the *insured* is entitled to be indemnified by the *SIF* or under a professional indemnity insurance contract for a period earlier than the *period of insurance*, whether by reason of notification of *circumstances* to *SIF* or under the earlier contract or otherwise.

6.2   *Death or bodily injury*

Any liability of any *insured* for causing or contributing to death or bodily injury, except that the insurance must nonetheless cover liability for psychological injury or emotional distress which arises from a breach of duty in the performance of (or failure to perform) legal work.

6.3   *Property damage*

Any liability of any *insured* for causing or contributing to damage to, or destruction or physical loss of, any property (other than property in the care, custody or control of any *insured* in connection with the *insured firm's practice* and not occupied or used in the course of the *insured firm's practice*), except that the insurance must nonetheless cover liability for such damage, destruction or loss which arises from breach of duty in the performance of (or failure to perform) legal work.

6.4   *Partnership disputes*

Any actual or alleged breach of the *insured firm's partnership* or shareholder agreement or arrangements, including any equivalent agreement or arrangement where the *insured firm* is an *LLP* or a company without a share capital.

6.5   *Employment breaches, discrimination, etc.*

Wrongful dismissal, repudiation or breach of an employment contract or arrangement, termination of a training contract, harassment, discrimination or like conduct in relation to any *partnership* or shareholder agreement or arrangement or the equivalent where the *insured firm* is an *LLP* or a company without a share capital, or in relation to any employment or training agreement or arrangement.

6.6   *Debts and trading liabilities*

Any:

(a)   trading or personal debt of any *insured*; or

(b)   legal liability assumed or accepted by an *insured* or an *insured firm* under any contract or agreement for the supply to, or use by, the *insured* or *insured firm* of goods or services in the course of the *insured firm's practice*, save that this exclusion 6.6(b) will not apply to any legal liability arising in the course of an *insured firm's practice* in connection with its or any *insured's* use of or access to the HM Land Registry network (including, without limitation, access under a Network Access Agreement made under the Land Registration (Network Access) Rules and the Land Registration (Electronic Communications) Order 2007) other than an obligation to pay search fees or other charges for searches or services provided by HM Land Registry to the *insured firm*; or

(c)   guarantee, indemnity or undertaking by any particular *insured* in connection with the provision of finance, property, assistance or other benefit or advantage directly or indirectly to that *insured*.

6.7   *Fines, penalties, etc*

Any:

(a)   fine or penalty; or

(b)   award of punitive, exemplary or like damages under the law of the United States of America or Canada, other than in respect of defamation; or

(c)   order or agreement to pay the costs of a complainant, regulator, investigator or prosecutor of any professional conduct complaint against, or investigation into the professional conduct of, any *insured*.

6.8 *Fraud or dishonesty*

The insurance may exclude liability of the *insurer* to indemnify any particular *person* to the extent that any civil liability or related *defence costs* arise from dishonesty or a fraudulent act or omission committed or condoned by that *person*, except that:

(a) the insurance must nonetheless cover each other *insured*; and

(b) the insurance must provide that no dishonesty, act or omission will be imputed to a body corporate unless it was committed or condoned by, in the case of a company, all directors of that company, or in the case of an *LLP*, all members of that *LLP*.

6.9 *Directors' or officers' liability*

The insurance may exclude liability of the *insurer* to indemnify any natural person in their capacity as a director or officer of a body corporate (other than a *recognised body*, *licensed body* (in respect of its *regulated activities*) or a service, administration, trustee or nominee company referred to in clauses 1.3(b), 1.5(b) or 1.7(b)) except that:

(a) the insurance must nonetheless cover any liability of that *person* which arises from a breach of duty in the performance of (or failure to perform) legal work; and

(b) the insurance must nonetheless cover each other *insured* against any vicarious or joint liability.

6.10 *War and terrorism, and asbestos*

The insurance may exclude, by way of an exclusion or endorsement, liability of the *insurer* to indemnify any *insured* in respect of, or in any way in connection with:

(a) terrorism, war or other hostilities; and/or

(b) asbestos, or any actual or alleged asbestos-related injury or damage involving the use, presence, existence, detection, removal, elimination or avoidance of asbestos or exposure to asbestos,

provided that any such exclusion or endorsement does not exclude or limit any liability of the *insurer* to indemnify any *insured* against civil liability or related *defence costs* arising from any actual or alleged breach of duty in the performance of (or failure to perform) legal work or failure to discharge or fulfil any duty incidental to the *insured firm's practice* or to the conduct of *private legal practice*.

7   General conditions

7.1 *As agreed*

The insurance may contain such general conditions as are agreed between the *insurer* and the *insured firm*, but the insurance must provide that the special conditions required by clause 4 prevail to the extent of any inconsistency.

7.2 *Reimbursement*

The insurance may provide that each *insured* who:

    (a) committed or condoned (whether knowingly or recklessly):

        (i)   non-disclosure or misrepresentation; or

        (ii) any breach of the terms or conditions of the insurance; or

        (iii) dishonesty or any fraudulent act or omission; or

    (b) undertakes, either itself or by any of its principals, employees, consultants or agents or any person on its behalf, any activity during the *cessation period* in connection with *private legal practice* save to the extent that the activity is undertaken to discharge any of its obligations within the scope of its *existing instructions* or is necessary in connection with the discharge of any such obligation,

will reimburse the *insurer* to the extent that is just and equitable having regard to the prejudice caused to the *insurer's* interests by such non-disclosure, misrepresentation, breach, dishonesty, act or omission, provided that no *insured* shall be required to make any such reimbursement to the extent that any such breach of the terms or conditions of the insurance was in order to comply with any applicable rules or codes laid down from time to time by the *Society*, or in the *Society* publication *Your Clients – Your Business*, as amended from time to time.

The insurance must provide that no non-disclosure, misrepresentation, breach, dishonesty, act or omission will be imputed to a body corporate unless it was committed or condoned by, in the case of a company, all directors of that company, or in the case of an *LLP*, all members of that *LLP*. The insurance must provide further that any right of reimbursement contemplated by this clause 7.2 against any *person* referred to in clauses 1.3(d), 1.5(d) or 1.7(d) (or against the estate or legal personal representative of any such *person* if they die or become legally incapacitated) is limited to the extent that is just and equitable having regard to the prejudice caused to the *insurer's* interests by that *person* having committed or condoned (whether knowingly or recklessly) the non-disclosure, misrepresentation, breach, dishonesty, act or omission.

7.3   *Reimbursement of defence costs*

The insurance may provide that each *insured* will reimburse the *insurer* for *defence costs* advanced on that *insured's* behalf which the *insurer* is not ultimately liable to pay.

7.4   *Reimbursement of the excess*

The insurance may provide for those *persons* who are at any time during the *period of insurance principals* of the *insured firm*, together with, in relation to a *sole practitioner*, any *person* held out as a *partner* of that practitioner, to reimburse the *insurer* for any *excess* paid by the *insurer* on an *insured's* behalf. The *sum insured* must be reinstated to the extent of reimbursement of any amount which eroded it as contemplated by clause 3.4.

7.5 *Reimbursement of moneys paid pending dispute resolution*

The insurance may provide that each *insured* will reimburse the *insurer* following resolution of any coverage dispute for any amount paid by the *insurer* on that *insured's* behalf which, on the basis of the resolution of the dispute, the *insurer* is not ultimately liable to pay.

7.6 *Withholding assets or entitlements*

The insurance may require the *insured firm* to account to the *insurer* for any asset or entitlement of any *person* who committed or condoned any dishonesty or fraudulent act or omission, provided that the *insured firm* is legally entitled to withhold that asset or entitlement from that *person*.

7.7 *Premium*

The premium may be calculated on such basis as the *insurer* determines and the *insured firm* accepts including, without limitation, a basis which recognises *claims* history, categories of work performed by the *insured firm*, numbers of *principals* and *employees*, revenue derived from the *insured firm's practice* and other risk factors determined by the *insurer*.

8   Definitions and interpretation

8.1   The SRA Handbook Glossary 2012 (the Glossary) shall apply and, unless the context otherwise requires:

   (a)   all italicised terms shall be defined in accordance with the Glossary;

   (b)   terms shall be interpreted in accordance with the Glossary;

   (c)   references to the *Society* include the *SRA* and any body or *person* which succeeds in whole or in part to the functions of the *Society* or the *SRA* and any delegate of the *Society*, the *SRA* or any such body or *person*; and

   (d)   a reference to a director includes a member of an *LLP*.

8.2   These *MTC* shall be, and the insurance shall be expressed to be, governed by and interpreted in accordance with English law.

APPENDIX 2

[Deleted]

APPENDIX 3 – SPECIAL PROVISIONS FOR RELS

1   If:

   (a)   one or more of the *principals* of an *insured firm* are RELs who claim that professional indemnity insurance, or a professional indemnity fund, under their home professional rules provides the *insured firm's practice* with professional indemnity cover in all respects equivalent in its conditions and extent to that which would be provided under the *MTC* (**Full Home State Cover**); and

   (b)   the *Council* is so satisfied, (including, without limitation, by reason of any provider of the Full Home State Cover entering into such agreement as the *Council* may require from time to time but provided that the *Council* shall not be so satisfied if more than 25% of the *principals* are *solicitors*),

the *insured firm* and its *principals* shall for so long as such cover continues (and, where the *Council* has required such agreement, for so long as such agreement remains in force and its requirements are complied with by the provider(s) of the Full Home State Cover that are party to it) be exempted from the obligation to take out and maintain *qualifying insurance*.

2   If on an application by one or more *RELs* who are *principals* in an *insured firm*, the *Council* is satisfied that the *insured firm's practice* has professional indemnity cover under home professional rules but that the equivalence is only partial (**Partial Home State Cover**) (including, without limitation, by reason of the provider of the Partial Home State Cover entering into such agreement as the *Council* may require from time to time), the *insured firm* and its *principals* shall for so long as such cover continues (and, where the *Council* has required such agreement, for so long as such agreement remains in force and its requirements are complied with by the provider(s) of the Partial Home State Cover that are party to it) be exempted from the obligation to take out and maintain *qualifying insurance*, on condition that they take out and maintain a *difference in conditions policy*, which shall provide cover including the *MTC* as modified by the following changes (but not otherwise):

   (a)   Clause 4.5 shall be deleted and replaced with the following:

   4.5 No "other insurance" provision

   The insurance must not provide that the liability of the *insurer* is reduced or excluded by reason of the existence or availability of any other insurance other than as contemplated by clauses 6.2 or 6.12. For the avoidance of doubt, this requirement is not intended to affect any right of the *insurer* to claim contribution from any other *insurer* which is also liable to indemnify any *insured*.

   (b)   Clause 4.9 shall be deleted and replaced with the following:

   4.9 Resolution of disputes

   The insurance must provide that, if there is a dispute as to whether a *practice* is a *successor practice* for the purposes of clauses 1.4, 1.6 or 5.6, the *insured* and the *insurer* will take all reasonable steps (including, if appropriate, referring the dispute to arbitration) to resolve the dispute in conjunction with any related dispute between any other party which has insurance complying with these *MTC* and that party's insurer, and in conjunction with the provider of the Partial Home State Cover.

   (c)   Clause 4.10 shall be deleted and replaced with the following:

4.10 Conduct of a claim pending dispute resolution

The insurance must provide that, pending resolution of any coverage dispute and without prejudice to any issue in dispute, the *insurer* will, if so directed by the *Society*, conduct any *claim*, advance *defence costs* and, if appropriate, compromise and pay the *claim* (whether alone or in conjunction with the provider of the Partial Home State Cover). If the *Society* is satisfied that:

(a) the party requesting the direction has taken all reasonable steps to resolve the dispute with the other party/ies; and

(b) there is a reasonable prospect that the coverage dispute will be resolved or determined in the *insured's* favour; and

(c) it is fair and equitable in all the circumstances for such direction to be given;

it may in its absolute discretion make such a direction.

(d) Clause 4.12 shall be added:

4.12 Period of insurance

The *period of insurance* must not expire prior to the the date with effect on which the Partial Home State Cover expires or is avoided.

(e) The following clause shall be added:

6.11 Partial Home State Cover

The insurance may exclude any liability of the *insurer* to the extent that any such liability is covered under the terms of the Partial Home State Cover irrespective of whether recovery is actually made in respect of such liability.

and in these Rules the following definition shall be added:

Partial Home State Cover has the meaning given in Appendix 3 to the SRA Indemnity Insurance Rules 2013.

3   In the event of an *insured firm* which has the benefit of an exemption under paragraph 1 or paragraph 2 of this Appendix ceasing for whatever reason to enjoy that exemption but continuing to carry on a *practice* it shall be treated for all the purposes of these Rules as though it had commenced the *practice* on the date when such exemption ceased.

4   Rule 6 (Insolvency Event) shall apply to an *insured firm* which has the benefit of an exemption under paragraph 1 or paragraph 2 of this Appendix in like manner as though the insurance company or entity or fund providing professional indemnity cover under its home professional rules, on the basis of which exemption or partial exemption was granted, was a *participating insurer*.

5   In the case of an *insured firm* which has the benefit of an exemption under paragraph 2 of this Appendix all the provisions of these Rules shall apply to the

additional professional indemnity insurance required under that paragraph to be taken out with a *participating insurer*.

SRA Indemnity (Enactment) Rules 2012

These rules consist of one part split into two rules. The SRA Indemnity Rules 2012 form the annex to these rules.

PART 1: THE ENACTMENT RULES

Rule 1: Authority

1.1   These Rules are made on 22 June 2012 by the Solicitors Regulation Authority Board under sections 37, 79 and 80 of the Solicitors Act 1974, section 9 of the Administration of Justice Act 1985, and paragraph 19 of Schedule 11 to the Legal Services Act 2007, with the approval of the Legal Services Board under paragraph 19 of Schedule 4 to the Legal Services Act 2007.

Rule 2: Commencement and application

2.1   The Solicitors' Indemnity Rules 1987 as amended from time to time shall be further amended with effect from 1 October 2012 and shall continue in force thereafter in the form annexed hereto in which form they may be known as the SRA Indemnity Rules 2012.

2.2   The Solicitors' Indemnity (Incorporated Practice) Rules 1991 as amended from time to time shall continue in force only in respect of the *indemnity periods* commencing on 1 September 1991 and 1 September 1992.

2.3   The *contributions* payable in respect of the *indemnity periods* commencing prior to 1 September 1996 shall remain unaltered.

2.4   In respect of any *indemnity periods* commencing on or after 1 September 1996 the *Society* shall retain the power under Rule 35 of the Solicitors' Indemnity Rules 1996 to determine supplementary *contributions* in respect of any such period.

2.5   The indemnity available in respect of the *indemnity periods* commencing prior to 1 October 2012 shall remain unaltered.

2.6   In these Rules the terms in italics will have the meaning set out in Rule 3.1 of the SRA Indemnity Rules 2012 annexed hereto.

Client Protection

[F.2A] SRA Indemnity Rules 2012

These rules form the annex to the SRA Indemnity (Enactment) Rules 2012.

PART 1: GENERAL PROVISIONS AND INTERPRETATION

Rule 1: Authority

1.1   These Rules are made on 22 June 2012 by the Solicitors Regulation Authority Board under sections 37, 79 and 80 of the Solicitors Act 1974, section 9 of the Administration of Justice Act 1985, and paragraph 19 of Schedule 11 to the Legal Services Act 2007, with the approval of the Legal Services Board under paragraph 19 of Schedule 4 to the Legal Services Act 2007.

1.2   These Rules regulate indemnity provision in respect of the practices of *solicitors*, *recognised bodies*, *RELs*, *RFLs*, and *licensed bodies* in respect of their *regulated activities* and certain other European lawyers, carried on wholly or in part in England and Wales.

Rule 2: Citation

2.1   These Rules may be cited as the SRA Indemnity Rules 2012.

Rule 3: Definitions and interpretation

3.1   The SRA Handbook Glossary 2012 (the *Glossary*) shall apply and unless the context otherwise requires:

    (a)   all italicised terms shall be defined in accordance with the *Glossary*;

    (b)   terms shall be interpreted in accordance with the *Glossary*;

    (c)   a reference to a Rule is to a Rule forming part of these Rules, except in relation to Schedule 1 where a reference to a rule is to a rule in the Solicitors' Indemnity Rules 1999;

    (d)   the Schedule to these Rules forms part of these Rules; and

    (e)   these Rules will be governed by and interpreted in accordance with English law.

Rule 4: Establishment and maintenance of fund

4.1   The *Society* shall maintain the *fund* in accordance with these Rules.

4.2   The purpose of the *fund* is to provide indemnity against loss as mentioned in section 37 of the *SA* as extended by section 9 of the *AJA*, Schedule 4 paragraph 1(3) of the European Communities (Lawyer's Practice) Regulations 2000 and section 89 of the

Courts and Legal Services Act 1990 in the circumstances, to the extent and subject to the conditions and exclusions specified by the Solicitors' Indemnity Rules 1987 as the same have been and are in force and amended and applied from time to time and by any future Rules continuing, amending, adding to, applying or re-enacting such or other Rules to provide such indemnity in respect of annual *indemnity periods* (starting in 1987) unless and until otherwise determined by future Rules.

4.3   The *fund* shall be maintained by *contributions* previously made by or on behalf of *solicitors*, *recognised bodies*, *RELs* and *RFLs* in respect of each *indemnity period* in accordance with Part III of the SRA Indemnity Rules 2011 (or any earlier corresponding provisions), and by any additional *contributions* in accordance with Rule 16.

4.4   The *Society* may maintain the *fund* as a single continuous *fund*, and any deficiency in respect of one *indemnity period* may be met in whole or part from *contributions* in respect of another *indemnity period* or *indemnity periods* and any balance in respect of one *indemnity period* may be applied to the benefit of any other *indemnity period* or *indemnity periods*.

4.5   The *fund* shall be held, managed and administered in accordance with Part IV of these Rules by Solicitors Indemnity Fund Limited, a company set up by the *Society* for this purpose, or by such other *person* or *persons* (including the *Society* itself) as the *Society* may designate for such purpose, in place of Solicitors Indemnity Fund Limited. References in these Rules to Solicitors Indemnity Fund Limited shall include any such other *person* or *persons*.

Rule 5: Indemnity Periods before 1 September 1987

5.1   The policies taken out and maintained and the certificates issued by the *Society* pursuant to the Solicitors' Indemnity Rules 1975 to 1986 shall continue to provide cover subject to and in accordance with their terms in respect of their respective periods up to and including 31 August 1987. They shall not provide cover in respect of any subsequent period.

Rule 6: Application of the Rules

6.1   These Rules shall apply to a *practice* carried on by:

   (a)   a sole *solicitor*;

   (b)   an *REL* practising on or before 31 March 2012 or the date on which an order made pursuant to section 69 of the *LSA* relating to the status of sole practitioners comes into force, whichever is the later, as a *sole practitioner*;

   (c)   a *recognised body*;

   (d)   a *partnership* consisting of one or more *solicitors* and/or *RELs* and/or *recognised bodies* and/or *licensed bodies*;

   (e)   a *partnership* consisting of one or more *solicitors* and/or *RELs*, together with one or more *RFLs*;

   (f)   a *partnership* consisting of one or more *RELs* with or without one or more

RFLs, together with one or more *non-registered European lawyers* practising from one or more offices in any state to which the *Establishment Directive* applies, but outside England and Wales; and

(g) a *licensed body* in respect of its *regulated activities*.

Rule 7: Scope of indemnity

7.1 The following *persons*, namely:

(a) *solicitors*, former *solicitors*, *RELs*, *persons* formerly practising as *RELs*, *RFLs* practising in *partnership* with *solicitors* or *RELs*, *persons* formerly practising as *RFLs* in *partnership* with *solicitors* or *RELs*, *non-registered European lawyers* practising in *partnership* with *RELs*, and *persons* formerly practising as *non-registered European lawyers* in *partnership* with *RELs*;

(b) employees and former employees of the above;

(c) *recognised bodies* and former *recognised bodies*;

(d) officers and employees and former officers and employees of *recognised bodies* and former *recognised bodies*;

(e) *licensed bodies* and former *licensed bodies* in respect of their *regulated activities*; and

(f) *regulated persons*, including officers and employees and former officers and employees of *licensed bodies*,

shall be provided with indemnity out of the *fund* against loss arising from claims in respect of civil liability incurred in *private practice* in their aforesaid capacities or former capacities in the manner set out in Rule 10 and in the circumstances, to the extent and subject to the conditions and exclusions set out in Part II of these Rules and not otherwise.

PART 2: INDEMNITY COVER

Rule 8: Indemnity

Indemnity for ceased practices

8.1 Any *member* of a *previous practice* which ceased on or before 31 August 2000 who has at any time been either:

(a) an assured as a result of the issue of a certificate under one or more of the *master policies*, or

(b) a *person* entitled to be indemnified by virtue of the issue of a receipt under the Solicitors' Indemnity Rules 1987–1990 or a payment of Contribution and Value Added Tax thereon as stated in the Solicitors' Indemnity Rules 1991–1999, and who is not, at the time during the *indemnity period* when a claim is first made or intimated against him or her or when circumstances which might give rise to such a claim are first notified by him or her to Solicitors Indemnity Fund Limited, a *person* entitled or required to be indemnified in respect of claims arising from that *previous practice* by a policy of *qualifying insurance* or otherwise under the *SIIR*,

and the *previous practice*

shall be entitled to indemnity out of the *fund* in the manner, to the extent and subject to the conditions and exclusions set out in these Rules against:

(c) all loss (including liability for third party claimants' costs) incurred by the *previous practice* or any *member* thereof at any time arising directly from:

    (i) any claim(s) first made or intimated against the *previous practice* or any *member* thereof during the *indemnity period* in respect of any description of civil liability whatsoever which may have been incurred in *private practice* by the *previous practice* or by a *member* as a *member* of such *previous practice*;

    (ii) any claim in respect of any such description of civil liability as aforesaid, made or intimated against the *previous practice* or any *member* thereof, whether during or subsequent to the *indemnity period* arising out of circumstances notified to Solicitors Indemnity Fund Limited during the *indemnity period* as circumstances which might give rise to such a claim; and

(d) all costs and expenses incurred with the consent of Solicitors Indemnity Fund Limited (such consent not to be unreasonably withheld) in the defence or settlement or compromise of any such claim as aforesaid.

Eligible former principals

8.2   Rule 8.1 shall apply in addition in respect of any *principal* of a *previous practice* that is an *eligible former principal*.

8.3   In respect of any claim referred to in Rule 8.2 made by an *eligible former principal*, the extent of the indemnity (if any) to be provided by Solicitors Indemnity Fund Limited shall be limited to an amount equal to the lesser of:

(a) the Due Proportion of the Deductible (excluding any Penalty Deductible) in respect of the *eligible former principal* that would have been disregarded by Solicitors Indemnity Fund Limited in relation to the claim had it been made under the Solicitors' Indemnity Rules 1999; and

(b) such amount if any which the *relevant successor practice* is entitled to and seeks to recover from the *eligible former principal* in relation to the claim.

8.4   For the purposes of Rule 8.3, "Due Proportion", "Deductible" and "Penalty Deductible" shall have the meanings respectively given to them by the Solicitors' Indemnity Rules 1999, as set out in Schedule 1 to these Rules.

Expired run-off claims

8.5   Any firm or *person* shall be entitled to indemnity out of the *fund* in the manner, to the extent and subject to the conditions and exclusions set out in this Rule 8.5, in relation to an *expired run-off claim*, provided that:

(a)   such claim is first notified to Solicitors Indemnity Fund Limited at any time between 1 September 2007 and 30 September 2020; and

(b)   there is no *preceding qualifying insurance* which provides cover for such claim; and

(c)   such claim does not relate to or arise out of any *claim* first made against an *insured* or *circumstances* first notified to the provider of such *preceding qualifying insurance*, in either case at a time when such *preceding qualifying insurance* was required to provide cover in respect thereof; and

(d)   such *person* was an *insured* under the relevant *preceding qualifying insurance*.

Notwithstanding any other provision of these Rules:

(e)   the obligations of the *fund* and/or any *insured* in respect of an *expired run-off claim* shall be in accordance with, and limited to, the *expired run-off cover*; and

(f)   any obligation owed by any *insured* under the *preceding qualifying insurance* to the qualifying insurer which issued such insurance shall be deemed to be owed to Solicitors Indemnity Fund Limited in place of such qualifying insurer, unless and to the extent that Solicitors Indemnity Fund Limited in its absolute discretion otherwise agrees.

Rule 9: Exclusions from cover

9.1   The *fund* shall not afford any indemnity in respect of any loss arising out of any claim:

(a)   for death, bodily injury, physical loss or physical damage to property of any kind whatsoever (other than property in the care, custody and control of the *previous practice* or *member* thereof in connection with its, his or her *private practice* for which it, he or she is responsible, not being property occupied or used by it, him or her for the purposes of the *previous practice*);

(b)   for any alleged breach or other relief in respect of any *partnership* or *partnership* agreement between the *principals* in the *previous practice* or between any *principal* therein and any other *person* as *principals* in any other *previous practice*;

(c)   for wrongful dismissal or termination of articles of clerkship or training contract or any other alleged breach or any other relief by either party in respect of any contract of employment by the *previous practice* or any *member* thereof; and/or for wrongful termination or any other alleged breach or any other relief by either party in respect of any contract for supply to or use by the *previous practice* or any *member* thereof of services and/or materials and/or equipment and/or other goods;

(d) for the payment of a trading debt incurred by the *previous practice* or any *member* thereof;

(e) in respect of any undertaking given by any *principal* in the *previous practice* or by a *recognised body* or *licensed body* or on his, her or its behalf (whether in his, her or its own name or in the name of the *previous practice*) to any *person* in connection with the provision of finance, property, assistance or other advantage whatsoever to or for the benefit of such *principal* or any other *principal* or of his or her or any other *principal's* spouse or children or of such *recognised body* or *licensed body* or of any business, firm, company, enterprise, association or venture owned or controlled by him, her or it or any other *principal* or in a beneficial capacity whether alone or in concert with others, EXCEPT to the extent that the *person* seeking indemnity shall establish that he, she or it was unaware that the undertaking was or was likely to be connected with the provision of any such finance, property, assistance or other advantage;

(f) in respect of any dishonest or fraudulent act or omission, but nothing in this exclusion shall prevent any particular *member* of the *previous practice* who was not concerned in such dishonesty or fraud being indemnified in accordance with these Rules in respect of any loss arising out of any claim in respect of any dishonest or fraudulent act or omission by any other such *member*;

(g) in respect of any liability incurred in connection with an *overseas practice*. In relation to a *previous practice* having any *overseas* offices deemed by paragraph (ii) of the definition of *separate practice* in Rule 3.1 to form a *separate practice*, a liability shall be deemed to have been incurred in connection with the office where or from which the major part of the work out of which the loss arose in respect of which indemnity is sought was being done. In the event of doubt as to which (if any) office satisfies this requirement, the liability shall be deemed to have been incurred in connection with the office to which the *person* who accepted the initial instructions was most closely connected;

(h) in respect of any liability incurred in connection with a *previous practice* in relation to which the obligation to pay *contribution* has been exempted under Rule 27 of the Solicitors' Indemnity Rules 2006 (or any earlier corresponding Rule) or, unless otherwise provided by the terms of the waiver, waived by the *Council* under Rule 19 (or under any corresponding earlier Rule);

(i) arising out of any circumstances or occurrences which have been notified under the *master policy* or any certificate issued under the *master policy* or any other insurance existing prior to 1 September 1987;

(j) in respect of any adjustment by way of claims loading or loss of discount which may at any future date or in respect of any future period be made by reference to any claim or claims first made or intimated during any *indemnity period*;

(k) in respect of any liability incurred by any *person* in his, her or its capacity as a shareholder or beneficial owner of a share in a body corporate that is either a *recognised body* or *licensed body* notwithstanding the definition of *principal* in Rule 3.1;

(l) in respect of any act or omission on the part of any *principal* whilst acting on behalf of the *previous practice* or any *member* thereof in connection with any matter affecting the business of the *previous practice* provided that at the time of such act or omission such *principal* was a *principal* in the *previous practice*;

(m) where the *previous practice* or any *member* thereof is entitled to indemnity under any insurance except in respect of any amount greater than the amount which would have been payable under such insurance in the absence of the indemnity provided by the *fund*.

9.2 For the avoidance of doubt, any claim or claims by any *member* or former *member* of any *previous practice* against any *member* or former *member* of any such *previous practice* for the payment of the whole or any part of the deductible paid or due in respect of a claim already notified or made under these Rules or any previous Rules is not a loss arising within the meaning of Rule 8 and shall in no event be recoverable hereunder.

9.3 The exclusions set out in this Rule 9 shall not apply in relation to an *expired run-off claim*, in respect of which the provisions of Rule 8.5 shall apply.

Rule 10: Manner of indemnity

10.1 Such indemnity shall be provided, according to the decision of Solicitors Indemnity Fund Limited as set out in Rule 10.2, in any one or any combination of the following ways:

(a) by payment, in or towards satisfaction of the claim and/or claimant's costs and expenses, to or to the order of the claimant making the claim;

(b) by payment, in respect of the claim and/or claimant's costs and expenses and/or costs and expenses incurred in respect of the defence or settlement or compromise of the claim, to or to the order of the *person* against whom the claim is made;

(c) by payment, in or towards discharge of costs and expenses incurred in respect of the defence or settlement or compromise of the claim, to or to the order of the legal advisers, adjusters or other persons by whom or in respect of whose services such costs and expenses were incurred;

(d) by payment to any firm or *person* in relation to an *expired run-off claim* who was an *insured* under the relevant *preceding qualifying insurance*.

Client Protection

10.2   Solicitors Indemnity Fund Limited shall in any particular case, and notwithstanding the insolvency or bankruptcy of any *person* for whom indemnity is provided, have the sole and absolute right to decide in which way or combination of ways indemnity is provided.

Rule 11: Source of indemnity

11.1   Any such indemnity shall be provided and any claim thereto shall lie and be made exclusively out of and against the *fund*.

11.2   Solicitors Indemnity Fund Limited shall have no obligation to provide indemnity save to the extent that the same can be provided out of the *fund*.

11.3   In no circumstances shall any claim to indemnity lie or be made against the *Society* or the *Council* or the Legal Services Board.

11.4   Save as provided in Rule 21, the *fund* shall be available exclusively for the purpose specified in Rule 4.2.

11.5   In no circumstances shall the *fund* or any part thereof be available or be treated by any *person* as available (whether by virtue of any claim, attachment, execution or proceeding or otherwise howsoever) for or in connection with any other purpose.

Rule 12: Maximum liability of the fund

12.1   The liability of the *fund* as stated in Rule 8.1(c) shall in no event exceed in respect of each such claim the indemnity limit for the *relevant indemnity period*.

12.2   All claims arising from the same act or omission (whether or not made or intimated or arising out of circumstances notified during the same *indemnity period* and whether or not involving the same or any number of different *practices* or *previous practices* and/or *members* of such *practices* or *previous practices*) shall be regarded as one claim.

12.3   If a payment exceeding the indemnity limit is made to dispose of any such claim (or, in circumstances within Rule 12.2, claims) for loss (including claimants' costs) such as stated in Rule 8.1(c), then any liability of the *fund* for costs and expenses under Rule 8.1(d) shall be limited to such proportion of such costs and expenses as the indemnity limit bears to the amount of the payment so made.

12.4   The provisions of this Rule 12 shall not apply in relation to an *expired run-off claim*, in respect of which the provisions of Rule 8.5 shall apply.

Rule 13: Indemnity limit

13.1   Save in relation to an *expired run-off claim*, in respect of which the provisions of Rule 8.5 shall apply, the indemnity limit shall be £1,000,000 each and every claim (including claimants' costs).

Rule 14: Conditions

14.1   The *previous practice* and each *member* thereof shall procure that notice to Solicitors Indemnity Fund Limited shall be given in writing as soon as practicable of:

(a)   any claim(s) the subject of Rule 8 made or intimated during the *relevant indemnity period* against it, him or her of any claim for or likely to be for more than £500; or

(b)   the receipt by it, him or her of notice of any intention to make any such claim(s).

14.2   The *previous practice* and any *member* thereof may also give notice in writing to Solicitors Indemnity Fund Limited of any circumstances of which it, he or she shall become aware which may (whether during or after the *relevant indemnity period*) give rise to any such claim(s).

14.3   Any notice given under Rule 14.2, will be effective only if, at the date when such notice was given, the circumstances known to and notified by the *previous practice* and/or *member* thereof, represent sufficient ground for a genuine and reasonable supposition on the part of the *previous practice* or *member* that those circumstances may give rise to a claim the subject of indemnity under Rule 8.

14.4   If notice is given to Solicitors Indemnity Fund Limited under Rule 14.1(b) or 14.2, any claim subsequently made (whether during or after the *relevant indemnity period*) pursuant to such an intention to claim or arising from circumstances so notified shall be deemed to have been made at the date when such notice was given.

14.5   The *previous practice* and each *member* thereof shall not admit liability for, or settle, any claim falling within Rule 8 or incur any costs or expenses in connection therewith without the prior consent of Solicitors Indemnity Fund Limited (such consent not to be unreasonably withheld).

14.6   Subject to Rule 14.7:

(a)   the *previous practice* and each *member* thereof shall procure that Solicitors Indemnity Fund Limited shall be entitled at the *fund's* own expense at any time to take over the conduct in the name of the *previous practice* or *member* of the defence or settlement of any such claim, including any claim in respect of which the *previous practice* or *member* may become entitled to partial indemnity under any insurance with any insurers; and

(b)   Solicitors Indemnity Fund Limited may after taking over the defence or settlement of any such claim conduct the same as it may in its absolute discretion think fit notwithstanding any dispute or difference, whether or not referred to arbitration under Rule 15, which may exist or arise between it and the *previous practice* or *member*.

14.7   No *previous practice* or *member* thereof shall be required to contest any legal proceedings unless a Queen's Counsel (to be mutually agreed upon or failing agreement

Client Protection

to be appointed by the President of the *Society* for the time being) shall advise that such proceedings should be contested.

14.8   Without prejudice to Rules 14.5, 14.6 and 14.7, the *previous practice* and each *member* thereof shall keep Solicitors Indemnity Fund Limited informed in writing at all times, whether or not Solicitors Indemnity Fund Limited shall specifically so request, as to the development and handling of any claim, intimated claim, notice or circumstances the subject of or arising subsequent to any notice given to Solicitors Indemnity Fund Limited under Rule 14.1 or 14.2; and shall consult and co-operate with Solicitors Indemnity Fund Limited in relation thereto as Solicitors Indemnity Fund Limited may request, whether or not Solicitors Indemnity Fund Limited shall take over the conduct thereof.

14.9   The *fund* waives any rights of subrogation against any *member* of the *previous practice* save where those rights arise in connection with

(a)   a dishonest or criminal act by that *member*; or

(b)   the provision of indemnity under the exception to Rule 9.1(e); or

(c)   a claim to indemnity in circumstances where that *member* has received a net benefit to which he or she was not entitled as a consequence of another *member* being provided with indemnity out of the *fund*;

and save as otherwise expressly provided in these Rules.

14.10   If the *previous practice* or any *member* thereof shall prefer any claim to indemnity out of the *fund* knowing the same to be false or fraudulent as regards amount or otherwise, it, he or she shall forfeit any claim to any such indemnity in respect of any claim or future claim against the *previous practice* or *member* to which the false or fraudulent claim to indemnity out of the *fund* may have related or relate.

14.11   Where there has been a failure to pay any instalment of any *contribution* due or any Value Added Tax payable in accordance with the Solicitors' Indemnity Rules 1987 to 2007 or the SRA Indemnity Rules 2011 or 2012 and a claim has been made or intimated against the *previous practice* or any *member* thereof in respect of which such *previous practice* or *member* would otherwise have been entitled to be provided with indemnity, Solicitors Indemnity Fund Limited shall provide such indemnity by payment (up to the indemnity limit) in or towards satisfying, or enabling the *previous practice* or *member* concerned to satisfy, the claim and claimants' costs and such *previous practice* shall thereafter upon request reimburse to Solicitors Indemnity Fund Limited on behalf of the *fund* the whole or such part as Solicitors Indemnity Fund Limited may request of any payment so made and of any costs and expenses incurred in its defence, settlement or compromise, and each *principal* therein shall be jointly and severally responsible to Solicitors Indemnity Fund Limited for such reimbursement accordingly. Provided always that Solicitors Indemnity Fund Limited shall require such reimbursement only to the extent of (a) any increase which in its opinion may have occurred in the total payable out of the *fund* (including costs and expenses) as a result of such failure, together with (b) such amount as may be necessary to satisfy any unpaid *contribution* and Value Added Tax and interest thereon at the rate of 4% above Barclays Bank base rate with quarterly rests or at such other rate as the *Society* may from time to time publish in the Law Society's Gazette.

14.12   Where non-compliance with any provision of these Rules by any *previous practice* or any *member* thereof claiming to be entitled to indemnity out of the *fund* has resulted in prejudice to the handling or settlement of any claim in respect of which such *previous practice* or *member* is entitled to indemnity hereunder, such *previous practice* or *member* shall reimburse to Solicitors Indemnity Fund Limited on behalf of the *fund* the difference between the sum payable out of the *fund* in respect of that claim and the sum which would have been payable in the absence of such prejudice. Provided always that it shall be a condition precedent of the right of the *fund* to such reimbursement that it shall first have provided full indemnity for such *previous practice* or *member* by payment (up to the indemnity limit) in or towards satisfying, or enabling such *previous practice* or *member* to satisfy, the claim and claimants' costs in accordance with the terms hereof.

14.13   In respect of any loss arising from any claim or claims as described by Rule 8.1(c) arising out of any dishonest or fraudulent act or omission of any *member* of the *previous practice*, the *fund* shall nonetheless be available to afford indemnity in accordance with these Rules to the *previous practice* and any *member* thereof, other than and excluding in each case the particular *member* concerned in such dishonesty or fraud. Provided always that at the request of Solicitors Indemnity Fund Limited, the *previous practice* or *member* being indemnified shall:

(a)   take or procure to be taken at the *fund's* expense all reasonable steps to obtain reimbursement for the benefit of the *fund* from or from the personal representatives of any such *member* concerned in such dishonesty or fraud, and

(b)   procure that any reimbursement so obtained together with any monies which but for such fraud or dishonesty would be due to such *member* concerned in such dishonesty or fraud shall be paid to the *fund* up to but not exceeding the amounts paid by the *fund* in respect of such claim together with any expenditure reasonably incurred by the *fund* in obtaining such reimbursement.

14.14   In the event of indemnity being afforded under the exception to Rule 9.1(e), the *previous practice* or *member* being indemnified shall take or procure to be taken at the *fund's* expense all reasonable steps to obtain reimbursement for the benefit of the *fund* from any *person* to whom any benefit arising from the giving of any undertaking accrues in the circumstances set out in Rule 9.1(e). Provided always that such reimbursement shall not exceed:

(a)   the amount paid by the *fund* by way of indemnity together with any expenditure reasonably incurred by the *fund* in obtaining such reimbursement, or

(b)   the amount of any benefit accruing to such *person*,

whichever is the lesser.

Client Protection

14.15   In respect of any claim to indemnity, Solicitors Indemnity Fund Limited may appoint *panel solicitors* to act on its behalf and on behalf of the *previous practice* or any *member* thereof, and *panel solicitors* shall:

(a)   act at the sole direction of the *fund* for any purpose falling within the scope of these Rules, including acting on the Court record for the *previous practice* or any *member* thereof, and

(b)   disclose to Solicitors Indemnity Fund Limited as required any statement or information given to or which becomes known to *panel solicitors* in the course of so acting, and such disclosure shall be treated as having been made directly to Solicitors Indemnity Fund Limited by the *previous practice* or *member*.

14.16   The provisions of this Rule 14 shall not apply in relation to an *expired run-off claim*, in respect of which the provisions of Rule 8.5 shall apply.

Rule 15: Arbitration

15.1   Any dispute or difference concerning any claim or the quantum of any claim to be provided with indemnity in accordance with these Rules shall be referred to the sole arbitrament, which shall be final and binding, of a *person* to be appointed on the application of either party in default of agreement by the President of the *Society* for the time being. Any such arbitration shall take place and be conducted between, on the one hand, the *person* for whom indemnity is provided, the party to the dispute or difference and, on the other hand, Solicitors Indemnity Fund Limited for and in respect of the *fund*.

PART 3: CONTRIBUTIONS

Rule 16: Power to require contributions

16.1   The *Society* shall have power to require *principals* to make *contributions* of such amount and on such basis as the *Society* may from time to time determine. Value Added Tax, to the extent chargeable on any relevant supply which takes or may be treated as taking place under or by virtue of these Rules, will be charged and payable in addition to and at the same time as any *contributions* payable hereunder.

16.2   Solicitors Indemnity Fund Limited may at any time give to any *practice* written notice correcting any inaccuracy in the calculation of any *contribution* under these Rules. Any reimbursement or any payment of *contribution* hereby required shall be made forthwith upon, respectively, issue or receipt of such a notice, together with any Value Added Tax applicable and (in the case of any amount payable to Solicitors Indemnity Fund Limited upon correction of an inaccuracy in calculation) interest at a rate of 4% above Barclays Bank base rate with quarterly rests or at such other rate as the *Society* may from time to time determine and publish in the Law Society's Gazette.

16.3   Solicitors Indemnity Fund Limited may at any time, to the extent that it is reasonably practicable for it to do so, recalculate any claims adjustment applicable to any *practice* under the Solicitors' Indemnity Rules 2006 (or any earlier corresponding

Rules) as a result of the receipt by Solicitors Indemnity Fund Limited of any sum from any third party relating to any indemnity provided to that *practice* out of the *fund* under these Rules or any earlier corresponding Rules, after deduction of the reasonable costs and expenses incurred by Solicitors Indemnity Fund Limited.

16.4   Solicitors Indemnity Fund Limited shall not be entitled, at any time after 30 September 2008, to require any *practice* to make any *contribution* under the Solicitors' Indemnity Rules 2006 (or any earlier corresponding Rules) which would otherwise be payable by reason of an inaccuracy in calculation, unless that inaccuracy is attributable to a failure to provide information or to a material inaccuracy in information provided by or on behalf of that *practice* under Part III of the Solicitors' Indemnity Rules 2006 (or any earlier corresponding Rules).

16.5   The *Society's* decision shall be final and binding on all affected on any question arising as to:

(a)   any obligation to make a *contribution*; or

(b)   any sum due to any *person* out of the *fund*;

under this Rule 16.

PART 4: MANAGEMENT AND ADMINISTRATION OF THE FUND

Rule 17: Powers of the Society

17.1   Solicitors Indemnity Fund Limited shall hold, and have full power to manage and administer, the *fund*, subject only to:

(a)   such directions, conditions and/or requirements as the *Society* may from time to time issue to or impose upon it expressly pursuant to this provision, and/or

(b)   such further detailed arrangements as the *Society* may from time to time agree with it.

17.2   Without limiting the generality of Rule 17.1, the management and administration of the *fund* shall include power to:

(a)   collect and recover *contributions* due to the *fund* in accordance with these Rules;

(b)   deposit or invest in such manner as Solicitors Indemnity Fund Limited may determine all or any part of the *fund*, including any interest, dividends, profits, gains or other assets accruing to or acquired by the *fund*;

(c)   arrange such insurances as Solicitors Indemnity Fund Limited may determine in respect of the *fund* and/or its assets and/or the *fund's* liability under these Rules to afford indemnity in respect of claims and costs and expenses; and to handle all aspects of any such insurances, including the payment of premiums thereon out of the *fund* and the making and recovery of claims thereunder;

(d) receive, investigate and handle claims to indemnity and other notices prescribed to be given to Solicitors Indemnity Fund Limited by these Rules,
including settlement and compromise and making of ex gratia payments out
of the *fund* in respect thereof and conduct of any dispute or difference
referred to arbitration under Rule 15;

(e) receive, investigate and handle any claim made or intimated against any
person in respect of which they are or may be entitled to be provided with
indemnity out of the *fund* (whether or not a claim to indemnity hereunder
has been made) and/or in respect of which the conduct is by these Rules
assigned to Solicitors Indemnity Fund Limited, including settlement and
compromise and making of ex gratia payments and conduct of any proceedings arising in respect of such claim;

(f) claim and recover reimbursement in respect of any sums paid by way of
indemnity in any circumstances in which such reimbursement may under
these Rules be claimed;

(g) exercise any right of subrogation save where such rights are waived in
accordance with these Rules;

(h) maintain full and proper records and statistics (which subject to Rule 18,
shall at all reasonable times be available on request to the *Society* for
inspection and copying) as to the *fund* and all aspects of its management and
administration;

(i) make to and review with the Council of the *Society* annually and at any other
time that the *Council* may require, written and (if the *Council* so requires)
oral reports as to the *fund* and, subject to Rule 18, its management and
administration, including inter alia recommendations as to the *contributions*
which are or may be required in respect of past, present and/or future
indemnity periods and the circumstances in which, extent to which and
conditions and exclusions subject to which indemnity should in any future
indemnity period be afforded out of the *fund*;

(j) engage the assistance of any third party in respect of all or any aspect(s) of the
management and administration of the *fund*;

(k) delegate to any third party all or any aspect(s) of the management and
administration of the *fund*;

(l) institute and/or conduct such proceedings as it may consider necessary or
appropriate for the due management and administration of the *fund* in its
own name or (subject to prior consent of the *Society*) in the name of the
Society;

(m) disburse and/or reimburse out of the *fund* all administrative and legal and
other costs, overheads, fees and other expenses and liabilities incurred in
respect of the *fund*, including without prejudice to the generality of the
foregoing any such costs, overheads, fees and other expenses and liabilities
incurred by the *Society* in respect of the establishment or maintenance, or the
management, administration or protection, of the *fund*;

(n) disburse and/or reimburse out of the *fund* payments for any educational, charitable or other useful purpose which in its opinion is likely directly or indirectly to lead to the reduction or prevention of claims on the *fund* or otherwise to further the purpose or interests of the *fund*;

(o) disburse and/or reimburse out of the *fund* the costs, fees and expenses of the handling after 31 August 1987 of claims and potential claims against assureds notified under the *master policies* and *master policy* certificates;

(p) effect out of the *fund* or by arrangement with third parties the funding pending reimbursement by *master policy insurers* of such claims and potential claims and to bear out of the *fund* the costs, fees and expenses incurred thereby.

Rule 18: Use of information

18.1   Without prejudice to the *Society's* power under Rule 4.5 to designate itself as the *person* responsible for holding, managing and administering the *fund*, information and documents obtained by Solicitors Indemnity Fund Limited about any particular *practice* or *member* thereof in the course of investigating and handling any claim made or intimated or any circumstances notified as mentioned in Rule 21, may be utilised by Solicitors Indemnity Fund Limited for the purpose of preparation of general records, statistics, reports and recommendations (not identifying the particular *practice* or *member*) for or to the *Society*.

18.2   Solicitors Indemnity Fund Limited may bring to the attention of the *Society* at any time and without notice to the *practice* or *person* concerned:

(a) any failure to provide information in respect of any *practice* as required by Part III of the Solicitors' Indemnity Rules 2006 (or any earlier corresponding provisions) or any material omission or inaccuracy in such information;

(b) any failure to pay any *contribution* or other sum due when required to do so under these Rules (or any earlier corresponding Rules) or to reimburse any amount due by way of a Deductible, Due Proportion or Penalty Deductible, or (in the case of an *expired run-off claim*) which falls within a policy excess;

(c) a material inaccuracy in any proposal form submitted by or on behalf of a *practice*;

(d) (in the case of an *expired run-off claim*) any matter or circumstances that would permit the *expired run-off cover* to be avoided or but for the provisions of clause 4.1 of the *MTC* (and/or the corresponding of the *expired run-off cover*);

(e) any dishonesty or fraud suspected on the part of any *person* in relation to any *practice* or *member* thereof, or any other person subject to these Rules or any earlier corresponding Rules, or any *insured*; and

(f) any claim of inadequate professional services of which it becomes aware made against any such *practice*, *member* or *person* or any *insured*.

Client Protection

18.3   Such information and documents shall not otherwise be disclosed or available to the *Society* without the prior consent of the *practice* (or any subsequent or successor *practice* thereto) or *member* concerned, except where Solicitors Indemnity Fund Limited or the *Society* have reason to suspect dishonesty on the part of any *practice*, *previous practice*, subsequent or successor *practice* or any *member* or former *member* thereof, or *insured*.

18.4   Any information and documents held by Solicitors Indemnity Fund Limited about a particular *practice* or *member* thereof may be disclosed or available to the *Society* without the prior consent of the *practice* (or any subsequent or successor *practice* thereto) or *member* concerned where the *Society* has been requested by any *practice*, subsequent or successor *practice* or *member* thereof to grant, amend or revoke any waiver under Rule 19 or to make a determination under Rule 20.

18.5   Solicitors Indemnity Fund Limited may pass to the *Society* the name of any *practice* (including any subsequent, successor or *previous practice*) or any *member* or former *member* thereof in circumstances where Solicitors Indemnity Fund Limited has cause for concern having regard to:

(a)   the nature, incidence or value of paid and/or reserved claims in respect of any such *practice* or *member*; or

(b)   the existence of circumstances which are considered by the *fund* to create an increased risk of claims occurring in respect of that *practice* or *member*; or

(c)   failure on the part of a *practice* or *member* thereof, or any *insured*, to comply with their obligations under these Rules (or any earlier corresponding Rules);

and for the purposes of paragraphs (b) and (c) above Solicitors Indemnity Fund Limited shall have the power to determine criteria which would indicate the likelihood of an increased risk of claims occurring and to specify those obligations in respect of which a failure to comply could form the basis for Solicitors Indemnity Fund Limited to pass on information.

18.6   In the exercise of the powers set out in Rule 18.5 Solicitors Indemnity Fund Limited may give details to the *Society* of the reasons for the decision to pass the name of the *practice* or *member* thereof to the *Society* including, in appropriate cases, releasing documentary information provided that no such documentary information will be released which could breach the general duty of confidentiality owed by a *practice* or *member* thereof to a client or former client.

18.7   In respect of any information that may be brought to the attention of the *Society* in accordance with Rules 18.1 to 18.6:

(a)   the *Society* shall keep all such information confidential;

(b)   the *Society* shall not (except where and to the extent required by law or in the proper performance by the *Society* of its regulatory functions) at any time reveal any such information to any *person* other than a duly authorised employee of the *Society* or any of its subsidiaries; and

(c) any privilege attaching to such information shall not be regarded as having been waived whether by virtue of such information having been provided to the *Society* or otherwise;

but the provisions of this Rule 18.7 shall not prevent the *Society* from making use of any such information for the purpose of bringing disciplinary proceedings against any *person*.

Rule 19: Waivers

19.1   The *Society* shall have power in any case or class of cases to waive in writing prospectively or retrospectively any obligation on any *solicitor*, *recognised body*, *licensed body* or *foreign lawyer* under these Rules and to amend or revoke any such waiver.

19.2   Any application by any *person* for:

(a) a waiver of any obligation under these Rules or under the Solicitors' Indemnity Rules 2001 or any Rules subsequent thereto; or

(b) a correction or recalculation of any sum paid or payable to the *fund* under these Rules, or under the Solicitors' Indemnity Rules 2001 or any Rules subsequent thereto;

must be made in writing to the *Society* no later than 3 calendar months from the date on which the relevant obligation has effect in relation to that *person*, or the date on which that *person* is notified thereof by Solicitors Indemnity Fund Limited, whichever is the earlier.

19.3   No application by any *person* for:

(a) a waiver of any obligation under the Solicitors' Indemnity Rules 2000 or any Rules made prior thereto; or

(b) a correction or recalculation of any sum paid or payable to the *fund* under the Solicitors' Indemnity Rules 2000 or any Rules made prior thereto;

may be considered unless it was made in writing to the *Society* as soon as practicable, and in any event no later than 28 February 2002.

19.4   Any appeal against any decision made by the *Society* in respect of any application for a waiver of any obligation under these Rules or any previous Rules, or in respect of any correction or recalculation of any sum paid or payable to the *fund* under these Rules or any previous Rules, must be made in writing to the *Society* within 21 days from the date of the decision.

19.5   An application for a waiver as contemplated by this Rule 19 or the making of an appeal against any decision made by the *Society* in respect of such application shall not relieve any *person* from any obligation under these Rules or any previous Rules pending the determination of any such application or appeal.

Client Protection

Rule 20: Decisions by the Society

20.1   The *Society* shall have power to treat any *person* as complying with any provision of these Rules for the purposes of the *SA* notwithstanding that the *person* has failed to comply with any provision of these Rules where such non-compliance is regarded by the *Society* in a particular case or cases as being insignificant.

PART 5: MAINTENANCE AND TERMINATION OF THE FUND

Rule 21: Maintenance and termination of the fund

21.1   The *fund* shall continue to be held, managed and administered by Solicitors Indemnity Fund Limited for so long as and to the extent that the *Society*, in the light of the reports made to it by Solicitors Indemnity Fund Limited, may consider necessary or appropriate for the purpose of providing indemnity in respect of any claim(s) made or intimated during any *indemnity period* and/or during or subsequent to any *indemnity period* arising out of circumstances notified during any *indemnity period* as circumstances which might give rise to such claim(s).

21.2   As and when the *Society* no longer considers it necessary or appropriate that all or any part of the *fund* should be so held, managed and administered, the *Society* may require all or any part of the *fund* not so required to be released to the *Society* which shall apply the same if and to the extent the *Society* considers it reasonably practicable for the purpose of providing indemnity in any other way permitted by section 37(2) of the *SA* and otherwise for the overall benefit of the *solicitors'* profession in such manner as it may decide.

SCHEDULE 1: EXTRACT FROM THE SOLICITORS' INDEMNITY RULES 1999

The definitions set out below are provided for convenience only. For the purposes of these Rules, the full text of the Solicitors' Indemnity Rules 1999 prevails and should be consulted when interpreting the extracts contained in this Schedule.

21   Deductibles

21.1   For the purposes of these Rules:

(a)   the "Deductible" means in respect of any claim either:

(i)   the sum calculated by reference to the total number of Relevant Principals and shall be the amount set out in Table I which corresponds to a Practice with the same number of Principals as there are Relevant Principals; or

(ii)   the amount of the increased deductible under Rule 22.2 applicable to the Practice in which the majority of Relevant Principals practise at the Date of Notification;

(b)   a "Relevant Principal" means a Principal or former Principal who is liable for the claim by virtue of having been a Principal in the Practice which was concerned with the matters giving rise to the claim at the date when such matters occurred;

(c) "Due Proportion of the Deductible" means a sum equal to the amount of the Deductible divided by the number of Relevant Principals except where the number of Relevant Principals exceeds fifty when it means a sum equal to the amount of the Deductible divided by the number of Relevant Principals still in practice as Principals at the Date of Notification (provided such number still exceeds fifty);

(d) the "Date of Notification" means either the date of receipt by Solicitors Indemnity Fund Limited of the first of any notices given under either Rule 19.1 or 19.2, or the date of receipt by Solicitors Indemnity Fund Limited of any claim or intimation of claim in respect of which there is or may be an entitlement to indemnity out of the Fund, whichever is the earlier. Provided however that if in either case such date is subsequent to the Relevant Indemnity Period, the Date of Notification shall be deemed to be the date any claim was first made or intimated against the Practice or any Member thereof;

(e) the "Aggregate Deductible" is the amount set out in Table II corresponding to the number of Principals in the Practice as at 1st September 1999 or, where applicable, the date of commencement given in any notice required to be delivered under either Rule 26 or 27 during the Relevant Indemnity Period or the amount of the amended aggregate effected under Rule 22.2.

22   Amending the deductible or aggregate deductible

22.1   In respect of any claim not yet made or intimated and not arising from circumstances already known to the Practice or any Member thereof or notified to Solicitors Indemnity Fund Limited:

(a) the Deductible applicable to the Practice in accordance with Table I may be reduced to 50% or to nil (such reduction also having the effect of reducing the Aggregate Deductible applicable to the Practice in accordance with Table II to 50% or to nil);

(b) the Aggregate Deductible applicable to the Practice in accordance with Table II may be reduced as follows:

   (i)   to one third or two thirds;

   (ii) to one third or two thirds, of any aggregate calculated in accordance with Rule 22.1(a);

in each case upon payment by the Practice to the Fund of an additional Contribution in an amount calculated on a scale approved by the Society from time to time taking into account the claims record of such Practice and of any other Practice(s) in which any Principal therein was previously a Member.

22.2   In respect of any claim not yet made or intimated and not arising from circumstances already notified to Solicitors Indemnity Fund Limited, the Deductible and Aggregate Deductible applicable to the Practice may be increased specifically to sums of:

   (i)   £250,000 subject to an aggregate of two or three times;

(ii) £500,000 subject to an aggregate of one, two or three times;

(iii) £750,000 subject to an aggregate of one, two or three times;

(iv) £1,000,000 subject to an aggregate of one, two or three times

by any Practice in respect of which Gross Fees in excess of £15 million have been disclosed in the Certificate or Notice of Succession, whichever may be appropriate, delivered under Rule 27 save that the amount of the Aggregate Deductible after amendment shall not exceed 3% of the said Gross Fees, in return for a reduced Contribution or repayment by the Fund of any part of any Contribution paid, in an amount determined by the Society either generally or in respect of the particular Practice or any Successor Practice.

22.3 Without prejudice to Rule 22.1, where a claim arises out of circumstances known to the Practice or any Member thereof but not notified prior to the Relevant Indemnity Period and an amendment to the Deductible or Aggregate Deductible was in force during the Indemnity Period when such knowledge was acquired, Solicitors Indemnity Fund Limited may apply the benefit of any Deductible or Aggregate Deductible amendment effected for the Relevant Indemnity Period under Rule 22.1 to any such claim, but shall not be required to do so in any circumstances.

TABLE I
Deductible (Rule 21.1(a))

Number of Principals in Practice	Amount per Practice (£)
1	3,000
2	3,000
3	4,500
4	6,000
5	7,500
6	10,500
7	12,250
8	14,000
9	18,000
10	20,000
11	22,000
12	24,000
13	26,000
14	28,000
15	30,000
16	32,000
17	36,000

Number of Principals in Practice	Amount per Practice (£)
18	40,000
19	44,000
20	48,000
21	52,000
22	56,000
23	60,000
24	64,000
25	68,000
26	71,500
27	74,250
28	77,000
29	79,750
30	82,500
31	93,000
32	96,000
33	99,000
34	102,000
35	105,000
36	108,000
37	111,000
38	114,000
39	117,000
40	120,000
41	123,000
42	126,000
43	129,000
44	132,000
45	135,000
46	138,000
47	141,000
48	144,000
49	147,000
50	150,000
Over 50	150,000

Client Protection

TABLE II
Aggregate Deductible (Rule 21.1(e))

Number of Principals in Practice	Amount per Practice (£)
1	9,000
2	9,000
3	13,500
4	18,000
5	22,500
6	31,500
7	36,750
8	42,000
9	54,000
10	60,000
11	66,000
12	72,000
13	78,000
14	84,000
15	90,000
16	96,000
17	108,000
18	120,000
19	132,000
20	144,000
21	156,000
22	168,000
23	180,000
24	192,000
25	204,000
26	214,500
27	222,750
28	231,000
29	239,250
30	247,500
31	279,000
32	288,000
33	297,000
34	306,000

Number of Principals in Practice	Amount per Practice (£)
35	315,000
36	324,000
37	333,000
38	342,000
39	351,000
40	360,000
41	369,000
42	378,000
43	387,000
44	396,000
45	405,000
46	414,000
47	423,000
48	432,000
49	441,000
50	450,000
Over 50	450,000

23   Penalty deductibles

23.1   For the purposes of these Rules:

(a)   the "Penalty Deductible" means in respect of any claim arising out of the circumstances referred to in Rule 23.2 such sum as is equal to 50% of the amount set out in Table I which corresponds to a Practice with the same number of Principals as there are Relevant Principals;

(b)   "Due Proportion of the Penalty Deductible" means a sum equal to the amount of the Penalty Deductible divided by the number of Relevant Principals except where the number of Relevant Principals exceeds fifty when it means a sum equal to the amount of the Penalty Deductible divided by the number of Relevant Principals still in practice as Principals at the Date of Notification (provided such number still exceeds fifty);

(c)   the "Aggregate Penalty Deductible" is the sum equivalent to 50% of the amount set out in Table II corresponding to the number of Principals in the Practice as at 1st September 1999 or, where applicable, the date of commencement given in any notice required to be delivered under either Rule 26 or 27 during the Relevant Indemnity Period.

23.2   Each and every claim that

(a)   arises from a failure to:

(i) commence proceedings within the time permitted under sections 2, 5 or 11 of the Limitation Act 1980 or any statutory re-enactment thereof;

(ii) commence proceedings within the time permitted under section 111 of the Employment Rights Act 1996 or any statutory re-enactment thereof;

(iii) serve civil proceedings within the time permitted under Part 7.5 of the Civil Procedure Rules 1998 or any statutory re-enactment thereof;

(iv) serve a notice or issue an application within the periods permitted under Part II of the Landlord and Tenant Act 1954 or any statutory re-enactment thereof;

(v) register at Companies House a charge against the assets of a company within the time permitted by section 395 of the Companies Act 1985 or any statutory re-enactment thereof;

(vi) apply to register a protected transaction within the priority period afforded under the Land Registration (Official Searches) Rules 1993 or any statutory re-enactment thereof;

(vii) execute a Deed of Variation within the two years permitted under section 142(1) of the Inheritance Tax Act 1984 and/or to give written notice to the Inland Revenue within the six months permitted under section 142(2) or any statutory re-enactment thereof; or

(b) falls within Rule 19.15(c);

shall, in addition to any Deductible applicable, be subject to a Penalty Deductible in respect of which the Fund shall not afford indemnity under Rule 13(a) PROVIDED THAT such failure occurred on or after 1st September 1996.

23.3 Each Relevant Principal shall be liable for a Due Proportion of the Penalty Deductible PROVIDED THAT:

(a) in the case of any Relevant Principal practising in the same Practice as any other Relevant Principal(s) at the Date of Notification such Relevant Principal shall be jointly and severally liable for such sum as is equal to the total sum of the Due Proportions of the Penalty Deductible payable by all Relevant Principals in that Practice.

(b) Solicitors Indemnity Fund Limited shall disregard the Due Proportion(s) of the Penalty Deductible payable by:

(i) any insolvent or bankrupt Relevant Principal;

(ii) any Relevant Principal in a Practice where the total sum of Penalty Deductible payments in respect of claims to which the Relevant Indemnity Period applies is equal to that Practice's Aggregate Penalty Deductible;

(iii) any Relevant Principal who as at the Date of Notification has ceased to be a Principal in any Practice and who does not become a Principal in any Practice within 12 months of that date;

PROVIDED ALWAYS THAT where the number of Relevant Principals exceeds fifty, the definition in Rule 23.1(b) shall apply and (i) and (iii) above shall not apply unless the number of Principals in practice as Principals at the Date of Notification is fifty or less.

(c) Where an increased Deductible under Rule 22.2 is applicable to the Practice in which the majority of Relevant Principals practise at the Date of Notification, the Principals in such Practice shall be jointly and severally liable for the whole of any Penalty Deductible due PROVIDED ALWAYS THAT if the number of Principals in the Originating Practice is not more than ten then any Penalty Deductible payable shall be due and payable in such Due Proportions as would apply in the absence of any increased Deductible under Rule 22.2.

(d) Solicitors Indemnity Fund Limited may pay, or include in any payment made, out of the Fund in respect of any claim, the whole or any part of any Penalty Deductible applicable thereto, and in that event the Penalty Deductible or any Due Proportion of the Penalty Deductible shall be reimbursed forthwith to the Fund by the appropriate Relevant Principal(s) in accordance with Rule 23.3(a).

23.4 Every Practice shall have an Aggregate Penalty Deductible.

Client Protection

SRA Compensation Fund Rules 2011

Rules dated 17 June 2011 made by the Solicitors Regulation Authority Board, subject to the coming into force of relevant provisions of an Order made under section 69 of the Legal Services Act 2007, S.I. 2011 No. 1716, under sections 36, 36A, 79 and 80 of the Solicitors Act 1974, section 9 of the Administration of Justice Act 1985, section 83(5)(e) of, and paragraph 19 of Schedule 11 to, the Legal Services Act 2007, and the aforementioned Order, with the approval of the Legal Services Board under paragraph 19 of Schedule 4 to the Legal Services Act 2007.

PART 1: GENERAL

Rule 1: Interpretation

1.1   The SRA Handbook Glossary 2012 shall apply and, unless the context otherwise requires:

(a)   all italicised terms shall be defined; and

(b)   terms shall be interpreted,

in accordance with the *Glossary*.

PART 2: THE FUND

Rule 2: Maintenance of and contributions to the Fund

2.1   The *Society* shall establish and maintain the fund called the Solicitors' Compensation Fund ("the Fund") for making grants in respect of compensation claims.

2.2   The *Society* may hold monies raised for the purposes of the Fund in a single fund, and may distribute any monies, pursuant to the provisions of the *SA*, *LSA* and these rules, out of such fund.

2.3   Every *solicitor*, *REL*, *RFL*, *recognised body* and *licensed body* shall make contributions to the Fund in such amounts, at such times and in such circumstances, as may be prescribed from time to time by the *SRA*. Any unpaid contributions may be recovered as a debt due to the *Society*.

2.4   Rule 2.3 shall not apply to a *solicitor*, *REL* or *RFL* who is a Crown Prosecutor.

2.5   The *Society* may invest any money which forms part of the Fund in any investments in which trustees may invest under the general power of investment in section 3 of the Trustee Act 2000 (as restricted by sections 4 and 5 of that Act).

Client Protection

2.6   The *Society* may insure with authorised insurers, in relation to the Fund, for such purposes and on such terms as it considers appropriate.

2.7   The *Society* may

(a) borrow for the purposes of the Fund;

(b) charge investments which form part of the Fund as security for borrowing by the *Society* for the purposes of the Fund.

2.8   The Fund may be applied by the *SRA* for the following purposes (in addition to the making of grants in respect of compensation claims):

(a) payment of premiums on insurance policies effected under rule 2.6;

(b) repayment of money borrowed by the *Society* for the purposes of the Fund and payment of interest on any money so borrowed under rule 2.7;

(c) payment of any other costs, charges or expenses incurred by the *Society* in establishing, maintaining, protecting, administering or applying the Fund;

(d) payment of any costs, charges or expenses incurred by the *SRA* in exercising its powers under Part 2 of Schedule 1 to the *SA* or Schedule 14 to the *LSA* (intervention powers);

(e) payment of any costs or damages incurred by the *Society*, the *SRA*, their *employees* or agents as a result of proceedings against any or either of them for any act or omission of its or theirs in good faith and in the exercise or purported exercise of such powers.

PART 3: GRANTS AND APPLICATIONS

Rule 3: Grants which may be made from the Fund

3.1   The primary object of the Fund is to replace money which a *defaulting practitioner* or a *defaulting practitioner's employee* or *manager* has misappropriated or otherwise failed to account for. The *applicant* need not necessarily be or have been the *defaulting practitioner's* client.

3.2   It is also an object of the Fund to provide compensation in respect of the civil liability of a *defaulting practitioner* or a *defaulting practitioner's employee* or *manager* who in accordance with the *SRA Indemnity Insurance Rules* should have had, but did not have, in place a *policy* of *qualifying insurance* against which a *claim* could be made in respect of such civil liability.

3.3   A grant out of the Fund is made wholly at the discretion of the *SRA*. No person has a right to a grant enforceable at law.

3.4   For any grant to be made out of the Fund (save in respect of a grant made under rule 5), an *applicant* must satisfy the *SRA* that:

(a)   he has suffered or is likely to suffer loss in consequence of the dishonesty of a *defaulting practitioner* or the *employee* or *manager* or *owner* of a *defaulting practitioner*; or

(b)   he has suffered or is likely to suffer loss and hardship in consequence of a failure to account for money which has come into the hands of a *defaulting practitioner* or the *employee* or *manager* or *owner* of a *defaulting practitioner*, which may include the failure by a *defaulting practitioner* to complete work for which he was paid;

in the course of an activity of a kind which is part of the usual business of a *defaulting practitioner* and, in the case of a *defaulting licensed body*, the act or default arose in the course of performance of a *regulated activity*.

3.5   For the purposes of rule 3.4(b):

(a)   an individual whose dealings with the *defaulting practitioner* have been in a personal capacity and who has suffered or is likely to suffer loss due to a failure to account shall be deemed to have suffered hardship; and

(b)   a body corporate, or an individual whose dealings with the *defaulting practitioner* have been in a business capacity and who has suffered or is likely to suffer loss due to a failure to account must provide evidence to satisfy the *SRA* that it, he or she (the body or individual) has suffered or is likely to suffer hardship.

3.6   A grant may, at the sole discretion of the *SRA*, be made as an interim measure.

Rule 4: Grants in respect of persons in default of regulatory requirements

4.1   A grant may be made in respect of a *defaulting solicitor* even if the *defaulting solicitor* had no practising certificate in force at the date of the relevant act or default, provided that the *SRA* is reasonably satisfied that the *applicant* was unaware of the absence of a valid practising certificate.

4.2   A grant may be made in respect of a *defaulting REL* even if, at the date of the relevant act or default, the registration of that lawyer in the *SRA's* register of European lawyers had expired or been revoked under the SRA Practising Regulations, provided that the *SRA* is reasonably satisfied that the *applicant* was unaware of the expiry or revocation.

4.3   A grant may be made in respect of a *defaulting recognised body* even if the recognition of that body was suspended or was revoked under the SRA Recognised Bodies Regulations or the *SRA Authorisation Rules* (as the case may be) on or before the date of the relevant act or default, provided that the *SRA* is reasonably satisfied that the *applicant* was unaware of such suspension or revocation.

4.4   A grant may be made in respect of a *defaulting licensed body* even if the licence issued to that body under the *SRA Authorisation Rules* has been suspended or revoked on or before the date of the relevant act or default, provided that the *SRA* is reasonably satisfied that the *applicant* was unaware of the suspension or revocation.

4.5   A grant may be made in respect of a *defaulting RFL* even if, at the date of the relevant act or default, the registration of that lawyer in the register of foreign lawyers had expired or been revoked under the SRA Practising Regulations, provided that the *SRA* is reasonably satisfied that the *applicant* was unaware of the expiry or revocation.

Rule 5: Grants in respect of uninsured defaulting practitioners

5.1   A grant may be made to provide compensation for loss suffered as a result of the civil liability of a *defaulting practitioner* or a *defaulting practitioner's employee* or *manager* who in accordance with the *SRA Indemnity Insurance Rules* should have had, but did not have, in place a *policy* of *qualifying insurance* against which a *claim* could be made in respect of such civil liability.

5.2   Where an application for a grant is made under rule 5.1 a grant will only be made in circumstances where:

(a)   the *defaulting practitioner* should have had, but did not have, in place a *policy* of *qualifying insurance* against which a *claim* could be made in respect of the civil liability of the *defaulting practitioner* or the *defaulting practitioner's employee* or *manager*;

(b)   the liability of the *defaulting practitioner* or the *defaulting practitioner's employee* or *manager* arises from *private legal practice* in connection with the *defaulting practitioner's practice*; and

(c)   the loss is not covered by the *SIF*.

5.3   Any grant made under this rule 5 will be made in accordance with these rules and otherwise will be assessed and determined in accordance with the terms, conditions and exclusions of the *MTC* as though the *defaulting practitioner* had a *policy* of *qualifying insurance* against which a *claim* in respect of the loss had been made.

5.4   Rules 4, 6, 7, 8.1, 9, 10.3, 14, 15.3 and 20 shall not apply to any grant made under this rule 5.

Rule 6: Grants to practitioners

6.1   A grant may be made to a *defaulting practitioner* who or which has suffered or is likely to suffer loss by reason of his, her or its liability to any client in consequence of some act or default of:

(a)   in the case of a *defaulting solicitor*, *defaulting REL* or *defaulting RFL*, any of his or her *employees* or any fellow *manager*;

(b)   in the case of a *defaulting recognised body*, any of its *managers* or *employees* or any fellow *manager*;

(c)   in the case of a *defaulting licensed body*, any of its *managers* or *employees* or any fellow *manager*, provided that such act or default arose in the course of performance of a *regulated activity*;

in circumstances where but for the liability of that *defaulting practitioner* a grant might have been made from the Fund to some other person.

6.2   No grant shall be made under rule 6.1 unless the *SRA* is satisfied that no other means of making good the loss is available and that the *defaulting practitioner* is fit and proper to receive a grant.

6.3   A grant under rule 6.1 shall normally be made by way of a loan and shall be repayable by the recipient at the time and upon such terms as shall be specified by the *SRA*.

6.4   In the case of a *defaulting recognised body* or a *defaulting licensed body*, such grant may be payable to one or more of the *managers* of the *defaulting recognised body* or *defaulting licensed body*. If a loan is made to more than one *manager*, they shall be jointly and severally liable for the repayment of the loan to the *Society*.

Rule 7: Foreign lawyers

7.1   If an *REL* is exempted from contributing to the Fund on the basis that he or she has completely equivalent cover under home state rules, no grant shall be made:

(a)   in respect of any act or default of the *REL* or his or her *employee* unless, in the case of an *employee*, the *employee* is:

    (i)   a *solicitor*; or

    (ii) the *employee* of a *partnership* which includes at least one person who or which contributes to the Fund; or

(b)   under rule 6, to the *REL*.

7.2   No grant shall be made in respect of any act or default of an *REL* or an *EEL*, or the *employee* of an *REL*, where such act or default took place outside the United Kingdom, unless the *SRA* is satisfied that the act or default was, or was closely connected with, the act or default of a *solicitor* or the *employee* of a *solicitor*, or that the act or default was closely connected with the *REL's practice* in the United Kingdom.

7.3   No grant shall be made in respect of the act or default of an *RFL*, or of the *employee* of an *RFL*, where such act or default took place outside England and Wales, unless the *SRA* is satisfied that the act or default was, or was closely connected with, the act or default of a *solicitor* or the *employee* of a *solicitor*, or that the act or default was closely connected with *practice* in England and Wales.

Rule 8: Losses outside the remit of the Fund

8.1   For the avoidance of doubt, a grant will not be made in respect of the following:

(a)   Losses arising solely by reason of professional negligence by a *defaulting practitioner*, or the *employee* or *manager* of a *defaulting practitioner*.

Client Protection

(b) Losses which are the personal debts of a *defaulting practitioner* and where the facts would not otherwise give rise to a claim on the Fund.

(c) The loss results from, but does not form part of, any misappropriation of, or failure to account for, money or money's worth.

(d) The loss results from the trading debts or liabilities of the *defaulting practitioner*.

(e) The loss amounts to a claim for contractually agreed interest between the *applicant* and the *defaulting practitioner*.

(f) The *SRA* was not notified of the *applicant's* loss in accordance with rule 11.

(g) The loss occurred in relation to an overseas partnership which does not fall within rule 50.1(c) or 50.2(b) of the *SRA Accounts Rules*, unless:

    (i) the loss occurred as a result of a *solicitor's* dishonesty; or

    (ii) the loss occurred as a result of failure to account by a *solicitor* acting as a named trustee.

(h) The application is by the Legal Aid Agency for loss occasioned through making regular payments under the Agency's contracting schemes for civil and/or criminal work.

(i) In the case of a *defaulting licensed body*, losses incurred other than in the course of performance of a *regulated activity*.

8.2   For the avoidance of doubt, a grant will not be made under rule 5 in respect of the following:

(a) Where there is a *policy* or *policies* of *qualifying insurance* against which a *claim* could be or has been made in respect of the civil liability of the *defaulting practitioner* or the *defaulting practitioner's employee* or *manager*.

(b) Any losses that would not be covered under the terms, conditions and exclusions of the *MTC* had the loss been subject to a *claim* under a *policy* of *qualifying insurance*.

Rule 9: Undertakings

9.1   A grant in respect of a failure by a *defaulting practitioner* to comply with an undertaking will be considered if it can be shown that the undertaking was given in the course of the *defaulting practitioner's* usual business acting on behalf of a client, that the recipient acted reasonably in accepting the undertaking and placing reliance on the undertaking and that:

(a) the undertaking was given with dishonest intent for the purpose of procuring money or money's worth; or

(b) the undertaking, although not given with dishonest intent, is subsequently dishonestly not performed for the purpose of procuring money or money's worth.

9.2   The *SRA* does not consider the giving of an undertaking in circumstances which amount to the giving of a bare guarantee of the *defaulting practitioner's* personal liabilities, or the financial obligations and liabilities of a client or third party, to form part of the usual business of a *solicitor* or other legal practitioner, and in the case of a *defaulting licensed body* the *SRA* does not consider such an undertaking to be part of its *regulated activities*.

Rule 10: Multi-party and multi-profession issues

10.1   Where the loss has been sustained as a result of the combined activities of more than one party (e.g. a *defaulting practitioner* conspires with an accountant or surveyor, or is assisted by a negligent accountant or valuer), the *SRA* will consider the role of each contributing factor in causing the *applicant's* loss. The *SRA* will base any grant on its assessment of that portion of the loss primarily attributable to the acts of the *defaulting practitioner* as opposed to that portion which is primarily attributable to the acts or omissions of the other parties, or to other factors. The *SRA* may decide to make a grant on a pro-rata basis in accordance with its assessment of the importance of each contributing factor in the loss, or may reject an application in its entirety if it is of the opinion that the loss was primarily due to other factors rather than the *defaulting practitioner's* conduct.

10.2   When a *solicitor*, *REL* or *RFL* is practising as the *manager* or *employee* of a body authorised not by the *SRA* but by another *approved regulator*, the *SRA* will not consider any claim in respect of that individual's act or default, or his or her *employee's* act or default.

10.3   When an individual authorised not by the *SRA* but by another *approved regulator* is practising as the *manager* or *employee* of a *recognised body*, the *SRA* will in its discretion consider a claim in respect of that individual's act or default.

10.4   In the case of a *defaulting licensed body*, the *SRA* will assess the extent (if any) to which the loss is attributable to an act or default in the course of performance of a *regulated activity* (as opposed to an activity not regulated by the *SRA* or to other factors). The *SRA* will take that assessment into account in deciding whether to make a grant and, if so, in what amount. The *SRA* may refuse to make any grant in a case where it assesses that the loss was primarily attributable to an act or default in the course of performance of an activity not regulated by the *SRA* or to other factors.

Rule 11: Applications: form and time limit

11.1   Every application must be delivered to the *SRA*, in such form as may from time to time be prescribed by the *SRA*, within twelve months after the loss, or likelihood of loss, or failure to account, as the case may be, first came, or reasonably should have come, to the knowledge of the *applicant*. The *SRA* may extend this period if satisfied that there are circumstances which justify the extension of the time limit.

Client Protection

Rule 12: Documentation in support

12.1   The burden of proving a claim rests with the *applicant* who must provide such documentation as may be required by the *SRA* including when requested, a statement of truth. Failure to provide such documentation or to co-operate with the *SRA* will be taken into account when determining the merits of the application.

Rule 13: Exhausting other remedies

13.1   A grant may be refused or limited where the loss or part of the loss is an insured risk or where the loss is capable of being made good by some other means.

13.2   The *SRA* may, before deciding whether to make a grant, require the *applicant*:

(a) to pursue any civil remedy which may be available to the *applicant* in respect of the loss;

(b) to commence insolvency proceedings;

(c) to make a formal complaint to the Police in respect of any dishonesty on the part of the *defaulting practitioner*; or

(d) to assist in the taking of any action against the *defaulting practitioner*.

13.3   In respect of an application for a grant under rule 5, the *SRA* may, before deciding whether to make a grant, require the *applicant* and/or the *defaulting practitioner* to seek indemnity from one or more qualifying insurers under a *policy* or *policies* of *qualifying insurance*.

13.4   In the absolute discretion of the *SRA*, a grant may be made before requiring the *applicant* to resort to other means of recovery.

Rule 14: Notice to defaulting practitioner

14.1   The *SRA* shall not make a grant unless:

(a) a communication has been sent to the *defaulting practitioner* at his, her or its last known correspondence address or to his, her or its representative informing the *defaulting practitioner* of the nature and value of the application; and

(b) not less than eight days have elapsed since the date of receipt of such communication, which shall be regarded as the day following the date of the communication.

14.2   If it appears to the *SRA* that:

(a) any communication sent under rule 14.1 will not come to the attention of the *defaulting practitioner* or his, her or its *representative*; or

(b) a grant should be made urgently as an interim measure to protect the interests of an *applicant* or potential *applicant* to the Fund, then the *SRA* may make a grant notwithstanding failure to comply with the provisions of this rule.

14.3 Where the *SRA* has made a grant as an interim measure in accordance with rule 14.2(b), the *SRA* shall as soon as practicable send the communication referred to in rule 14.1(a) and may (insofar as the failure to communicate before the making of the grant has prejudiced the *defaulting practitioner*) waive in whole or in part the Fund's right of recovery against the *defaulting practitioner*.

Rule 15: Costs

Litigation

15.1 Where an *applicant* intends to or has already instituted proceedings for recovery of his loss and wishes to apply for a grant in respect of the costs of the proceedings, the *SRA* will only consider such costs where:

    (a) they can be shown to be proportionate to the loss and the amount likely to be recovered; or

    (b) the proceedings were necessary for the making of an application to the Fund.

Application

15.2 Where a grant is made, the *SRA* may consider an application for a further grant in respect of the reasonable costs properly incurred by the *applicant* with either his *solicitor* or other professional adviser, provided that such costs were incurred wholly, necessarily and exclusively in connection with the preparation, submission and proof of the application.

Costs where the defaulting practitioner has failed to complete work

15.3 If the *defaulting practitioner* did not complete the work for which he was paid, a failure to account shall be deemed to have arisen within the meaning of rule 3.3(b) of these rules. In such circumstances, the *SRA* may consider making a grant in respect of the additional reasonable legal costs incurred by the *applicant* in completing the outstanding work or a grant by way of contribution towards those costs.

Rule 16: Interest

16.1 The *SRA* may consider an application for a supplementary grant by way of a sum in lieu of lost interest on a principal grant. Such interest will be calculated in accordance with the rates prescribed from time to time by the *SRA*. This will normally be calculated from the day the loss which was the subject of the principal grant was incurred, up to the next working day after payment of the principal grant. Such payment will take into account that a grant is a gift and is therefore not subject to tax.

Client Protection

16.2   Where the application for the principal grant is in respect of a failure to redeem a mortgage, the *SRA* may also make a grant in respect of the additional interest accrued to the mortgage account as a result of the *defaulting practitioner's* failure to redeem.

Rule 17: Maximum grant

17.1   Subject to rule 24 the maximum grant that may be made is £2 million.

Rule 18: Recovery and subrogation

18.1   Where a grant is made otherwise than by way of loan or if by way of a loan repayment of the loan is waived or otherwise the borrower has failed to repay part or all of the loan, the *Society* shall be subrogated to the rights and remedies of the person to whom or on whose behalf the grant is made (the recipient) to the extent of the amount of the grant. In such event the recipient shall if required by the *SRA* whether before or after the making of a grant and upon the *SRA* giving to the recipient a sufficient indemnity against costs, prove in any insolvency and/or winding-up of the *defaulting practitioner* and sue for recovery of the loss in the name of the recipient but on behalf of the *Society*. The recipient shall also comply with all proper and reasonable requirements of the *SRA* for the purpose of giving effect to the *Society's* rights and shall permit the *SRA* to have conduct of such proceedings.

Rule 19: Reduction in grants

19.1   Where an *applicant* or the *applicant's* servant or agent has contributed to the loss as a result of his, her or its activities, omissions or behaviour whether before, during or after the event giving rise to the application, the *SRA* may, in the exercise of discretion and to the extent that such activity, omission or behaviour has contributed to the loss, reduce the amount of any grant that may be authorised or reject the application in its entirety.

Rule 20: Deduction from grants

20.1   The *SRA* may deduct from any grant the costs that would have been legally due to the *defaulting practitioner* so that the *applicant* will not be in a better position by reason of a grant than he, she or it would otherwise have been in.

20.2   The *SRA* may within its discretion deduct from any grant all monies already recovered by an *applicant* and monies which either will be or should have been recovered.

Rule 21: Refusal of an application

21.1   If the *SRA* refuses to make a grant of either the whole or part of the amount applied for, the *applicant* will be informed in writing of the reasons for the decision.

21.2   The fact that an application has been rejected does not prevent a further application being submitted provided that substantial new relevant evidence, information or submissions are produced in support of the new application.

Rule 22: Appeals

22.1   Should the *applicant* wish to appeal against refusal of an application, written notice of intention to appeal must be delivered to the *SRA* within thirty days of the date of receipt of the decision, which shall be regarded as the day following the date of the written communication of the decision. Such notice must be accompanied by details of the grounds of appeal together with any additional evidence in support.

Rule 23: Notice of requirements

23.1   Any requirement of the *SRA* under these rules will be communicated in writing.

Rule 24: Waivers

24.1   The *SRA* may waive any of the provisions of these rules except rules 14 and 21 to 25.

PART 4: REPEALS AND COMMENCEMENT PROVISIONS

Rule 25: Repeals and commencement

25.1   These rules shall come into effect on 6 October 2011, whereupon the Solicitors' Compensation Fund Rules 2009 ("the 2009 Rules") shall cease to have effect save in respect of applications submitted before that date, which shall continue to be subject to the 2009 Rules.

[F.4] SRA Intervention Powers (Statutory Trust) Rules 2011

Rules dated 17 June 2011 made by the Solicitors Regulation Authority Board under sections 79 and 80 of and paragraph 6B of Schedule 1 to the Solicitors Act 1974, paragraphs 32 to 34 of Schedule 2 to the Administration of Justice Act 1985, and paragraph 6 of Schedule 14 to the Legal Services Act 2007, with the approval of the Legal Services Board under paragraph 19 of Schedule 4 to the Legal Services Act 2007, governing the treatment of sums vested in the Law Society under paragraphs 6 or 6A of Schedule 1 to the Solicitors Act 1974, and under paragraphs 3 or 4 of Schedule 14 to the Legal Services Act 2007.

PART 1: GENERAL

Rule 1: Interpretation

1.1   The SRA Handbook Glossary 2012 shall apply and, unless the context otherwise requires:

(a)   all italicised terms shall be defined; and

(b)   terms shall be interpreted,

in accordance with the *Glossary*.

Rule 2: Holding statutory trust monies

2.1   The *SRA* will place all *statutory trust monies* in identifiable *statutory trust accounts*.

2.2   All interest earned on any *statutory trust account* will be added to that account.

Rule 3: Proportionality

3.1   Nothing in these rules shall require the *SRA* to take any action which it considers unreasonable or disproportionate in the context of any *statutory trust account*.

3.2   The *SRA* may apply a level to beneficial entitlements within a *statutory trust account* below which it will not attempt to identify and/or locate potential *beneficiaries* where in the opinion of the *SRA* it would be unreasonable or disproportionate to do so. The level applies to the principal sum identified as relating to a particular *beneficiary*, after the application of any pro-rata adjustment which may be made under rule 7.2 and ignoring the addition of any interest as set out in rule 8.1.

Client Protection

Rule 4: Identifying beneficial entitlements

4.1   In respect of the *statutory trust monies* held following an *intervention*, the *SRA* will create a *reconciled list* or a *best list* from the evidence which it has available, including documents and other evidence provided by or on behalf of *claimants*.

4.2   In creating a *reconciled list* or a *best list*, any sums of money which are identified within a *statutory trust account* as being payments on account of costs, or which are equivalent to the costs incurred in the matter to which the funds relate, will be treated as due to the client rather than the *intervened practitioner*, unless there is sufficient evidence of a bill or other written notification of costs having been sent to the client.

4.3   The *SRA* will attempt to contact all *persons* identified as having a potential beneficial interest in the *statutory trust monies* inviting them to submit a claim in accordance with rule 5.

PART 2: CLAIMS

Rule 5: Claimants to money

5.1   Every *claimant* must deliver to the *SRA* a completed and signed claim form. The claim form shall require such information as may be prescribed by the *SRA* from time to time.

5.2   A *claimant* must provide such documentation and other evidence as may be requested by the *SRA* in order to support the claim including a statement of truth and proof of identity. Failure to provide such documentation or evidence will be taken into account by the *SRA* when deciding whether to make a payment in respect of a claim.

5.3   The *SRA* may, in its discretion, waive the requirements of rules 5.1 and/or 5.2.

Rule 6: Verification of claims

6.1   Subject to rule 6.2, the *SRA* will verify the individual potential beneficial entitlements claimed under rule 5 by examining all available evidence.

6.2   The extent of verification work will be determined by the *SRA* by considering, but not limited to, the circumstances of the *intervention*, the reliability of the accounts of the *intervened practitioner* and the perceived integrity of the list of beneficial entitlements prepared.

Rule 7: Shortfall in statutory trust account

7.1   In cases where a shortfall is revealed between the *statutory trust monies* held and the beneficial entitlements shown in a *reconciled list* or *best list*, the *SRA* may rectify the position, in whole or in part, by the use of other monies taken into its possession following the *intervention* to which that account relates.

7.2   Where a shortfall still exists on a *statutory trust account* after the application of the additional funds set out in rule 7.1, the *SRA* will decide on the method for distribution of the deficient account.

Rule 8: Distribution of beneficial entitlements

8.1   Any interest which has accrued on the *statutory trust account* under rule 2.2 will be distributed to *beneficiaries* on a pro-rata basis in proportion to the payments made to them or on such other basis as the *SRA* may decide.

8.2   In a case where the accounting records of the *intervened practitioner* are *reconciled accounts*, payments to *beneficiaries* will be made on the basis of the *reconciled list*.

8.3   In a case where the accounting records of the *intervened practitioner* are not *reconciled accounts*, payments to *beneficiaries* will be made on the basis of the *best list*.

Rule 9: Residual balances

9.1   The *SRA* may use any funds which remain in a *statutory trust account* following the distribution to *beneficiaries* under rule 8 to offset any costs, charges or other expenses which it has incurred in establishing the beneficial entitlements to the *statutory trust monies* and in distributing the monies accordingly.

9.2   If funds remain in a *statutory trust account* after payment to *beneficiaries* and the deduction of costs, charges and expenses in accordance with rule 9.1, the *SRA* may transfer such remaining funds into the compensation fund held by the *SRA* in respect of the activities carried on by the *intervened practitioner* and thereupon any claim to such funds shall be extinguished.

Rule 10: Miscellaneous

10.1   The *SRA* may make an interim payment to a *beneficiary* before the full distribution on a *statutory trust account* takes place. This will be done only where the *SRA* is satisfied that the circumstances are such that the payment can be made without prejudicing other claims on the *statutory trust account*.

10.2   The *SRA* may issue guidance notes to *claimants* to assist in the making of a claim and to explain the steps and processes which the *SRA* takes in dealing with a *statutory trust account*.

Rule 11: Commencement and application

11.1   These rules shall apply to all *statutory trust accounts*, whether such accounts were created before or after the 6 October 2011.

Rule 12: Transitional provisions

12.1   These rules shall not apply to *licensed bodies* until such time as the *Society* is designated as a *licensing authority* under Part 1 of Schedule 10 to the *LSA* and all definitions shall be construed accordingly.

Client Protection

12.2   In these rules references in the preamble to the rules being made under paragraph 6 of Schedule 14 to the Legal Services Act 2007 shall have no effect until the *Society* is designated as a *licensing authority* under Part 1 of Schedule 10 to the *LSA*.

[G]   Discipline and Costs Recovery

[G.0] Introduction to Discipline and Costs Recovery

This section of the Handbook contains the following rules:

- SRA Disciplinary Procedure Rules; and
- SRA Cost of Investigations Regulations

These rules must be read in conjunction with the Principles. The Principles underpin all aspects of practice, including how you respond to any regulatory investigation or action.

The desired outcomes that apply to the disciplinary and costs recovery provisions are that:

- clients and the general public are confident that the SRA will take appropriate action to discipline firms that do not comply with the Principles, do not achieve the outcomes in the Code, or otherwise breach the SRA's regulatory requirements;
- firms and individuals are aware of the SRA's procedures for disciplining and fining them, and for recovering costs, and the circumstances in which such action will be taken;
- persons subject to disciplinary action by the SRA provide the SRA with all relevant information and comply with all reasonable requests of the SRA;
- the SRA is able to take appropriate disciplinary action where there has been a failure to comply with a regulated person's duties; and
- persons subject to disciplinary action by the SRA contribute to the cost of the disciplinary action.

[G.1] SRA Disciplinary Procedure Rules 2011

Rules dated 17 June 2011 commencing 6 October 2011 made by the Solicitors Regulation Authority Board, after consultation with the Solicitors Disciplinary Tribunal, under sections 31, 44D, 79 and 80 of the Solicitors Act 1974, section 9 of and paragraph 14B of Schedule 2 to the Administration of Justice Act 1985 and section 83 and Schedule 11 of the Legal Services Act 2007, with the approval of the Legal Services Board under paragraph 19 of Schedule 4 to the Legal Services Act 2007.

PART 1: GENERAL

Rule 1: Interpretation

1.1   The SRA Handbook Glossary 2012 shall apply to these rules and, unless the context otherwise requires:

(a)   all italicised terms within these rules shall be defined; and

(b)   terms within these rules shall be interpreted,

in accordance with the *Glossary*.

Rule 2: Scope

2.1   These rules govern the procedure for the *SRA* to:

(a)   give a *regulated person* a written rebuke;

(b)   direct a *regulated person* to pay a penalty;

(c)   publish details of a written rebuke or a direction to pay a penalty;

(d)   *disqualify* a *person* from acting as a *HOLP* or *HOFA*, or being a manager or employee; and

(e)   make an application to the *Tribunal*.

2.2   These rules shall not prevent, prohibit or restrict the exercise of any other powers or other action by the *SRA*.

Rule 3: Disciplinary powers

3.1   The circumstances in which the *SRA* may make a *disciplinary decision* to give a *regulated person* a written rebuke or to direct a *regulated person* to pay a penalty are when the following three conditions are met:

(a)   the first condition is that the *SRA* is satisfied that the act or omission by the *regulated person* which gives rise to the *SRA finding* fulfils one or more of the following in that it:

(i) was deliberate or reckless;

(ii) caused or had the potential to cause loss or significant inconvenience to any other *person*;

(iii) was or was related to a failure or refusal to ascertain, recognise or comply with the *regulated person's* professional or regulatory obligations such as, but not limited to, compliance with requirements imposed by legislation or rules made pursuant to legislation, the *SRA*, the Law Society, the Legal Ombudsman, the *Tribunal* or the court;

(iv) continued for an unreasonable period taking into account its seriousness;

(v) persisted after the *regulated person* realised or should have realised that it was improper;

(vi) misled or had the potential to mislead clients, the court or other *persons*, whether or not that was appreciated by the *regulated person*;

(vii) affected or had the potential to affect a vulnerable *person* or child;

(viii) affected or had the potential to affect a substantial, high-value or high-profile matter; or

(ix) formed or forms part of a pattern of misconduct or other regulatory failure by the *regulated person*;

(b) the second condition is that a proportionate outcome in the public interest is one or both of the following:

(i) a written rebuke;

(ii) a direction to pay a penalty; and

(c) the third condition is that the act or omission by the *regulated person* which gives rise to the *SRA finding* was neither trivial nor justifiably inadvertent.

3.2 Where the *SRA* has decided to direct a *regulated person* to pay a penalty:

(a) in considering the level of penalty to direct the *SRA* shall take into account the financial penalty criteria in appendix 1 to these rules; and

(b) the penalty shall not exceed the maximum permitted by law.

3.3 The circumstances in which the *SRA* may make a *disciplinary decision* to *disqualify* a *person* from acting as a *HOLP* or *HOFA*, or being a manager or employee are when the following two conditions are met:

(a) the *SRA* is satisfied that it is undesirable for the *person* to engage in the relevant activity or activities; and

(b) the *SRA* is satisfied that *disqualification* is a proportionate outcome in the public interest.

3.4   In considering whether to make a *disciplinary decision* to *disqualify* a *person* from acting as a *HOLP* or *HOFA*, or being a manager or employee, the *SRA* shall take into account:

(a)   the criteria at appendix 3; and

(b)   any indicative guidance published by the *SRA* from time to time.

3.5   The *SRA* may make a *disciplinary decision* to publish details of a written rebuke or a direction to pay a penalty when it considers it to be in the public interest to do so in accordance with the publication criteria in appendix 2 to these rules.

3.6   Nothing in this rule shall prevent the *SRA* making an application to the *Tribunal* in accordance with rule 10.

PART 2: PRACTICE AND PROCEDURE

Rule 4: Investigations

4.1   The parties to a *discipline investigation* are the *SRA* and the *person under investigation*.

4.2   The *SRA* may exercise any investigative or other powers at any time including those arising from:

(a)   sections 44B, 44BA, 44BB of the *SA*;

(b)   sections 93 and 94 of the *LSA*; or

(c)   rules made by the Law Society or the *SRA* for the production of documents, information or explanations.

4.3   Subject to rule 4.4, the *SRA* may disclose any information or documents (including the outcome) arising from its *discipline investigation*:

(a)   to an informant;

(b)   to a *person* who is under investigation;

(c)   to any *person* in order to facilitate its investigation and in particular to identify and obtain evidence, comments or information;

(d)   to other regulators, law enforcement agencies, or other *persons*, in the public interest.

4.4   The *SRA* may restrict disclosure of information to protect another *person's* right of confidentiality or privilege.

Discipline and Costs Recovery

Rule 5: Seeking explanations

5.1   The *SRA* will give the *person under investigation* the opportunity to provide an explanation of the *person's* conduct.

5.2   When seeking an explanation from the *person* as referred to in rule 5.1 above, the *SRA* will warn the *person* that:

    (a)   failure to reply to the *SRA* may in itself lead to disciplinary action;

    (b)   the reply and other information may be disclosed to other *persons* pursuant to rule 4.3; and

    (c)   the reply may be used by the *SRA* for regulatory purposes including as evidence in any investigation, decision by the *SRA*, or proceedings brought by or against the *SRA*.

5.3   The *person* must provide the explanation referred to in rule 5.1 or any other information within a time period specified by the *SRA*, which shall be no less than 14 calendar days from the request for an explanation and where no explanation or information is received within the specified time, the *SRA* may proceed to decision in the absence of an explanation.

Rule 6: Report stage

6.1   Before making a *disciplinary decision*, the *SRA* will prepare a report for disclosure to the *person under investigation*.

6.2   The report will summarise the allegations against the *person under investigation*, explain the supporting facts and evidence, and attach documentary evidence that the *SRA* considers to be relevant.

6.3   The report may also include evidence of the *person's* propensity to particular behaviour and a summary of the regulatory and disciplinary history of the *person under investigation* and of any other *person* that the *SRA* considers relevant.

6.4   The report will be provided to the *person under investigation* for the *person* to provide written comments upon it within a time period specified by the *SRA*, which shall be no less than 14 calendar days from the date on which the report has been sent to the *person*.

6.5   The *person under investigation* will also be invited to make submissions on whether any decision which is made by the *SRA*, in respect of the matters in the report, should be published. Any such submissions must be made within a time specified by the *SRA*, which shall be no less than 14 calendar days from the date on which the report has been sent to the *person*.

6.6   The report may be disclosed by the *SRA* to any other *person* with a legitimate interest in the matter to enable that *person* to comment upon it. Any such comments shall be disclosed to the *person under investigation* if they are to be included in the documents referred for adjudication.

6.7 The *SRA* may restrict disclosure of part of the report or all or part of the attached documents in the public interest or in the interests of efficiency and proportionality, such as:

(a) by only providing to the *person under investigation* or any other *person* documents that are not already in their possession;

(b) by not providing to a *person* other than the *person under investigation* the report or documents if they include information that is or might be subject to another *person's* right of confidentiality or privilege.

6.8 The *SRA* may recommend an outcome or advocate a particular position in the report or otherwise.

6.9 The report and comments received shall be referred for consideration within a reasonable time after receipt of any comments or the expiry of any time period specified for the provision of comments.

6.10 The *SRA* is not required to adopt the procedure in rules 5 and 6 in order to make an *SRA finding* or an application to the *Tribunal* under rule 10 below.

6.11 Where the *SRA* considers that it is just and in the public interest to do so the *SRA* may dispense with or vary the procedure and the time limits set out in rules 5 and 6.

6.12 Where the *SRA* dispenses with or varies the procedure or the time limits in accordance with rule 6.11, the *SRA* shall, so far as practicable, notify the *person under investigation* that it has done so.

PART 3: DECISIONS

Rule 7: Decisions: general

7.1 An *SRA finding* may be made by:

(a) agreement between the *person under investigation* and the *SRA*;

(b) a *person* duly authorised by the *SRA*;

(c) a single *adjudicator*; or

(d) an adjudication panel.

7.2 A *disciplinary decision* may be made by:

(a) agreement between the *person under investigation* and the *SRA*;

(b) a single *adjudicator*; or

(c) an adjudication panel.

7.3   An *SRA finding* which does not involve a consequential *disciplinary decision* may incorporate or be accompanied by:

   (a)   advice to the *person* as to the *person's* regulatory obligations;

   (b)   a warning to the *person* as to future conduct.

7.4   An adjudication panel shall be properly constituted if at least two members are present.

7.5   Where an adjudication panel is comprised of three or more members, a decision may be made by a majority.

7.6   The strict rules of evidence shall not apply to decisions of the *SRA*.

7.7   The standard of proof shall be the civil standard.

7.8   Subject to rule 7.9, decisions will be made on consideration of the report described in rule 6.

7.9   An adjudicator or adjudication panel may give directions for the just, expeditious and effective conduct of a *discipline investigation*, which may include but are not limited to:

   (a)   the provision of further evidence (including formal disclosure of documents which are relevant to the *discipline investigation* and certification that disclosure is full, frank and complete), representations or formal statements of case analogous to pleadings;

   (b)   the admission of oral evidence;

   (c)   where oral evidence is to be admitted, whether the evidence is to be considered in public or in private; and

   (d)   the consequences of failure by a *regulated person* to comply with a direction, which may include the exclusion of evidence relevant to that direction from the *discipline investigation*.

7.10   The decision shall be made when it is sent to the *person* in writing. The decision will be accompanied with information in writing about any right of appeal within the *SRA* and any external right of appeal.

Rule 8: Decisions to impose a penalty

8.1   Where the *SRA* is minded to direct a *regulated person* to pay a penalty, it may request from that *person* a statement as to their financial means, and such statement shall:

   (a)   include a statement of truth signed by the person or a person duly authorised to sign on their behalf; and

(b) be provided within 14 days from the date of the request or such longer period as the *SRA* may specify.

8.2 Where the *SRA* has decided to direct a *regulated person* to pay a penalty, the *SRA* may direct that the payment of all or part of the penalty be suspended on terms to be specified by the *SRA* in accordance with rule 8.3.

8.3 Any decision to suspend a penalty shall specify:

(a) the payment which is being suspended;

(b) the period of time for which the payment is suspended; and

(c) the circumstances in which the payment is and is not payable, which may include that it shall become payable if the *SRA* makes a further *SRA finding* in respect of the *person* concerned in the period for which the payment has been suspended.

8.4 Where the *SRA* has directed a *regulated person* to pay a penalty, subject to rule 8.2 above, such penalty shall be paid within a time and in the manner specified by the *SRA* but shall not become payable until:

(a) the end of the period during which an appeal may be made under rules 11 or 12, section 44E of the *SA* or paragraph 14C of Schedule 2 to the *AJA* or section 96 of the *LSA*; or

(b) if such an appeal is made, such time as the appeal is determined or withdrawn.

Rule 9: Decisions to disqualify, and to review a disqualification

9.1 Subject to rule 9.6, any decision to *disqualify* a *person* from acting as a *HOLP* or *HOFA* or being a manager or employee shall continue to have effect until such time as it is brought to an end:

(a) by the *SRA* following a review under rule 9.4 or an internal appeal or reconsideration under rule 11 or 13; or

(b) by the *appellate body* following an appeal under rule 12.

9.2 A *person* who has been *disqualified* from acting as a *HOLP* or *HOFA*, or being a manager or employee, may apply to the *SRA* for a review of the *disqualification* only:

(a) after a period of 12 months from the date of the decision to *disqualify*, or after such other period as may be specified in the decision to *disqualify*; or

(b) where there has been one or more prior unsuccessful applications to review the *disqualification*, after a period of 12 months from the date of the decision of the most recent application, or after such other period as may be specified in that decision.

9.3 Where the *SRA* has received an application under rule 9.2:

   (a) rule 6 shall apply save that:

      (i) before making a decision in respect of the application a report shall instead be prepared in relation to the matters leading to the decision to *disqualify* and any information or evidence relating to the *person's* conduct or behaviour in the period since that decision was made;

      (ii) rule 6.5 shall not apply and rules 6.10 to 6.12 shall apply only to the extent that they refer to the application of rule 6;

      (iii) reference to a *person under investigation* in rule 6 should be read as a reference to a *person* who has made an application under rule 9.2; and

      (iv) reference to a *disciplinary decision* should be read as a reference to a decision as to whether to bring a *disqualification* to an end in accordance with rule 9.4;

   (b) the *SRA* may:

      (i) exercise any investigative or other powers at any time; and

      (ii) request from the applicant documents or other information relevant to the application.

9.4   The *SRA* shall decide to bring a *disqualification* to an end if it is satisfied that:

   (a) it is no longer undesirable for the *disqualified person* to engage in the relevant activity or activities; and

   (b) it is proportionate and otherwise in the public interest to do so.

9.5   In considering whether to bring a *disqualification* to an end, the *SRA* shall take into account all of the circumstances including:

   (a) the criteria at appendix 3; and

   (b) any indicative guidance published by the *SRA* from time to time.

9.6   Any decision to *disqualify* a *person* from acting as a *HOLP* or *HOFA* or being a manager or employee may include a direction that the *disqualification* shall not take effect until any internal or external appeals made under rules 11 or 12 have been withdrawn or determined.

Rule 10: Applications to the Tribunal

10.1   The *SRA* may make an application to the *Tribunal* in respect of a *regulated person* at any time, if the *SRA* is satisfied that:

   (a) there is sufficient evidence to provide a realistic prospect that the application will be upheld by the *Tribunal*;

   (b) the allegation to be made against the *person under investigation* either in itself or in the light of other allegations is sufficiently serious that the *Tribunal* is likely to order that the *person*:

(i) be struck off;

(ii) be suspended;

(iii) be subject to an order revoking its recognition;

(iv) pay a penalty exceeding the maximum that can be imposed from time to time by the *SRA*; or

(v) be subject to any other order that the *SRA* is not empowered to make; and

(c) it is in the public interest to make the application.

10.2 The *SRA* will apply rule 10.1 in accordance with a code for referral to the *Tribunal* as promulgated by the *SRA* from time to time.

10.3 An application to the *Tribunal* under rule 10.1 may be authorised by:

(a) agreement between the *person under investigation* and the *SRA*;

(b) a *person* duly authorised by the *SRA*;

(c) a single *adjudicator*; or

(d) an adjudication panel.

10.4 There is no right of appeal against authorisation of an application to the *Tribunal*.

10.5 Subject to any contrary order of the *Tribunal*, the *SRA* may exercise any investigative or other powers at any time before a final hearing of an application at the *Tribunal*, including those arising from:

(a) sections 44B, 44BA, 44BB of the *SA*;

(b) rules made by the Law Society or the *SRA* for the production of documents, information or explanations.

10.6 Nothing in these rules shall permit the *SRA* to make an application to the *Tribunal* in respect of a *person* over whom the *Tribunal* has no jurisdiction.

PART 4: APPEALS, REVIEWS AND RECONSIDERATION

Rule 11: Internal appeals

11.1 A *person* who is subject to an *SRA finding* or a *disciplinary decision* or a decision to determine an application made to the *SRA* under rule 9.2 may appeal under this rule against all or any part of such an *SRA finding*, or *disciplinary decision* (or both) or against all or any part of a decision to determine such an application.

11.2 There is no appeal under this rule against:

(a) any decision other than those specified in rule 11.1;

(b) a decision on an appeal; or

(c) any decision which has been made by agreement with the *SRA*.

11.3 An appeal under this rule must be made within 14 calendar days of the date of the letter or electronic communication informing the *person* of the decision appealed against or within a longer time period specified by the *SRA*.

11.4 An appeal shall:

(a) be in writing; and

(b) provide reasoned arguments in support.

11.5 Appeals will be determined as follows:

(a) where the decision was made by a *person* authorised by the *SRA*, the appeal will be decided by a single *adjudicator*;

(b) where the decision was made by a single *adjudicator*, the appeal will be decided by an adjudication panel;

(c) where the decision was made by an adjudication panel, the appeal will be decided by a differently constituted panel.

11.6 Appeals will be limited to a review of the decision which is being appealed, taking into account the reasoned arguments provided by the *person* bringing the appeal. Failure to provide reasoned arguments either at all or in sufficient or clear terms may result in summary dismissal of the appeal.

11.7 All powers available to the *SRA* on adjudication are exercisable on appeal and for the avoidance of doubt this means that, in relation to an appeal brought under rule 11.1, an appeal decision may include findings or sanctions more severe than those made or applied in the decision being appealed.

11.8 Nothing in these rules shall affect a *person's* right of appeal to the *Tribunal* under section 44E of the *SA* or paragraph 14C of Schedule 2 to the *AJA* or to the *appellate body* under section 96 of the *LSA* or rule 12 below.

Rule 12: Appeals to the Tribunal and the appellate body

12.1 Subject to any rules made by the *appellate body* or Legal Services Board, where the *SRA* has:

(a) directed a *licensed body*, or the manager or employee of a *licensed body*, to pay a penalty;

(b) decided to *disqualify* a *person* from acting as a *HOLP* or *HOFA* or from being a manager or employee;

(c) decided not to bring a *disqualification* to an end following a review held under rule 9.4; or

(d)   decided to publish details of a written rebuke given to a *licensed body*, or the manager or employee of a *licensed body*;

the *person* subject to the direction or decision may appeal to the *appellate body* within the period of 28 days from the date on which the notice of the direction or decision is given to the appellant, or, if there has been a decision following an internal appeal, within the period of 28 days from the date on which the notice of that decision is given to the appellant.

12.2   Subject to any rules made by the *Tribunal* pursuant to section 46(9)(b) of the *SA*, an appeal to the *Tribunal* must be made within the period of 28 days from the date on which the notice of the direction or decision appealed against is given to the appellant or, if there has been a direction or decision following an internal appeal, the period of 28 days from the date on which the notice of that decision is given to the appellant.

12.3   If an appeal is made to the *appellate body* in relation to a direction or decision to *disqualify* a *person* from acting as a *HOLP* or *HOFA* or being a manager or employee, the appellant may apply to the *appellate body* for a stay of such decision pending the determination or discontinuance of the appeal.

12.4   If the *appellate body* imposes an order for a stay in relation to a decision in accordance with rule 12.3, the *SRA* shall stay the decision accordingly.

Rule 13: Reconsideration

13.1   The *SRA* may reconsider or rescind any decision made under these rules with the agreement of the *person* in respect of whom the decision was made.

13.2   In its absolute discretion the *SRA* may also reconsider any decision including an *SRA finding*, a *disciplinary decision* or authorisation of an application to the *Tribunal* when it appears that the *person* or panel who made the decision:

(a)   was not provided with material evidence that was available to the *SRA*;

(b)   was materially misled by any *person*;

(c)   failed to take proper account of material facts or evidence;

(d)   took into account immaterial facts or evidence;

(e)   made a material error of law;

(f)   made a decision which was otherwise irrational or procedurally unfair;

(g)   made a decision which was ultra vires; or

(h)   failed to give sufficient reasons.

13.3   The *SRA*, when considering the exercise of its powers under this rule, may also give directions for:

(a)   further investigations to be undertaken;

(b)   further information or explanation to be obtained from any *person*;

(c)　consideration of whether to authorise an application to the *Tribunal*;

(d)　the reconsideration of the decision to be undertaken by the original decision maker or adjudication panel or by a different decision maker or a differently constituted adjudication panel.

13.4　Nothing in these rules requires the *SRA* to commence or continue with any proceedings or prospective proceedings in the *Tribunal* or any other court or tribunal. A duly authorised *person* may rescind a decision to take proceedings in the *Tribunal*.

PART 5: NOTIFICATION, PUBLICATION AND COMMENCEMENT

Rule 14: Notification of Disqualification decisions

14.1　Where the *SRA* has:

(a)　decided to *disqualify* a *person* from acting as a *HOLP* or *HOFA*, or being a manager or employee;

(b)　reached a decision following an internal appeal or reconsideration of a decision to *disqualify* a *person* from acting as a *HOLP* or *HOFA*, or being a manager or employee; or

(c)　decided that a *person's disqualification* to act as a *HOLP* or *HOFA*, or to be a manager or employee, should cease to apply,

it shall, as soon as reasonably practicable, notify the Legal Services Board of the decision reached.

Rule 15: Publication of decisions

15.1　This rule governs the publication of details of a written rebuke or a direction to pay a penalty.

15.2　Subject to rule 15.4, publication in accordance with this rule:

(a)　will include a short statement of the *disciplinary decision* including brief details of its factual basis and the reasons for the decision;

(b)　will identify the *person* who has been subject to a relevant *disciplinary decision*;

(c)　will take reasonable steps to avoid the publication of information relating to other identifiable *persons*;

(d)　will provide the practising details of the *person* who has been subject to a relevant *disciplinary decision* at the time of the matters giving rise to the decision and at the time of decision if different;

(e)　will be in such form as the *SRA* may from time to time decide;

(f)　may include provision of a copy of the publishable information upon request by any *person*;

(g) will be made promptly after the decision has been made, provided that the *SRA* may delay or withhold publication in the public interest.

15.3   The *SRA* may vary or dispense with any of the requirements in rule 15.2 in the public interest.

15.4   The *SRA* may not publish details of a written rebuke or a direction to pay a penalty:

(a) during the period in which an appeal may be made under rules 11 or 12 above, section 44E of the *SA*, paragraph 14C of Schedule 2 to the *AJA* or section 96 of the *LSA*; or

(b) if such an appeal has been made, until such time as it is determined or withdrawn.

15.5   For the avoidance of doubt, the *SRA* may also publish information about other decisions or investigations.

Rule 16: Application and repeal

16.1   Save for those matters to which the SRA Disciplinary Procedure Rules 2010 (the 2010 rules) apply in accordance with rule 16.2, these rules apply to acts or omissions whenever they occur, unless occurring wholly before 1 June 2010.

16.2   These rules repeal the 2010 rules, save that the 2010 rules shall continue to apply to matters in which an explanation has been sought or a report issued in accordance with rule 5 or 6 of those rules, or in which an *SRA finding* or application to the *Tribunal* has been made without an explanation having been sought or a report issued in accordance with rule 6(11) of those rules.

Rule 17: Transitional Provisions

17.1   These rules shall not apply to licensed bodies until such time as the Society is designated as a licensing authority under Part 1 of Schedule 10 to the *LSA* and all definitions shall be construed accordingly.

17.2   The rules shall not apply to the exercise of disciplinary powers in relation to:

(a) *licensed bodies*, or managers or employees of *licensed bodies*; or

(b) former managers or employees of *licensed bodies*;

until such time as the Society is designated as a licensing authority under Part 1 of Schedule 10 to the *LSA*.

17.3   In these rules references in the preamble to the rules being made under section 83 and Schedule 11 of the Legal Services Act 2007 shall have no effect until such time as the Law Society is designated as a licensing authority under Part 1 of Schedule 10 to the Legal Services Act 2007.

Discipline and Costs Recovery

APPENDIX 1 – FINANCIAL PENALTY CRITERIA (RULE 3.2)

1   In this appendix, the term "misconduct" shall mean conduct or behaviour resulting in an *SRA finding*.

2   In deciding the amount of a financial penalty, the *SRA* will take into account all relevant circumstances, including that any financial penalty should, so far as practicable:

   (a)   be proportionate to the misconduct;

   (b)   be proportionate to any harm done;

   (c)   be of an amount that is likely to deter repetition of the misconduct by the *person* directed to pay the penalty and to deter misconduct by others;

   (d)   eliminate any financial gain or other benefit obtained as a direct or indirect consequence of the misconduct;

   (e)   be proportionate to the means of the *person* directed to pay it;

   (f)   take into account the intent, recklessness or neglect that led to the misconduct;

   (g)   take into account any mitigating or aggravating circumstances; and

   (h)   take into account indicative guidance published by the *SRA* from time to time.

3   Aggravating circumstances include:

   (a)   failure to correct, or delay in correcting, any harm caused as a result of the misconduct;

   (b)   failure to co-operate with the *SRA* investigation or the investigation of any other regulator or ombudsman;

   (c)   failure to admit, or delay in admitting, any misconduct;

   (d)   that the *regulated person* has been the subject of other findings by the *SRA*, the *Tribunal*, or any other approved regulator or the *appellate body*.

4   Mitigating circumstances include:

   (a)   prompt correction of any harm caused as a result of the misconduct;

   (b)   prompt admission of any misconduct;

   (c)   taking steps to prevent future misconduct.

5   When considering a *regulated person's* means the *SRA* shall take into account:

   (a)   all relevant information of which the *SRA* is aware; and

   (b)   any statement of means, verified by a statement of truth, which has been provided by the *regulated person*.

6   The *SRA* may take into account in considering a *regulated person's* means any failure to provide a statement of means following a reasonable request by the *SRA* to do so under rule 8(1).

APPENDIX 2 – PUBLICATION CRITERIA (RULE 3.5)

1   In deciding whether or not to publish a decision to give a *person* a written rebuke or direct that *person* to pay a penalty, the *SRA* will take into account all relevant circumstances including the following factors when relevant.

2   Each case will be decided on its own merits.

3   The following support a decision to publish:

(a)   the circumstances leading to the rebuke or penalty, or the rebuke or penalty itself, are matters of legitimate public concern or interest;

(b)   the importance of transparency in the regulatory and disciplinary process;

(c)   the existence or details of the rebuke or penalty will or might be relevant to a client or prospective client of a *person* who has been subject to a relevant *disciplinary decision* in deciding whether to instruct or continue to instruct that *person*, or as to the instructions to be given;

(d)   the existence or details of the rebuke or penalty will or might be relevant as to how any other *person* will deal with a *person* who has been subject to a relevant *disciplinary decision*;

(e)   the seriousness of the finding against the *person*;

(f)   the rebuke or penalty has been given to a *person* who has previously been the subject of disciplinary or regulatory decisions whether private or published;

(g)   the rebuke or penalty arises from facts that affected or may affect or have affected a number of clients or other *persons*;

(h)   the rebuke or penalty arises from facts that relate to the administration of justice.

4   The following support a decision not to publish:

(a)   publication would disclose a *person's* confidential or legally privileged information;

(b)   publication would disclose a *person's* confidential medical condition or treatment;

(c)   publication may prejudice legal proceedings or legal, regulatory or disciplinary investigations;

(d)   publication would involve a significant risk of breaching a *person's* rights under Article 8 of the European Convention on Human Rights;

Discipline and Costs Recovery

   (e) in all the circumstances the impact of publication on the individual or the firm would be disproportionate.

5   In deciding whether to publish, the *SRA* may also take into account:

   (a) the overall disciplinary and regulatory history of another *person* when relevant;

   (b) whether any disciplinary or regulatory action by another body is being or has been taken against the *person* who has been subject to a relevant *disciplinary decision*.

6   The factors set out above are not exhaustive and do not prevent the *SRA* from taking into account other factors that it considers to be relevant.

7   The *SRA* will from time to time publish indicative guidance about the application of these criteria.

APPENDIX 3 – DISQUALIFICATION AND DISQUALIFICATION REVIEW CRITERIA (RULES 3.4 AND 9.5)

1   In this appendix, the term "misconduct" shall mean conduct or behaviour resulting in an *SRA finding*.

2   This criteria is to be used in conjunction with the tests set out at rules 3.3 and 9.4.

3   In deciding whether to *disqualify* a *person* or to bring a *disqualification* to an end, the *SRA* will take into account all relevant circumstances, including that the aim of any *disqualification* should be:

   (a) for the *disqualification* to deter the *regulated person* or other *persons* from engaging in similar conduct in the future; or

   (b) to protect the public from a *regulated person*.

4   Where there has been misconduct, the following support a decision to *disqualify*:

   (a) the conduct of the *regulated person* has caused significant loss or harm;

   (b) the *regulated person* has abused a position of trust;

   (c) the conduct of the *regulated person* has caused harm to or to the interests of a vulnerable *person*;

   (d) the conduct of the *regulated person* was motivated by any form of discrimination;

   (e) the conduct was deliberate, pre-meditated, repeated or reckless;

   (f) the conduct has put the public confidence in the regulation of the profession at risk; or

(g) the conduct of the *regulated person* indicates that the *person* is unsuitable for the role being undertaken.

5   Where there has been misconduct, the following support a decision not to *disqualify*:

(a) the conduct was committed as a result of a genuine mistake or misunderstanding;

(b) the *regulated person* has cooperated fully with the *SRA*;

(c) the conduct was trivial; or

(d) there is a low likelihood of repetition of the conduct.

6   In deciding the appropriate duration of a *disqualification* without review in accordance with rule 9.2, the *SRA* shall take account of the factors set out at paragraphs 4 and 5 above.

7   The following, collectively, support a decision to bring a *disqualification* to an end:

(a) the *disqualification* has achieved any intended deterrent effect;

(b) to do so would not present a risk to the public, which could include consideration of any complete and demonstrable rehabilitation on the part of the *regulated person*; and

(c) to do so would not have an adverse impact upon the public confidence in the regulation of the profession.

8   An absence of any one of the factors set out at paragraph 7(a)–(c) would support a decision not to bring a *disqualification* to an end.

9   The factors set out above are not exhaustive and do not prevent the *SRA* from taking into account other factors that it considers to be relevant.

[G.2] SRA Cost of Investigations Regulations 2011

Rules and regulations about charging for the costs of investigations carried out by the Solicitors Regulation Authority dated 17 June 2011 commencing 6 October 2011 made by the Solicitors Regulation Authority Board, subject to the coming into force of relevant provisions of an Order made under section 69 of the Legal Services Act 2007, S.I. 2011 No. 1716, under sections 31, 43, 44C, 79 and 80 of the Solicitors Act 1974, the aforementioned Order, section 9 of and paragraph 14A of Schedule 2 to the Administration of Justice Act 1985 and section 83 of the Legal Services Act 2007 with the approval of the Legal Services Board under paragraph 19 of Schedule 4 to the Legal Services Act 2007.

PART 1: GENERAL

Regulation 1: Interpretation

1.1   The SRA Handbook Glossary 2012 shall apply to these rules and, unless the context otherwise requires:

(a)   all italicised terms within these rules shall be defined; and

(b)   terms within these rules shall be interpreted,

in accordance with the *Glossary*.

Regulation 2: Scope

2.1   These regulations prescribe the charges to be paid to the *SRA* by:

(a)   *regulated persons* who are the subject of a *discipline investigation*;

(b)   persons who are the subject of a *section 43 investigation*.

2.2   These regulations shall not prevent, prohibit or restrict the exercise of any other powers or other action by the *SRA*.

PART 2: SUBSTANTIVE PROVISIONS

Regulation 3: Discipline investigations

3.1   A *regulated person* who is the subject of a *discipline investigation* may be required by the *SRA* to pay a charge in accordance with these regulations provided that there has been an *SRA finding* against the *regulated person*.

3.2   An *SRA finding* may be made by:

    (a)   agreement between the *regulated person* and the *SRA*;

    (b)   a *person* duly authorised by the *SRA*;

    (c)   a single *adjudicator*; or

    (d)   an adjudication panel.

Regulation 4: Section 43 investigations

4.1   A person who is the subject of a *section 43 investigation* may be required by the *SRA* to pay a charge in accordance with these regulations provided that the *SRA* has made an order under section 43(2) of the *SA*.

4.2   An order under section 43(2) of the *SA* may be made by:

    (a)   agreement between the person and the *SRA*;

    (b)   a single *adjudicator*; or

    (c)   an adjudication panel.

Regulation 5: Decision to require payment of charges

5.1   The amount of charges payable by any *person* in the circumstances falling within regulation 3.1 or 4.1 above will be determined by the *person*, *adjudicator* or adjudication panel making the relevant *SRA finding* or decision to make an order under section 43(2) of the *SA*, or where such a finding or order is made by agreement, the *person* duly authorised by the *SRA* to enter into such an agreement.

5.2   Where a *person* is required to pay any charges under these regulations, such charges shall be paid within a time and in the manner specified by the *SRA*.

Regulation 6: Basis of charges

6.1   Subject to regulation 6.2 below, the amount payable under regulation 5 will be determined in accordance with the schedule of charges in appendix 1 to these regulations.

6.2   In exceptional circumstances, the *SRA* may charge less than the amount that would be payable in accordance with the schedule of charges in appendix 1 to these regulations provided that it is considered by the *SRA* to be fair and reasonable to do so.

6.3   The *SRA* may require any *person* in the circumstances falling within regulation 3.1 or 4.1 above to pay an additional charge where such *person* has made an unsuccessful appeal to the *SRA* against the *SRA finding* or the order made under section 43(2) of the *SA*.

6.4   The additional amount payable under regulation 6.3 shall be in accordance with the schedule of charges in appendix 1 to these regulations.

6.5   For the purposes of this regulation an appeal will be unsuccessful if, after the appeal has been heard, any *SRA finding* remains or the order made under section 43(2) of the *SA* has not been quashed.

Regulation 7: Recovery of charges

7.1   Any charge which a *person* is required to pay under these regulations is recoverable by the *SRA* as a debt due to the *SRA* from that *person*.

PART 3: REPEALS AND TRANSITIONAL PROVISIONS

Regulation 8: Repeals

8.1   These regulations repeal the SRA (Cost of Investigations Regulations) 2009 (the 2009 regulations), save that the 2009 regulations shall continue to apply to any decisions that were made before that date.

8.2   From 31 March 2012 or the date on which an order made pursuant to section 69 of the*LSA* relating to the status of sole practitioners comes into force, whichever is the later, the definition of "recognised body" in regulation 1.1 shall have effect as if the words "sole practitioner or" were inserted after "means".

Regulation 9: Transitional Provisions

9.1   These regulations shall not apply to *licensed bodies* until such time as the Society is designated as a licensing authority under Part 1 of Schedule 10 to the *LSA* and all definitions shall be construed accordingly.

9.2   In these regulations references in the preamble to the Rules being made:

(a)   subject to the coming into force of relevant provisions of an Order made under section 69 of the Legal Services Act 2007, S.I. 2011 No. 1716; and

(b)   under section 83 of the Legal Services Act 2007

shall have no effect until the Society is designated as a licensing authority under Part 1 of Schedule 10 to the *LSA*.

APPENDIX 1 – SCHEDULE OF CHARGES

1   This Schedule of charges sets out the basis of calculating the amount of charges payable under regulations 5 and 6.

2   The *SRA* will record the amount of time spent investigating and considering each case and the amount payable under the regulations will vary depending on the amount of time spent on that matter.

3   The standard levels of charges are as follows:

Discipline and Costs Recovery

Number of hours spent on matter	Standard Charge
Under 2 hours	£300
2 hours or more but under 8 hours	£600
8–16	£1350

4   In addition to the fixed charge of £1350, where investigations take more than 16 hours, an extra charge of £75 for every hour (£37.50 for every half hour) will be applied (rounded up or down to the nearest half hour).

5   For the purposes of regulations 6.3 and 6.4, the additional fixed charge for an appeal shall be £250.

[H]   Overseas Rules

[H.0] **Introduction to the Overseas Rules**

This section of the Handbook contains the SRA Overseas Rules.

Although the SRA primarily regulates the provision of legal services by solicitors, firms and other authorised persons practising in England and Wales, it also needs to provide a regulatory framework for authorised persons and bodies established overseas in order to take account of the regulatory risk they pose in England and Wales. This must be proportionate, reflecting the different level and type of risks posed to the SRA's regulatory objectives by practising overseas, as well as the existence, in many jurisdictions, of local regulatory requirements.

These rules apply to regulated individuals practising overseas and to responsible authorised bodies. Subject to Rule 2 of these rules, the SRA Code of Conduct does not apply to regulated individuals and authorised bodies practising overseas since its requirements are, in many cases, not relevant to, or may have a disproportionate impact, on them.

These rules are the starting point for the conduct of SRA regulated individuals and authorised bodies providing legal services outside England and Wales. They apply to those regulated individuals who are established in practice overseas and those authorised bodies or recognised sole practitioners with responsibility for or control over, bodies or branch offices overseas. They do not apply to those engaged in temporary practice overseas or authorised bodies established overseas to whom the Principles and relevant sections of the SRA Code of Conduct and the SRA Handbook apply.

The Overseas Principles are modified from the general SRA Principles, in order to take account of the different legal, regulatory and cultural context of practice in other jurisdictions, which may require different standards of conduct to those required in England and Wales. There is no intention to imply a lower standard of general behaviour; regulated individuals practising overseas and responsible authorised bodies are therefore required to ensure that they, or those for whom they are responsible, under these rules, behave in a way which meets both the SRA's Overseas Rules and its character and suitability requirements. For guidance on the SRA's approach to factors relevant to the assessment of an individual's suitability see the SRA Suitability Test.

Regulators in many other jurisdictions rely on certificates of good standing granted by the SRA to regulated individuals and authorised businesses who wish to practise overseas and, in many cases, they will also expect and require that the SRA's regulatory oversight will continue to operate alongside the local regulatory regime. Nonetheless, applicable law and local regulation should prevail in circumstances in which compliance with the Overseas Principles would create difficulties, with the exception of principle 6 which must be observed at all times, even if to do so would result in a breach of local law or regulation.

In addition to the obligations of those regulated individuals practising overseas, the SRA also requires that a recognised sole practitioner or authorised body in England and Wales will identify, monitor and manage risks arising from its overseas practices and connected practices to ensure they do not undermine its financial viability, or its ability to fulfil its compliance and regulatory obligations, its reputation and that of SRA regulation and the legal profession of England and Wales in general. These obligations are also present in the domestic SRA Code of Conduct.

A failure to meet these obligations may result in the SRA taking regulatory action against a regulated individual or an authorised body and its managers. Such action may include limiting, or removing, the right to practise as an authorised body or individual regulated by the SRA.

[H.1] **SRA Overseas Rules 2013**

Rules dated 30 August 2013 made by the Solicitors Regulation Authority Board under sections 31, 79 and 80 of the Solicitors Act 1974, sections 9 and 9A of the Administration of Justice Act 1985 and section 83 of the Legal Services Act 2007, with the approval of the Legal Services Board under paragraph 19 of Schedule 4 to the Legal Services Act 2007 regulating the conduct of solicitors and their employees, registered European lawyers and their employees, registered foreign lawyers, recognised bodies and their managers and employees and licensed bodies and their managers and employees.

PART 1: THE OVERSEAS PRINCIPLES

Rule 1: Overseas Principles

1.1   You

   (a)   as a *regulated individual practising overseas* must ensure that you; or

   (b)   as a *responsible authorised body* must ensure that your *overseas practice*, and individual *managers*, and *members* and *owners* of your *overseas practice* (who are, for the purposes of these rules, 'those for whom you are responsible');

comply with the Overseas Principles stated below.

1.2   Each of the Overseas Principles stated below, is supplemented by a note to assist individuals and bodies to determine how best to comply with each Principle. These notes do not form part of the Principles and are for guidance only.

1.3   Overseas Principle 1: You must uphold the rule of the law and the proper administration of justice in England and Wales.

   Guidance note

   (i)   Your obligations to *clients*, the *court* and third parties in England and Wales with whom you are dealing on behalf of your *clients* are unaffected by the location outside England and Wales from which you practise or by the location of your *overseas practice*.

1.4   Overseas Principle 2: You must act with integrity.

   Guidance note

   (i)   Personal integrity is central to your role as the *client's* trusted adviser and should characterise all of your professional dealings with *clients*, the *court*, other *lawyers* and the public, wherever they are being conducted. You should use your judgment when considering how best to maintain your integrity at all times and avoid any behaviour outside England and Wales which undermines your character and suitability to be an *authorised person*. A *responsible authorised body* should ensure that its *overseas practices* observe comparable standards.

1.5   Overseas Principle 3: You must not allow your independence or the independence of your *overseas practice* to be compromised.

Guidance note

(i)   "Independence" means your own independence and that of your firm and your *overseas practice*, and not merely your ability to give independent advice to a *client*. You should avoid giving control of your *overseas practice* to a third party beyond any local legal or regulatory ownership requirements.

1.6   Overseas Principle 4: You must act in the best interests of each *client*.

Guidance note

(i)   You should act in good faith and do your best for each of the *clients* for whom you are (or your *overseas practice* is) acting. In particular, you should follow the local legal or regulatory requirements of the jurisdiction in which you or your *overseas practice* are practising in relation to confidentiality and conflicts of interest. If no such requirements exist, you should be guided by what you consider to be the best interests of each *client* in the circumstances.

1.7   Overseas Principle 5: You must provide a proper standard of service to your *clients*/the *clients* of your *overseas practice*.

Guidance note

(i)   You should provide a proper standard of client care and work. This includes exercising competence, skill and diligence and taking into account the individual needs and circumstances of each *client* as well as the particular requirements and circumstances of the jurisdiction in which you are working. If your *client* meets the definition of a complainant under Section 128(3) of the Legal Services Act 2007 or the Legal Services Act 2007 (Legal Complaints) (Parties) Order 2010, you should inform the *client* who is regulating the legal services you or your *overseas practice* is providing to the *client*, what client protections are in place and whether they have the benefit of professional indemnity insurance or other indemnity.

1.8   Overseas Principle 6: You must not do anything which will or will be likely to bring into disrepute the *overseas practice*, yourself as a *regulated individual* or *responsible authorised body* or, by association, the legal profession in and of England and Wales.

Guidance note

(i)   This includes any behaviour which occurs within or outside your professional *practice* which undermines your own reputation, that of the *practice* within which you are a *manager* or solicitor employee, or the wider reputation of the legal profession in and of England and Wales.

1.9   Overseas Principle 7: You must comply with your legal and regulatory obligations in England and Wales, and deal with your regulators and ombudsmen in England and Wales in an open, timely and co-operative manner and assist and not impede any *authorised person* or *authorised body* practising in England and Wales in complying with their legal and regulatory obligations and dealings with their regulators and ombudsmen.

Guidance note

(i)   As a *responsible authorised body*, you should ensure that you, and those for whom you are responsible, comply with all of the reporting and notification requirements that apply to you and respond promptly and substantively to communications. You should ensure that you (and those for whom you are responsible) do not cause, contribute or facilitate a failure to comply with the *SRA's* regulatory arrangements by any *authorised person* or *authorised body* practising in England and Wales. *Regulated individuals practising overseas* should assist their *responsible authorised body* to comply with its regulatory obligations to the *SRA*.

1.10   Overseas Principle 8: You must run your business/the business of your *overseas practice* or carry out your/their role in the business effectively and in accordance with proper governance and sound financial and risk management principles.

Guidance note

(i)   As a *responsible authorised body* you are required to ensure that your relations with your *overseas practice* accord with sound governance, financial and risk management principles. You should ensure that those for whom you are responsible under these rules assist you in meeting your obligations to the *SRA* in relation to managing any risks that your *overseas practice* might pose to your operations.

1.11   Overseas Principle 9: You must run your business/the business of your *overseas practice* or carry out your/their role in the business in a way that encourages equality of opportunity and respect for diversity.

Guidance note

(i)   Every jurisdiction has its own legal, regulatory and cultural framework for equality and diversity. The *SRA* does not expect, or require, *regulated individuals* or bodies *practising overseas* to approach these issues as they would in England and Wales. It does, however, expect that *SRA regulated individuals* and bodies will do what they reasonably can to encourage equality of opportunity and respect for diversity, within the legal, regulatory and cultural context in which they are *practising overseas*.

1.12   Overseas Principle 10: You must protect *client money* and assets.

Guidance note

(i) You and those for whom you are responsible should comply with local regulatory requirements in relation to *client money*, documents and assets and, in any event, you should ensure that they are protected appropriately.

PART 2: APPLICATION

Rule 2: Application

2.1 With regard to the Overseas Principles set out in Rule 1:

(a) they apply to you if you are a *regulated individual practising overseas*, or a *responsible authorised body* in relation to each of its *overseas practices*;

(b) you will be committing a breach if you permit another person to do anything on your behalf which, if done by you, would constitute a breach of these rules;

(c) you should ensure that you and those for whom you are responsible under these rules comply with all legal and regulatory obligations applicable in the jurisdiction outside England and Wales in which you or they are practising. You, and those for whom you are responsible under these rules, should not cause, contribute to or facilitate a failure to comply with those legal or regulatory obligations by any other person or body subject to them;

(d) where there is a conflict between compliance with the Overseas Principles set out in Rule 1 and/or the Reporting Requirements set out in Rule 3 on the one hand, and any requirements placed upon you or those for whom you are responsible under these rules by local law or regulation on the other hand, the latter shall prevail, with the exception of Overseas Principle 6, which must be observed at all times;

(e) *Reserved legal activities* may only be conducted overseas from an *authorised body*. However, *regulated individuals* may conduct *reserved legal activities* overseas in the following circumstances:

(i) on an occasional basis from an *Overseas Practice* for clients in England and Wales provided that they comply with the *SRA Principles* and the provisions in Chapter 13A.3 to 13A.6 of the *SRA Code of Conduct* when conducting those *reserved legal activities*.

(ii) from an *Overseas Practice* under the Overseas Principles provided that this work is undertaken for clients based outside England and Wales.

(f) Notwithstanding (e) above, if you are a *solicitor* or a *REL*, and your *practice* predominantly and consistently comprises the provision of legal services to clients, or in relation to assets located in England and Wales, then regardless of where you are *established*, the *SRA Principles* and Chapter 13A of the *SRA Code of Conduct* will apply;

(g) if you are a *regulated individual practising overseas*, or a *responsible authorised body*, you must ensure that you, or those for whom you are responsible under these rules, comply with any requirements under:

  (i) the SRA Property Selling Rules 2011;

  (ii) the *SRA Insolvency Practice Rules*;

  (iii) the *SRA European Cross-border Practice Rules*;

  (iv) the *SRA Financial Services (Scope) Rules*;

  (v) the SRA Financial Services (Conduct of Business) Rules 2001; and

  (vi) the SRA Quality Assurance Scheme for Advocates (Crime) Regulations [2013];

which apply to you or your *overseas practice*.

PART 3: REPORTING REQUIREMENTS

Rule 3: Reporting requirements

3.1　The *SRA* does not expect or require the same level of detailed monitoring, reporting and notification from those *practising overseas* as it would expect of *authorised persons* and *authorised bodies* in England and Wales. The level of reporting the *SRA* expects is proportionate to the level of regulatory risk posed by an *overseas practice*.

3.2　You, as a *regulated individual practising overseas* or as a *responsible authorised body*, must monitor any material or systemic breaches of the Overseas Principles that apply to you or to those for whom you are responsible and report them to the *SRA* when they occur, or as soon as reasonably practicable thereafter. In relation to an *overseas practice*, a material or systemic breach will relate either to the character and suitability of an individual, the financial vulnerability of an *overseas practice* outside of established business planning, or a pattern of behaviour within an *overseas practice* that infringes Overseas Principle 6. Notifications by the compliance officer of a *responsible authorised body*, or by another person on behalf of an *overseas practice* will satisfy these requirements without separate notifications from each individual or body who has knowledge of the breach. For example, you will be required to:

(a) notify the *SRA*, if you, or any of the *partners, members, managers*, solicitor employees or other professionally qualified employees in your *overseas practice*, are convicted by any *court* of a criminal offence or become subject to disciplinary action by another regulator;

(b) notify the *SRA* immediately if you believe that your firm or your *overseas practice* is in serious financial difficulty;

(c) provide the *SRA* with documents held by you or your *overseas practice*, to which it is entitled, and any necessary permissions to access information as soon as possible following a notice from the *SRA* to do so.

   (d) provide the *SRA*, if you are a *responsible authorised body*, with an annual return which:

      (i) identifies the contact details of the office(s) from which you are, or your *overseas practice* is, practising, and

      (ii) confirms that you have fulfilled your reporting and notification obligations.

PART 4: COMMENCEMENT

Rule 4: Commencement

4.1 These Rules shall come into force as follows:

   (a) Rule 1, 2 and 4 of these rules shall come into force on 1 October 2013, for:

      (i) *regulated individuals* falling within the definition of *practising overseas*, and

      (ii) persons falling within paragraph (i)(a) and (e) of the definition of *overseas practice*,

   (b) Otherwise, these rules shall come into force on 1 October 2014.

[I] Specialist Services

Introduction to Specialist Services

This section of the Handbook contains the following rules which apply when you provide certain specialist services to your clients:

- SRA Property Selling Rules – these apply when you provide property selling services through your law firm;

- SRA Financial Services (Scope) Rules and the SRA Financial Services (Conduct of Business) Rules – these apply when you are not authorised by the Financial Conduct Authority and carry on exempt regulated activities for your clients;

- SRA European Cross-border Practice Rules – these apply to your European cross-border practice; and

- SRA Insolvency Practice Rules – these apply when you carry on insolvency practice.

These rules must be read in conjunction with the Principles. The Principles underpin all aspects of practice, including your European cross-border practice, insolvency practice and the provision of property selling and financial services.

The desired outcomes that apply to these specialist services are that:

- clients receive a proper standard of service, and are treated fairly, when they purchase specialist services;

- you uphold the reputation of the legal profession in England and Wales by co-operating with European lawyers in the spirit of the CCBE Code;

- you maintain trust in the legal profession by providing estate agency services in the spirit of the legislation governing estate agents;

- your financial services are provided to the same standard as required by the Financial Conduct Authority and in a manner that maintains confidence in the legal profession; and

- you carry on your insolvency practice to the same standard required for all insolvency practitioners, by complying with the Joint Insolvency Committee's Code of Ethics.

[I.1] SRA Property Selling Rules 2011

The SRA Property Selling Rules dated 17 June 2011 commencing 6 October 2011 made by the Solicitors Regulation Authority Board under sections 31, 79 and 80 of the Solicitors Act 1974 and sections 9 and 9A of the Administration of Justice Act 1985 with the approval of the Legal Services Board under paragraph 19 of Schedule 4 to the Legal Services Act 2007 regulating the conduct of solicitors and their employees, registered European lawyers and their employees, recognised bodies, their managers and employees.

PART 1: RULES

Rule 1: Purpose

1.1 The purpose of these rules is to set out the standards which must be met by *solicitors* and others when they carry on *property selling*, either themselves or through their *employees*.

Rule 2: Application and interpretation

2.1 These rules apply to:

(a) *solicitors*;

(b) *recognised bodies*;

(c) *RELs* or *partners* of *RELs*; and

(d) *persons employed* by *RELs*, their *partners*, *solicitors* or *recognised bodies*,

in any part of the *UK*.

2.2 The SRA Handbook Glossary 2012 shall apply and, unless the context otherwise requires:

(a) all italicised terms shall be defined; and

(b) all terms shall be interpreted,

in accordance with the *Glossary*.

Rule 3: Standards of property selling services

3.1 When providing *property selling* services, you must:

(a) ensure that you, or any *employees* through whom the work is carried out, are competent to do so, and meet any standards of competence set by the Secretary of State under section 22 of the Estate Agents Act 1979;

(b) not seek from any *buyer* a *pre-contract deposit* in excess of any limit prescribed by the Secretary of State under section 19 of the Estate Agents Act 1979; and

(c) if you receive from any *buyer* a *pre-contract deposit* which exceeds the prescribed limit, so much of that deposit as exceeds the prescribed limit shall be either repaid to the *buyer* or paid to such other *person* as the *buyer* may direct.

Note

(i) The requirements of rule 3 are in addition to the requirements in the SRA Code of Conduct in Chapter 1 in respect of client care.

Rule 4: Statement of agreement

4.1 When accepting instructions to act in the sale of a *property*, you must, at the outset of communication between you and the *client*, or as soon as is reasonably practicable, and before the *client* is committed to any liability towards you, give the *client* a written statement setting out whether or not you are to have "sole agency" or "sole selling rights". The statement must also include a clear explanation of the intention and effect of those terms, or any similar terms used, which shall, subject to (4.3) below, take the following form:

(a) "Sole agency: You will be liable to pay a fee to us, in addition to any other costs or charges agreed, if unconditional contracts for the sale of the *property* are exchanged at any time: with a buyer introduced by us with whom we had negotiations about the *property* in the period during which we have sole agency; or with a buyer introduced by another agent during the period of our sole agency."

(b) "Sole selling rights: You will be liable to pay a fee to us, in addition to any other costs or charges agreed, in each of the following circumstances:

(i) if unconditional contracts for the sale of the *property* are exchanged in the period during which we have sole selling rights, even if the buyer was not found by us but by another agent or by any other person, including yourself; or

(ii) if unconditional contracts for the sale of the *property* are exchanged after the expiry of the period during which we have sole selling rights but to a buyer who was introduced to you during that period or with whom we had negotiations about the *property* during that period."

4.2 If the statement refers to a "ready, willing and able" buyer (or similar term), you must include a clear explanation of the term, which shall, subject to (4.3) below, take the following form:

(a) "A buyer is a "ready, willing and able" buyer if he or she is prepared and is able to exchange unconditional contracts for the purchase of your *property*. You will be liable to pay a fee to us, in addition to any other costs or charges agreed, if such a buyer is introduced by us in accordance with your

Specialist Services

instructions and this must be paid even if you subsequently withdraw and unconditional contracts for sale are not exchanged, irrespective of your reasons."

4.3   If, by reason of the provisions of the statement in which any of the terms referred to in (4.1) or (4.2) above appear, any of the prescribed explanations is in any way misleading, you should alter the content of the explanation so as accurately to describe the liability of the *client* to pay a fee in accordance with those provisions. Subject to this requirement, you should reproduce the explanations prominently, clearly and legibly without any material alterations or additions. They should be given no less prominence than that given to any other information in the statement apart from the heading, firm names, names of the parties, numbers or lettering subsequently inserted.

Note

(i)   The requirements of rule 4 correspond to those in the Estate Agents (Provision of Information) Regulations 1991 (SI 1991/859) and the Schedule to those Regulations. The requirements of rule 4 are in addition to the requirements in the SRA Code of Conduct in Chapter 1 in respect of client care.

Rule 5: Transactions in which you have a personal interest

5.1   When selling *property* you must comply with the following requirements:

(a)   If you have, or, to your *knowledge*, any *connected person* has, or is seeking to acquire, a beneficial interest in the *property* or in the proceeds of sale of any interest in the *property*, you must promptly inform your *client* in writing.

(b)   If you have, or to your *knowledge* any *connected person* has, a beneficial interest in a *property* or in the proceeds of sale of any interest in it, you must promptly inform in writing any person negotiating to acquire or dispose of any interest in that *property*. You must make this disclosure before entering into any negotiations with that *person*, whether or not you are negotiating on your own behalf or on that of a *client*.

Note

(i)   The requirements in rule 5 are in addition to the need to comply with the requirements in the SRA Code of Conduct in Chapter 3 about conflicts. The requirements in rule 5 are similar to those imposed on estate agents by the Estate Agents (Undesirable Practices) (No.2) Order 1991 (SI 1991/1032).

Rule 6: Waivers

6.1   The Board of the Solicitors Regulation Authority shall not have power to waive any of the provisions of these rules.

Note

(i)   The exemption from the Estate Agents Act 1979 is on the basis that the standards in these rules are complied with in all circumstances. For this reason there is no power to waive.

[I.2] SRA Financial Services (Scope) Rules 2001

These rules, dated 18 July 2001, are made by the Solicitors Regulation Authority Board under sections 31, 79 and 80 of the Solicitors Act 1974, sections 9 and 9A of the Administration of Justice Act 1985 and section 83 of the Legal Services Act 2007, with the approval of the Legal Services Board under paragraph 19 of schedule 4 to the Legal Services Act 2007, and for the purposes of section 332 of the Financial Services and Markets Act 2000 regulating the practices of:

- *Authorised bodies* and *recognised sole practitioners* in any part of the world,

- *RELs* in any part of the United Kingdom, and

- *RFLs* in England and Wales,

in carrying out *regulated activities* in, into or from the United Kingdom.

PART 1: RULES

Rule 1: Purpose

1.1　The Law Society is a designated professional body under Part XX of *FSMA*, and *firms* may therefore carry on certain *regulated activities* without being regulated by the *FCA*, if they can meet the conditions specified in section 327 of *FSMA*. As a designated professional body the Law Society is required to make rules governing the carrying on by *firms* of *regulated activities*. The purpose of these rules is to set out the scope of the *regulated activities* which may be undertaken by *firms* which are not regulated by the *FCA*.

1.2　These rules:

(a)　prohibit firms which are not regulated by the *FCA* from carrying on certain *regulated activities*;

(b)　set out the basic conditions which those *firms* must satisfy when carrying on any *regulated activities*;

(c)　set out other restrictions on *regulated activities* carried on by those *firms*.

Note

(i)　*FSMA* makes the *FCA* and the Prudential Regulation Authority (PRA) the statutory regulators of financial services business. Under *FSMA* anyone carrying on *regulated activities* needs to be regulated by the *FCA*. Part XX of *FSMA* enables *firms* authorised and regulated by the *SRA* to be treated as exempt professional firms and to carry on activities known as exempt regulated activities provided that these *firms* are able to comply with the SRA Financial Services (Scope) Rules 2001 as these Rules set out the scope of the activities which may be undertaken.

Rule 2: Application

2.1   These rules apply only to *firms* which are not regulated by the *FCA*.

2.2   Where a *firm* is a *licensed body*, these rules apply only in respect of:

(a)   any *reserved legal activity*;

(b)   any other *legal activity*;

(c)   any other activity in respect of which the *licensed body* is regulated pursuant to Part 5 of the *LSA*.

Note

(i)   Any *firm* which undertakes *regulated activities* and cannot comply with the Part XX exemption must be authorised by the *FCA* and comply with the *FCA's* requirements.

Rule 3: Prohibited activities

3.1   A *firm* must not carry on, or agree to carry on, any of the following activities:

(a)   *market making* in *investments*;

(b)   buying, selling, subscribing for or underwriting *investments* as principal where the *firm*:

(i)   holds itself out as engaging in the business of buying such *investments* with a view to selling them;

(ii)   holds itself out as engaging in the business of underwriting *investments* of the kind to which the transaction relates; or

(iii)   regularly solicits members of the public with the purpose of inducing them, as principals or agents, to enter into transactions and the transaction is entered into as a result of the *firm* having solicited members of the public in that manner.

(c)   buying or selling *investments* with a view to stabilising or maintaining the market price of the *investments*;

(d)   acting as a *stakeholder pension scheme* manager;

(e)   entering into a *broker funds arrangement*;

(f)   effecting and carrying out *contracts of insurance* as principal;

(g)   establishing, operating or winding up a *collective investment scheme*;

(h)   establishing, operating or winding up a *stakeholder pension scheme* or a *personal pension scheme*;

(i) managing the underwriting capacity of a Lloyds syndicate as a managing agent at Lloyds;

(j) advising a person to become a member of a particular Lloyd's syndicate;

(k) entering as provider into a *funeral plan contract*;

(l) entering into a *regulated mortgage contract* as lender or administering a *regulated mortgage contract* (unless this is in the *firm's* capacity as a trustee or personal representative and the borrower is a beneficiary under the trust, will or intestacy);

(m) entering into a *regulated home purchase plan* as provider or administering a *regulated home purchase plan* (unless this is in the *firm's* capacity as a trustee or personal representative and the *home purchaser* is a beneficiary under the trust, will or intestacy);

(n) entering into a *regulated home reversion plan* as a provider or administering a *regulated home reversion plan* (unless this is in the *firm's* capacity as a trustee or personal representative and the reversion seller is a beneficiary under the trust, will or intestacy); or

(o) entering into a *regulated sale and rent back agreement* as an *agreement provider* or administering a *regulated sale and rent back agreement* (unless this is in the *firm's* capacity as a trustee or personal representative and the *agreement seller* is a beneficiary under the trust, will or intestacy).

Note

(i) The Treasury has made the Financial Services and Markets Act 2000 (Professions) (Non-Exempt Activities) Order 2001 which sets out those activities which cannot be provided by professional firms under the Part XX exemption. These activities are also restricted in Rules 3 and 5 of the SRA Financial Services (Scope) Rules 2001.

Rule 4: Basic conditions

4.1 A *firm* which carries on any *regulated activities* must ensure that:

(a) the activities arise out of, or are complementary to, the provision of a particular *professional service* to a particular *client*;

(b) the manner of the provision by the *firm* of any service in the course of carrying on the activities is incidental to the provision by the *firm* of *professional services*;

(c) the *firm* accounts to the *client* for any pecuniary reward or other advantage which the *firm* receives from a third party;

(d) the activities are not of a description, nor do they relate to an investment of a description, specified in any order made by the Treasury under section 327(6) of *FSMA*;

(e) the *firm* does not carry on, or hold itself out as carrying on, a *regulated activity* other than one which is allowed by these rules or one in relation to which the firm is an *exempt person*;

(f) there is not in force any order or direction of the *FCA* under sections 328 or 329 of *FSMA* which prevents the *firm* from carrying on the activities; and

(g) the activities are not otherwise prohibited by these rules.

Notes

(i)   In order to comply with rule 4(a) you must ensure that the *regulated activity* in question arises out of, or is complementary to, other *professional services* to a particular *client*. The effect of this is that it is not possible to undertake a *regulated activity* in isolation for a *client*.

(ii)   In order to comply with rule 4(b) the exempt *regulated activities* cannot be a major part of the practice of the *firm*. The FCA considers that the following factors are relevant to this: the scale of *regulated activity* in proportion to other *professional services* provided; whether and to what extent activities that are *regulated activities* are held out as separate services; and the impression given of how the *firm* provides *regulated activities*, for example through its advertising or other promotion of its services.

(iii)   In order to comply with rule 4(c) you must account for any commission or other *financial benefit* to the *client*. Accounting to the *client* does not mean simply telling the *client* that the *firm* will receive commission. It means that the commission etc must be held to the order of the *client* and the *client* gives you informed consent to keep it. To comply with the rule you should, in advance of the arrangement and/or provision of the third party financial service:

(a) inform the *client* of their rights to any commission etc;

(b) inform the *client* that the arrangement and/or provision of the service is not dependant on their agreement to waive their right to any commission etc;

(c) seek and record agreement from the *client* as to whether any commission etc should be passed to the *client*, retained by the *firm* to offset client fees, or retained by the *firm* with the *client* waiving their right to it.

Rule 5: Other restrictions

5.1   Retail investment products (except personal pension schemes)

(a) A *firm* must not recommend, or make arrangements for, a *client* to buy a *retail investment product* except where:

(i) recommending, or arranging for, a *client* to buy a *retail investment product* by means of an assignment;

(ii) the arrangements are made as a result of a *firm* managing assets within the exception to rule 5(4) below; or

(iii) arranging a transaction for a *client* where the *firm* assumes on reasonable grounds that the *client* is not relying on the *firm* as to the merits or suitability of that *transaction*.

5.2 Personal pension schemes

(a) A *firm* must not recommend a *client* to buy or dispose of any rights or interests in a *personal pension scheme*.

(b) A *firm* must not make arrangements for a *client* to buy any rights or interests in a *personal pension scheme* except where the *firm* assumes on reasonable grounds that the *client* is not relying on the *firm* as to the merits or suitability of that *transaction* but this exception does not apply where the *transaction* involves:

(i) a *pension transfer*; or

(ii) an *opt-out*.

5.3 Securities and *contractually based investments* (except *retail investment products*)

(a) A *firm* must not recommend a *client* to buy or subscribe for a *security* or a *contractually based investment* where the *transaction* would be made:

(i) with a person acting in the course of carrying on the business of buying, selling, subscribing for or underwriting the *investment*, whether as principal or agent;

(ii) on an investment exchange or any other market to which that *investment* is admitted for dealing; or

(iii) in response to an invitation to subscribe for an *investment* which is, or is to be, admitted for dealing on an investment exchange or any other market.

(b) This rule does not apply where the *client* is:

(i) not an individual;

(ii) an individual who acts in connection with the carrying on of a business of any kind by himself or by an undertaking of which the *client* is, or would become as a result of the *transaction* to which the recommendation relates, a *controller*; or

(iii) acting in his capacity as a trustee of an *occupational pension scheme*.

5.4 Discretionary management

(a) A *firm* must not manage assets belonging to another person in circumstances which involve the exercise of discretion except where the *firm* or a *manager* or *employee* of the *firm* is a trustee, personal representative, donee of a power of attorney or receiver appointed by the Court of Protection, and either:

(i) all routine or day to day decisions, so far as relating to that activity, are taken by an *authorised person* with permission to carry on that activity or an *exempt person*; or

(ii) any decision to enter into a *transaction*, which involves buying or subscribing for an *investment*, is undertaken in accordance with the advice of an *authorised person* with permission to give advice in relation to such an activity or an *exempt person*.

5.5 Corporate finance

(a) A *firm* must not act as any of the following:

(i) sponsor to an issue in respect of *securities* to be admitted for dealing on the London Stock Exchange; or

(ii) nominated adviser to an issue in respect of *securities* to be admitted for dealing on the Alternative Investment Market of the London Stock Exchange; or

(iii) corporate adviser to an issue in respect of *securities* to be admitted for dealing on the PLUS Market.

5.6 Insurance mediation activities

(a) Unless a *firm* is registered in the *Financial Services Register* it must not carry on any *insurance mediation activities*;

(b) Any *firm* undertaking *insurance mediation activities* must appoint an *insurance mediation officer* whose details will be made known to the *FCA* and who will be responsible for the *firm's insurance mediation activities*.

5.7 Regulated mortgage contracts

(a) A *firm* must not recommend a *client* to enter as borrower into a *regulated mortgage contract* but can endorse a recommendation given by an *authorised person* with permission to advise on *regulated mortgage contracts* or an *exempt person* in relation to the giving of such advice.

5.8 Regulated home purchase plans

(a) A *firm* must not recommend a *client* to enter as *home purchaser* into a *regulated home purchase plan* with a particular person but can endorse a recommendation given by an *authorised person* with permission to advise on *regulated home purchase plans* or an *exempt person* in relation to the giving of such advice.

5.9 Regulated home reversion plans

(a) A *firm* must not recommend a *client* to enter as *reversion seller* or *plan provider* into a *regulated home reversion plan* with a particular person but can endorse a recommendation given by an *authorised person* with permission to advise on *regulated home reversion plans* or an *exempt person* in relation to the giving of such advice.

5.10   Regulated sale and rent back agreements

(a)   A *firm* must not recommend a *client* to enter as *agreement seller* or *agreement provider* into a *regulated sale and rent back agreement* with a particular person but can endorse a recommendation given by an *authorised person* with permission to advise on *regulated sale and rent back agreements* or an *exempt person* in relation to the giving of such advice.

5.11   Credit-related regulated activities

(a)   Where a *firm* carries on a *credit-related regulated activity* or a connected activity it must comply with the provisions and guidance set out in Rule 1.3R of the transitional provisions in the *FCA's CONC* as they were in force immediately before 1 April 2014 in relation to that activity, with any appropriate modification to take into account the coming into force of HM Treasury Orders that give effect to the transfer of consumer credit regulation from the OFT to the *FCA*.

Note

(i)   A *firm* which relies on the Part XX exemption cannot carry on *insurance mediation activities* unless they are on the *FCA's* Exempt Professional Firms (EPF) Register and appoint an *insurance mediation officer*. *Firms* wishing to be on this Register should notify the *SRA* (contactcentre@sra.org.uk and 0370 606 2555) and provide details of their *insurance mediation officer*. The EPF Register can be accessed on the *FCA* website – see **www.fca.org.uk**.

(ii)   During the transitional period between 1 April 2014 and 1 April 2015, *firms* carrying on *credit-related regulated activities* will be required to comply with the guidance and other provisions listed in the transitional provisions in the *FCA's CONC*. These provisions should not impose any new obligations as *firms* should already be complying with them but *firms* will need to adopt a common sense approach in interpreting them, for example, references to the OFT in these provisions and guidance should be read as if they referred to the *FCA* and references to the relevant supervisory authority mean the *SRA*.

Rule 6: Effect of a breach of these rules

6.1   The *SRA* may exercise its statutory powers in respect of any *firm* which breaches these rules.

6.2   In determining whether or not there has been a breach of these rules the *SRA* will take account of whether the *firm* has given due regard to the guidance issued by the Law Society or the *SRA* on how to determine whether *regulated activities* are carried on in accordance with these rules.

6.3   A *firm* which breaches these rules may:

(a)   be committing a criminal offence under section 23 of *FSMA*; and

(b) be made subject to an order by the *FCA* under section 329 of *FSMA* which
could prevent the *firm* from carrying on any *regulated activities*.

PART 2: REPEAL, COMMENCEMENT AND TRANSITIONAL PROVISIONS

Rule 7: Repeal, commencement and transitional provisions

7.1   These rules repeal the Solicitors' Investment Business Rules 1995.

7.2   These rules come into force on 1 December 2001.

7.3   From 31 March 2012 or the date on which an order made pursuant to section 69
of the LSA relating to the status of sole practitioners comes into force, whichever is the
later, these rules shall have effect subject to the following amendments:

(a) in the preamble the words "and *recognised sole practitioners*" shall be
omitted.

7.4   The rules shall not apply to licensed bodies until such time as the Law Society is
designated as a licensing authority under Part 1 of Schedule 10 to the Legal Services Act
2007 and all definitions shall be construed accordingly.

7.5   In these rules references in the preamble to the Rules being made under section 83
of the Legal Services Act 2007 shall have no effect until the Law Society is designated as
a licensing authority under Part 1 to Schedule 10 of the Legal Services Act 2007.

Rule 8: Interpretation

8.1   The SRA Handbook Glossary 2012 shall apply and, unless the context otherwise
requires:

(a) all italicised terms shall be defined; and:

(b) all terms shall be interpreted,

in accordance with the *Glossary*.

8.2   In these rules references to statutes, rules, codes or regulations, statements or
principles etc other than these rules include any modification or replacement thereof.

8.3   As the context requires, other words and expressions shall have the meanings
assigned to them by the Interpretation Act 1978, *FSMA* and the *SA*.

8.4   References in these rules to activities carried on by a *firm* include activities carried
on by an individual as sole principal, *manager* or *employee* of the *firm*.

SRA Financial Services (Conduct of Business) Rules 2001

These rules, dated 18 July 2001, are made by the Solicitors Regulation Authority Board under sections 31, 79 and 80 of the Solicitors Act 1974, sections 9 and 9A of the Administration of Justice Act 1985 and section 83 of the Legal Services Act 2007, with the approval of the Legal Services Board under paragraph 19 of schedule 4 to the Legal Services Act 2007, regulating the practices of:

- *Authorised bodies* and *recognised sole practitioners* in any part of the world,
- *RELs* in any part of the United Kingdom, and
- *RFLs* in England and Wales,

in carrying out *regulated activities* in, into or from the United Kingdom.

PART 1: RULES

Rule 1: Purpose

1.1   The Law Society is a designated professional body under Part XX of *FSMA*, and *firms* may therefore carry on certain *regulated activities* without being regulated by the *FCA*.

1.2   The SRA Financial Services (Scope) Rules 2001 set out the scope of the *regulated activities* which may be undertaken by *firms* which are not regulated by the *FCA*. These rules regulate the way in which *firms* carry on such exempt *regulated activities*.

Rule 2: Application

2.1   Where a *firm* is a *licensed body*, these rules apply only in respect of:

(a)   any *reserved legal activity*;

(b)   any other *legal activity*;

(c)   any other activity in respect of which the *licensed body* is regulated pursuant to Part 5 of the *LSA*.

2.2   Apart from rule 3 (status disclosure), these rules apply to:

(a)   *firms* which are not regulated by the *FCA*; and

(b)   *firms* which are regulated by the *FCA* but these rules only apply to such *firms* in respect of their *non-mainstream regulated activities*.

Rule 3: Status disclosure

3.1   This rule applies only to *firms* which are not regulated by the *FCA*.

3.2   A *firm* shall give the *client* the following information in writing in a manner that is clear, fair and not misleading before the *firm* provides a service which includes the carrying on of a *regulated activity*:

  (a)   a statement that the *firm* is not authorised by the *FCA*;

  (b)   the name and address of the *firm*;

  (c)   the nature of the *regulated activities* carried on by the *firm*, and the fact that they are limited in scope;

  (d)   a statement that the *firm* is authorised and regulated by the Solicitors Regulation Authority; and

  (e)   a statement explaining that complaints and redress mechanisms are provided through the Solicitors Regulation Authority and the Legal Ombudsman;

3.3   Before a *firm* provides a service which includes the carrying on of an *insurance mediation activity* with or for a *client*, it must make the following statement in writing to the *client* in a way that is clear, fair and not misleading:

> "[This firm is]/[We are] not authorised by the Financial Conduct Authority. However, we are included on the register maintained by the Financial Conduct Authority so that we can carry on insurance mediation activity, which is broadly the advising on, selling and administration of insurance contracts. This part of our business, including arrangements for complaints or redress if something goes wrong, is regulated by Solicitors Regulation Authority. The register can be accessed via the Financial Conduct Authority website at www.fca.org.uk/register."

Notes

(i)   Where the status disclosure relates to *insurance mediation activities* then the statement in rule 3(3) must be used. The status disclosure need not be tailored to the needs of the individual *client*. The disclosures may be provided alongside or integrated with other material provided to the *client*. These disclosures may be made in the *firm's* client care letter or in a separate letter.

(ii)   Outcome (8.5) in Chapter 8 of the SRA Code of Conduct is that your letterhead, website and e-mails must show the words "authorised and regulated by the Solicitors Regulation Authority" which will assist in meeting the requirements of rule 3(2).

(iii)   The provisions of rule 3(2)(d) and rule 3(3) reflect the requirements of the outcomes in Chapter 1 of the SRA Code of Conduct in respect of complaints handling.

Rule 4: Execution of transactions

4.1   A *firm* shall ensure that where it has agreed or decided in its discretion to effect a *transaction*, it shall do so as soon as possible, unless it reasonably believes that it is in the *client's* best interests not to do so.

Note

(i)   Principle 4 sets out your duty to act in the best interests of the *client*. Accordingly, in cases where there is any doubt on the point, *firms* should ensure that transactions are effected on the best terms reasonably available.

Rule 5: Records of transactions

5.1   Where a *firm* receives instructions from a *client* to effect a *transaction*, or makes a decision to effect a *transaction* in its discretion, it shall keep a record of:

(a)   the name of the *client*;

(b)   the terms of the instructions or decision; and

(c)   in the case of instructions, the date when they were received.

5.2   Where a *firm* gives instructions to another person to effect a transaction, it shall keep a record of:

(a)   the name of the *client*;

(b)   the terms of the instructions;

(c)   the date when the instructions were given; and

(d)   the name of the other person instructed.

Note

(i)   It is not necessary for the *firm* to make a separate record. Normal file notes or letters on the file will meet the requirements of this rule provided that they include the appropriate information. If instructions are given or received over the telephone, an appropriate attendance note would satisfy this rule.

Rule 6: Record of commissions

6.1   Where a *firm* receives commission which is attributable to *regulated activities* carried on by the *firm*, it shall keep a record of:

(a)   the amount of the commission; and

(b)   how the *firm* has accounted to the *client*.

Notes

(i)   Any *financial benefit* has to be dealt with in accordance with Outcome (1.15) in Chapter 1 of the SRA Code of Conduct. However, *firms* should bear in mind that in the case of commissions attributable to *regulated activities*, *firms* must also comply with the requirements of the SRA Financial Services (Scope) Rules 2001, rule 4 (c).

(ii)   The record could be a letter or bill of costs provided the information is clear.

Rule 7: Safekeeping of clients' investments

7.1   Where a *firm* undertakes the *regulated activity* of safeguarding and administering investments, the *firm* must operate appropriate systems, including the keeping of appropriate records, which provide for the safekeeping of assets entrusted to the *firm* by *clients* and others.

7.2   Where such assets are passed to a third party:

(a)   an acknowledgement of receipt of the property should be obtained; and

(b)   if they have been passed to a third party on the *client's* instructions, such instructions should be obtained in writing.

Rule 8: Packaged products – execution-only business

8.1   If a *firm* arranges for a *client* on an *execution-only* basis any *transaction* involving a *retail investment product*, the *firm* shall send the *client* written confirmation to the effect that:

(a)   the *client* had not sought and was not given any advice from the *firm* in connection with the *transaction*; or

(b)   the *client* was given advice from the *firm* in connection with that *transaction* but nevertheless persisted in wishing the *transaction* to be effected; and in either case the *transaction* is effected on the *client's* explicit instructions.

Rule 9: Insurance mediation activities

9.1   Where a *firm* undertakes *insurance mediation activities* for a *client*, it must comply with appendix 1 to these rules.

Rule 10: Retention of records

10.1   Each record made under these rules shall be kept for at least six years.

Note

(i)   The six years shall run from the date on which the relevant record has been made.

Rule 11: Waivers

11.1   In any particular case or cases the *SRA* shall have power to waive in writing any of the provisions of these rules, but shall not do so unless it appears that:

(a) compliance with them would be unduly burdensome having regard to the benefit which compliance would confer on investors; and

(b) the exercise of the power would not result in any undue risk to investors.

11.2   The *SRA* shall have power to revoke any waiver.

Rule 12: Commencement

12.1   These rules come into force on 1 December 2001.

12.2   From 31 March 2012 or the date on which an order made pursuant to section 69 of the *LSA* relating to the status of sole practitioners comes into force, whichever is the later, these rules shall have effect subject to the following amendment:

(a) in the preamble the words "and *recognised sole practitioners*" shall be omitted.

12.3   These rules shall not apply to licensed bodies until such time as the Law Society is designated as a licensing authority under Part 1 of Schedule 10 to the Legal Services Act 2007 and all definitions shall be construed accordingly.

12.4   In these rules references in the preamble to the Rules being made under section 83 of the Legal Services Act 2007 shall have no effect until the Law Society is designated as a licensing authority under Part 1 of Schedule 10 to the Legal Services Act 2007.

Rule 13: Interpretation

13.1   The SRA Handbook Glossary 2012 shall apply and, unless the context otherwise requires:

(a) all italicised terms shall be defined; and

(b) all terms shall be interpreted,

in accordance with the *Glossary*.

Notes

(i)   Whether a transaction is *execution-only* will depend on the existing relationship between the *client* and the *firm* and the circumstances surrounding that *transaction*. Generally, a *transaction* will be *execution-only* if the *client* instructs the *firm* to effect it without having received advice from the *firm*. Even though this is the case, however, the *transaction* may still not qualify as *execution-only* because, in view of the relationship, the *client* may reasonably expect the *firm* to indicate if the *transaction* is inappropriate. In any event, a *firm* may be negligent (and possibly in breach of Principle 4) if it fails to advise on the appropriateness or otherwise.

(ii)   A *transaction* will also be *execution-only* if the *firm* has advised the *client* that the *transaction* is unsuitable, but the *client* persists in wishing the *transaction* to be carried out. In those circumstances it is good practice (and in some cases a requirement) for the *firm* to confirm in writing that its advice has not been accepted, and that the *transaction* is being effected on an *execution-only* basis.

(iii)   Where the *transaction* involves a *retail investment product*, there is a specific requirement to confirm in writing the *execution-only* nature of a *transaction* (see Rule 8 above).

13.2   These rules are to be interpreted in the light of the notes.

PART 2: APPENDIX

APPENDIX 1: Insurance Mediation Activities

1   *Disclosure of information*

(a)   Where a *firm* undertakes *insurance mediation activities* for a *client*, it must take reasonable steps to communicate information to the *client* in a way that is clear, fair and not misleading.

(b)   Where a *firm* recommends a *contract of insurance* (other than a *life policy*) to a *client*, the *firm* must inform the *client* whether the *firm* has given advice on the basis of a fair analysis of a sufficiently large number of insurance contracts available on the market to enable the *firm* to make a recommendation in accordance with professional criteria regarding which *contract of insurance* would be adequate to meet the *client's* needs.

(c)   If the *firm* does not conduct a fair analysis of the market, the *firm* must:

(i)   advise the *client* whether the *firm* is contractually obliged to conduct *insurance mediation activities* in this way;

(ii)   advise the *client* that the *client* can request details of the *insurance undertak-ings* with which the firm conducts business; and

(iii)   provide the *client* with such details on request.

(d)   The information referred to in paragraphs 1(2) and 1(3) above must be provided to the *client* on paper or on any other durable medium available and accessible to the *client*.

Notes

(i)   Paragraph 1(1) covers all communications with the *client*, including oral statements and telephone calls.

(ii)   Indicative behaviours arising in respect of Chapter 6 (Your Client and Introductions to third parties) of the SRA Code of Conduct provides that you ought not in connection with *regulated activities* have any *arrangement* with other persons under which you could be constrained to recommend to *clients* or effect for them (or refrain from doing so) transactions in some *investments* but not others, or with some persons but not others, or through the agency of some persons but not others; or to introduce or refer *clients* or other persons with whom the *firm* deal to some persons but not others. However, these provisions do not apply to arrangements in connection with *regulated mortgage contracts*, *general insurance contracts* or *pure protection contracts*.

(iii)   Paragraphs 1(2) and 1(3) apply to *contracts of insurance* other than *life policies*. *Firms* who are not authorised by the *FCA* are not allowed to recommend the buying of *life policies*, but they can make recommendations and advise on other *contracts of insurance*.

(iv)   Reference to a durable medium in paragraph 1(4) is to a form that allows for the storage of information to be reproduced without changes. This includes floppy disks, CD-roms, DVDs and hard drives where emails are stored.

2   *Suitability*

(a)   Before a *firm* recommends a *contract of insurance* (other than a *life policy*) the *firm* must take reasonable steps to ensure that the recommendation is suitable to the *client's* demands and needs by:

    (i)   considering relevant information already held;

    (ii)   obtaining details of any relevant existing insurance;

    (iii)   identifying the *client's* requirements and explaining to the *client* what the *client* needs to disclose;

    (iv)   assessing whether the level of cover is sufficient for the risks that the *client* wishes to insure; and

    (v)   considering the relevance of any exclusions, excesses, limitations or conditions.

(b)   Where the *firm* recommends a *contract of insurance* that does not meet the needs of the *client* because there is no such contract available in the market, this should be disclosed to the *client*.

3   *Demands and needs statement*

(a)   Where a *firm* recommends a *contract of insurance* (other than a *life policy*) or arranges a *contract of insurance*, the *firm* must, before the contract is finalised, provide the *client* with a written demands and needs statement that:

    (i)   sets out the *client's* demands and needs on the basis of the information provided by the *client*;

    (ii)   where a recommendation has been made, explains the reason for recommending that *contract of insurance*;

    (iii)   reflects the complexity of the insurance contract being proposed; and

(iv) is on paper or on any other durable medium available and accessible to the *client*.

(b)   Where a *firm* arranges a *contract of insurance* on an *execution-only* basis, the demands and needs statement need only identify the *contract of insurance* requested by the *client*, confirm that no advice has been given and state that the *firm* is undertaking the arrangement at the *client's* specific request.

(c)   The requirement in paragraph 3(1) to provide the *client* with a written demands and needs statement before the contract is finalised will not apply in the following circumstances:

   (i)   where the *firm* acts on the renewal or amendment of a *contract of insurance* other than a *life policy* if the information given to the *client* in relation to the initial contract is still accurate and up-to-date. If the information previously disclosed has changed, the *firm* must draw the attention of the *client* to the matters which have changed before the renewal or amendment takes place;

   (ii)   where the information is provided orally at the request of the *client*;

   (iii)   where immediate cover is required;

   (iv)   where the contract is concluded by telephone; or

   (v)   where the *firm* is introducing the *client* to an *authorised person* or an *exempt person* and taking no further part in arranging the *contract of insurance*;

save that in (b), (c) and (d) above the information contained in the written demands and needs statement must be provided to the *client* immediately after the conclusion of the *contract of insurance*.

Notes

(i)   Reference to a durable medium in paragraph 3(1)(d) is to a form that allows for the storage of information and allows the information to be reproduced without changes. This includes floppy disks, CD-Roms, DVDs and hard drives where emails are stored.

(ii)   Paragraph 2 and 3(1) apply to *contracts of insurance* other than life policies. *Firms* who are not authorised by the *FCA* are not allowed to recommend the buying of *life policies*, but they can make recommendations and advise on other *contracts of insurance*.

4   Exclusion for large risks

(a)   Paragraphs 1–3 above do not apply where a *firm* carries on *insurance mediation activities* for commercial *clients* in relation to *contracts of insurance* covering risks within the following categories:

   (i)   railway rolling stock, aircraft, ships (sea, lake, river and canal vessels), goods in transit, aircraft liability and liability of ships (sea, lake, river and canal vessels);

(ii) credit and suretyship, where the policyholder is engaged professionally in an industrial or commercial activity or in one of the liberal professions, and the risks relate to such activity;

(iii) land vehicles (other than railway rolling stock), fire and natural forces, other damage to property, motor vehicle liability, general liability, and miscellaneous financial loss, in so far as the policyholder exceeds the limits of at least two of the following three criteria:

    (A) balance sheet total: €6.2 million;

    (B) net turnover: €12.8 million;

    (C) average number of employees during the financial year: 250.

5   *Notification of establishment and services in other Member States*

If a *firm* wishes to exercise the right conferred by Article 6 of the Insurance Mediation Directive to establish a branch or provide cross-border services in another EEA state, an appropriate application must be made directly to the *FCA*. The Rules under the *FCA's* Supervision Manual, SUP 13, Exercise of Passport Rights by *UK* firms, contain details of the applicable process. A *firm* proposing to provide such services must comply with the applicable provisions of the Act, as laid down in the *FCA's* Professional Firms' Sourcebook Chapter 7 as amended from time to time.

Specialist Services

Rules dated 17 June 2011 commencing 6 October 2011 made by the Solicitors Regulation Authority Board under sections 31, 79 and 80 of the Solicitors Act 1974, sections 9 and 9A of the Administration of Justice Act 1985 and section 83 of the Legal Services Act 2007, with the approval of the Legal Services Board under paragraph 19 of Schedule 4 to the Legal Services Act 2007.

PART 1: GENERAL

Rule 1: Purpose

1.1   The purpose of these rules is to set the standard for professional conduct in the context of European cross-border practice.

Rule 2: Application

2.1   In these rules:

   (a)   European cross-border practice means:

   (i)   *professional activity* in a *CCBE state* other than the *UK*, whether or not you are physically present in that *CCBE state*; and

   (ii)   any *professional contact* with a *lawyer* of a *CCBE state* other than the *UK*.

   (b)   *Professional contacts* and *professional activities* taking place within a *firm* or in-house legal department do not constitute *European cross-border practice*.

2.2   These rules apply to *European cross-border practice* from any office by:

   (a)   *solicitors*;

   (b)   *managers* of *authorised bodies* who are *lawyers of England and Wales*;

   (c)   *non-lawyer managers* of *authorised bodies*;

   (d)   *managers* of *authorised bodies* who are registered with the Bar Standards Board under the Establishment Directive; and

   (e)   *authorised bodies*.

2.3   These rules also apply to *European cross-border practice* from an office in England and Wales by:

   (a)   *RELs*; and

(b) any *RFL* who is a *manager* or an employee of an *authorised body*.

PART 2: SUBSTANTIVE PROVISIONS

Rule 3: Occupations considered incompatible with legal practice

3.1 If you act in legal proceedings or proceedings before public authorities in a *CCBE state* other than the *UK*, you must, in that state, comply with any rules regarding occupations incompatible with the practice of law, as if you were a lawyer of that state, whether or not you are based at an office in that state.

3.2 If you are a solicitor based at an office in a *CCBE state* other than the *UK*, you must respect any rules regarding participation in commercial or other activities not connected with the practice of law, as they are applied to *lawyers* of that state.

Rule 4: Fee sharing with non-lawyers

4.1 You must not share your professional fees with a *non-lawyer* situated in a *CCBE state* other than the *UK* except:

(a) within a *firm* and only as permitted under the SRA Practice Framework Rules 2011; or

(b) with a retired *manager, member, owner* or predecessor of the *firm*, or the dependants or personal representatives of a deceased *manager, member, owner* or predecessor.

4.2 If you are *practising* from an office in a *CCBE state* other than the *UK*, whether or not you are actually present at that office, you must not share your professional fees from that practice with a *non-lawyer*, except:

(a) within a *firm*, and only as permitted under the SRA Practice Framework Rules 2011; or

(b) with a retired *manager, member, owner* or predecessor of the *firm*, or the dependants or personal representatives of a deceased *manager, member, owner* or predecessor.

Rule 5: Co-operation between lawyers of different CCBE states

5.1 If you are approached by a *lawyer* of a *CCBE state* other than the *UK* to undertake work which you are not competent to undertake, you must assist that *lawyer* to obtain the information necessary to find and instruct a *lawyer* capable of providing the service asked for.

5.2 When co-operating with a *lawyer* of a *CCBE state* other than the *UK* you must take into account the differences which may exist between your respective legal systems and the professional organisations, competencies and obligations of *lawyers* in your respective states.

Rule 6: Correspondence between lawyers in different CCBE states

6.1   If you are *practising* from an office in a *CCBE state* and you want to send to a *lawyer* in a different *CCBE state* (with the exception of the *UK*) a communication which you wish to remain "confidential" or "without prejudice", you must, before sending the communication, clearly express your intention in order to avoid misunderstanding, and ask if the *lawyer* is able to accept the communication on that basis. When you send the communication you must express your intention clearly at the head of the communication or in a covering letter.

6.2   If you are the intended recipient of a communication from a *lawyer* in another *CCBE state* which is stated to be "confidential" or "without prejudice", but which you are unable to accept on the basis intended by that *lawyer*, you must inform the sender accordingly without delay. If the communication has already been sent you must return it unread without revealing the contents to others. If you have already read the communication and you are under a professional duty to reveal it to your *client* you must inform the sender of this immediately.

Rule 7: Paying referral fees to non-lawyers

7.1   You must not pay a fee, commission or any other compensation to a *non-lawyer* as a consideration for referring a *client* to you:

(a)   if the *non-lawyer* is situated in a *CCBE state* other than the *UK*; or

(b)   if you are *practising* from an office in a *CCBE state* other than the *UK*, whether or not you are physically present at that office.

Rule 8: Disputes between lawyers in different member states

8.1   If you consider that a *lawyer* in a *CCBE state* other than the *UK* has acted in breach of a rule of professional conduct you must draw the breach to the other *lawyer's* attention.

8.2   Before commencing any form of proceedings against the other *lawyer*, you must inform the Law Society and the other *lawyer's* bar or law society in order to allow them an opportunity to assist in resolving the matter.

Rule 9: Fee of lawyers of other CCBE states

9.1   If in the course of practice you instruct a *lawyer* of a *CCBE state* other than the *UK* you must, as a matter of professional conduct, pay the lawyer's proper fees unless the lawyer is *practising* as a *lawyer of England and Wales*; or

(a)   you have expressly disclaimed that responsibility at the outset, or at a later date you have expressly disclaimed responsibility for any fees incurred after that date;

(b)   the *lawyer* is an *REL* or is registered with the Bar of England and Wales under the *Establishment Directive*; or

(c)   the *lawyer* is an *RFL* based in England and Wales and *practising* in a *firm*.

9.2   If in the course of *practice* you instruct a business carrying on the *practice of a lawyer of a CCBE state* other than the *UK* you must, as a matter of professional conduct, pay the proper fees for the work that *lawyer* does, unless:

(a)   you have expressly disclaimed that responsibility at the outset, or at a later date you have expressly disclaimed responsibility for any fees incurred after that date; or

(b)   the business is a *firm*.

PART 3: INTERPRETATION AND TRANSITIONAL PROVISIONS

Rule 10: Interpretation

10.1   The SRA Handbook Glossary 2012 shall apply and, unless the context otherwise requires:

(a)   all italicised terms shall be defined; and

(b)   all terms shall be interpreted,

in accordance with the *Glossary*.

Rule 11: Transitional Provisions

11.1   These rules shall not apply to licensed bodies until such time as the Society is designated as a licensing authority under Part 1 of Schedule 10 to the *LSA* and all definitions shall be construed accordingly.

11.2   References in the preamble to the rules being made under section 83 of the Legal Services Act 2007 shall have no effect until such time as the Society is designated as a licensing authority under Part 1 of Schedule 10 to the *LSA*.

SRA Insolvency Practice Rules 2012

The SRA Insolvency Practice Rules dated 18 April 2012 commencing on 18 April 2012 made by the Solicitors Regulation Authority Board under sections 31, 79 and 80 of the Solicitors Act 1974 with the approval of the Legal Services Board under paragraph 19 of Schedule 4 to the Legal Services Act 2007.

PART 1: RULES

Rule 1: Purpose

1.1   The purpose of these Rules is to set out the standards which must be met by *solicitors* and *RELs* when carrying on *insolvency practice*.

Rule 2: Interpretation

2.1   The SRA Handbook Glossary 2012 shall apply and, unless the context otherwise requires:

(a)   all italicised terms shall be defined; and

(b)   terms shall be interpreted,

in accordance with the *Glossary*.

Rule 3: Standard of insolvency practice

3.1   When engaged in *insolvency practice*, you must comply with the *Insolvency Code of Ethics*.

Rule 4: Waivers

4.1   In any particular case or cases the *SRA* Board shall have the power, in exceptional circumstances, to waive in writing the provisions of these Rules for a particular purpose or purposes expressed in such waiver, to place conditions on and to revoke such a waiver.

Notes

(i)   You must comply with the requirements of the Insolvency Act 1986 and other relevant legislation in relation to accepting appointments and acting as an appointment holder.

(ii)   You should have regard to the other guidance and best practice issued from time to time by the SRA as a recognised professional body on all issues relating to appointment holding, including professional independence.

[J]   Glossary

[J.1]   SRA Handbook Glossary 2012

PART 1: INTRODUCTION AND PREAMBLE

Introduction

This section of the Handbook contains the SRA Handbook Glossary.

The SRA Handbook Glossary comprises a set of defined terms which are used in the SRA Handbook. Terms being used in their defined sense appear as italicised text within the individual sets of provisions of the SRA Handbook. The same terms in the SRA Handbook may appear as italicised text in some cases but not in others. Where they are not italicised, for reasons relating to the specific context, they are not being used in their defined sense and take their natural meaning in that context.

The Glossary also contains interpretation and transitional provisions.

Preamble

The SRA Handbook Glossary dated 18 April 2012 made by the Solicitors Regulation Authority Board.

Made under Part I, Part II, section 79 and 80 of, and paragraph 6B of Schedule 1 to, the Solicitors Act 1974; and section 9 and 9A of, and paragraphs 14A, 14B and 32 to 34 of Schedule 2 to, the Administration of Justice Act 1985; and section 83 of, and Schedule 11 to and paragraph 6 of Schedule 14 to, the Legal Services Act 2007; and paragraphs 2 and 3 of Schedule 14 to the Courts and Legal Services Act 1990.

Subject to the approval of the Legal Services Board under paragraph 19 of Schedule 4 to the Legal Services Act 2007 and coming into force on the day it is approved.

PART 2: GENERAL

Rule 1: Application

1.1   Subject to Rule 1.2 below:

    (a)   the definitions set out at Rule 2 below shall apply to the corresponding term where this appears in italics in the *SRA Handbook*; and

    (b)   the interpretation provisions set out at Rule 3 below shall apply to the *SRA Handbook*.

1.2   This Rule shall not apply to the SRA Indemnity Insurance Rules 2011, the SRA Indemnity (Enactment) Rules 2011 and the SRA Indemnity Rules 2011 until 1 October 2012.

Rule 2: Definitions

academic stage of training means the undertaking by an individual of the following programmes of study which satisfy the requirements of the *Joint Statement*:

    (i) a *QLD*;

    (ii) a *CPE*; or

    (iii) an *Exempting Law Degree*;

at an *approved education provider*.

accounting period has the meaning given in Rule 33 of the *SRA Accounts Rules*.

accreditation means either *full accreditation* or *provisional accreditation* under the *SRA QASA Regulations*, and references to "accredited" should be construed accordingly.

actively participate in means, in relation to a *separate business*, having any active involvement in the *separate business*, and includes:

    (i) any direct control over the business, and any indirect control through another *person* such as a spouse; and

    (ii) any active participation in the business or the provision of its services to customers.

adequate training during a period of *recognised training* means training:

    (i) and experience in at least three distinct areas of English law and practice;

    (ii) to enable a *trainee* to develop the skills needed to activities set out in the *Practice Skills Standards* and comply with the *Principles*;

    (iii) which is appropriately supervised; and

    (iv) which meets the requirements of regulation 12 of the *SRA Training Regulations* – Qualification and Provider Regulations.

adjudicator

    (i) in the *SRA Cost of Investigations Regulations* means a person not involved in the investigation or preparation of a case who is authorised by the *SRA* to make an *SRA finding*; and

    (ii) in the *SRA Disciplinary Procedure Rules* means a person not involved in the investigation or preparation of a case who is authorised by the *SRA* to take *disciplinary decisions*.

agreed fee has the meaning given in Rule 17.5 of the *SRA Accounts Rules*.

agreement provider has the meaning given by article 63J(3) of the *Regulated Activities Order* read with paragraphs (6) and (7) of that article.

agreement seller has the meaning given by article 63J(3) of the *Regulated Activities Order*.

AJA means the Administration of Justice Act 1985.

appellate body means the body with the power, by virtue of an order under section 80(1) of the *LSA*, to hear and determine appeals against decisions made by the *SRA* acting as a *licensing authority*.

applicant means a *person* or *persons* applying for a grant out of the Compensation Fund under Rule 3 of the *SRA Compensation Fund Rules*.

applicant body means a *licensable body* or a *legal services body* which makes an application to the *SRA* for *authorisation* in accordance with the *SRA Authorisation Rules*.

application for admission means application to *us* for a *certificate of satisfaction* under section 3(1) of the *SA* and for admission as a *solicitor* under section 3(2) of the *SA*.

appointed person in the *SRA Indemnity Insurance Rules*, means any person who is designated as a fee-earner in accordance with any arrangements made from time to time between the *firm* and the Legal Services Commission pursuant to the provisions of the Access to Justice Act 1999 or the Lord Chancellor (or any body established by the Lord Chancellor to provide or facilitate the provision of services) pursuant to the provisions of the Legal Aid, Sentencing and Punishment of Offenders Act 2012, regardless of whether the services performed for the *firm* by that person in accordance with Rule 4.1 of those Rules are performed pursuant to such arrangements or otherwise, and who is engaged by the *firm* under a contract for services in the course of the *private practice* of the *firm*.

appointed representative has the meaning given in *FSMA*.

approved education provider means a provider recognised by *us* as providing a *QLD*, *CPE* and/or an *Exempting Law Degree*.

approved regulator means any body listed as an approved regulator in paragraph 1 of Schedule 4 to the *LSA* or designated as an approved regulator by an order under paragraph 17 of that Schedule.

ARP means the Assigned Risks Pool, namely, the arrangements by which certain *firms* obtained professional indemnity insurance against civil liability up to 30 September 2013 pursuant to and on the terms set out in the SRA Indemnity Insurance Rules 2012 (and prior variations thereof).

ARP manager means the manager of the *ARP* being any *person* from time to time appointed by the *SRA* to carry out all or any particular functions of the manager of the *ARP* or the *SRA* and any such *person*.

Glossary

arrangement in relation to financial services, fee sharing and *referrals* in Chapters 1, 6 and 9 of the *SRA Code of Conduct*, means any express or tacit agreement between you and another *person*, whether contractually binding or not.

assessment organisation in the *QLTSR* means the organisation awarded the initial three year contract to provide the *QLTS assessments*, together with any other organisations subsequently authorised to provide the *QLTS assessments* after the initial three year period has expired.

assets includes money, documents, wills, deeds, investments and other property.

associate has the meaning given in paragraph 5 to Schedule 13 of the *LSA*, namely:

(i) "associate", in relation to a person ("A") and:

    (A) a shareholding in a body ("S"); or

    (B) an entitlement to exercise or control the exercise of voting power in a body ("V");

means a person listed in sub-paragraph (ii).

(ii) The persons are:

    (A) the spouse or civil partner of A;

    (B) a child or stepchild of A (if under 18);

    (C) the *trustee* of any settlement under which A has a life interest in possession (in Scotland a life interest);

    (D) an undertaking of which A is a *director*;

    (E) an *employee* of A;

    (F) a *partner* of A (except, where S or V is a *partnership* in which A is a *partner*, another *partner* in S or V);

    (G) if A is an undertaking:

        (I) a *director* of A;

        (II) a subsidiary undertaking of A; or

        (III) a *director* or *employee* of such a subsidiary undertaking;

    (H) if A has with any other person an agreement or arrangement with respect to the acquisition, holding or disposal of shares or other interests in S or V (whether or not they are interests within the meaning of section 72(3) of the *LSA*), that other person; or

    (I) if A has with any other person an agreement or arrangement under which they undertake to act together in exercising their voting power in relation to S or V, that person.

associated firm means:

(i)   a *partnership* with whom you have one *partner* in common;

(ii) an *LLP* or a *company* without shares with whom you have one *member* in common; or

(iii) a *company* with shares with whom you have one *owner* in common.

authorisation granted to a body under Rule 6 of the *SRA Authorisation Rules* means:

(i)   recognition under section 9 of the *AJA*, if it is granted to a *legal services body*; and

(ii) a licence under Part 5 of the *LSA*, if it is granted to a *licensable body*;

and the term "*certificate of authorisation*" shall be construed accordingly.

authorised activities means:

(i)   any *reserved legal activity* in respect of which the body is authorised;

(ii) any *non-reserved legal activity* except, in relation to an *MDP*, any such activity that is excluded from *regulated activity* on the terms of the licence;

(iii) any other activity in respect of which a *licensed body* is regulated pursuant to Part 5 of the *LSA*; and

(iv) any other activity a *recognised body* carries out in connection with its *practice*.

authorised body means a body that has been authorised by the *SRA* to practise as a *licensed body* or a *recognised body*.

authorised CPD course providers means those providers authorised by *us* to provide training that attracts *CPD* hours as a result of attendance.

authorised distance learning providers means those providers authorised by *us* to provide distance learning courses delivered by methods including correspondence, webinar, webcast, podcast, DVD, video and audio cassettes, television or radio broadcasts and computer based learning programmes.

authorised education provider means a provider recognised by *us* as providing the *LPC* and/or the *PSC*.

authorised insurer means:

(i)   a *person* who has permission under Part IV of *FSMA* to effect or carry out contracts of insurance of a relevant class;

(ii) a *person* who carries on an insurance market activity, within the meaning of section 316(3) of *FSMA*;

(iii) an *EEA* firm of the kind mentioned in paragraph 5(d) of Schedule 3 to *FSMA*, which has permission under paragraph 15 of that Schedule (as a result of qualifying for authorisation under paragraph 12 of that Schedule) to effect or carry out contracts of insurance of a relevant class; or

(iv) a *person* who does not fall within paragraph (i), (ii) or (iii) and who may lawfully effect or carry out contracts of insurance of a relevant class in a member state other than the *UK*,

where "relevant class" has the meaning set out in section 87(1B) of the *SA* provided that this definition must be read with section 22 of *FSMA*, any relevant order under that section, and Schedule 2 to *FSMA*.

authorised non-SRA firm means a firm which is authorised to carry on *legal activities* by an *approved regulator* other than the *SRA*.

authorised person

(i) subject to sub-paragraph (ii) below, means a *person* who is authorised by the *SRA* or another *approved regulator* to carry on a *legal activity* and for the purposes of the *SRA Authorisation Rules* and the *SRA Practice Framework Rules* includes a *solicitor*, a *sole practitioner*, an *REL*, an *EEL*, an *RFL*, an *authorised body*, an *authorised non-SRA firm* and a *European corporate practice* and the terms "*authorised individual*" and "non-authorised person" shall be construed accordingly; and

(ii) in the *SRA Financial Services (Scope) Rules*, has the meaning given in section 31 of *FSMA*.

authorised role holder means *COLP*, *COFA*, *owner* or *manager* under Rules 8.5 and 8.6 of the *SRA Authorisation Rules* or *COLP* or *COFA* under Regulation 4.8 of the *SRA Practising Regulations*, and "authorised role" should be construed accordingly.

authorised training provider means an organisation, body, firm, company, in-house practice or individual authorised by *us* under the *SRA Training Regulations* to take and train a *trainee solicitor*.

bank has the meaning given in section 87(1) of the *SA*.

barrister means a person called to the Bar by one of the Inns of Court and who has completed pupillage and is authorised by the General Council of the Bar to practise as a barrister.

beneficiary means a *person* with a beneficial entitlement to funds held by the *Society* on *statutory trust*.

best list means a list of potential beneficial entitlements to *statutory trust monies* which, in cases where it is not possible to create a *reconciled list*, is, in the view of the *SRA*, the most reliable that can be achieved with a reasonable and proportionate level of work taking into account the circumstances of the *intervention* and the nature of the evidence available.

body corporate means a company, an *LLP* or a partnership which is a legal person in its own right.

broker funds arrangement means an arrangement between a *firm* and a *life office* (or operator of a *regulated collective investment scheme*) under which the *life office* (or operator of the *regulated collective investment scheme*) agrees to establish a separate fund whose composition may be determined by instructions from the *firm* and in which it is possible for more than one *client* to invest.

BSB means the Bar Standards Board.

building society means a building society within the meaning of the Building Societies Act 1986.

buyer includes a prospective buyer.

CAEF means a criminal advocacy evaluation form completed by a judge to record the competence of a *solicitor* or an *REL* to conduct *criminal advocacy* against the Statement of Standards contained in the *QASA*.

candidate means a *person* who is assessed by the *SRA* for approval as an *owner*, *manager* or *compliance officer* under Part 4 of the *SRA Authorisation Rules*.

CCBE means the Council of the Bars and Law Societies of Europe.

CCBE Code means the *CCBE's* Code of Conduct for European lawyers.

CCBE state means any state whose legal profession is a full member, an associate member or an observer member of the *CCBE*.

certificate of eligibility means a certificate issued by *us* confirming eligibility to take assessments under *QLTSR*, or the *QLTT* under *QLTR*, or an authorisation under those regulations to apply for admission as a *solicitor* without taking any test or assessment.

certificate of satisfaction means a certificate or a certifying letter from *us* confirming that *you* have satisfied the *SRA Training Regulations* and are of the proper *character and suitability* to be admitted as a *solicitor*.

cessation means where the *insured firm's practice* ceases during or on expiry of the *period of insurance* and the *insured firm* has not obtained succeeding insurance in compliance with the *MTC*.

cessation period means the period commencing on the expiry of the *extended indemnity period* where, during the *extended indemnity period* the relevant *firm* has not ceased *practice* or obtained a *policy* of *qualifying insurance* incepting with effect on and from the day immediately following expiration of the *policy period*, and ending on the date which is the earlier to occur of:

(i) the date, if any, on which the *firm* obtains a *policy* of *qualifying insurance* incepting with effect on and from the day immediately following expiration of the *policy period*;

(ii) the date which is 90 days after the commencement of the *extended indemnity period*; or

(iii) the date on which the *insured firm's practice* ceases.

character and suitability satisfies the requirement of section 3 of the *SA* in order that an individual shall be admitted as a *solicitor*.

charity has the meaning given in section 1 of the Charities Act 2011.

circumstances means an incident, occurrence, fact, matter, act or omission which may give rise to a *claim* in respect of civil liability.

claim means a demand for, or an assertion of a right to, civil compensation or civil damages or an intimation of an intention to seek such compensation or damages. For these purposes, an obligation on an *insured firm* and/or any *insured* to remedy a breach of the Solicitors' Accounts Rules 1998 (as amended from time to time), or any rules (including, without limitation, the *SRA Accounts Rules*) which replace the Solicitors' Accounts Rules 1998 in whole or in part, shall be treated as a claim, and the obligation to remedy such breach shall be treated as a civil liability for the purposes of clause 1 of the *MTC*, whether or not any *person* makes a demand for, or an assertion of a right to, civil compensation or civil damages or an intimation of an intention to seek such compensation or damages as a result of such breach, except where any such obligation may arise as a result of the insolvency of a bank (as defined in section 87 of the *SA*) or a *building society* which holds client money in a client account of the *insured firm* or the failure of such bank or *building society* generally to repay monies on demand.

claim for redress has the meaning given in section 158 of the *LSA*.

claimant means:

(i) in the *SRA Statutory Trust Rules*, a *person* making a claim to *statutory trust monies*; and

(ii) in the *SRA Indemnity Insurance Rules*, a *person* or entity which has made or may make a *claim* including a *claim* for contribution or indemnity.

client means:

(i) the *person* for whom you act and, where the context permits, includes prospective and former clients;

(ii) in Parts 1–6 of the *SRA Accounts Rules*, the person for whom *you* act; and

(iii) in the *SRA Financial Services (Scope) Rules*, in relation to any *regulated activities* carried on by a *firm* for a trust or the estate of a deceased person (including a controlled trust), the trustees or personal representatives in their capacity as such and not any *person* who is a beneficiary under the trust or interested in the estate.

client account has the meaning given in Rule 13.2 of the *SRA Accounts Rules*.

client account (overseas) means an account at a bank or similar institution, subject to supervision by a public authority, which is used only for the purpose of holding *client money (overseas)* and/or *trust* money, and the title or designation of which indicates that the funds in the account belong to the client or clients of a *solicitor* or *REL* or are held subject to a *trust*.

client conflict for the purposes of Chapter 3 of the *SRA Code of Conduct*, means any situation where you owe separate duties to act in the best interests of two or more *clients* in relation to the same or related matters, and those duties conflict, or there is a significant risk that those duties may conflict.

client money has the meaning given in Rule 12 of the *SRA Accounts Rules*.

client money (overseas) means money received or held for or on behalf of a client or *trust* (but excluding money which is held or received by a multi-disciplinary practice – a *licensed body* providing a range of different services – in relation to those activities for which it is not regulated by the *SRA*).

COFA means a compliance officer for finance and administration in accordance with Rule 8.5 of the *SRA Authorisation Rules*, or Regulation 4.8 of the *SRA Practising Regulations*, and in relation to a *licensable body* is a reference to its *HOFA*.

collective investment scheme means (in accordance with section 235 of *FSMA* (Collective Investment Schemes)) any arrangements with respect to property of any description, including money, the purpose or effect of which is to enable *persons* taking part in the arrangements (whether by becoming owners of the property or any part of it or otherwise) to participate in or receive profits or income arising from the acquisition, holding, management or disposal of the property or sums paid out of such profits or income, which are not excluded by the Financial Services and Markets Act (Collective Investment Schemes) Order 2001 (SI 2001/1062).

COLP means compliance officer for legal practice in accordance with Rule 8.5 of the *SRA Authorisation Rules* or Regulation 4.8 of the *SRA Practising Regulations*, and in relation to a *licensable body* is a reference to its *HOLP*.

Companies Acts means the Companies Act 1985 and the Companies Act 2006.

company means a company incorporated in an *Establishment Directive state* and registered under the *Companies Acts* or a *societas Europaea*.

competing for the same objective for the purposes of Chapter 3 of the *SRA Code of Conduct* means any situation in which two or more *clients* are competing for an "objective" which, if attained by one *client*, will make that "objective" unattainable to the other *client* or *clients*, and "objective" means, for the purposes of Chapter 3, an asset, contract or business opportunity which two or more *clients* are seeking to acquire or recover through a liquidation (or some other form of insolvency process) or by means of an auction or tender process or a bid or offer which is not public.

complaint means an oral or written expression of dissatisfaction which alleges that the complainant has suffered (or may suffer) financial loss, distress, inconvenience or other detriment.

compliance officer is a reference to a body's *COLP* or its *COFA*.

compulsory professional indemnity insurance means the insurance you are required to have in place under the *SIIR*.

CONC means the *FCA's* Consumer Credit sourcebook.

conflict of interests means any situation where:

(i) you owe separate duties to act in the best interests of two or more *clients* in relation to the same or related matters, and those duties conflict, or there is a significant risk that those duties may conflict (a "client conflict"); or

(ii) your duty to act in the best interests of any *client* in relation to a matter conflicts, or there is a significant risk that it may conflict, with your own interests in relation to that or a related matter (an "own interest conflict").

connected person means:

(i) any *associated firm*;

(ii) anyone with whom you are related by blood, marriage or adoption, or with whom you are living together in a civil or domestic partnership;

(iii) any *owner* or *employee* of your *firm* or of an *associated firm*, or anyone with whom that *owner* or *employee* is related by blood, marriage or adoption, or with whom they are living together in a civil or domestic partnership;

(iv) any *company* of which you are a *director* or *employee*, or any *LLP* of which you are a *member* or *employee*, or any *company* in which you, either alone or with any other connected person or persons, are entitled to exercise, or control the exercise of, one-third or more of the voting power at any general meeting;

(v) any *company* of which any of the *persons* mentioned in (i) and (ii) above is a *director* or *employee*, or any *LLP* of which any of them is a *member* or *employee*, or any *company* in which any of them, either alone or with any other connected person or persons, is entitled to exercise, or control the exercise of, one-third or more of the voting power at any general meeting; and

(vi) any other "associate" as defined in section 32 of the Estate Agents Act 1979.

connected practice means a body providing legal services, established outside England and Wales which is not an *overseas practice* or an *excluded body* but is otherwise connected to an *authorised body* in England and Wales, or a *recognised sole practitioner* in England and Wales, by virtue of:

(i) being a parent undertaking, within the meaning of section 1162 of the Companies Act 2006, of the *authorised body*;

(ii) being jointly managed or owned, or having a partner, member or owner in common, or controlled by or, with the *authorised body*;

(iii) participating in a joint enterprise or across its practice generally, sharing costs, revenue or profits related to the provision of legal services with the *authorised body* or *recognised sole practitioner*; or

(iv) common branding;

and in this definition:

(A) a "body" means a natural person or company, limited liability partnership or partnership or other body corporate or unincorporated association or business entity; and

(B) an "excluded body" means a body which is part of:

(I) a Verein or similar group structure involving more than one body providing legal services in respect of which the *authorised body* in England and Wales connected to it is not regarded as being the body which is the headquarters of that Verein or similar group structure or a significant part of it; or

(II) a joint practice, alliance or association or association with the *authorised body* in England and Wales connected to it which is controlled by a body providing legal services outside of England and Wales; or

(III) a group of affiliated bodies providing legal services which is not managed or controlled by an *authorised body* in England and Wales.

(C) A "joint enterprise" means any contractual arrangements between two or more independent bodies which provide legal services, for profit and/or other defined purpose or goal which apply generally between them, not just agreed on a matter by matter basis.

(D) "Common branding" means the use of a name, term, design, symbol, words or a combination of these that identifies two or more legal practices as distinct from other legal practices or an express statement that a legal practice is practising in association with one or more other named firms.

connected with means in relation to a *separate business* for the purpose of Chapter 12 of the *SRA Code of Conduct*:

(i) having one or more *partner(s)*, *owner(s)*, *director(s)* or *member(s)* in common with the *separate business*;

(ii) being a *subsidiary company* of the same *holding company* as the *separate business*; or

(iii) being a *subsidiary company* of the *separate business*.

contract of insurance means (in accordance with article 3(1) of the *Regulated Activities Order*) any contract of insurance which is a *long-term insurance contract* or a *general insurance contract*.

contractually based investment has the meaning given by article 3(1) of the *Regulated Activities Order* but does not include an *investment* which falls within the definition of a packaged product.

contributions means contributions previously made to the *fund* in accordance with Part III of the Solicitors' Indemnity Rules 2007 (or any earlier corresponding provisions), and any additional sums paid in accordance with Rule 16 of the *SRA Indemnity Rules*.

controller has the meaning given in section 422 of *FSMA*.

costs means *your fees* and *disbursements*.

Council has the meaning given in section 87 of the *SA*.

court means any court, tribunal or inquiry of England and Wales, or a British court martial, or any court of another jurisdiction.

Court of Protection deputy

(i) for the purposes of the *SRA Accounts Rules* includes a deputy who was appointed by the Court of Protection as a receiver under the Mental Health Act 1983 before the commencement date of the Mental Capacity Act 2005; and

(ii) for the purposes of the *SRA Authorisation Rules* also includes equivalents in other *Establishment Directive states*.

CPD means continuing professional development, namely, the training requirement(s) set by *us* to ensure *solicitors* and *RELs* maintain competence.

CPD training record means a record of all *CPD* undertaken to comply with the *SRA Training Regulations* Part 3 – CPD Regulations.

CPD year means each year commencing 1 November to 31 October.

CPE means the Common Professional Examination, namely, a course, including assessments and examinations, approved by the JASB for the purposes of completing the *academic stage of training* for those who have not satisfactorily completed a *QLD*.

credit-related regulated activity means any of the following activities specified in Part 2 or 3A of the *Regulated Activities Order*:

   (i)   entering into a regulated credit agreement as lender (article 60B(1);

   (ii) exercising, or having the right to exercise, the lender's rights and duties under a regulated credit agreement (article 60B(2));

   (iii) credit broking (article 36A);

   (iv) debt adjusting (article 39D(1) and (2));

   (v) debt counselling (article 39E(1) and (2));

   (vi) debt collecting (article 39F(1) and (2));

   (vii) debt administration (article 39G(1) and (2));

   (viii) entering into a regulated consumer hire agreement as owner (article 60N(1));

   (ix) exercising, or having the right to exercise, the owner's rights and duties under a regulated consumer hire agreement (article 60N(2));

   (x) providing credit information services (article 89A);

   (xi) providing credit references (article 89B);

   (xii) operating an electronic system in relation to lending (article 36H);

   (xiii) agreeing to carry on a regulated activity (article 64) so far as relevant to any of the activities in (i) to (xii);

which is carried on by way of business and relates to a specified investment applicable to that activity or, in the case of (x) and (xi), relates to information about a person's financial standing.

criminal advocacy means advocacy in all hearings arising out of a police-led or Serious Fraud Office-led investigation and prosecuted in the criminal courts by the Crown Prosecution Service or the Serious Fraud Office but does not include hearings brought under the Proceeds of Crime Act 2002.

date of notification the date of any notification or notice given is deemed to be:

   (i)   the date on which the communication is sent electronically to the recipient's e-mail or fax address;

   (ii) the date on which the communication is delivered to or left at the recipient's last notified *practising address* if the recipient is *practising*, or to the recipient's last notified contact address if the recipient is not *practising*; or

   (iii) seven days after the communication has been sent by post or document exchange to the recipient's last notified *practising address* if the recipient is *practising*, or to the recipient's last notified contact address if the recipient is not *practising*.

decision period is the period specified in Rule 5 of the *SRA Authorisation Rules*.

defaulting practitioner means:

    (i)   a *solicitor* in respect of whose act or default, or in respect of whose *employee's* act or default, an application for a grant is made;

    (ii) an *REL* in respect of whose act or default, or in respect of whose *employee's* act or default, an application for a grant is made;

    (iii) a *recognised body* in respect of whose act or default, or in respect of whose *manager's* or *employee's* act or default, an application for a grant is made;

    (iv) an *RFL* who is a *manager* of a *partnership*, *LLP* or *company* together with a *solicitor*, an *REL* or a *recognised body*, and in respect of whose act or default or in respect of whose *employee's* act or default, an application for a grant is made; or

    (v) a *licensed body* in respect of whose act or default, or in respect of whose *owner's*, or *manager's* or *employee's* act or default, an application for a grant is made;

and the expressions "defaulting solicitor", "defaulting *REL*", "defaulting recognised body", "defaulting *RFL*" and "defaulting licensed body" shall be construed accordingly.

defence costs means legal costs and disbursements and investigative and related expenses reasonably and necessarily incurred with the consent of the *insurer* in:

    (i)   defending any proceedings relating to a *claim*; or

    (ii) conducting any proceedings for indemnity, contribution or recovery relating to a *claim*; or

    (iii) investigating, reducing, avoiding or compromising any actual or potential *claim*; or

    (iv) acting for any *insured* in connection with any investigation, inquiry or disciplinary proceeding (save in respect of any disciplinary proceeding under the authority of the *Society* (including, without limitation, the *SRA* and the *Tribunal*));

and does not include any internal or overhead expenses of the *insured firm* or the *insurer* or the cost of any *insured's* time.

difference in conditions policy means a contract of professional indemnity insurance, made between one or more *participating insurers* and a *firm*, which provides cover including the *MTC* as modified in accordance with paragraph 2 of Appendix 3 to the *SRA Indemnity Insurance Rules*.

director means a director of a company; and in relation to a *societas Europaea* includes:

    (i)   in a two-tier system, a member of the management organ and a member of the supervisory organ; and

    (ii) in a one-tier system, a member of the administrative organ.

disbursement means, in respect of those activities for which the practice is regulated by the *SRA*, any sum spent or to be spent on behalf of the *client* or trust (including any VAT element).

disciplinary decision means a decision, following an *SRA finding*, to exercise one or more of the powers provided by:

(i)   section 44D(2) and (3) of the *SA*;

(ii) paragraph 14B(2) and (3) of Schedule 2 to the *AJA*; or

(iii) section 95 or section 99 of the *LSA*;

or otherwise to give a *regulated person* a written rebuke or to publish details of a written rebuke or a direction to pay a penalty in accordance with the *SRA Disciplinary Procedure Rules*.

discipline investigation means:

(i)   subject to sub-paragraph (ii), an investigation by the *SRA* to determine whether a person should be subject to an *SRA finding*, a *disciplinary decision* or an application to the *Tribunal* under Rule 10 of the *SRA Disciplinary Procedure Rules*; and

(ii) for the purposes of the *SRA Cost of Investigations Regulations*, an investigation by the *SRA* to determine whether a *regulated person* should be subject to an *SRA finding* or an application to the *Tribunal*.

discrimination has the meaning set out in the Equality Act 2010, namely if, because of a protected characteristic as set out in that Act, *person* A treats *person* B less favourably than A treats or would treat others.

disqualified refers to a *person* who has been disqualified under section 99 of the *LSA* by the *SRA* or by any other *approved regulator*,

and references to "disqualify" and "disqualification" should be construed accordingly.

document in Chapter 10 of the *SRA Code of Conduct*, includes documents, whether written or electronic, relating to the *firm's client accounts* and *office accounts*.

EEA means European Economic Area.

EEL means exempt European *lawyer*, namely, a member of an *Establishment Directive profession*:

(i)   registered with the *BSB*; or

(ii) based entirely at an office or offices outside England and Wales,

who is not a *lawyer of England and Wales* (whether entitled to *practise* as such or not).

eligible former principal means a *principal* of a *previous practice* where:

(i) that *previous practice* ceased on or before 31 August 2000; and

(ii) a *relevant claim* is made in respect of any matter which would have given rise to an entitlement of the *principal* to indemnity out of the *fund* under the Solicitors' Indemnity Rules 1999 had the claim been notified to Solicitors Indemnity Fund Limited on 31 August 2000; and

(iii) the *principal* has not at any time been a "principal" of the *relevant successor practice* ("principal" having the meaning applicable to the *SIIR*); and

(iv) at the time that the *relevant claim* is made the *principal* is not a "principal" in "private practice" ("principal" and "private practice" having the meanings applicable to the *SIIR*).

employee means an individual who is:

(i) engaged under a contract of service by a *firm* or its wholly owned service company;

(ii) engaged under a contract for services, made between a *firm* or organisation and:

(A) that individual;

(B) an employment agency; or

(C) a *company* which is not held out to the public as providing legal services and is wholly owned and directed by that individual; or

(iii) a *solicitor*, *REL* or *RFL* engaged under a contract of service or a contract for services by an *authorised non-SRA firm*;

(iv) a *solicitor*, *REL* or *RFL* engaged under a contract of service or a contract for services by a person, business or organisation,

under which the *firm*, *authorised non-SRA firm*, person, business, or organisation has exclusive control over the individual's time for all or part of the individual's working week; or in relation to which the *firm* or organisation has designated the individual as a fee earner in accordance with arrangements between the *firm* or organisation and the Lord Chancellor (or any body established by the Lord Chancellor to provide or facilitate the provision of services) pursuant to the provisions of the Legal Aid, Sentencing and Punishment of Offenders Act 2012, save that:

(A) for the purposes of the *SRA Financial Services (Scope) Rules*, means an individual who is employed in connection with the *firm's regulated activities* under a contract of service or under a contract for services such that he or she is held out as an employee or consultant of the *firm*; and

(B) for the purposes of the *SRA Indemnity Insurance Rules*, means any person other than a *principal*:

(I) employed or otherwise engaged in the *insured firm's practice* (including under a contract for services) including, without limitation, as a *solicitor*, lawyer, *trainee solicitor* or trainee lawyer, consultant, associate, locum tenens, agent, *appointed person*, office or clerical staff member or otherwise;

(II)   seconded to work in the *insured firm's practice*; or

(III) seconded by the *insured firm* to work elsewhere;

but does not include any person who is engaged by the *insured firm* under a contract for services in respect of any work where that person is required, whether under the *SRA Indemnity Insurance Rules* or under the rules of any other professional body, to take out or to be insured under separate professional indemnity insurance in respect of that work.

employer means a:

(i)   *firm* which engages an individual under a contract of service either on its own behalf or through its wholly-owned service company;

(ii) *firm* or organisation which has engaged an individual under a contract for services made between the firm or organisation and:

(A)   that individual;

(B)   an employment agency; or

(C)   a company which is not held out to the public as providing legal services and is wholly owned and directed by that individual; or

(iii) an *authorised non-SRA firm* which engages a *solicitor*, *REL* or *RFL* under a contract of service or a contract for services;

(iv) a person, business or organisation which engages a *solicitor*, *REL* or *RFL* under a contract of service or a contract for services,

under which the *firm*, *authorised non-SRA firm*, person, business or organisation has exclusive control over the individual's time for all or part of the individual's working week; or in relation to which the *firm* or organisation has designated the individual as a fee earner in accordance with arrangements between the *firm* or organisation and the Lord Chancellor (or any body established by the Lord Chancellor to provide or facilitate the provision of services) pursuant to the provisions of the Legal Aid, Sentencing and Punishment of Offenders Act 2012.

entitled to practise for the purposes of the *QLTSR* means having the right to practise without restrictions or conditions as a *qualified lawyer* of the *recognised jurisdiction*.

equivalent means means learning which is assessed and for which qualification(s) or certificates have been granted and/or work based experiential learning which *we* determine is of at least an equivalent level and standard of that required by all or any part of the *solicitor* qualification and training framework as set out in the *SRA Training Regulations*. *We* will assess equivalence in accordance with guidance *we* may issue from time to time.

established

    (i)   For the purpose of the definition of "overseas practice", the status of an individual as being established outside England and Wales may be indicated by any of the following factors:

        (A) a requirement for a work permit;

        (B) the intention to reside outside England and Wales for a period of six months or longer;

        (C) a requirement for authorisation with local regulatory body;

        (D) an overseas practising address nominated in mySRA;

        (E) an employment contract with a legal practice established outside England and Wales.

    (ii) An individual who is temporarily seconded, assigned or transferred to work in an overseas practice, being supervised and managed for the duration of his or her secondment, transfer or assignment, by *managers* in the overseas practice, will be treated as *practising overseas*.

Establishment Directive means the Establishment of Lawyers Directive 98/5/EC.

Establishment Directive profession means any profession listed in Article 1.2(a) of the *Establishment Directive*, including a solicitor, barrister or advocate of the *UK*.

Establishment Directive state means a state to which the *Establishment Directive* applies.

European corporate practice means a *lawyers'* practice which is a body incorporated in an *Establishment Directive state*, or a partnership with separate legal identity formed under the law of an *Establishment Directive state* and which is regulated as a *lawyers'* practice:

    (i)   which has an office in an *Establishment Directive state* but does not have an office in England and Wales;

    (ii) whose ultimate beneficial owners include at least one individual who is not a *lawyer of England and Wales* but is, and is entitled to practise as, a *lawyer* of an *Establishment Directive profession*;

    (iii) whose *managers* include at least one such individual, or at least one *body corporate* whose *managers* include at least one such individual; and

    (iv) of which *lawyers* are entitled to exercise, or control the exercise of, more than 90% of the *voting rights*.

European cross-border practice has the meaning set out in Rule 2.1 of the *SRA European Cross-border Practice Rules*.

excess means the first amount of a *claim* which is not covered by the insurance.

execution-only means a *transaction* which is effected by a *firm* for a *client* where the *firm* assumes on reasonable grounds that the *client* is not relying on the *firm* as to the merits or suitability of that *transaction*.

exempt person in the *SRA Financial Services (Scope) Rules* means a *person* who is exempt from the *general prohibition* as a result of an exemption order made under section 38(1) or as a result of section 39(1) or 285(2) or (3) of *FSMA* and who, in engaging in the activity in question, is acting in the course of business in respect of which that *person* is exempt.

Exempting Law Degree means a *QLD* incorporating an *LPC*, approved by *us*.

existing instructions means instructions to carry out *legal activities* received by a *firm* from a client, which the *firm* has accepted, on terms that have been agreed by the client, prior to the *firm* becoming subject to cover under the *cessation period*.

expired run-off claim means any claim made against the *fund* for indemnity under the *SRA Indemnity Rules* in respect of which no *preceding qualifying insurance* remains in force to cover such claim, by reason only of:

(i) the run-off cover provided or required to be provided under the policy having been activated; and

(ii) the sixth anniversary of the date on which cover under such *qualifying insurance* would have ended but for the activation of such run-off cover having passed; or

(iii) (in the case of a firm in default or a *run-off firm*) the period of run-off cover provided or required to be provided under arrangements made to cover such claim through the *ARP* having expired.

expired run-off cover means either:

(i) (unless (ii) below applies) the terms of the ARP policy in force at the time immediately prior to the date on which run-off cover was triggered under the *preceding qualifying insurance*, excluding clause 5 (Run-off cover) of the *MTC*, as if it were a contract between Solicitors Indemnity Fund Limited and the firm or person making an *expired run-off claim*; or

(ii) where they are provided to Solicitors Indemnity Fund Limited prior to payment of the *claim*, the terms of the *preceding qualifying insurance*, provided that:

(A) references in the *preceding qualifying insurance* to the qualifying insurer that issued such insurance shall be read as references to Solicitors Indemnity Fund Limited;

(B) any obligation owed by any *insured* under the *preceding qualifying insurance* to the qualifying insurer which issued such insurance shall be deemed to be owed to Solicitors Indemnity Fund Limited in place of

Glossary

such qualifying insurer, unless and to the extent that Solicitors Indemnity Fund Limited in its absolute discretion otherwise agrees;

(C) the obligations of the *fund* and/or any *insured* in respect of an *expired run-off claim* shall neither exceed nor be less than the requirements of the *MTC* which, in accordance with the applicable *SIIR*, such *preceding qualifying insurance* included or was required to include.

Solicitors Indemnity Fund Limited shall be under no obligation to take any steps to obtain the terms of any such *preceding qualifying insurance*, which for these purposes includes the terms on which it was written in respect of the *insured firm* or person in question, and not merely a standard policy wording.

extended indemnity period means the period commencing at the end of the *policy period* and ending on the date which is the earlier to occur of:

(i) the date, if any, on which the *firm* obtains a *policy* of *qualifying insurance* incepting on and with effect from the day immediately following the expiration of the *policy period*;

(ii) the date which is 30 days after the end of the *policy period*; or

(iii) the date on which the *insured firm's practice* ceases.

FCA means the Financial Conduct Authority.

fees means *your* own charges or profit costs (including any VAT element).

fee sharer means another *person* or business who or which shares *your* fees.

financial benefit includes any commission, discount or rebate, but does not include your *fees* or interest earned on any *client account*.

financial institution means any undertaking or unincorporated association which carries on a business of lending money (which may include mortgage lending) or otherwise providing or issuing credit including, without limitation, any bank or *building society*.

Financial Services Register means the record maintained by the *FCA* as required by section 347 of *FSMA* and including those *persons* who carry on, or are proposing to carry on, *insurance mediation activities*.

firm means:

(i) save as provided in paragraphs (ii) and (iii) below, an *authorised body*, a *recognised sole practitioner* or a body or *person* which should be authorised by the *SRA* as a *recognised body* or *recognised sole practitioner* (but which could not be authorised by another *approved regulator*); and for the purposes of the *SRA Code of Conduct* and the *SRA Accounts Rules* can also include in-house practice;

(ii) in the *SRA Indemnity Insurance Rules*:

    (A)   any *recognised body* (as constituted from time to time); or

    (B)   any *solicitor* or *REL* who is a *sole practitioner*, unless that *sole practitioner* is a *non-SRA firm*; or

    (C)   any *partnership* (as constituted from time to time) which is eligible to become a *recognised body* and which meets the requirements applicable to *recognised bodies* set out in the *SRA Practice Framework Rules* and the *SRA Authorisation Rules*, unless that *partnership* is a *non-SRA firm*; or

    (D)   any *licensed body* in respect of its *regulated activities*;

    whether before or during any relevant *indemnity period*;

(iii) in the *SRA European Cross-border Practice Rules*, means any business through which a *solicitor* or *REL* carries on *practice* other than *in-house practice*.

firm (overseas) means any business through which a *solicitor* or *REL* carries on practice other than in-house practice.

foreign lawyer means an individual who is not a *solicitor* or barrister of England and Wales, but who is a member, and entitled to practise as such, of a legal profession regulated within a jurisdiction outside England and Wales.

foundations of legal knowledge means those foundations of law the study of which is prescribed by *us* and the *BSB* for the purpose of completing the *academic stage of training* by undertaking a *QLD* or *CPE* and passing the assessments and examinations set during that course.

FSMA means the Financial Services and Markets Act 2000.

full accreditation means *accreditation* to conduct *criminal advocacy* under the *SRA QASA Regulations*, and references to "fully accredited" should be construed accordingly.

full route to qualification means that the applicant has not completed a shortened or fast-track route to qualification, which would be evidenced if non-domestic lawyers are not assessed on all the same outcomes/subjects/practices in the law of that jurisdiction as domestic candidates, prior to qualification.

full time in relation to a period of *recognised training*, means working 32 hours a week or more.

fund means the fund maintained in accordance with the *SRA Indemnity Rules*.

funeral plan contract has the meaning given in article 59 of the *Regulated Activities Order*.

general client account has the meaning given in Rule 13.5(b) of the *SRA Accounts Rules*.

general insurance contract means any *contract of insurance* within Part I of Schedule 1 to the *Regulated Activities Order*.

general prohibition has the meaning given in section 19(2) of *FSMA*.

higher courts means the Crown Court, High Court, Court of Appeal and Supreme Court in England and Wales.

higher courts advocacy qualification means, subject to regulation 6 of the *SRA Higher Rights of Audience Regulations*, one of the qualifications referred to in regulation 3 of those regulations to exercise extended rights of audience in the *higher courts*.

HOFA means a Head of Finance and Administration within the meaning of paragraph 13(2) of Schedule 11 to the *LSA*.

holding company has the meaning given in the Companies Act 2006.

HOLP means a Head of Legal Practice within the meaning of paragraph 11(2) of Schedule 11 to the *LSA*.

home purchaser has the meaning given by article 63F(3) of the *Regulated Activities Order*.

immigration work means the provision of immigration advice and immigration services, as defined in section 82 of the Immigration and Asylum Act 1999.

indemnity period means:

    (i)   in the *SRA Indemnity Insurance Rules*, the period of one year starting on 1 September 2000, 2001 or 2002, the period of 13 calendar months starting on 1 September 2003, or the period of one year starting on 1 October in any subsequent calendar year; and

    (ii) in the *SRA Indemnity Rules*, the period of one year commencing on 1 September in any calendar year from 1987 to 2002 inclusive, the period of 13 calendar months commencing on 1 September 2003, and the period of one year commencing on 1 October in any subsequent calendar year.

independent financial adviser means an adviser who provides unbiased and unrestricted advice based on a comprehensive and fair analysis of the relevant market and discloses this in writing to the *client*.

individual pension contract means a *pension policy* or *pension contract* under which contributions are paid to:

    (i)   a *personal pension scheme* approved under section 630 of the Income and

Corporation Taxes Act 1988, whose sole purpose is the provision of annuities or lump sums under arrangements made by individuals in accordance with the scheme; or

(ii) a retirement benefits scheme approved under section 591(2)(g) of the Income and Corporation Taxes Act 1988, for the provision of relevant benefits by means of an annuity contract made with an insurance company of the *employee's* choice.

in-house practice means *practice* as a *solicitor*, *REL* or *RFL* (as appropriate) in accordance with Rules 1.1(c)(ii), 1.1(d)(ii), 1.1(e), 1.2(f), 2.1(c)(ii), 2.1(d)(ii), 2.1(e), 2.2(f), 3.1(b)(ii) or 3.1(c)(ii) of the *SRA Practice Framework Rules* and "in-house" shall be construed accordingly.

Insolvency Code of Ethics means the Code of Ethics produced by the *Joint Insolvency Committee* and adopted by the *SRA*.

insolvency event means in relation to a *participating insurer*:

(i) the appointment of a provisional liquidator, administrator, receiver or an administrative receiver; or

(ii) the approval of a voluntary arrangement under Part I of the Insolvency Act 1986 or the making of any other form of arrangement, composition or compounding with its creditors generally; or

(iii) the passing of a resolution for voluntary winding up where the winding up is or becomes a creditors' voluntary winding up under Part IV of the Insolvency Act 1986; or

(iv) the making of a winding up order by the court; or

(v) the making of an order by the court reducing the value of one or more of the *participating insurer's* contracts under section 377 of *FSMA*; or

(vi) the occurrence of any event analogous to any of the foregoing insolvency events in any jurisdiction outside England and Wales.

insolvency practice means accepting an appointment or acting as an appointment holder as an insolvency practitioner within the terms of the Insolvency Act 1986 and other related legislation.

insurance mediation activity means any of the following activities specified in the *Regulated Activities Order* which is carried on in relation to a *contract of insurance* or rights to or interests in a *life policy*:

(i) dealing in *investments* as agent;

(ii) arranging (bringing about) deals in *investments*;

(iii) making arrangements with a view to *transactions* in *investments*;

(iv) assisting in the administration and performance of a *contract of insurance*;

(v)   advising on *investments*;

(vi) agreeing to carry on a *regulated activity* in (i) to (v) above.

insurance mediation officer means the individual within the management structure of the *firm* who is responsible for an *insurance mediation activity*.

insurance undertaking means an undertaking, whether or not an *insurer*, which carries on insurance business.

insured in the *SRA Indemnity Insurance Rules* means each person and entity named or described as a person to whom the insurance extends and includes, without limitation, those referred to in clause 1.3 in the *MTC* and, in relation to *prior practices* and *successor practices* respectively, those referred to in clauses 1.5 and 1.7 of the *MTC*.

insured firm means the *firm* (as defined for the purposes of the *SRA Indemnity Insurance Rules*) which contracted with the *insurer* to provide the insurance.

insured firm's practice means:

(i)   the legal *practice* carried on by the *insured firm* as at the commencement of the *period of insurance*; and

(ii) the continuous legal *practice* preceding and succeeding the *practice* referred to in paragraph (i) (irrespective of changes in ownership of the *practice* or in the composition of any *partnership* which owns or owned the *practice*).

insurer means:

(i)   for the purposes of the SRA Financial Services (Conduct of Business) Rules 2001 a firm with permission to effect or carry out *contracts of insurance* (other than a bank); and

(ii) for the purposes of the *SRA Indemnity Insurance Rules* the underwriter(s) of the insurance.

interest includes a sum in lieu of interest.

interest holder means a *person* who has an interest or an indirect interest, or holds a *material interest*, in a body (and "indirect interest" and "interest" have the same meaning as in the *LSA*), and references to "holds an interest" shall be construed accordingly.

international lawyers means lawyers who are not basing their application on a professional qualification as a *qualified lawyer* gained within the *UK* or within the EEA or Switzerland.

intervened practitioner means the *solicitor*, *recognised body*, *licensed body*, *REL* or *RFL* whose *practice* or *practices* are the subject of an *intervention*.

intervention means the exercise of the powers specified in section 35 of and Schedule 1 to the *SA*, or section 9 of and paragraphs 32 to 35 of Schedule 2 to the *AJA*, or section 89 of and paragraph 5 of Schedule 14 to the Courts and Legal Services Act 1990, or section 102 of and Schedule 14 to the *LSA*.

introducer means any person, business or organisation who or that introduces or refers *clients* to your business, or recommends your business to *clients* or otherwise puts you and *clients* in touch with each other.

investment means any of the *investments* specified in Part III of the *Regulated Activities Order*.

investment trust means a closed-ended *company* which is listed in the *UK* or another member state and:

(i)   is approved by HM Revenue and Customs under section 842 of the Income and Corporation Taxes Act 1988 (or, in the case of a newly formed *company*, has declared its intention to conduct its affairs so as to obtain approval); or

(ii) is resident in another member state and would qualify for approval if resident and listed in the *UK*.

investment trust savings scheme means a dedicated service for investment in the securities of one or more *investment trusts* within a particular marketing group (and references to an "investment trust savings scheme" include references to securities to be acquired through that scheme).

ISA means an Individual Savings Account, namely, an account which is a scheme of investment satisfying the conditions prescribed in the Individual Savings Account Regulations 1998 (S.I. 1998/1870).

Joint Insolvency Committee means the Committee formed by the Insolvency Service, the recognised professional bodies under the Insolvency Act 1986 and other related legislation, and appointed lay representatives.

Joint Statement means the Joint Statement on Qualifying Law Degrees, prepared jointly by *us* and the *BSB*, setting out the conditions a law degree course must meet in order to be recognised by *us* as a *QLD*.

knowledge of any matter, includes any matter of which you may reasonably be expected to have knowledge.

LASPO means the Legal Aid, Sentencing and Punishment of Offenders Act 2012.

lawyer means a member of one of the following professions, entitled to practise as such:

(i)   the profession of solicitor, barrister or advocate of the *UK*;

(ii) a profession whose members are authorised to carry on *legal activities* by an *approved regulator* other than the *SRA*;

(iii) an *Establishment Directive profession* other than a *UK* profession;

(iv) a legal profession which has been approved by the *SRA* for the purpose of *recognised bodies* in England and Wales; and

(v) any other regulated legal profession specified by the *SRA* for the purpose of this definition.

lawyer-controlled body means:

(i) an *authorised body* in which *lawyers of England and Wales* constitute the national group of *lawyers* with the largest (or equal largest) share of control of the body either as individual *managers* or by their share in the control of bodies which are *managers*;

(ii) for the purposes of Part 7 (Overseas practice) of the *SRA Accounts Rules* the definition at sub-paragraph (i) above applies save that the second reference to "lawyers" is to be given its natural meaning and the references to *managers* are to be read as *managers (overseas)*.

lawyer of England and Wales means:

(i) a *solicitor*; or

(ii) an individual who is authorised to carry on *legal activities* in England and Wales by an *approved regulator* other than the *SRA*, but excludes a member of an *Establishment Directive profession* registered with the *BSB* under the *Establishment Directive*.

lead insurer means the insurer named as such in the contract of insurance, or, if no lead insurer is named as such, the first-named insurer on the relevant certificate of insurance.

legal activity has the meaning given in section 12 of the *LSA*, and includes any *reserved legal activity* and any other activity which consists of the provision of legal advice or assistance, or representation in connection with the application of the law or resolution of legal disputes.

Legal Ombudsman means the scheme administered by the Office for Legal Complaints under Part 6 of the *LSA*.

legally qualified body means any of the following:

(i) a *recognised body*;

(ii) a *licensed body* of which *lawyers* are entitled to exercise, or control the exercise of, 90% or more of the *voting rights* of that *licensed body*;

(iii) an *authorised non-SRA firm* of which *lawyers* are entitled to exercise, or control the exercise of, 90% or more of the *voting rights* of that *authorised non-SRA firm*; or

(iv) a *European corporate practice*,

and for the purposes of section 9A(6)(h) and (6C) of the *AJA* means a body which would meet the requirement in Rule 13.2 of the *SRA Practice Framework Rules*.

legal services body means a body which meets the criteria in Rule 13 (Eligibility criteria and fundamental requirements for recognised bodies) of the *SRA Practice Framework Rules*.

licensable body means a body which meets the criteria in Rule 14 (Eligibility criteria and fundamental requirements for licensed bodies) of the *SRA Practice Framework Rules*.

licensed body means a body licensed by the *SRA* under Part 5 of the *LSA*.

licensing authority means an *approved regulator* which is designated as a licensing authority under Part 1 of Schedule 10 to the *LSA*, and whose licensing rules have been approved for the purposes of the *LSA*.

life office means a *person* with permission to effect or carry out *long-term insurance contracts*.

life policy means a *long-term insurance contract* other than a *pure protection contract* or a *reinsurance contract*, but including a *pension policy*.

LLP means a limited liability partnership incorporated under the Limited Liability Partnerships Act 2000.

local authority means any of those bodies which are listed in section 270 of the Local Government Act 1972 or in section 21(1) of the Local Government and Housing Act 1989.

long-term care insurance contract has the meaning given in Part II of Schedule 1 to the *Regulated Activities Order*.

long-term insurance contract has the meaning given in Part II of Schedule 1 to the *Regulated Activities Order*.

LPC means a Legal Practice Course, namely, a course, the satisfactory completion of which is recognised by *us* as satisfying, in part, the vocational stage of training.

LSA means the Legal Services Act 2007.

manager means:

    (i)   a *member* of an *LLP*;

    (ii) a *director* of a *company*;

    (iii) a *partner* in a *partnership*; or

    (iv) in relation to any other body, a member of its governing body.

manager (overseas) means:

    (i)   a member of an *LLP*;

    (ii) a director of a company;

    (iii) a *partner* in a *partnership*; or

    (iv) in relation to any other body, a member of its governing body.

market making means where a *firm* holds itself out as willing, as principal, to buy, sell or subscribe for *investments* of the kind to which the *transaction* relates at prices determined by the *firm* generally and continuously rather than in respect of each particular *transaction*.

master policy means a policy referred to in Rule 5 of the *SRA Indemnity Rules*.

master policy insurer means an insurer under a *master policy*.

material interest has the meaning given to it in Schedule 13 to the *LSA*; and a person holds a "material interest" in a body ("B"), if that person:

    (i)   holds at least 10% of the shares in B;

    (ii) is able to exercise significant influence over the management of B by virtue of the person's shareholding in B;

    (iii) holds at least 10% of the shares in a parent undertaking ("P") of B;

    (iv) is able to exercise significant influence over the management of P by virtue of the person's shareholding in P;

    (v) is entitled to exercise, or control the exercise of, voting power in B which, if it consists of *voting rights*, constitutes at least 10% of the *voting rights* in B;

    (vi) is able to exercise significant influence over the management of B by virtue of the person's entitlement to exercise, or control the exercise of, *voting rights* in B;

    (vii) is entitled to exercise, or control the exercise of, voting power in P which, if it consists of *voting rights*, constitutes at least 10% of the *voting rights* in P; or

    (viii)is able to exercise significant influence over the management of P by virtue of the person's entitlement to exercise, or control the exercise of, *voting rights* in P;

and for the purpose of this definition, "person" means:

    (i)   the *person*,

    (ii) any of the *person's* associates, or

    (iii) the *person* and any of the *person's* associates taken together;

and "parent undertaking" and "voting power" are to be construed in accordance with paragraphs 3 and 5 of Schedule 13 to the *LSA*.

MDP means a *licensed body* which is a multi-disciplinary practice providing a range of different services, only some of which are regulated by the *SRA*.

member

(i) means:

(A) in relation to a *company*, a *person* who has agreed to be a member of the *company* and whose name is entered in the *company's* register of members; and

(B) in relation to an *LLP*, a member of that *LLP*; save that

(ii) for the purposes of the *SRA Indemnity Rules*, means a member of a practice, being:

(A) any principal (including any *principal*) therein;

(B) any *director* or officer thereof, in the case of a *recognised body* or a *licensed body* which is a *company*;

(C) any member thereof in the case of a *recognised body* or a *licensed body* which is an *LLP*;

(D) any *recognised body* or a *licensed body* which is a *partner* or held out to be a *partner* therein and any officer of such *recognised body* or a *licensed body* which is a *company*, or any member of such *recognised body* or a *licensed body* which is an *LLP*;

(E) any person employed in connection therewith (including any *trainee solicitor*);

(F) any *solicitor* or *REL* who is a consultant to or associate in the practice;

(G) any *foreign lawyer* who is not an *REL* and who is a consultant or associate in the practice; and

(H) any *solicitor* or *foreign lawyer* who is working in the practice as an agent or locum tenens, whether he or she is so working under a contract of service or contract for services;

and includes the estate and/or personal representative(s) of any such persons.

members of the public for the purposes of Chapter 8 of the *SRA Code of Conduct*, does not include:

(i) a current or former *client*;

(ii) another *firm* or its *manager*;

(iii) an existing or potential professional or business connection; or

(iv) a commercial organisation or public body.

mixed payment has the meaning given in Rule 18.1 of the *SRA Accounts Rules*.

MTC means the minimum terms and conditions with which a *policy* of *qualifying insurance* is required by the *SRA Indemnity Insurance Rules* to comply, a copy of which is annexed as Appendix 1 to those Rules.

non-lawyer means:

(i) an individual who is not a *lawyer* practising as such; or

(ii) a *body corporate* or *partnership* which is not:

    (A) an *authorised body*;

    (B) an *authorised non-SRA firm*; or

    (C) a business, carrying on the practice of *lawyers* from an office or offices outside England and Wales, in which a controlling majority of the *owners* and *managers* are *lawyers*;

save in Part 7 (Overseas) of the *SRA Accounts Rules* where the term "lawyer" is to be given its natural meaning.

non-mainstream regulated activity means a *regulated activity* of a *firm* regulated by the *FCA* in relation to which the conditions in the Professional Firms' Sourcebook (5.2.1R) are satisfied.

non-registered European lawyer means:

(i) in the *SRA Indemnity Rules*, a member of a legal profession which is covered by the *Establishment Directive*, but who is not:

    (A) a *solicitor*, *REL* or *RFL*,

    (B) a barrister of England and Wales, Northern Ireland or the Irish Republic, or

    (C) a Scottish advocate; and

(ii) in the *SRA Financial Services (Scope) Rules*, a member of a profession covered by the *Establishment Directive* who is based entirely at an office or offices outside England and Wales and who is not a solicitor, *REL* or *RFL*.

non-reserved legal activity means a legal activity that falls within section 12(3)(b) of the *LSA*.

non-solicitor employer means any *employer* other than a *recognised body*, *recognised sole practitioner*, *licensed body* or *authorised non-SRA firm*.

non-SRA firm means a *sole practitioner*, *partnership*, *LLP* or *company* which is not authorised to practise by the *SRA*, and which is either:

(i) authorised or capable of being authorised to practise by another *approved regulator*; or

(ii) not capable of being authorised to practise by any *approved regulator*.

occupational pension scheme means any scheme or arrangement which is comprised in one or more documents or agreements and which has, or is capable of having, effect in relation to one or more descriptions or categories of employment so as to provide benefits, in the form of pensions or otherwise, payable on termination of service, or on death or retirement, to or in respect of earners with qualifying service in an employment of any such description or category.

office account means an account of the *firm* for holding *office money* and/or *out-of-scope money*, or other means of holding *office money* or *out-of-scope money* (for example, the office cash box or an account holding money regulated by a regulator other than the *SRA*).

office money has the meaning given in Rule 12 of the *SRA Accounts Rules*.

opt-out means a *transaction* resulting from a decision by an individual to opt-out of or decline to join a final salary or money-purchase *occupational pension scheme* of which he or she is a current member, or which he or she is, or at the end of a waiting period will become, eligible to join, in favour of an *individual pension contract* or contracts.

out-of-scope money means money held or received by an *MDP* in relation to the *MDP's regulated activities*.

overseas means outside England and Wales.

overseas practice

   (i)   means:

      (A)   a branch office of an *authorised body*;

      (B)   a *subsidiary company* of an *authorised body*;

      (C)   a subsidiary undertaking, within the meaning of section 1162 of the Companies Act 2006, of an *authorised body*;

      (D)   an entity whose business, management or ownership are otherwise in fact or law controlled by an *authorised body* or *recognised sole practitioner*;

      (E)   an individual acting as a representative (whether as an employee or agent) of an *authorised body* or *recognised sole practitioner*; or

      (F)   a sole principal whose business, management or ownership are otherwise in fact or law controlled by an *authorised body* or *recognised sole practitioner*,

     established outside England and Wales and providing legal services; and

   (ii) in the *SRA Indemnity Rules* means a *practice* carried on wholly from an *overseas* office or offices, including a *practice* deemed to be a *separate practice* by virtue of paragraph (ii) of the definition of *separate practice*.

own interest conflict for the purpose of Chapter 3 of the *SRA Code of Conduct*, means any situation where your duty to act in the best interests of any *client* in relation to a matter conflicts, or there is a significant risk that it may conflict, with your own interests in relation to that or a related matter.

owner means, in relation to a body, a *person* with any interest in the body, save that:

(i)   in the *SRA Authorisation Rules*, the *SRA Practice Framework Rules* and the *SRA Practising Regulations* owner means any *person* who holds a *material interest* in an *authorised body*, and in the case of a *partnership*, any *partner* regardless of whether they hold a *material interest* in the *partnership*; and

(ii) for the purposes of the *SRA Principles* and the *SRA Code of Conduct* means a *person* who holds a *material interest* in the body; and

(iii) for the purposes of the *SRA Suitability Test* includes owners who have no active role in the running of the business as well as owners who do,

and "own" and "owned by" shall be construed accordingly.

panel solicitors means any solicitors appointed by the Solicitors Indemnity Fund in accordance with Rule 14.15 of the *SRA Indemnity Rules*.

participating insurer means an *authorised insurer* which has entered into a *participating insurer's agreement* with the *Society* which remains in force for the purposes of underwriting new business at the date on which the relevant contract of *qualifying insurance* is made.

participating insurer's agreement means an agreement in such terms as the *Society* may prescribe setting out the terms and conditions on which a *participating insurer* may provide professional indemnity insurance to *solicitors* and others in *private practice* in England and Wales.

partner means a *person* who is or is held out as a partner in a *partnership*.

partnership means a body that is not a *body corporate* in which *persons* are, or are held out as, *partners*, save that in the *MTC* means an unincorporated *insured firm* in which *persons* are or are held out as *partners* and does not include an *insured firm* incorporated as an *LLP*.

participation for the purposes of regulation 8 of the *SRA Training Regulations* Part 3 – CPD Regulations includes preparing, delivering and/or attending accredited courses and "participating" should be construed accordingly.

part-time in relation to a *period of recognised training* means working fewer than 32 hours a week.

payment includes any form of consideration whether any benefit is received by you or by a third party (but does not include the provision of hospitality that is reasonable in the circumstances) and "pay" and "paid" shall be construed accordingly.

pension contract means a right to benefits obtained by the making of contributions to an *occupational pension scheme* or to a *personal pension scheme*, where the contributions are paid to a *regulated collective investment scheme*.

pension policy means a right to benefits obtained by the making of contributions to an *occupational pension scheme* or to a *personal pension scheme*, where the contributions are paid to a *life office*.

pension transfer means a *transaction* resulting from a decision by an individual to transfer deferred benefits from a final salary *occupational pension scheme*, or from a money-purchase *occupational pension scheme*, in favour of an *individual pension contract* or contracts.

PEP means a personal equity plan within the Personal Equity Plan Regulations 1989.

period of insurance means the period for which the insurance operates.

permitted separate business means for the purpose of Chapter 12 of the *SRA Code of Conduct*, a *separate business* offering any of the following services:

(i)   alternative dispute resolution;

(ii) financial services;

(iii) estate agency;

(iv) management consultancy;

(v)   company secretarial services;

(vi) acting as a parliamentary agent;

(vii) practising as a lawyer of another jurisdiction;

(viii)acting as a bailiff;

(ix) acting as nominee, *trustee* or executor outside England and Wales;

(x)   the services of a wholly owned nominee *company* in England and Wales, which is operated as a subsidiary but necessary part of the work of a *separate business* providing financial services;

(xi) providing legal advice or drafting legal documents not included in (i) to (x) above, where such activity is provided as a subsidiary but necessary part of some other service which is one of the main services of the *separate business*; and

(xii) providing any other business, advisory or agency service which could be provided through a *firm* or *in-house practice* but is not a *prohibited separate business activity*.

person includes a body of persons (corporate or unincorporated).

person under investigation means a *person* subject to a *discipline investigation*.

person who has an interest in a licensed body means a *person* who has an interest or an indirect interest in a *licensed body* as defined by sections 72(3) and (5) of the *LSA*.

person who lacks capacity under Part 1 of the Mental Capacity Act 2005 includes a "patient" as defined by section 94 of the Mental Health Act 1983 and a person made the subject of emergency powers under that Act, and equivalents in other *Establishment Directive states*.

personal pension scheme means any scheme or arrangement which is not an *occupational pension scheme* or a *stakeholder pension scheme* and which is comprised in one or more instruments or agreements, having or capable of having effect so as to provide benefits to or in respect of people on retirement, or on having reached a particular age, or on termination of service in an employment.

plan provider has the meaning given by article 63B(3) of the *Regulated Activities Order* read with paragraphs (7) and (8) of that article.

policy means a contract of professional indemnity insurance made between one or more *persons*, each of which is a *participating insurer*, and a *firm*.

policy default

    (i)   means in the *SRA Indemnity Insurance Rules* a failure on the part of a *firm* or any *principal* of that *firm*:

        (A)   to pay for more than two months after the due date for payment all or any part of the premium or any other sum due in respect of a *policy*; or

        (B)   to reimburse within two months a *participating insurer* in respect of any amount falling within a *firm's policy* excess which has been paid on an *insured's* behalf to a *claimant* by a *participating insurer*;

    (ii) for the purposes of this definition, the due date for payment means, in respect of any *policy* or any payment to be made under any *policy*:

        (A)   the date on which such payment fell due under the terms of the *policy* or any related agreement or arrangement; or

        (B)   if a *firm* was first required under the *SIIR* to effect such a *policy* prior to the date on which it did so, the date if earlier on which such payment would have fallen due had such *policy* been effected by the *firm* when it was first required to do so under the *SIIR*.

policy period means the *period of insurance* in respect of which risks may attach under a *policy*, but excluding the *extended indemnity period* and the *cessation period*.

practice means the activities, in that capacity, of:

    (i)   a *solicitor*;

    (ii) an *REL*, from an office or offices within the *UK*;

(iii) a member of an *Establishment Directive profession* registered with the *BSB* under the *Establishment Directive*, carried out from an office or offices in England and Wales;

(iv) an *RFL*, from an office or offices within England and Wales, as:

  (A) an *employee* of a *recognised sole practitioner*; or

  (B) a *manager, employee, member* or *interest holder* of an *authorised body* or a *manager, employee* or owner of an *authorised non-SRA firm*;

(v) an *authorised body*;

(vi) a *manager* of an *authorised body*;

(vii) a person employed in England and Wales by an *authorised body* or *recognised sole practitioner*;

(viii) a *lawyer of England and Wales*; or

(ix) an *authorised non-SRA firm*;

and "practise" and "practising" should be construed accordingly; save for in:

(i) the *SRA Indemnity Insurance Rules* where "practice" means the whole or such part of the *private practice* of a *firm* as is carried on from one or more offices in England and Wales;

(ii) the *SRA Indemnity Rules* where it means a practice to the extent that:

  (A) in relation to a *licensed body*, it carries on *regulated activities*; and

  (B) in all other cases, it carries on *private practice* providing professional services as a sole *solicitor* or *REL* or as a *partnership* of a type referred to in Rule 6.1(d) to 6.1(f) and consisting of or including one or more *solicitors* and/or *RELs*, and shall include the business or practice carried on by a *recognised body* in the providing of professional services such as are provided by individuals practising in *private practice* as *solicitors* and/or *RELs* or by such individuals in *partnership* with *RFLs*, whether such practice is carried on by the *recognised body* alone or in *partnership* with one or more *solicitors*, *RELs* and/or other *recognised bodies*; and

(iii) in the *SRA Overseas Rules* where it shall be given its natural meaning.

practice from an office includes *practice* carried on:

(i) from an office at which you are based; or

(ii) from an office of a *firm* in which you are the *sole practitioner*, or a *manager*, or in which you have an ownership interest, even if you are not based there,

save that for the purposes of Part 7 (Overseas) of the *SRA Accounts Rules* the term "practice" is to be given its natural meaning, and references to "firm" and "manager" are to be read as references to "*firm (overseas)*" and to "*manager (overseas)*";

and "practising from an office" and "practises from an office" should be construed accordingly.

practice of a lawyer of a CCBE state means the activities of a *lawyer* of a *CCBE state* in that capacity.

Practice Skills Standards means the standards published by *us* which set out the practice skills *trainees* will develop during the *period of recognised training* and use when qualified.

practising address means, in relation to an *authorised body*, an address from which the body provides services consisting of or including the carrying on of activities which it is authorised to carry on.

practising overseas means the conduct of a practice:

(i) of an overseas practice;

(ii) of a manager, member or owner of an overseas practice in that capacity;

(iii) of a solicitor *established* outside England and Wales for the purpose of providing legal services in an overseas jurisdiction; and

(iv) of an REL *established* in Scotland or Northern Ireland for the purpose of providing legal services in those jurisdictions.

preceding qualifying insurance means, in the case of any *firm* or person who makes an *expired run-off claim*, the policy of *qualifying insurance* which previously provided run-off cover in respect of that *firm* or person, or which was required to provide such cover, or (in the case of a firm in default or a *run-off firm*) arrangements to provide such run-off cover through the *ARP*.

pre-contract deposit means the aggregate of all payments which constitute pre-contract deposits from a *buyer* in relation to the proposed sale of a *property*.

prescribed means prescribed by the *SRA* from time to time.

previous practice means any *practice* which shall have ceased to exist as such for whatever reason, including by reason of:

(i) any death, retirement or addition of *principals*; or

(ii) any split or cession of the whole or part of its practice to another without any change of *principals*.

previous regulations in the *SRA Higher Rights of Audience Regulations* means either the Higher Courts Qualification Regulations 1992, the Higher Courts Qualification Regulations 1998, or the Higher Courts Qualification Regulations 2000, or the Solicitors Higher Rights of Audience Regulations 2010.

principal

(i) subject to paragraphs (ii) to (iv) means:

    (A) a *sole practitioner*;

    (B) a *partner* in a *partnership*;

    (C) in the case of a *recognised body* which is an *LLP* or *company*, the *recognised body* itself;

    (D) in the case of a *licensed body* which is an *LLP* or *company*, the *licensed body* itself;

    (E) the principal *solicitor* or *REL* (or any one of them) employed by a *non-solicitor employer* (for example, in a law centre or in commerce and industry); or

    (F) in relation to any other body, a member of its governing body;

(ii) in the *SRA Authorisation Rules*, *SRA Practice Framework Rules* and *SRA Practising Regulations*, means a *sole practitioner* or a *partner* in a *partnership*;

(iii) in the *SRA Indemnity Insurance Rules* means:

    (A) where the *firm* is or was:

        (I) a *sole practitioner* – that practitioner;

        (II) a *partnership* – each *partner*;

        (III) a *company* with a share capital – each *director* of that *company* and any *person* who:

            (01) is held out as a *director*; or

            (02) beneficially owns the whole or any part of a share in the *company*; or

            (03) is the ultimate beneficial owner of the whole or any part of a share in the *company*;

        (IV) a *company* without a share capital – each *director* of that *company* and any *person* who:

            (01) is held out as a *director*; or

            (02) is a *member* of the *company*; or

            (03) is the ultimate owner of the whole or any part of a *body corporate* or other legal person which is a *member* of the *company*;

        (V) an *LLP* – each *member* of that *LLP*, and any *person* who is the ultimate owner of the whole or any part of a *body corporate* or other legal person which is a *member* of the *LLP*;

    (B) where a *body corporate* or other legal person is a *partner* in the *firm*, any *person* who is within paragraph (A)(III) of this definition (including sub-paragraphs (01) and (03) thereof), paragraph (A)(IV) of this definition (including sub-paragraphs (01) and (03) thereof), or paragraph (A)(V) of this definition;

(iv) in the *SRA Indemnity Rules*, means:

(A) a *solicitor* who is a *partner* or a sole *solicitor* within the meaning of section 87 of the *SA*, or an *REL* who is a *partner*, a *recognised body* or who on or before 31 March 2012 or the date on which an order made pursuant to section 69 of the *LSA* relating to the status of *sole practitioners* coming into force, whichever was the latter, was a sole practitioner, or an *RFL* or *non-registered European lawyer* who is a *partner*, and includes any *solicitor*, *REL*, *RFL* or *non-registered European lawyer* held out as a principal; and

(B) additionally in relation to a *practice* carried on by a *recognised body* or a *licensed body* alone, or a *practice* in which a *recognised body* or a *licensed body* is or is held out to be a *partner*:

(I) a *solicitor*, *REL*, *RFL* or *non-registered European lawyer* (and in the case of a *licensed body* any other person) who:

(01) beneficially owns the whole or any part of a share in such *recognised body* or *licensed body* (in each case, where it is a *company* with a share capital); or

(02) is a member of such *recognised body* or *licensed body* (in each case, where it is a *company* without a share capital or an *LLP* or a *partnership* with legal personality); or

(II) a *solicitor*, *REL*, *RFL* or *non-registered European lawyer* (and in the case of a *licensed body* any other person) who is:

(01) the ultimate beneficial owner of the whole or any part of a share in such *recognised body* or *licensed body* (in each case, where the *recognised* body or *licensed body* is a *company* with a share capital); or

(02) the ultimate owner of a member or any part of a member of such *recognised body* or *licensed body* (in each case, where the *recognised body* or *licensed body* is a *company* without a share capital or an *LLP* or a *partnership* with legal personality).

prior practice means each *practice* to which the *insured firm's practice* is ultimately a *successor practice* by way of one or more mergers, acquisitions, absorptions or other transitions, but does not include any such *practice* which has elected to be insured under run-off cover in accordance with clause 5.6(a) of the *MTC*.

private legal practice means the provision of services in *private practice* as a *solicitor* or *REL* including, without limitation:

(i)   providing such services in England, Wales or anywhere in the world, whether alone or with other lawyers in a *partnership* permitted to practise in England and Wales by Rule 12 of the Solicitors' Code of Conduct 2007 or by the *SRA Practice Framework Rules*, a *recognised body* or a *licensed body* (in respect of its *regulated activities*); and

(ii) the provision of such services as a secondee of the *insured firm*; and

(iii) any *insured* acting as a personal representative, *trustee*, attorney, notary, insolvency practitioner or in any other role in conjunction with a *practice*; and

(iv) the provision of such services by any *employee*; and

(v)   the provision of such services pro bono publico;

but does not include:

(vi) practising as an *employee* of an employer other than a *solicitor*, an *REL*, a *partnership* permitted to practise in England and Wales by Rule 12 of the Solicitors' Code of Conduct 2007 or by the *SRA Practice Framework Rules*, a *recognised body* or a *licensed body* (in respect of its *regulated activities*); or

(vii) discharging the functions of any of the following offices or appointments:

    (A)   judicial office;

    (B)   Under Sheriffs;

    (C)   members and clerks of such tribunals, committees, panels and boards as the *Council* may from time to time designate but including those subject to the Tribunals and Inquiries Act 1992, the Competition Commission, Legal Services Commission Review Panels, Legal Aid Agency Review Panels and Parole Boards;

    (D)   Justices' Clerks; or

    (E)   Superintendent Registrars and Deputy Superintendent Registrars of Births, Marriages and Deaths and Registrars of Local Crematoria.

private loan means a loan other than one provided by an institution which provides loans on standard terms in the normal course of its activities.

private practice

(i)   for the purposes of the *SRA Indemnity Insurance Rules*:

    (A)   in relation to a *firm* which is a *licensed body* means its *regulated activities*; and

    (B)   subject to paragraph (A) of this definition, in relation to all *firms* includes without limitation all the professional services provided by the *firm* including acting as a personal representative, trustee, attorney, notary, insolvency practitioner or in any other role in conjunction with a *practice*, and includes services provided pro bono publico, but does not include:

(C) *practice* carried on by a *solicitor* or *REL* in the course of employment with an employer other than a *firm*; or

(D) *practice* carried on through a *non-SRA firm*; or

(E) discharging the functions of any of the following offices or appointments:

    (I) judicial office;

    (II) Under Sheriffs;

    (III) members and clerks of such tribunals, committees, panels and boards as the *Council* may from time to time designate but including those subject to the Tribunals and Inquiries Act 1992, the Competition Commission, Legal Services Commission Review Panels, Legal Aid Agency Review Panels and Parole Boards;

    (IV) Justices' Clerks;

    (V) Superintendent Registrars and Deputy Superintendent Registrars of Births, Marriages and Deaths and Registrars of Local Crematoria; or

    (VI) such other offices as the *Council* may from time to time designate;

(F) *practice* consisting only of providing professional services without remuneration for friends, relatives, or to companies wholly owned by the *solicitor* or *REL's* family, or registered charities; or

(G) in respect of a sole *solicitor* or a sole *REL*, *practice* consisting only of:

    (I) providing professional services without remuneration for friends, relatives, or to companies wholly owned by the *solicitor* or *REL's* family, or registered charities; and/or

    (II) administering oaths and statutory declarations; and/or

    (III) activities which could constitute *practice* but are done in the course of discharging the functions of any of the offices or appointments listed in paragraphs (E)(I) to (VI) above.

(ii) for the purposes of the *SRA Indemnity Rules* "private practice" shall be deemed to include:

(A) the acceptance and performance of obligations as trustees; and

(B) notarial practice where a solicitor notary operates such notarial practice in conjunction with a solicitor's practice, whether or not the notarial fees accrue to the benefit of the solicitor's practice;

but does not include:

(C) practice to the extent that any fees or other income accruing do not accrue to the benefit of the *practice* carrying on such practice (except as provided by paragraph (B) in this definition);

(D) practice by a *solicitor* or *REL* in the course of his or her employment with an employer other than a *solicitor*, *REL*, *recognised body*, *licensed body* or *partnership* such as is referred to in Rule 6.1(d) to 6.1(f); in which connection and for the avoidance of doubt:

  (I) any such *solicitor* or *REL* does not carry on private practice when he or she acts in the course of his or her employment for persons other than his or her employer;

  (II) any such *solicitor* or *REL* does not carry on private practice merely because he or she uses in the course of his or her employment a style of stationery or description which appears to hold him or her out as a *principal* or *solicitor* or *foreign lawyer* in private practice; or

  (III) any practice carried on by such a *solicitor* outside the course of his or her employment will constitute private practice;

(E) discharging the functions of the following offices:

  (I) judicial office;

  (II) Under Sheriffs;

  (III) members and clerks of such tribunals, committees, panels and boards as the *Council* may from time to time designate but including those subject to the Tribunals and Inquiries Act 1992, the Competition Commission, Legal Services Commission Review Panels and Parole Boards;

  (IV) Justices' Clerks;

  (V) Superintendent Registrars and Deputy Superintendent Registrars of Births, Marriages and Deaths and Registrars of Local Crematoria;

  (VI) such other offices as the *Council* may from time to time designate.

professional activity means a professional activity which is regulated by the *SRA*.

professional contact means professional contact which is regulated by the *SRA*.

professional disbursement means, in respect of those activities for which the practice is regulated by the *SRA*, the fees of counsel or other *lawyer*, or of a professional or other agent or expert instructed by *you*, including the fees of interpreters, translators, process servers, surveyors and estate agents but not travel agents' charges.

professional principles are as set out in section 1(3) of the *LSA*:

  (i) that authorised persons should act with independence and integrity;

(ii) that authorised persons should maintain proper standards of work;

(iii) that authorised persons should act in the best interests of their *clients*;

(iv) that persons who exercise before any *court* a right of audience, or conduct litigation in relation to proceedings in any *court*, by virtue of being authorised persons should comply with their duty to the *court* to act with independence in the interests of justice; and

(v) that the affairs of *clients* should be kept confidential,

and in this definition "authorised persons" has the meaning set out in section 18 of the *LSA*.

professional services means, for the purposes of the *SRA Financial Services (Scope) Rules*, services provided by a *firm* in the course of its *practice* and which do not constitute carrying on a *regulated activity*.

prohibited referral fee means

(i) a *payment* prohibited by section 56 of *LASPO*; or

(ii) a *payment* made to or by you which appears to the *SRA* to be a referral fee for the purposes of section 57(7) of *LASPO*, unless you show that the *payment* was made as consideration for the provision of services or for another reason and not as a referral fee.

prohibited separate business activities means, for the purpose of Chapter 12 of the *SRA Code of Conduct*:

(i) the conduct of any matter which could come before a *court*, whether or not proceedings are started;

(ii) advocacy before a *court*;

(iii) instructing counsel in any part of the *UK*;

(iv) *immigration work*;

(v) any activity in relation to conveyancing, applications for probate or letters of administration, or drawing *trust* deeds or *court* documents, which is reserved to *solicitors* and others under the *LSA*;

(vi) drafting wills;

(vii) acting as a nominee, *trustee* or executor in England and Wales, except for the services of a wholly owned nominee *company* where such services are provided as a subsidiary but necessary part of the work of a *separate business* providing financial services; and

(viii) providing legal advice or drafting legal documents not included in (i) to (vii) above where such activity is not provided as a subsidiary but necessary part of some other service which is one of the main services of the *separate business*.

property includes an interest in property.

property selling means things done by any person in the course of a business (including a business in which they are *employed*) pursuant to instructions received from another person (in this definition referred to as the "*client*") who wishes to dispose of or acquire an interest in land:

(i)   for the purpose of, or with a view to, effecting the introduction to the *client* of a third person who wishes to acquire or, as the case may be, dispose of such an interest; and

(ii) after such an introduction has been effected in the course of that business, for the purpose of securing the disposal or, as the case may be, the acquisition of that interest.

provisional accreditation means accreditation to conduct *criminal advocacy* under the *SRA QASA Regulations* but which requires further steps to be taken to obtain *full accreditation*, and references to "provisionally accredited" should be construed accordingly.

PSC means the Professional Skills Course, namely, a course normally completed during the training contract, building upon the *LPC*, providing training in Financial and Business Skills, Advocacy and Communication Skills, and Client Care and Professional Standards. Satisfactory completion of the PSC is recognised by *us* as satisfying, in part, the vocational stage of training.

publicity includes all promotional material and activity, including the name or description of your *firm*, stationery, advertisements, brochures, websites, directory entries, media appearances, promotional press releases, and direct approaches to potential *clients* and other *persons*, whether conducted in person, in writing, or in electronic form, but does not include press releases prepared on behalf of a *client*.

pure protection contract means:

(i)   a *long-term insurance contract*:

(A) under which the benefits are payable only in respect of death or of incapacity due to injury, sickness or infirmity;

(B) which has no surrender value or the consideration consists of a single premium and the surrender value does not exceed that premium; and

(C) which makes no provision for its conversion or extension in a manner which would result in its ceasing to comply with (A) or (B); or

(ii) a *reinsurance contract* covering all or part of a risk to which a *person* is exposed under a *long-term insurance contract*.

QASA means the Quality Assurance Scheme for Advocates (Crime) developed by the Joint Advocacy Group and described in full in the QASA Handbook published from time to time and available at: **http://www.sra.org.uk**.

QLD means a qualifying law degree, namely, a degree or qualification awarded by a body approved by the JASB for the purposes of completing the *academic stage of training*, following a course of study which includes:

    (i)   the study of the *foundations of legal knowledge*; and

    (ii) the passing of appropriate assessments set in those foundations.

QLTR means the Qualified Lawyers Transfer Regulations 1990 and 2009.

QLTR certificate of eligibility means a certificate issued under the *QLTR*.

QLTSR means the *SRA* Qualified Lawyers Transfer Scheme Regulations 2010 and 2011.

QLTT means the Qualified Lawyers Transfer Test, namely, the test which some lawyers are required to pass under the *QLTR*.

QLTS assessments means the suite of assessments approved by *us* and provided by the *assessment organisation*.

QLTS certificate of eligibility means a certificate of eligibility to take the *QLTS assessments* under the *QLTSR*, or an authorisation under the *QLTSR* to apply for admission as a *solicitor* without taking any of the *QLTS assessments*.

qualified lawyer means either:

    (i)   a lawyer whose qualification *we* have determined:

        (A)   gives the lawyer rights of audience;

        (B)   makes the lawyer an officer of the court in the *recognised jurisdiction*; and

        (C)   has been awarded as a result of a generalist (non-specialist) legal education and training; or

    (ii) any other lawyer to whom *we* determine Directive 2005/36/EC on the recognition of professional qualifications applies.

qualified to supervise means a person complying with the requirements of Rule 12.2 of the *SRA Practice Framework Rules*.

qualifying insurance means a single *policy* which includes the *MTC*, or more than one *policy* which, taken together, include the *MTC*, and each of which includes the *MTC* except only in relation to the *sum insured*.

re-accreditation means the process by which a *solicitor* or an *REL* demonstrates their competence and renews their *accreditation* under the *SRA QASA Regulations* at their existing level for a further five years.

recognised body means a body recognised by the *SRA* under section 9 of the *AJA*.

recognised jurisdiction means a jurisdiction where *we* have determined that:

(i) to become a *qualified lawyer* applicants have completed specific education and training at a level that is at least equivalent to that of an English/Welsh H-Level (e.g. Bachelor's) degree;

(ii) members of the *qualified lawyer's* profession are bound by an ethical code that requires them to act without conflicts of interest and to respect their client's interests and confidentiality; and

(iii) members of the *qualified lawyer's* profession are subject to disciplinary sanctions for breach of their ethical code, including the removal of the right to practise, and

all European jurisdictions to which Directive 2005/36/EC on the recognition of professional qualifications apply are "recognised jurisdictions" for the purposes of the *QLTSR*.

recognised sole practitioner means a *solicitor* or *REL* authorised by the *SRA* under section 1B of the *SA* to practise as a *sole practitioner*.

recognised training means training required under *SRA Training Regulations* Regulation 5.1, and "period of recognised training" and "recognise training" should be construed accordingly.

reconciled accounts means that all elements of the accounting records of an *intervened practitioner's practice* are consistent with each other.

reconciled list means a list of beneficial entitlements to *statutory trust monies* created from a set of *reconciled accounts*.

record of training means a record created and maintained by a *trainee*, which contains details of the work he or she has performed, how the *trainee* has acquired, applied and developed his or her skills by reference to the *Practice Skills Standards* and the *Principles*, and the *trainee's* reflections on his or her performance and development plans, and is verified by the individual(s) supervising the *trainee*.

referral includes any situation in which another person, business or organisation introduces or refers a *client* to your business, recommends your business to a *client* or otherwise puts you and a *client* in touch with each other.

register of European lawyers means the register of European lawyers maintained by the *SRA* under regulation 15 of the European Communities (Lawyer's Practice) Regulations 2000 (SI 2000/1119).

register of foreign lawyers means the register of foreign lawyers maintained by the *SRA* under the Courts and Legal Services Act 1990.

regular payment has the meaning given in Rule 19 of the *SRA Accounts Rules*.

Regulated Activities Order means the Financial Services and Markets Act 2000 (Regulated Activities) Order 2001.

regulated activity means:

> (i) subject to sub-paragraph (ii) below:
>
>> (A) any *reserved legal activity*;
>>
>> (B) any *non-reserved legal activity* except, in relation to an *MDP*, any such activity that is excluded on the terms of the licence;
>>
>> (C) any other activity in respect of which a *licensed body* is regulated pursuant to Part 5 of the *LSA*; and
>
> (ii) in the *SRA Financial Services (Scope) Rules*, an activity which is specified in the *Regulated Activities Order*.

regulated collective investment scheme means:

> (i) an investment *company* with variable capital;
>
> (ii) an authorised unit trust scheme as defined in section 237(3) of *FSMA*; or
>
> (iii) a scheme recognised under sections 264, 270 or 272 of *FSMA*.

regulated home purchase plan has the meaning given by article 63F(3) of the *Regulated Activities Order*.

regulated home reversion plan has the meaning given by article 63B(3) of the *Regulated Activities Order*.

regulated individual means:

> (i) a solicitor;
>
> (ii) an REL; and
>
> (iii) a manager, member or owner of an *overseas practice*.

regulated mortgage contract has the meaning given by article 61(3) of the *Regulated Activities Order*.

regulated person

> (i) in the *SRA Indemnity Rules* has the meaning given in section 21 of the *LSA*;
>
> (ii) means, in the *SRA Disciplinary Procedure Rules*:
>
>> (A) a *solicitor*;
>>
>> (B) an *REL*;
>>
>> (C) an *RFL*;

(D) a *recognised body*;

(E) a *manager* of a *recognised body*;

(F) a *licensed body*;

(G) a *manager* of a *licensed body*;

(H) an *employee* of a *recognised body*, a *licensed body*, a *solicitor*, or an *REL*; or

(I) to the extent permitted by law, any person who has previously held a position or role described in (A) to (H) above;

(iii) for the purposes of the *SRA Cost of Investigations Regulations* means the persons at paragraph (ii) (A) to (I) above and also includes a *person who has an interest in a licensed body* and, to the extent permitted by law, any person who has previously held an interest in a *licensed body*.

regulated sale and rent back agreement has the meaning given by article 63J(3) of the *Regulated Activities Order*.

regulatory arrangements has the meaning given to it by section 21 of the *LSA*, and includes all rules and regulations of the *SRA* in relation to the authorisation, *practice*, conduct, discipline and qualification of persons carrying on *legal activities* and the accounts rules and indemnification and compensation arrangements in relation to their *practice*.

regulatory objectives has the meaning given to it by section 1 of the *LSA* and includes the objectives of protecting and promoting the public interest, supporting the constitutional principle of the rule of law, improving access to justice, protecting and promoting the interests of consumers, promoting competition in the provision of *legal activities* by *authorised persons*, encouraging an independent, strong, diverse and effective legal profession, increasing public understanding of the citizen's legal rights and duties, and promoting and maintaining adherence to the *professional principles*.

reinsurance contract means a *contract of insurance* covering all or part of a risk to which a *person* is exposed under a *contract of insurance*.

REL means registered European lawyer, namely, an individual registered with the *SRA* under regulation 17 of the European Communities (Lawyer's Practice) Regulations 2000 (SI 2000/ no.1119).

REL-controlled body means an *authorised body* in which *RELs*, or *RELs* together with *lawyers of England and Wales* and/or European lawyers registered with the *BSB*, constitute the national group of lawyers with the largest (or equal largest) share of control of the body, either as individual *managers (overseas)* or by their share in the control of bodies which are *managers (overseas)*, and for this purpose *RELs* and European lawyers registered with the *BSB* belong to the national group of England and Wales.

related authorised body means an *authorised body* or *recognised sole practitioner's firm* which has a *manager, owner* or *sole practitioner* in common with another *authorised body* or *recognised sole practitioner's firm*.

related body in relation to *in-house practice* means a body standing in relation to your *employer* as specified in Rule 4.7(a) to (d) or 4.15(c) of the *SRA Practice Framework Rules*.

relevant claim means a claim made on or after 1 September 2000 against a *relevant successor practice*.

relevant indemnity period in relation to *contributions* or indemnity means that *indemnity period* in respect of which such *contributions* are payable or such indemnity is to be provided in accordance with the *SRA Indemnity Rules*.

relevant insolvency event occurs in relation to a body if:

    (i)   a resolution for a voluntary winding up of the body is passed without a declaration of solvency under section 89 of the Insolvency Act 1986;

   (ii)   the body enters administration within the meaning of paragraph 1(2)(b) of Schedule B1 to that Act;

  (iii)   an administrative receiver within the meaning of section 251 of that Act is appointed;

  (iv)   a meeting of creditors is held in relation to the body under section 95 of that Act (creditors' meeting which has the effect of converting a *members'* voluntary winding up into a creditors' voluntary winding up);

   (v)   an order for the winding up of the body is made;

  (vi)   all of the *managers* in a body which is unincorporated have been adjudicated bankrupt; or

 (vii)   the body is an overseas company or a *societas Europaea* registered outside England, Wales, Scotland and Northern Ireland and the body is subject to an event in its country of incorporation analogous to an event as set out in paragraphs (i) to (vi) above.

relevant licensed body means a *licensed body* other than:

    (i)   an unlimited company, or an *overseas* company whose members' liability for the company's debts is not limited by its constitution or by the law of its country of incorporation; or

   (ii)   a nominee company only, holding *assets* for clients of another *practice*; and

       (A)   it can act only as agent for the other *practice*; and

       (B)   all the individuals who are *principals* of the *licensed body* are also *principals* of the other *practice*; and

(C) any fee or other income arising out of the *licensed body* accrues to the benefit of the other *practice*; or

(iii) a *partnership* in which none of the *partners* is a limited company, an *LLP* or a legal person whose *members* have limited liability.

relevant recognised body means a *recognised body* other than:

(i) an unlimited company, or an *overseas* company whose members' liability for the company's debts is not limited by its constitution or by the law of its country of incorporation; or

(ii) a nominee company only, holding *assets* for clients of another *practice*; and

(A) it can act only as agent for the other *practice*; and

(B) all the individuals who are *principals* of the *recognised body* are also *principals* of the other *practice*; and

(C) any fee or other income arising out of the *recognised body* accrues to the benefit of the other *practice*; or

(iii) a *partnership* in which none of the *partners* is a limited company, an *LLP* or a legal person whose *members* have limited liability; or

(iv) a *sole practitioner* that is a *recognised body*.

relevant successor practice means in respect of a *previous practice*, a *successor practice* or a "successor practice" (as defined in Appendix 1 to the *SIIR*) (as may be applicable) against which a *relevant claim* is made.

relevant work-based experience means experience which an *authorised training provider* may recognise as satisfying up to six months of the period of *recognised training*, and which:

(i) has been gained in the preceding three years;

(ii) was in English and Welsh law and practice and in one or more areas of law;

(iii) enabled the acquisition of one or more of the *Practice Skills Standards* and/or the *Principles*; and

(iv) was adequately supervised and appraised.

representative in the *SRA Compensation Fund Rules*, means the personal representative of a deceased *defaulting practitioner*; the *trustee* of a bankrupt *defaulting practitioner*; the administrator of an insolvent *defaulting practitioner*, or other duly appointed representative of a *defaulting practitioner*.

reserved legal activity has the meaning given in section 12 of the *LSA*, and includes the exercise of a right of audience, the conduct of litigation, reserved instrument activities, probate activities, notarial activities and the administration of oaths, as defined in Schedule 2 to the *LSA*.

reserved work means activities which *persons* are authorised by the *SRA* to carry out, or prohibited from carrying out, under the *SRA Practice Framework Rules*.

responsible authorised body in respect of an overseas practice means the authorised body or recognised sole practitioner referred to in whichever of paragraph (i)(A) to (F) of the definition of "overseas practice" is applicable to that practice.

retail investment product has the meaning given in the Financial Conduct Authority Handbook.

reversion seller has the meaning given by article 63B(3) of the *Regulated Activities Order*.

revocation in relation to a practising certificate or registration under the *SRA Practising Regulations* includes withdrawal of a practising certificate or registration for the purposes of the *SA* and cancellation of registration for the purposes of Schedule 14 to the Courts and Legal Services Act 1990.

RFL means registered foreign lawyer, namely, an individual registered with the *SRA* under section 89 of the Courts and Legal Services Act 1990.

run-off firm means a *firm* or former *firm* which has ceased to practise in circumstances where, in accordance with paragraph 5.1 of the *MTC*, run-off cover is not required to be provided by any *participating insurer*.

SA means the Solicitors Act 1974.

secondment means the temporary transfer of a *trainee* to an organisation other than his or her *authorised training provider*, the *authorised training provider* remaining responsible for ensuring that the requirements of the *SRA Training Regulations* are met.

section 43 investigation means an investigation by the *SRA* as to whether there are grounds for the *SRA*:

    (i)   to make an order under section 43(2) of the *SA*; or

    (ii) to make an application to the *Tribunal* for it to make such an order.

security has the meaning given by article 3(1) of the *Regulated Activities Order* but does not include an *investment* which falls within the definition of a packaged product.

separate business means a business, wherever situated, which is not an *authorised body*, a *recognised sole practitioner*, an *authorised non-SRA firm*, or an *overseas practice*, or comprises *in-house practice* or practice overseas which is permitted by the *SRA Practice Framework Rules*.

separate designated client account has the meaning given in Rule 13.5(a) of the *SRA Accounts Rules*.

separate practice means:

(i) a *practice* in which the number and identity of the *principals* is not the same as the number and identity of the *principals* in any other *practice*. When the same *principals* in number and identity carry on *practice* under more than one name or style, there is only one *practice*;

(ii) in the case of a *practice* of which more than 25% of the *principals* are *foreign lawyers*, any *overseas* offices shall be deemed to form a separate practice from the offices in England and Wales;

(iii) in the case of an *overseas* office of a *practice*, the fact that a *principal* or a limited number of *principals* represent all the *principals* in the *practice* on a local basis shall not of itself cause that *overseas* office to be a separate practice provided that any fee or other income arising out of that office accrues to the benefit of the *practice*; and

(iv) in the case of a *recognised body* or *licensed body* the fact that all of the shares in the *recognised body* or *licensed body* (as the case may be) are beneficially owned by only some of the *principals* in another *practice*, shall not, of itself, cause such a *recognised body* or *licensed body* (as the case may be) to be a separate practice provided that any fee or other income arising out of the *recognised body* or *licensed body* accrues to the benefit of that other *practice*.

shareowner means:

(i) a *member* of a company with a share capital, who owns a share in the body; or

(ii) a *person* who is not a *member* of a company with a share capital, but owns a share in the body, which is held by a *member* as nominee.

SIF means the Solicitors Indemnity Fund.

SIIR means the Solicitors' Indemnity Insurance Rules 2000 to 2010, the SRA Indemnity Insurance Rules 2011 to 2012 or the *SRA Indemnity Insurance Rules* or any rules subsequent thereto.

societas Europaea means a European public limited liability company within the meaning of Article 1 of Council Regulation 2157/2001/EC.

Society means the Law Society, in accordance with section 87 of the *SA*.

sole practitioner means a *solicitor* or an *REL practising* as a sole principal and does not include a *solicitor* or an *REL practising in-house*, save for the purposes of the *SRA Accounts Rules*, the *SRA Indemnity Insurance Rules* where references to "practising" are to be given their natural meaning.

solicitor means a person who has been admitted as a solicitor of the Senior Courts of England and Wales and whose name is on the roll kept by the *Society* under section 6 of the *SA*, save that in the *SRA Indemnity Insurance Rules* includes a person who *practises* as a solicitor whether or not he or she has in force a practising certificate, and also includes *practice* under home title of a former *REL* who has become a solicitor.

SRA means the Solicitors Regulation Authority, and reference to the SRA as an *approved regulator* or *licensing authority* means the SRA carrying out regulatory functions assigned to the *Society* as an *approved regulator* or *licensing authority*.

SRA Accounts Rules means the SRA Accounts Rules 2011.

SRA Admission Regulations means the SRA Admission Regulations 2011.

SRA Authorisation Rules means the SRA Authorisation Rules for Legal Services Bodies and Licensable Bodies 2011.

SRA Code of Conduct means the SRA Code of Conduct 2011.

SRA Compensation Fund Rules means the SRA Compensation Fund Rules 2011.

SRA Cost of Investigations Regulations means the SRA Cost of Investigations Regulations 2011.

SRA Disciplinary Procedure Rules means the SRA Disciplinary Procedure Rules 2011.

SRA European Cross-border Practice Rules means the SRA European Cross-border Practice Rules 2011.

SRA Financial Services (Scope) Rules means the SRA Financial Services (Scope) Rules 2001.

SRA finding means:

    (i) for the purposes of the *SRA Disciplinary Procedure Rules*, a decision that the *SRA* is satisfied:

        (A) that a *regulated person* (which for the avoidance of doubt, shall include a *solicitor*) has failed to comply with a requirement imposed by or made under the *SA*, the *AJA* or the *LSA*;

        (B) in relation to a *solicitor*, that there has been professional misconduct; or

        (C) that a *HOLP, HOFA, manager, employee, person who has an interest in a licensed body*, or any other person has (intentionally or through neglect) caused or substantially contributed to a significant breach of the terms of the *licensed body's* licence, or has failed to comply with duties imposed by section 90, 91, 92 or 176 of the *LSA* as appropriate,

and for the avoidance of doubt does not include:

        (D) investigatory decisions such as to require the production of information or *documents*;

(E)   directions as to the provision or obtaining of further information or explanation;

(F)   decisions to stay or adjourn;

(G)   authorisation of the making of an application to the *Tribunal*;

(H)   authorisation of an *intervention* pursuant to the *SA*, the *AJA*, the Courts and Legal Services Act 1990 or Schedule 14 to the *LSA*;

(I)   a letter of advice from the *SRA*;

and

(ii) for the purposes of the *SRA Cost of Investigations Regulations*, a decision that the *SRA* is satisfied:

(A)   that a *regulated person* has failed to comply with a requirement imposed by or made under the *SA*, the *AJA* or the *LSA*;

(B)   in relation to a *solicitor*, that there has been professional misconduct.

SRA Handbook means the handbook published from time to time by the *SRA* and containing its *regulatory arrangements*.

SRA Handbook Glossary means the SRA Handbook Glossary 2012, and references to the "Glossary" shall be interpreted accordingly.

SRA Higher Rights of Audience Regulations means the SRA Higher Rights of Audience Regulations 2011.

SRA Indemnity Insurance Rules means the SRA Indemnity Insurance Rules 2013.

SRA Indemnity Rules means the SRA Indemnity Rules 2012.

SRA Insolvency Practice Rules means the SRA Insolvency Practice Rules 2012.

SRA Overseas Rules means the SRA Overseas Rules 2013.

SRA Practice Framework Rules means the SRA Practice Framework Rules 2011.

SRA Practising Regulations means the SRA Practising Regulations 2011.

SRA Principles means the SRA Principles in the *SRA Handbook* and "Principles" shall be interpreted accordingly.

SRA QASA Regulations means the SRA Quality Assurance Scheme for Advocates (Crime) Regulations 2013.

SRA Quality Assurance Scheme for Advocates (Crime) Notification Regulations means the SRA Quality Assurance Scheme for Advocates (Crime) Notification Regulations 2012.

SRA Statutory Trust Rules means the SRA Intervention Powers (Statutory Trust) Rules 2011.

SRA Suitability Test means the SRA Suitability Test 2011.

SRA Training Regulations means the SRA Training Regulations 2014.

stakeholder pension scheme means a scheme established in accordance with Part I of the Welfare and Pensions Reform Act 1999 and the Stakeholder Pension Scheme Regulations 2000.

statement of standards means the "statement of standards for solicitor higher court advocates" issued by *us*.

statutory trust means the trust created by Schedule 1 of the *SA*, or Schedule 14 of the *LSA*, over monies vesting in the *Society* following an *intervention*.

statutory trust account means an account in which *statutory trust monies* are held by the *Society*.

statutory trust monies means the monies vested in the *Society* under the *statutory trust*.

statutory undertakers means:

(i)   any persons authorised by any enactment to carry on any railway, light railway, tramway, road transport, water transport, canal, inland navigation, dock, harbour, pier or lighthouse undertaking or any undertaking for the supply of hydraulic power; and

(ii)   any licence holder within the meaning of the Electricity Act 1989, any public gas supplier, any water or sewerage undertaker, the Environment Agency, any public telecommunications operator, the Post Office, the Civil Aviation Authority and any relevant airport operator within the meaning of Part V of the Airports Act 1986.

subsidiary company has the meaning given in the Companies Act 2006.

substantially common interest for the purposes of Chapter 3 of the *SRA Code of Conduct*, means a situation where there is a clear common purpose in relation to any matter or a particular aspect of it between the *clients* and a strong consensus on how it is to be achieved and the *client conflict* is peripheral to this common purpose.

successor practice

(i)   means a *practice* identified in this definition as 'B', where:

(A)   'A' is the *practice* to which B succeeds; and

(B)   'A's owner' is the owner of A immediately prior to transition; and

(C)   'B's owner' is the owner of B immediately following transition; and

(D) 'transition' means merger, acquisition, absorption or other transition which results in A no longer being carried on as a discrete legal *practice*.

(ii) B is a successor practice to A where:

(A) B is or was held out, expressly or by implication, by B's owner as being the successor of A or as incorporating A, whether such holding out is contained in notepaper, business cards, form of electronic communications, publications, promotional material or otherwise, or is contained in any statement or declaration by B's owner to any regulatory or taxation authority; and/or

(B) (where A's owner was a *sole practitioner* and the transition occurred on or before 31 August 2000) – the *sole practitioner* is a *principal* of B's owner; and/or

(C) (where A's owner was a *sole practitioner* and the transition occurred on or after 1 September 2000) – the *sole practitioner* is a *principal* or *employee* of B's owner; and/or

(D) (where A's owner was a *recognised body* or a *licensed body* (in respect of its *regulated activities*)) – that body is a *principal* of B's owner; and/or

(E) (where A's owner was a *partnership*) – the majority of the *principals* of A's owner have become *principals* of B's owner; and/or

(F) (where A's owner was a *partnership* and the majority of *principals* of A's owner did not become *principals* of the owner of another legal *practice* as a result of the transition) – one or more of the *principals* of A's owner have become *principals* of B's owner and:

(I) B is carried on under the same name as A or a name which substantially incorporates the name of A (or a substantial part of the name of A); and/or

(II) B is carried on from the same premises as A; and/or

(III) the owner of B acquired the goodwill and/or *assets* of A; and/or

(IV) the owner of B assumed the liabilities of A; and/or

(V) the majority of staff employed by A's owner became *employees* of B's owner.

(iii) Notwithstanding the foregoing, B is not a successor practice to A under paragraph (ii) (B), (C), (D), (E) or (F) if another *practice* is or was held out by the owner of that other *practice* as the successor of A or as incorporating A, provided that there is insurance complying with the *MTC* in relation to that other *practice*.

sum insured means the aggregate limit of liability of each *insurer* under the insurance.

supplementary run-off cover means run-off cover provided by the Solicitors Indemnity Fund following the expiry of run-off cover provided to a *firm* in accordance with the *SRA Indemnity Insurance Rules* or otherwise under a *policy* (but subject to compliance with the *MTC*).

temporary practice overseas means the situation where:

    (i)   a *solicitor* is practising but not established overseas; or

    (ii) an *REL* is practising from an office in Scotland or Northern Ireland,

but the solicitor or REL is not *practising overseas*.

trainee solicitor means any person receiving *recognised training* with the express purpose of qualification as a *solicitor*, at an *authorised training provider* and "trainee" should be construed accordingly.

training principal means a *solicitor* or *barrister* nominated by an *authorised training provider* and who meets the requirements of regulation 13 of the SRA Training Regulations 2014 – Qualification and Provider Regulations to oversee *recognised training* within that organisation.

transaction in the *SRA Financial Services (Scope) Rules* means the purchase, sale, subscription or underwriting of a particular *investment*.

Tribunal means the Solicitors Disciplinary Tribunal which is an independent statutory tribunal constituted under section 46 of the *SA* but references to the Tribunal do not include the Tribunal when it is performing any function as an *appellate body*.

trustee includes a personal representative, and "trust" includes the duties of a personal representative.

UK means United Kingdom.

UK qualified lawyer in the *QLTSR*, means solicitors and barristers qualified in Northern Ireland, solicitors and advocates qualified in Scotland and *barristers* qualified in England and Wales.

unadmitted person means a person who:

    (i)   has requested us to assess a *character and suitability* issue under regulation 6 of the SRA Training Regulations 2014 – Qualification and Provider Regulations;

    (ii) has commenced a period of *recognised training* under regulation 5 of the SRA Training Regulations 2014 – Qualification and Provider Regulations;

    (iii) is seeking to establish eligibility to apply for admission under regulation 2 of the *QLTSR*; or

    (iv) is seeking admission pursuant to Directive 2005/36/EC;

but who has not been admitted as a *solicitor*, and "unadmitted persons" should be construed accordingly.

undertaking means a statement, given orally or in writing, whether or not it includes the word "undertake" or "undertaking", made by or on behalf of you or your *firm*, in the course of *practice*, or by you outside the course of *practice* but as a *solicitor* or *REL*, to someone who reasonably places reliance on it, that you or your *firm* will do something or cause something to be done, or refrain from doing something.

us means the *SRA*, and "our" and "ourselves" should be construed accordingly.

vocational stage means:

    (i)   the *LPC*;

    (ii) a required period of *recognised training*; and

    (iii) the *PSC*.

voting rights in a body includes the right to vote in a partners', members', directors' or shareholders' meeting, or otherwise in relation to the body, and "control the exercise of voting rights" shall be interpreted as including de facto as well as legal control over such rights.

we means the *SRA*, and "our" and "ourselves" should be construed accordingly.

without delay means, in normal circumstances, either on the day of receipt or on the next working day.

you means:

    (i)   for the purposes of the *SRA Training Regulations* any person intending to be a *solicitor*, other than those seeking admission under the *QLTSR*;

    (ii) for the purposes of the SRA Training Regulations 2011 Part 3 a *solicitor* or an *REL*;

    (iii) for the purposes of the *SRA Admission Regulations* any person intending to be a *solicitor*;

    (iv) for the purpose of the *QLTSR* a person seeking admission as a *solicitor* via transfer in accordance with those regulations;

    (v) for the purpose of the *SRA Suitability Test* any individual intending to be a *solicitor*, and any person seeking authorisation as an *authorised role holder* under the *SRA Authorisation Rules*;

    (vi) for the purposes of the *SRA Accounts Rules* (save for Part 7 (Overseas practice)):

        (A) a *solicitor*; or

        (B) an *REL*;

in either case who is:

(I)   a *sole practitioner*;

(II)   a *partner* in a *partnership* which is a *recognised body*, *licensed body* or *authorised non-SRA firm*, or in a *partnership* which should be a *recognised body* but has not been recognised by the *SRA*;

(III) an assistant, associate, professional support lawyer, consultant, locum or person otherwise employed in the practice of a *recognised body*, *licensed body*, *recognised sole practitioner* or *authorised non-SRA firm*; or of a *partnership* which should be a *recognised body* but has not been recognised by the *SRA*, or of a *sole practitioner* who should be a *recognised sole practitioner* but has not been authorised by the *SRA*; and "employed" in this context shall be interpreted in accordance with the definition of "employee" for the purposes of the *SRA Code of Conduct*;

(IV) employed as an in-house lawyer by a *non-solicitor employer* (for example, in a law centre or in commerce and industry);

(V)   a *director* of a *company* which is a *recognised body*, *licensed body* or *authorised non-SRA firm*, or of a *company* which is a *manager* of a *recognised body*, *licensed body* or *authorised non-SRA firm*;

(VI) a member of an *LLP* which is a *recognised body*, *licensed body* or *authorised non-SRA firm*, or of an *LLP* which is a *manager* of a *recognised body*, *licensed body* or *authorised non-SRA firm*; or

(VII)a *partner* in a *partnership* with separate legal personality which is a *manager* of a *recognised body*, *licensed body* or *authorised non-SRA firm*;

(C)   an *RFL* practising:

(I)   as a *partner* in a *partnership* which is a *recognised body*, *licensed body* or *authorised non-SRA firm*, or in a *partnership* which should be a *recognised body* but has not been recognised by the *SRA*;

(II)   as the *director* of a *company* which is a *recognised body*, *licensed body* or *authorised non-SRA firm*, or as the *director* of a *company* which is a *manager* of a *recognised body*, *licensed body* or *authorised non-SRA firm*;

(III) as a member of an *LLP* which is a *recognised body*, *licensed body* or *authorised non-SRA firm*, or as a member of an *LLP* which is a *manager* of a *recognised body*, *licensed body* or *authorised non-SRA firm*;

(IV) as a *partner* in a *partnership* with separate legal personality which is a *manager* of a *recognised body*, *licensed body* or *authorised non-SRA firm*;

(V) as an employee of a *recognised body*, *licensed body* or *recognised sole practitioner*; or

(VI) as an employee of a *partnership* which should be a *recognised body* but has not been authorised by the *SRA*, or of a *sole practitioner* who should be a *recognised sole practitioner* but has not been authorised by the *SRA*;

(D) a *recognised body*;

(E) a *licensed body*;

(F) a *manager* or employee of a *recognised body* or *licensed body*, or of a *partnership* which should be a *recognised body* but has not been authorised by the *SRA*; or

(G) an employee of a *recognised sole practitioner*, or of a *sole practitioner* who should be a *recognised sole practitioner* but has not been authorised by the *SRA*;

(vii) for the purposes of the *SRA Higher Rights of Audience Regulations* means a *solicitor* or an *REL*;

(viii) for the purposes of the *SRA Insolvency Practice Rules* means a *solicitor* or an *REL*;

(ix) for the purposes of the *SRA Quality Assurance Scheme for Advocates (Crime) Notification Regulations* means a *solicitor* or an *REL*; and

(x) for the purposes of the *SRA QASA Regulations* means a *solicitor* or an *REL*;

and references to "your" and "yourself" should be construed accordingly.

Rule 3: General Interpretation

3.1 Unless the context otherwise requires:

(a) the singular includes the plural and vice versa;

(b) words importing the masculine gender include the feminine and vice versa and references to the masculine or feminine include the neuter;

(c) the word "body" includes a *sole practitioner*, and a special body within the meaning of section 106 of the *LSA*;

(d) any explanatory notes, guidance notes and/or commentary are for the purposes of guidance only;

(e) any headings are for ease of reference only;

(f) any appendices to the provisions within the *SRA Handbook* will form part of the *SRA Handbook*;

(g) "in writing" includes any form of written electronic communication normally used for business purposes, such as emails;

(h) references to certificates, letters or other forms of written communication include references to those in both electronic and hard copy format; and

(i) a reference to any statute, statutory provision, code or regulation includes any subordinate legislation (as defined by section 21(1) of the Interpretation Act 1978) made under it.

Alphabetical index of headings